# *Classic*
# SITCOMS

# *Classic* SITCOMS

A Celebration of the Best in Prime-Time Comedy

2nd Edition • Revised and Expanded

## *Vince Waldron*

SILMAN-JAMES PRESS          LOS ANGELES

10 9 8 7 6 5 4 3 2 1

Library of Congress Cataloging-in-Publication Data

Waldron, Vince.
Classic sitcoms : a celebration of
the best prime-time comedy / by Vince Waldron.—[2nd ed.]
p.     cm.
Includes bibliographical references and index.
1. Television comedies—United States.  I. Title.
PN1992.8.C66W35   1998        791.45′617—dc21        98–10431

ISBN: 1-879505-25-8

Cover drawing by Drew Friedman ©1997
Author drawing by Drew Friedman

Cover design by Wade Lageose, Art Hotel

Photographs courtesy The Howard Frank Archives

Printed and bound in the United States of America

**SILMAN-JAMES PRESS**
1181 Angelo Drive
Beverly Hills, CA 91210

*For Buddy and Mary*

# Contents

# Foreword
# by Bob Newhart

When I look back on the days when we were making *The Bob Newhart Show* on the MTM lot in the 1970s, what immediately comes to mind is how lucky I was to find myself in such good company. When Grant Tinker, Mary Tyler Moore, and Arthur Price founded MTM, they created what was, in my estimation, the most creative and nurturing atmosphere in which I've ever worked; and also one of the most productive. During the time we were shooting *The Bob Newhart Show*, our neighbors on the MTM lot included not only *The Mary Tyler Moore Show* but *Rhoda*, *Phyllis*, and *The Tony Randall Show*. It was an extremely good time to be in the business of making television comedy.

And it wasn't such a bad time to be watching it, either. I remember there was a period in the mid-'70s when you could turn on your TV set on a Saturday night and watch brand-new episodes of *All in the Family*, *M*A*S*H*, *The Mary Tyler Moore Show*, and *The Bob Newhart Show*, one right after the other. And while I'm sure that all of us who worked on those shows were proud of what we were doing, I doubt if anyone involved in any of those four series ever dreamed that we would one day find ourselves reunited between the covers of a book titled *Classic Sitcoms*.

But here we are, nestled comfortably in the middle of this remarkable study, with Lucy, Jackie Gleason, and Dick Van Dyke on one side and the talented casts of *Barney Miller*, *Taxi*, and *Cheers* on the other. Of course, I should probably point out that we also share these pages with a lot of other important people as well. One of the nicest things about Vince's book is that he doesn't just write about all the glamorous and funny people who appeared in front of the cameras; he also acknowledges the contributions of the many writers, directors, and producers who worked so hard to make sure that all of us glamorous and funny people managed to find our ways into your living rooms every week without stumbling over the carpet on our way in.

And I'm equally happy that this book finds the space to recognize so many of the supporting players and guest stars who brought so much to our shows, a surprising number of whom later went on to become stars themselves. I find it great fun to browse through these pages trying to spot the names of all the bit players and guest stars who later became household names on their own. Where else would you go to find out that the late Broadway and film star Raul Julia once played Jerry the dentist's brother on our show? Or that, long before he starred in *Amadeus*, F. Murray Abraham showed up on an episode of *All in the Family*? Or that future movie stars Tom Hanks, Tom Selleck, and Mandy Patinkin all appeared as guest stars on *Taxi*?

I suppose everyone who buys this book will find their own favorite use for it. Some readers will no doubt find it an invaluable tool for research; others might see it as an endless source of obscure trivia and show-business lore. But for me, I suppose this book will always serve as a kind of memory album of a very exciting period of my life—of six very happy years that I spent in the company of some very wonderful people indeed.

—BOB NEWHART

*December, 1997*
*Los Angeles, California*

# Acknowledgements

This volume would have been much less interesting—and a lot thinner—had it not been'for the generous cooperation of the producers, writers, directors, actors, and executives, who agreed to be interviewed for this book. For sharing their insights and anecdotes, I'm indebted to Danny Arnold, Glen Charles, Les Charles, Frank Dungan, Lynne Farr, Ron Jacobs, Burt Metcalfe, Lorenzo Music, John Rich, Tony Sheehan, Jeff Stein, Alan Wagner, Ed. Weinberger, and Michael Zinberger. Thanks also to Sheldon Leonard and Carl Reiner for answering specific queries about their long and illustrious careers in television; and to Norman Lear for sharing his memories, and for letting me view rare material from his collection. I'm also obliged to Carroll O'Connor and Rob Reiner for helping me nail down the elusive creative credits for the historic pilot episodes of *All in the Family*.

I'd also like to extend my heartfelt thanks to all the other writers, actors, researchers, and concerned television professionals who helped me track down specific background information on the many shows in this volume: Hal Biard and Jim Behrens at CBS; *Daily Variety*'s Tom Bierbaum; Bob Braithwaite at 20th Century-Fox Television; George Faber and Betsy Vorce, the friendly voices at Viacom International; Abby Nelson; Linda Frank at Danny Thomas Productions; Jackie Koch and Mark Pollack at Act III Communications; Jerry Leichter and the staff of *The Television Index*; Carol Navratil at Charles/Burrows/Charles; Paramount's Mike Novall; Jeff Thomas; and Tise Vahimagi, one of the British Film Institute's tireless television historians. I'm also grateful to the A.C. Nielsen Company for allowing me to print ratings figures compiled from their audience measurement services; to Howard Frank for making the marvelous photos in this book available for my use; to Vicki

XII ACKNOWLEDGMENTS

Siamas and Nita Boyum, Malibu's sharpest photographic team; and, of course, to all the TV columnists who responded to my original critic's choice pole.

I'm also indebted to that small group of genuine television experts who prevented me from making any serious blunders when they reviewed the finished chapters of this book for accuracy. Thanks to Brenda L. Fraunfelter, who seems to know all there is to know about *All in the Family* and *M*A*S*H*; Brenda Scott Royce, whose encyclopedic knowledge of television belies her tender age; Bill Ginch, a *Honeymooners* aficionado with a keen eye for detail; and a big thank you to Diane Albert, the able editor of *The TV Collector*, and Richard Tharp, the publisher of *Reruns: The Magazine of Television History*, who each shared invaluable material from their substantial personal archives. I also extend my deepest appreciation to the authors of other television books who so unselfishly shared their inspiration and advice: Wally Podrazik, co-author of *Watching TV*; John Javna, the writer of *Cult TV*; Cheryl L. Blythe, co-author of *The Official Cheers Scrapbook*; Coyne Steven Sanders, co-author of *The Dick Van Dyke Show: Anatomy of a Classic*; Donna McCrohan, the author of *The Honeymooners Companion*, and Bart Andrews, author of *The "I Love Lucy" Book*.

I must also express my gratitude to the helpful staff of the Margaret Herrick Library of the Academy of Motion Picture Arts and Sciences; Dan Einstein and Eleanor Tanin of the UCLA Motion Picture and Television Archives; Anne Schlosser of the American Film Institute's Louis B. Mayer Library; and Sharon Farb and Leah R. Smith of UCLA's Theater Arts Library, whose cheerful enthusiasm never wavered as they guided me through thousands and thousands of back issues of *TV Guide*. I owe a similar debt to the curators of New York's Museum of Broadcasting—Ron Simon, Jeff Fuerst, and Randy Dolnick—for the gracious hospitality they extended during my visits to their splendid stronghold of TV arcana.

My warm regards to those friends whose enthusiasm for this project kept me going throughout the uncertain early days of its genesis: Joanna Monks, Dan Castellaneta, Richard Kuhlman, Gordon Flagg, Cynthia Berry, David Meyer, Jeremiah Bosgang, and Helen MacEachron. And a special salute to Eileen Sutton, whose early confidence brought this book to life.

Finally, a solid round of applause to the individuals who made such major contributions to *Classic Sitcoms* that they practically deserve co-creator credit: Howard Prouty, a film and television historian whose boundless enthusiasm is matched only by his intelligence and taste; my pal Nancy Giles, whose genuine affection for the classic comedies in this book provided consistent inspiration; and my brother, Robert Waldron, who would've written this book himself—probably in half the time—if I hadn't beaten him to it. And I've reserved my last and loudest ovation for my original editor, Bill Whitehead, whose wisdom guided the project safely into open waters, and his assistant, Kathy Zuckerman, who shored up all the loose ends with patience and grace.

—VINCE WALDRON

*April 29, 1987*
*Los Angeles, California*

# Acknowledgements for the Second Edition

It seems only fitting that I open my acknowledgments to this second, expanded edition of *Classic Sitcoms* by expressing my gratitude to those readers of the first edition who took the time to share their thoughts, opinions, and corrections with me, an estimable roster of armchair TV scholars that includes Janice Barclay, Phil Bowling, Walter Bruley, Dave Chapman, Mike Doyle, Bob Gassel, Joe Isham, Michael B. Kassel, Don Murphy, Roger Patrick, Alan Sepinwall, Joakim Skog, James E. Smith III, Daniel J. Styer, Peter Vassilakis, and Gerry Wright. I'd also like to extend my special thanks to reader Erich P. Wise for his many helpful suggestions and corrections, a large percentage of which have been incorporated into this edition.

My warm regards also to all the actors, writers, directors, and producers who were kind enough to offer their comments and suggestions on the first edition of this work, with special thanks to those television professionals who so kindly consented to lend their endorsement to the present volume: Danny Arnold, Howard Gewirtz, Sheldon Leonard, Carl Reiner, John Rich, Dan Staley, and Jay Sandrich. And, of course, I am also deeply indebted to Bob Newhart for contributing the marvelous Foreword that launches the current edition of this book.

One area where this updated edition of *Classic Sitcoms* offers a significant improvement over its predecessor is in its coverage of *Cheers*, a series that had barely completed four seasons on the air when the first edition of this book went to press in 1987. But, thanks in no small measure to the kind assistance I received from the staff at Charles/Burrows/Charles Productions in Hollywood, I'm happy to report that this new edition of *Classic Sitcoms* contains the most complete and accurate guide to that show's near-record eleven-season run yet published. Naturally, the act of compiling, updating, and fact-checking that much data on a single series was no slight undertaking. But fortunately, I had quite a bit of help. And though it would be practically impossible to cite each and every individual who aided me in those efforts, I would like to single out a few of them for special mention here.

For generously sharing their memories and impressions of the creation and evolution of *Cheers* throughout its first fledgling seasons, I'm deeply indebted to the show's creators, Glen Charles, Les Charles, and James Burrows. And, for allowing me the benefit of their unique backstage perspectives on the show's middle and later seasons, I'm equally beholden to *Cheers* writer/producers Peter Casey, Dan Staley, and Phoef Sutton. I'd also like to extend special thanks to Chris Connor and David Reid for the many courtesies extended me during the course of my investigations into the long and colorful history of that remarkable series.

Finally, for their unfailing support—and other acts of kindness too numerous to list in the limited space I have here—I'd also like to express my gratitude to Diane Albert, Dirk Burhans, Dona Chernoff, Rick Copp, Gordon Flagg, Cheryl Giraud, David Goodman, Katy Hickman, Pete Johnston, Edie Magoun, Wally Podrazik, Rich Reetz, Brenda Scott-Royce, Steve Sheridan, Max D. Staley, Mindy Staley, and Kim Witherspoon. And last, though certainly not least, I'd like to offer a final tip of the hat to Jim Fox and Gwen Feldman, my publishers at Silman-James Press. To all of you—and anyone I may have inadvertently failed to mention—my deepest thanks for making this volume so much richer for your efforts.

—VINCE WALDRON

*December 19, 1997*
*Los Angeles, California*

# INTRODUCTION

·

*The better the quality of the show, the
longer it will take to catch on with the
general public.*
—SHELDON LEONARD, TV Producer

PRACTICALLY EVERY SHOW in this book started out—or ended up—a flop.

The pilot episodes of *All in the Family* and *Barney Miller* were initially rejected by the networks that financed them. First-season ratings for *The Dick Van Dyke Show* were so low that it was actually canceled after a single season, and its eleventh-hour revival was considered nothing short of miraculous; *Cheers* was one of the lowest-rated programs of the year when it started; *M\*A\*S\*H* barely squeaked into a second season; and two different networks gave *Taxi* the heave-ho while the series was still in its prime.

Clearly, prime-time television has not been the most hospitable breeding ground for classic situation comedy. Today, all of these shows—along with *The Honeymooners*, *The Bob Newhart Show*, *The Mary Tyler Moore Show*, and *I Love Lucy*—are revered as time-honored television classics. But each one of them owes its survival to a handful of determined visionaries who repeatedly defied the whims of a billion-dollar industry in their stubborn efforts to craft a few half hours of television that mattered.

These are their stories.

The producers most responsible for the classic TV comedy that have kept us laughing for nearly four decades form an honor roll of television's most distinguished creators: Desi Arnaz, Danny Arnold, James Brooks,

1

Allan Burns, James Burrows, Glen Charles and Les Charles, Stan Daniels, David Davis, Larry Gelbart, Jackie Gleason, Norman Lear, Sheldon Leonard, Lorenzo Music, Jess Oppenheimer, Carl Reiner, Gene Reynolds, John Rich, and Ed Weinberger. Without them, prime-time comedy might still be holding out for a punchline from *Lum and Abner Abroad*.

Of course, it's the characters, not the creators, that come to mind when we think of these classic comedies. And that's as it should be. Over the years, the inhabitants of the peculiar universe of the situation comedy have become so familiar that they've practically written their own chapter in our modern American folklore.

From Ralph Kramden to Barney Miller, they've mirrored our fondest hopes and dreams—though that never stopped them from taking merciless potshots at our silly foibles as well. From Lucy Ricardo's assault on the blandness of the Eisenhower fifties to Mary Richards' gentle struggle to stay afloat in the liberated seventies, their stories were our stories. How could we help but love them?

There's a common misconception that we welcomed each of them into our living rooms every week—but that's not exactly true. Few of us relished the thought of inviting Archie Bunker into *our* parlors; and we had better sense than to let a madman like Louie De Palma run amok among our knickknacks. But we welcomed the opportunity to accompany our favorite characters on regularly scheduled excursions into their habitats. And those journeys took us to some pretty fascinating locales.

We've gone conga dancing at the Club Babalu and stood behind bars at the Twelfth Precinct. We've suffered the stifling heat of a Korean medical compound and whiled away more hours than we care to remember hanging out with a gang of compassionate New York cabbies—without even once looking at the meter. We also spent quieter half hours in cozy parlors from Queens to Minneapolis—living rooms that we remember far more clearly than our own.

And the characters we met along the way were just as hard to forget. From the outraged Queens dockworker to the befuddled Chicago airline navigator, they all had the capacity to think and feel—and their passions rarely failed to touch us. Looking back on the friends we made—from the Cuban bandleader to that erudite barmaid in Boston—it's hard to believe we got to know them all so well in just a half hour a week.

The ten classic situation comedies that make up the present volume were chosen by a poll of American television critics, so it's not surprising that their choices reflect the wide breadth of achievement of this much-maligned art form. It's another happy coincidence that the consensus traces the history of the American situation comedy from its humble beginnings in a cold-water flat in Brooklyn to its more recent stronghold in an upscale Boston bar.

In the early 1950s, before *I Love Lucy* or *The Honeymooners*, TV's earliest comedies—*Amos 'N' Andy*, *The Goldbergs*, *The Life of Riley*—were holdovers from radio, and their scripts usually worked just as well whether you watched the picture or not. Then, out of nowhere, an impetuous redhead barreled into prime time—with a headstrong bus driver close on her heels. Suddenly, we found it nearly impossible to take our eyes off the old Philco in the corner.

By the 1960s, Rob Petrie regularly engaged our wit as well as our imagination when *The Dick Van Dyke Show* combined the vaudeville of the fifties sitcom with an urbane charm that would become the hallmark of quality comedy in the seventies.

*The Mary Tyler Moore Show* ushered in the next decade with a whole new school of comedy, with sharp humor based on the gentle observation of ordinary people who find themselves trapped in the absurd circumstances of everyday life. *The Bob Newhart Show* twisted that formula to create a view of the modern world as Lewis Carroll might have described it had he worked in Studio City instead of at Oxford.

But it was *All in the Family* that finally broke down the remaining barriers when it exposed prime time to the screaming headlines of our daily newspapers. Before anyone realized what was happening, a rowdy gang of doctors and nurses from the *M\*A\*S\*H* 4077th took the creative license that Archie Bunker had pried loose and parlayed it into eleven seasons of deeply felt comic drama. The day's headlines also figured in the station-house humor of *Barney Miller*, though the Twelfth Precinct detectives usually paid more attention to the little stories buried on page six.

Finally, the decade of the 1970s drew to a close, and with it, the Golden Age of situation comedy. *Taxi* and *Cheers*—both created by producers schooled at MTM during the studio's glory days—proved that the goal of quality television didn't completely evaporate when Mary Richards closed up shop in 1977, though few comedies would have a lasting impact in the lean period that kicked off the 1980s.

And then came Cosby.

Spurred on by the tremendous success of *The Cosby Show* in 1984, the situation comedy reclaimed its grasp on the American imagination with a boom in half-hour comedy that has already continued well past the mid-point of the following decade. In recent years, *The Golden Girls*, *Newhart*, *Roseanne*, and *Murphy Brown* have proven their enduring appeal, while *Seinfeld*, *The Simpsons*, and an upstart from cable TV called *The Larry Sanders Show* have demonstrated an especially high regard for the intelligence of the TV audience, which certainly bodes well for the immediate future. Of course, whether this latest sitcom renaissance will have a lasting impact as television moves into its second forty years remains to be seen.

But we'll be watching.

# I LOVE LUCY

•

*Maybe television would be good for a*
*year or two . . .*
—LUCILLE BALL

THEY TOLD HER the show would never work.

The audience would never buy Lucille Ball as the wacky wife of a Cuban bandleader, the network insisted. But Lucy persevered, and her efforts resulted in a television show that has probably had a more lasting impact than any other series in the history of the medium.

Yet, ironically, *I Love Lucy* began as a last-ditch effort to save a crumbling show-biz marriage—the same marriage CBS insisted that no one would believe in the first place.

Lucille Ball had come a long way from her humble start as one of the Goldwyn Girls of 1933. She'd worked her way up from contract player to starring roles in films like *Dubarry Was a Lady* and *The Big Street*. But by the late forties, she was convinced that the studio casting agents had no idea what to do with her. She'd been saddled with a succession of women's pictures and frivolous comedies, when all she really wanted was to play comic roles that were closer to herself—she wanted to develop a consistent screen personality, the way Cary Grant or Clark Gable had. "After fifteen years in motion pictures, I'd always been playing someone else," she complained. "I *wanted* to be typecast."

When she finally achieved that goal, it wasn't in a feature film at all. The actress found her first near-perfect role in radio, when she was cast as the screwball wife in *My Favorite Husband*, a CBS radio sitcom that co-starred Richard Denning. It was good work, and it came along at just the right time. But then, the actress had discovered long before that things always seemed to fall into place in her professional life.

Unfortunately, she didn't have nearly so much luck at home.

After ten stormy years with Desi Arnaz, the actress was ready to throw in the towel. The marriage had been plagued almost from the start. She'd married the Cuban bandleader shortly after they met on an RKO set in 1940. But the honeymoon ended soon after, when Desi left Hollywood to tour the country with his orchestra while she stayed on to resume her film career. The strain of their long separations began to take its toll, and by the end of the decade, Lucy was convinced that they had but two options—they could find a way to work together professionally or they could file for divorce.

When Harry Ackerman approached Lucy with a business proposition early in 1950, the CBS program executive had no idea that his offer would save her marriage. But when Ackerman told her of the network's plan to star her in a television version of *My Favorite Husband*, the actress recognized a golden opportunity. She would be glad to do the series, with one stipulation—Desi Arnaz would have to play her husband.

Ackerman hadn't anticipated signing a package deal. But he was confident enough in the comedienne's talents to give the matter some thought. He had seen Lucy's rapport with live audiences when he was the executive in charge of her radio series, and he was convinced that she had a quality that could easily make the transition to television. He finally presented the case to William S. Paley, the chairman and elder statesman of the powerful network. If CBS wanted Lucy, Ackerman explained, they would have to take the Cuban as well.

Paley, who thought the idea sounded like madness, personally pleaded with his star to reconsider. But Lucy would not budge. As she remembers it, "CBS said, 'We want you to go into television, but we think your husband, well, no one would believe *he* was your husband.' And I said, 'Why not? We're married!'"

The negotiations were stalled, but Lucy and Desi refused to give up. The series would be a godsend, even if it lasted only a season or two, and the couple was determined to see it through. If the skeptical CBS executives needed proof of the pair's creative compatibility, they would get it. Lucy and Desi put together a vaudeville variety show, and in the summer of 1950 they set off on a personal-appearance tour.

The hunch paid off. They returned to Hollywood with glowing reviews, and the enthusiastic response they got from audiences all across the country proved that the public was actually quite taken by the unusual chemistry of the handsome Latin and his bubbly, clowning wife.

On the basis of that success, Harry Ackerman convinced CBS to foot the bill for a pilot film based on an entirely new series concept. The new format would be dreamed up by Lucy's radio producer, Jess Oppenheimer—who would also produce the new venture with Desi Arnaz—and scripted by Oppenheimer and Madelyn Pugh and Bob Carroll, Jr., the chief writers of *My Favorite Husband*.

The classic format of the show that would become *I Love Lucy* was finally arrived at by a combination of equal parts inspiration and expedience. The idea of casting Desi as a bandleader was a natural response to the network's fears that Arnaz might not be able to handle any sterner acting demands. The writers were also careful not to stray far from the format that had worked so well on *My Favorite Husband*, so they decided to cast Lucy as an ordinary housewife—with the twist that she was always trying to horn in on her husband's glamorous show-biz life.

Lucy loved the idea of playing a domestic role. As she later observed, in her entire film career "there were only three or four scenes that I cared anything about. When I put them all together, I found out they were all domestic scenes where I played a housewife."

The pilot episode that was filmed in 1951 bore little more than passing resemblance to the series that eventually premiered the following fall. The writers combined large chunks of the previous summer's vaudeville show with a storyline Carroll and Pugh cribbed from one of their old *My Favorite Husband* scripts. But the results were promising enough to attract a sponsorship offer from the Phillip Morris Tobacco Company, and the series was slated to begin production.

Even so, the writers still weren't entirely satisfied with the show's format. They felt they needed more characters to enhance the story possibilities, and—turning once again to their radio show for inspiration—they introduced a second, older couple to act as friendly foils for their leading players. They had used the same basic structure to good effect on *My Favorite Husband*, and Oppenheimer, like any good TV writer, was loath to abandon a workable idea just because he'd already used it. It was in this offhanded fashion that two of the most durable and well-loved characters in the entire realm of the situation comedy were born—Fred and Ethel Mertz.

When Oppenheimer and Arnaz discovered that Gale Gordon and Bea Benaderet—the actors who had played equivalent roles on the radio show—were unavailable, William Frawley and Vivian Vance were cast. There was some network opposition to Frawley, whose drinking problems had earned him an unsavory reputation in Hollywood; and Vance was another unlikely choice, with scarcely any film work to her credit. But with more than four decades' hindsight, it's impossible to imagine any other actors filling the Mertzes' well-worn shoes.

There was one element of the pilot show that everyone agreed should be retained when they shot the series—the live studio audience. Harry Ackerman remembered how favorably the audience reaction affected Lucy's work on *My Favorite Husband*. "Her performance without a live audience was ghastly," he recalls. "When I brought in a dress-rehearsal audience, I could see that she lifted immediately. I just knew she would be nothing without that live audience."

Oppenheimer concurred. "We talked about shooting it like a movie, and then dubbing in the laughs. But there is that quality, that response, that comes only from a live experience."

Everything was falling into place for the fall premiere. Naturally, the new series had been given a fresh name: *I Love Lucy*. The title pleased Lucy because it gave an equal emphasis to Desi—the presumed speaker of the title phrase—while CBS was satisfied that it imparted top billing to their more well-known star.

For Lucy, it was like a dream come true. She and Desi had finally created a professional life that made it possible to build the home life she'd always wanted. She couldn't have been happier.

Until she found out that CBS wanted her and Desi to move to New York.

In those pioneering days of broadcasting—before satellites and high-quality videotape—most TV shows were telecast live from the East Coast, while the western time zones had to settle for crude kinescope films that were shot directly from TV monitors for later broadcast west of the Rockies. CBS and the sponsors had no intention of disrupting this system to suit Lucille Ball and Desi Arnaz. If they wanted to do their show in front of a live audience, they would have to do it from New York.

The Arnazes were practically in a state of shock. The whole point of doing the show initially was so that they'd be able to work close to home. When they refused to pull up stakes and move to New York, it looked as though things had reached yet another creative impasse.

The compromise that was finally reached—to film the half-hour episodes live before a Hollywood studio audience—seems a terribly obvious solution by today's standards. But in 1951, it was a revolutionary—and very risky—idea.

In the first place, no one had ever attempted to conquer the rigorous demands of shooting 35mm movie film with a noisy and distracted audience in attendance. And even if the technical problems could be ironed out, film was certainly a far costlier medium than the alternative of a live broadcast.

Desi tackled the financial complications by volunteering a salary cut for himself and his wife, in exchange for complete ownership of the show—lock, stock, and conga drum. It was a shrewd deal that only hinted at the financial acumen Desi would eventually use to build Desilu Productions into one of the wealthiest and most successful production outfits in television.

To solve the technical problems, Arnaz and Oppenheimer hired a production wizard named Al Simon, who simply adapted a system he'd used to film TV game shows—a multicamera arrangement that allowed the action to proceed onstage, almost as if the actors were performing a play. Lucy than cajoled the legendary Czech cinematographer Karl Freund into devising a system for lighting the entire stage without creating unwanted shadows—no mean feat. With minor adjustments, the method that Simon and Freund improvised for the first season of I Love Lucy remains the standard technique for filming live situation comedy to this day.

At long last, the show was in production. All that remained now was to see how the public responded to the series that had been labored over by so many for so long.

And that response was not slow in arriving. On Monday, October 15, 1951, we got our first glimpse of Lucy and Ricky and Fred and Ethel, and the living rooms of America haven't been the same since. For the first time ever, a sitcom showed us people we felt we really knew. And before long, we wanted to know them better.

The show had a galvanizing effect on the television audience. By May of that first season, the comedy already commanded an astonishing 11.5 million television sets each Monday evening—in the days when there were barely 15 million sets in existence! It was the dawn of a new era in broadcasting. The situation comedy had come into its own.

It's practically impossible to explain why the escapades of this kooky redhead and her family so riveted the audience of her day, or how she continues to enchant audiences today. But a close look at the 180 episodes listed here offers a clue.

Quite simply, the show was better written, performed, and photographed than anything else the audience had ever seen. Even today—more than four decades after the series ended its run—few situation comedies can match the look, pacing, and precision of the best episodes of I Love Lucy, television's first classic sitcom.

# A Critical Guide to All 180 Episodes

# 1951    THE PILOT EPISODE

**Pilot**   *I Love Lucy* Audition                          April 30, 1990
  **Writers:** Jess Oppenheimer, Madelyn Pugh, Bob Carroll, Jr.
  **Director:** Ralph Levy
  **Guest Stars:** Jerry Hausner, Pepito the Clown

Determined to break into show business, Lucy schemes to replace the ailing clown in her husband's nightclub act.

This embryonic tryout episode was substantially different from the final series format. Arnaz and Ball play Larry and Lucy Lopez, and the Mertzes are nowhere to be found. The script was actually a rewrite of the Lucy/Desi vaudeville touring show, patched together with an old *My Favorite Husband* script. Kinescoped on March 2, 1951, as an audition for potential backers, the film was presumed lost for nearly four decades when a copy resurfaced and was broadcast as a CBS-TV special.

# 1951-52    THE FIRST SEASON

*Year-End Rating: 50.9 (3rd place)*

First-season scripts explore the screwball possibilities of a Manhattan housewife's efforts to break out of her routine and share the spotlight with her husband, Ricky Ricardo, bandleader at the Tropicana Club. Lucy's comical complications are skillfully orchestrated by the show's creators, Jess Oppenheimer, Madelyn Pugh, and Bob Carroll, Jr., the team that will chronicle Lucy's misadventures throughout her first five seasons.
  Oppenheimer will serve as producer for the first five years, and Desi Arnaz will be executive producer for the entire run. Marc Daniels is staff director for the first season, and Al Simon is associate producer.

**1**   The Girls Want to Go to a Nightclub      October 15, 1951
  **Writers:** Jess Oppenheimer, Madelyn Pugh, Bob Carroll, Jr.
  **Director:** Marc Daniels

Fred and Ricky decide they'd rather attend the fights than go to a fancy nightclub on the Mertzes' anniversary.

This episode provides the cast with an early display of the show's broad farce, when the wives dress up as hicks and try to pass themselves off as their husbands' blind dates. Such stock plots were used ad nauseam in radio, but as Jess Oppenheimer told TV historian Alex C.

MacKenzie, "We were the first to do them on television. Certain things were done so much on radio that no one had the guts to do them anymore. But on television, those tired bits were great."

**2    Be a Pal**                                        October 22, 1951
**Writers:** Jess Oppenheimer, Madelyn Pugh, Bob Carroll, Jr.
**Director:** Marc Daniels
**Guest Stars:** Richard J. Reeves, Tony Michaels

Fearing that the honeymoon is over, Lucy follows the advice of a self-help text and tries to revive Ricky's interest by becoming his pal.

**3    The Diet**                                        October 29, 1951
**Writers:** Jess Oppenheimer, Madelyn Pugh, Bob Carroll, Jr.
**Director:** Marc Daniels
**Guest Star:** Marco Rizo

Lucy has to shed twelve pounds in two days to qualify for a part in the chorus line of Ricky's nightclub act.

**4    Lucy Thinks Ricky is Trying**                    November 5, 1951
         **to Murder Her**
**Writers:** Jess Oppenheimer, Madelyn Pugh, Bob Carroll, Jr.
**Director:** Marc Daniels
**Guest Star:** Jerry Hausner

Her imagination spurred by a mystery novel, Lucy is convinced that Ricky's plotting to poison her.

Telecast a month after the series began, this show was actually the very first episode filmed—and it shows. The lighting, pacing—even the makeup—look primitive compared with that in episodes filmed in succeeding weeks, after the cast and crew got their bearings in the pioneering three-camera system.

    For this inaugural episode, the crew actually crammed a fourth back-up camera onto the crowded soundstage so they could shoot the entire script straight through—from start to finish—the method used in live television of that era. It wasn't until the second week that they realized the studio audience *would* sit patiently through the short breaks that were necessary to reposition the cameras, and the technical quality of the shows made a giant leap in subsequent episodes. Significantly, the three-camera, stop-and-start method adopted in the second week allowed the writers

greater flexibility to engineer the complicated prop and costume
sequences that would become Lucy's comedic trademark.

**5    The Quiz Show**                              November 12, 1951
**Writers:** Jess Oppenheimer, Madelyn Pugh, Bob Carroll, Jr.
**Director:** Marc Daniels
**Guest Star:** Frank Nelson, John Emery, Phil Ober

To qualify for a thousand-dollar prize on a radio quiz show, Lucy
must convince Ricky that she was once married to another man.

The first of many guest appearances by Frank Nelson. Here he plays
Freddie Fillmore, the emcee in a parody of *Truth or Consequences*, a popular
quiz show of the day.

**6    The Audition**                               November 19, 1951
**Writers:** Jess Oppenheimer, Madelyn Pugh, Bob Carroll, Jr.
**Director:** Marc Daniels
**Guest Stars:** Harry Ackerman, Jess Oppenheimer

In an all-out effort to be seen by visiting TV talent scouts, Lucy
schemes to replace an ailing clown in Ricky's big circus number.

This episode was adapted from the series's original pilot film, which
was itself based on material from Lucy and Desi's vaudeville act.
     The network honchos are played by producer Jess Oppenheimer and
Harry Ackerman, CBS vice president and longtime supporter of the series.

**7    The Seance**                                 November 26, 1951
**Writers:** Jess Oppenheimer, Madelyn Pugh, Bob Carroll, Jr.
**Director:** Marc Daniels
**Guest Star:** Jay Novello

Lucy and Ethel stage a phony seance for the benefit of an eccentric producer.

**8    Men are Messy**                              December 3, 1951
**Writers:** Jess Oppenheimer, Madelyn Pugh, Bob Carroll, Jr.
**Director:** Marc Daniels
**Guest Stars:** Kenny Morgan, Harry Shannon

To teach their sloppy husbands a lesson, Lucy and Ethel turn the
Ricardo apartment into a hillbilly shanty.

**9**    The Fur Coat                             December 10, 1951
**Writers:** Jess Oppenheimer, Madelyn Pugh, Bob Carroll, Jr.
**Director:** Marc Daniels
**Guest Star:** Ben Weldon

When Ricky brings home a rented mink for his act, Lucy assumes it's a surprise gift for her.

A prime example of how Lucy's total commitment as a performer contributed immeasurably to otherwise pedestrian storylines. When the actress squeals in abandon at the prospect of getting a fur coat, the gesture seems remarkably genuine, and when she weeps as the fur is taken away, her conviction renders her crocodile tears real. Through sheer force of personality, Lucy actually engages our sympathy in a character's pathological need to have a mink coat!

**10**    Lucy is Jealous of Girl Singer          December 17, 1951
**Writers:** Jess Oppenheimer, Madelyn Pugh, Bob Carroll, Jr.
**Director:** Marc Daniels
**Guest Star:** Helen Silver

Lucy joins the chorus line to keep an eye on things after Ricky hires an attractive new dancing partner.

**11**    Drafted                                December 24, 1951
**Writers:** Jess Oppenheimer, Madelyn Pugh, Bob Carroll, Jr.
**Director:** Marc Daniels

The wives are convinced that Fred and Ricky are headed for boot camp after they overhear the boys rehearsing a military number for a benefit show.

**12**    The Adagio                             December 31, 1951
**Writers:** Jess Oppenheimer, Madelyn Pugh, Bob Carroll, Jr.
**Director:** Marc Daniels
**Guest Star:** Shepard Menken

Lucy's desire to perform an Apache routine at the club cools considerably after she sparks romantic desires in her French dance coach.

**13**   The Benefit                         January 7, 1952
**Writers:** Jess Oppenheimer, Madelyn Pugh, Bob Carroll, Jr.
**Director:** Marc Daniels

Lucy blackmails Ethel into letting her perform at a women's club benefit after Lucy promises Ricky's services as headliner.


**14**   The Amateur Hour                    January 14, 1952
**Writers:** Jess Oppenheimer, Madelyn Pugh, Bob Carroll, Jr.
**Director:** Marc Daniels
**Guest Stars:** Gail Bonney, David Stollery, Sammy Ogg

Lucy has her hands full when she baby-sits two mischievous twins at an amateur talent competition.


**15**   Lucy Plays Cupid                    January 21, 1952
**Writers:** Jess Oppenheimer, Madelyn Pugh, Bob Carroll, Jr.
**Director:** Marc Daniels
**Guest Stars:** Bea Benaderet, Edward Everett Horton

Matchmaker Lucy tries to unite the grocery man with a spinster neighbor, but only succeeds in igniting the elderly clerk's passion for redheads.


**16**   Lucy Fakes Illness                  January 28, 1952
**Writers:** Jess Oppenheimer, Madelyn Pugh, Bob Carroll, Jr.
**Director:** Marc Daniels
**Guest Star:** Hal March

Lucy feigns a nervous breakdown after Ricky refuses to hire her for his nightclub act.


**17**   Lucy Writes a Play                  February 4, 1952
**Writers:** Jess Oppenheimer, Madelyn Pugh, Bob Carroll, Jr.
**Director:** Marc Daniels
**Guest Stars:** Myra Marsh, Maury Thompson

Ricky plays the lead in *A Tree Grows in Havana,* Lucy's entry in an amateur writing competition.

**18**    Breaking the Lease                          February 11, 1952
**Writers:** Jess Oppenheimer, Madelyn Pugh, Bob Carroll, Jr.
**Director:** Marc Daniels
**Guest Stars:** Barbara Pepper, Bennett Green, Hazel Pierce

Lucy and Ricky attempt to break their lease after a disagreement with the Mertzes develops into all-out war.

In the scene where Ethel confronts Lucy the morning after their blowup, the redhead haughtily puffs a cigarette—not an uncommon occurrence in the show's early years. Not surprisingly, the show's original sponsor was the Phillip Morris Tobacco Company.

**19**    The Ballet                                  February 18, 1952
**Writers:** Jess Oppenheimer, Madelyn Pugh, Bob Carroll, Jr.
**Director:** Marc Daniels
**Guest Stars:** Mary Wickes, Frank Scannell

Ricky has openings for a ballet singer and a burlesque comic— and naturally, Lucy tries out for both parts.

**20**    The Young Fans                              February 25, 1952
**Writers:** Jess Oppenheimer, Madelyn Pugh, Bob Carroll, Jr.
**Director:** William Asher
**Guest Stars:** Janet Waldo, Richard Crenna

Lucy comes to the rescue when a swooning bobby-soxer develops a crush on Ricky.

William Asher's debut as *I Love Lucy* director. Coincidentally, Asher had just directed guest star Richard Crenna in the TV pilot of Desilu's *Our Miss Brooks*.

**21**    New Neighbors                               March 3, 1952
**Writers:** Jess Oppenheimer, Madelyn Pugh, Bob Carroll, Jr.
**Director:** Marc Daniels
**Guest Stars:** K. T. Stevens, Hayden Rorke, Allen Jenkins

Lucy and Ethel jump to alarming conclusions after they spy on the new couple who've just moved into the building.

**22**    Fred and Ethel Fight                                    March 10, 1952
**Writers:** Jess Oppenheimer, Madelyn Pugh, Bob Carroll, Jr.
**Director:** Marc Daniels
**Guest Star:** Hazel Pierce

The Ricardos attempt to reunite Fred and Ethel after a lover's spat, only to wind up in a marital row of their own.

**23**    The Mustache                                    March 17, 1952
**Writers:** Jess Oppenheimer, Madelyn Pugh, Bob Carroll, Jr.
**Director:** Marc Daniels
**Guest Star:** John Brown

Lucy's scheme to convince Ricky to shave off his new mustache backfires when she finds herself unable to remove a set of false whiskers.

**24**    The Gossip                                    March 24, 1952
**Writers:** Jess Oppenheimer, Madelyn Pugh, Bob Carroll, Jr.
**Director:** Marc Daniels
**Guest Stars:** Richard J. Reeves, Robert Jellison

Fred and Ricky wager that they can refrain from gossiping longer than their wives.

**25**    Pioneer Women                                    March 31, 1952
**Writers:** Jess Oppenheimer, Madelyn Pugh, Bob Carroll, Jr.
**Director:** Marc Daniels
**Guest Stars:** Florence Bates, Ruth Perrott

Fred and Ricky challenge their wives to a contest to see who can survive the longest without modern conveniences.

One of the series' most memorable sight gags results when Lucy unwittingly adds too much yeast to her bread dough, and the gargantuan loaf practically fills the kitchen. It doesn't take a psychologist to interpret the symbolism of a twelve-foot loaf of bread that suddenly emerges from a hot oven to pin a housewife to the sink. Even disregarding the hilarious Freudian connotation, the scene makes us laugh because the unexpected sight gag meshes perfectly with the logic of the situation as it offers a wry commentary on the contemporary domestic condition.

**26**    The Marriage License                          April 7, 1952
   **Writers:** Jess Oppenheimer, Madelyn Pugh, Bob Carroll, Jr.
   **Director:** Marc Daniels
   **Guest Stars:** Elizabeth Patterson, Irving Bacon

When she finds out that their marriage license is not legally binding, Lucy insists that Ricky reenact their entire courtship.

In later episodes, Elizabeth Patterson would portray Little Ricky's
baby-sitter, Mrs. Trumbull.


**27**    The Kleptomaniac                            April 14, 1952
   **Writers:** Jess Oppenheimer, Madelyn Pugh, Bob Carroll, Jr.
   **Director:** Marc Daniels
   **Guest Star:** Joseph Kearns

Ricky suspects Lucy is a kleptomaniac after he uncovers a stash
of goods she's collected for a charity bazaar.

Veteran character actor Joseph Kearns plays Lucy's psychiatrist. Kearns
made occasional guest appearances on *Lucy*, but he would be better
known as Mr. Wilson on *Dennis the Menace*.


**28**    Cuban Pals                                  April 21, 1952
   **Writers:** Jess Oppenheimer, Madelyn Pugh, Bob Carroll, Jr.
   **Director:** Marc Daniels
   **Guest Stars:** Alberto Morin, Rita Convy, Lita Baron

Lucy is jealous of the gorgeous Latin dancer who was Ricky's first
dancing partner in Cuba.


**29**    The Freezer                                 April 28, 1952
   **Writers:** Jess Oppenheimer, Madelyn Pugh, Bob Carroll, Jr.
   **Director:** Marc Daniels
   **Guest Stars:** Frank Sully, Bennett Green, Fred Aldrich

Lucy and Ethel unwittingly set themselves up in the meat business
when they grossly overestimate the capacity of their new walk-in
freezer.

A classic *Lucy* situation. From the moment the walk-in freezer is introduced, the audience is waiting for the impetuous redhead to get herself locked in—and naturally, they aren't disappointed.

**30**    Lucy Does a TV Commercial                          May 5, 1952
      **Writers:** Jess Oppenheimer, Madelyn Pugh, Bob Carroll, Jr.
      **Director:** Marc Daniels
      **Guest Stars:** Ross Elliott, Jerry Hausner

Lucy is the TV pitchwoman for Vitameatavegamin, a cure-all
tonic that packs a kick—since it's twenty-three percent alcohol!

The sequence where Lucy rehearses her pitch until she's absolutely
bombed offers a rich example of her character's fundamental appeal—
her recklessness always leads to disaster, but she's invariably the one
who suffers most. And Lucy suffers brilliantly. Here, she slowly, and
believably, descends into a drunken stupor, no easy acting feat.
   The inspiration for this comic gem may well have been Red Skelton,
another movie clown who found his greatest success on CBS. In MGM's
1946 *Ziegfield Follies,* in which Lucy also appeared, Skelton did a burlesque comedy bit where he became progressively drunk as he pitched a
product called Guzzler's Gin.

**31**    The Publicity Agent                               May 12, 1952
      **Writers:** Jess Oppenheimer, Madelyn Pugh, Bob Carroll, Jr.
      **Director:** Marc Daniels
      **Guest Stars:** Peter Leeds, Bennett Green, Richard J. Reeves, Gil
Herman

As a publicity stunt, Lucy masquerades as a Middle Eastern prin-
cess who claims to be Ricky Ricardo's greatest fan.

**32**    Lucy Gets Ricky on the Radio                     May 19, 1952
      **Writers:** Jess Oppenheimer, Madelyn Pugh, Bob Carroll, Jr.
      **Director:** Marc Daniels
      **Guest Stars:** Frank Nelson, Bobby Ellis, Roy Rowan

Ricky and Lucy are ill-prepared contestants on a radio quiz show.

Frank Nelson returns as quizmaster Freddie Fillmore, an emcee who
delights in making Lucy's life miserable.

**33**    Lucy's Schedule                                  May 26, 1952
      **Writers:** Jess Oppenheimer, Madelyn Pugh, Bob Carroll, Jr.
      **Director:** Marc Daniels
      **Guest Stars:** Gale Gordon, Edith Meiser

Inspired by Ricky's efficient new boss, the boys impose a rigid
household schedule on Ethel and Lucy.

Gale Gordon makes the first of two appearances as Alvin Littlefield, the new owner of the Club Tropicana.

**34** Ricky Thinks He's Getting Bald                    June 2, 1952
**Writers:** Jess Oppenheimer, Madelyn Pugh, Bob Carroll, Jr.
**Director:** Marc Daniels
**Guest Stars:** Milton Parsons

Lucy administers a series of crackpot cures to allay Ricky's fear that he's going bald.

**35** Ricky Asks for a Raise                    June 9, 1952
**Writers:** Jess Oppenheimer, Madelyn Pugh, Bob Carroll, Jr.
**Director:** Marc Daniels
**Guest Stars:** Gale Gordon, Maurice Marsac, Edith Meiser

After Ricky's request for a raise backfires, Lucy concocts an elaborate scheme to convince the Tropicana management of her husband's immense popularity.

## 1952-53    THE SECOND SEASON

*Year-End Rating: 67.3 (1st place)*

The Ricardos and the Mertzes swing into a second year on the wave of unprecedented popularity as producer Jess Oppenheimer and writers Madelyn Pugh and Bob Carroll, Jr., seize upon their star's real-life pregnancy for some of the series' best-remembered episodes.

William Asher assumes the show's directorial reins in the second year, and Argyle Nelson takes on the duties of production manager.

**36** Job Switching                    September 15, 1952
**Writers:** Jess Oppenheimer, Madelyn Pugh, Bob Carroll, Jr.
**Director:** William Asher
**Guest Stars:** Alvin Hurwitz, Elvia Allman, Amanda Milligan

Lucy and Ethel discover they've bitten off more than they can chew after they take assembly-line jobs at a candy factory.

The memorable sequence where Lucy and Ethel unsuccessfully cope with a relentless conveyor belt is a comic gem—reminiscent of Chaplin's bout with technology in *Modern Times,* and just as funny.

**37**   The Saxophone                         September 22, 1952
**Writers:** Jess Oppenheimer, Madelyn Pugh, Bob Carroll, Jr.
**Director:** Marc Daniels
**Guest Stars:** Herb Vigran, Charles Victor

Lucy auditions for Ricky's orchestra, despite a saxophone repertoire that consists of but a single tune.

**38**   The Anniversary Present                September 29, 1952
**Writers:** Jess Oppenheimer, Madelyn Pugh, Bob Carroll, Jr.
**Director:** Marc Daniels
**Guest Stars:** Gloria Blondell, Herb Vigran

Disguised as house painters, Lucy and Ethel spy on a neighbor
they suspect is having an affair with Ricky.

**39**   The Handcuffs                          October 6, 1952
**Writers:** Jess Oppenheimer, Madelyn Pugh, Bob Carroll, Jr.
**Director:** Marc Daniels
**Guest Stars:** Paul Dubov, Will Wright

Ricky finds himself handcuffed to Lucy on the eve of his appearance on a gala television special.

**40**   The Operetta                           October 13, 1952
**Writers:** Jess Oppenheimer, Madelyn Pugh, Bob Carroll, Jr.
**Director:** Marc Daniels
**Guest Star:** Myra Marsh

After they're elected to stage the big musicale for their women's
club, Lucy and Ethel attempt to save royalty expenses by writing
their own operetta.

**41**   Vacation from Marriage                 October 27, 1952
**Writers:** Jess Oppenheimer, Madelyn Pugh, Bob Carroll, Jr.
**Director:** William Asher

In an effort to invigorate their routine married lives, the Mertzes
and Ricardos each embark on week-long separations.

William Asher signed on as the regular *Lucy* director with this episode, a role he would become identified with for most of the show's long
run. He later produced and directed *Bewitched*, the long-running sitcom
that starred his wife, Elizabeth Montgomery.

**42**   The Courtroom                    November 10, 1952
**Writers:** Jess Oppenheimer, Madelyn Pugh, Bob Carroll, Jr.
**Director:** William Asher
**Guest Stars:** Moroni Olsen, Harry Bartell, Robert B. Williams

Fred and Ethel take the Ricardos to court to settle a petty squabble over a broken television set.

**43**   Redecorating                    November 24, 1952
**Writers:** Jess Oppenheimer, Madelyn Pugh, Bob Carroll, Jr.
**Director:** William Asher
**Guest Star:** Hans Conried

Convinced that she's won a home-furnishings contest, Lucy enlists Ethel's help in redecorating her apartment.

**44**   Ricky Loses His Voice                    December 1, 1952
**Writers:** Jess Oppenheimer, Madelyn Pugh, Bob Carroll, Jr.
**Director:** William Asher
**Guest Stars:** Arthur Q. Bryan, Hazel Pierce, Barbara Pepper

Lucy and the Mertzes stage a vaudeville burlesque show at the Tropicana while Ricky's bedridden with a case of laryngitis.

**45**   Lucy is Enceinte                    December 8, 1952
**Writers:** Jess Oppenheimer, Madelyn Pugh, Bob Carroll, Jr.
**Director:** William Asher
**Guest Stars:** William R. Hamel, Richard J. Reeves

Lucy is bursting with the news that she's going to have a baby, but she finds it impossible to get Ricky alone so that she can tell him.

When Lucille Ball announced that she was pregnant at the close of the first season, the writers wisely worked her blessed event into the second-year continuity. This inspiration allowed the actress to appear on the show throughout most of her pregnancy, while it provided the writers with a raft of fresh storylines.

Today, it's hard to imagine what a stir was created by Lucy's 1952 pregnancy, but CBS and her sponsor balked loudly at the idea of depicting a pregnant mother on network television. After protracted discussions that were probably funnier than anything Carroll and Pugh could've thought up, the show's producers reached a compromise with the nervous broadcasters. They would not use the word pregnant in any of the episodes—and for good measure, prominent members of the clergy would be allowed to screen all the finished scripts that dealt with the stork's impending arrival.

**46** Pregnant Women are Unpredictable     December 15, 1952
**Writers:** Jess Oppenheimer, Madelyn Pugh, Bob Carroll, Jr.
**Director:** William Asher

Lucy begins to feel unloved and overlooked after Ricky makes a big fuss over naming the baby.

**47** Lucy's Show-Biz Swan Song     December 22, 1952
**Writers:** Jess Oppenheimer, Madelyn Pugh, Bob Carroll, Jr.
**Director:** William Asher
**Guest Stars:** Jerry Hausner, Pepito the Clown

Lucy schemes to become the fourth member of Ricky's barbershop quartet.

**48** Lucy Hires an English Tutor     December 29, 1952
**Writers:** Jess Oppenheimer, Madelyn Pugh, Bob Carroll, Jr.
**Director:** William Asher
**Guest Star:** Hans Conried

Lucy enlists the aid of a diction expert to coach the Mertzes and Ricardos in proper English usage so that they'll set a good example for the baby.

**49** Ricky Has Labor Pains     January 5, 1953
**Writers:** Jess Oppenheimer, Madelyn Pugh, Bob Carroll, Jr.
**Director:** William Asher
**Guest Stars:** Louis D. Merrill, Jerry Hausner

Lucy's afraid Ricky might be growing jealous of the baby after he begins to suffer psychosomatic morning sickness.

**50** Lucy Becomes a Sculptress     January 12, 1953
**Writers:** Jess Oppenheimer, Madelyn Pugh, Bob Carroll, Jr.
**Director:** William Asher
**Guest Stars:** Shepard Menken, Leon Belasco, Paul Harvey

In her continued efforts to bring culture into the Ricardo home, Lucy tries her hand at sculpting.

**51**    Lucy Goes to the Hospital                    January 19, 1953
  **Writers:** Jess Oppenheimer, Madelyn Pugh, Bob Carroll, Jr.
  **Director:** William Asher
  **Guest Stars:** Charles Lane, Adele Longmire, Ralph Montgomery, Peggy Rea

Despite careful rehearsal, Fred, Ethel, and Ricky unleash chaos as they try to get Lucy to the maternity ward when the great moment arrives.

Desi Arnaz, Jr., was born on the day this show first aired, a happy coincidence that helped make this episode the highest-rated program of its day.

**52**    Sales Resistance                    January 26, 1953
  **Writers:** Jess Oppenheimer, Madelyn Pugh, Bob Carroll, Jr.
  **Director:** William Asher
  **Guest Stars:** Sheldon Leonard, Verna Felton

Lucy is unable to fend off a persuasive salesman and gets stuck with an overpriced vacuum cleaner, which she then tries to palm off on a neighbor.

Sheldon Leonard was well known for playing Damon Runyonesque types in countless films and TV appearances, but he would achieve even greater success in partnership with Danny Thomas as one of the most successful sitcom producers of the fifties and sixties.

**53**    The Inferiority Complex                    February 2, 1953
  **Writers:** Jess Oppenheimer, Madelyn Pugh, Bob Carroll, Jr.
  **Director:** William Asher
  **Guest Star:** Gerald Mohr

Ricky objects when a handsome psychiatrist attempts to bolster Lucy's sagging confidence with a particularly strong dose of flattery.

**54**    The Club Election                    February 16, 1953
  **Writers:** Jess Oppenheimer, Madelyn Pugh, Bob Carroll, Jr.
  **Director:** William Asher
  **Guest Stars:** Lurene Tuttle, Ida Moore, Doris Singleton

It's a close race when Lucy and Ethel both vie for the presidency of their women's club.

**55**   The Black Eye                             March 9, 1953
**Writers:** Jess Oppenheimer, Madelyn Pugh, Bob Carroll, Jr.
**Director:** William Asher
**Guest Star:** Bennett Green

Ricky sets off a comedy of errors when he accidentally gives Lucy
a black eye.

**56**   Lucy Changes Her Mind                     March 30, 1953
**Writers:** Jess Oppenheimer, Madelyn Pugh, Bob Carroll, Jr.
**Director:** William Asher
**Guest Stars:** Frank Nelson, Phil Arnold

Lucy attempts to make Ricky jealous when she pays a visit to an
old boyfriend who's gone into the fur trade.

**57**   No Children Allowed                       April 20, 1953
**Writers:** Jess Oppenheimer, Madelyn Pugh, Bob Carroll, Jr.
**Director:** William Asher
**Guest Star:** Elizabeth Patterson

Ethel defends the Ricardos after another tenant complains about
the baby's crying—and then won't let them forget it.

The question must've occurred to the writers the moment Lucy announced her pregnancy—what would they do with the baby when Lucy
Ricardo had to go off to stomp grapes or climb the side of a building
somewhere? The answer would be Mrs. Trumbull, Little Ricky's all-purpose baby-sitter, introduced as an irate neighbor in this episode.

**58**   Lucy Hires a Maid                         April 27, 1953
**Writers:** Jess Oppenheimer, Madelyn Pugh, Bob Carroll, Jr.
**Director:** William Asher
**Guest Star:** Verna Felton

The Ricardos regret hiring a domineering domestic after she takes
charge of the entire household.

**59**   The Indian Show                           May 4, 1953
**Writers:** Jess Oppenheimer, Madelyn Pugh, Bob Carroll, Jr.
**Director:** William Asher
**Guest Stars:** Carol Richards, Jerry Hausner

Lucy is determined to don a feathered headdress and join Ricky's
act when he stages an Indian number at the Tropicana.

**60**   Lucy's Last Birthday                          May 11, 1953
**Writers:** Jess Oppenheimer, Madelyn Pugh, Bob Carroll, Jr.
**Director:** William Asher
**Guest Stars:** Jerry Hausner, Elizabeth Patterson

Lucy is convinced she hasn't a friend in all the world after Ricky and the Mertzes apparently forget her birthday.

At Lucy's party, Ricky surprises her by singing the *I Love Lucy* theme song, with lyrics written especially for this episode by Harold Adamson.

**61**   The Ricardos Change Apartments              May 18, 1953
**Writers:** Jess Oppenheimer, Madelyn Pugh, Bob Carroll, Jr.
**Director:** William Asher
**Guest Star:** Norma Varden

Yearning for more space for the baby's nursery, the Ricardos move to a larger apartment.

**62**   Lucy the Matchmaker                          May 25, 1953
**Writers:** Jess Oppenheimer, Madelyn Pugh, Bob Carroll, Jr.
**Director:** William Asher
**Guest Stars:** Hal March, Doris Singleton, Phil Arnold

Lucy tries to fix up one of her friends with a handsome lingerie salesman she meets at the Mertzes.

**63**   Lucy Wants New Furniture                      June 1, 1953
**Writers:** Jess Oppenheimer, Madelyn Pugh, Bob Carroll, Jr.
**Director:** William Asher

Lucy buys new living-room furniture and then hides it in the kitchen until she works up the nerve to tell Ricky how much it cost.

**64**   The Camping Trip                              June 8, 1953
**Writers:** Jess Oppenheimer, Madelyn Pugh, Bob Carroll, Jr.
**Director:** William Asher
**Guest Star:** Jerry Hausner

Ethel and Lucy plot to outshine their husbands when they tag along on a weekend hunting trip.

**65**   Ricky and Fred Are TV Fans                        June 22, 1953
**Writers:** Jess Oppenheimer, Madelyn Pugh, Bob Carroll, Jr.
**Director:** William Asher
**Guest Stars:** Larry Dobkin, Allen Jenkins, Frank Nelson

After their husbands abandon them for TV's Wednesday-night fights, Lucy and Ethel attempt to sabotage the broadcast from the rooftop antenna.

**66**   Never Do Business With Friends                    June 29, 1953
**Writers:** Jess Oppenheimer, Madelyn Pugh, Bob Carroll, Jr.
**Director:** William Asher
**Guest Stars:** Herb Vigran, Elizabeth Patterson

Lucy and Ricky sell their old washing machine to Fred and Ethel just before it breaks down, igniting a battle royal between the Mertzes and the Ricardos.

This dispute, like so many others, springs from Fred's incredible miserliness, one of the curmudgeon's more durable traits. Frawley invested his character with an uncanny believability, though he was certainly no Method actor. "He never knew what the story was about," Lucy confessed some years later. "He just tore out the pages he was supposed to do! But he was a funny, irascible, wonderful man whom the writers wrote for perfectly."

## 1953-54   THE THIRD SEASON

*Year-End Rating: 58.8 (1st place)*

Producer Jess Oppenheimer heads a creative staff that remains largely unchanged as the series moves into a third season of uninterrupted critical and popular success.

**67**   Ricky's Life Story                                October 5, 1953
**Writers:** Jess Oppenheimer, Madelyn Pugh, Bob Carroll, Jr.
**Director:** William Asher
**Guest Star:** Louis Nicoletti

*Life* magazine does a big story on Ricky, but leaves Lucy out of the picture.

**68**    The Girls Go Into Business                October 12, 1953
**Writers:** Jess Oppenheimer, Madelyn Pugh, Bob Carroll, Jr.
**Director:** William Asher
**Guest Stars:** Mabel Paige, Emory Parnell

Lucy and Ethel figure to make a killing when they buy a dress shop, but revise their optimistic projections when they sell only five outfits—to each other.

**69**    Lucy and Ethel Buy the Same Dress        October 19, 1953
**Writers:** Jess Oppenheimer, Madelyn Pugh, Bob Carroll, Jr.
**Director:** William Asher
**Guest Stars:** Shirley Mitchell, Doris Singleton

Lucy and Ethel are horrified to discover that they both plan to wear the same outfit on a TV talent show.

**70**    Equal Rights                             October 26, 1953
**Writers:** Jess Oppenheimer, Madelyn Pugh, Bob Carroll, Jr.
**Director:** William Asher
**Guest Stars:** Lawrence Dobkin, Fred Aldrich, Louis A. Nicoletti

Lucy and Ethel demand equal rights, but their protest backfires when Fred and Ricky stick them with an equal portion of the dinner check at a restaurant.

**71**    Baby Pictures                            November 2, 1953
**Writers:** Jess Oppenheimer, Madelyn Pugh, Bob Carroll, Jr.
**Director:** William Asher
**Guest Stars:** Doris Singleton, Hy Averback

Caroline and Charlie Appleby arouse Lucy's competitive instincts when they brag endlessly about their son, Stevie, who was born the same day as Little Ricky.

The Applebys seem well suited to provide the writers with fresh plot springboards: They have a boy the same age as Little Ricky; Charlie runs a local TV station; and Caroline is involved with the wives in the women's club. Oddly, Charlie Appleby rarely figures in future stories, and the character is soon dropped. But his wife, Caroline, would prove a frequent and worthy foil for Lucy and Ethel during this and ensuing seasons.

**72    Lucy Tells the Truth**                    November 9, 1953
  **Writers:** Jess Oppenheimer, Madelyn Pugh, Bob Carroll, Jr.
  **Director:** William Asher
  **Guest Stars:** Doris Singleton, Shirley Mitchell, Charles Lane,
  Mario Siletti

Lucy alienates practically everyone she knows when she attempts
to go twenty-four hours without telling a single lie.

**73    The French Revue**                    November 16, 1953
  **Writers:** Jess Oppenheimer, Madelyn Pugh, Bob Carroll, Jr.
  **Director:** William Asher
  **Guest Stars:** Alberto Morin, Louis A. Nicoletti

Lucy hires a French waiter to teach her the language after Ricky
announces his plans to stage a French revue at the club.

**74    Redecorating the Mertzes' Apartment**    November 23, 1953
  **Writers:** Jess Oppenheimer, Madelyn Pugh, Bob Carroll, Jr.
  **Director:** William Asher

Lucy wreaks her usual quotient of disaster when she organizes a
painting party to redecorate the Mertzes' apartment.

**75    Too Many Crooks**                    November 30, 1953
  **Writers:** Jess Oppenheimer, Madelyn Pugh, Bob Carroll, Jr.
  **Director:** William Asher
  **Guest Stars:** Elizabeth Patterson, Allen Jenkins, Alice Wills

Lucy and Ethel mistake each other for Madame X, the neighborhood cat burglar.

No matter how ludicrous the situation, according to head writer Jess
Oppenheimer, logic remained the key to the comedy of *I Love Lucy*. "I
insisted on starting every show with a very basic, utterly believable
premise," the producer explained to broadcast historian Alex C.
Mackenzie. "If you motivate your audience in a series of small steps,
you can go to absolute heights."

**76**    Changing the Boys' Wardrobe                December 7, 1953
**Writers:** Jess Oppenheimer, Madelyn Pugh, Bob Carroll, Jr.
**Director:** William Asher
**Guest Stars:** Oliver Blake, Alberto Calderone, Jerry Hausner,
Lee Millar

Indignant over their husbands' utter disregard for fashion, Lucy
and Ethel donate the boys' cherished old clothes to a second-
hand store.

**77**    Lucy Has Her Eyes Examined               December 14, 1953
**Writers:** Jess Oppenheimer, Madelyn Pugh, Bob Carroll, Jr.
**Director:** William Asher
**Guest Stars:** Arthur Walsh, Dayton Lummis, Shepard Menken

Lucy valiantly auditions for the part of a jitterbugging coed, even
though eyedrops have left her temporarily blind.

**78**    Ricky's Old Girlfriend                   December 21, 1953
**Writers:** Jess Oppenheimer, Madelyn Pugh, Bob Carroll, Jr.
**Director:** William Asher
**Guest Stars:** Rosa Turich, Lillian Molieri, Jerry Hausner

Ricky is more surprised than anyone when the old flame he invented to make Lucy jealous suddenly arrives in New York.

**79**    The Million-Dollar Idea                   January 11, 1954
**Writers:** Jess Oppenheimer, Madelyn Pugh, Bob Carroll, Jr.
**Director:** William Asher
**Guest Star:** Frank Nelson

Lucy and Ethel are convinced that they've finally struck it rich
when they're deluged with orders for homemade salad dressing.

**80**    Ricky Minds the Baby                      January 18, 1954
**Writers:** Jess Oppenheimer, Madelyn Pugh, Bob Carroll, Jr.
**Director:** William Asher

Concerned that Ricky isn't spending enough time with his son,
Lucy leaves the new father to baby-sit Little Ricky.

**81**   The Charm School                          January 25, 1954
**Writers:** Jess Oppenheimer, Madelyn Pugh, Bob Carroll, Jr.
**Director:** William Asher
**Guest Stars:** Tyler McVey, Vivi Janiss, Natalie Schafer,
Maury Hill

Lucy and Ethel enroll in charm school after an attractive young
bombshell overwhelms their husbands.

Natalie Schafer later found considerable recognition when she was
stranded with six other castaways on *Gilligan's Island* in the 1960s.

**82**   Sentimental Anniversary                   February 1, 1954
**Writers:** Jess Oppenheimer, Madelyn Pugh, Bob Carroll, Jr.
**Director:** William Asher
**Guest Stars:** Barbara Pepper, Bennett Green, Hazel Pierce

Lucy and Ricky plan to commemorate their anniversary with a romantic, candlelight supper, but the Mertzes have other ideas.

**83**   Fan Magazine Interview                    February 8, 1954
**Writers:** Jess Oppenheimer, Madelyn Pugh, Bob Carroll, Jr.
**Director:** William Asher
**Guest Stars:** Joan Banks, Jerry Hausner, Kathryn Card

The Ricardos and Mertzes put on airs for the benefit of a reporter
who arrives to do a magazine piece on a day in the life of Ricky
Ricardo.

**84**   Oil Wells                                 February 15, 1954
**Writers:** Jess Oppenheimer, Madelyn Pugh, Bob Carroll, Jr.
**Director:** William Asher
**Guest Stars:** Harry Cheshire, Ken Christy, Sandra Gould

The Ricardos and Mertzes buy shares in an oil well but have second thoughts when they suspect they've been swindled.

**85**   Ricky Loses His Temper                    February 22, 1954
**Writers:** Jess Oppenheimer, Madelyn Pugh, Bob Carroll, Jr.
**Director:** William Asher
**Guest Stars:** Madge Blake, Byron Kane, Max Terhune

To win a $50 bet, Lucy has to force Ricky to blow his top within
twenty-four hours.

**86**    Home Movies                                    March 1, 1954
**Writers:** Jess Oppenheimer, Madelyn Pugh, Bob Carroll, Jr.
**Director:** William Asher
**Guest Star:** Stanley Farrar

Lucy and the Mertzes create an unintentional comedy when they splice scenes from their home movies into the workprint of Ricky's new TV pilot.

**87**    Bonus Bucks                                    March 8, 1954
**Writers:** Jess Oppenheimer, Madelyn Pugh, Bob Carroll, Jr.
**Director:** William Asher
**Guest Stars:** Tony Michaels, Don Garner, Frank Jacquet

Lucy loses a lucky buck that's worth $300 in a newspaper contest and then sets off on a mad chase as she tracks the bill across the city.

**88**    Ricky's Hawaiian Vacation                      March 22, 1954
**Writers:** Jess Oppenheimer, Madelyn Pugh, Bob Carroll, Jr.
**Director:** William Asher
**Guest Star:** Frank Nelson

Lucy once again suffers abuse from radio quizmaster Freddie Fillmore when she attempts to qualify for an all-expenses-paid trip to Hawaii.

**89**    Lucy Is Envious                                March 29, 1954
**Writers:** Jess Oppenheimer, Madelyn Pugh, Bob Carroll, Jr.
**Director:** William Asher
**Guest Stars:** Mary Jane Croft, Herb Vigran, Dick Elliott, Kay Wiley

Lucy tries to earn $500 to cover an impossibly large charity pledge by performing a dangerous publicity stunt atop the Empire State Building.

Mary Jane Croft appears as Lucy's society friend, Cynthia Harcourt—a role she would reprise when she played Lucy's sidekick, under various names, on later variations of the star's sitcoms over the next two decades.

**90**   Lucy Writes a Novel                              April 5, 1954
  **Writers:** Jess Oppenheimer, Madelyn Pugh, Bob Carroll, Jr.
  **Director:** William Asher
  **Guest Stars:** Pierre Watkin, Dayton Lummis

Ricky, Fred, and Ethel are less than flattered to find themselves depicted in Lucy's novel—a *roman à clef* about life around the Ricardo household.

**91**   Lucy's Club Dance                               April 12, 1954
  **Writers:** Jess Oppenheimer, Madelyn Pugh, Bob Carroll, Jr.
  **Director:** William Asher
  **Guest Stars:** Shirley Mitchell, Doris Singleton

Ricky is drafted into service to conduct the would-be musicians in Lucy's all-girl band.

**92**   The Black Wig                                   April 19, 1954
  **Writers:** Jess Oppenheimer, Madelyn Pugh, Bob Carroll, Jr.
  **Director:** William Asher
  **Guest Stars:** Eva McVeagh, Douglas Evans

Ethel and Lucy test their husbands' fidelity by disguising themselves as a pair of exotic foreigners.

Another sturdy plot line enters the lexicon of situation comedy when Lucy discovers the invigorating effect a different-colored coiffure can have on a jaded marriage. The tactic would be used by countless sitcom wives, from Laura Petrie on *The Dick Van Dyke Show* to Gloria Stivic, who donned a black wig of her own on *All in the Family* some twenty years later.

**93**   The Diner                                       April 26, 1954
  **Writers:** Jess Oppenheimer, Madelyn Pugh, Bob Carroll, Jr.
  **Director:** William Asher
  **Guest Stars:** James Burke, Fred Sherman, Don Garner

The Mertzes and Ricardos pool their finances to buy a diner, but soon find themselves competing with each other for a single customer.

**94**    Tennessee Ernie Visits                    May 3, 1954
**Writers:** Jess Oppenheimer, Madelyn Pugh, Bob Carroll, Jr.
**Director:** William Asher
**Guest Star:** Tennessee Ernie Ford

The Ricardos play reluctant hosts to Cousin Ernest Ford, a backwoods rube with a powerful yen for big-city life.

**95**    Tennessee Ernie Hangs On                    May 10, 1954
**Writers:** Jess Oppenheimer, Madelyn Pugh, Bob Carroll, Jr.
**Director:** William Asher
**Guest Star:** Tennessee Ernie Ford

The Ricardos' schemes to rid themselves of their unwanted houseguest backfire, and they end up performing with Cousin Ernie on a hayseed amateur hour.

This two-parter, featuring the popular hillbilly performer Tennessee Ernie Ford, scored ratings that were far above average, a fact that was not lost on the network or the producers. From that moment on, special guest stars became an integral part of the Lucy formula.

**96**    The Golf Game                    May 17, 1954
**Writers:** Jess Oppenheimer, Madelyn Pugh, Bob Carroll, Jr.
**Director:** William Asher
**Guest Stars:** Jimmy Demaret, George Pirrone

To discourage Lucy and Ethel from tagging along to the golf course, Fred and Ricky conspire to make their wives' day on the green as difficult as possible.

**97**    The Sublease                    May 24, 1954
**Writers:** Jess Oppenheimer, Madelyn Pugh, Bob Carroll, Jr.
**Director:** William Asher
**Guest Stars:** Virginia Brissac, Jay Novello

Skinflint Fred foils Ricky's efforts to sublease the Ricardo apartment for the summer after he discovers that his tenants will make a small profit.

# 1954-55    THE FOURTH SEASON

*Year-End Rating: 49.3 (1st place)*

It's westward ho, Ricardo, when Ricky lands a movie role and moves to California with Lucy and the Mertzes—a slant that provides fresh inspiration for producer Jess Oppenheimer and writers Madelyn Pugh and Bob Carroll, Jr., as they embark on their fourth consecutive year as Lucy's preeminent scripters. William Asher once again directs every episode in the season.

**98**   The Business Manager                    October 4, 1954
**Writers:** Jess Oppenheimer, Madelyn Pugh, Bob Carroll, Jr.
**Director:** William Asher
**Guest Stars:** Charles Lane, Elizabeth Patterson

Lucy invigorates her sagging household finances with a novel cash-flow system: She buys the neighbors' groceries on credit and keeps the cash.

Charles Lane plays Ricky's accountant in one of his frequent TV guest spots. His stint as Homer Bedloe, the villain of Paul Henning's *Petticoat Junction*, would assure the actor's lasting fame—for better or worse.

**99**   Mertz and Kurtz                         October 11, 1954
**Writers:** Jess Oppenheimer, Madelyn Pugh, Bob Carroll, Jr.
**Director:** William Asher
**Guest Stars:** Charles Winninger, Stephen Wootton

After trying to impress an old vaudeville chum with his prosperity, Fred discovers that his former partner is no better off than he and Ethel.

**100**   Lucy Cries Wolf                        October 18, 1954
**Writers:** Jess Oppenheimer, Madelyn Pugh, Bob Carroll, Jr.
**Director:** William Asher
**Guest Stars:** Beppy DeVries, Fred Aldrich, Louis A. Nicoletti

Lucy tests Ricky's devotion by calling him home from the club for a series of phony emergencies.

**101**   The Matchmaker                    October 25, 1954
   **Writers:** Jess Oppenheimer, Madelyn Pugh, Bob Carroll, Jr.
   **Director:** William Asher
   **Guest Stars:** Sarah Selby, Milton Frome

Lucy hopes to inspire an engaged couple to finally tie the knot when she invites them to share an evening of domestic bliss at the Ricardos.


**102**   Ricky's Movie Offer                    November 8, 1954
   **Writers:** Jess Oppenheimer, Madelyn Pugh, Bob Carroll, Jr.
   **Director:** William Asher
   **Guest Stars:** Frank Nelson, James Dobson, Elizabeth Patterson

The entire neighborhood shows up to audition after word leaks out that a Hollywood talent scout plans to pay a call on Ricky.


**103**  Ricky's Screen Test                    November 15, 1954
   **Writers:** Jess Oppenheimer, Madelyn Pugh, Bob Carroll, Jr.
   **Director:** William Asher
   **Guest Stars:** Clinton Sundberg, Ray Kellogg

Lucy is assigned a bit role in Ricky's Hollywood screen test—but there's no such thing as a small part for this actress, and she sets out to prove it.


**104**   Lucy's Mother-In-Law                    November 22, 1954
   **Writers:** Jess Oppenheimer, Madelyn Pugh, Bob Carroll, Jr.
   **Director:** William Asher
   **Guest Stars:** Mary Emery, Fortunio Bonanova

The arrival of Ricky's mother spells trouble in two languages when Lucy tries to make her Cuban mother-in-law at home in New York City.

Lucy so earnestly wants to impress Mother Ricardo with her command of Spanish that she plants a bilingual translator in the kitchen to coach her by secret microphone. Of course the ruse backfires, but—as was often the case—Lucy's touching emotional investment in the harebrained scheme makes us laugh even harder at her pathetic attempt to fake her way through the conversation.

**105**   Ethel's Birthday                          November 29, 1954
   **Writers:** Jess Oppenheimer, Madelyn Pugh, Bob Carroll, Jr.
   **Director:** William Asher

Fred and Ricky plan to take the girls out for Ethel's birthday, even
though the wives aren't speaking to each other.

**106**   Ricky's Contract                          December 6, 1954
   **Writers:** Jess Oppenheimer, Madelyn Pugh, Bob Carroll, Jr.
   **Director:** William Asher

After weeks of waiting by the phone, Ricky finally gets the fateful summons to Hollywood, and the great trip begins.

**107**   Getting Ready                             December 13, 1954
   **Writers:** Jess Oppenheimer, Madelyn Pugh, Bob Carroll, Jr.
   **Director:** William Asher

Ricky invites the Mertzes to join them on the drive to Hollywood,
and then makes the mistake of letting Fred pick out the car.

**108**   Lucy Learns to Drive                        January 3, 1955
   **Writers:** Jess Oppenheimer, Madelyn Pugh, Bob Carroll, Jr.
   **Director:** William Asher

Lucy has barely learned the rules of the road when she decides
to teach Ethel to drive—behind the wheel of Ricky's brand-new
convertible!

**109**   California, Here We Come!                    January 10, 1955
   **Writers:** Jess Oppenheimer, Madelyn Pugh, Bob Carroll, Jr.
   **Director:** William Asher
   **Guest Stars:** Kathryn Card, Elizabeth Patterson

When the departing travelers encounter a flurry of last-minute
complications, Ricky begins to wonder if they'll ever make it out
of their parking space.

Kathryn Card joins the cast as Lucy's mother, Mrs. McGillicuddy, in
this finely structured sitcom episode. Like most of the best *Lucy* scripts,
a perfectly ordinary situation—packing the family car—soon blossoms,
in small, logical steps, to heights of absurdity. And as always, the complications are ironed out by the end of the half hour as the foursome
drive off singing "California, Here I Come" in the euphoric finale.

**110**   First Stop                           January 17, 1955
   **Writers:** Jess Oppenheimer, Madelyn Pugh, Bob Carroll, Jr.
   **Director:** William Asher
   **Guest Star:** Olin Howlin

At the end of their first day, the intrepid travelers are bilked by a canny roadside innkeeper.


**111**   Tennessee Bound                      January 24, 1955
   **Writers:** Jess Oppenheimer, Madelyn Pugh, Bob Carroll, Jr.
   **Director:** William Asher
   **Guest Stars:** Tennessee Ernie Ford, Will Wright, Rosalyn and Marilyn Borden

The tourists are glad to see their old friend Cousin Ernie after a backwoods sheriff snags them in a speed trap.


**112**   Ethel's Hometown                     January 31, 1955
   **Writers:** Jess Oppenheimer, Madelyn Pugh, Bob Carroll, Jr.
   **Director:** William Asher
   **Guest Stars:** Irving Bacon, Chick Chandler

Arriving in Ethel's hometown, the gang is surprised to discover that all of Albuquerque thinks of little Ethel Mae Potter as a Hollywood-bound celebrity.

Ethel is the comic foil when Fred, Lucy, and Ricky decide to upstage the darling of Albuquerque as she performs her big comeback number, "Short'nin' Bread."


**113**   L.A. at Last                         February 7, 1955
   **Writers:** Jess Oppenheimer, Madelyn Pugh, Bob Carroll, Jr.
   **Director:** William Asher
   **Guest Stars:** William Holden, Eve Arden, Robert Jellison

Lucy makes a mess of things when she spies actor William Holden at the Brown Derby.

Eve Arden, Lucy's old cohort at RKO, takes a break from filming her own Desilu series, *Our Miss Brooks*, to make a cameo appearance.

Movie stars like Holden generally appeared on the show for minimum pay in exchange for the chance to plug their latest film before *Lucy's* vast television audience, which explains why the guest stars invariably announce their latest release in none-too-subtle tones somewhere in each episode's script. The big studios still kept an arm's distance from television as late as the mid-1950s, but that didn't prevent them from climbing into bed with TV's most popular couple when the opportunity arose.

**114**   Don Juan and the Starlets                     February 14, 1955
**Writers:** Jess Oppenheimer, Madelyn Pugh, Bob Carroll, Jr.
**Director:** William Asher
**Guest Stars:** Ross Elliot, Dolores Donlon, Beverly Thompson, Shirlee Tigge

Lucy is jealous when Ricky's studio publicist insists that he escort a bevy of beautiful starlets to a Hollywood premiere.

**115**   Lucy Gets Into Pictures                       February 21, 1955
**Writers:** Jess Oppenheimer, Madelyn Pugh, Bob Carroll, Jr.
**Director:** William Asher
**Guest Stars:** Lou Krugman, Onna Conners, Robert Jellison

Lucy makes the director's life miserable when she lands a small part as a showgirl in an MGM musical.

Lucy's burning desire to prove her talents takes on even greater urgency when Fred and Ethel—and even the hotel bellboy—all land movie roles. Of course, she milks her moment in the spotlight for all it's worth as she totters down a long staircase with an immense feathered headdress balanced atop her head.

**116**   The Fashion Show                             February 28, 1955
**Writers:** Jess Oppenheimer, Madelyn Pugh, Bob Carroll, Jr.
**Director:** William Asher
**Guest Stars:** Don Loper, Amzie Strickland

Lucy decides to get a California tan—and quickly—after she finagles her way into a celebrity wives' fashion show.

The wives of Alan Ladd, Forrest Tucker, Dean Martin, William Holden, Van Heflin, Gordon MacRae, and Richard Carlson make cameo appearances here.

**117**   The Hedda Hopper Story                    March 14, 1955
   **Writers:** Jess Oppenheimer, Madelyn Pugh, Bob Carroll, Jr.
   **Director:** William Asher
   **Guest Stars:** Hedda Hopper, Hy Averback, Kathryn Card

A studio press agent convinces Lucy and Ricky to pull a poolside
rescue stunt, hoping Ricky's mock heroics will earn a mention in
Hedda Hopper's gossip column.

**118**   Don Juan Is Shelved                       March 21, 1955
   **Writers:** Jess Oppenheimer, Madelyn Pugh, Bob Carroll, Jr.
   **Director:** William Asher
   **Guest Stars:** Kathryn Card, Robert Jellison, Phil Ober

When MGM cancels Ricky's picture, Lucy schemes to trick studio
head Dore Schary into renewing her husband's contract.

Dore Schary actually was the head of production at MGM, though
Vivian Vance's husband, Phil Ober, was called in to play him after the
executive begged off at the last minute.

**119**   Bullfight Dance                           March 28, 1955
   **Writers:** Jess Oppenheimer, Madelyn Pugh, Bob Carroll, Jr.
   **Director:** William Asher
   **Guest Stars:** Ross Elliot, Ray Kellogg

Lucy threatens to feed an exposé of Ricky Ricardo to the fan press
unless he promises her a role in his TV special.

**120**   Hollywood Anniversary                     April 4, 1955
   **Writers:** Jess Oppenheimer, Madelyn Pugh, Bob Carroll, Jr.
   **Director:** William Asher
   **Guest Stars:** Ross Elliot, Robert Jellison, Kathryn Card

Ricky surprises Lucy with a gala anniversary party at a fancy Hollywood nightclub.

**121**   Mr. and Mrs. TV Show                      April 11, 1955
   **Writers:** Jess Oppenheimer, Madelyn Pugh, Bob Carroll, Jr.
   **Director:** William Asher
   **Guest Stars:** John Litel, Lee Millar

Ricky is excited when he's offered the chance to host a TV talk
show, until he discovers that the producers expect his wife to act
as co-host.

**122**   The Star Upstairs                          April 18, 1955
**Writers:** Jess Oppenheimer, Madelyn Pugh, Bob Carroll, Jr.
**Director:** William Asher
**Guest Stars:** Cornel Wilde, Robert Jellison

Cornel Wilde is the latest object of Lucy's star-struck enthusiasm
when she discovers he's staying in the suite directly above theirs.

**123**   In Palm Springs                            April 25, 1955
**Writers:** Jess Oppenheimer, Madelyn Pugh, Bob Carroll, Jr.
**Director:** William Asher
**Guest Stars:** Rock Hudson, Kathryn Card

Lucy and Ethel meet Rock Hudson during a Palm Springs getaway
vacation.

Hudson's guest shot here marked the first time Universal Studios allowed one of their contract players to appear in a filmed teleplay. Their
resistance to such guest shots is ironic—in a few short years, their willingness to exploit the hungry market for television films would make
Universal one of the strongest studios in Hollywood.

**124**   The Dancing Star                           May 2, 1955
**Writers:** Jess Oppenheimer, Madelyn Pugh, Bob Carroll, Jr.
**Director:** William Asher
**Guest Stars:** Van Johnson, Doris Singleton

Caroline Appleby unexpectedly arrives in California to call Lucy's
bluff after the redhead brags about her friendship with film star
Van Johnson.

**125**   Harpo Marx                                 May 9, 1955
**Writers:** Jess Oppenheimer, Madelyn Pugh, Bob Carroll, Jr.
**Director:** William Asher
**Guest Stars:** Harpo Marx, Doris Singleton

Lucy's ruse to convince Caroline that the Ricardos' suite is the
hub of Hollywood's social scene is further complicated by the
unexpected arrival of Harpo Marx.

The justly lauded mirror scene, where Lucy mimes Harpo's actions
perfectly through a doorway, is an homage to a similar scene Harpo performed in the early Marx Brothers feature *Duck Soup*.

**126**   Ricky Needs an Agent                    May 16, 1955
   **Writers:** Jess Oppenheimer, Madelyn Pugh, Bob Carroll, Jr.
   **Director:** William Asher
   **Guest Stars:** Parley Baer, Helen Kleeb

Lucy masquerades as Ricky's agent, and in no time at all she negotiates him right out of a job.

**127**   The Tour                               May 30, 1955
   **Writers:** Jess Oppenheimer, Madelyn Pugh, Bob Carroll, Jr.
   **Director:** William Asher
   **Guest Stars:** Richard Widmark, Juney Ellis, Benny Rubin

Lucy is determined to snatch a souvenir grapefruit from a tree in Richard Widmark's backyard.

## 1955-56   THE FIFTH SEASON

*Year-End Rating: 46.1 (2nd place)*

The Mertzes and Ricardos travel to Europe in fifth-year episodes written once again by producer Jess Oppenheimer, Madelyn Pugh, and Bob Carroll, Jr., who welcome newcomers Bob Schiller and Bob Weiskopf to their overworked writing staff at the top of the season. And James V. Kern replaces William Asher as the show's regular director.

**128**   Lucy Visits Grauman's                October 3, 1955
   **Writers:** Jess Oppenheimer, Madelyn Pugh, Bob Carroll, Jr.,
   Bob Schiller, Bob Weiskopf
   **Director:** James V. Kern
   **Guest Stars:** Gege Pearson, Hal Gerard

Lucy cons Ethel into helping her remove a chunk of the historic sidewalk in front of Grauman's Chinese Theatre as the ultimate Hollywood souvenir.

Writers Schiller and Weiskopf had acquired a respectable résumé of sitcom assignments when they began a long association with Lucy, which would last well into the mid-1960s. The writing team eventually bridged two generations of situation comedy when they applied the skills they'd honed on *I Love Lucy* to a long run of memorable scripts for Norman Lear's *Maude* and *All in the Family* in the mid-1970s.

**129**   Lucy and John Wayne                    October 10, 1955
   **Writers:** Jess Oppenheimer, Madelyn Pugh, Bob Carroll, Jr.,
   Bob Schiller, Bob Weiskopf
   **Director:** James V. Kern
   **Guest Stars:** John Wayne, Ralph Volkie

Lucy finds out how difficult it is to refill John Wayne's boots after she destroys the star's concrete slab from Grauman's Chinese Theatre.

**130**   Lucy and the Dummy                     October 17, 1955
   **Writers:** Jess Oppenheimer, Madelyn Pugh, Bob Carroll, Jr., Bob
   Schiller, Bob Weiskopf
   **Director:** James V. Kern
   **Guest Star:** Lee Millar

Ricky declines an invitation to perform at a studio party, but Lucy volunteers her services—along with those of a stuffed "Ricky."

Lucy's inspired dance with a determined mannequin provides ample evidence of the broad physical business that writers Schiller and Weiskopf favored in their story contributions during the show's final seasons.

**131**   Ricky Sells the Car                    October 24, 1955
   **Writers:** Jess Oppenheimer, Madelyn Pugh, Bob Carroll, Jr.,
   Bob Schiller, Bob Weiskopf
   **Director:** James V. Kern
   **Guest Stars:** Donald Brodie, Bennett Green

Ricky books return passage home by rail, but the Mertzes feel abandoned when he forgets to buy their tickets as well.

**132**   The Great Train Robbery                October 31, 1955
   **Writers:** Jess Oppenheimer, Madelyn Pugh, Bob Carroll, Jr.,
   Bob Schiller, Bob Weiskopf
   **Director:** James V. Kern
   **Guest Stars:** Frank Nelson, Lou Krugman, Joseph Crehan

Lucy's quotient for confusion on the train ride home involves a flustered conductor, two jewel thieves, and one slightly abused emergency brake.

The train ride provides yet another opportunity for the systematic pandemonium that Schiller and Weiskopf reintroduced to the series.

**133** Homecoming November 7, 1955
**Writers:** Jess Oppenheimer, Madelyn Pugh, Bob Carroll, Jr.,
Bob Schiller, Bob Weiskopf
**Director:** James V. Kern
**Guest Stars:** Elvia Allman, Elizabeth Patterson

Lucy is jealous of all the attention lavished on Ricky, until finally
even she starts to believe her husband's press.

**134** The Ricardos Are Interviewed November 14, 1955
**Writers:** Jess Oppenheimer, Madelyn Pugh, Bob Carroll, Jr.,
Bob Schiller, Bob Weiskopf
**Director:** James V. Kern
**Guest Stars:** John Gallaudet, Elliot Reid

Fred and Ethel are offended when Ricky's agent suggests that he
find an apartment more befitting his celebrity status.

Latter-day viewers of *Lucy* reruns are unlikely to recognize the live
interview show that hosts the tearful reconciliation of the Ricardos and
the Mertzes as a parody of Edward R. Murrow's ground-breaking *Person
to Person*.

**135** Lucy Goes to a Rodeo November 28, 1955
**Writers:** Jess Oppenheimer, Madelyn Pugh, Bob Carroll, Jr.,
Bob Schiller, Bob Weiskopf
**Director:** James V. Kern
**Guest Stars:** Dub Taylor, John Gallaudet, Doyle O'Dell

Ricky gets roped into performing in a rodeo show with Lucy and
the Mertzes.

**136** Nursery School December 5, 1955
**Writers:** Jess Oppenheimer, Madelyn Pugh, Bob Carroll, Jr.,
Bob Schiller, Bob Weiskopf
**Director:** James V. Kern
**Guest Stars:** Olan E. Soule, Howard Hoffman, Iva Shepard

The Ricardos argue over modern child-rearing methods when
Lucy refuses to let Little Ricky attend nursery school.

**137**   Ricky's European Booking                December 12, 1955
   **Writers:** Jess Oppenheimer, Madelyn Pugh, Bob Carroll, Jr.,
   Bob Schiller, Bob Weiskopf
   **Director:** James V. Kern
   **Guest Stars:** Harry Antrim, Barney Phillips, Dorothea Wolbert

After Ricky offers Fred a job on his band's European tour, Ethel
and Lucy stage an illegal charity raffle to raise money for their
own passage.

**138**   The Passports                        December 19, 1955
   **Writers:** Jess Oppenheimer, Madelyn Pugh, Bob Carroll, Jr.,
   Bob Schiller, Bob Weiskopf
   **Director:** James V. Kern
   **Guest Stars:** Sheila Bromley, Robert Forrest, Sam Hearn

When her passport application gets bogged down in red tape,
Lucy decides to stow away in a steamer trunk all the way to
Europe.

**139**   Staten Island Ferry                      January 2, 1956
   **Writers:** Jess Oppenheimer, Madelyn Pugh, Bob Carroll, Jr.,
   Bob Schiller, Bob Weiskopf
   **Director:** James V. Kern
   **Guest Stars:** Charles Lane, Stanley Farrar

Lucy tries to cure Fred of his chronic seasickness by spending the
day with him on the Staten Island Ferry.

**140**   Bon Voyage                           January 16, 1956
   **Writers:** Jess Oppenheimer, Madelyn Pugh, Bob Carroll, Jr.,
   Bob Schiller, Bob Weiskopf
   **Director:** James V. Kern
   **Guest Stars:** Kathryn Card, Elizabeth Patterson, Tyler McVey,
   Jack Albertson

Ricky and the Mertzes are ready to set sail when Lucy misses the
boat.

Jack Albertson plays the helicopter dispatcher who gets Lucy to her
ship on time. The veteran supporting player became an unlikely sitcom
star when he was cast opposite comic Freddie Prinze in the 1974 NBC
series *Chico and the Man*.

**141**   Second Honeymoon                    January 23, 1956
   **Writers:** Jess Oppenheimer, Madelyn Pugh, Bob Carroll, Jr.,
   Bob Schiller, Bob Weiskopf
   **Director:** James V. Kern
   **Guest Stars:** Tyler McVey, Harvey Grant, Virginia Barbour, Louis
   A. Nicoletti

Neptune plays Cupid when the sea air rekindles a romantic spark
in the Mertzes, and Lucy's jealous of the ardor.

The Mertzes cooing like lovebirds was a rare sight indeed. Frawley's
offscreen dislike for his TV wife was long a well-kept secret, but in *The "I
Love Lucy" Book*, Bart Andrews reveals that the two actors couldn't stand
each other. Frawley referred to his co-star as an "old sack of doorknobs,"
and Vivian Vance was convinced that the sixty-four-year-old actor
would've been more appropriately cast as her father than her husband.
The offscreen animosity certainly never harmed their performances—in
fact, it may have accounted for their utter believability as a couple who've
been married for twenty-five years.

**142**   Lucy Meets the Queen                    January 30, 1956
   **Writers:** Jess Oppenheimer, Madelyn Pugh, Bob Carroll, Jr.,
   Bob Schiller, Bob Weiskopf
   **Director:** James V. Kern
   **Guest Stars:** Sam Edwards, Robert Shafter, Nancy Kulp

Lucy works her way into Ricky's routine at the London Palladium
in order to gain an audience with the queen.

**143**   The Fox Hunt                    February 6, 1956
   **Writers:** Jess Oppenheimer, Madelyn Pugh, Bob Carroll, Jr.,
   Bob Schiller, Bob Weiskopf
   **Director:** James V. Kern
   **Guest Stars:** Walter Kingsford, Hilary Brooke, Trevor Ward

Lucy's plans for a pleasant weekend in the country are dashed
when she becomes a reluctant participant in a fox hunt.

**144**   Lucy Goes to Scotland                        February 20, 1956
   **Writers:** Jess Oppenheimer, Madelyn Pugh, Bob Carroll, Jr.,
   Bob Schiller, Bob Weiskopf
   **Director:** James V. Kern
   **Guest Stars:** Larry Orenstein, John Gustafson, Norma Zimmer

Ricky, Fred, and Ethel each assume mythic roles when Lucy dreams of visiting her ancestral stomping grounds in Scotland.

**145**   Paris at Last                              February 27, 1956
   **Writers:** Jess Oppenheimer, Madelyn Pugh, Bob Carroll, Jr.,
   Bob Schiller, Bob Weiskopf
   **Director:** James V. Kern
   **Guest Stars:** Lawrence Dobkin, Shepard Menken, Fritz Feld,
   Maurice Marsac

Lucy inflicts more havoc on the streets of Paris than Marie Antoinette, and almost meets the same fate when she makes an unscheduled stop at the Bastille.

**146**   Lucy Meets Charles Boyer                      March 5, 1956
   **Writers:** Jess Oppenheimer, Madelyn Pugh, Bob Carroll, Jr.,
   Bob Schiller, Bob Weiskopf
   **Director:** James V. Kern
   **Guest Stars:** Charles Boyer, Jack Chefe

Lucy and Ethel spot Charles Boyer at a sidewalk café, and before long he finds himself mixed up in the usual shenanigans.

**147**   Lucy Gets a Paris Gown                       March 19, 1956
   **Writers:** Jess Oppenheimer, Madelyn Pugh, Bob Carroll, Jr.,
   Bob Schiller, Bob Weiskopf
   **Director:** James V. Kern
   **Guest Star:** John Bliefer

Lucy and Ethel threaten a hunger strike to extort Paris designer gowns from their practical husbands.

**148**   Lucy in the Swiss Alps                    March 26, 1956
   **Writers:** Jess Oppenheimer, Madelyn Pugh, Bob Carroll, Jr.,
   Bob Schiller, Bob Weiskopf
   **Director:** James V. Kern
   **Guest Star:** Torben Meyer

Lucy, the Alps, avalanche.

An irresistible exchange occurs when the foursome, facing almost certain death in an avalanche, confess their darkest secrets: Fred has been quietly bilking the Ricardos on their monthly rent, while Ethel admits she'd been secretly returning it each month. When it's Ricky's turn to bare his soul, he defers, insisting, "I'm no fool . . . we might be saved!"

**149**   Lucy Gets Homesick in Italy                    April 9, 1956
   **Writers:** Jess Oppenheimer, Madelyn Pugh, Bob Carroll, Jr.,
   Bob Schiller, Bob Weiskopf
   **Director:** James V. Kern
   **Guest Stars:** Vincent Padula, Bart Bradley, Kathryn Card

Lucy, homesick for Little Ricky, throws the toddler a long-distance birthday party with an Italian shoeshine boy as his stand-in.

Perhaps nowhere in the Lucy chronicles is her patented crying jag used to better effect than here, when she repeatedly breaks down at the mere thought of her baby so many miles away on his birthday.
   Crocodile tears were an effective tool in Lucy's bag of tricks, though she probably didn't realize she was creating a monster—the blubbering sitcom wife became a self-perpetuating TV convention that stubbornly hung on for decades to come. The bit was used to good effect by Mary Tyler Moore on *The Dick Van Dyke Show* and by Marlo Thomas on *That Girl* in the 1960s, and also—with less effective results—by Sally Struthers on *All in the Family*.

**150**   Lucy's Italian Movie                    April 16, 1956
   **Writers:** Jess Oppenheimer, Madelyn Pugh, Bob Carroll, Jr.,
   Bob Schiller, Bob Weiskopf
   **Director:** James V. Kern
   **Guest Stars:** Franco Corsaro, Saverio Lo Medico, Ernesto
   Molinari, Teresa Tirelli

When Lucy is unexpectedly cast in an Italian epic, her character research leads her to the grape-stomping vat of an old-fashioned vineyard.

This memorable later episode demonstrates how Lucy could transform the broad slapstick of a fight in a giant vat of grapes into a hilarious bit of comic choreography.

**151**  Lucy's Bicycle Trip                    April 23, 1956
**Writers:** Jess Oppenheimer, Madelyn Pugh, Bob Carroll, Jr., Bob Schiller, Bob Weiskopf
**Director:** James V. Kern
**Guest Stars:** Mario Siletti, Francis Ravel

The Ricardos and Mertzes bicycle all the way to the French border before Lucy realizes she's misplaced her passport.

**152**  Lucy Goes to Monte Carlo                    May 7, 1956
**Writers:** Jess Oppenheimer, Madelyn Pugh, Bob Carroll, Jr., Bob Schiller, Bob Weiskopf
**Director:** James V. Kern
**Guest Stars:** John Mylong, Gordon Clark, Jacques Villon

Lucy inadvertently wins a small fortune at Monte Carlo, even though Ricky has forbidden her to enter the gaming casino.

**153**  Return Home From Europe                    May 14, 1956
**Writers:** Jess Oppenheimer, Madelyn Pugh, Bob Carroll, Jr., Bob Schiller, Bob Weiskopf
**Director:** James V. Kern
**Guest Stars:** Mary Jane Croft, Mildred Law, Frank Nelson, Ray Kellogg

Bound for home at last, Lucy attempts to smuggle a twenty-five-pound hunk of Italian cheese aboard the plane to avoid excess baggage fees.

This would be the last episode written and produced by Jess Oppenheimer, who left the series at the end of the fifth year for an executive post at NBC. In his long tenure as *Lucy's* head writer, producer, and co-creator, Oppenheimer's contribution had been enormous—a factor that would become obvious as the show moved into a final uneven season without the unifying vision of the man who had steered the Ricardos' fate for the past five years.

# 1956-57    THE SIXTH SEASON

*Year-End Rating: 43.7 (1st place)*

The show ends its phenomenally successful run as a half-hour sitcom at the close of the sixth year, as the Ricardos and the Mertzes settle down to a new life in Connecticut during the final thirteen installments. New cast members include Keith Thibodeaux as the five-year-old Little Ricky and Frank Nelson and Mary Jane Croft, who play neighbors Ralph and Betty Ramsey in the Connecticut episodes.

Desi Arnaz is the producer of the show's final year, and writers Madelyn Pugh Martin, Bob Carroll, Jr., Bob Schiller, and Bob Weiskopf continue to pen all of the scripts. William Asher replaces James V. Kern as staff director for the final thirteen episodes.

**154**   Lucy and Bob Hope                    October 1, 1956
   **Writers:** Madelyn Pugh Martin, Bob Carroll, Jr., Bob Schiller,
   Bob Weiskopf
   **Director:** James V. Kern
   **Guest Stars:** Bob Hope, Lou Krugman, Peter Leeds, Dick Elliott,
   Maxine Semon

Lucy tries to talk Bob Hope into appearing as the opening-night act at Ricky's new nightclub.

Bob Hope was an old friend of the Arnazes. Desi had been his orchestra leader in radio, and Lucy co-starred with him in *Sorrowful Jones* and *Fancy Pants*.

**155**   Little Ricky Learns to Play the Drums      October 8, 1956
   **Writers:** Madelyn Pugh Martin, Bob Carroll, Jr., Bob Schiller,
   Bob Weiskopf
   **Director:** James V. Kern
   **Guest Stars:** Elizabeth Patterson, Keith Thibodeaux

Ricky decides to give his son a head start in show business when he buys the five-year-old a snare drum.

Keith Thibodeaux, officially the world's tiniest professional drummer— and a dead ringer for the senior Arnaz—was brought in to play the five-year-old Little Ricky in the sixth season.

**156**   Lucy Meets Orson Welles                October 15, 1956
  **Writers:** Madelyn Pugh Martin, Bob Carroll, Jr., Bob Schiller,
  Bob Weiskopf
  **Director:** James V. Kern
  **Guest Stars:** Orson Welles, Ellen Corby, Lou Krugman

When Orson Welles invites Lucy to take part in his act, she starts brushing up on her Shakespeare—only to discover that the director has other plans for her.

Welles uses Lucy in his magic act, much as he called on the services of two other redheads—Marlene Dietrich and Rita Hayworth—to fill the role when he performed the novelty act for USO troupes during World War II.

Clearly demonstrating how the ambitions of Desilu had grown beyond *I Love Lucy*, in 1956 Arnaz engaged Welles to direct a proposed series of classic short-story adaptations for television. The director fashioned a Peabody Award-winning adaptation of John Collier's *Fountain of Youth* as a pilot film, but the series never sold.

**157**   Little Ricky Gets Stage Fright                October 22, 1956
  **Writers:** Madelyn Pugh Martin, Bob Carroll, Jr., Bob Schiller,
  Bob Weiskopf
  **Director:** James V. Kern
  **Guest Stars:** Howard McNear, Marjorie Bennett

Little Ricky gets cold feet on the eve of his first music-school recital.

Ricky's drum teacher is played by Howard McNear, the lovable character actor who later portrayed Floyd the barber on *The Andy Griffith Show*.

**158**   Visitor from Italy                October 29, 1956
  **Writers:** Madelyn Pugh Martin, Bob Carroll, Jr., Bob Schiller,
  Bob Weiskopf
  **Director:** James V. Kern
  **Guest Stars:** Jay Novello, Eduardo Ciannelli, Aldo Formica

The Ricardos offer a helping hand to a visiting gondolier they met during their tour of Venice.

**159**   Off to Florida                          November 12, 1956
   **Writers:** Madelyn Pugh Martin, Bob Carroll, Jr., Bob Schiller,
   Bob Weiskopf
   **Director:** James V. Kern
   **Guest Stars:** Elsa Lanchester, Strother Martin

When Lucy loses the train tickets for her trip to Florida, she and
Ethel are forced to share a ride with an eccentric old woman.

**160**   Deep-Sea Fishing                     November 19, 1956
   **Writers:** Madelyn Pugh Martin, Bob Carroll, Jr., Bob Schiller,
   Bob Weiskopf
   **Director:** James V. Kern
   **Guest Stars:** James Hayward, Billy McLean

Ricky and Fred stage a fishing competition with the wives to see
who can hook the largest catch on a deep-sea-fishing expedition.

Jay Sandrich, the son of RKO director Mark Sandrich, signed on as
assistant director with this episode. After a stint as director of *He and She*
in the late sixties, Sandrich distinguished himself as the Emmy-winning
director of *The Mary Tyler Moore Show* in the seventies and of *The Cosby
Show* in the eighties, making him one of the few directors whose career
has spanned three generations of superior TV comedy.

**161**   Desert Island                         November 26, 1956
   **Writers:** Madelyn Pugh Martin, Bob Carroll, Jr., Bob Schiller,
   Bob Weiskopf
   **Director:** James V. Kern
   **Guest Stars:** Claude Akins, Jil Jarmyn, Joi Lansing

The wives go to extreme measures to prevent their husbands from
participating as judges in a Miami Beach beauty pageant.

**162**   The Ricardos Visit Cuba               December 3, 1956
   **Writers:** Madelyn Pugh Martin, Bob Carroll, Jr., Bob Schiller,
   Bob Weiskopf
   **Director:** James V. Kern
   **Guest Stars:** George Trevino, Nacho Galindo, Mary Emery

Lucy is a nervous wreck at the prospect of meeting Ricky's Uncle
Alberto at the Ricardos' family reunion in Cuba.

**163**   Little Ricky's School Pageant          December 17, 1956
   **Writers:** Madelyn Pugh Martin, Bob Carroll, Jr., Bob Schiller,
   Bob Weiskopf
   **Director:** James V. Kern
   **Guest Star:** Candy Rogers Schoenberger

The Mertzes and Ricardos are the improbable supporting players
in Little Ricky's kindergarten production of *The Enchanted Forest*.


**164**   I Love Lucy Christmas Show          December 24, 1956
   **Writers:** Madelyn Pugh Martin, Bob Carroll, Jr., Bob Schiller,
   Bob Weiskopf
   **Director:** James V. Kern
   **Guest Star:** Cameron Grant

As the Ricardos and Mertzes trim the tree on Christmas Eve, they
reminisce how much their lives have changed since the arrival of
Little Ricky.

Here's one for video archaeologists. Because of its seasonal theme and
an uncharacteristic reliance on flashbacks, this show was left out of the
bundle when the series was later packaged for syndication, and would
not be rerun until CBS rebroadcast it as a prime time special on December 18, 1989.


**165**   Lucy and the Loving Cup              January 7, 1957
   **Writers:** Madelyn Pugh Martin, Bob Carroll, Jr., Bob Schiller,
   Bob Weiskopf
   **Director:** James V. Kern
   **Guest Stars:** Robert Foulk, Johnny and Hazel Longden,
   Jesslyn Fax

Lucy gets lost on the New York subway system with a loving-cup
trophy stuck on her head.


**166**   Lucy and Superman                   January 14, 1957
   **Writers:** Madelyn Pugh Martin, Bob Carroll, Jr., Bob Schiller,
   Bob Weiskopf
   **Director:** James V. Kern
   **Guest Stars:** George Reeves, Doris Singleton, George O'Hanlon,
   Steven Kay

Lucy impersonates Superman at Little Ricky's birthday party when she's unable to arrange an appearance by the real man of steel.

**167**   Little Ricky Gets a Dog                    January 21, 1957
**Writers:** Madelyn Pugh Martin, Bob Carroll, Jr., Bob Schiller,
Bob Weiskopf
**Director:** James V. Kern
**Guest Star:** John Emery

Lucy schemes to let Little Ricky keep a puppy, despite the no pets clause in their lease agreement with Fred and Ethel.

June Foray, the voice of Rocky the flying squirrel, provided the yelps of Little Ricky's dog, Fred. Unlike most sitcom pups, who vanish unaccountably from subsequent episodes, Fred did manage another appearance in the final episode of the series.

**168**   Lucy Wants to Move to the Country        January 28, 1957
**Writers:** Madelyn Pugh Martin, Bob Carroll, Jr., Bob Schiller,
Bob Weiskopf
**Director:** William Asher
**Guest Stars:** Frank Wilcox, Eleanor Audley

The Ricardos make plans to forsake Manhattan's grit and grime for a new home in suburban Connecticut.

The decision to remove the Ricardos from the familiar surroundings of their New York apartment house seems almost sacrilegious, but after five and a half years, and close to 170 scripts, the writers had finally run out of movie stars for Lucy to pester, and they'd long since exhausted her repertoire of material for Ricky's nightclub.

Of course, the Mertzes and Ricardos weren't alone in their urban flight. By the late 1950s, the colorful melting pot of Ralph Kramden's Bensonhurst, Amos 'n' Andy's Harlem, and Molly Goldberg's Bronx would give way to a half dozen bucolic and geographically undefined towns with names such as Mayfield, Hilldale, and Springfield. By the mid-1960s, TV's prime-time atlas would read like the *Farmer's Almanac*, with the most popular sitcoms set in exotic rural communities such as Mayberry, Pixley, and Hooterville—all far from the harsh urban reality that had typified the shows of Lucy's era.

**169**   Lucy Hates to Leave                        February 4, 1957
**Writers:** Madelyn Pugh Martin, Bob Carroll, Jr., Bob Schiller,
Bob Weiskopf
**Director:** William Asher
**Guest Stars:** Gene Reynolds, Mary Ellen Kaye

Lucy and Ricky double up and cram in with the Mertzes until
their new home in Connecticut is ready.

Guest star Gene Reynolds, a former child actor, discovered far greener
pastures as a producer of such acclaimed series as *Room 222*, *M\*A\*S\*H*,
and *Lou Grant*.


**170**   Lucy Misses the Mertzes                  February 11, 1957
**Writers:** Madelyn Pugh Martin, Bob Carroll, Jr., Bob Schiller,
Bob Weiskopf
**Director:** William Asher
**Guest Stars:** William Coffin, Jesse Kirkpatrick, Robert Brice

After less than eight hours in their new home, Lucy and Ricky find
life almost unbearable without the Mertzes.


**171**   Lucy Gets Chummy With the Neighbors   February 18, 1957
**Writers:** Madelyn Pugh Martin, Bob Carroll, Jr., Bob Schiller,
Bob Weiskopf
**Director:** William Asher
**Guest Stars:** Frank Nelson, Mary Jane Croft

The Ricardos decide to redecorate with the help of their new
neighbors, Ralph and Betty Ramsey.


**172**   Lucy Raises Chickens                       March 4, 1957
**Writers:** Madelyn Pugh Martin, Bob Carroll, Jr., Bob Schiller,
Bob Weiskopf
**Director:** William Asher
**Guest Stars:** Tyler McVey, Mary Alan Hokenson, Mary
Jane Croft

Fred and Ethel join the Ricardos in their newest venture as Connecticut chicken ranchers.

**173**   Lucy Does the Tango                       March 11, 1957
  **Writers:** Madelyn Pugh Martin, Bob Carroll, Jr., Bob Schiller,
  Bob Weiskopf
  **Director:** William Asher
  **Guest Stars:** Ray Ferrell

When the Mertzes and Ricardos invest in 200 laying hens, Lucy
ends up with egg on her face—and everywhere else.

**174**   Ragtime Band                              March 18, 1957
  **Writers:** Madelyn Pugh Martin, Bob Carroll, Jr., Bob Schiller,
  Bob Weiskopf
  **Director:** William Asher

Ricky is enlisted as reluctant bandleader when Lucy and the
Mertzes combine their meager musical talents to form a band to
play at a charity bazaar.

**175**   Lucy's Night in Town                      March 25, 1957
  **Writers:** Madelyn Pugh Martin, Bob Carroll, Jr., Bob Schiller,
  Bob Weiskopf
  **Director:** William Asher
  **Guest Stars:** Joseph Kearns, Gladys Hurlbut, Doris Packer, John
  Eldredge

The Mertzes and Ricardos plan to see the latest Broadway hit,
until Lucy realizes that she bought the wrong tickets.

**176**   Housewarming                              April 1, 1957
  **Writers:** Madelyn Pugh Martin, Bob Carroll, Jr., Bob Schiller,
  Bob Weiskopf
  **Director:** William Asher
  **Guest Stars:** Ray Ferrell, Mary Jane Croft

Ethel is jealous of Lucy's burgeoning friendship with her new
neighbor, Betty Ramsey.

**177**   Building a Barbecue                       April 8, 1957
  **Writers:** Madelyn Pugh Martin, Bob Carroll, Jr., Bob Schiller,
  Bob Weiskopf
  **Director:** William Asher

Lucy is convinced that she's lost her wedding ring in the wet cement of their freshly constructed backyard barbecue.

The episode provided Lucy and Ethel with one of their last comic set pieces—a huge brick barbecue that they stay up all night to dismantle and then rebuild, brick by brick.

**178**   Country Club Dance                            April 22, 1957
   **Writers:** Madelyn Pugh Martin, Bob Carroll, Jr., Bob Schiller,
   Bob Weiskopf
   **Director:** William Asher
   **Guest Stars:** Frank Nelson, Mary Jane Croft, Barbara Eden,
   Tristam Coffin, Ruth Brady

Lucy and Ethel decide to give a local glamour girl some mature competition.

**179**   Lucy Raises Tulips                            April 29, 1957
   **Writers:** Madelyn Pugh Martin, Bob Carroll, Jr., Bob Schiller,
   Bob Weiskopf
   **Director:** William Asher
   **Guest Stars:** Peter Brocco, Eleanor Audley

Lucy tries her hand at gardening when she competes with Betty Ramsey to win a tulip-judging competition.

**180**   The Ricardos Dedicate a Statue                May 6, 1957
   **Writers:** Madelyn Pugh Martin, Bob Carroll, Jr., Bob Schiller,
   Bob Weiskopf
   **Director:** William Asher

Lucy accidentally destroys a statue that Ricky is supposed to dedicate during Westport's Yankee Doodle Days.

The Mertzes and Ricardos would return in a series of thirteen hour-long specials over the next few years, but no episodes of *I Love Lucy* would be made after the show left the air on May 6, 1957, while still the highest-rated series on television.

Of course, *I Love Lucy* didn't really end there.

In 1957, Desi Arnaz sold the rerun rights to CBS, and the series began what is probably the most successful afterlife in TV history. To this day it remains one of the most durable half-hour sitcoms in syndication, appearing almost perpetually in every major market in the country.

Finally, in 1986, the most innovative comedy of the 1950s was ushered into the new video age, when *I Love Lucy* became one of the first TV series to be made widely available on home videocassette. It's not hard to imagine historians from some far-distant age stumbling across one of these odd little videotapes as they explore the remains of the third planet from the sun. If that happens, assuming they're able to dig up a videoplayer—VHS format— it's almost certain that those explorers from that faraway era will find the antics of this twentieth-century Earthling as worthy of repeated viewing as we did.

And before long, it's a sure bet, they'll love Lucy, too.

## EMMY AWARDS

The following is a complete listing of the Emmy Awards bestowed on *I Love Lucy* by the National Academy of Television Arts and Sciences.

**1952**      Best Situation Comedy
            Best Comedienne: Lucille Ball

**1953**      Best Situation Comedy
            Best Series Supporting Actress: Vivian Vance

**1955**      Best Actress, Continuing Performance: Lucille Ball

# THE HONEYMOONERS

.

*People like the show because* we *are*
*them.*
—JACKIE GLEASON

THE INSPIRATION for the longest honeymoon in television history was
very simple—a couple of writers wanted to come up with a sketch that
would round out an hour of live TV.

Joe Bigelow and Harry Crane, staff writers for *Cavalcade of Stars*—the
flagship variety show of the tiny Dumont network—listened as the up-
and-coming comic who'd been brought in to host the show a few weeks
earlier described his latest brainstorm. Jackie Gleason had an idea for
the week's final comedy sketch. He wanted to play an ordinary guy, an
everyday working stiff who lived with his wife in Brooklyn. "This dame
is very wise and very tired. She knows this guy inside out, see, and he's
always got a gripe. They got a little flat in Brooklyn. Flatbush Avenue,
maybe."

The writers had to admit that the idea sounded like a keeper.

In his first few weeks as host of the Dumont network variety show,
the rotund comedian had already developed a popular cast of comic alter
egos—Joe the Bartender, The Poor Soul, and the expansive Reginald Van
Gleason III, among others. Each one was just a little bit bigger than life,
but the star and his writers agreed there was no reason why they couldn't
mine just as many laughs from the less-exotic routine of an ordinary guy
living an ordinary life.

Bigelow and Crane worked up a sketch that described a domestic squabble between Ralph and Alice Kramden of Brooklyn, USA. The scene was short—the Kramdens had barely enough time to finish the round—but in less than twelve minutes, Jackie Gleason's immortality was assured.

Of course, in 1950, no one guessed the eventual impact that that short sketch would have on American television. Even Jackie Gleason ventured no more than a smile when he told his writers, "You know, maybe we got something here."

The honeymoon had begun.

"Make it real," Gleason told his writers. "Make it the way people live. If it isn't credible, nobody's going to laugh." And if anyone was qualified to act as technical adviser on the everyday reality of working-class Brooklyn, it was Jackie Gleason. He'd grown up in the same neighborhood as Ralph Kramden and then quit school to hustle pool before he finally worked his way into show business via nightclubs and bit parts in World War II programmers at Warner Bros.

He first hit television in 1949, when he allowed himself to be miscast as the lead in the first TV version of *The Life of Riley*. The disastrous experience convinced him of one thing—if he was going to make it in television, he would have to trust his own instincts. Gleason resolved that on his next television series—if there was one—*he* would be the one to call the shots.

And call the shots he did. As host of the fledgling *Cavalcade of Stars*, Gleason lavished loving attention on each of his growing cast of characters, but he was particularly fond of the recurring sketch about his battling couple from Brooklyn, Ralph and Alice Kramden. Gleason and his writers flirted with the notion of giving Ralph a job as a cop, but they finally put him to work behind the wheel of a bus, since, as the star remembers it, "Bus drivers get aggravated, and I was delighted with anything that would aggravate Ralph."

But it was Kramden's tender side that most appealed to the actor. When the writers proposed calling the segment "The Beast," Gleason nixed the idea. He had a better title—"The Honeymooners." In his mind, the story of the Kramdens was basically an old-fashioned romance. "The guy really loves this broad," he maintained. "They fight, sure. But they always end in a clinch."

That "clinch"—the embrace that ended so many episodes—was the demonstrative flourish of a healthy physical attraction, something that was rare on fifties' television. As played by Audrey Meadows, Alice's smoldering allure wasn't hard to see through Ralph's eyes. And, as

Gleason hinted in a later interview, the attraction was certainly more erotic than anyone acknowledged in the Eisenhower era. "You never got to see the bedroom," recalled the star. "I felt it was best to leave that to the imagination. But at the end of each show, when they'd kiss—you could imagine that they must get along pretty good."

Even stronger than the Kramdens' conjugal ties—and perhaps even more crucial, finally, to the show's delicate chemistry—was the strange, spiritual bond shared by lodge brothers Ralph Kramden and Ed Norton. Wiry, even-tempered, and reasonably satisfied with his life, Art Carney's Norton was everything Ralph wasn't. And yet, the hapless sewer worker sympathized with his neighbor's absurd obsessions as Alice never could. In Norton's childlike devotion, Kramden found strength.

Jackie Gleason once remarked that Art Carney was responsible for ninety percent of *The Honeymooners'* success. Even allowing for the star's characteristic exaggeration, it *is* very difficult to overestimate Carney's contribution to the series. Like Gleason, he was a gifted physical actor. In his hands, the simplest physical shtick—chalking a pool cue, sleepwalking, even signing his name!—became a graceful comic choreography. The chemistry of his pairing with Gleason was instant, and unmistakable. "The first time I worked with him I saw that this guy knew what the hell he was doing," Gleason remembers. "Every move he made was the right move."

It's entirely possible that Carney's comic influence on television may prove even greater than Gleason's. Stretching far beyond *The Honeymooners*, Ed Norton's comic legacy continues to inspire television's most sophisticated situation comedy even today. It's difficult to watch such latter-day loons as Howard Borden on *The Bob Newhart Show*, "Reverend Jim" Ignatowski on *Taxi*, or Ernie "Coach" Pantusso on *Cheers* without acknowledging the inspired clowning of their distant cousin, a guy who worked beneath the streets of Brooklyn.

The popular *Honeymooners* sketches continued as a staple of Gleason's variety show throughout the early 1950s, even after he moved his comic caravan to CBS in 1952. By the time the Buick Motor Company approached Gleason with an offer to sponsor the sketch as a freestanding sitcom in 1955, it had been running, in one form or another, since 1950. It's not surprising that *The Honeymooners* emerged as one of TV's all-time classics in the space of a single season—they'd already been rehearsing for more than four years!

The Buick deal was the largest sponsorship commitment in television's brief history. The motor company paid more than $6 million for the privilege of bringing us two years of half-hour *Honeymooners*, with an option for a third season of thirty-nine more shows after that. Gleason also arranged for the episodes to be shot live on film, mainly so that his company could reap a few extra bucks when the programs were rerun while he took the summer off. It was a crucial detail in what turned out to be the most fortunate marriage of commerce and art in the history of the situation comedy.

It was also one of the shortest. After only thirty-nine weeks, Gleason called the whole deal off.

But, what a thirty-nine weeks they were!

The 1100 people who crowded into New York's Adelphi Theatre for the twice-weekly filming of live *Honeymooners* episodes probably never guessed that they were watching television history in the making—most of them were too busy laughing. Just as audiences have continued laughing at those same thirty-nine timeless half-hour films for well over four decades.

The show has a timeless appeal that's as mysterious as it is unarguable. It's practically impossible to watch an episode without getting drawn in—once again—to the relentless comic drama of the indefatigable bus driver who somehow managed to keep his head in the clouds, even when the rest of him was sinking fast.

Whether he's trying to foist off a warehouse full of useless can openers on late-night TV or causing Alice heartache by withholding a five-dollar rent increase, his foolhardy shortcuts to self-fulfillment invariably end in some poetically appropriate disaster. And yet, no matter how brutal his fate, we're comforted by the knowledge that Ralph will always bounce back to attempt one of the thirty-eight other schemes in his perpetually replenished bag of tricks.

By all accounts, events behind the scenes of *The Honeymooners* were often as chaotic as anything that happened to the Kramdens and Nortons onstage. Gleason maintained that too much rehearsal—which, for him, amounted to anything beyond a cursory run-through—destroyed the show's spontaneity. As a result, the actors often found themselves relying on prayer and their raw instincts to get them through live performances where almost anything could happen.

And despite his near-photographic memory, Gleason himself got lost more frequently than most people guessed. According to legend, when the star did blank out, he would pace back and forth and pat his stomach—the prearranged distress signal that told the other actors to start winging it. Of course, some performers adjusted to the star's unorthodox rehearsal procedures more quickly than others.

"I came close to walking out on Jackie Gleason before the show even got off the ground," Audrey Meadows told *TV Guide* many years later. "I felt totally unprepared and desperate. Standing in the wings, ready to go on, I'd tell him, 'You are a simply dreadful man.'"

But like everyone else on the series, Meadows adapted, and soon developed a great trust for her fellow actors' unerring instincts, particularly Gleason's. "I've always maintained that there's no way you could play a scene wrong with Jackie," she told an interviewer. "He is so good, and so real."

That sense of reality permeated every fiber of the series, from Norton's dusty felt hat—a relic that Carney had carried with him since high-school days—to the Kramdens' ill-furnished apartment, which was itself an only slightly exaggerated model of the flat where Gleason grew up. The burden of re-creating the Kramdens' little universe each week fell to a staff of six dedicated writers—Marvin Marx and Walter Stone, Andy Russell and Herbert Finn, and Leonard Stern and Sydney Zelinka—all unsung heroes of *The Honeymooners* classic episodes.

Since the shows were cranked out and filmed—two each week—until all thirty-nine were shot, the pressure to supply the insatiable demand for top-grade material could be grueling. "We'd be there twelve to fourteen hours each day, Monday through Friday," Leonard Stern told *Honeymooners* historian Donna McCrohan. "No social life. No escape. It probably was more painful than I remember."

And yet, in the entire season, there was barely a clinker in the bunch. Given the show's breakneck pace, it's not surprising that the scribes kept their catalog of stock situations close at hand. But the characters were so genuine—and the scripts so inventive—that the plays transcended the occasional shopworn premise to create a fully developed world that remains convincing—and alluring—to this day.

But Gleason wasn't so sure at the time.

Convinced that "the excellence of the material could not be maintained," the quixotic comedian pulled the plug after a single season. "We had done every script you could think of," the star later complained. The show's ratings might have been another persuasive factor. Despite the audience's obvious affection for the series, *The Honeymooners* barely broke into the year's top twenty. Whatever his reasons, Gleason irrevocably returned to his more successful variety-show format, and the Kramdens and Nortons were relegated to supporting status once again.

But the honeymoon didn't end there.

The series began a second, far more profitable life as a TV rerun when Gleason sold the syndication rights to those thirty-nine half hours in 1957. And since that time, a day hasn't passed when the Kramdens and the

Nortons haven't invoked bellows of laughter in some corner of the United States. Perhaps the only real secret of *The Honeymooners'* durability is that it remains just as funny, if not funnier, on the third, fourth—or tenth—viewing, as it was on the first.

Like a fine symphony that reveals new depth and coloration with each performance, *The Honeymooners* has proved impervious to age. The show's classic status grows stronger each year, as new generations are charmed by the simple comic premise that began life as a throwaway sketch on an obscure variety show and climaxed in the most enduring—and endearing—season of situation comedy ever made.

# A Critical Guide to the Classic 39 Episodes

REGULAR CAST

| | |
|---|---|
| Ralph Kramden | Jackie Gleason |
| Ed Norton | Art Carney |
| Alice Kramden | Audrey Meadows |
| Trixie Norton | Joyce Randolph |

SUPPORTING CAST

| | |
|---|---|
| Mrs. Angelina Manicotti | Zamah Cunningham |
| Mrs. Gibson (Alice's mother) | Ethel Owen |

STOCK COMPANY

George Petrie, Frank Marth, Dick Bernie, John Griggs, Les Damon, Eddie Hanley, Jack Davis, Sammy Birch, Vic Rendina, John Seymour, Ned Glass

Created by Joe Bigelow, Harry Crane, Jackie Gleason
Music by Sammy Spear and his orchestra
Theme ("You're My Greatest Love") by Jackie Gleason
Director of photography was Jack Etra
Principal director was Frank Satenstein

## THE 1955-56 SEASON

*Year-End Rating: 30.2 (19th place)*

Jack Philbin was executive producer for *The Honeymooners'* single, bountiful season as a half-hour situation comedy, and all thirty-nine were produced by Jack Hurdle. Three of Gleason's veteran writing teams traded off scripting chores throughout the season—Marvin Marx and Walter Stone, A.J. Russell and Herbert Finn, and Leonard Stern and Sydney Zelinka. Frank Satenstein was the director, and the entire production was supervised by Jackie Gleason.

**1** TV or Not TV                    October 1, 1955
**Writers:** Marvin Marx, Walter Stone
**Director:** Frank Satenstein

The wonders of television disrupt life in the Kramden household when Ed and Ralph share custody of a brand-new TV set.

Marvin Marx and Walter Stone scripted more classic *Honeymooners* dialogue than any other two men on Earth. They first teamed up in the writers' pool on Gleason's *Cavalcade of Stars* and soon found themselves resident scribes of the chronicles of Kramden and Norton—a task to which they were ideally suited, according to the series's executive producer. "Marx and Walter Stone were Ralph and Ed's counterparts," observed Jack Philbin, "Marx thought like Ralph, Stone thought like Norton."

**2** Funny Money                    October 8, 1955
**Writers:** Marvin Marx, Walter Stone
**Director:** Frank Satenstein
**Guest Stars:** Boris Aplon, Frank Marth, Eddie Hanley, Ethel Owen, Vic Rendina, Jack Davis

There's no extravagance too grand for the Kramdens after Ralph discovers a satchel filled with $50,000—all of it counterfeit.

**3** The Golfer                    October 15, 1955
**Writers:** A.J. Russell, Herbert Finn
**Director:** Frank Satenstein
**Guest Stars:** Frank Marth, John Griggs, John Gibson, George Petrie, Jack Davis

To curry favor with his boss, Ralph brags about his skill on the green—a boast the non-golfer lives to regret when Mr. Harper invites him to play that weekend.

**4** A Woman's Work Is Never Done                    October 22, 1955
**Writers:** Marvin Marx, Walter Stone
**Director:** Frank Satenstein
**Guest Stars:** Betty Garde, Frank Marth

Tired of Ralph's endless domestic complaints, Alice takes a job and leaves a maid to take care of the housework.

**5    A Matter of Life and Death**                    October 29, 1955
**Writers:** Marvin Marx, Walter Stone
**Director:** Frank Satenstein
**Guest Stars:** George Petrie, Les Damon

Convinced that he's only got six months to live, Ralph sells his
deathbed story to a weekly magazine.

Ralph is worried when he contracts the fictitious malady arterial
monochromia, but he'd already survived *cerebral* monochromia in an
earlier *Honeymooners* variety show sketch, a vignette that would serve as
the inspiration for this script. As authors Donna McCrohan and Peter
Crescenti reveal in *The Honeymooners Lost Episodes*, Gleason's writers
thought nothing of filching whole sequences—and sometimes entire
plots—from scenes they'd written in the early fifties. At least two other
episodes from the classic 1955-56 season, "The Loudspeaker" and "'Twas
the Night Before Christmas," were virtual remakes of earlier sketches
that eventually reappeared when many of the "lost episodes" resurfaced—to the delight of *Honeymooners* fans everywhere—in early 1985.

**6    The Sleepwalker**                              November 5, 1955
**Writers:** A.J. Russell, Herbert Finn
**Director:** Frank Satenstein
**Guest Star:** George Petrie

Norton's sleepwalking wreaks havoc with Ralph's well-ordered
routine after Trixie appoints him caretaker for her husband's
somnambulant strolls.

**7    Better Living Through TV**                     November 12, 1955
**Writers:** Marvin Marx, Walter Stone
**Director:** Frank Satenstein
**Guest Star:** Eddie Hanley

Ralph is the tongue-tied "chef-of-the-future" in an ill-fated late-
night TV commercial that he and Norton concoct to sell 2000
Happy Housewife Helpers.

One of the funniest episodes in a very funny season. Norton and
Kramden's chefs of the past and future create even greater pandemonium than Lucy did with her classic Vitameatavegamin pitch. Here the
boys practically topple an entire TV studio in their efforts to demonstrate
the superior way to "core a apple."

**8  Pal O'Mine**                                   November 19, 1955
**Writers:** Leonard Stern, Sydney Zelinka
**Director:** Frank Satenstein
**Guest Stars:** John Seymour, Abbie Lewis, Ned Glass

Ralph's feelings are bruised when Ed buys a friendship ring for one of his pals on the sewer crew.

Veteran comedy scribes Stern and Zelinka wrote their first "Honeymooners" sketch for *The Jackie Gleason Show* in 1954. Leonard Stern continued to create classic television comedy as a writer for *The Phil Silvers Show* and later as creator of the influential 1967 sitcom *He and She*.

**9  Brother Ralph**                                 November 26, 1955
**Writers:** Marvin Marx, Walter Stone
**Director:** Frank Satenstein

Ralph's insecurity gets the better of him after Alice lands a job with a handsome employer, who thinks she's a single girl.

The tempest is short-lived, and by the fade-out, Ralph once again intones, "Baby, you're the greatest," and envelops Alice in an embrace capable of propelling the show's broad slapstick into the realm of divine romantic comedy. "That kiss was very important," Gleason told interviewer Bill Zehme. "Without it, people would have hated *The Honeymooners*. They would have thought, 'Jesus, it's just arguing all the time.'"

**10  Hello, Mom**                                   December 3, 1955
**Writers:** Marvin Marx, Walter Stone
**Director:** Frank Satenstein

Ralph seeks sanctuary with the Nortons when he and Alice have a major row over an impending visit from her mother.

**11  The Deciding Vote**                            December 10, 1955
**Writers:** A.J. Russell, Herbert Finn
**Director:** Frank Satenstein
**Guest Stars:** George Petrie, John Gibson

Ralph regrets his most recent outburst at Norton when his pal suddenly holds the deciding vote in an important election at the Raccoon Lodge.

**12**     Something Fishy           December 17, 1955
**Writers:** Leonard Stern, Sydney Zelinka
**Director:** Frank Satenstein
**Guest Stars:** Dick Bernie, Joseph Ruskin, Sammy Birch, Eddie Hanley, John Gibson

Ralph and Ed easily persuade the lodge brothers to ban their wives from the Raccoons' annual fishing trip—now all they have to do is convince Trixie and Alice.

**13**     'Twas the Night Before Christmas     December 24, 1955
**Writers:** Marvin Marx, Walter Stone
**Director:** Frank Satenstein
**Guest Star:** Anne Seymour

Ralph trades in his bowling ball to buy Alice's Christmas gift in this modern revamp of O. Henry's "Gift of the Magi."

The episode ends with a priceless moment that preserves forever the spontaneity of the show's theatrical origins, when Gleason—obviously buoyed by holiday cheer—stops the final curtain to introduce the cast in an impromptu curtain call.

**14**     The Man From Space          December 31, 1955
**Writers:** A.J. Russell, Herbert Finn
**Director:** Frank Satenstein
**Guest Stars:** Eddie Hanley, Vic Rendina

Hoping to win a $50 prize, Ralph attends the annual Raccoon Lodge costume ball dressed as a man from space.

**15**     A Matter of Record          January 7, 1956
**Writers:** A.J. Russell, Herbert Finn
**Director:** Frank Satenstein
**Guest Stars:** Ralph Robertson, Ethel Owen
Ralph is at loose ends when Alice moves in with her mother after his latest outburst, until Norton convinces him to transcribe his apology onto a record.

**16**    Oh, My Aching Back                     January 14, 1956
   **Writers:** Leonard Stern, Sydney Zelinka
   **Director:** Frank Satenstein
   **Guest Stars:** George Petrie, Frank Marth

Ralph goes bowling on the eve of his company physical—against
Alice's warning—and returns home with a sore sacroiliac.

**17**    The Baby-Sitter                       January 21, 1956
   **Writers:** Leonard Stern, Sydney Zelinka
   **Director:** Frank Satenstein
   **Guest Stars:** Vic Rendina, Frank Marth, Sid Raymond

When Alice takes on baby-sitting jobs to pay for the phone she's
secretly installed, Ralph suspects she's having an affair.

Telephones and children were both taboo in the Kramdens' cold-water walk-up. The gross misunderstandings that fueled many *Honeymooners* plots could too easily have been cleared up with a simple phone call,
and who wanted that? Gleason and his writers were also aware that the
show's stringent production demands practically mandated that the
Kramdens remain childless. "Kids can't time jokes or lines or dialogue,"
Gleason explained. "To do a live show with them, you'd be dead. So I
decreed it—no kids."

**18**    The $99,000 Answer                    January 28, 1956
   **Writers:** Leonard Stern, Sydney Zelinka
   **Director:** Frank Satenstein
   **Guest Stars:** Jay Jackson, Rita Colton, Ethel Owen, Bill Zuckert,
   Zamah Cunningham, Jack Davis

Ralph is a man obsessed when he lands a chance to break the
bank on a big-money quiz show.

**19**    Ralph Kramden, Inc.                   February 4, 1956
   **Writers:** A.J. Russell, Herbert Finn
   **Director:** Frank Satenstein
   **Guest Star:** John Seymour

Con-man Ralph sells Ed a percentage of his entire future earnings,
but has second thoughts after an eccentric old woman bequeaths
him a fortune in her will.

**20**   Young at Heart                    February 11, 1956
   **Writers:** Marvin Marx, Walter Stone
   **Director:** Frank Satenstein
   **Guest Star:** Ronnie Burns

Inspired by a pair of teenagers, the Kramdens and Nortons decide to recapture their lost youth at a skating rink.

The writers rarely passed an opportunity to exact a sight gag from Gleason's graceful girth, whether it meant dressing him up as a man from space for a costume ball or, as in this episode, setting him loose at a skating rink to make a spectacle of himself on wheels.

Ronnie Burns, George and Gracie's son, took a break from *The Burns and Allen Show* to make a guest appearance in this episode.

**21**   A Dog's Life                    February 18, 1956
   **Writers:** Leonard Stern, Sydney Zelinka
   **Director:** Frank Satenstein
   **Guest Stars:** George Petrie, John Griggs, Eddie Hanley, Frank Marth, Les Damon

Only after Ralph convinces his boss to invest in his new snack-food sensation does he discover that Kram–Mar's Delicious Mystery Appetizer is dog food.

**22**   Here Comes the Bride                    February 25, 1956
   **Writers:** Marvin Marx, Walter Stone
   **Director:** Frank Satenstein
   **Guest Stars:** John Gibson, Treva Frazee

Ralph ruins his sister-in-law's wedding night when he convinces her mild-mannered groom to assume his rightful place as lord of the manor.

**23**   Momma Loves a Mambo                    March 3, 1956
   **Writers:** Marvin Marx, Walter Stone
   **Director:** Frank Satenstein
   **Guest Stars:** Charles Korvin, Louis Sorin, Zamah Cunningham

The husbands are jealous when a Latin lover moves into the building and sweeps the wives off their feet with suave manners and free mambo lessons.

**24**    Please Leave the Premises                 March 10, 1956
  **Writers:** Marvin Marx, Walter Stone
  **Director:** Frank Satenstein
  **Guest Star:** Luis Van Rooten

The Kramdens are evicted after Ralph stubbornly refuses to pay a five-dollar rent increase.

**25**    Pardon My Glove                           March 17, 1956
  **Writers:** A.J. Russell, Herbert Finn
  **Director:** Frank Satenstein
  **Guest Star:** Alexander Clark

Ralph suspects hanky-panky when Alice postpones his surprise birthday party to arrange a clandestine meeting with a genteel interior decorator.

**26**    Young Man With a Horn                     March 24, 1956
  **Writers:** A.J. Russell, Herbert Finn
  **Director:** Frank Satenstein
  **Guest Stars:** Charles Eggleston, Nel Harrison

A chance meeting with a self-made millionaire inspires Ralph to embark on a rigorous self-improvement program.

**27**    Head of the House                         March 31, 1956
  **Writers:** Leonard Stern, Sydney Zelinka
  **Director:** Frank Satenstein
  **Guest Stars:** Frank Marth, Dick Bernie

Ralph thinks he's king of his castle, but it's Alice who lays down the law when the local paper prints his inflammatory views on a woman's place in the home.

**28**    The Worry Wart                            April 7, 1956
  **Writers:** Marvin Marx, Walter Stone
  **Director:** Frank Satenstein
  **Guest Star:** Warren Parker

A summons from the IRS has Ralph imagining the worst.

**29**   Trapped                              April 14, 1956
**Writers:** Leonard Stern, Sydney Zelinka
**Director:** Frank Satenstein
**Guest Stars:** Frank Marth, Larry Barton, Ken Lynch, Ralph
Robertson, Sammy Birch, George Petrie, Eddie Hanley

A pair of thugs holds Ed and the Kramdens hostage after Ralph
witnesses a robbery outside Harry's pool hall.

**30**   The Loudspeaker                      April 21, 1956
**Writers:** Marvin Marx, Walter Stone
**Director:** Frank Satenstein
**Guest Star:** Jock MacGregor

Ralph is so sure that he's about to be named Raccoon of the Year
that he drives Alice mad rehearsing his acceptance speech.

**31**   Onstage                              April 28, 1956
**Writers:** Leonard Stern, Sydney Zelinka
**Director:** Frank Satenstein
**Guest Stars:** George Neise, Alexander Clark, George Petrie

Ralph is delighted to be cast as the lead in the Lodge's annual
fund-raiser, until he finds out that Norton is slated to appear as his
co-star.

**32**   Opportunity Knocks, But
                                             May 5, 1956
**Writers:** Leonard Stern, Sydney Zelinka
**Director:** Frank Satenstein
**Guest Stars:** John Griggs, George Petrie

Ralph attempts to schmooze his boss over a game of pool, but it's
Norton who scores all the points.

**33**   Unconventional Behavior              May 12, 1956
**Writers:** Marvin Marx, Walter Stone
**Director:** Frank Satenstein
**Guest Star:** Humphrey Davis

A long train ride gets even longer after Norton accidentally handcuffs himself to Ralph during their trip to the Raccoon Convention
in Minneapolis.

This episode is fondly remembered for the classic handcuff routine, but in *The Official Honeymooners Treasury,* authors Peter Crescenti and Bob Columbe revealed that the entire bit was a last-minute improvisation devised to fill time after another gag was cut at dress rehearsal. "Jackie and Art played this incredible routine of trying to sleep in the upper and lower berths with their hands locked together in these handcuffs," reports actor Humphrey Davis. "And five minutes was used up just like that, with absolutely incredible comic invention."

**34**   The Safety Award                          May 19, 1956
   **Writers:** Leonard Stern, Sydney Zelinka
   **Director:** Frank Satenstein
   **Guest Stars:** Eddie Hanley, Frank Marth, George Petrie, Les Damon

Ralph has his first traffic accident—on the way to accept an award for being the safest bus driver in the city.

**35**   Mind Your Own Business                    May 26, 1956
   **Writers:** Leonard Stern, Sydney Zelinka
   **Director:** Frank Satenstein

Norton follows Ralph's advice to gain a promotion at work, and soon finds himself selling irons door-to-door.

**36**   Alice and the Blonde                       June 2, 1956
   **Writers:** Leonard Stern, Sydney Zelinka
   **Director:** Frank Satenstein
   **Guest Stars:** Freda Larsen, Frank Behrens

Alice and Trixie are abandoned by their husbands at a dinner party while Ed and Ralph heap lavish attention on a vapid blonde.

**37**   Bensonhurst Bomber                    September 8, 1956
   **Writers:** Marvin Marx, Walter Stone
   **Director:** Frank Satenstein
   **Guest Stars:** Leslie Barrett, George Mathews

After Ralph is challenged to a boxing match by a local tough, he and Ed devise a scheme to force the bus driver's flinty opponent to back down.

**38**   Dial J for Janitor                    September 15, 1956
**Writers:** A.J. Russell, Herbert Finn
**Director:** Frank Satenstein
**Guest Stars:** Luis Van Rooten, Zamah Cunningham

With dreams of free rent, a salary—and tips!—Ralph signs on as building superintendent at 328 Chauncey Street.

**39**   A Man's Pride                         September 22, 1956
**Writers:** Leonard Stern, Sydney Zelinka
**Director:** Frank Satenstein
**Guest Stars:** Dick Bernie, Vic Rendina

Ralph brags about his success to one of Alice's old suitors and then has to make good on his boast when the man unexpectedly arrives at the garage.

The series came to an abrupt end with this episode.

After Gleason voluntarily retired the half-hour *Honeymooners* at the end of the 1955-56 season, the Kramdens and Nortons continued to make occasional appearances on his variety show until it, too, was finally canceled in 1970—an incidental casualty in the CBS housecleaning that cleared the way for the network's bold new comedies, including a new show called *All in the Family.*

Within a few months, Ralph's traditional Saturday-night spot would be occupied by another bellicose, blue-collar Everyman. He was a little older than Ralph, but they shared similar tastes in interior decoration. Like the diligent bus driver, Archie Bunker worked hard at his job—though he was quick to spot any scheme that might net him a quick profit. And like Ralph, he was utterly dependent on the patience and wisdom of his long-suffering wife—though he never understood just how much.

They created quite a stir, this new family on the block. They were often loud, usually abrasive, and really very much in love. We were certain we'd never met anyone quite like Archie and Edith Bunker.

And yet, in so many ways, we'd known them all along.

## EMMY AWARDS

The following is a complete listing of the Emmy Awards bestowed on *The Honeymooners* by the National Academy of Television Arts and Sciences.

**1953**     Best Actor in a Supporting Role: Art Carney

(Carney and Audrey Meadows were also honored for their work on "The Honeymooners" while it was part of *The Jackie Gleason Show*. Carney received the Best Supporting Actor Award in 1953 and 1954, and Meadows walked off with the Best Supporting Actress Award in 1954.)

# THE DICK VAN DYKE SHOW

•

*It was like a lovely party you never wanted to end.*
—MOREY AMSTERDAM

IN THE SUMMER OF 1958, Carl Reiner packed his typewriter for the trip to Fire Island but left the suntan lotion behind. It would be nice to spend a few weeks in the cool ocean breeze of the Long Island community, far from the stifling inferno of summertime Manhattan—but he knew he would scarcely see the beach. While his neighbors tanned, the writer would spend his holiday polishing off a baker's dozen of the most innovative comedy scripts ever written.

And yet, just a few months earlier, Carl Reiner never dreamed he'd spend his summer vacation writing his own sitcom. When the performer told his agent he was anxious to give situation comedy a try—after nine seasons in the cast of *Your Show of Shows* and Sid Caesar's subsequent variety shows—he envisioned starring in one, not writing it.

But the inspiration to build a better sitcom came from his wife, Estelle, after she'd leafed through the pile of lackluster sitcom scripts his agent had sent over. "She told me, 'You can write better than this!'" explains Reiner. "Of course, I'd never written a sitcom. But when your wife thinks you can—you can."

With little more preparation than that, he set out for Fire Island, determined to stay until he'd finished a series of scripts that would reflect his unique view of the world, and no one else's. He started by asking himself, "On what piece of ground do I stand that no one else occupies?"

The answer was quite simple. The New York comedy writer would simply write about a New York comedy writer. The idea was a natural. After all, explained Reiner, "I had a nine-year backlog of material from *Your Show of Shows*."

He had little trouble examining his own life through the comic prism of a situation comedy. "I wrote a script every four days," he remembers. And in a remarkable burst of creative energy, he didn't stop until he had finished a full thirteen episodes of *Head of the Family*, as he would call his new series.

The writer bundled the scripts together and presented them to his agent, Harry Kalcheim, who immediately recognized their enormous potential. He showed the scripts to film star and TV producer Peter Lawford, who was then married to Patricia Kennedy, of the powerful Boston political clan.

According to Reiner, Lawford submitted one of the scripts to his father-in-law, Joseph P. Kennedy, who insisted on approval of any venture that involved the family money. Finally, with the blessing of the father of the next president of the United States, the pilot for *Head of the Family* was filmed with Carl Reiner in the starring role. It was like a dream come true.

But the writer would wake up soon enough. With Barbara Britton as his co-star, Reiner shot the first—and, as it would turn out, only—episode of *Head of the Family*. Then he waited for the offers to come pouring in.

But nobody was buying.

Westerns were in that year—family sitcoms were out. Reiner finally saw *Head of the Family* air as an unsold pilot during the summer of 1960, after which he resolved to forget the whole painful affair.

But Harry Kalcheim wouldn't let him. The agent was so convinced of the quality of Reiner's unsold scripts that he sought a second opinion from another of his clients, Sheldon Leonard—a veteran actor who had found considerable success as a TV producer and director. The former movie gangster read the thirteen scripts Reiner had written during his summer on Fire Island and was mightily impressed.

"I thought that basketful of scripts was the best body of material it had been my good luck to find," enthused Leonard, "and I had worked on some pretty good shows."

The director of *The Danny Thomas Show* and producer of *The Andy Griffith Show* and *The Real McCoys*, Leonard was one of the most powerful creators in television. So, naturally, Carl Reiner was intrigued when the producer offered to help revamp the concept of *Head of the Family* into an all-new series that he thought he could sell to CBS. But, the producer hastened to add, he did have one strong suggestion—one that might not be popular with the show's creator.

In Leonard's opinion, they would have to recast the lead—Carl Reiner was completely wrong for the part of Rob Petrie.

"I wondered how to break the news," Leonard explained. "How do you tell an actor he's just not the type to play himself?" But when he finally suggested that Reiner would be better off behind the cameras than in front of them, the writer appeared almost relieved. "I'll always be grateful to Sheldon Leonard," Reiner later exclaimed, "for telling me I was a producer when I thought I was an actor."

Leonard offered his services as executive producer, despite the advice of well-meaning friends who warned him not to get involved with a series that was so clearly destined for failure. Leonard chose to follow his instincts and eventually convinced his business partner, Danny Thomas, to finance a new pilot.

And so Carl Reiner and his new executive producer began the delicate process of casting the reborn series. For the crucial role of Rob Petrie, Leonard suggested that Reiner look at an actor who was already making a name for himself on Broadway—a lanky comedian named Dick Van Dyke.

Long before he made it to the Great White Way, Van Dyke paid his rent with the usual assortment of show-biz jobs—he'd been a record pantomimist and radio talk-show host before he signed with CBS-TV in the mid-1950s, where he spent most of television's Golden Age in a succession of thankless assignments ranging from game-show emcee to host of the *CBS Cartoon Theater*. His break finally came when he landed a part in *The Girls Against the Boys*, a revue that starred Bert Lahr and Nancy Walker.

Van Dyke's performance in that revue left an indelible impression on Sheldon Leonard, who considered offering the actor a supporting part on *The Danny Thomas Show*. Pat Harrington got that role, and Van Dyke went on to even greater acclaim on Broadway in *Bye Bye Birdie*. But there was never any doubt in the producer's mind that Dick Van Dyke would be dynamite on television.

And when Reiner finally saw the actor in *Bye Bye Birdie*, he was quick to agree.

The only other serious contender for the role of Rob Petrie had been Johnny Carson, but finally, the producers decided that Van Dyke was unmistakably right for the part. "We wanted a guy who was shy—like a writer," Reiner insists, "but who was also a naturally funny performer. And Dick Van Dyke had those qualities."

The producers then hired Rose Marie and Morey Amsterdam in supporting roles and discovered—to their delight—that the veteran character actors invested their roles with such depth that distinctions between star players and secondary roles soon vanished. The serendipity continued when the producers signed Richard Deacon and Larry Mathews; and finally, Ann Morgan Guilbert and Jerry Paris would round out one of the most inspired ensembles ever to grace a half-hour comedy.

But that ensemble maintained a conspicuous gap as the deadline to begin shooting loomed, and Reiner and Leonard still hadn't found their Laura Petrie. The producers had seen scores of actresses but couldn't envision any of them in the pivotal role of Rob's wife. They finally came close to signing Eileen Brennan—by far the best of the actresses they'd looked at—but decided against her, because, Reiner admits, "We knew she would be too strong for Dick."

With time running short, they consulted Leonard's partner, Danny Thomas, who had fronted the money for the new pilot. Thomas recalled an actress he'd recently auditioned for the part of his older daughter on *The Danny Thomas Show*. She didn't get that role, but Thomas thought she would make a perfect Laura Petrie. The only problem was that neither he nor Sheldon Leonard could remember her name.

At the tender age of twenty-four, lack of recognition seemed to be Mary Tyler Moore's professional curse. In her most memorable role to date—as Sam, the leggy secretary on *Richard Diamond, Private Detective*—the camera never even showed her face! It was not the most promising start for an ambitious young actress, and by the time Sheldon Leonard finally tracked her down, her professional enthusiasm was clearly on the wane.

But when she walked though Carl Reiner's door for the first time, Mary Tyler Moore had no way of knowing that her career was about thirty seconds away from being turned completely inside out.

"I had her read three lines," Reiner remembers, and "Hello, Rob" was one of them. "That was all it took. I grabbed her by the top of her head and dragged her over to Sheldon. 'This is her!' I told him. 'She said *hello* like a real person!'"

By January 1961, with all the pieces finally in place, Leonard directed Reiner's "The Sick Boy and the Sitter" script as the pilot episode of the newly christened *Dick Van Dyke Show*. On the basis of that outstanding opener, Procter & Gamble offered to sponsor the show as a weekly series on CBS.

But even with that sponsorship commitment, the producers allowed themselves only guarded optimism. Before the show found a spot on the network's fall schedule, they would have to counter an ominous resistance from a most unlikely source—the president of CBS himself.

Jim Aubrey was not an affable man. His cold-hearted demeanor had earned him the nickname "The Smiling Cobra," and the show's producers learned early on that he had no particular affection for *The Dick Van Dyke Show*. According to Leonard, at one point the executive even suggested that they change Rob Petrie's job from that of a writer to an insurance agent.

But in the early 1960s, powerful sponsors like Procter & Gamble still exerted a considerable influence over which programs did—or did not—make it to the network schedules. And in 1961, the soap manufacturer wanted *The Dick Van Dyke Show* on the air.

Carl Reiner recalls vividly the exact moment when he realized that the show was actually going to make it, when he happened to notice a high-ranking executive from Procter & Gamble sitting across from him on a commuter train from Manhattan. "He sat across the aisle from me and didn't say a word. Then I noticed that he made a little 'okay' sign with his hand. That was when I knew we were going to be all right."

Procter & Gamble's demands formed an edict that even a network president couldn't ignore, and finally Aubrey slated *The Dick Van Dyke Show* to premiere in early October. But despite his acquiescence, maintains Sheldon Leonard, the executive saddled their show with one of the worst time slots available—Tuesday nights at eight o'clock, far too early to reach the sophisticated adult audience they were counting on.

And there it languished, proving Sheldon Leonard's axiom that "the higher the quality of a show, the longer it will take to catch on with the general public." By that standard, *The Dick Van Dyke Show* must have been of very high quality indeed. The first year's ratings were so low that the series was actually canceled at the end of the season.

And yet, even as the cast and crew staged their farewell party, Sheldon Leonard refused to abandon hope.

He insisted that *The Dick Van Dyke Show* was on the brink of finding its audience and that—if given time—it would succeed. But the only ones who could buy that time were the executives at Procter & Gamble, and they had already withdrawn their sponsorship for the second season. The executive producer resolved to change their minds—even if he had to fly to the soap company's doorstep in Cincinnati, Ohio.

Which is exactly what he did.

Bleary-eyed after the all-night flight to Ohio, Sheldon Leonard made his eleventh-hour pitch in the office of a slightly astonished Procter & Gamble executive early one morning. Reaching deep into his actor's bag of tricks, Sheldon Leonard poured on the charm, drawing on the charisma that had made his countless portrayals of self-assured con men so lovably persuasive. In his own words, "I went back east, got down on one knee, and sang 'Mammy.'"

And it worked.

Procter & Gamble put up half the cash for a second season of *The Dick Van Dyke Show*, and Leonard repeated his performance for executives of the Lorillard Tobacco Company, who agreed to sign on as co-sponsors. And, sure enough, by the end of the second year, the series had caught on—beyond anyone's wildest dreams.

By the time *The Dick Van Dyke Show* left the air in 1966, it would be widely hailed as a masterpiece in the admittedly thin annals of television art. The show's unique combination of warmth, intelligence, and believability finally forced television comedy to grow out of a painful adolescence, setting a standard of excellence that would remain a dominant influence on quality television comedy for decades to come.

# A Critical Guide to All 158 Episodes

REGULAR CAST

| | |
|---:|:---|
| Rob Petrie | Dick Van Dyke |
| Laura Petrie | Mary Tyler Moore |
| Sally Rogers | Rose Marie |
| Buddy Sorrell | Morey Amsterdam |
| Mel Cooley | Richard Deacon |
| Jerry Helper | Jerry Paris |
| Millie Helper | Ann Morgan Guilbert |
| Ritchie Petrie | Larry Mathews |
| Alan Brady | Carl Reiner |


SUPPORTING CAST

| | |
|---:|:---|
| Fiona "Pickles" Sorrell | Barbara Perry |
| | Joan Shawlee |
| Sam Pomeroy (a.k.a. Pomerantz) | Allan Melvin |
| Sol Pomeroy | Marty Ingels |
| Freddie Helper | Peter Oliphant |
| | David Fresco |
| Herman Glimscher | Bill Idelson |
| Sam Petrie (Rob's father) | Tom Tully |
| | J. Pat O'Malley |
| Edward Petrie (Rob's father) | Will Wright |
| Clara Petrie (Rob's mother) | Isabel Randolph |
| | Carol Veasie |
| Mr. Meehan (Laura's father) | Carl Benton Reid |
| Mrs. Meehan (Laura's mother) | Geraldine Wall |
| Stacey Petrie (Rob's brother) | Jerry Van Dyke |


STOCK PLAYERS

Allan Melvin, Frank Adamo, Jamie Farr, Isabel Randolph, Herbie Faye,
Jerry Hausner, Johnny Silver, Doris Singleton, Amzie Strickland

Created by Carl Reiner
Music and theme song by Earle Hagen
Director of photography was Robert de Grasse
Principal directors were John Rich, Jerry Paris

## 1960    THE PILOT EPISODE

**Pilot**  Head of the Family                    July 19, 1960
  **Writer:** Carl Reiner
  **Director:** Don Weis
  **Guest Stars:** Carl Reiner, Barbara Britton, Gary Morgan, Sylvia
  Miles, Morty Gunty, Jack Wakefield, Milt Kamen, Nancy
  Kenyon

Comedy writer Rob Petrie tries to convince his skeptical son that
writing for TV is as exciting as the jobs held by any of the other
kids' dads.

A better-than-average one-camera sitcom, Carl Reiner's prototype for
*The Dick Van Dyke Show* was no more than a rough blueprint for the series that followed, so direct comparisons are unfair—if irresistible.
Reiner's aggressive interpretation of Rob Petrie as a slightly confused—
but well-intentioned—dad is not without its charm, though there's far
less warmth in the office scenes than we would later come to expect.
And the romantic sparks that would soon ignite Rob and Laura's domestic interplay are almost entirely lacking in this embryonic version.

The episode, which aired on CBS's *Comedy Spot* anthology series, also
starred Barbara Britton as Laura, and Gary Morgan as a surprisingly
winning Ritchie Petrie; Morty Gunty and Sylvia Miles played Buddy and
Sally; and Jack Wakefield essayed the positively demonic Alan Sturdy.
    Stuart Rosenberg and Martin Poll were the credited producers, and
Bernard Green composed the musical score.

## 1961-62    THE FIRST SEASON

*Year-End Rating: 16.1 (80th place)*

The triumphs and struggles of TV writer Rob Petrie and his wife, Laura,
are chronicled in a first season of exceptional scripts written or super-

vised by Carl Reiner, who will shepherd the series through its first three seasons as head writer, story consultant, and producer.

Sheldon Leonard serves as executive producer throughout each of the show's five seasons, and Ron Jacobs is associate producer for the entire run. John Rich signs on as regular director, and he will continue to direct most episodes through the show's first two seasons. Jay Sandrich is assistant director in the first year.

**1**　The Sick Boy and the Sitter　　　　　October 3, 1961
**Writer:** Carl Reiner
**Director:** Sheldon Leonard
**Guest Stars:** Mary Lee Dearing, Barbara Eiler, Stacy Keach, Sr.

Rob talks Laura into going to a party at Alan Brady's apartment, even though she'd rather stay home and look after their ailing five-year-old.

Rob and Laura Petrie emerge as believable human beings from the very first episode, as we watch them argue, cook liver, and fret about leaving their boy with the baby-sitter—just like real people. They also share a physical attraction that was remarkably frank for television, a direct result of Carl Reiner's refusal to let the couple telegraph their devotion in words. In five years, the pair rarely uttered the words "I love you" onscreen—because they never had to.

**2**　My Blonde-Haired Brunette　　　　　October 10, 1961
**Writer:** Carl Reiner
**Director:** John Rich
**Guest Star:** Benny Rubin

Laura dyes her hair blonde to rekindle Rob's interest after she becomes convinced that the romance has left their marriage.

Confronted with a disastrous dye job and a thoroughly confused husband, Laura finally breaks down and sobs her exasperation in a string of barely coherent phrases that communicate her poignant needs in a seemingly indecipherable code. Finally, at her wit's end, she collapses in Rob's arms—and somehow, he gets the message loud and clear. And so do we.

This script was actually the ninth episode filmed, but the producers scheduled it to run in the second week to better spotlight the quickly emerging talents of Mary Tyler Moore. As Reiner told a reporter for *TV Guide*, "It was obvious from the first that we had accidentally stumbled on a kid of twenty-three who could do comedy."

**3    Sally and the Lab Technician**                    October 17, 1961
**Writer:** Carl Reiner
**Director:** John Rich
**Guest Stars:** Eddie Firestone, Jamie Farr

Laura plays matchmaker for Sally—with disastrous results—when she pairs the talkative comedy writer with her shy cousin.

The first episode filmed by John Rich, the series's regular director through the start of the third season. A veteran director of *Our Miss Brooks* and scores of TV westerns in the 1950s, he had a knack for getting involved with classic comedies; a decade later he would direct four years of *All in the Family*, and he was also a key figure in the genesis of *Barney Miller*.

**4    Washington Versus the Bunny**                    October 24, 1961
**Writer:** Carl Reiner
**Director:** John Rich
**Guest Stars:** Jesse White, Jamie Farr

Rob is plagued by fatherly guilt when he's forced to take a business trip on the night of Ritchie's debut in the school play.

**5    Oh, How We Met the Night**                    October 31, 1961
      **That We Danced**
**Writer:** Carl Reiner
**Director:** Robert Butler
**Guest Stars:** Marty Ingels, Glenn Turnbull, Jennifer Gillespie, Chickie James

Rob recalls his frustrated attempts to date Laura when she was a USO showgirl and he was an over-eager sergeant in the Special Services.

The saga of the Petries takes on an epic quality in the first of many flashback episodes that describe significant moments in Rob and Laura's life together.

**6** Harrison B. Harding                    November 6, 1961
   of Camp Crowder, Mo.
**Writer:** Carl Reiner
**Director:** John Rich
**Guest Stars:** Allan Melvin, Peter Leeds, June Dayton

Rob is too embarrassed to admit that he doesn't remember the mysterious stranger who arrives and claims to be an old Army pal from Camp Crowder.

Ironically, Allan Melvin actually would play Rob's best Army pal in numerous later episodes. The well-known character actor also held down regular roles on *The Phil Silvers Show*, *Gomer Pyle*, and *All in the Family*, among others.

**7** Jealousy!                    November 7, 1961
**Writer:** Carl Reiner
**Director:** Sheldon Leonard
**Guest Star:** Joan Staley

Laura's jealousy gets the better of her when Rob begins working overtime with Alan Brady's gorgeous guest star.

**8** To Tell or Not to Tell                    November 14, 1961
**Writer:** David Adler
**Director:** John Rich
**Guest Star:** Jamie Farr

When Mel offers Laura an opportunity to dance on *The Alan Brady Show*, Rob worries that she might be tempted back into show business full-time.

David Adler, the first writer other than Carl Reiner to contribute scripts to the series, was actually a pseudonym for Frank Tarloff, a Hollywood screenwriter blacklisted as a Communist sympathizer in the fifties. A decade later, his son, Erik, would be a regular contributor to *All in the Family*.

**9** The Unwelcome Houseguest                    November 21, 1961
**Writer:** Carl Reiner
**Director:** Robert Butler

The Petries' plans for a weekend in the country are spoiled after

Buddy suckers Rob into looking after his family pet—Larry, a giant German shepherd.

**10    The Meershatz Pipe**                          November 28, 1961
  **Writer:** Carl Reiner
  **Director:** Sheldon Leonard
  **Guest Star:** Jon Silo

Rob worries about his job security when Buddy and Sally polish off an entire script while he's out sick.

**11    Forty-Four Tickets**                          December 5, 1961
  **Writer:** Carl Reiner
  **Director:** John Rich
  **Guest Stars:** Eleanor Audley, Opal Euard, Joe Devlin, Paul Bryar

Rob turns to scalpers as a last resort after he forgets to reserve forty-four tickets to *The Alan Brady Show* for his local PTA.

**12    Empress Carlotta's Necklace**                          December 12, 1961
  **Writer:** Carl Reiner
  **Director:** James Komack
  **Guest Stars:** Gavin MacLeod, Carol Veasie, Will Wright

Rob surprises Laura with an unexpected gift—a thoroughly tasteless necklace that she's far too embarrassed to wear.

Gavin MacLeod plays Maxwell, the jewelry salesman, in a role that predates his memorable stint as Murray Slaughter on the *Mary Tyler Moore Show* by almost a decade.

**13    Sally Is a Girl**                          December 19, 1961
  **Writer:** David Adler
  **Director:** John Rich
  **Guest Stars:** Jamie Farr, Paul Tripp, Barbara Perry

Buddy and Mel jump to conclusions when Rob decides to start treating Sally like a lady.

**14    Buddy, Can You Spare a Job?**                          December 26, 1961
  **Writer:** Walter Kempley
  **Director:** James Komack
  **Guest Star:** Len Weinrib

When Buddy's plan to leave for greener pastures backfires, Rob and Sally face the difficult task of convincing Mel to let him return.

Director James Komack became a successful TV producer in the 1970s, with a string of hits that included *The Courtship of Eddie's Father*, *Welcome Back, Kotter*, and *Chico and the Man*.

**15    Where Did I Come From?**                    January 3, 1962
**Writer:** Carl Reiner
**Director:** John Rich
**Guest Stars:** Herbie Faye, Jerry Hausner, Tiny Brauer

Rob recalls the final frantic days of Laura's pregnancy, which culminated in her arrival at the maternity ward in a laundry truck.

**16    The Curious Thing About Women**                    January 10, 1962
**Writer:** David Adler
**Director:** John Rich
**Guest Star:** Frank Adamo

Unable to control her curiosity, Laura can't resist opening a mysterious package that contains a large, self-inflating life raft.

**17    Punch Thy Neighbor**                    January 17, 1962
**Writer:** Carl Reiner
**Director:** John Rich
**Guest Stars:** Frank Adamo, Peter Oliphant, Jerry Hausner, Peter Leeds

Rob gets fighting mad after Jerry thoughtlessly broadcasts his low opinion of *The Alan Brady Show* throughout the neighborhood.

**18    Who Owes Who What?**                    January 24, 1962
**Writer:** Carl Reiner
**Director:** John Rich

Buddy remains oblivious to Rob's efforts to collect an old debt.

**19**   The Talented Neighborhood                    January 31, 1962
   **Writer:** Carl Reiner
   **Director:** John Rich
   **Guest Stars:** Doris Singleton, Ken Lynch, Michael Davis, Jack
   Davis, Barry Livingston, Anne Marie Hediger, Ilana Dowding,
   Kathleen Green, Christian Van Dyke, Barry Van Dyke, Cornell
   Chulay

When Alan Brady announces a juvenile talent competition, Rob
is besieged by pushy stage mothers and their would-be child stars.

**20**   A Word a Day                              February 7, 1962
   **Writer:** Jack Raymond
   **Director:** John Rich
   **Guest Stars:** William Schallert, Lia Waggner

Rob and Laura are disturbed when Ritchie's vocabulary expands
to include a small glossary of four-letter words.

**21**   The Boarder Incident                     February 14, 1962
   **Writers:** Norm Liebmann, Ed Haas
   **Director:** John Rich

Rob invites Buddy to spend a few days at his house while Pickles is out of town.

**22**   Father of the Week                       February 21, 1962
   **Writers:** Arnold and Lois Peyser
   **Director:** John Rich
   **Guest Stars:** Isabel Randolph, Allan Fielder, Patrick Thompson

Rob is crushed when he's not invited to speak on career day at
Ritchie's school because his son is embarrassed to admit how his
dad makes his living.

A rewrite of Carl Reiner's pilot script for *Head of the Family*. In the
original, Reiner's Rob Petrie redeemed himself with a clever poem composed for Ritchie's class, but in this version—adapted to emphasize the
unique talents of Dick Van Dyke—Rob wins the kids over with an impromptu demonstration of physical clowning.

**23**   The Twizzle                              February 28, 1962
   **Writer:** Carl Reiner
   **Director:** John Rich
   **Guest Stars:** Jerry Lanning, Jack Albertson, Tony Stag, Freddie
Blassie

Sally drags Mel and the writing staff to a bowling alley to audition
her latest discovery—a reluctant pop singer who's invented a new
dance craze.

Jerry Lanning sings "The Twizzle," written by pop tunesmiths Mack
David and Jerry Livingston.

**24**   One Angry Man                            March 7, 1962
   **Writers:** Leo Solomon, Ben Gershman
   **Director:** John Rich
   **Guest Stars:** Sue Ane Langdon, Dabbs Greer, Lee Bergere,
Doodles Weaver, Herb Vigran, Herbie Faye, Patsy Kelly,
Howard Wendell

Laura is convinced that a pretty face has tipped the scales of justice when Rob—on jury duty—sides with the attractive defendant.

**25**   Where You Been, Fassbinder?             March 14, 1962
   **Writer:** John Whedon
   **Director:** John Rich
   **Guest Stars:** George Neise, Barbara Perry

Sally pins her romantic dreams on Leo Fassbinder, an old ac-
quaintance she hopes will arrive to brighten a lonely birthday
celebration.

**26**   I Am My Brother's Keeper                March 21, 1962
   **Writer:** Carl Reiner
   **Director:** John Rich
   **Guest Star:** Jerry Van Dyke

Rob knows something's wrong when his brother arrives telling
jokes and singing songs—shy, retiring Stacey Petrie acts that way
only when he's sleepwalking.

Jerry Van Dyke's two-part appearance led to a checkered TV career for the star's younger brother that included starring parts in two sitcoms—*My Mother the Car* and *Accidental Family*—and a supporting role on *The Judy Garland Show* the following season. He later became a household name for his role as Luther Van Dam on *Coach*.

**27**    The Sleeping Brother                              March 28, 1962
  **Writer:** Carl Reiner
  **Director:** John Rich
  **Guest Star:** Jerry Van Dyke

Rob's somnambulant brother lands a guest spot on *The Alan Brady Show* and then wonders how he'll get through the show if he happens to be awake.

Whenever Rob and the gang break into song at a party—which they did quite often, particularly in the early seasons—the show reveals its strong ties to *The Danny Thomas Show*, which, like *I Love Lucy*, regularly incorporated music and dancing into its show-biz format. It was a happy coincidence that Reiner ended up filming his show on Danny Thomas's stages, since the writer identified Thomas's program as one of the primary models—along with *Leave It to Beaver*—that inspired him when he sat down to create his own series.

**28**    The Bad Old Days                                  April 4, 1962
  **Writers:** Norm Liebmann, Ed Haas
  **Director:** John Rich

Rob rebels against Laura's domestic tyranny after Buddy convinces him that he's become hopelessly henpecked.

**29**    Sol and the Sponsor                               April 11, 1962
  **Writer:** Walter Kempley
  **Director:** John Rich
  **Guest Stars:** Marty Ingels, Patty Regan, Roy Roberts, Isabel Randolph

Rob can't bring himself to tell a boisterous old Army buddy that he's not invited to stay for the fancy dinner the Petries are hosting for an important sponsor.

Marty Ingels left the occasional role of Sol Pomeroy to star in *I'm Dickens, He's Fenster* in 1962. Allan Melvin assumed the role of Rob's Army pal in later episodes.

**30**   The Return of Happy Spangler                April 18, 1962
  **Writer:** Carl Reiner
  **Director:** John Rich
  **Guest Star:** Jay C. Flippen

Rob runs into the old-timer who gave him his first break in show business and makes the mistake of trying to return the favor.

## 1962-63   THE SECOND SEASON

*Year-End Rating: 27.1 (9th place)*

Carl Reiner continues as producer and head writer in the show's second year, once again contributing most of the season's scripts, with a welcome assist from Sheldon Keller and Howard Merrill, who would continue to write for the show through the fourth season. John Rich returns as staff director, and John C. Chulay signs on as assistant director—a position he maintains for the remainder of the show's run.

**31**   Never Name a Duck                    September 26, 1962
  **Writer:** Carl Reiner
  **Director:** John Rich
  **Guest Stars:** Jerry Hausner, Jane Dulo, Geraldine Wall, Frank Adamo

Ritchie is grief-stricken by the death of his pet duck.

**32**   The Two Faces of Rob                    October 3, 1962
  **Writers:** Sheldon Keller, Howard Merrill
  **Director:** John Rich
  **Guest Star:** Herbie Faye

Posing as a mysterious stranger, Rob calls Laura and asks for a date—a prank that backfires when she accepts his invitation.

**33**   The Attempted Marriage                    October 10, 1962
  **Writer:** Carl Reiner
  **Director:** John Rich
  **Guest Stars:** Sandy Kenyon, Ray Kellogg, Dabbs Greer

Rob recalls the disastrous circumstances that led to his beleaguered arrival at his own wedding—battered, bruised, and three hours late.

Carl Reiner fondly recalls the sequence where Rob shudders as he summons the courage to propose to Laura in an open Jeep. "That was my proposal! When I asked my wife to marry me, I got chills just like that." The producer took pride that most of the stories on the show sprang from events that had actually happened to him, or someone on the staff. "I would always ask writers," he explained, "'What happened to you today?' and not, 'What have you seen lately—and how can we change it around for a story?'"

Writer Bill Persky found that the search for storylines could become a comical obsession. In *Look* magazine, he recalled getting a flat tire on a deserted Mexican roadway. "I was scared to death, but I was thinking, how can I put this in the show?"

**34**  Bank Book 6565696                                   October 17, 1962
  **Writers:** Ray Allen Saffian, Harvey Bullock
  **Director:** John Rich

Rob's imagination runs rampant when he discovers a sizable sum of cash stowed away in Laura's secret bank account.

**35**  Hustling the Hustler                                October 24, 1962
  **Writer:** Carl Reiner
  **Director:** John Rich
  **Guest Star:** Phil Leeds

Buddy worries that his incorrigible brother plans to fleece Rob when the supposedly reformed gambler challenges the head writer to a friendly game of pool.

**36**  My Husband Is Not a Drunk                           October 31, 1962
  **Writer:** Carl Reiner
  **Director:** Al Rafkin
  **Guest Stars:** Charles Aidman, Roy Roberts

Rob suffers from a post-hypnotic suggestion that forces him to act hopelessly inebriated every time he hears a bell ring.

**37**  What's in a Middle Name?                            November 7, 1962
  **Writer:** Carl Reiner
  **Director:** John Rich
  **Guest Stars:** Carl Benton Reid, Geraldine Wall, Cyril Delevanti, J. Pat O'Malley, Isabel Randolph

Rob tells Ritchie how he was given the middle name Rosebud in order to settle a feud that raged among his grandparents before he was born.

**38    Like a Sister**                    November 14, 1962
**Writer:** Carl Reiner
**Director:** Hal Cooper
**Guest Star:** Vic Damone

Rob is concerned that Sally may be developing romantic illusions about Ric Vallone, the handsome singer who's been flirting with her all week.

**39    The Night the Roof Fell In**                    November 21, 1962
**Writer:** John Whedon
**Director:** Hal Cooper
**Guest Star:** Peter Oliphant

Rob and Laura recount vastly different versions of a spat that sent Rob storming out of the house.

**40    The Secret Life of Buddy and Sally**       November 28, 1962
**Writer:** Lee Erwin
**Director:** Coby Ruskin
**Guest Star:** Phil Arnold

Rob suspects foul play when Buddy and Sally mysteriously disappear together every weekend.

**41    A Bird in the Head Hurts**                    December 5, 1962
**Writer:** Carl Reiner
**Director:** John Rich
**Guest Star:** Cliff Norton

Rob and Laura worry that Ritchie may be suffering from an overactive imagination when he complains that he's been attacked by a giant woodpecker.

**42    Gesundheit, Darling**                    December 12, 1962
**Writer:** Carl Reiner
**Director:** John Rich
**Guest Star:** Sandy Kenyon

A sudden fit of uncontrollable sneezing has Rob worried that he's developed an allergic reaction to Laura.

**43**    A Man's Teeth Are Not His Own        December 19, 1962
   **Writer:** Carl Reiner
   **Director:** John Rich

Rob is afraid that Jerry will never forgive him after he lets another dentist perform emergency work on his teeth.

**44**    Somebody Has to Play Cleopatra        December 26, 1962
   **Writer:** Martin A. Ragaway
   **Director:** John Rich
   **Guest Stars:** Valerie Yerke, Eleanor Audley, Bob Crane, Shirley Mitchell

Rob has his hands full directing the latest neighborhood variety show; none of the husbands are too keen on letting *their* wife play Cleopatra.

Guest star Bob Crane would move on to a regular spot on *The Donna Reed Show* before he assumed the lead role in CBS's long-running wartime sitcom *Hogan's Heroes*.

**45**    The Cat Burglar                        January 2, 1963
   **Writer:** Carl Reiner
   **Director:** John Rich
   **Guest Stars:** Barney Phillips, Johnny Silver

Rob and Laura are unable to unravel the mystery of how a cat burglar stole their living-room set without leaving any clues.

**46**    The Foul-Weather Girl                  January 9, 1963
   **Writer:** Carl Reiner
   **Director:** John Rich
   **Guest Star:** Joan O'Brien

The TV weather girl from Rob's hometown asks him to help her land a role on *The Alan Brady Show*—a proposition that Laura eyes with suspicion.

Rob responds to Laura's jealousy by accusing her of sounding "exactly like one of those wives in a situation comedy." That such a comment could be delivered without self-consciousness offers a clue to the show's growing sophistication. The world of the Petries had become so real that we could easily envision Rob and Laura sitting through annoying half-hour comedies, just as we did.

**47**   Will You Two Be My Wife?                January 16, 1963
   **Writer:** Carl Reiner
   **Director:** John Rich
   **Guest Stars:** Barbara Bain, Ray Kellogg, Allan Melvin

Rob faces the fury of a woman scorned in a flashback that recounts how he lowered the boom on his hometown sweetheart after his engagement to Laura.

**48**   Ray Murdock's X-Ray                January 23, 1963
   **Writer:** Carl Reiner
   **Director:** Jerry Paris
   **Guest Stars:** Gene Lyons, Jerry Hausner

Laura feels betrayed when Rob tells a TV interviewer how she inspired most of the outlandish domestic situations featured on *The Alan Brady Show*.

Jerry Paris began his long tenure as the primary director of *The Dick Van Dyke Show* with this episode. John Rich recalls how he came to appoint the actor as his successor when he left the series to direct feature films. "Carl and Sheldon were worried about what would happen to the show," he remembers. "But it was already firmly on the tracks. The cast and the writing were so solid, I told them, that anyone could direct the show—I looked around, and Jerry happened to be standing there—even *him*. Actually, Jerry turned out to be a fine director. He did an excellent job."

The show's creator recalls a different account of how the talented director found his calling. According to Carl Reiner, Paris had been anxious to direct from the very start. "But he was such a fidgety guy, no one thought he'd be very good as a director. After John left, we finally gave Jerry a chance, and he did better than anyone dreamed. He finally surprised us all."

**49**   I Was a Teenage Head Writer                January 30, 1963
   **Writers:** Sheldon Keller, Howard Merrill
   **Director:** Jerry Paris

When Buddy and Sally refuse to join Rob in an impulsive walkout, he recalls his tempestuous early days as a writer on *The Alan Brady Show*.

**50**    It May Look Like a Walnut!              February 6, 1963
   **Writer:** Carl Reiner
   **Director:** Jerry Paris
   **Guest Star:** Danny Thomas

A late-show thriller gives Rob a nightmare about a world-domina-
tion plot cooked up by an alien who looks exactly like Danny
Thomas.

**51**    My Husband Is a Check-Grabber          February 13, 1963
   **Writer:** Carl Reiner
   **Director:** Al Rafkin
   **Guest Stars:** Phil Arnold, Bill Idelson, Joan Shawlee

The Petries' latest skirmish springs from Rob's annoying habit of
always picking up the check when they're out with friends.

Laura gives Rob the silent treatment on the ride home from the restaurant as he tries to figure out just what he did that got her so riled.
"Well," she finally volunteers, "I think it's pretty terrible not to be able
to send our son to college." And from that marvelous leap in logic, the
quarrel escalates in a funny, dizzying spiral, and we laugh as we recognize how in comedy—as well as in marriage—what isn't said often reveals more than what is.

**52**    Don't Trip Over That Mountain          February 20, 1963
   **Writer:** Carl Reiner
   **Director:** Coby Ruskin
   **Guest Stars:** Jean Allison, Ray Kellogg

Fearing disaster, Laura warns Rob not to go on a weekend ski trip
and then blames herself for the inevitable accident.

**53**    Give Me Your Walls!                    February 27, 1963
   **Writer:** Carl Reiner
   **Director:** Jerry Paris
   **Guest Star:** Vito Scotti

Laura hires a flamboyant artist to paint the living-room walls but
has second thoughts when the ingratiating con man takes over the
entire household.

**54**    The Sam Pomerantz Scandals                    March 6, 1963
**Writer:** Carl Reiner
**Director:** Claudio Guzman
**Guest Stars:** Henry Calvin, Len Weinrib, Joan Shawlee

Rob convinces Laura and the gang to stage a variety show at an old pal's Catskills resort.

Rob and his old Army pal revive their old Laurel and Hardy routine in what amounts to Dick Van Dyke's own heartfelt homage to the movie comedy team. The star frequently acknowledged Stan Laurel's influence on his work, especially the screen comedian's talent for "taking one simple prop and doing fifteen minutes with it"—a gift that would also prove to be Van Dyke's forte in the many extended solo bits that would appear in later episodes.

**55**    The Square Triangle                    March 20, 1963
**Writer:** Bill Idelson
**Director:** Jerry Paris
**Guest Star:** Jacques Bergerac

Buddy and Sally are puzzled when Rob vanishes every time the show's handsome French guest star walks in.

Writer Bill Idelson also appeared in a handful of episodes as Sally's forlorn boyfriend, Herman Glimscher. He continued to forge a distinguished career as a comedy writer and eventually produced much of the first year of MTM's *The Bob Newhart Show*.

**56**    I'm No Henry Walden!                    March 27, 1963
**Writer:** Carl Reiner
**Story By:** Ray Brenner, Jack Guss
**Director:** Jerry Paris
**Guest Stars:** Everett Sloane, Doris Packer, Roxanne Berard, Betty Lou Gerson, Frank Adamo, Howard Wendell, Carl Reiner

Rob feels self-conscious when he discovers that he's the only comedy writer at a literary gathering.

Carl Reiner does a lively bit as Yale Sampson, an English philosopher prone to double-talk. The canny producer supplied himself with ample opportunities to chew scenery, even after he assumed the on camera role of Alan Brady in the show's third year.

**57**   Racy Tracy Rattigan                                    April 3, 1963
   **Writers:** Ronald Alexander, Carl Reiner
   **Director:** Sheldon Leonard
   **Guest Star:** Richard Dawson

Alan Brady's summer replacement is Tracy Rattigan, a lecherous flirt who tests Rob's patience when he zeroes in on Laura.

Richard Dawson later discovered enormous popularity as a game-show host, though not before he would log scores of sitcom appearances—including regular roles on *Hogan's Heroes* and in the final incarnation of *The New Dick Van Dyke Show* in the early seventies.

**58**   Divorce                                             April 10, 1963
   **Writer:** Carl Reiner
   **Director:** Jerry Paris
   **Guest Stars:** Joan Shawlee, Charles Cantor, Marian Collier

Rob plays amateur marriage counselor when Buddy threatens to divorce Pickles over a silly misunderstanding.

**59**   It's a Shame She Married Me                          April 17, 1963
   **Writers:** Sheldon Keller, Howard Merrill
   **Director:** James Niver
   **Guest Star:** Robert Vaughn

Rob makes a fool of himself by attempting to outdo Laura's old boyfriend, a suave and wealthy industrialist.

**60**   A Surprise Surprise Is a Surprise                   April 24, 1963
   **Writer:** Carl Reiner
   **Director:** Jerry Paris

Rob tries to second-guess Laura's plan to surprise him on his birthday.

**61**   Jilting the Jilter                                    May 1, 1963
   **Writer:** Ronald Alexander
   **Director:** Jerry Paris
   **Guest Star:** Guy Marks

Sally's latest heartthrob is a stand-up comic who's badly in need of a new writer, which is exactly what Rob and Buddy suspect he's after.

**62**   When a Bowling Pin Talks, Listen                May 8, 1963
   **Writer:** Martin A. Ragaway
   **Director:** Jerry Paris
   **Guest Stars:** Jon Silo, Herbie Faye, Carl Reiner

Ritchie helps his dad overcome a bout with writer's block when the boy inadvertently causes Rob to plagiarize a sketch idea from a TV kid's show.

## 1963-64   THE THIRD SEASON

*Year-End Rating: 33.3 (3rd place)*

The creative team expands with the permanent addition of Bill Persky and Sam Denoff, who—along with Jerry Belson and Garry Marshall—make their first significant story contributions in the third year. The new writers work under the close supervision of Carl Reiner, who continues as producer, story consultant, and head writer in the third season.

Jerry Paris succeeds John Rich as the series's regular director, a position he will maintain for the final three seasons.

**63**   That's My Boy???                September 25, 1963
   **Writers:** Bill Persky, Sam Denoff
   **Director:** John Rich
   **Guest Stars:** Greg Morris, Mimi Dillard, Amzie Strickland

Rob recalls Ritchie's birth and a series of mix-ups that had him convinced he'd brought the wrong baby home from the hospital.

Of course, as Rob discovers when he finally meets them, it's unlikely that Mr. and Mrs. Peters could've confused the Petries' baby for their own, since they're black. Strange as it seems now, this relatively innocuous topper caused great controversy in 1963. After being rejected by both CBS and the sponsor, the script was only filmed after executive producer Sheldon Leonard offered to reshoot the ending if it didn't play to the live studio audience. The producers were vindicated when the gag received the longest ovation in the show's history.

Writers Persky and Denoff began their long tenure on the show with this script, after a false start the previous year. In *The Dick Van Dyke Show: Anatomy of a Classic*, authors Ginny Weissman and Coyne Steven Sanders recount how Carl Reiner rejected the team's first submission outright. When they returned a few months later with "That's My Boy???" the producer was so impressed that he offered them permanent jobs. "If I hadn't found Persky and Denoff in the third year," Reiner observed, only half joking, "I think I would have had a heart attack."

**64**    The Masterpiece                              October 2, 1963
   **Writers:** Sam Denoff, Bill Persky
   **Director:** John Rich
   **Guest Stars:** Howard Morris, Alan Reed, Amzie Strickland, Ray Kellogg

The Petries become instant art collectors when Rob accidentally places the high bid at an art auction.

Guest star Howard Morris—an old crony from Carl Reiner's days with Sid Caesar in the 1950s—also directed a handful of episodes in the show's third and fourth seasons.

**65**    Laura's Little Lie                             October 9, 1963
   **Writers:** Carl Reiner, Howard Merrill
   **Director:** John Rich
   **Guest Star:** Charles Aidman

The Petries discover that their marriage may not be legally binding after Laura confesses that she lied about her age on their marriage license.

**66**    Very Old Shoes, Very Old Rice                  October 16, 1963
   **Writer:** Carl Reiner
   **Director:** John Rich
   **Guest Stars:** Burt Mustin, Madge Blake, Russell Collins

Rob and Laura renew their vows in a hastily arranged ceremony, even though neither is speaking to the other.

This was the farewell episode directed by John Rich, who left the series to direct feature films.

**67**    All About Eavesdropping                        October 23, 1963
   **Writers:** Sheldon Keller, Howard Merrill
   **Director:** Stanley Cherry

The Petries get an earful when they accidentally listen in on Millie and Jerry over Ritchie's toy intercom.

**68**  Too Many Stars                                    October 30, 1963
   **Writers:** Sheldon Keller, Howard Merrill
   **Director:** Jerry Paris
   **Guest Stars:** Sylvia Lewis, Eleanor Audley, Jerry Hausner, Eddie
   Ryder

Rob has to choose between Laura and a beautiful new neighbor
for the lead role when he directs the annual PTA revue.

**69**  Who and Where Was Antonio              November 6, 1963
       Stradivarius?
   **Writer:** Carl Reiner
   **Director:** Jerry Paris
   **Guest Stars:** Sallie Janes, Betty Lou Gerson, Hal Peary, Amzie
   Strickland, Chet Stratton

Rob finds himself the life of the party in Red Hook, New Jersey,
during a temporary bout with amnesia, while Laura waits up nervously in New Rochelle.

**70**  Uncle George                              November 13, 1963
   **Writer:** Bill Idelson
   **Director:** Jerry Paris
   **Guest Stars:** Denver Pyle, Bill Idelson, Elvia Allman

Rob's exuberant Uncle George comes to New York to find a wife
and sets his sights on Sally.

**71**  Big Max Calvada                           November 20, 1963
   **Writers:** Bill Persky, Sam Denoff
   **Director:** Jerry Paris
   **Guest Stars:** Sheldon Leonard, Art Batanides, Jack Larson, Sue
   Casey, Tiny Brauer, Johnny Silver

Rob, Buddy, and Sally's latest assignment finds them under the
gun—perhaps literally—when a mobster asks them to pen a comedy routine for his nephew.

Executive producer Sheldon Leonard was a natural for the role of Big
Max, having played scores of Runyonesque tough guys in his career as
an actor in films and TV. The character's name was also an in-joke—
Calvada Productions was the company that owned *The Dick Van Dyke
Show*.

**72**    The Ballad of the Betty Lou              November 27, 1963
     **Writer:** Martin A. Ragaway
     **Director:** Howard Morris
     **Guest Star:** Danny Scholl

Landlubbers Rob and Jerry buy a sailboat, but run aground due to their petty squabbles on deck.

**73**    Turtles, Ties, and Toreadors              December 4, 1963
     **Writer:** John Whedon
     **Director:** Jerry Paris
     **Guest Stars:** Miriam Colon, Tiny Brauer, Alan Dexter

Rob hires a maid to help out around the house, but the incompetent domestic who arrives only makes Laura's life more complicated.

Maria offers the Petries an unusual gift—a box turtle with the family's caricature painted on its shell. The actual cartoon was sketched by Van Dyke himself, an enthusiastic doodler.

**74**    The Sound of the Trumpets              December 11, 1963
          of Conscience Falls Deafly
          on a Brain That Holds Its Ears
     **Writers:** Bill Persky, Sam Denoff
     **Director:** Jerry Paris
     **Guest Stars:** Ken Lynch, Bernie Hamilton, Edward Holmes

Rob can't decide whether to testify when he discovers he's the only witness to a jewelry-store holdup.

**75**    The Alan Brady Show Presents              December 18, 1963
     **Writers:** Bill Persky, Sam Denoff
     **Director:** Jerry Paris
     **Guest Stars:** Carl Reiner, Cornell Chulay, Brendan Freeman

Alan Brady revamps his Christmas show into a Yuletide extravaganza starring Rob, Laura, and the rest of his show's talented writing staff.

Carl Reiner makes his first full onscreen appearance as Alan Brady, after hiding in the shadows for his occasional cameos during the first two seasons. The producer resisted casting an actor in the role because he didn't think a bit player would be convincing enough playing a star of Alan Brady's magnitude. "I wanted the audience to think of Milton Berle or Danny Thomas," Reiner said, "not some guy I hired for $600."

**76**    The Third One From the Left                January 1, 1964
**Writer:** John Whedon
**Director:** Jerry Paris
**Guest Stars:** Cheryl Holdridge, Jimmy Murphy

Rob seeks Laura's advice when he finds himself the reluctant object of an enthusiastic young dancer's affections.

**77**    My Husband Is the Best One                January 8, 1964
**Writer:** Martin A. Ragaway
**Director:** Jerry Paris
**Guest Stars:** Valerie Yerke, Carl Reiner, Frank Adamo

Rob faces a frigid reception from his co-workers after Laura convinces a journalist that her husband is the brains behind *The Alan Brady Show*.

**78**    The Lady and the Tiger and the Lawyer    January 15, 1964
**Writers:** Garry Marshall, Jerry Belson
**Director:** Jerry Paris
**Guest Stars:** Anthony Eisley, Lyla Graham

The Petries stage a matchmaking competition to see whether a new bachelor in the neighborhood prefers Sally to Laura's cousin, Donna.

An early script from Garry Marshall and Jerry Belson, the talented pair who later turned Neil Simon's *Odd Couple* into a hit series. Garry Marshall would eventually forge one of the most formidable dynasties in sitcom history with *Happy Days* and its family of spin-offs in the 1970s.

**79**    The Life and Love of Joe Coogan          January 22, 1964
**Writer:** Carl Reiner
**Director:** Jerry Paris
**Guest Stars:** Michael Forrest, Johnny Silver

Rob is overcome with jealousy when he meets one of Laura's old beaus at the golf club and then discovers that she saved a box of his old love poems.

**80**    A Nice Friendly Game of Cards              January 29, 1964
**Writer:** Ernest Chambers
**Director:** Howard Morris
**Guest Stars:** Edward C. Platt, Shirley Mitchell

Rob is a big winner in poker, though it nearly costs him his friends after they discover he's been dealing from a marked deck.

**81**    Happy Birthday and Too Many More          February 5, 1964
**Writers:** Bill Persky, Sam Denoff
**Director:** Jerry Paris
**Guest Stars:** Michael Chulay, Cornell Chulay, Brendan Freeman, Tony Paris, Johnny Silver

After Rob scotches Laura's elaborate plans for Ritchie's birthday party, he faces the challenge of entertaining sixty-three screaming kids in the Petrie living room.

**82**    The Brave and the Backache                February 12, 1964
**Writers:** Sheldon Keller, Howard Merrill
**Director:** Jerry Paris
**Guest Stars:** Ken Berry, Ross Elliott

Laura is convinced that Rob's recurring backache is a subconscious sign that he really doesn't want to spend the weekend alone with her.

**83**    The Pen Is Mightier Than the Mouth        February 19, 1964
**Writers:** Bill Persky, Sam Denoff
**Director:** Jerry Paris
**Guest Stars:** Dick Patterson, Herb Vigran, Johnny Silver

Sally considers leaving her job on *The Alan Brady Show* after she makes a big splash on a late-night talk show.

**84**    My Part-Time Wife                         February 26, 1964
**Writers:** Bill Persky, Sam Denoff
**Director:** Jerry Paris
**Guest Star:** Jackie Joseph

Rob reluctantly hires Laura as interim secretary during Sally's absence.

Buddy and Rob's inability to cope with Sally's temporary absence underscores the creative symbiosis the trio enjoyed under normal circumstances. Not surprisingly, Carl Reiner's fictional staff had real-life counterparts in the writers' room of *Your Show of Shows*. "Alan Brady was Sid Caesar," the creator admits. "Sally was a combination of Lucille Kallen and Selma Diamond, and Buddy was Mel Brooks."

**85**     Honeymoons Are for the Lucky        March 4, 1964
**Writer:** Carl Reiner
**Director:** Jerry Paris
**Guest Stars:** Johnny Silver, Kathleen Freeman, Allan Melvin, Peter Hobbs

Rob recalls how he and Laura spent their honeymoon in a dilapidated wedding suite when he went AWOL from Camp Crowder.

**86**     How to Spank a Star        March 11, 1964
**Writers:** Nathaniel Curtis, Bill Idelson
**Director:** Jerry Paris
**Guest Star:** Lola Albright

Laura is jealous when Rob is appointed producer of *The Alan Brady Show* as a sop to the show's beautiful, but spoiled, guest star.

This episode offers a vivid comic portrait of marital discord in the painfully funny sequence where Laura chews her pot roast and potatoes alone while Rob feebly explains how he dined on chicken fricassee with the flirtatious starlet. Laura's fuming anger suggests a more complex motivation than petty jealousy: She also resents that Rob gets to travel through a world of movie stars and romantic temptation while she's stuck at home with a faulty garbage disposal. Mary Tyler Moore once observed, "Laura Petrie was nothing more than an extension of her husband and child, but she didn't question it." But if Laura never questioned her role, she was certainly no stranger to the frustrations of its limitations.

The actress presumably had no such complaints about the character she played in her own series a few years later. And yet, it's doubtful that Mary Richards would ever have considered trying to make it on her own if the seeds of her independence hadn't been planted so many years earlier by a headstrong young housewife in Capri pants.

**87**   The Plots Thicken                    March 18, 1964
   **Writers:** Carl Reiner, Bill Persky, Sam Denoff
   **Director:** Jerry Paris
   **Guest Stars:** J. Pat O'Malley, Isabel Randolph, Geraldine Wall,
   Carl Benton Reid

The Petries are caught in a raging debate as their in-laws fight to
determine where Rob and Laura will make their final resting
place.

**88**   Scratch My Car and Die                March 25, 1964
   **Writer:** John Whedon
   **Director:** Howard Morris

Rob is obsessed with his new sports car, which doesn't make it
any easier for Laura to confess when she brings it home with a
brand-new scratch.

Dick Van Dyke had a similar weakness for fancy sports cars. When
the episode was written, he had recently indulged himself with the pur-
chase of a Jaguar XKE.

**89**   The Return of Edwin Carp                April 1, 1964
   **Writer:** Carl Reiner
   **Director:** Howard Morris
   **Guest Stars:** Richard Haydn, Arlene Harris, Bert Gordon

Rob attempts to coax a legendary radio star out of retirement for
a guest spot on a TV special.

**90**   October Eve                            April 8, 1964
   **Writers:** Bill Persky, Sam Denoff
   **Director:** Jerry Paris
   **Guest Stars:** Carl Reiner, Howard Wendell, Genevieve Griffin

Laura encounters a long-forgotten skeleton from her closet when
a nude oil portrait bearing her face surfaces at a prominent gallery.

A classic episode that features Carl Reiner in one of his best guest
roles, as the newly respectable bohemian artist Serge Carpetna.

**91**   Dear Mrs. Petrie, Your Husband Is in Jail       April 15, 1964
   **Writers:** Jerry Belson, Garry Marshall
   **Director:** Jerry Paris
   **Guest Stars:** Herkie Styles, Barbara Stuart, Jackie Joseph, Johnny Silver, Art Batanides, Henry Scott

Rob ventures into a steamy honky-tonk to catch an old buddy's nightclub act and winds up in jail on vice charges.

**92**   My Neighbor's Husband's Other Life       April 22, 1964
   **Writers:** Carl Reiner, Bill Persky, Sam Denoff
   **Director:** Jerry Paris
   **Guest Star:** Johnny Silver

Laura and Rob suspect the worst after they spot Jerry having dinner at a fancy restaurant with a beautiful blonde.

**93**   I'd Rather Be Bald Than Have No Head at All   April 29, 1964
   **Writers:** Bill Persky, Sam Denoff
   **Director:** Jerry Paris
   **Guest Star:** Ned Glass

Worried that he might be going prematurely bald, Rob consults a quack who administers a bizarre vinegar-and-oil treatment.

**94**   Teacher's Petrie                          May 13, 1964
   **Writers:** Jerry Belson, Garry Marshall
   **Director:** Jerry Paris
   **Guest Stars:** Bernard Fox, Cheerio Meredith

Rob is unable to share Laura's enthusiasm for a creative-writing course after he begins to suspect her attentive instructor's motives.

## 1964-65   THE FOURTH SEASON

*Year-End Rating: 27.1 (7th place)*

Carl Reiner continues as producer of the series's fourth season of popular and critical acclaim. Story consultants Bill Persky and Sam Denoff write a majority of the season's scripts, with notable contributions from

Reiner, Garry Marshall, Jerry Belson, and Joseph C. Cavella, among others.

**95**    My Mother Can Beat Up My Father          September 23, 1964
   **Writers:** Bill Persky, Sam Denoff
   **Director:** Jerry Paris
   **Guest Stars:** Paul Gilbert, Ken Berry, Tom Avera, Imelda de Martin, Lou Cutell

Laura flattens an obnoxious drunk after he slugs Rob, but mainly succeeds in wounding her husband's delicate pride.

**96**    The Ghost of A. Chantz                  September 30, 1964
   **Writers:** Bill Persky, Sam Denoff
   **Director:** Jerry Paris
   **Guest Stars:** Maurice Brenner, Milton Parsons

Rob and Laura share an unsettling night with Buddy and Sally in a haunted cabin.

**97**    The Lady and the Baby-Sitter              October 7, 1964
   **Writers:** Bill Persky, Sam Denoff
   **Director:** Jerry Paris
   **Guest Star:** Eddie Hodges

The Petries' teenage baby-sitter develops an adolescent crush on Laura.

**98**    A Vigilante Ripped My Sports Coat        October 14, 1964
   **Writer:** Carl Reiner
   **Director:** Peter Baldwin

Rob and Jerry lock horns when Rob refuses to join the vigilante group Jerry formed to police the neighborhood lawns.

Carl Reiner, himself a former resident of the sleepy suburb of New Rochelle, concocts a sly satire of suburban life in his dark tale of how one man's unruly crabgrass very nearly incites the neighborhood to mob action.

**99**    The Man From Emperor                    October 21, 1964
**Writers:** Bill Persky, Sam Denoff, Carl Reiner
**Director:** Jerry Paris
**Guest Stars:** Lee Philips, Gloria Neil, Nadia Sanders, Sally
Carter, Tracy Butler

Rob is tempted by an offer to join the editorial staff of a glossy
men's magazine, though Laura has other ideas.

**100**    Romance, Roses, and Rye Bread                    October 28, 1964
**Writers:** Garry Marshall, Jerry Belson
**Director:** Jerry Paris
**Guest Stars:** Sid Melton, Jeri Lou James, Frank Adamo

Sally discovers an unlikely admirer when the local deli man delivers a single red rose along with her chicken salad.

**101**    4½                    November 4, 1964
**Writers:** Garry Marshall, Jerry Belson
**Director:** Jerry Paris
**Guest Star:** Don Rickles

Rob recalls the story of Lyle Delp—a hapless stickup man who
had the misfortune to rob the Petries in a stalled elevator.

The holdup man is played by Don Rickles, who had known Bill Persky
and Sam Denoff since the days when they wrote material for his nightclub act.

**102**    *The Alan Brady Show* Goes to Jail       November 11, 1964
**Writers:** Bill Persky, Sam Denoff
**Director:** Jerry Paris
**Guest Stars:** Don Rickles, Robert Strauss, Arthur Batanides, Ken
Lynch, Allan Melvin, Vincent Barbi

The gang's all set to perform a show inside prison gates when
Rob is mistaken for one of the inmates.

**103**    Three Letters From One Wife                    November 18, 1964
**Writers:** Bill Persky, Sam Denoff
**Director:** Jerry Paris
**Guest Stars:** Carl Reiner, Valerie Yerke

Millie and Laura wage an ill-fated write-in campaign to bolster Rob's standing in Alan Brady's eyes.

**104**   Pink Pills and Purple Parents              November 25, 1964
   **Writers**: Garry Marshall, Jerry Belson
   **Director:** Alan Rafkin
   **Guest Stars:** Isabel Randolph, Tom Tully

Rob recalls Laura's first disastrous encounter with his parents, after she'd taken a few too many of Millie's little pink pills to relax her nerves.

Director Alan Rafkin went on to become one of TV's most prolific comedy directors; his later credits include early episodes of *The Andy Griffith Show*, *One Day at a Time*, and MTM's *The Bob Newhart Show*, among many others.

**105**   It Wouldn't Hurt Them              December 2, 1964
            to Give Us a Raise
   **Writers:** Jay Burton, Ernest Chambers
   **Director:** Peter Baldwin
   **Guest Star:** Roger C. Carmel
   Rob enters the labyrinth of corporate finance when he tries to squeeze a raise for Buddy and Sally from Alan Brady's tightfisted accountant.

**106**   The Death of the Party              December 9, 1964
   **Writers:** Bill Persky, Sam Denoff
   **Director:** Alan Rafkin
   **Guest Stars:** Willard Waterman, Jane Dulo, Patty Regan, Pitt Herbert

Despite chills and a raging fever, Rob is determined to get through Laura's family reunion without anyone guessing that he's deathly ill.

**107**   My Two Show-Offs and Me              December 16, 1964
   **Writers:** Sheldon Keller, Howard Merrill
   **Director:** Jerry Paris
   **Guest Star:** Doris Singleton

The attentions of a visiting reporter transform Alan Brady's writing staff into a trio of bickering grandstanders.

**108** Stretch Petrie Versus Kid Schenk   December 30, 1964
**Writers:** Garry Marshall, Jerry Belson
**Director:** Jerry Paris
**Guest Stars:** Jack Carter, Peter Hobbs, Lynn Borden, Albert
Carrier, Judy Taylor, Sally Carter

Rob finds it impossible to stand up to Neil Schenk, an opportunistic old friend who comes fishing for a job in return for an ancient
favor.

**109** Brother, Can You Spare $2,500?   January 6, 1965
**Writers:** Garry Marshall, Jerry Belson
**Director:** Jerry Paris
**Guest Stars:** Gene Baylos, Herbie Faye, Jimmy Cross, Tiny
Brauer, Larry Blake, Brian Nash, Sheila Rogers

A lost *Alan Brady Show* script is recovered by a vagrant, who demands that Rob pay $2,500 in exchange for its safe return.

**110** The Impractical Joke   January 13, 1965
**Writers:** Bill Persky, Sam Denoff
**Director:** Jerry Paris
**Guest Stars:** Lennie Weinrib, Alvy Moore, Johnny Silver

Wary of being taken in by a practical joke, Buddy refuses to heed
a visit from an agent of the Internal Revenue Service.

**111** Stacey Petrie—Part I   January 20, 1965
**Writer:** Carl Reiner
**Director:** Jerry Paris
**Guest Stars:** Jerry Van Dyke, Howard Wendell, Bill Idelson

Rob talks Sally into coaching his withdrawn brother, Stacey,
through a practice date at her apartment.

**112** Stacey Petrie—Part II   January 27, 1965
**Writers:** Carl Reiner, Bill Persky, Sam Denoff
**Director:** Jerry Paris
**Guest Stars:** Jerry Van Dyke, Jane Wald, Kendrick Huxham,
Herbie Faye, Carl Reiner

Rob and Laura help Stacey recover from a cold rejection by the
woman of his dreams.

**113**    Boy Number 1 Versus Boy Number 2          February 3, 1965
   **Writer:** Martin A. Ragaway
   **Director:** Jerry Paris
   **Guest Stars:** Peter Oliphant, Colin Male

Millie and Laura become overnight stage mothers when Ritchie and Freddie are chosen to play small parts on *The Alan Brady Show*.

**114**    The Redcoats Are Coming               February 10, 1965
   **Writers:** Bill Persky, Sam Denoff
   **Director:** Jerry Paris
   **Guest Stars:** Chad Stuart, Jeremy Clyde, Mollie Howerton, Bill Beckley, Wendy Wilson, Ellie Sommers, Trudi Ames

The Petrie home becomes a potential mob scene when Rob and Laura offer secret asylum to the Redcoats, a pair of teen idols from England.

The Redcoats were played by the British folk-rock duo Chad and Jeremy, who would repeat their performance in similar roles on ABC's *Patty Duke Show* a few weeks later.

**115**    The Case of the Pillow                 February 17, 1965
   **Writers:** Bill Persky, Sam Denoff
   **Director:** Howard Morris
   **Guest Stars:** Ed Begley, Alvy Moore, Joel Fluellen, Amzie Strickland

Rob fancies himself a crusading lawyer when he takes an unscrupulous pillow salesman to small claims court.

**116**    Young Man With a Shoehorn              February 24, 1965
   **Writers:** Garry Marshall, Jerry Belson
   **Director:** Jerry Paris
   **Guest Stars:** Lou Jacobi, Milton Frome, LaRue Farlow, Amzie Strickland, Jane Dulo

Rob and Buddy sign on as silent partners in a discount shoe store, but before long, they're pushing pumps on the sales floor.

**117**   Girls Will Be Boys                         March 3, 1965
   **Writers:** Garry Marshall, Jerry Belson
   **Director:** Jerry Paris
   **Guest Stars:** Bernard Fox, Tracy Stratford, Doris Singleton

Ritchie runs into girl trouble when he comes home with bruises inflicted by a bully named Priscilla.

**118**   Bupkiss                                    March 10, 1965
   **Writers:** Bill Persky, Sam Denoff
   **Director:** Lee Philips
   **Guest Stars:** Robert Ball, Greg Morris, Patty Regan, Tim Herbert, Charles Dugdale

Rob is surprised when a novelty song he penned with an old Army buddy pops up on the radio, but is dismayed to find out that his partner took all the credit.

Writers Persky and Denoff wrote "Bupkiss," which was recorded for the show by pop singers Dick and Dee Dee.

**119**   Your Home Sweet Home Is My Home      March 17, 1965
   **Writers:** Howard Ostroff, Joan Darling
   **Director:** Lee Philips
   **Guest Stars:** Stanley Adams, Eddie Ryder

Rob recalls the day he and Laura decided to buy their dream house, even after they discovered a massive rock in its basement.

**120**   Anthony Stone                             March 24, 1965
   **Writer:** Joseph C. Cavella
   **Director:** Jerry Paris
   **Guest Stars:** Richard Angarola, Bob Hoffman

Rob and Buddy make the startling discovery that Sally's mysterious new boyfriend is a mortician—and a married one, at that.

**121**   Never Bathe on Saturday                 March 31, 1965
   **Writer:** Carl Reiner
   **Director:** Jerry Paris
   **Guest Stars:** Bernard Fox, Bill Idelson, Kathleen Freeman, Arthur Malet, Johnny Silver

Laura finds herself in an embarrassing fix when she gets her toe stuck in the water spout of a fancy hotel bathtub—with the door locked from the inside.

**122**   A Show of Hands                                April 14, 1965
   **Writer:** Joseph C. Cavella
   **Director:** Theodore J. Flicker
   **Guest Stars:** Joel Fluellen, Henry Scott, Herkie Styles

Rob and Laura are forced to wear gloves to a prestigious awards banquet after they accidentally dye their hands an indelible shade of black.

**123**   Baby Fat                                      April 21, 1965
   **Writers:** Garry Marshall, Jerry Belson
   **Director:** Jerry Paris
   **Guest Stars:** Strother Martin, Carl Reiner, Sandy Kenyon, Richard Erdman

After agreeing to doctor the script for Alan Brady's Broadway debut, Rob has second thoughts about performing the thankless task without recognition.

**124**   100 Terrible Hours                            May 5, 1965
   **Writers:** Bill Persky, Sam Denoff
   **Director:** Theodore J. Flicker
   **Guest Stars:** Carl Reiner, Fred Clark, Howard Wendell, Dabbs Greer, Harry Stanton.

Rob recalls the time he broadcast a radio show for 100 hours straight before he stumbled in to meet Alan Brady for the first time.

Rob's early career as a disc jockey was another facet of his character borrowed from real life. Dick Van Dyke hosted popular radio talk shows in Atlanta and New Orleans before he moved into television in the mid-1950s.

**125**   Br-room, Br-room                              May 12, 1965
   **Writers:** Dale McRaven, Carl Kleinschmitt
   **Director:** Jerry Paris
   **Guest Stars:** Sandy Kenyon, Jimmy Murphy, Johnny Silver, Bob Random, Carl Reindel, Linda Marshall

Rob takes his new motorcycle out for a spin and unwittingly falls in with a gang of teenage bikers.

**126**   There's No Sale Like Wholesale                May 26, 1965
**Writers:** Garry Marshall, Jerry Belson
**Director:** Jerry Paris
**Guest Stars:** Lou Krugman, Jane Dulo, Peter Brocco, A. G. Vitanza

Rob decides to save a few bucks on Laura's new fur coat by letting Buddy order it wholesale—a decision he lives to regret.

## 1965-66    THE FIFTH SEASON

*Year-End Rating: 23.6 (16th place)*

After the show's creators announce their intention to quit while they're ahead of the game, the series ends its celebrated run at the close of the fifth year. Carl Reiner trades off producer's chores with story consultants Bill Persky and Sam Denoff, who maintain the show's high standards in a final season that includes some of the show's most fondly remembered episodes.

Fifth-year scripts are contributed by a wide array of writers, including notable efforts from Garry Marshall and Jerry Belson, Carl Kleinschmitt and Dale McRaven, John Whedon, and, as usual, Bill Persky and Sam Denoff.

**127**   Coast-to-Coast Big Mouth                September 15, 1965
**Writers:** Bill Persky, Sam Denoff
**Director:** Jerry Paris
**Guest Stars:** Carl Reiner, Dick Curtis

Laura faces Alan Brady's wrath after a fast-talking game-show host goads her into admitting that the star wears a toupee.

**128**   A Farewell to Writing                September 22, 1965
**Writers:** Fred Freeman, Lawrence J. Cohen
**Director:** Jerry Paris
**Guest Star:** Guy Raymond

Rob hopes a few days of seclusion in a mountain cabin will motivate him to complete his novel, but it nearly drives him stir-crazy instead.

Rob expends most of his efforts on avoiding writing, as he perfects his paddle-ball swing and horses around with a pair of cowboy six-shooters he finds in the cabin. The producers knew Van Dyke well enough to know they couldn't go wrong by leaving Rob Petrie alone in a room filled with funny props.

**129**    Uhny Uftz                              September 29, 1965
  **Writers:** Carl Kleinschmitt, Dale McRaven
  **Director:** Jerry Paris
  **Guest Stars:** Karl Lukas, Ross Elliott, Madge Blake, John Mylong

No one seems to believe Rob's claim that he's seen a flying saucer hovering outside the office window.

**130**    The Ugliest Dog in the World            October 6, 1965
  **Writers:** Bill Persky, Sam Denoff
  **Director:** Lee Philips
  **Guest Stars:** Billy De Wolfe, George Tyne, Michael Conrad, Florence Halop, Barbara Dodd

A homely mongrel becomes the temporary ward of the Petries after his abbreviated appearance on *The Alan Brady Show*.

**131**    No Rice at My Wedding                   October 13, 1965
  **Writers:** Garry Marshall, Jerry Belson
  **Director:** Lee Philips
  **Guest Stars:** Van Williams, Bert Remsen, Johnny Silver, Allan Melvin

Rob recalls his only serious competition for Laura's hand, a charming Army corporal who won a date with her in a USO charity auction.

**132**    Draw Me a Pear                          October 20, 1965
  **Writers:** Art Baer, Ben Joelson
  **Director:** Jerry Paris
  **Guest Stars:** Ina Balin, Jackie Joseph, Frank Adamo, Jody Gilbert, Dorothy Neumann

Laura suspects that Rob's comely drawing instructor may be interested in something other than her husband's artistic abilities.

**133**  The Great Petrie Fortune                      October 27, 1965
  **Writers:** Ernest Chambers, Jay Burton
  **Director:** Jerry Paris
  **Guest Stars:** Dan Tobin, Herb Vigran, Forrest Lewis, Elvia Allman, Amzie Strickland, Howard Wendell, Tiny Brauer

Rob discovers that he's the heir to a mysterious fortune that's hidden somewhere in his Uncle Hezekiah's rolltop desk.

**134**  Odd But True                      November 3, 1965
  **Writers:** Garry Marshall, Jerry Belson
  **Director:** Jerry Paris
  **Guest Stars:** James Millhollin, Hope Summers, Peter Oliphant, David Fresco, Bert May, Ray Kellogg

Rob becomes a reluctant candidate for the "Odd But True" newspaper column when Ritchie connects the freckles on his back and discovers the Liberty Bell.

Bill Persky and Sam Denoff begin their stint as producers with this episode, after Carl Reiner takes a temporary leave to appear in *The Russians Are Coming, The Russians Are Coming.*

**135**  Viva Petrie                      November 10, 1965
  **Writer:** John Whedon
  **Director:** Jerry Paris
  **Guest Stars:** Joby Baker, Jack Bernardi

Rob and Laura attempt to find work for a newly landed immigrant whose only occupational skill is professional bullfighting.

**136**  Go Tell the Birds and Bees                      November 17, 1965
  **Writer:** Rick Mittleman
  **Director:** Jerry Paris
  **Guest Stars:** Alberta Nelson, Peter Hobbs

After Ritchie regales his schoolmates with tall tales about where babies come from, Rob sits him down and tells him the real story.

**137**  Body and Sol                      November 24, 1965
  **Writers:** Carl Kleinschmitt, Dale McRaven
  **Director:** Jerry Paris
  **Guest Stars:** Allan Melvin, Ed Peck, Michael Conrad, Garry Marshall, Barbara Dodd, Paul Stader, Burt Taylor

Rob recalls his short-lived career as Pitter Patter Petrie—middle-weight champ of the U.S. Army Special Services.

Writer Garry Marshall has a cameo as the referee of Rob's boxing match.

**138**   See Rob Write, Write Rob, Write          December 8, 1965
   **Writers:** Lawrence J. Cohen, Fred Freeman
   **Director:** Jerry Paris
   **Guest Star:** John McGiver

The Petries find themselves locked in literary competition after Rob volunteers his help on a children's book that Laura's writing.

**139**   You're Under Arrest          December 15, 1965
   **Writer:** Joseph C. Cavella
   **Director:** Jerry Paris
   **Guest Stars:** Phillip Pine, Lee Krieger, Sandy Kenyon, Ed McCready, Bella Bruck, Tiny Brauer, Johnny Silver

Rob has difficulty coming up with a plausible alibi when the police accuse him of taking part in a barroom brawl.

**140**   Fifty-two Forty-five or Work          December 29, 1965
   **Writer:** Rick Mittleman
   **Director:** Jerry Paris
   **Guest Stars:** Reta Shaw, Dabbs Greer, Al Ward, John Chulay, Jerry Hausner, James Frawley

Rob recalls the financial strain that forced him to take a job writing copy for an electronics catalog during his first hiatus from *The Alan Brady Show*.

**141**   Who Stole My Watch?          January 5, 1966
   **Writer:** Joseph Bonaduce
   **Director:** Jerry Paris
   **Guest Star:** Milton Frome

Rob plays amateur sleuth when his new watch turns up missing and he becomes convinced it was stolen by one of his friends.

**142**   I Do Not Choose to Run                    January 19, 1966
   **Writers:** Dale McRaven, Carl Kleinschmitt
   **Director:** Jerry Paris
   **Guest Stars:** Arte Johnson, Philip Ober, George Tyne, Peter
   Brocco, Howard Wendell, Helen Spring

Rob's stirring speech at a citizen's meeting brings him an unexpected nomination for a seat on the New Rochelle City Council.

Arte Johnson, later a star of NBC's *Laugh-In*, has a role as the high-
powered media coordinator of Rob's political campaign.

**143**   The Making of a Councilman                    January 26, 1966
   **Writers:** Carl Kleinschmitt, Dale McRaven
   **Director:** Jerry Paris
   **Guest Stars:** Wally Cox, George Tyne, Margaret Muse, Lia
   Waggner, Arthur Adams, Remo Pisani, James Henaghan, Jr., Kay
   Stewart, Holly Harris, Marilyn Hare, Lorna Thayer

Rob has second thoughts about running for city council after he
meets his eminently more qualified opponent.

Wally Cox, star of TV's *Mr. Peepers* in the early 1950s, plays Rob's well-
versed competitor, Lincoln Goodheart.

**144**   The Curse of the Petrie People                    February 2, 1966
   **Writers:** Dale McRaven, Carl Kleinschmitt
   **Director:** Jerry Paris
   **Guest Stars:** Tom Tully, Isabel Randolph, Leon Belasco

Laura single-handedly destroys generations of Petrie family tradition when she accidentally crunches a garish heirloom brooch in
the garbage disposal.

**145**   The Bottom of Mel Cooley's Heart                    February 9, 1966
   **Writer:** John Whedon
   **Director:** Jerry Paris
   **Guest Star:** Carl Reiner

Mel loses his job after Rob convinces him to stand up to Alan
Brady's bullying.

**146**   Remember the Alimony                    February 16, 1966
  **Writers:** Dale McRaven, Carl Kleinschmitt
  **Director:** Jerry Paris
  **Guest Stars:** Lee Krieger, Allan Melvin, Don Diamond, Bernie
  Kopell, Shelah Hackett, Jose Nieto, Guillermo DeAnda

Rob and Laura recall a hectic trip to Mexico that almost spelled
the end of their new marriage.

**147**   Dear Sally Rogers                    February 23, 1966
  **Writer:** Ronald Axe
  **Director:** Richard Erdman
  **Guest Stars:** Richard Schaal, Bill Idelson, Bert Remsen

Sally's televised plea for a husband on a late-night talk show
yields unexpected results—including a letter from Mr. Right.

This episode suggests one possible conclusion to the bittersweet saga
of Sally's oft-stalled love life when her secret admirer is revealed to be
Herman Glimscher.
Dick Schaal plays talk-show host Stevie Parsons. The talented charac-
ter actor would hit his stride a few years later as a recurring player on
*The Mary Tyler Moore Show* and its offspring.

**148**   Buddy Sorrell—Man and Boy                    March 2, 1966
  **Writers**: Ben Joelson, Art Baer
  **Director:** Richard Erdman
  **Guest Stars:** Pippa Scott, Ed Peck, Arthur Ross Jones, Sheldon
  Golomb, Maria Sokolov

Buddy's strange behavior has Rob and Sally completely puzzled
until they discover he's been nervously preparing for his belated
bar mitzvah.

**149**   Bad Reception in Albany                    March 9, 1966
  **Writers:** Garry Marshall, Jerry Belson
  **Director:** Jerry Paris
  **Guest Stars:** Bert Remsen, Tom D'Andrea, Joseph Mell, Johnny
  Haymer, Robert Nichols, Chanin Hale, Bella Bruck, Lorraine
  Bendix, Joyce Wellington, Tiny Brauer

Rob encounters endless difficulties at a hotel in Albany when he
tries to find a functioning TV set during the annual convention of
the Seals Lodge.

**150**   Talk to the Snail                           March 23, 1966
   **Writers:** Jerry Belson, Garry Marshall
   **Director:** Jerry Paris
   **Guest Stars:** Paul Winchell, Henry Gibson, Carl Reiner

Fearing that network budget cuts might cost him his job, Rob interviews for a position as staff writer for a talking snail.

As Sally's date, Henry Gibson recites "Keep A-Goin'," the poem that would be his trademark on NBC's *Laugh-In*. Jellybean the Snail is brought to life by ventriloquist Paul Winchell.


**151**   A Day in the Life of Alan Brady             April 6, 1966
   **Writer:** Joseph Bonaduce
   **Director:** Jerry Paris
   **Guest Stars:** Carl Reiner, Kim Ford, Lou Wills, John Chulay,
   Joyce Jameson

Pandemonium results when Alan Brady arrives at Millie and Jerry's anniversary party with a documentary-film crew recording his every move.

Assistant director John C. Chulay has a cameo as the director of the documentary crew.


**152**   Obnoxious, Offensive, Egomaniac, Etc.       April 13, 1966
   **Writers:** Carl Kleinschmitt, Dale McRaven
   **Director:** Jerry Paris
   **Guest Stars:** Forrest Lewis, Carl Reiner

Rob, Buddy, and Sally try to retrieve a script that contains less-than-flattering descriptions of their arrogant boss before he has a chance to see it.


**153**   The Man From My Uncle                       April 20, 1966
   **Writers:** Garry Marshall, Jerry Belson
   **Director:** Jerry Paris
   **Guest Stars:** Godfrey Cambridge, Biff Elliott, Steve Geray

The Petries' dull weekend is enlivened by the arrival of an unlikely secret agent who wants to conduct a stakeout from Ritchie's bedroom.

**154**   You Ought to Be in Pictures                    April 27, 1966
    **Writer:** Jack Winter
    **Director:** Jerry Paris
    **Guest Stars:** Michael Constantine, Jayne Massey, Frank Adamo

When Rob is cast opposite a voluptuous Italian in an underground film, Laura keeps a close watch on the star chemistry.

Jack Winter won a Writer's Guild Award for this script, which features Rob at his most endearing as a would-be actor who can barely stammer out a line and fumbles even worse when he's called on to kiss the beautiful starlet. Ever the dutiful husband, he first asks his wife, "May I?"

**155**   Love Thy Other Neighbor                        May 4, 1966
    **Writers:** Dale McRaven, Carl Kleinschmitt
    **Director:** Jerry Paris
    **Guest Stars:** Joby Baker, Sue Taylor

Jerry and Millie fly into a jealous fit when Rob and Laura begin spending time with a new couple on the block.

Joby Baker, a favorite of writers Persky and Denoff, made his second appearance of the season in this episode. In 1967, the writers would co-star the actor in *Good Morning World*, a series that bore distinct echoes of *Dick Van Dyke*—including a set design that afforded an unsettling glimpse of what the Petries' living room might have looked like in full color.

**156**   Long Night's Journey Into Day                  May 11, 1966
    **Writers:** Jerry Belson, Garry Marshall
    **Director:** Jerry Paris
    **Guest Star:** Ogden Talbot

Laura and Millie spend a terrifying night with only a mynah bird to keep them company after Rob and Jerry go off for a weekend fishing trip.

**157**   The Gunslinger                                 May 25, 1966
    **Writers:** Bill Persky, Sam Denoff
    **Director:** Jerry Paris
    **Guest Stars:** Carl Reiner, Allan Melvin

Under Jerry's anesthetic, Rob dreams that he's a sheriff in the Old West, the only man who can save the town from the threat of Big Bad Brady.

For the last episode of the series filmed, the cast and crew allowed themselves the final indulgence of this irreverent parody of the Old West—a well-earned release of all the silly gags and priceless puns they managed to restrain during five seasons of the most deceptively disciplined comedy on television.

**158** The Last Chapter               June 1, 1966
**Writers:** Carl Reiner, Bill Persky, Sam Denoff
**Directors:** Jerry Paris, John Rich
**Guest Stars:** Carl Reiner, Dabbs Greer, Herbie Faye, Frank Adamo, Tiny Brauer, Greg Morris, Mimi Dillard

Laura excitedly reads the completed manuscript of Rob's autobiography, a comical look at the life and times of a TV comedy writer and his loving wife.

High points in the colorful saga of Rob and Laura Petrie are recounted in flashbacks of Rob's stuttering marriage proposal, his faltering stumble down the aisle, and Laura's eventful trip to the maternity ward. The show finally ends where it began, as Carl Reiner's Alan Brady announces his plan to produce and star in a TV show based on the real-life story of a TV comedy writer.

When *The Dick Van Dyke Show* voluntarily left the air in 1966, it had already distinguished itself as the most-honored show of its time, and its demise would be lamented by viewers in living rooms all across the country. With intelligence and keen wit, the show proved that a sitcom for grown-ups could not only survive, it could thrive.

Thankfully, the lesson wasn't lost on the next generation of TV creators. When Mary Richards, Archie Bunker, and Barney Miller arrived to burst the floodgates of intelligent, meaningful TV comedy in the 1970s, all they had to do was fling open the door that Rob Petrie had so thoughtfully left ajar in 1966.

## EMMY AWARDS

The following is a complete listing of the Emmy Awards bestowed on *The Dick Van Dyke Show* by the National Academy of Television Arts and Sciences.

**1961-62**  Outstanding Writing Achievement in Comedy: Carl Reiner

**1962-63**  Outstanding Program Achievement in the Field of Humor
Outstanding Writing Achievement in Comedy: Carl Reiner
Outstanding Directorial Achievement in Comedy: John
Rich

**1963-64**  Outstanding Program Achievement in the Field Of Comedy
Outstanding Continued Performance by an Actor in a
Series (Lead): Dick Van Dyke
Outstanding Continued Performance by an Actress in a
Series (Lead): Mary Tyler Moore
Outstanding Writing Achievement in Comedy or Variety:
Carl Reiner, Sam Denoff, Bill Persky
Outstanding Directorial Achievement in Comedy: Jerry
Paris

**1964-65**  Outstanding Program Achievement in Entertainment
Outstanding Individual Achievement in Entertainment
(Actors and Performers): Dick Van Dyke

**1965-66**  Outstanding Comedy Series
Outstanding Continued Performance by an Actor in a
Leading Role in a Comedy Series: Dick Van Dyke
Outstanding Continued Performance by an Actress in a
Leading Role in a Comedy Series: Mary Tyler Moore
Outstanding Writing Achievement in Comedy: Bill Persky,
Sam Denoff, "Coast-to-Coast Big Mouth"

# THE MARY TYLER MOORE SHOW

·

*Perhaps perkiness will save the world.*
—JOHN LEONARD, TV Critic

THANK GOD for *Thoroughly Modern Millie.*

If it hadn't been for that thoroughly forgettable 1967 Julie Andrews movie, America's most popular and critically acclaimed situation comedy might never have made it to our twelve-inch diagonally measured screens. The film is notable mainly because it featured the big-screen debut of Mary Tyler Moore, fresh from a successful five-year stint on the popular early-sixties TV series *The Dick Van Dyke Show.* Her beguiling characterization of the perky and impulsive Laura Petrie—she was just like Jackie Kennedy, except that *she* wasn't afraid to wear Capri pants around the house—had earned her a matched set of Emmys while it established her as one of the most popular performers on television. By the time the series voluntarily left the air, Mary Tyler Moore was perched at the very top of the television industry.

But in 1966, none of that mattered to her. You see, what she *really* wanted was to be a musical-comedy star—a modern-day Ginger Rogers. The young actress didn't realize that the road to Forty-Second Street, like the pathway to hell, was paved with good intentions.

Her first setback came when she starred in a Broadway musical version of Truman Capote's *Breakfast at Tiffany's.* Luckily, no one remembers it because it closed before lunch. Undaunted, the star was certain that *Thoroughly Modern Millie* would be different. Hadn't Universal Pictures already begun its campaign to groom her for movie stardom? Weren't they starting her out as second lead in this big-budget musical spoof of the Roaring Twenties, starring Julie Andrews? How could it fail? Surely, she would never again face the daily grind of a weekly television series! Unfortunately, what no one counted on was the public's widespread lack of interest in big-budget musical spoofs of the Roaring Twenties in 1967. The film didn't exactly catch fire; it just sort of fumed. And Mary's fantasy of becoming a latter-day Ginger Rogers was fading very, very quickly.

Meanwhile, the CBS-TV network was having troubles of its own. By late 1960s, the network had developed a highly successful prime-time schedule that relied heavily on corn-pone silliness like *Petticoat Junction*, *Green Acres*, and *Gomer Pyle*. Though they all delivered consistently high ratings, it was clear to the advertisers of that era that CBS's hayseed comedies weren't being watched by the audience that the ad men most wanted to reach: the urban men and women who annually spend much more money on a given sponsor's products than do their country cousins. In order to keep Madison Avenue happy, CBS desperately needed to upgrade their programming image by replacing the scent of hush puppies and haywagons with the more profitable fragrance of urbane, sophisticated, adult entertainment.

Enter Mary Tyler Moore.

In 1969, her screen career having steadfastly refused to move out of third gear, she agreed to return to CBS for a musical-comedy special that reunited her with her old friend and mentor, Dick Van Dyke. The special was very well received. Quicker than you can say *I Love Lucy*, CBS realized all over again that Mary Tyler Moore was a potential gold mine. Here was a star who could attract the bright, upscale audience they so desperately wanted to reach.

Suddenly, the network was willing to forgive her string of unmemorable movies—even the one in which she played a nun in love with Elvis Presley—if only she would return to CBS in a brand-new sitcom. They offered her the moon atop the Hollywood Hills, gambling that lightning would strike twice and the network would end up with another *Dick Van Dyke Show*.

Mary wasn't so sure. She knew as well as anyone that the success of the original *Dick Van Dyke* series resulted from a rare confluence of talent that would be very difficult to duplicate. Where would she find a tightly knit ensemble of veteran actors and writers capable of creating sophisticated and witty adult situation comedy in an era when *The Beverly*

*Hillbillies* regularly rode shotgun over the weekly Nielsen ratings?

But still, the specter of *Thoroughly Modern Millie* hovered over the star's perky and impulsive brow.

She consulted her husband, Grant Tinker, a successful executive at Twentieth Century-Fox. Together, they came up with a solution. She would return to CBS in a new sitcom, but only on the condition that she and Tinker would maintain total responsibility for creating, casting, and producing the series. Only in an atmosphere free of network interference could they reasonably expect to create a truly original series for prime-time television. CBS happily agreed, and in any event, they were in no position to argue. And so, *The Mary Tyler Moore Show* was announced on the CBS lineup for fall 1970.

Tinker and Moore wasted no time inaugurating MTM Productions, a production house where the new series would grow and flourish in a creative environment that was unique in television. To create the new show's format and produce the series, Tinker hired two young writers, James L. Brooks and Allan Burns. Brooks, a former CBS newswriter, had created *Room 222* for ABC the year before, a warm classroom comedy set in a somewhat idealized inner-city high school. Allan Burns had an equally varied Hollywood background: after a rocky start writing Bullwinkle cartoons, he'd written scripts for *Get Smart* and CBS's landmark sitcom *He and She*. Ironically, he was also co-creator of *My Mother the Car*, a series that is probably as reviled as *Mary Tyler Moore* is revered.

It's impossible to say whether Tinker knew then that this most unlikely pair would create one of television's all-time classics, but there's no doubt that he had confidence in the team from the very start. When CBS program executives objected to his offbeat choice of producers and suggested that he hire a more reliable creative team, Tinker refused to waver—an early indication of the strong executive leadership that Tinker himself feels was his single most important contribution to the eventual success of the fledgling production company.

Whether by design or happenstance, for the format of the new series, the producers created a pastiche that contained distinct echoes of practically every great sitcom that had come before it. Like *The Dick Van Dyke Show*, the new series would feature a dual emphasis on the leading character's home and work environments. Like *The Honeymooners*, Mary's new show would be filmed on very few sets before a live audience, with each episode enlivened by the contributions of a tightly knit ensemble of established character actors. And, like the creators of *I Love Lucy*—who were canny enough to furnish their star player with an equally game second banana in Ethel Mertz, the producers of Mary's new series wisely provided her with a feisty comic counterpart and confidant in the indelible form of Rhoda Morgenstern. And yet, despite the new show's surface similarities to its illustrious predecessors, there could be little doubt that *The Mary Tyler Moore Show* was a truly original creation: a hybrid of great ideas, infused with enough fresh inspiration to propel it soundly into uncharted territory.

Next, the producers cast an inspired—and until then, largely unheralded—group of character actors to fill the roles that they had created. Valerie Harper, Ed Asner, Gavin MacLeod, Cloris Leachman, and Ted Knight formed the nucleus of this well-matched actors' ensemble—none of whom would be likely to dispute the assertion that they did the best work of their careers on the show.

Finally, and perhaps most significantly, Tinker and his producers hired a roster of young and talented writers—many of them women—all of whom were familiar enough with authentic human behavior to portray the show's characters as real, believable people. In Mary's Minneapolis, it was decided, they would banish the sitcom zombies that ran rampant through the towns and cities of practically every other comedy on television.

And so, MTM Productions was born. By bringing together such a formidable group of talented writers, performers, and directors—and then building a framework that made it easy for each one of them to contribute their very best work—Tinker and Moore had secured a running start toward creative success long before the first episode was even filmed.

When the show finally premiered on Saturday, September 19, 1970, there was little doubt in anyone's mind that *The Mary Tyler Moore Show* was not just another sitcom. Clearly, this show heralded a new commitment to television entertainment that took as a given the intelligence and experience of an adult audience—an audience that had been largely ignored by network programmers during the previous decade.

The first few bars of the opening theme song set the tone for the series and gave a clue that this show would indeed be different. For the first time ever, television was going to show us a beautiful young woman who was single—not by chance, but by choice.

> How will you make it on your own?
> This world is awfully big,
> And, girl, this time you're all alone . . .

Ironically, the creators of the show had originally planned to make Mary Richards a recently divorced woman who strikes out on her own. But, in one of the few instances where the network did manage to exert influence on the series, CBS insisted that Mary Richards be an unmarried single girl. Apparently they felt that the American audience wasn't yet ready to laugh at a sitcom based on the comic possibilities in the life of a divorced woman. And besides, they reasoned, wouldn't people remember Mary as Laura Petrie and think that she had really just divorced Dick Van Dyke?

Whatever the reason for the adjustment, changing Mary to a single woman who freely chooses her independence made for a much more interesting and contemporary character. This is borne out in a marvelous scene from the premiere episode where the boyfriend who has jilted Mary arrives to talk her out of her foolhardy plan to start a new life on her own. It's clear that Mary still has her doubts about the move, and at least a part of her hopes that her old boyfriend will provide the easy answer of a marriage proposal.

But when the manipulative Lothario proves unable even to speak the words "I love you," Mary realizes his only interest in getting her back is to salvage his own ego. In that moment of painful recognition, she finds the strength to finally end the affair. "Take care of yourself," he blurts out, as she ushers him into the hallway. "I think I just did" is her parting shot as she closes the door on her past, ready to begin a new life without ever looking back.

The scene is a masterpiece of comic surprise and invention. Mary's confrontation with the man from her past is unexpected. And even when we eventually see where the scene is inexorably headed, we are so wrapped up in the drama of the situation that we remain engrossed until Mary's final, pivotal line. We are surprised, amused, and touched—all at the same time. Suddenly we feel a kinship with this confused, vulnerable, and ultimately wise young woman. In an instant, understand that there's a little bit of Mary Richards in all of us.

The eloquence of that one short scene is typical of the skill and subtlety that the writers, performers, and directors unfailingly brought to the show. The scene also serves to demonstrate what must have been the unwritten dictum of everyone connected with the series: When in doubt, have the character act like a real person.

From the very start, the characters on *The Mary Tyler Moore Show* always behaved like real people; and the situations they found themselves in, no matter how absurd, were always plausible. And that's what made the world of Mary's Minneapolis such a compelling and completely believable place. It was a world that often looked a lot like the one we live in, with all the confusion, embarrassments—and yes, the unexpected joys—intact.

All of which goes a long way toward explaining the almost universal acclaim that was lavished on *The Mary Tyler Moore Show* throughout its long run—and, thanks to syndication, continues even today.

Remarkably, the writing, directing, and performances on the show hardly diminished over the entire seven years the series was on the air. On the contrary, as the critical episode guide that follows demonstrates in great detail, the series never stopped developing and maturing. Eventually, the show reached a peak of sophistication in theme, performance, and subject matter that had rarely been attempted in television comedy. Indeed, to this day, *The Mary Tyler Moore Show* remains the benchmark for judging quality television entertainment programming of any kind.

# A Critical Guide to All 168 Episodes

| | |
|---|---|
| Mary Richards | Mary Tyler Moore |
| Lou Grant | Ed Asner |
| Rhoda Morgenstern | Valerie Harper |
| Murray Slaughter | Gavin MacLeod |
| Ted Baxter | Ted Knight |
| Phyllis Lindstrom | Cloris Leachman |
| Georgette Franklin Baxter | Georgia Engel |
| Sue Ann Nivens | Betty White |

SUPPORTING CAST

| | |
|---|---|
| Ida Morgenstern (Rhoda's mother) | Nancy Walker |
| Martin Morgenstern (Rhoda's father) | Harold Gould |
| Marie Slaughter | Joyce Bulifant |
| Bess Lindstrom | Lisa Gerritsen |
| Edie Grant (Lou's wife) | Priscilla Morrill |
| Gordy the Weatherman | John Amos |
| Dottie Richards (Mary's mother) | Nanette Fabray |
| Walter Richards (Mary's father) | Bill Quinn |
| Flo Meredith (Mary's aunt) | Eileen Heckart |
| David Baxter (Ted's son) | Robbie Rist |

Created by James L. Brooks, Allan Burns
Music by Pat Williams
Theme song ("Love Is All Around") written and sung by Sonny Curtis
Directors of photography were Paul Uhl, William T. Cline
Principal director was Jay Sandrich

## 1970-71 THE FIRST SEASON

*Year-End Rating: 20.3 (22nd place)*

Mary's first season on CBS finds her settling into Minneapolis and the WJM newsroom, with equal emphasis on the trials and tribulations that she and Rhoda face as contemporary single women in their thirties. Many of these episodes are written with the knowing eye of Treva Silverman, who, along with James L. Brooks and Allan Burns, David Davis, Lorenzo Music, and Steve Pritzker, wrote most of the scripts aired during the first season.

Jay Sandrich becomes firmly established as the series's most prominent director, a role he will hold for the next seven years. David Davis is producer for the first two seasons, assisted by his partner, Lorenzo Music. The show's creators, James L. Brooks and Allan Burns, serve as executive producers for the run of the series.

**1**   Love Is All Around                      September 19, 1970
**Writers:** James L. Brooks, Allan Burns
**Director:** Jay Sandrich
**Guest Stars:** Angus Duncan, Dave Morick

Mary Richards gets a fresh start in Minneapolis when she moves into a new apartment and takes a job as associate producer of the city's bottom-rated TV news show.

The show had been in preproduction for nine months by the time this episode aired. Producer Allan Burns recently recalled that this gestation period, so rare in television, contributed immeasurably to the overall quality of the series because it allowed the producers time to refine and adjust the backlog of scripts to reflect new developments as the series evolved.

This premiere episode offers ample evidence of just how sharp the series was from the very start. Already, the characters are well-rounded enough to carry a number of classic scenes, not the least of which depicts Mary's WJM job interview. Here, Mary first experiences Lou Grant's peculiar worldview when he tells her she's got spunk . . . and he *hates* spunk.

**2**   Today I Am a Ma'am                      September 26, 1970
**Writer:** Treva Silverman
**Director:** Jay Sandrich
**Guest Stars:** Richard Schaal, Jack DeMave, Sheila Wells

When a man in his twenties addresses Mary as "ma'am," she panics at the prospect of being an old maid; finally she and Rhoda invite two unlikely bachelors over for dinner, one of whom brings his wife!

This episode features Richard Schaal's first guest appearance. Schaal, then Valerie Harper's real-life husband, got his start at Chicago's Second City improvisational theater in the 1960s and later worked with his wife in *Paul Sills' Story Theatre*. He would appear semi-regularly on *Mary Tyler Moore* throughout the first few seasons, invariably playing one of Mary's, uh, "less sensitive" suitors.

This was also the first episode written by Treva Silverman, one of the many women who would script for the show and also one of the most prolific writers for the series. Though Silverman contributed many uniformly strong scripts essential to the development of the series and its characters, she is best remembered as the author of many of the early episodes that explored and defined the friendship of Mary and Rhoda.

There always seemed to be a sting of truth in those early scripts that centered on the pair's struggles to find success and gain independence as two thirtyish single women. Silverman invested her observations of these often painful situations with an authenticity that had rarely been seen on sitcoms—and has been seen far too infrequently since.

This humorous approach to looking at the ways we cope with all the painful indignities of everyday life would come to define the comic philosophy of *The Mary Tyler Moore Show* and would eventually be adopted as a kind of house style for all MTM Productions.

**3    Bess, You Is My Daughter Now**               October 3, 1970
**Writer:** John D. F. Black
**Director:** Jay Sandrich

When Mary is asked to baby-sit for Phyllis, she soon finds herself losing a friend and gaining a daughter.

**4    Divorce Isn't Everything**                   October 10, 1970
**Writer:** Treva Silverman
**Director:** Alan Rafkin
**Guest Stars:** Shelley Berman, Jane Connell, Pat Finley, Dave Ketchum, Gino Conforti, Vernon Weddle

Rhoda and Mary deceptively join a group of divorced singles to qualify for a cut-rate trip to Europe.

Another painfully funny Treva Silverman script. This time Silverman takes the desperation shared by members of a support group for divorced people and milks it for every laugh. The fact that Mary and Rhoda seem willing to exploit these people so that they might save money on a vacation only makes the situation all the more painful—and that much funnier. The dark humor of the mildly maladjusted therapy group is territory that was to be mined more fully on MTM's *The Bob Newhart Show*.

**5  Keep Your Guard Up**                                    October 17, 1970
**Writer:** Steve Pritzker
**Director:** Alan Rafkin
**Guest Stars:** John Schuck, Tim Brown

A sensitive but incompetent ex-football player wants a job as WJM's sportscaster and won't leave Mary alone until he gets it.

**6  Support Your Local Mother**                            October 24, 1970
**Writers:** James L. Brooks, Allan Burns
**Director:** Alan Rafkin
**Guest Star:** Nancy Walker

Rhoda's mother pays a visit but ends up spending all her time with Mary when Rhoda refuses to see her.

Incredibly, CBS initially refused to allow this script to be shot, insisting that a story about a daughter who turns her back on her mother was not suitable for a comedy. "Their hair turned white," Allan Burns told journalist Paul Weingarten. "They said 'This is not funny. You can't shoot this show. You can't.'" The writers finally appealed to Grant Tinker, who calmly okayed the script, despite the network veto. Later, this classic episode—one of the funniest of all the early scripts—went on to earn an Emmy Award for writers Brooks and Burns.

**7  Toulouse-Lautrec Is One of My**                        October 31, 1970
**    Favorite Artists**
**Writers:** Lloyd Turner, Gordon Mitchell
**Director:** Jay Sandrich
**Guest Star:** Hamilton Camp

Mary's fledgling romance with a professional writer hits a snag when Mary discovers that she's at least a foot taller than he is.

**8**  The Snow Must Go On                          November 7, 1970
**Writers:** David Davis, Lorenzo Music
**Director:** Jay Sandrich
**Guest Stars:** Richard Schaal, Ivor Francis, Robert Rothwell

Snowbound in the WJM newsroom, Mary faces the challenge of producing an up-to-the-minute election broadcast without any incoming results.

**9**  Bob and Rhoda and Teddy and Mary  November 14, 1970
**Writer:** Bob Rodgers
**Director:** Peter Baldwin
**Guest Stars:** Greg Mullavey, Henry Corden

It's professional glory but personal strife for Mary when she's nominated for a Teddy Award at the same time that Rhoda's new boyfriend appears to be more attracted to her than to Rhoda.

The first of many shows to revolve around the durable premise of the local Minneapolis broadcast award, the Teddy. Here the comic potential of the Ted Baxter character is in full swing as he is once again left at the starting gate in the Teddy derby.

Guest star Greg Mullavey would later appear as Mary Hartman's husband in Norman Lear's soap-opera spoof, *Mary Hartman, Mary Hartman.*

**10**  Assistant Wanted, Female                  November 21, 1970
**Writer:** Treva Silverman
**Director:** Peter Baldwin
**Guest Star:** John Amos

Mary unwisely hires Phyllis as her new assistant.

John Amos debuts as Gordy the Weatherman in the first of many appearances. The show's creators thought that it would be funny to have a black weatherman at a time when most blacks in broadcasting were still relegated to the sports booth. Amos later achieved far greater fame as the star of Norman Lear's *Good Times*, as well as in the immensely popular miniseries *Roots*.

**11**    1040 or Fight                                November 28, 1970
   **Writers:** David Davis, Lorenzo Music
   **Director:** Jay Sandrich
   **Guest Star:** Paul Sand

Mary's tax return is audited by a romantically inclined IRS man.

The auditor is played by Paul Sand, though the part was originally tailored for the talents of Bob Newhart. Writers Music and Davis were undaunted when the nightclub comic passed on the role—they would get a second chance two years later when they created and produced *The Bob Newhart Show* for MTM.

And Paul Sand was certainly a worthy substitute. Yet another talented comic actor who—like Valerie Harper and Ed Asner—got his start with improvisational theater director Paul Sills in Chicago. In 1974, Sand also landed his own MTM series, when Jim Brooks and Allan Burns created the highly regarded, but short-lived, *Paul Sand in Friends and Lovers*.

**12**    Anchorman Overboard                          December 5, 1970
   **Writer:** Lorenzo Music
   **Director:** Jay Sandrich
   **Guest Star:** Bill Fiore

Mary tries to bolster Ted's sagging confidence after he bombs at a women's club speaking engagement.

Mary's role as den mother to the WJM staff is by now firmly established in this first of many episodes to explore her paradoxical, but characteristically protective, attitude toward the newsroom's terror, Ted Baxter.

**13**    He's All Yours                               December 12, 1970
   **Writer:** Bob Rodgers
   **Director:** Jay Sandrich
   **Guest Star:** Wes Stern

A young cameraman is so enchanted with Mary that he invents tall tales describing their romantic involvements.

**14**    Christmas and the Hard-Luck Kid              December 19, 1970
   **Writers:** James L. Brooks, Allan Burns
   **Director:** Jay Sandrich
   **Guest Star:** Ned Wertimer

Depressed because she has to work on Christmas Day, Mary tries to create some Yuletide spirit in the WJM newsroom.

**15**    Howard's Girl                          January 2, 1971
   **Writer:** Treva Silverman
   **Director:** Jay Sandrich
   **Guest Stars:** Richard Schaal, Henry Jones, Mary Jackson

Mary dates her former boyfriend's brother, much to the consternation of his parents.

**16**    Party Is Such Sweet Sorrow             January 9, 1971
   **Writer:** Martin Cohan
   **Director:** Jay Sandrich
   **Guest Star:** Dick Clair

Mary faces the prospect of leaving WJM when she's offered a promotion by a rival station.

**17**    Just a Lunch                           January 16, 1971
   **Writers:** James L. Brooks, Allan Burns
   **Director:** Bruce Bilson
   **Guest Stars:** Monte Markham, Joyce Bulifant

Mary becomes involved with a charming newsman—the only problem is that he's married.

Joyce Bulifant makes her first appearance in the semi-regular role of Marie Slaughter, Murray's faithful and understanding wife. The faithful and understanding wife is the most thankless role in television, but Bulifant held her own throughout all six remaining seasons. Before signing on with MTM, she had been a regular on Bill Cosby's first NBC sitcom, *The Bill Cosby Show*.

**18**    Second-Story Story                     January 23, 1971
   **Writer:** Steve Pritzker
   **Director:** Jay Sandrich
   **Guest Stars:** Bob Dishy, Burt Mustin, Vic Tayback

Mary is the victim of a rare Minneapolis crime spree when her apartment is burglarized twice in as many days.

**19** We Closed in Minneapolis                              January 30, 1971
  **Writers:** Kenny Solms, Gail Parent
  **Director:** Jay Sandrich
  **Guest Star:** Elliot Street

Murray is given good news, and bad—his play about life in a newsroom is finally going to be produced, but Ted Baxter will play a featured role.

**20** Hi!                                                        February 6, 1971
  **Writer:** Treva Silverman
  **Director:** Jay Sandrich
  **Guest Stars:** Pat Carroll, Bruce Kirby, Robert Casper

When Mary is hospitalized for a minor operation, she finds that even her sunny disposition can't dispel the clouds that hang over her curmudgeonly roommate.

Veteran actress Pat Carroll, late of *The Danny Thomas Show*, portrays the disagreeable patient.

**21** The Boss Isn't Coming to Dinner            February 13, 1971
  **Writers:** David Davis, Lorenzo Music
  **Director:** Jay Sandrich
  **Guest Star:** Paul Micale

Mary is shocked to learn that Lou and his wife, Edie, are separating.

Though the series wouldn't really tackle Lou's divorce for another two years, the seeds of compassion that Mary will feel for Mr. Grant are very clearly planted in this episode. The writers probably didn't realize it then, but they were setting the stage for what was to become one of the most graceful love affairs in popular fiction—the unconsummated romance of Mary Richards and Lou Grant.

**22** A Friend in Deed                                    February 20, 1971
  **Writer:** Susan Silver
  **Director:** Jay Sandrich
  **Guest Star:** Pat Finley

Mary's long-forgotten childhood friend arrives and begins ingratiating herself with each of Mary's newsroom friends.

Pat Finley would later play Bob's sister, Ellen, on *The Bob Newhart Show*.

**23** Smokey the Bear Wants You February 27, 1971
**Writer:** Steve Pritzker
**Director:** Jay Sandrich
**Guest Star:** Michael Callan

Rhoda falls in love with a successful businessman who plans to drop out of society and sign up as a forest ranger.

**24** The Forty-Five-Year-Old Man March 6, 1971
**Writer:** George Kirgo
**Director:** Herbert Kenwith
**Guest Stars:** Slim Pickens, Richard Libertini, Richard Roat

Lou Grant is the scapegoat when the show's ratings falter, but Mary tries to convince WJM's eccentric station owner to give him his job back.

Western character actor Slim Pickens plays the cowboy station owner with such reckless abandon that it's a pity his character was used only as a one-shot in this single episode.

## 1971-72 THE SECOND SEASON

*Year-End Rating: 23.7 (10th place)*

As the series enters its second season, plots that offer insight into the personalities of the regular characters set the stage for the strong ensemble company that will be in full flower by the middle of the following year.

David Davis continues as producer, and Jay Sandrich shares directing chores with Peter Baldwin and Jerry Paris. Primary writers for the season are David Davis, Lorenzo Music, Treva Silverman, Susan Silver, and Steve Pritzker.

**25** The Birds . . . And . . . Um . . . Bees September 18, 1971
**Writer:** Treva Silverman
**Director:** Jay Sandrich
**Guest Star:** Lisa Gerritsen

Phyllis decides that Mary is the person best suited to tell her daughter, Bess, the facts of life.

**26**    I Am Curious Cooper                          September 25, 1971
   **Writers:** David Davis, Lorenzo Music
   **Director:** Jay Sandrich
   **Guest Stars:** Michael Constantine, Shizuko Iwamatsu

Lou plays Cupid when he tries to orchestrate a romance between Mary and one of his middle-aged friends.

**27**    He's No Heavy, He's My Brother              October 2, 1971
   **Writer:** Allan Burns
   **Director:** Jerry Paris
   **Guest Star:** Frank Ramirez

When Mary and Rhoda decide to take a midwinter vacation in Mexico, they get involved in a mysterious plot involving the owner of a Mexican restaurant.

This episode represented a creative family reunion of sorts. Director Jerry Paris played the next-door neighbor and directed Mary Tyler Moore in many classic episodes of *The Dick Van Dyke Show*. He would later sign on as director of *Happy Days*, Garry Marshall's long-running hit.

**28**    Room 223                                    October 9, 1971
   **Writer:** Susan Silver
   **Director:** Jay Sandrich
   **Guest Stars:** Michael Tolan, Florida Friebus, Val Bisoglio

Mary dates her professor in a night-school class.

Handsome Dan Whitfield, played by Michael Tolan, was one of Mary's more persistent suitors. He would return, still carrying a torch, as late as the sixth season.

**29**    A Girl's Best Mother Is Not Her Friend      October 16, 1971
   **Writers:** David Davis, Lorenzo Music
   **Director:** Jay Sandrich
   **Guest Star:** Nancy Walker

Rhoda's mother returns, and this time she's determined to be friends with her daughter.

Writers David Davis and Lorenzo Music continue to expand the comic possibilities of Rhoda's character. The groundwork they lay here will serve them well in 1974 when they produce the successful spinoff series *Rhoda*.

**30**   Cover Boy                                    October 23, 1971
   **Writer:** Treva Silverman
   **Director:** Jay Sandrich
   **Guest Star:** Jack Cassidy

Ted tries to impress his visiting brother, Hal, by pretending that Mary is his sweetheart.

In his portrayal of Ted's brother, Jack Cassidy draws heavily on Oscar North, the arrogant actor he played in the highly regarded CBS series *He and She*. In fact, there are enough echoes of Oscar North in the character of Ted Baxter himself to suggest that the creators of MTM drew at least a passing inspiration from that short-lived 1967 series. Of course, it's not exactly an airtight case of creative larceny, since most of the *Mary Tyler Moore* creative staff also labored on *He and She*, including director Jay Sandrich, writers David Davis and Allan Burns, as well as the writer of this particular episode, Treva Silverman.

**31**   Didn't You Used to Be. . . Wait. . .        October 30, 1971
         Don't Tell Me!
   **Writer:** Allan Burns
   **Director:** Jay Sandrich
   **Guest Stars:** Richard Schaal, Jack Riley, Kermit Murdock, Ron Masak, Pippa Scott

Mary learns that you can never go home again when she attends her high school reunion and runs into her old boyfriend Howard Arnell.

Jack Riley is featured in his first MTM guest spot. The actor's excellent timing and delivery were particularly well-suited to the MTM style, and he would later be used to good advantage in the role of Elliot Carlin on MTM's *Bob Newhart Show*.

**32**   Thoroughly Unmilitant Mary                  November 6, 1971
   **Writer:** Martin Cohan
   **Director:** Jay Sandrich
   **Guest Stars:** Dick Balduzzi, Larry Gelman, Paul Micale

The WJM newsroom goes on strike, leaving Mary and Lou to produce the entire show by themselves.

**33**   And Now, Sitting in for Ted Baxter       November 13, 1971
   **Writer:** Steve Pritzker
   **Director:** Jerry Paris
   **Guest Stars:** Jed Allen, Bill Woodson

Ted worries about his job security when he sees the more competent anchorman who is brought in as his vacation replacement.

**34**   Don't Break the Chain       November 20,1971
   **Writers:** David Davis, Lorenzo Music
   **Director:** Jerry Paris
   **Guest Stars:** Jack DeMave, Gino Conforti

Mary must decide whether to answer a chain letter sent to her by Lou.

**35**   The Six-and-a-Half-Year Itch       November 27,1971
   **Writer:** Treva Silverman
   **Director:** Jay Sandrich
   **Guest Stars:** Lawrence Pressman, Elizabeth Berger

Lou suspects his son-in-law of philandering when he spots him at a movie with a strange woman.

**36**   . . . Is a Friend in Need       December 4, 1971
   **Writer:** Susan Silver
   **Director:** Jay Sandrich
   **Guest Star:** Beverly Sanders

When Rhoda loses her job as a department store window dresser, Mary tries to help her land another one.

**37**   The Square-Shaped Room       December 11, 1971
   **Writer:** Susan Silver
   **Director:** Jay Sandrich

Mary talks Lou into letting Rhoda redecorate his house, though he soon lives to regret it.

**38**    Ted Over Heels                     December 18, 1971
**Writers:** David Davis, Lorenzo Music
**Director:** Peter Baldwin
**Guest Star:** Arlene Golonka

Ted develops a crush on the daughter of Chuckles the Clown.

Guest star Arlene Golonka has appeared in scores of sitcom episodes since the late 1960s, when she had a featured role on *The Andy Griffith Show.*

**39**    The Five-Minute Dress              January 1, 1972
**Writers:** Pat Nardo, Gloria Banta
**Director:** Jay Sandrich

Mary's new boyfriend is a politician who can't seem to find time in his schedule to see her.

**40**    Feeb                               January 8, 1972
**Writers:** Dick Clair, Jenna McMahon
**Director:** Peter Baldwin
**Guest Star:** Barbara Sharma

Mary feels guilty when she causes an incompetent waitress to be fired, so she hires the girl to work in the newsroom.

Director Peter Baldwin had previously worked with Mary Tyler Moore on *The Dick Van Dyke Show* in the early 1960s.

**41**    The Slaughter Affair               January 15, 1972
**Writer:** Rick Mittleman
**Director:** Peter Baldwin
**Guest Star:** Joyce Bulifant

When Murray takes a second job to help pay for his wife's anniversary present, Marie suspects that he's having an affair with Mary.

**42**    Baby Sitcom                        January 22, 1972
**Writer:** Treva Silverman
**Director:** Jay Sandrich
**Guest Stars:** Joshua Bryant, Leslie Graves

When Mary has to back out of an agreement to baby-sit Bess, she talks Lou into pinch-hitting for her.

**43**    More Than Neighbors                    January 29, 1972
  **Writer:** Steve Pritzker
  **Director:** Jay Sandrich
  **Guest Star:** Jack Bender

Mary and Rhoda try to talk Ted out of becoming their neighbor after he decides to move into their building.

**44**    The Care and Feeding of Parents          February 5, 1972
  **Writers:** Dick Clair, Jenna McMahon
  **Director:** Jay Sandrich
  **Guest Stars:** Jon Locke, Brad Trumbull

Mary finds herself playing literary agent for an eleven-year-old after Phyllis hears her compliment Bess's school composition.

**45**    Where There's Smoke, There's Rhoda      February 12, 1972
  **Writer:** Martin Cohan
  **Director:** Peter Baldwin

After Rhoda's apartment is destroyed by a fire, Mary offers to put her up for a few days—a favor that nearly ruins their friendship.

**46**    You Certainly Are a Big Boy              February 19, 1972
  **Writer:** Martin Cohan
  **Director:** Jay Sandrich
  **Guest Stars:** Bradford Dillman, John Rubinstein, Beverly Saunders

Mary is unnerved to discover that the handsome architect she's been dating has a son who's practically her age.

**47**    Some of My Best Friends Are Rhoda       February 26, 1972
  **Writer:** Steve Pritzker
  **Director:** Peter Baldwin
  **Guest Star:** Mary Frann

Mary forms a kinship with a woman she meets in a minor traffic accident, but the friendship quickly sours after Mary discovers that the woman is prejudiced.

An atypical foray into the Norman Lear social-consciousness arena, this episode delves into Mary's staunch liberalism and Rhoda's Jewishness—two themes that weren't often confronted in such a head-on fashion. A comparison of MTM's humanist approach to politics and the more didactic approach adopted by Norman Lear for his contemporary sitcoms would make an interesting study indeed.

A decade later, Mary Frann would play Bob Newhart's second TV wife on *Newhart*.

**48**   His Two Right Arms                    March 4, 1972
  **Writers:** Jim Parker, Arnold Margolin
  **Director:** Jay Sandrich
  **Guest Stars:** Bill Daily, Carol Androsky, Janet MacLachlan, Wally Taylor, Isabel Sanford, Patrick Campbell

Mary schedules an ignorant politician on a WJM talk show and then tries to groom him so that he doesn't make a complete fool of himself.

This episode was designed as a pilot for a proposed spinoff series that was to star Bill Daily as befuddled politician Pete Peterson. When that series failed to sell, MTM producers wisely tapped the talented actor for the role of Howard Borden, the equally confused navigator on *The Bob Newhart Show*.

## 1972-73   THE THIRD SEASON

*Year-End Rating: 23.6 (7th place)*

The characters are by now so familiar that the writers are able to base many episodes on previously unknown facets of their personalities—Murray's occasional feelings of inadequacy; Rhoda's newly blossomed beauty; and, of course, Mary's slowly maturing relationships with the men in her life. Even Ted Baxter is taken more seriously when he gets involved with Georgette, played by Georgia Engel, who would join the regular cast during the third season.

Ed. Weinberger signs on to produce in a season that features scripts from the widest variety of writers yet, including primary contributions from Weinberger, Dick Clair and Jenna McMahon, Martin Cohan, as well as the occasional gem from regulars Steve Pritzker and Treva Silverman, who also serves as story editor.

**49**   The Good-Time News                September 16, 1972
   **Writers:** James L. Brooks, Allan Burns
   **Director:** Hal Cooper
   **Guest Stars:** Robert Hogan, John Amos

Lou cringes when Mary is assigned to develop a new happy-talk format for *The Six O'Clock News.*

**50**   What Is Mary Richards Really Like?    September 23, 1972
   **Writer:** Susan Silver
   **Director:** Jerry Belson
   **Guest Star:** Peter Haskell

Mary dates a muckraking columnist who happens to be doing a story on her.

Director Jerry Belson was one of the staff writers of *The Dick Van Dyke Show* and a co-creator, with Garry Marshall, of TV's *Odd Couple.*

**51**   Who's in Charge Here?                September 30, 1972
   **Writer:** Martin Cohan
   **Director:** Jay Sandrich

Confusion ensues when Lou is promoted to program director and Murray is put in charge of the newsroom.

**52**   Enter Rhoda's Parents               October 7, 1972
   **Writer:** Martin Cohan
   **Director:** Jay Sandrich
   **Guest Stars:** Nancy Walker, Harold Gould, Leanna Roberts

Rhoda's parents come for a visit and end up tackling their marital difficulties.

Harold Gould and Nancy Walker continued to play Rhoda's parents on Valerie Harper's spinoff series, *Rhoda,* in 1974.

**53**   It's Whether You Win or Lose         October 14, 1972
   **Writer:** Martin Donovan
   **Director:** Jay Sandrich
   **Guest Star:** Patrick Campbell

Mary arranges a friendly poker game for the newsroom staff, only to discover that Murray has a compulsive gambling streak.

**54**   Rhoda the Beautiful                    October 21, 1972
  **Writer:** Treva Silverman
  **Director:** Jay Sandrich

Rhoda, still lacking confidence in her looks even after she's lost twenty pounds, is chosen to compete in a store-sponsored beauty contest.

Treva Silverman confronts Rhoda's metamorphosis from a pudgy duckling to an attractive single woman with a script that is so sensitive to the character's emotional plight that it is both funny and surprisingly touching at the same time.

**55**   Just Around the Corner                October 28, 1972
  **Writer:** Steve Pritzker
  **Director:** Jay Sandrich
  **Guest Stars:** Nanette Fabray, Bill Quinn

Mary is apprehensive when her parents move to Minneapolis to be near her.

Nanette Fabray and Bill Quinn were brought in as semi-regulars to play Mary's parents, but judging by how few episodes the writers were able to work them into, it must have been clear early on that they had no real need for the characters. They were never seen after the third season.

**56**   But Seriously, Folks                  November 4, 1972
  **Writer:** Phil Mishkin
  **Director:** Peter Baldwin
  **Guest Stars:** Jerry Van Dyke, John Fox

Mary tries to help a frustrated comedian who has higher aspirations than writing material for Chuckles the Clown.

Van Dyke appeared with Mary Tyler Moore a decade earlier as an occasional guest star on his brother's series *The Dick Van Dyke Show*.

**57**   Farmer Ted and the News              November 11, 1972
  **Writer:** Martin Donovan
  **Director:** Jay Sandrich
  **Guest Star:** Lurene Tuttle

Ted becomes a pitchman on local TV commercials, to the chagrin of Lou and the rest of the newsroom staff.

**58**    Have I Found a Guy for You                November 18, 1972
   **Writer:** Charlotte Brown
   **Director:** Hal Cooper
   **Guest Stars:** Bert Convy, Beth Howland

Mary is faced with an awkward situation when two married friends split up and she finds out that the husband is interested in her.

**59**    You've Got a Friend                        November 25, 1972
   **Writer:** Steve Pritzker
   **Director:** Jerry Belson
   **Guest Stars:** Nanette Fabray, Bill Quinn

When Mary's father retires, she decides he should form a new friendship—with Lou.

**60**    It Was Fascination, I Know                  December 2, 1972
   **Writer:** Ed. Weinberger
   **Director:** Jay Sandrich
   **Guest Stars:** Gerald Michenaud, Lisa Gerritsen

Mary unwittingly gets involved in an odd triangle with Phyllis's daughter, Bess.

An early *Mary* script by Ed. Weinberger, who—with partner Stan Daniels—would write and produce many of the finest episodes of the series. Weinberger joined MTM after writing and producing Bill Cosby's first NBC sitcom, the soft-spoken and intelligent *Bill Cosby Show*. In 1978, Weinberger and Daniels would team up with Jim Brooks and Dave Davis to create *Taxi* for ABC.

**61**    Operation: Lou                              December 9, 1972
   **Writers:** Elias Davis, David Pollack
   **Director:** Jay Sandrich
   **Guest Stars:** Florida Friebus, Michael McGinnis

Lou undergoes minor surgery and reluctantly leaves the newsroom in Mary's tentative care.

**62**    Rhoda Morgenstern: Minneapolis             December 16, 1972
          to New York
   **Writer:** Treva Silverman
   **Director:** Jay Sandrich
   **Guest Stars:** Jack Riley, Robert Casper

Rhoda decides to move back to New York City but has second thoughts when all her friends arrive for a farewell party.

This episode introduces the character of Georgette Franklin, played by Georgia Engel. Though Rhoda's exit from the show wouldn't occur for another two seasons, the producers were obviously aware that they'd have to build a second generation of supporting players if they were to keep the series strong over the long haul. The introduction of Georgette as a love interest for Ted Baxter indicated yet another radical shift: The show's creators were finally going to build Ted into something more than pure comic relief.

**63**   The Courtship of Mary's                    December 23, 1972
         Father's Daughter
**Writers:** Elias Davis, David Pollack
**Director:** Jay Sandrich
**Guest Stars:** Michael Tolan, Barra Grant, Steve Franken, Bill Quinn, Gordon Jump, Arthur Abelson

Mary attends the engagement party of an old boyfriend and ends up on the receiving end of his awkward proposal.

**64**   Lou's Place                               January 6, 1973
**Writer:** Ed. Weinberger
**Director:** Jay Sandrich
**Guest Stars:** Dick Balduzzi, Jack Spritt, Arthur Abelson, Lew Horn

Lou enters into an ill-advised partnership with Ted to buy a bar.

**65**   My Brother's Keeper                       January 13, 1973
**Writers:** Dick Clair, Jenna McMahon
**Director:** Jay Sandrich
**Guest Star:** Robert Moore

Phyllis is surprised when her visiting brother seems more interested in Rhoda than Mary, though it never occurs to her that he's gay.

Gay-rights groups applauded the show for presenting a nonstereotypical gay characterization, but producer James Brooks confesses that it was largely unintentional, since Phyllis's brother wasn't even gay in the original script! The twist was added at a last-minute rewrite session after a previous ending fell flat during rehearsal.

**66**   The Georgette Story                          January 20, 1973
  **Writer:** Ed. Weinberger
  **Director:** Peter Baldwin

Ted and Georgette's blossoming romance gets off to a rocky start when Georgette starts to think that Ted is taking advantage of her.

**67**   Romeo and Mary                              January 27, 1973
  **Writers:** Jim Mulholland, Mike Barrie
  **Director:** Peter Baldwin
  **Guest Stars:** Stuart Margolin, Joe Warfield, Bo Kaprall

Rhoda fixes Mary up with a zany obsessive who insists on marrying her.

**68**   What Do You Do When the Boss Says,      February 3, 1973
         "I Love You"?
  **Writers:** David Pollack, Elias Davis
  **Director:** Jay Sandrich
  **Guest Stars:** Lois Nettleton, Dick Balduzzi

Lou panics when the attractive new station manager appears to have designs on him.

**69**   Murray Faces Life                          February 10, 1973
  **Writer:** Martin Cohan
  **Director:** Jay Sandrich

Murray becomes depressed when he begins to fear that he hasn't accomplished anything important in his life.

**70**   Remembrance of Things Past                February 17, 1973
  **Writers:** Dick Clair, Jenna McMahon
  **Director:** Jay Sandrich
  **Guest Star:** Joseph Campanella

An old boyfriend of Mary's pays a visit, but she's afraid to rekindle the flame of a painful romance.

Joseph Campanella plays the ingratiating former lover, a role that he was to repeat in the semi-regular part of Ann Romano's former husband on Norman Lear's long-running sitcom *One Day at a Time.*

**71**   Put on a Happy Face                     February 24, 1973
   **Writers:** Marilyn Suzanne Miller, Monica Magowan
   **Director:** Jay Sandrich
   **Guest Stars:** Steve Franken, Art Gilmore, Herbie Faye

Mary is nominated for a Teddy Award, but her personal life seems jinxed when everything she does turns out wrong.

**72**   Mary Richards and the Incredible Plant Lady March 3, 1973
   **Writer:** Martin Cohan
   **Director:** John C. Chulay
   **Guest Stars:** Louise Lasser, Robert Karvelas, Henry Corgen

Rhoda decides to open a plant store—with Mary's savings as seed money.

## 1973-74   THE FOURTH SEASON

*Year-End Rating: 23.1 (9th place)*

The fourth season sees the characters and situations developed to a level of depth and sophistication that few thought possible on a network sitcom. Lou Grant's separation and eventual divorce were a recurring plot springboard that demonstrated the show's remarkable ability to deal with sobering issues of real life in a funny, but not frivolous, way.

Other developments during this peak middle period of the show's development include the addition of Sue Ann Nivens to the regular cast. Betty White's verbally assaultive and sexually voracious character would provide a potent source of fresh plot ideas throughout the remaining three years of the series.

Ed. Weinberger continues to serve as producer, while Jay Sandrich once again directs most of the episodes; and Treva Silverman is executive story consultant in the fourth year.

**73**   The Lars Affair                         September 15, 1973
   **Writer:** Ed. Weinberger
   **Director:** Jay Sandrich
   **Guest Star:** Betty White

Phyllis discovers that her husband, Lars, is having an affair with WJM's *Happy Homemaker*, Sue Ann Nivens.

This episode marks the introduction of Betty White as Sue Ann Nivens, host of *The Happy Homemaker Show*. Legend has it that the show's creators wanted to add a bitchy, bright, and sexually omnivorous female character to the series and thought that it would be a funny twist to cast against type and use a clean-living, all-American "Betty White type" in the role. On a lark, they sent her the script, she loved the idea, and no male in the WJM newsroom has been safe since.

Cloris Leachman, whose star had risen meteorically since the series began, was busy pursuing other avenues of her career, and so was seen less frequently on the show by this time. However, she did make occasional guest appearances, such as her performance here—for which she was awarded an Emmy.

**74**   Angels in the Snow                         September 22, 1973
   **Writers:** Marilyn Suzanne Miller, Monica Magowan Johnson
   **Director:** Jay Sandrich
   **Guest Stars:** Peter Strauss, Elayne Heilveil

Mary's new boyfriend is in his twenties, which suddenly makes her feel very old.

**75**   Rhoda's Sister Gets Married                September 29, 1973
   **Writer:** Karyl Geld
   **Director:** Jerry Belson
   **Guest Stars:** Liberty Williams, Nancy Walker, Harold Gould

Mary and Rhoda fly to New York for the marriage of Rhoda's sister, Debbie.

This prototype version of Rhoda's sister was not the same one used in the spinoff series *Rhoda*. It must've been some honeymoon: Poor Debbie vanished and was never heard from again.

**76**   The Lou and Edie Story                     October 6, 1973
   **Writer:** Treva Silverman
   **Director:** Jay Sandrich
   **Guest Stars:** Priscilla Morrill, Darrel Zwerling

Lou and his wife, Edie, separate after raising a family, leaving Lou heartbroken.

A compassionate development in the life of one of the show's most interesting, and real, characters. The relationship of Mary and Lou continues to develop in subtle and complex ways that mirror the way two real people might grow close—by building a fond attachment, without ever really identifying their shared emotion as love. The script would win a well-deserved Emmy, surely a sign that the television industry was keenly aware of the show's ever-blossoming level of sophistication.

**77**    Hi There, Sports Fans                    October 13, 1973
    **Writer:** Jerry Mayer
    **Director:** Jay Sandrich
    **Guest Stars:** Dick Gautier, Gordon Jump, John Gabriel
Mary wants more responsibility, so Lou awards her the task of firing the WJM sportscaster.

**78**    Father's Day                    October 20, 1973
    **Writers:** Ed. Weinberger, Stan Daniels
    **Director:** Jay Sandrich
    **Guest Stars:** Liam Dunn, John Holland

Ted is nervous at the prospect of a reunion with his long-lost father.

**79**    Son of "But Seriously, Folks"                    October 27, 1973
    **Writer:** Phil Mishkin
    **Director:** Jay Sandrich
    **Guest Star:** Jerry Van Dyke

When Mary's old comedy-writer boyfriend joins the newsroom staff, he concentrates more on Mary than his work.

**80**    Lou's First Date                    November 3, 1973
    **Writers:** Ed. Weinberger, Stan Daniels
    **Director:** Jay Sandrich
    **Guest Stars:** Florence Lake, Priscilla Morrill, Jeff Thompson

Lou, now a bachelor, asks Mary to drum him up a date for an awards banquet.

**81**    Love Blooms at Hempel's                    November 10, 1973
  **Writers:** Sybil Adelman, Barbara Gallagher
  **Director:** Jay Sandrich
  **Guest Stars:** William Burns, Barbara Barrett, Meg Wyllie, Roy West

Rhoda falls head over heels for the manager of the department store where she works.

**82**    The Dinner Party                    November 17,1973
  **Writer:** Ed. Weinberger
  **Director:** Jay Sandrich
  **Guest Stars:** Irene Tedrow, Henry Winkler

Mary is surprised when a congresswoman accepts her rhetorical invitation to a dinner party.

Henry Winkler plays one of the dinner guests in a role that predates his imminent fame as a star of *Happy Days*.

**83**    Just Friends                    November 24,1973
  **Writer:** William Wood
  **Director:** Nancy Walker
  **Guest Star:** Priscilla Morrill

When Lou becomes Mary's perennial dinner guest, she decides to reunite him with Edie.

Directed by Nancy Walker, the actress we usually thought of as Rhoda's mother.

**84**    We Want Baxter                    December 1, 1973
  **Writer:** David Lloyd
  **Director:** Jay Sandrich
  **Guest Star:** John Amos

Phyllis convinces Ted to forgo his news career and run for city council.

This is the first *Mary Tyler Moore* episode written by David Lloyd, who had once written jokes for both Jack Paar and Merv Griffin. Lloyd's daughter, a fan of *The Mary Tyler Moore Show*, suggested that he submit a script—which he did, without ever watching the show! Working from character descriptions his daughter gave him, Lloyd constructed a sample script that was good enough to land him a regular spot on the writers' roster. A gifted comedy writer, Lloyd would contribute many of the show's most memorable later episodes.

**85**    I Gave at the Office          December 8, 1973
   **Writers:** Don Reo, Allan Katz
   **Director:** Jay Sandrich
   **Guest Stars:** Tammi Bula, Bruce Boxleitner

Mary hires Murray's daughter, Bonnie, to work in the newsroom.

**86**    Almost a Nun's Story          December 15, 1973
   **Writers:** Ed. Weinberger, Stan Daniels
   **Director:** Jay Sandrich
   **Guest Star:** Gail Strickland

Georgette is prepared to join a convent after she spies Ted with another woman in his dressing room.

**87**    Happy Birthday, Lou          December 22, 1973
   **Writer:** David Lloyd
   **Director:** George Tyne
   **Guest Star:** Priscilla Morrill

Mary plans an unwanted surprise party for Lou's birthday.

The decision to separate Lou from his wife has become a bonanza for new plots involving Lou and Mary. Actor Ed Asner rises to the challenge by developing the irascible old news-hawk into a compelling portrait of a man facing middle age, suddenly alone.

**88**    WJM Tries Harder          January 5, 1974
   **Writer:** Karyl Geld
   **Director:** Jay Sandrich
   **Guest Stars:** Anthony Eisley, Ned Wertimer, Regis Cordic

Mary begins to have doubts about the integrity of her own show after she dates the anchorman at a competing station.

**89**    Cottage for Sale          January 12, 1974
   **Writer:** George Atkins
   **Director:** Jay Sandrich
   **Guest Star:** Michele Nichols

Phyllis tries to convince Lou to let her sell his house, despite his sentimental attachment to it.

**90**    The Co-Producers                           January 19, 1974
      **Writers:** David Pollack, Elias Davis
      **Director:** Jay Sandrich

Mary and Rhoda become producers of a show that features the
unlikely team of Ted and Sue Ann.


**91**    Best of Enemies                            January 26, 1974
      **Writers:** Marilyn Suzanne Miller, Monica Magowan Johnson
      **Director:** Jay Sandrich

Mary and Rhoda have a blowup that threatens to devastate their
friendship.


**92**    Better Late . . . That's a Pun. . .        February 2, 1974
          Than Never
      **Writer:** Treva Silverman
      **Director:** John C. Chulay
      **Guest Star:** Jennifer Leak

Mary writes a joke obituary that Ted reads on the air, forcing Lou
to punish her with a suspension.


**93**    Ted Baxter Meets Walter Cronkite           February 9, 1974
      **Writer:** Ed. Weinberger
      **Director:** Jay Sandrich
      **Guest Stars:** Walter Cronkite, John Gabriel, John Pringle

Ted develops delusions of network stardom when Walter Cronkite
drops by the newsroom.


**94**    Lou's Second Date                          February 16, 1974
      **Writer:** Ed. Weinberger
      **Director:** Jerry London

Lou dates Rhoda, causing all sorts of speculation in the newsroom.

Valerie Harper left the cast after this episode to star in *Rhoda*, which
would begin the following fall.

**95** Two Wrongs Don't Make a Writer February 23, 1974
**Writer:** David Lloyd
**Director:** Nancy Walker
**Guest Star:** Shirley O'Hara

Ted horns in on a creative-writing course that Mary's attending and then has the nerve to paraphrase and plagiarize her touching personal reminiscence.

Writer David Lloyd seemed to possess an understanding of Ted Baxter's character that few of the show's other writers could touch. The episodes that he wrote with Ted as a central character are among the funniest ever aired, as this particular show aptly demonstrates. Ted's boyish malevolence is exploited in a chilling fashion in the scene where Ted claims Mary's assignment as his own and then reinterprets it aloud in class, leaving her to stammer out a new composition on the spot. A comic masterpiece that presents actor Ted Knight at his finest.

**96** I Was a Single for WJM March 2, 1974
**Writer:** Treva Silverman
**Director:** Mel Ferber
**Guest Stars:** Richard Schaal, Penny Marshall, Arlene Golonka, Robert Riesel

Mary goes on location for an in-depth report on the singles scene.

The scene where Mary and Lou must improvise an entire half-hour show on location from the suddenly deserted single's bar is another hilarious example of a staple MTM situation—as a well-intentioned Lou and Mary find themselves struggling to endure a magnificently embarrassing predicament while trying not to reveal the slightest discomfort.
Penny Marshall, who plays one of the singles, would soon achieve lasting notoriety as one half of *Laverne and Shirley*.

## 1974-75   THE FIFTH SEASON

*Year-End Rating: 24.0 (11th place)*

The show practically glides into a fifth season, buoyed aloft by critical and popular acclaim, as well as a cast and creative team that are among the finest ever assembled for the production of a weekly situation comedy.

Major developments in the continuing story include the engagement of Ted and Georgette and the final appearance of Phyllis, who will move to San Francisco and her own series the following fall.

The show continues to benefit from the contributions of many talented scripters, with stalwart David Lloyd acting as executive story editor. Prolific scripters Ed. Weinberger and Stan Daniels also serve as producers in season five, a position they will hold for the remainder of the series. Jay Sandrich continues to head the roster of directors, though Mary Tyler Moore herself directs an episode this season—her single venture behind the camera.

**97**    Will Mary Richards Go to Jail?          September 14, 1974
**Writers:** Ed. Weinberger, Stan Daniels
**Director:** Jay Sandrich
**Guest Stars:** Barbara Colby, James Randolph

Mary spends the night in jail after she refuses to reveal a news source.

**98**    Not Just Another Pretty Face          September 21, 1974
**Writers:** Ed. Weinberger, Stan Daniels
**Director:** Jay Sandrich
**Guest Star:** Robert Wolders

Mary dates a man because of his striking looks, even though she knows they have nothing in common.

An episode that takes the risk of exploring Mary's apparently shallow ability to date a rather dull man merely because he happens to be very good-looking. In fact, her actions actually reflect a newfound maturity in Mary's character, who makes the refreshingly adult realization that she is capable of dating a great-looking man for purely physical reasons—and why, she wonders, shouldn't she? This sophisticated treatment of an essentially feminist issue wouldn't have been possible in an earlier phase of the series's development, when Mary was still constrained by the rules of what good girls did, and didn't do, on sitcoms.

**99**   You Sometimes Hurt                    September 28, 1974
         the One You Hate
**Writer:** David Lloyd
**Director:** Jackie Cooper

After he tosses Ted from the newsroom in an angry fit, Lou takes stock of his temper and begins to treat Ted with kid gloves.

**100**   Lou and That Woman                    October 5, 1974
**Writer:** David Lloyd
**Director:** Jay Sandrich
**Guest Stars:** Sheree North, Fred Festinger

Lou gets involved with a lounge singer of dubious reputation.

**101**   The Outsider                          October 12, 1974
**Writer:** Jack Winter
**Director:** Peter Bonerz
**Guest Star**: Richard Masur

A consultant tries to bolster the ratings of *The Six O'Clock News*, but succeeds only in enraging the newsroom staff.

**102**   I Love a Piano                        October 19, 1974
**Writer:** Treva Silverman
**Director:** Jay Sandrich
**Guest Star:** Barbara Barrie

Murray comes very close to having an affair with an attractive woman.

Barbara Barrie would play Liz on *Barney Miller* when the station-house comedy premiered in 1975.

**103**   A New Sue Ann                         October 26, 1974
**Writer:** David Lloyd
**Director:** Jay Sandrich
**Guest Stars:** Linda Kelsey, Ron Rifkin

Sue Ann meets her match when a manipulative young woman tries to take over *The Happy Homemaker Show*.

Linda Kelsey guests as the unscrupulous girl—a far cry from Billie Newman, the earthy reporter she would later play on *Lou Grant*.

**104**   Ménage à Phyllis                    November 2, 1974
   **Writer:** Treva Silverman
   **Director:** Jay Sandrich
   **Guest Star:** John Saxon

Phyllis dates a man for purely intellectual stimulation but is alarmed when he begins dating Mary for a different kind of exhilaration.

**105**   Not a Christmas Story                    November 9, 1974
   **Writers:** Ed. Weinberger, Stan Daniels
   **Director:** John C. Chulay

Sue Ann attempts to introduce a little Yuletide cheer, a month and a half too early, when the staff gets snowbound at work in early November.

**106**   What Are Friends For?                    November 16, 1974
   **Writer:** David Lloyd
   **Director:** Allan Rafkin
   **Guest Stars:** Noble Willingham, David Huddleston, Dan Barrows, Robert Karvelas

Sue Ann tries to nudge Mary into the fast lane when they attend a broadcasters' convention together in Chicago.

**107**   A Boy's Best Friend                    November 23, 1974
   **Writer:** David Lloyd
   **Director:** Mary Tyler Moore
   **Guest Star:** Nolan Leary

Ted is shocked when his mother announces that she intends to move in with her boyfriend.

**108**   A Son for Murray                    November 30, 1974
   **Writers:** Ed. Weinberger, Stan Daniels
   **Director:** Jay Sandrich
   **Guest Stars:** Michael Higa, John Gabriel

Murray desperately wants a son but can't convince Marie to have another child after she's already had three girls.

**109** Neighbors                                    December 7,1974
  **Writer:** Ziggy Steinberg
  **Directors:** James Burrows, John C. Chulay
  **Guest Star:** Clifford Davis

When Lou decides to move out of his house and into Rhoda's old apartment, Mary is afraid that she'll lose all sense of privacy.

One of director James Burrows' apprentice assignments. His later association with *Taxi* and *Cheers* would eventually establish his credentials as one of the brightest TV directors in the business.

**110** A Girl Like Mary                             December 14, 1974
  **Writers:** Ann Gibbs, Joel Kimmel
  **Director:** Jay Sandrich
  **Guest Star:** Rosalind Cash

When Lou decides to add a female newscaster to the show, he's faced with two unlikely candidates—Sue Ann and Mary.

**111** An Affair to Forget                          December 21, 1974
  **Writers:** Ed. Weinberger, Stan Daniels
  **Director:** Jay Sandrich

Ted convinces the newsroom that he and Mary are having a torrid affair.

A perfect example of the kind of character comedy that was to become the trademark of the early MTM sitcoms. The absurd situation arises organically from the personalities of the characters; it was inevitable that Ted would try this stunt sooner or later. And it was equally inevitable that Mary would be unable to rationally cope with the galling repercussions of Ted's innuendo.

Because we're so familiar with Mary's and Ted's personalities, we can see instantly that both are merely victims of their own character. We sympathize with Ted's desperate plight just as much as we identify with Mary's utter mortification. The entire embarrassing situation is made funny largely because we are convinced that it could conceivably happen to any one of us.

**112**    Mary Richards: Producer        January 4, 1975
**Writer**: David Lloyd
**Director:** Norman Campbell
**Guest Stars:** Anthony Holland, Phillip R. Allen

Mary feels dissatisfied with the scope of her job and asks for the chance to produce *The Six O'Clock News*.

**113**   The System         January 11, 1975
**Writers:** Ed. Weinberger, Stan Daniels
**Director:** Jay Sandrich

Ted invents a seemingly foolproof scheme for betting on the football pools, luring Lou into partnership with him.

**114**   Phyllis Whips Inflation        January 18, 1975
**Writers:** Ed. Weinberger, Stan Daniels
**Director:** Jay Sandrich
**Guest Star:** Doris Roberts

When Lars takes away her credit cards, Phyllis is dismayed at the prospect of actually having to look for a job.

Cloris Leachman won an Emmy for her role in this episode, her last regular appearance on the series. She would begin filming her spinoff series, *Phyllis*, the following season.

**115**   The Shame of the Cities        January 25, 1975
**Writers:** Michael Elias, Arnie Kogen
**Director:** Jay Sandrich
**Guest Stars:** Sheree North, Robert Emhardt, Chuck Bergansky, James Jeter

Lou rashly mounts a tough exposé of a Minneapolis civic leader who turns out to have a spotless reputation.

**116**   Marriage: Minneapolis-Style        February 1, 1975
**Writer:** Pamela Russell
**Director:** Jay Sandrich
**Guest Star:** Eileen McDonough

Ted proposes to Georgette in the middle of his *Six O'Clock News* broadcast.

**117**   You Try to Be a Nice Guy                    February 8, 1975
   **Writer:** Michael Leeson
   **Director:** Jay Sandrich
   **Guest Star:** Barbara Colby

Mary agrees to lend a hand when the woman she met in jail is finally released.

Barbara Colby reprises her role as Sherry, the inmate Mary first met when she was jailed for contempt of court in episode 97.

**118**   You Can't Lose Them All                    February 15, 1975
   **Writer:** David Lloyd
   **Director:** Marjorie Mullen

Lou is indignant when he is honored with an award that is usually bestowed on broadcasters who have outlived their usefulness.

Director Marjorie Mullen was the show's regular script supervisor, a job she'd also performed throughout five seasons of *The Dick Van Dyke Show* a decade before.

**119**   Ted Baxter's Famous Broadcasters School   February 22, 1975
   **Writer:** Michael Zinberg
   **Director:** Jay Sandrich
   **Guest Stars:** Bernie Kopell, Leonard Frey, Norman Bartold

Ted is conned into endorsing a shady broadcasting school that turns out to have a total student enrollment of one.

Another classic episode. The strange fabric of the newsroom staff's paternal relationship with Ted Baxter is demonstrated as they each endure undeniable embarrassment in order to bail Ted out of a jam. The scene where Lou, Murray, and Mary take turns lecturing to the lone student is an absolute gem.

**120**   Anyone Who Hates Kids and Dogs             March 8, 1975
   **Writer:** Jerry Mayer
   **Director:** Jay Sandrich
   **Guest Stars:** Laurence Luckinbill, Lee H. Montgomery, Mabel Albertson, Ian Wolfe

Mary must face the difficult fact that she can't stand her new boyfriend's young son.

## 1975-76    THE SIXTH SEASON

*Year-End Rating: 21.9 (19th place)*

With both Phyllis and Rhoda gone from the series, the dual focus on Mary's home and work-life environments is diminished. With fewer characters to serve, the writers are free to increase the interaction among the surviving members of Mary's TV family, a shift that will yield substantial comic dividends in the show's final seasons.

On the creative end, Ed. Weinberger and Stan Daniels return as sixth-year producers. And Bob Ellison signs on as executive story editor, replacing David Lloyd, who will assume the position of creative consultant for the final two seasons of the series.

**121**   Edie Gets Married                        September 13, 1975
**Writer:** Bob Ellison
**Director:** Jay Sandrich
**Guest Stars:** Priscilla Morrill, Nora Heflin

Lou can't bring himself to attend the ceremony when Edie gets remarried.

**122**   Mary Moves Out                           September 20, 1975
**Writer:** David Lloyd
**Director:** Jay Sandrich
**Guest Star:** John Lehne

Convinced that she's in a rut, Mary moves into a new apartment.

The scene where Mary demonstrates her tedium by accurately predicting every word the newsroom staff will utter is even more compelling when one realizes that the creators of the show must've found themselves in a very similar rut. How could they keep the series fresh when they were going into a sixth season with characters and situations that by now must've seemed completely familiar to every man, woman, and child in the country?

One way they faced the challenge was to move Mary out of her old apartment. Since it was clear that Rhoda and Phyllis would not be replaced, it made sense to finally close the book on that part of her life.

There is a touching moment in this episode when Mary seems to acknowledge the evolution her character has undergone. She is trying to hang the big letter M that she brought over from the old apartment, but she can't get it to hang the same way in the newer, more sterile high-rise.

She finally puts down her hammer and nails and whirls around in frustration. Suddenly, she realizes how much she misses her old life, her old friends, and her old apartment—and how much she hates the new place.

Finally, she walks from the room, struck by the irony of her new independence. Mary Richards no longer wonders how she will make it on her own—she already has. Now she's left to ponder if the struggle was worth it.

**123**   Mary's Father                          September 27, 1975
**Writer:** Earl Pomerantz
**Director:** Jay Sandrich
**Guest Star:** Ed Flanders

Mary fears that a dynamic Catholic priest may leave the church because he's fallen in love with her.

An episode that explores a rarely exposed area of Mary's character. When the priest reveals that his infatuation with Mary existed largely in her mind, her ego takes a slight trouncing. "I'm not *un*attractive," she exclaims, affording us a rare glimpse at the insecurity and vanity that lurk deep in the heart of every former prom queen. The show's creators took a risk depicting Mary in this unfavorable light—but it was a gamble that paid off. By the end of this half hour, we better understood Mary, and we liked her all the more for revealing this very human side of her character.

The scene where Lou tries to warn the priest of the moral danger of his actions is a masterpiece of comic misunderstanding, offering Ed Asner one of his best monologues of the series. When he starts to launch into a story that begins when he was twelve years old, the impatient priest interrupts him: "Lou, give me a hint. How old are you at the end of the story?"

**124**   Murray in Love                          October 4, 1975
**Writer:** David Lloyd
**Director:** Jay Sandrich
**Guest Stars:** Penny Marshall, Mary Kay Place, Peter Hobbs

Murray confides to Mary that he's fallen deeply in love with her.

A probing and surprisingly touching episode. When Mary reveals the nature of her love toward Murray—"I don't know what tomorrow morning may bring, but the last five years have been the most important of my life"—the actress and her character become one. The scene where Murray, the idealist, realizes that he must learn to accept himself—and not his dreams—is a powerful moment of recognition that suddenly makes worthy the five-year journey of this most sophisticated of "supporting" characters.

**125**   Ted's Moment of Glory                    October 11, 1975
   **Writers:** Charles Lee, Gig Henry
   **Director:** Jay Sandrich
   **Guest Stars:** Richard Balin, Marilyn Roberts

Ted plans to move to New York to accept an offer to host a game show, until Lou and Mary convince him to stay at WJM.

A character exploration of Ted Baxter that doesn't quite add up. There is nothing in Ted's personality that allows him the integrity to forgo an extra $1000 a week in salary just to stay in Minneapolis. The scene where Mary and Lou decide they want to keep Ted at WJM seems a little forced as well. At least the writers were smart enough to keep Murray out of the picture when Mary and Lou decide to convince Ted not to take the other offer.

**126**   Mary's Aunt                            October 18, 1975
   **Writer:** David Lloyd
   **Director:** Jay Sandrich
   **Guest Star:** Eileen Heckart

Mary's Aunt Flo—a world-class foreign correspondent—drops in for a visit and begins a friendly rivalry with Lou.

Mary's Aunt Flo, played by Oscar-winner Eileen Heckart, was the only character from *The Mary Tyler Moore Show* ever to make a crossover, however brief, to the more serious *Lou Grant* series of the late 1970s.

**127**   Chuckles Bites the Dust                 October 25, 1975
   **Writer:** David Lloyd

**Director:** Joan Darling
**Guest Stars:** John Harkins, Helen Kleeb

The death of Chuckles the Clown under the most ridiculous of circumstances prompts a nervous rash of gallows humor in the newsroom.

Director Joan Darling and writer David Lloyd both earned Emmy Awards for an outstanding episode that questions our culture's sanctimonious attitude toward death and dying with predictable irreverence. The plot bears echoes of a scene in an old Second City revue where a family is similarly convulsed by the absurd death of their father—which only shows how much *The Mary Tyler Moore Show*, like *Saturday Night Live* in the 1970s, drew from the same comic vein as the improvisational comedians of the 1960s.

**128**  Mary's Delinquent                    November 1, 1975
  **Writers:** Mary Kay Place, Valerie Curtin
  **Director:** Jay Sandrich
  **Guest Stars:** Mackenzie Phillips, Tamu, Phillip R. Allen

Mary and Sue Ann become big sisters to two wayward girls.

Writer Valerie Curtin would be one of the creators of the short-lived but critically acclaimed series *Square Pegs*.

**129**  Ted's Wedding                        November 8, 1975
  **Writer:** David Lloyd
  **Director:** Jay Sandrich
  **Guest Star:** John Ritter

Ted and Georgette are wed in an impulsive ceremony improvised in Mary's apartment.

There was really no chance of a June marriage for Ted and Georgette—sitcom weddings are invariably held in mid-November to boost viewership while the networks compete in their ratings sweeps.

**130**　　Lou Douses an Old Flame　　　November 15, 1975
**Writer:** David Lloyd
**Director:** Jay Sandrich
**Guest Star:** Beverly Garland

Lou has a rare opportunity to even the score with the woman who jilted him during the war.

**131**　Mary Richards Falls in Love　　　November 22, 1975
**Writers:** Ed. Weinberger, Stan Daniels
**Director:** Jay Sandrich
**Guest Stars:** Ted Bessell, Valerie Harper, David Groh, Beth Howland, Michael Perrotta

Mary thinks she may have finally found a man to settle down with but has second thoughts when he seems reluctant to make a commitment.

Mary could've saved about five years of looking for Mr. Right by watching reruns of *That Girl*. Long before he rode a white horse into Mary Richards' life as Joe Warner, Ted Bessell played the boyfriend on that late-sixties sitcom—a show that preceded *The Mary Tyler Moore Show* in theme, if not precisely in flavor. Bessell also shared billing with a chimpanzee in another sitcom—but that's a whole other story.

**132**　Ted's Tax Refund　　　　　　November 29, 1975
**Writer:** Bob Ellison
**Director:** Marjorie Mullen
**Guest Star:** Paul Lichtman

Ted is pleased when he gets an unusually large income tax refund, until he finds out he's scheduled to be audited by the IRS.

**133**　The Happy Homemaker Takes Lou　　December 6, 1975
　　　　Home
**Writer:** David Lloyd
**Director:** James Burrows
**Guest Stars:** Wynn Irwin, Titos Vandis

Lou is tricked into spending the evening in Sue Ann's desperate clutches.

**134**    One Boyfriend Too Many                December 13, 1975
   **Writer:** David Lloyd
   **Director:** Jay Sandrich
   **Guest Stars:** Michael Tolan, Ted Bessell

Mary is forced to choose between her current heartthrob and an old boyfriend who suddenly reenters her life.

**135**    What Do You Want to Do                December 20, 1975
       When You Produce?
   **Writers:** Shelley Nelbert, Craig Allen Hafner
   **Director:** Jay Sandrich
   **Guest Star:** Joyce Bulifant

Murray's life is transformed into a nightmare when he volunteers to become producer of domineering Sue Ann's *Happy Homemaker Show*.

**136**    Not With My Wife, I Don't                January 3, 1976
   **Writer:** Bob Ellison
   **Director:** Jay Sandrich
   **Guest Star:** Allan Manson

Georgette decides to seek professional marital counseling when she begins to feel that Ted no longer loves her.

**137**    The Seminar                January 10, 1976
   **Writers:** James MacDonald, Robert Gerlach
   **Director:** Stuart Margolin
   **Guest Stars:** Betty Ford, Dabney Coleman

Mary refuses to believe that Lou is on a first-name basis with Capitol Hill luminaries until he's paid a surprise visit by First Lady Betty Ford.

**138**    Once I Had a Secret Love                January 17, 1976
   **Writers**: Pat Nardo, Gloria Banta
   **Director:** Jay Sandrich

Lou's faith in Mary is tested when he confides that he once spent the night with Sue Ann.

**139**    Ménage à Lou                                    January 24, 1976
   **Writer:** Bob Ellison
   **Director:** Jay Sandrich
   **Guest Stars:** Janis Paige, Penny Marshall, Jeff Conaway

Lou is distraught when one of his old girlfriends arrives at Mary's party with her new beau.

**140**    Murray Takes a Stand                            January 31, 1976
   **Writer:** David Lloyd
   **Director:** Jay Sandrich
   **Guest Star:** Joyce Bulifant

Murray dares to speak out against the mercurial new station owner, but he soon finds himself out of a job.

**141** Mary's Aunt Returns                                February 7, 1976
   **Writer:** David Lloyd
   **Director:** Jay Sandrich
   **Guest Star:** Eileen Heckart

Lou once again locks horns with Mary's Aunt Flo when the pair squabble over the journalistic integrity of a documentary they're co-producing.

**142**    A Reliable Source                               February 21, 1976
   **Writer:** Richard M. Powell
   **Director:** Jay Sandrich
   **Guest Star:** Edward Winter

A conflict of ideals erupts when Lou decides to do an exposé on a politician who is also a good friend of Mary's.

**143**    Sue Ann Falls in Love                           February 28, 1976
   **Writer:** Bob Ellison
   **Director:** Doug Rogers
   **Guest Stars:** James Luisi, Pat Gaynor, Larry Wilde

Sue Ann falls in love and is finally nominated for a Teddy Award—both in the same week.

**144**   Ted and the Kid                                       March 6, 1976
   **Writer:** Bob Ellison
   **Director:** Marjorie Mullen
   **Guest Star:** Robbie Rist

After Ted finds out that he's unable to father a child, he and Georgette adopt a precocious young boy.

This episode demonstrates one of the more difficult attempts to expand and deepen a regular character on the series—the childlike anchorman Ted Baxter. When the role was created six years earlier, he was designed to offer the sort of broad comic relief that was a necessary and successful component of the show. A combination of good writing, as well as a perfect marriage of actor and role, soon made Ted one of the most popular characters on the show. But when the time came to humanize and expand his role, the show's creative staff ran into trouble. How could they humanize a character whose comic purpose was based on his lack of any believable human integrity? Essentially, they solved the problem by creating a new, more sympathetic character who still possessed the unsympathetic characteristics that made Ted so funny. It was an uneasy combination at best, and, as this episode indicates, a not entirely successful compromise.

## 1976-77   THE SEVENTH SEASON

*Year-End Rating: 19.2 (39th place)*

Acknowledging the pressures involved in maintaining the high standards of a series like *The Mary Tyler Moore Show*, the series's creators decide to bow out gracefully when they announce that the show's seventh season will be its last, ending the long run of one of the most popular and critically acclaimed series in television history.

Ed. Weinberger and Stan Daniels return as producers for the final season. Bob Ellison serves as executive story editor, while David Lloyd returns in the role of creative consultant.

**145**   Mary Midwife                                  September 25, 1976
   **Writer:** David Lloyd
   **Director:** Jay Sandrich
   **Guest Star:** Ford Rainey

Georgette unexpectedly has her baby in Mary's apartment.

**146**   Mary the Writer                    October 2, 1976
   **Writer:** Burt Prelutsky
   **Director:** James Burrows

Mary fulfills her desire to become a creative writer, despite Lou's harsh criticism of her abilities.

**147**   Sue Ann's Sister                   October 9, 1976
   **Writer:** David Lloyd
   **Director:** Jay Sandrich
   **Guest Star:** Pat Priest

Sue Ann's sister is hired as the hostess of a rival station's home-maker show.

**148**   What's Wrong With Swimming?        October 16, 1976
   **Writer:** David Lloyd
   **Director:** Marjorie Mullen
   **Guest Star:** Caren Kaye

Mary hires an Olympic swimmer as WJM's new sportscaster—against Lou's better judgment.

**149**   Ted's Change of Heart              October 23, 1976
   **Writer:** Earl Pomerantz
   **Director:** Jay Sandrich
   **Guest Stars:** Harvey Vernon, Jerry Fogel

After a brush with death, Ted decides to explore the joys of life—and he convinces the rest of the newsroom to join him.

**150**   One Producer Too Many              October 30, 1976
   **Writer:** Bob Ellison
   **Director:** Jay Sandrich
   **Guest Stars:** Richard Self, Murray Korda

Lou appoints Murray co-producer of *The Six O'Clock News*, which causes an unhealthy rivalry between Murray and Mary.

**151**   My Son, the Genius                 November 6, 1976
   **Writer:** Bob Ellison
   **Director:** Jay Sandrich
   **Guest Stars:** Robbie Rist, William Bogart, Ned Glass

Ted and Georgette discover that their adopted son has the IQ of a genius.

**152**   Mary Gets a Lawyer                    November 13, 1976
  **Writer:** Burt Prelutsky
  **Director:** Jay Sandrich
  **Guest Star:** John McMartin

Mary finally faces a judge for her contempt charges, but her defense lawyer seems more intent on winning *her* than defeating the case.


**153**   Lou Proposes                    November 20, 1976
  **Writer:** David Lloyd
  **Director:** Jay Sandrich
  **Guest Stars:** Eileen Heckart, T.J. Castronova

Lou finally musters the courage to propose to Mary's Aunt Flo.


**154**   Murray Can't Lose                    November 27, 1976
  **Writer:** David Lloyd
  **Director:** Jay Sandrich
  **Guest Stars:** Joyce Bulifant, Larry Wilde

Murray is convinced that he'll never be awarded a Teddy statuette until Lou builds his confidence with the implication that he's a shoo-in.


**155**   Mary's Insomnia                    December 4, 1976
  **Writer:** David Lloyd
  **Director:** James Burrows
  **Guest Star:** Sherry Hursey

Mary develops a dependence on sleeping pills, and Lou tries to force her off the habit.

An extraordinary look at an obsessive side of Mary's character that we never knew existed—and a revealing portrait of the true interdependency of Lou and Mary. This is a rare example of a sitcom episode that approaches successful human drama, largely due to the depth and believability the characters have developed during the later seasons.

**156**   Ted's Temptation                    December 11, 1976
**Writer:** Bob Ellison
**Director:** Harry Mastrogeorge
**Guest Star:** Trisha Noble

While in Hollywood for a newsmen's convention, Ted is almost seduced by a beautiful young reporter who's hoping for an in-depth interview.

**157**   Look at Us, We're Walking                    December 25, 1976
**Writer:** Bob Ellison
**Director:** Jay Sandrich
**Guest Star:** David Ogden Stiers

Lou and Mary decide to quit their jobs in order to bluff the new station manager into meeting their salary demands.

David Ogden Stiers played station manager Mel Price in only a few seventh-season episodes, but they would lead to the actor's far more lasting assignment as Major Charles Winchester of the 4077th after *M\*A\*S\*H* producer Burt Metcalfe spotted him on the show.

**158**   The Critic                    January 8, 1977
**Writer:** David Lloyd
**Director:** Martin Cohan
**Guest Stars:** Eric Braedon, David Ogden Stiers

WJM's new station manager hires a controversial critic for *The Six O'Clock News* as a ploy to boost the show's sagging ratings.

**159**   Lou's Army Reunion                    January 15, 1977
**Writer:** Bob Ellison
**Director:** Jay Sandrich
**Guest Star:** Alex Rocco

An old Army buddy of Lou's comes to town and decides to col-lect a favor—he wants a date with Mary.

**160**   The Ted and Georgette Show                    January 22, 1977
**Writer:** David Lloyd
**Director:** Jay Sandrich
**Guest Stars**: David Ogden Stiers, Alex Henteloff

Ted and Georgette host a successful variety show on WJM, until Georgette discovers that she can't stand the pressure.

**161**   Sue Ann Gets the Ax                    January 29, 1977
   **Writer:** Bob Ellison
   **Director:** Jay Sandrich
   **Guest Star:** Louis Guss

When Sue Ann's cooking show is canceled, she takes over as host of the afternoon kid's show.

**162**   Hail the Conquering Gordy                    February 5, 1977
   **Writer:** Earl Pomerantz
   **Director:** Jay Sandrich
   **Guest Star:** John Amos
Weatherman Gordy—now a well-known talk-show host—returns to WJM, only to face Ted, who volunteers his services as talk-show second banana.

**163**   Mary and the Sexagenarian                    February 12, 1977
   **Writers:** Les Charles, Glen Charles
   **Director:** Jay Sandrich
   **Guest Stars:** Lew Ayres, Jon Lormer

Mary goes out on a date with Murray's father, despite the ribbing she receives from the newsroom staff.

An early script from Glen Charles and Les Charles, two brothers who would one day create the popular and critically acclaimed NBC sitcom *Cheers*.

**164**   Murray Ghosts for Ted                    February 19, 1977
   **Writer:** David Lloyd
   **Director:** Jay Sandrich

Ted plans to take full credit—and make a large cash profit—when an article Murray has ghosted for him is picked up by a major magazine.

**165**   Mary's Three Husbands                    February 26, 1977
   **Writer:** Bob Ellison
   **Director:** Jay Sandrich
   **Guest Star:** Bill Darth

In dream sequences, we see what life would have been like had Mary become the wife of Lou, Ted, or Murray.

**166**   Mary's Big Party                              March 5, 1977
   **Writer:** Bob Ellison
   **Director:** Jay Sandrich
   **Guest Stars:** Johnny Carson, Irene Tedrow

To ensure that at least one of her parties will be a success, Mary invites Johnny Carson as guest of honor.

There are two sure signs that a sitcom is headed for the end of a long run on network TV. The first is when there's an entire episode devoted to flashbacks from earlier episodes, and the second is when a single show revolves around the surprise appearance of a special guest star. It's a credit to the ambition of the creative staff of *The Mary Tyler Moore Show* that they dared to dust off both those old sitcom chestnuts in a single audacious episode.

**167**   Lou Dates Mary                              March 12, 1977
   **Writer:** David Lloyd
   **Director:** Jan Sandrich
   **Guest Stars:** John Reilly, Kenny Waller

Lou and Mary finally have their first, and only, date.

Around the time this episode first aired, Ed Asner half-jokingly described the way that he thought this episode should end. Lou and Mary would be alone at the crest of the evening—in the dark, ensconced in a newly discovered bliss. As the credits begin to roll, there would be a long silence. Finally, the silence would be punctuated by Mary's familiar exclamation, "Oh, Mr. Grant!" Fade out . . . cut to commercial.

As tempting as that scenario must've seemed to Asner, it's not surprising that the show's creators opted for a more realistic ending to the big date, with Mary and Lou barely exchanging a goodnight kiss. The show's writers must've known all along that Lou and Mary were able to enjoy the most passionate love affair in TV history largely because it was unconsummated. Not sullied by carnal pleasure, they were free to exchange the passion of two thinking, feeling adults traveling together through seven years of highs and lows—through giddy pleasures and painful truths, through old divorces and new beginnings. Lou and Mary shared a respect for each other that was not unlike the respect that existed between the show's audience and its many creators—which gives some clue to the immense popularity of the series during its seven-year run.

Just as Mary grew to depend on Lou in her strange, ineffable way, so did we grow to expect the very best from this most unusual TV series. And right up to the very end, neither we, nor Mary, were ever disappointed.

**168**   The Last Show                                 March 19, 1977
    **Writers:** Allan Burns, James L. Brooks, Ed. Weinberger, Stan Daniels, David Lloyd, Bob   Ellison
    **Director:** Jay Sandrich
    **Guest Stars**: Robbie Rist, Vincent Gardenia, Cloris Leachman, Valerie Harper

WJM's new station owner decides to revamp *The Six O'Clock News*, so he fires everyone—except Ted Baxter.

It's a lucky thing that the show's creators decided to stage a final episode to end the series. The audience needed a proper occasion to say farewell to all those Saturday nights spent at home, often intentionally, with Mary Tyler Moore and the crew. The overall mood of this episode was that of a big, teary-eyed, good-bye kiss, and there was a built-in poignancy to this last hurrah that would be rarely equaled in series television.

Many viewers may still find it hard to stifle that lump in their throat when this episode is rerun on local TV at two or three in the morning. Although now that the show's in syndication, it must be a sobering consolation to know that Mary Richards will be back in Minneapolis the very next day, still tossing that silly hat in the air and finding out that Lou Grant thinks she's got spunk—and he hates spunk.

Fade out . . . cut to commercial.

## EMMY AWARDS

The following is a complete listing of the Emmy Awards bestowed on *The Mary Tyler Moore Show* by the National Academy of Television Arts and Sciences.

**1970-71**   Outstanding Performance by an Actor in a Supporting
            Role in Comedy: Edward Asner

            Outstanding Performance by an Actress in a Supporting
            Role in Comedy: Valerie Harper

            Outstanding Directorial Achievement in Comedy (Series):
            Jay Sandrich, "Toulouse-Lautrec Is One of My Favorite

Artists"

Outstanding Writing Achievement in Comedy: James L. Brooks, Allan Burns, "Support Your Local Mother"

**1971-72** Outstanding Performance by an Actor in a Supporting Role in Comedy: Edward Asner

Outstanding Performance by an Actress in a Supporting Role in a Comedy: Valerie Harper (tied with Sally Struthers)

**1972-73** Outstanding Continued Performance by an Actress in a Leading Role in a Comedy Series: Mary Tyler Moore

Outstanding Performance by an Actor in a Supporting Role in Comedy: Ted Knight

Outstanding Performance by an Actress in a Supporting Role in Comedy: Valerie Harper

Outstanding Directorial Achievement in Comedy: Jay Sandrich, "It's Whether You Win or Lose"

**1973-74** Best Lead Actress in a Comedy Series: Mary Tyler Moore

Actress of the Year, Series: Mary Tyler Moore

Best Supporting Actress in Comedy: Cloris Leachman, "The Lars Affair"

Best Writing in Comedy: Treva Silverman, "The Lou and Edie Story"

Writer of the Year, Series: Treva Silverman

**1974-75** Outstanding Comedy Series

Outstanding Continuing Performance by a Supporting Actor in a Comedy Series: Edward Asner

Outstanding Continuing Performance by a Supporting Actress in a Comedy Series: Betty White

Outstanding Single Performance by a Supporting Actress in a Comedy or Drama Series: Cloris Leachman, "Phyllis Whips Inflation"

Outstanding Writing in a Comedy Series: Ed. Weinberger, Stan Daniels, "Mary Richards Goes to Jail"

**1975-76** Outstanding Comedy Series

Outstanding Lead Actress in a Comedy Series: Mary Tyler Moore

Outstanding Continuing Performance by a Supporting Actor in a Comedy Series: Ted Knight

Outstanding Continuing Performance by a Supporting Actress in a Comedy Series: Betty White

Outstanding Writing in a Comedy Series: David Lloyd, "Chuckles Bites the Dust"

**1976-77** Outstanding Comedy Series

Outstanding Writing in a Comedy Series: Allan Burns, James L. Brooks, Ed. Weinberger, Stan Daniels, David Lloyd, Bob Ellison, "The Final Show" (a.k.a. "The Last Show")

# ALL IN THE FAMILY

·

*It was kind of like breaking
peanut brittle with a ballpeen
hammer.*
—ROBERT WOOD, former
president of CBS

STANDING in the dark, Norman Lear had an inspiration.

The balding, middle-aged movie producer had been cooped up in a New York editing room for the last few months of 1967, trying to make sense out of the disastrous first cut of *The Night They Raided Minsky's*. Standing in the shadows of the Moviola for what seemed like an eternity, he fondly recalled the manic pace he'd kept in the days of live television. As a scriptwriter for Dean Martin and Jerry Lewis in the early fifties, he could write a sketch on Wednesday morning and see it performed on *The Colgate Comedy Hour* the following Sunday night.

As he sweated out the endless months of postproduction on his fourth film in five years, he decided that his next project would be fast, cheap, and topical—everything a feature film wasn't. He resolved to return to television, where it was still possible to pick a story out of the headlines and put it up on the screen within weeks—not years.

It didn't matter to Norman Lear that, in the mid-1960s, prime-time TV ventured no closer to current events than the international intrigue of the latest world takeover bid on *The Man From U.N.C.L.E.* And it didn't faze the writer that the satirical venom he perfected in his screenplay for *Divorce American Style*—a scathing send-up of marriage rituals and family life—had no precedent on network television. He'd already found his inspiration in a TV program that no one in this country had even seen—himself included.

*Til Death Do Us Part* had been a hit in England for two years by 1966, when Norman Lear first read about it. According to the small item he saw in *TV Guide*, the BBC domestic comedy offered an uncensored look at British working-class life through the eyes of Alf Garnett, a bigoted dockworker who constantly locked horns with his nagging wife, vapid daughter, and deadbeat son-in-law. "My God," Lear thought, "if I could only get this kind of thing on American television."

Lear and Bud Yorkin, partners in Tandem Productions since the late fifties, quickly optioned the rights to do a U.S. adaptation of *Til Death Do Us Part*. As Lear continued to edit *Minsky's* throughout 1968, he spent every spare minute brainstorming *Those Were the Days*, as he named his version of the BBC comedy.

The Garnetts of England eventually landed in the states as the Bunkers of Queens, New York—although the writer's tempestuous clan had more in common with the Lears of Connecticut than the British originals. When he finally got to see a tape of Johnny Speight's *Til Death Do Us Part*, Lear discovered that the characters were too abrasive for his taste. For inspiration, he looked instead to his own family, where a surprising number of the heated exchanges that would eventually flare up between Archie Bunker and his meathead son-in-law had been played out years earlier by Norman Lear and his own father. "I'd accuse him of making racial slurs," Lear confessed, "and we'd get into real Mike-and-Archie shouting matches. And we were a nice *Jewish* family."

The unretouched family portrait that Lear painted in *Those Were the Days* offered a startling departure from the bucolic view of domestic life that still prevailed on most sitcoms—there was certainly no white-picket fence at 704 Hauser Street in Queens. The head of the family was Archie Bunker, described by the writer as "basically a horse's ass"; he was a seething mass of prejudice, half-truths, and malapropisms. In this family, father *never* knew best.

Playing a hunch that the third-place network had nothing to lose by taking a chance on his groundbreaker, Lear convinced ABC to finance a pilot episode. With a shooting date set for January 1969, Lear and Bud Yorkin scouted around for an actor to play Archie Justice—renamed Bunker after the original pilot was shot—a character who had to be both outrageous and likable.

Mickey Rooney was briefly considered, but Norman Lear recalls that the former child star didn't think much of Lear's concept when he pitched the show to Rooney during a transcontinental phone call in 1968. "It was one of those calls you never forget," chuckled Lear. "I told Mickey I wanted him to play a bigot, and he stopped me and said, 'Norman, if you go on the air with that, they're gonna kill you dead in the streets!'"

Apparently, Rooney had a different format in mind for his next television series. Remembers Lear, "He told me, 'You wanna do a show with the Mick? I'll give you the idea—Vietnam vet. Detective. Short. Blind. Big dog.'"

The pair never met.

Instead, Lear chose an accomplished character actor he first saw perform on a jet—during an in-flight screening of *What Did You Do in the War, Daddy?* Carroll O'Connor loved Lear's script, but, like Rooney, he didn't think the show had a chance. "I honestly thought it would be a big bomb," O'Connor later confessed. Jean Stapleton was the inspired choice to play Edith Bunker; the stage-trained actress invested Archie's dingbat wife with a comic depth that surprised even the writer. Together, O'Connor and Stapleton sparked an instantaneous chemistry, and the producers were delighted to discover the incongruous pair made an absolutely convincing married couple.

As portrayed by Carroll O'Connor, Archie Bunker was a comic figure of epic proportions, a colorful—if somewhat pathetic—folk hero. Lear would describe him as "the bigger-than-life epitome of something that's in all of us, like it or not." And yet, there was no doubt that Archie was a bigot, pure and simple. In the very first episode of the show, originally written as the pilot script, Archie vents his frustration with a vague assortment of "spics, spades, chinks, hebes"—and everyone else he holds responsible for the chaotic state of the Union, particularly his liberal son-in-law Michael, the "pinko polack atheist."

But beneath all the blustery polemics of Norman Lear's startling pilot script, the Bunkers quickly emerge as an ordinary, loving family who simply display their affection a little more loudly than most. When Gloria protests Archie's abuse by threatening to move out, Edith blurts out her deepest fears with logic only a mother could fathom, "If she leaves here, she'll be dead inside a year."

The comic desperation of Stapleton's delivery underscores the central irony of the show. Despite the apparent rancor, the Bunker living room still offers a reasonably attractive alternative to the cruel uncertainties that lie just beyond its portals. It's a point that's not lost on Archie—fixing the young couple in his gaze, he reassures his wife with the sarcastic understatement, "You don't have to worry, they ain't going nowhere."

Over the course of a single half hour, Lear and his cast seemed poised to launch a full-blown assault on the delicate sensibilities of a television audience that had grown soft on a steady diet of flying nuns and wise-cracking secret agents. Not surprisingly, the network executives who financed the original pilot wanted no part of it. "ABC didn't quite have the guts to put the show on," Lear recalled, "so they decided we had to shoot a second pilot, claiming they weren't happy with the kids."

The same script was shot again, four months later, with two different actors in the roles that would eventually be played by Sally Struthers and Rob Reiner. But no one was surprised when ABC quietly dropped their option on the series.

Norman Lear put the setback out of his mind and boarded a plane for Iowa to begin shooting his fifth feature film, *Cold Turkey*. He was editing it a few months later when his agent called with good news. CBS had been in touch, and they were suddenly *very* interested in *Those Were the Days*.

"Don't let that tape leave the building," Fred Silverman warned. He'd just left the CBS screening room after watching Lear's ABC pilot and was on his way to fetch Bob Wood, the network president. Silverman, the recently installed head of CBS programming, was unaware that his network had actually tried to option *Til Death Do Us Part* themselves two years earlier—ironically, as a potential Jackie Gleason vehicle. But in 1970, Silverman had very different reasons to be enthusiastic about this most unusual program.

He knew that Bob Wood was personally engineering a badly needed face-lift for the aging network. After a decade of hayseed hits like *The Beverly Hillbillies*, *Petticoat Junction*, and *Mayberry RFD*, CBS was in danger of losing the young, urban audience—those affluent viewers most prized by the advertisers. To lure this desirable demographic group back to the fold, the network needed a show so innovative that even the most sophisticated viewers would sit up and take notice. As he watched Lear's pilot, the CBS president laughed out loud. Not just because it was funny, but because it was exactly what he was looking for.

"It was very provocative if you consider what television was like in 1971 . . . kind of like breaking peanut brittle with a ballpeen hammer," Wood recalled. "I thought it might take some of the wrinkles out of the aging face of television. I knew it was a gamble, but I took a run at it."

The first person Wood had to convince was also his toughest audience. In 1970, William Paley, the sixty-nine-year-old monarch of CBS, still had the last word on what did—or did not—get on the air. He watched Lear's pilot impassively, as Bob Wood patiently explained how he thought prime time was finally ready to grow up, and how CBS was in a unique position to lead the pack. Paley leaned back in his chair and sniffed, "You may be right."

That was all the encouragement Wood needed. He ordered thirteen episodes of the new series, which was slated to debut in one of the network's January midseason replacement slots. At the same time, he offered Lear a list of changes that the network standards and practices department demanded before the show could go on the air. The producer reviewed the censor's suggestions and rejected every single one of them on the spot.

Lear refused to soften the show's impact by even one epithet. "I felt we had to get the network wet completely," was his negotiating stance. "Once you're completely wet, you can't get any wetter." And the producer clearly had the upper hand: If the CBS deal fell through, he could always return to his successful career as a screenwriter and director. Norman Lear stood firm; the show would be done his way, or not at all.

Bob Wood intervened and finally convinced the producer to make two small changes in the first episode. Lear excised a suggestive bit of business that showed Mike zipping his fly as he came downstairs from the bedroom; and the expletive "goddamn it" was deleted from Archie's dialogue. Lear incorporated one other change before the show premiered. CBS thought *Those Were the Days* sounded old-fashioned and suggested a new title, which Lear quickly adopted.

And so, on Tuesday, January 12, 1971, *All in the Family* was born.

The programming executives, understandably nervous on that fateful night, braced themselves for a deluge of irate phone calls, but were surprised when the network switchboard operators reported business as usual. "My God, I think we got twenty-three phone calls," remarked Bob Wood, puzzled at the public's massive indifference.

The mystery was solved when the first Nielsen returns came in. The reason so few people complained about *All in the Family* was that so few of them chose to watch.

Norman Lear was outwardly undaunted by the dismal ratings. "I knew we were going to be talked about," Lear declared, confident even then that positive word of mouth would help the show build an audience, eventually. But less optimistic observers conceded what the producer refused to acknowledge: The new show, buried—without advance publicity—at 9:30 on Tuesday night, would need a miracle to survive its first thirteen weeks.

The miracle arrived in May.

That's when the cast performed a sketch on the highly visible Emmy Awards broadcast on the same night that they walked off with three of the coveted statuettes. The sudden exposure to millions of new viewers quickly transformed the show's small cult following into a mass phenomenon. By the fall of 1971, there was scarcely a man, woman, or child anywhere in the country who didn't have an opinion, pro or con, about America's most vocal citizen—Archie Bunker.

*All in the Family* became a cause célèbre, simultaneously praised and vilified in editorial columns all across the country. *Ebony* accused the show of giving new currency to arcane racial slurs, and the Teamsters International lodged a protest against Archie's unflattering portrayal of the American working man as a bigoted slob. "Liberals were our first and loudest detractors," Carroll O'Connor observed, but "conservatives howled aplenty."

Norman Lear remained detached from the controversy. "The public is wise enough to take care of itself," he ventured. "If the bigots of America want to make Archie Bunker their hero—I think they deserve him."

"If Norman had continued to depend on the topical, he would not have succeeded," Fred Silverman observed. And of course, Lear and his talented staff of writers made sure that life with Archie, Edith, Mike, and Gloria wasn't all Sturm und Drang. The Bunkers confronted taboos such as racial prejudice, rape, and homosexuality head-on—but they also found time for the less dramatic activities that occupy any ordinary family. In between bouts with impotence and unemployment, they played Monopoly, fended off aluminum-siding salesmen, and came down with the flu.

Ironically, the family was often at its funniest during their most mundane moments. Today, long after the screaming headlines that fueled the Bunkers' fiercest battles look as dated as the yellowing newspapers they were printed on, what remains fresh is the show's affectionate portrait of a family whose members ate and slept, worked and played, fought and made love—just like the rest of us.

When *All in the Family* frightened television out of its lingering postadolescence in 1971, it heralded a bold new era of prime-time sophistication, intelligence, and sensitivity. By breaking down every established notion of how TV comedy should be written, performed, edited, and scored, the series almost single-handedly revolutionized the creative community's attitude toward the medium. By changing the way television looked, *All in the Family* changed forever the way we look at television.

# A Critical Guide to All 202 Episodes

REGULAR CAST

| | |
|---|---|
| Archie Bunker | Carroll O'Connor |
| Edith Bunker | Jean Stapleton |
| Gloria Bunker Stivic | Sally Struthers |
| Michael Stivic | Rob Reiner |
| Lionel Jefferson | Mike Evans |
| Louise Jefferson | Isabel Sanford |
| Stephanie Mills | Danielle Brisebois |
| Joey Stivic | Jason Draeger, Cory Miller |

SUPPORTING CAST

| | |
|---|---|
| Henry Jefferson | Mel Stewart |
| George Jefferson | Sherman Hemsley |
| Irene Lorenzo | Betty Garrett |
| Frank Lorenzo | Vincent Gardenia |
| Bert Munson | Billy Halop |
| Tommy Kelcy | Brendon Dillon, Bob Hastings |
| Barney Hefner | Allan Melvin |
| Harry the Bartender | Jason Wingreen |
| Hank Pivnik | Danny Dayton |
| Teresa Betancourt | Liz Torres |
| Justin Quigley | Burt Mustin |
| Jo Nelson | Ruth McDevitt |

Created by Norman Lear
Based on *Til Death Do Us Part*, created by Johnny Speight
Theme song ("Those Were the Days") by Lee Adams, Charles Strouse
Closing theme ("Remembering You") by Roger Kellaway, lyrics by
　　Carroll O'Connor
Principal directors were John Rich, Bob LaHendro, H. Wesley Kenney,
　　Paul Bogart

# 1968-69    THE PILOT EPISODES

**Pilot 1** Justice For All
  **Writer:** Norman Lear
  **Director:** Gordon Rigsby
  **Guest Stars:** Carroll O'Connor, Jean Stapleton, Tim McIntire, Kelly Jean Peters, D'Urville Martin

Archie and Edith Justice celebrate their twenty-second anniversary at an impromptu party thrown by their daughter, Gloria, and her husband, Richard.

**Pilot 2** Those Were the Days
  **Writer:** Norman Lear
  **Directors:** Bud Yorkin, Norman Lear
  **Guest Stars:** Carroll O'Connor, Jean Stapleton, Chip Oliver, Candy Azzara, D'Urville Martin

Generations clash in the Justice household when Richard and Gloria throw a surprise party for Archie and Edith.

Both ABC pilots were drawn from the exact same script that was eventually used, with minor revisions, for the show's broadcast premiere on CBS in 1971. The key differences were in casting—Kelly Jean Peters and Candy Azzara played Gloria before Sally Struthers finally landed the role, and Tim McIntire and Chip Oliver played Archie's son-in-law, then named Richard. Interestingly, no reference was made to the son-in-law's ethnic heritage until Rob Reiner adopted the role in the third and final version for CBS, when he was renamed Michael Stivic, and his Polish background was introduced as a further source of friction for the beleaguered family.

The original pilot was taped in October 1968 at the Dick Cavett Theater in New York City, and the second was shot a few months later, on February 16, 1969, at ABC's Hollywood studios, where it was produced by Edward Stephenson. The theme song, performed by Stapleton and O'Connor in both pilots, was written by Broadway composers Lee Adams and Charles Strouse, who decided on the spare arrangement after Lear informed them that he had only $800 left in his budget to record the title song.

# 1970-71    THE FIRST SEASON

*Year-End Rating: 18.9 (34th place)*

America meets its newest—and noisiest—neighbors, the Bunkers of Queens, New York, in thirteen trailblazing comic dramas that provide a Tuesday-night forum for the outspoken Archie Bunker. Producer Norman Lear presides over the raucous proceedings as head writer, aided and abetted in the first year by story editor Don Nicholl and writers Bryan Joseph and Jerry Mayer, among others.

Director John Rich is the dominant force behind the cameras for the first four seasons, and Jane Thompson is the associate producer for the initial thirteen shows.

**1**   Meet the Bunkers                              January 12, 1971
**Writer:** Norman Lear
**Director:** John Rich

A surprise anniversary party is the setting for the latest high-decibel debate between Archie Bunker and his son-in-law, Michael Stivic.

"I used the excuse of the Bunkers' wedding anniversary to go potshotting around—just to establish the people and the mood," Norman Lear told *TV Guide*, grossly understating the effect of a show that slew an entire herd of television's most sacred cows in its very first half hour. The language and controversy got all the press, but it was the less controversial—though no less radical—novelty of seeing a recognizably real family on television that brought the audience back week after week.

**2**   Writing the President                         January 19, 1971
**Writers:** Paul Harrison, Lennie Weinrib, Norman Lear
**Story:** Les Erwin, Fred Freiberger
**Director:** John Rich
**Guest Star:** Helen Page Camp

Mike writes a letter to the White House protesting the sorry state of the Union, prompting Archie to take pen in hand for his own rebuttal.

**3** Archie's Aching Back                     January 26, 1971
**Writer:** Stanley Ralph Ross
**Director:** John Rich
**Guest Stars:** George Furth, Salem Ludwig, Richard Stahl

Archie is convinced he'll collect a larger settlement from a petty traffic accident if a Jewish lawyer handles the case.

The stylistic minimalism of the Bunker's sparsely furnished set is on full display in this early episode. According to director John Rich, who grew up not far from Archie's neighborhood, the Spartan look of the Bunker's living room decor was achieved as a result of painstaking efforts. The director remembers personally supervising the cracking of windows and repainting of walls to give the place a run-down, lived-in look. "I told the set designers to take all the color out of it," remembers Rich. "Norman and I wanted to do the show in black and white, but CBS nearly went into a coma. So we decided to do the next best thing and shoot the entire show in muted sepia tones."

**4** Archie Gives Blood                       February 2, 1971
**Writer:** Norman Lear
**Director:** John Rich
**Guest Star:** Jeannie Linero

Archie refuses to donate blood because he's afraid that his vital fluids might get mixed in with those of a different race.

**5** Judging Books by Covers                  February 9, 1971
**Writers:** Burt Styler, Norman Lear
**Director:** John Rich
**Guest Stars:** Philip Carey, Tony Geary, Billy Halop, Linn Patrick

Archie scorns one of Mike's effeminate friends, unaware that one of his own beer-drinking buddies is actually a well-adjusted gay man.

Guest star Tony Geary became well known to daytime TV viewers as Luke Spencer on *General Hospital*.

**6**   Gloria Is Pregnant           February 16, 1971
**Writer:** Jerry Mayer
**Director:** John Rich
**Guest Stars:** Holly Near, Jon Silo

Archie's dream of becoming a grandfather is dashed when Gloria suffers a sudden miscarriage.

This landmark episode established Norman Lear's willingness to go beyond the boundaries of situation comedy in subject matter as well as language. And as he soon discovered, controversy attracted viewers. Before long, millions were tuning in each week just to see what taboo might bite the dust next.

**7**   Now That You Know the Way,     February 23, 1971
      Let's Be Strangers
**Writers:** Philip Mishkin, Rob Reiner, Don Nicholl, Bryan Joseph
**Story:** Philip Mishkin, Rob Reiner
**Director:** John Rich
**Guest Stars:** Jack Bender, Corey Fischer, Jenny Sullivan

Mike invites one of his hippie friends to spend the night in the living room, despite Archie's strenuous objections.

**8**   Lionel Moves Into the Neighborhood    March 2, 1971
**Writers:** Don Nicholl, Bryan Joseph
**Director:** John Rich
**Guest Stars:** Vincent Gardenia, Isabel Sanford

Archie does his best to keep a black family from buying the house next door, only to discover that the prospective buyers are Lionel's parents.

Louise Jefferson makes her first appearance, though husband George will remain an offscreen character for another two seasons. Their son, Lionel, had been a regular visitor to the Bunkers since the pilot episode, when the writers discovered how effective the street-smart black youth was at gently letting the air out of Archie's sails.

**9**   Edith Has Jury Duty                        March 9, 1971
**Writers:** Susan Harris, Don Nicholl, Bryan Joseph
**Story:** Susan Harris
**Director:** John Rich
**Guest Stars:** Holly Irving, Doris Singleton

Edith abandons the kitchen for the courtroom when she is chosen for jury duty, leaving Archie to fend for himself.

Susan Harris marks her writing debut by spotlighting Edith Bunker's innate intelligence and unflagging humanity in a script that casts the housewife as a juror with the integrity of Henry Fonda in *Twelve Angry Men*. Harris's knack for scripting interesting and intelligent roles for women flourished when she masterminded *Soap* for ABC in 1977 and NBC's *The Golden Girls* in 1985.

**10**   Archie Is Worried About His Job            March 16, 1971
**Writers:** Norman Lear, Don Nicholl, Bryan Joseph
**Story:** William Bickley, Jr.
**Director:** John Rich
**Guest Stars:** Holly Irving, Burt Mustin, Jack Perkins, Sandy Kenyon

No one in the family gets any sleep when Archie spends the night worrying that he might lose his job.

Holly Irving has a cameo as Clara Weidermeyer, the empty-headed next-door neighbor who stumbled into the Bunkers' living room to provide comic relief exactly two times before she was forever banished to sitcom limbo.

**11**   Gloria Discovers Women's Lib              March 23, 1971
**Writers:** Norman Lear, Sandy Stern
**Director:** John Rich

Gloria leaves the house in a rage after Mike refuses to recognize her as an equal partner in their marriage.

**12**   Success Story                             March 30, 1971
**Writer:** Burt Styler
**Director:** John Rich
**Guest Stars:** Len Lesser, Herbie Faye, George Savalas, Frank Ford, William Windom

Archie reevaluates his definition of success after he meets an old Army buddy who's become wealthy in the used-car trade.

**13**　　The First and Last Supper　　　　　　　　April 6, 1971
　**Writer:** Jerry Mayer
　**Director:** John Rich
　**Guest Stars:** Mel Stewart, Billy Benedict

The Jeffersons arrive for dinner at the Bunkers'—minus husband George, who refuses to socialize with his white neighbors.

Mel Stewart would play George's brother, Henry, until Sherman Hemsley finally graced the Bunkers' living room with his presence in the fourth season.

## 1971-72　　THE SECOND SEASON

*Year-End Rating: 34.0 (1st place)*

Archie's confounding opinions help anchor the series at the top of the ratings in the show's second year, but the family emerges as the star of the show in second-season episodes that paint a bizarre but believable portrait of one man's family, 1970's-style.

Joining producer Norman Lear are script supervisors Michael Ross and Bernie West, who, along with Don Nicholl, contribute most of the show's best early scripts. Writers Phil Mishkin and Lee Kalcheim also make significant contributions in the second year.

**14**　　The Saga of Cousin Oscar　　　September 18, 1971
　**Writers:** Burt Styler, Norman Lear
　**Story:** Burt Styler
　**Director:** John Rich
　**Guest Stars:** Jack Grimes, Will B. Able, Peggy Rea, Connie Sawyer, Billy Benedict

Archie is incensed when his sponging cousin Oscar has the nerve to drop dead in the upstairs bedroom.

**15**　　Gloria Poses in the Nude　　　September 25, 1971
　**Writers:** Michael Ross, Bernie West, Norman Lear
　**Director:** John Rich
　**Guest Star:** David Soul

Mike has second thoughts after he agrees to let Gloria pose as a nude model for one of his artist friends.

**16**   Archie in the Lock-Up                    October 2, 1971
  **Writers:** Paul Wayne, Michael Ross, Bernie West
  **Story:** Paul Wayne
  **Director:** John Rich
  **Guest Stars:** Allan Melvin, Ken Lynch, Kelly Houser, Corey
  Fischer

Archie suffers his ultimate indignity when he's arrested along with
a group of radicals at a protest rally.

**17**   Edith Writes a Song                    October 9, 1971
  **Writer:** Lee Kalcheim
  **Director:** John Rich
  **Guest Stars:** Cleavon Little, Demond Wilson

A pair of burglars holds the family at bay with Archie's own pistol.

The homebreakers are Tony Award winner Cleavon Little and Demond
Wilson, who would join Redd Foxx as co-star of NBC's midseason smash,
*Sanford and Son*.

**18**   Flashback: Mike Meets Archie          October 16, 1971
  **Writers:** Philip Mishkin, Rob Reiner
  **Director:** John Rich

On the Stivics' first wedding anniversary, the family recalls the
day Archie and Michael met.

Ironically, by the time Archie launches into a chorus of "God Bless
America" to defy his unwanted dinner guest, the script has already established that the pair's differences have little to do with their conflicting ideologies. Actually, Archie dislikes Mike far more for being the in-
terloper who's come to take away his little girl. As Norman Lear observed,
"It doesn't really matter what the men say—the audience is watching a
father and his son-in-law. The behavior is what's important."

By the second season, Archie has emerged in a more sympathetic light.
An insecure man facing middle age in a world that's changing much too
quickly, he's terrified of the new society that his son-in-law envisions,
afraid there won't be any place in it for him. In defense, he clings stubbornly to the prejudices of a bygone era that suddenly looks very rosy.
It's an attitude that makes the short verse he sings at the start of every
episode ring with plaintive irony: "Guys like us, we had it made. Those
were the days."

**19**   The Election Story                    October 30, 1971
**Writers:** Michael Ross, Bernie West
**Director:** John Rich
**Guest Stars:** Barbara Cason, Frank Whiteman, Ida McKenzie,
Robert Gibbons

Mike and Gloria campaign for the liberal candidate in a local
election, while Archie places himself in the opposing camp.

**20**   Edith's Accident                    November 6, 1971
**Writers:** Michael Ross, Bernie West
**Story:** Tom and Helen August
**Director:** John Rich
**Guest Star:** Barnard Hughes

A priest pays a call to reward Edith's honesty for leaving a note on
his car after she accidentally dents it with a large can of cling
peaches.

**21**   The Blockbuster                    November 13, 1971
**Writers:** Austin and Irma Kalish, Michael Ross, Bernie West
**Story:** Austin and Irma Kalish
**Director:** John Rich
**Guest Stars:** Jack Crowder, Peggy Rea

An unscrupulous black real-estate salesman tempts Archie to sell
his house to a black family at an inflated price.

**22**   Mike's Problem                    November 20, 1971
**Writers:** Alan J. Levitt, Philip Mishkin
**Story:** Alan J. Levitt
**Director:** John Rich
**Guest Stars:** Brendon Dillon, Mel Stewart

Gloria is upset when Mike's nervousness over his grades causes
him to become temporarily impotent.

This story met with greater network resistance than had any script
since the original pilot. "CBS didn't want that show done at all," Norman
Lear told interviewers Horace Newcomb and Robert Alley in their book
*The Producer's Medium.* "It was the first time that I said, 'If you know
what America wants and what America will fall apart over—then *you*
produce the show.' At the last moment they allowed us to make the show.

Nothing happened, the network didn't fall apart. States did not secede from the union. America even liked it."

**23    The Insurance Is Canceled**                November 27, 1971
    **Writers:** Lee Kalcheim, Michael Ross, Bernie West
    **Story:** Lee Kalcheim
    **Director:** John Rich
    **Guest Stars:** Philip Proctor, Rafael Campos

Archie lays off a Puerto Rican worker during a cutback at the dock; and his homeowner's policy is canceled when his neighborhood is redlined as a bad risk.

**24    The Man in the Street**                    December 4, 1971
    **Writers:** Lennie Weinrib, Paul Harrison, Don Nicholl
    **Story:** Lennie Weinrib, Paul Harrison
    **Director:** John Rich
    **Guest Stars:** Jack Griffin, Neil J. Schwartz, Bob Hastings

Archie Bunker anticipates becoming the voice of the American working man when his man-on-the-street interview is scheduled to appear on Walter Cronkite's *Evening News.*

Bob Hastings, the sniveling Lieutenant Carpenter from *McHale's Navy,* would appear as Tommy Kelcy, the proprietor of Archie's favorite watering hole, until it changed hands in the eighth year.

**25    Cousin Maude's Visit**                     December 11, 1971
    **Writers:** Philip Mishkin, Michael Ross, Bernie West
    **Story:** Philip Mishkin
    **Director:** John Rich
    **Guest Star:** Bea Arthur

Edith's feisty cousin, Maude, drops in for a visit during a flu epidemic at the Bunker House.

Like many *All in the Family* guest stars, Bea Arthur was a successful New York actress whom Norman Lear recruited to play a particularly juicy role—Edith's twice-divorced and fearlessly outspoken cousin, Maude, the first woman to fight Archie Bunker to a standoff. The sparks that erupted during their confrontation weren't lost on CBS program chief Fred Silverman, who convinced the producers that they'd stumbled onto something. *Maude* premiered the following fall, the first spin-off in what would become Norman Lear's prime-time dynasty.

**26**    Christmas Day at the Bunkers          December 18, 1971
  **Writer:** Don Nicholl
  **Director:** John Rich
  **Guest Stars:** Peggy Doyle, Noam Pitlik, Mel Stewart, Isabel
Sanford

Archie casts a pall on the family's Yuletide spirits when he complains that he was passed over for this year's Christmas bonus.

**27**    The Elevator Story                    January 1, 1972
  **Writer:** Alan J. Levitt
  **Director:** John Rich
  **Guest Stars:** Roscoe Lee Browne, Eileen Brennan, Hector
Elizondo, Edith Diaz

Archie gets caught in an elevator, along with a pregnant Puerto Rican and her husband, an aging hippie, and an erudite black businessman.

Naturally, the expectant mother gives birth while stranded in the elevator. But instead of the unbearable slapstick TV has taught us to expect from such stock situations, we're treated to a privileged moment. As each of the passengers succumbs to the charm of the newborn infant, even Archie Bunker drops his defenses long enough to join the spontaneous celebration of a new life, and we see the birth through his eyes.

According to Carroll O'Connor, that sublime moment wasn't even written into the original script. "The situation was thought to be a real howl," the actor wrote in *TV Guide.* "I was sure the way it was written, crudely and incredibly, would evoke audience revulsion." The solution came only after the actor stormed off the set, the pages of his script scattered on the floor. Producer Norman Lear intervened and finally convinced him to join the other actors in improvising a new ending, coached by Lear and director John Rich. Their revisions were incorporated into the final episode, and as O'Connor recalls, "We found a way to save the childbirth and make it a touching sequence."

**28**    Edith's Problem                       January 8, 1972
  **Writer:** Burt Styler
  **Story:** Burt Styler, Steve Zacharias
  **Director:** John Rich
  **Guest Star:** Jeannie Linero

Edith is suddenly moody and irritable with the approach of menopause.

A welcome stretch for Emmy winner Jean Stapleton. The actress had such a firm grasp on Edith's personality that even the severe mood swings brought on by her hot flashes seem absolutely in character. By the second year, the writers played catch-up to keep pace with Stapleton's portrayal, which had evolved to a depth that was barely suggested in the early scripts.

**29   Archie and the FBI**                          January 15, 1972
   **Writers:** Michael Ross, Bernie West, Susan Harris
   **Director:** John Rich
   **Guest Stars:** Graham Jarvis, Larry Grundy, John Korkes

Archie's paranoia during a mysterious government investigation drives him to betray a long-standing friendship.

What separates *All in the Family* from so many later, vastly inferior imitations—a few of them produced at Norman Lear's factory—was that the writers rarely felt compelled to tack on a tidy or simple resolution. This allegory of the McCarthy era witch-hunts is no exception. Once Archie and his neighbor betray each other over what amounts to a routine investigation, it's already too late to shake hands and make up. So they don't. Instead, Archie sits alone and contemplates his tragic folly with the halfhearted rationalization "All that best-buddy stuff . . . that's all for kids anyhow."

**30   Mike's Mysterious Son**                       January 22, 1972
   **Writer:** Warren Murray
   **Director:** John Rich
   **Guest Stars:** Marcia Rodd, Stephen Manley

An old girlfriend of Mike's suddenly arrives at the Bunkers' with a four-year-old boy who she claims is his son.

**31   Archie Sees a Mugging**                       January 29, 1972
   **Writers:** Philip Mishkin, Don Nicholl
   **Story:** Henry Garson
   **Director:** John Rich
   **Guest Stars:** Jack Somack, Val Bisoglio, Frank Campanella, Bill Macy

Archie refuses to get involved with the police, even though he's the only witness to a neighborhood mugging.

**32**   Archie and Edith Alone                    February 5, 1972
  **Writers:** Lee Kalcheim, Michael Ross, Bernie West
  **Story:** Tina and Les Pine
  **Director:** John Rich
  **Guest Star:** Connie Sawyer

The Bunkers are on their own for eight days after Mike and Gloria go off to spend a week at a commune.

The series's most accomplished comic drama to date, a twenty-three-minute sketch that offers a touching look at the rich fabric of a marriage that's still going strong after a quarter of a century. After Mike and Gloria go off to find their utopian dream of a week's stay at a mountain commune, the camera lingers behind on Archie and Edith as they settle down to face the more commonplace realities of their own life together. In the aftermath of a tense quarrel, they quietly share the litany of lost dreams and failed promises they've both endured over the years, as they come to realize what a gift their durable union has been. By the time Mike and Gloria come trudging home, disillusioned by their tour of Shangri-La, Archie and Edith are swaying to the strains of "The Moonlight Serenade" on Edith's phonograph. They may not have found utopia either, but they've come awfully close.

**33**   Edith Gets a Mink                    February 12, 1972
  **Writers:** Elias Davis, Dave Pollack, Don Nicholl
  **Story:** David Pollack, Elias Davis
  **Director:** John Rich
  **Guest Stars:** Rae Allen, Richard Dysart

Archie is too proud to let Edith accept a mink stole from her cousin Amelia, until he sees a chance to make a $300 profit.

**34**   Sammy's Visit                    February 19, 1972
  **Writer:** Bill Dana
  **Director:** John Rich
  **Guest Stars:** Sammy Davis, Jr., Billy Halop, Fay De Witt, Keri Shutleton

Sammy Davis, Jr., encounters Archie Bunker in all his glory when the star ventures out to Queens to retrieve a briefcase he left in Munson's taxicab.

When the producers discovered that Sammy Davis, Jr., was a big fan of the series, they couldn't resist inviting the diminutive star to meet Archie on camera. According to director John Rich, Archie's part-time job as a cab driver was introduced in an earlier episode largely to set up a plausible excuse for the famous nightclub performer to enter the Bunkers' Queens living room in this one.

**35**   Edith the Judge                        February 26, 1972
  **Writer:** Lee Kalcheim
  **Director:** John Rich
  **Guest Star:** Jack Weston

Edith arbitrates a dispute between Archie and the irate proprietor of a laundromat.

**36**   Archie Is Jealous                          March 4, 1972
  **Writer:** Rod Parker
  **Director:** John Rich
  **Guest Star:** Brendon Dillon

Archie is disturbed to discover that Edith once spent an entire weekend with an old beau.

**37**   Maude                                      March 11, 1972
  **Writer:** Rod Parker
  **Director:** John Rich
  **Guest Stars:** Beatrice Arthur, Bill Macy, Marcia Rodd, Bob Dishy, Bernie West

The Bunkers attend the wedding of cousin Maude's daughter, Carol.

This episode was the pilot for *Maude*. In the series, Maude's daughter would be played by Adrienne Barbeau.

## 1972-73   THE THIRD SEASON

*Year-End Rating: 33.3 (1st place)*

By the third year, the creators trust the material enough to downplay the earsplitting polemics in favor of scripts that chronicle the more mundane, though no less interesting, everyday hopes and frustrations of life at 704 Hauser Street.

Norman Lear assumes the role of executive producer when director John Rich takes over the show's production reins as well. Story editors Michael Ross and Bernie West continue to write most of the season's scripts, along with story consultant Don Nicholl.

**38**    Archie and the Editorial                    September 16, 1972
  **Writers:** George Bloom, Don Nicholl
  **Story:** George Bloom
  **Director:** Norman Campbell
  **Guest Stars:** Sorrell Booke, Val Bisoglio, Brendan Dillon, Diane Sommerfield, Lynnette Mettey

After he rails against gun control in a TV editorial, Archie meets his two biggest supporters—a pair of stickup artists who rob him at gunpoint.

John Rich takes a break from directing to get his bearings as the show's new producer. The veteran sitcom director never planned to stay with the show past the first episode. "When Norman and Bud Yorkin asked me to direct the pilot, I said I'd sign on for just two episodes," Rich recalled. But one season led to another, and by the show's third year, Rich found himself producing the show and directing the actors while associate director Bob LaHendro directed the cameras from the booth.

**39**    Archie's Fraud                    September 23, 1972
  **Writers:** Michael Ross, Bernie West
  **Director:** Norman Campbell
  **Guest Stars:** Billy Halop, James McEachin

Archie is audited by the IRS after he fails to report income he made driving Munson's taxicab.

**40**    The Threat                    September 30, 1972
  **Writers:** Michael Elias, Lila Garrett
  **Story:** Bill Manhoff, Michael Elias, Lila Garrett
  **Director:** John Rich
  **Guest Star:** Gloria LeRoy

Archie can barely contain himself when the attractive young wife of an old Army buddy spends an eventful night in the Bunker household.

**41** Gloria and the Riddle                    October 7, 1972
**Writer:** Don Nicholl
**Director:** Bob Livingston
**Guest Stars:** Patricia Stich, Brendon Dillon, Billy Sands, Allan Melvin

Gloria tests Mike and Archie's male chauvinism quotient with a riddle that stumps the men but is easily answered by Edith.

**42** Lionel Steps Out                    October 14, 1972
**Writers:** Michael Ross, Bernie West
**Story:** Terry Ryan, Michael Ross, Bernie West
**Director:** Michael Kidd
**Guest Stars:** Mike Evans, Diane Hull, Mel Stewart

Archie is aghast to find out that his visiting niece plans to go out dancing with Lionel Jefferson.

**43** Edith Flips Her Wig                    October 21, 1972
**Writers:** Sam Locke, Olga Vallance, Don Nicholl
**Director:** Hal Cooper
**Guest Stars:** Barnard Hughes, James Gregory

Edith is worried that she may be a kleptomaniac after she absent-mindedly takes a wig from a department store.

O'Connor and Stapleton get stiff competition from scene stealers Barnard Hughes and James Gregory in this episode. Both actors soon landed regular roles on a pair of other classic sitcoms: Gregory appeared as Inspector Luger in *Barney Miller*, and Hughes played Bob's father on *The Bob Newhart Show* before MTM featured him as *Doc* in his own CBS series in 1975.

**44** The Bunkers and the Swingers                    October 28, 1972
**Writers:** Lee Kalcheim, Michael Ross, Bernie West
**Story:** Norman Lear
**Directors:** John Rich, Bob LaHendro
**Guest Stars:** Vincent Gardenia, Rue McClanahan

Edith unwittingly invites a pair of wife-swapping swingers to dinner when she responds to a newspaper ad for pen pals.

This wasn't the last we'd see of the swingers. Vincent Gardenia would return the following season as the Bunkers' neighbor Frank Lorenzo, and

Rue McClanahan was Bea Arthur's best friend on *Maude*, a role she'd continue for six seasons before the pair renewed their friendship in 1985 as two of *The Golden Girls* on NBC.

**45**   Mike Comes Into Money                November 4, 1972
   **Writers:** Michael Ross, Bernie West
   **Directors:** John Rich, Bob LaHendro

Mike sparks the latest family feud when he donates $200 to George McGovern's presidential campaign instead of paying Archie for room and board.

**46**   Flashback: Mike and Gloria's Wedding November 11, 1972
      (Part 1)
   **Writers:** Rob Reiner, Philip Mishkin, Don Nicholl
   **Directors:** John Rich, Bob LaHendro
   **Guest Star:** Michael Conrad

On the Stivics' second anniversary, the family recalls the comedy of errors that transpired on their wedding day.

In the tradition of *The Dick Van Dyke Show*, the script illuminates the characters in an extended flashback that gives the writers an opportunity to take a revisionist look at events long past. The episode suggests that Archie has actually mellowed somewhat under Mike's influence— he was even more narrow-minded and stubborn in the flashback.

**47**   Flashback: Mike and Gloria's Wedding November 18, 1972
      (Part 2)
   **Writers:** Rob Reiner, Philip Mishkin
   **Directors:** John Rich, Bob LaHendro
   **Guest Stars:** Michael Conrad, Peter Hobbs

The Stivics' wedding is jeopardized when Michael's uncle insists, over Archie's virulent objections, that the marriage be performed by a Catholic priest.

The Meathead's Uncle Cas is played by the late Michael Conrad, best remembered as Sergeant Esterhaus of *Hill Street Blues*.

**48**   Mike's Appendix                December 2, 1972
**Writers:** Michael Ross, Bernie West
**Directors:** John Rich, Bob LaHendro
**Guest Stars:** John Zaremba, Ann Summers

Gloria is outraged when Mike insists that a male doctor perform his appendix operation.

**49**   Edith's Winning Ticket                December 9, 1972
**Writer:** Don Nicholl
**Directors:** John Rich, Bob LaHendro
**Guest Star:** Mel Stewart

Archie schemes to bilk the Jeffersons out of their winnings from a lottery ticket that Edith bought for Louise.

**50**   Archie and the Bowling Team                December 16, 1972
**Writers:** Allan Katz, Don Reo
**Story:** Don Nicholl
**Directors:** John Rich, Bob LaHendro
**Guest Stars:** Brad Logan, Allan Melvin

Archie loses his spot on a top bowling team to a black player.

**51**   The Locket                December 23, 1972
**Writers:** Robert Fisher, Arthur Marx
**Director:** Hal Cooper
**Guest Stars:** Liam Dunn, John Randolph, Louis Guss, Mario Roccuzzo

Archie tries to cheat the insurance company out of $300 after Edith misplaces her family-heirloom locket.

**52**   Archie in the Hospital                January 6, 1973
**Writer:** Don Nicholl
**Story:** Stanley Ralph Ross, Martin Cohan
**Directors:** John Rich, Bob LaHendro
**Guest Stars:** Roscoe Lee Browne, Priscilla Morrill, John Heffernan

Archie befriends the other patient in his semiprivate hospital room, unaware that he's black.

The comic shenanigans over Archie's black bunkmate merely underscore what we already know: Poor Archie gets along fine with his fellow man—until he sees the color of his skin. The producers let us in on the gag at the outset, placing the audience in a superior position to the folly of Archie's bigotry. But the results would have been more interesting had the show challenged our own prejudice by concealing the neighbor's color from the audience, as well as Archie, until the very end.

**53    Oh Say Can You See**                    January 20, 1973
   **Writers:** Michael Ross, Bernie West
   **Story:** Joe Kerr
   **Directors:** John Rich, Bob LaHendro
   **Guest Stars:** Larry Storch, Arlene Golonka

An old school chum tries to convince Archie that his fears of growing old are all in his mind.

**54    Archie Goes Too Far**                    January 27, 1973
   **Writers:** Austin and Irma Kalish
   **Directors:** John Rich, Bob LaHendro
   **Guest Stars:** Pamela Murphy, Mary Kay Place, Patty Weaver

Edith and Gloria end the latest family brawl when they storm out of the house to spend the night on their own.

The wives hide out at a sorority slumber party to await their husbands' overdue apologies, setting the scene for one of Edith's classic flights of fancy. After she and Gloria conjure romantic visions of their spouses returning the way Cary Grant always came back to Irene Dunne, or Bette Davis to Humphrey Bogart, Edith cautiously intones, "You were never sure about Bette Davis. Sometimes she'd come back. . . and sometimes she'd just die."

**55    Class Reunion**                    February 10, 1973
   **Writer:** Don Nicholl
   **Story:** Stanley Ralph Ross, Don Nicholl
   **Directors:** John Rich, Bob LaHendro
   **Guest Stars:** Harvey Lembeck, Rae Allen, Priscilla Morrill

Archie refuses to tag along to Edith's thirtieth high school reunion—until he finds out that one of her old beaus will be attending.

**56**   Hot Watch                          February 17, 1973
**Writers:** Sam Locke, Olga Vallance
**Directors:** John Rich, Bob LaHendro
**Guest Star:** Jack Tesler

Archie buys an expensive watch of dubious pedigree and has to find a jeweler who'll fix it with no questions asked.

As Archie schemes to profit from his blunder, he reveals his ancestral ties to Ralph Kramden, another blustery New Yorker who was similarly undone by his own greed.

**57**   Archie Is Branded                  February 24, 1973
**Writer:** Vincent Bogert
**Directors:** John Rich, Bob LaHendro
**Guest Stars:** Gregory Sierra, Billy Halop, Michael Gregory, John Putch, Patrick Campbell

Archie wakes up to find a swastika painted on his front door.

A classic episode in which Archie questions the basic tenets of his political extremism when he discovers just how much he has in common with the terrorist who defends them. In one of the series's most unsettling finales, the family's would-be protector is murdered outside their window as the family looks on in horror.

**58**   Everybody Tells the Truth          March 3, 1973
**Writer:** Don Nicholl
**Directors:** John Rich, Bob LaHendro
**Guest Stars:** Ron Glass, Ken Lynch, Maurice Marsac

It's *Rashomon* Bunker-style when the family recounts vastly different versions of their disastrous encounter with a pair of handymen in the Bunker kitchen.

**59**   Archie Learns His Lesson           March 10, 1973
**Writers:** Michael Ross, Bernie West
**Story:** John Christopher Strong III, Michael R. Stein
**Directors:** John Rich, Bob LaHendro

Archie attends night-school classes to qualify for a high-school diploma.

Mike and Archie discuss their differing perspectives on manifest destiny in a sharp scene that mines humor from Archie's desperate attempts to guard his ignorance in the face of his growing enlightenment.

**60**   Gloria, the Victim                           March 17, 1973
   **Writers:** Austin and Irma Kalish, Don Nicholl
   **Directors:** John Rich, Bob LaHendro
   **Guest Stars:** Charles Durning, Mel Stewart

After an attempted sexual assault, Gloria turns to the family for guidance as she suffers through the legal aftermath of reporting the crime.

**61**   The Battle of the Month                      March 24, 1973
   **Writers:** Michael Ross, Bernie West
   **Directors:** John Rich, Bob LaHendro

In a foul mood, Gloria lambasts Edith for her constant acquiescence to Archie's whims.

The writers clearly established that Gloria's irritation stemmed from premenstrual stress—a character motivation that brought more outraged mail than any other episode in the show's history. Writer Michael Ross defended his script when he told interviewer John Brady, "We didn't do the menstrual episode for shock value. We needed Gloria irritated to the point where she would blow up at Edith. In fact, we got the idea from Sally Struthers herself."

## 1973-74   THE FOURTH SEASON

*Year-End Rating: 31.2 (1st place)*

Archie is matched with two worthy new opponents in his fourth season of contentious controversy—Betty Garrett's Irene Lorenzo, a staunch believer in women's rights; and Sherman Hemsley's George Jefferson, an opinionated bigot with even less patience than Archie.

Once again, story consultant Don Nicholl and story editors Michael Ross and Bernie West are responsible for more than half the season's scripts. John Rappaport and Austin and Irma Kalish also make outstanding contributions in the fourth year.

**62**   We've Having a Heat Wave                September 15, 1973
   **Writer:** Don Nicholl
   **Directors:** John Rich, Bob LaHendro
   **Guest Stars:** Betty Garrett, Vincent Gardenia, Victor Argo

Henry Jefferson joins Archie in trying to prevent a Hispanic family from moving into the neighborhood.

Betty Garrett and Vincent Gardenia signed on as neighbors Irene and Frank Lorenzo during the show's most tempestuous period offscreen. *All in the Family* had become the most astonishing success story in CBS's history, and Carroll O'Connor thought that he deserved a bigger share of the stupendous profits the show was pulling in—which he got—as well as greater creative control, which Norman Lear and his producers staunchly refused to yield.

It was in the midst of this turbulence that the series gained—and lost—the services of Sada Thompson, the award-winning Broadway actress who later brought her gifts to the role of Kate Lawrence on ABC's *Family*. She'd been the producers' original choice to play the Bunkers' feisty neighbor, Irene, but O'Connor didn't share their enthusiasm. After less than a week on the tense set, she tired of O'Connor's cold shoulder and returned to New York. The part went to Betty Garrett, a musical-comedy star from MGM's heyday and a friend of O'Connor's who posed no threat to the testy star.

Vincent Gardenia, another New York transplant, also left the show after only a handful of appearances. He made his frustrations known at an infamous testimonial dinner for Norman Lear, where more than one actor voiced his opinion. As the producer stood at the podium, the actor heckled from his seat, shouting, "I love ya, Norman. I don't know what I'm doing in the show, but I love ya!" Not surprisingly, Gardenia left the series shortly thereafter.

**63**   We're Still Having a Heat Wave            September 22, 1973
   **Writers:** Michael Ross, Bernie West
   **Directors:** John Rich, Bob LaHendro

As the Lorenzos settle in, Archie grows jealous of Edith's friendship with Irene.

Betty Garrett's Irene gave Archie his first new female contender since Bea Arthur left to carve out her own prime-time grubstake. Less strident than Maude, Irene's even-tempered logic was her strongest weapon in the war against Archie. But his greatest fear was realized when, under

Irene's influence, Edith began to lash out against his petty household tyranny. To Archie's dismay, he discovered that he'd lost a dingbat and gained a partner in marriage.

**64**   Edith Finds an Old Man                  September 29, 1973
   **Writers:** Michael Ross, Bernie West
   **Story:** Susan Harris
   **Directors:** John Rich, Bob LaHendro
   **Guest Stars:** Burt Mustin, Ruth McDevitt

Edith befriends a lonely old man, though Archie is less than thrilled to have a constant reminder of his own advancing years hanging around the house.

Actor Burt Mustin had seemingly cornered the market on affable grandfather types from his very first appearance as Gus the fireman on *Leave It to Beaver*. He and Ruth McDevitt continued to make occasional visits throughout the fifth and sixth seasons.

**65**   Archie and the Kiss                       October 6, 1973
   **Writer:** John Rappaport
   **Directors:** John Rich, Bob LaHendro

Gloria brings home a Rodin replica for the living room, but the erotic sculpture makes Archie cringe.

A half-hour meditation on art and romance that begins with Edith's hilarious paean to Henry Mancini's "Moon River"—proof positive that beauty lies in the eye of the beholder.

**66**   Archie the Gambler                       October 13, 1973
   **Writers:** Michael Ross, Bernie West
   **Story:** Steve Zacharias, Michael Leeson
   **Directors:** John Rich, Bob LaHendro

Edith is deeply disturbed to find out that Archie's been playing the horses after he promised never to gamble again.

**67**   Henry's Farewell                         October 20, 1973
   **Writer:** Don Nicholl
   **Directors:** John Rich, Bob LaHendro
   **Guest Stars:** Mel Stewart, Sherman Hemsley

Archie finally meets George Jefferson at Henry's going-away party.

Sherman Hemsley inherited the part of Henry Jefferson's brother, George, after Mel Stewart opted out of the series to star in *Roll Out!*, a short-lived *M\*A\*S\*H*-style military sitcom.

**68**  Archie and the Computer            October 27, 1973
   **Writers:** Lloyd Turner, Gordon Mitchell, Don Nicholl
   **Directors:** John Rich, Bob LaHendro
   **Guest Star:** Jack Grimes

Edith receives a small fortune in quarters as a result of a computer error, while another computer informs Archie that he's been officially declared dead.

**69**  The Games Bunkers Play            November 3, 1973
   **Writers:** Michael Ross, Bernie West
   **Story:** Susan Perkis Haven, Dan Klein, Michael Ross, Bernie West
   **Directors:** John Rich, Bob LaHendro

Mike childishly refuses to accept criticism during an informal group therapy game.

"We're always looking for important subjects," writer Michael Ross once told a reporter, "but we've also found that a simple topic—like the family sitting around playing a little game of group therapy—often makes as funny and exciting a show as the big topic, if we do it right."

**70**  Edith's Conversion            November 10, 1973
   **Writers:** Ray Taylor, Don Nicholl
   **Directors:** John Rich, Bob LaHendro
   **Guest Stars:** Barnard Hughes, Phyllis Avery

Archie thinks that Irene Lorenzo is trying to convert Edith to Catholicism.

**71**  Archie in the Cellar            November 17, 1973
   **Writer:** Don Nicholl
   **Directors:** John Rich, Bob LaHendro
   **Guest Star:** Juan DeCarlos

Locked in his cellar with a bottle of vodka, Archie spends a long night contemplating his life through the haze of a drunken stupor.

**72**    Black Is the Color of My True Love's November 24, 1973
     Wig
**Writer:** Michael Morris
**Directors:** John Rich, Bob LaHendro

Gloria is insulted when Michael's ardor is renewed after she dons a cheap dime-store wig.

**73**    Second Honeymoon                    December 1, 1973
**Writers:** Warren S. Murray, Michael Ross, Bernie West
**Story:** Warren S. Murray
**Directors:** John Rich, Bob LaHendro
**Guest Star:** Mel Bryant

Archie and Edith rekindle their romance during a second honeymoon in Atlantic City.

**74**    The Taxi Caper                    December 8, 1973
**Writer:** Dennis Klein
**Directors:** John Rich, Bob LaHendro
**Guest Stars:** Michael Pataki, Al Stellone, Robert Mandan

An influential politician attempts to dissuade Archie from pressing charges against his son after the boy robs Archie in Munson's cab.

**75**    Archie Is Cursed                    December 15, 1973
**Writers:** John Rappaport, Michael Ross, Bernie West
**Directors:** John Rich, Bob LaHendro
**Guest Stars:** Bob Hastings, Sherman Hemsley

Irene challenges Archie to a pool match, but he begs off, complaining of a sore back.

**76**    Edith's Christmas Story                    December 22, 1973
**Writers:** Austin and Irma Kalish, Don Nicholl
**Story:** Austin and Irma Kalish
**Director:** John Rich

During the Christmas holidays, Edith tries to hide the fact that she may have breast cancer.

The Yuletide season was invariably a dramatic time around the Bunker household. Archie spent the series's first holiday show grousing that he was broke, and this year Edith nervously awaits the results of her cancer test. In a later Christmas episode, Edith's faith is shaken when she loses a dear friend to a gang of muggers; and in the series's final year, the Bunkers awake on Christmas morning only to discover that Mike and Gloria have separated. Makes you wonder why they didn't just leave town during the holidays.

**77**   Mike and Gloria Mix It Up                    January 5, 1974
   **Writers:** Michael Ross, Bernie West
   **Directors:** John Rich, Bob LaHendro

The Stivics' love life reaches another impasse when Michael is put off by Gloria's romantic aggressiveness.

**78**   Archie Feels Left Out                    January 12, 1974
   **Writers:** Paul Lichtman, Howard Storm, Don Nicholl
   **Directors:** John Rich, Bob LaHendro
   **Guest Stars:** Burt Mustin, Ruth McDevitt

Archie refuses to attend his own birthday party.

**79**   Et Tu, Archie                    January 26, 1974
   **Writers:** Mickey Rose, Lila Garrett
   **Directors:** John Rich, Bob LaHendro
   **Guest Stars:** Vic Tayback, David Doyle

Archie sabotages an old friend's efforts to land a job at the loading dock because he's afraid that the man might be in line for his position.

**80**   Gloria's Boyfriend                    February 2, 1974
   **Writers:** Bud Wiser, Don Nicholl
   **Director:** John Rich
   **Guest Stars:** Richard Masur, Joseph Mascolo

Archie's misconceptions run amok when Gloria befriends the retarded box boy from the local market.

**81**    Lionel's Engagement                    February 9, 1974
   **Writers:** Michael Ross, Bernie West
   **Director:** John Rich
   **Guest Stars:** Charles Aidman, Lynn Moody, Kim Hamilton,
   Samuel Olden, Jess Bolero, Eddie Carroll, Zara Cully

Archie squares off with George Jefferson's mother when he and
Edith attend Lionel's engagement party.

George Jefferson is as dismayed as Archie that Lionel's fiancée hails
from an interracial marriage. The basic situation would be retained when
the Jeffersons began their own series the following year, but most of the
roles would be recast—with the notable exception of Zara Cully as
George's acid-tongued mother.

**82**    Archie Eats and Runs                    February 16, 1974
   **Writers:** Paul Wayne, George Burditt
   **Director:** John Rich
   **Guest Stars:** Richard Stahl, Jane Dulo, Joseph George

The Bunkers are in a panic after Archie eats a stew made from
mushrooms that might have been contaminated.

**83**    Gloria Sings the Blues                    March 2, 1974
   **Writers:** Michael Ross, Bernie West
   **Director:** John Rich

Gloria is bewildered after she falls temporarily out of love with
Michael, until she discovers that her mother went through the
same thing with Archie.

A gentle episode that defied the series's popular conception as a show
where communication took place only above seventy-five decibels. "You
only have twenty-two minutes and thirty seconds to touch your audience," Lear once explained. "You have to hit them hard." And yet, many
of the show's finest moments take place in an atmosphere of quiet intro-
spection, as in this moving episode that contains nothing more strident
than a mother and daughter comparing notes at their kitchen table.

**84**   Pay the Twenty Dollars                           March 9, 1974
**Writers:** Robert L. Goodwin, Woody Kling
**Director:** John Rich

Archie unwittingly passes George Jefferson a counterfeit $20 bill
and sets off a string of hilarious exchanges as the family attempts
to rectify the error.

**85**   Mike's Graduation                               March 16, 1974
**Writer:** Don Nicholl
**Director:** John Rich

Archie's spirits soar on Mike's graduation day, until he discovers
that his meathead son-in-law has accepted a fellowship and won't
be moving out for another year.

## 1974-75   THE FIFTH SEASON

*Year-End Rating: 30.2 (1st place)*

As the series closes in on the midway point of its nine-year run, the
creative staff explores new territory when Mike and Gloria decide to move
into their own apartment at the end of the season.

After four years as director, John Rich is succeeded by H. Wesley
Kenney, who will direct all fifth-year episodes. Michael Ross and Bernie
West take over as producers, Bill Davenport and Lou Derman sign on as
story editors, and Don Nicholl is appointed executive producer.

**86**   The Bunkers and Inflation                    September 14, 1974
**Writers:** Don Nicholl, Michael Ross, Bernie West
**Director:** H. Wesley Kenney
**Guest Star:** Billy Halop

The Bunkers' breadwinner tries to avoid breaking the news that
his union has called a strike.

Lear's writers and producers pioneered the multipart episode as a
solution to the constraints imposed by the half-hour time slot. The extended format would rarely be used as effectively as in this four-part
reflection on the short-term impact and long-range effects of an infla-
tionary economy on the working-class Bunkers.

**87** The Bunkers and Inflation— September 21, 1974
    Archie Underfoot
**Writers:** Don Nicholl, Michael Ross, Bernie West
**Director:** H. Wesley Kenney

Tempers flare in the Bunker household when Archie finds himself with nothing to do but sit around the house.

**88** The Bunkers and Inflation— September 28, 1974
    Edith the Job Hunter
**Writers:** Don Nicholl, Michael Ross, Bernie West
**Director:** H. Wesley Kenney

When strike negotiations bog down, Archie grudgingly trades places with Edith and allows her to take a job at Jefferson's dry cleaners.

**89** The Bunkers and Inflation— October 5, 1974
    Archie's Raise
**Writers:** Don Nicholl, Michael Ross, Bernie West
**Director:** H. Wesley Kenney
**Guest Star:** James Cromwell

Archie's union settles the strike, but under terms that effectively leave him worse off than he was before the walkout.

James Cromwell appears as Stretch Cunningham, the bard of the loading dock, who was often referred to, but, until now, seldom seen.

**90** Lionel the Live-in October 12, 1974
**Writer:** Woody Kling
**Story:** Jeffrey Mackowsky
**Director:** H. Wesley Kenney

Lionel arrives to spend a few days with the Bunkers after a big blow-up with his father.

**91** Archie's Helping Hand October 19, 1974
**Writers:** Norman and Harriet Belkin
**Director:** H. Wesley Kenney

The rising tide of feminism confronts Archie on all sides when Edith joins a women's group and Irene lands a job alongside him on the loading dock.

Edith's gradual awakening was inevitable. As Norman Lear observed, once the women's movement caught the writers' awareness, it wasn't long before Edith's consciousness was also raised. Her slow but steady evolution invested the series with a certain suspense: With each passing week, we wonder how long Archie can resist the waves of enlightenment that seem to be washing up all around him.

**92**   Gloria's Shock                    October 26, 1974
   **Writer:** Dixie Brown Grossman
   **Director:** H. Wesley Kenney

Gloria is shocked when Mike announces that he doesn't plan on having children.

**93**   Where's Archie? (Part 1)          November 2, 1974
   **Writers:** Barry Harman, Harve Brosten
   **Director:** H. Wesley Kenney
   **Guest Stars:** Hector Elias, Charlotte Rae

Edith holds her first Tupperware party under a cloud of worry when Archie disappears on his way to a union convention in Buffalo.

This script was part of the producers' clever dodge to force the leading actor's hand after another contract dispute. When Carroll O'Connor failed to report to work at the start of the season, Lear taped this show without him. Then he vowed that Archie Bunker would be killed off in the very next episode—unless the actor returned to honor his contract.

Whether Norman Lear really had a plaid-jacketed, cigar-chomping stand-in for Archie Bunker waiting in the wings will never be known. By the third episode of this trilogy, O'Connor was back—at a substantially higher salary—and all was right on Hauser Street once more.

**94**   Archie Is Missing (Part 2)        November 9, 1974
   **Writers:** Lloyd Turner, Gordon Mitchell
   **Director:** H. Wesley Kenney
   **Guest Stars:** Allan Lurie, James Cromwell

With no word from Archie after twenty-four hours, the family faces the possibility that he might've run off with another woman.

**95**   The Longest Kiss (Part 3)            November 16, 1974
**Writers:** Lou Derman, Bill Davenport
**Story:** Dawn M. Stephens, Lou Derman, Bill Davenport
**Director:** H. Wesley Kenney

Archie returns from his sorry adventure—he got sidetracked to a podiatrists' convention in Rochester—to find his friends and family celebrating his return with kissing contests, Hula Hoops, and ballroom dancing.

**96**   Archie and the Miracle            November 23, 1974
**Writers:** Lloyd Turner, Gordon Mitchell
**Director:** H. Wesley Kenney
**Guest Star:** James Cromwell

After an accident on the loading dock brings Archie within inches of his life, he suddenly becomes a devout—if somewhat hypocritical—churchgoer.

**97**   George and Archie Make a Deal       November 30, 1974
**Writer:** David P. Harmon
**Director:** H. Wesley Kenney

George Jefferson seeks Archie's help when he runs for local political office.

**98**   Archie's Contract                   December 7, 1974
**Writer:** Ron Friedman
**Director:** H. Wesley Kenney
**Guest Stars**: Dennis Patrick, Mike Wagner, Ed Peck

Irene and the Jeffersons bail the Bunkers out after Archie buys $2000 worth of aluminum siding from a fast-talking salesman.

**99**   Mike's Friend                       December 14, 1974
**Writers:** Roger Shulman, John Baskin
**Director:** H. Wesley Kenney
**Guest Star:** Greg Mullavey

Gloria is made to feel like an intellectual outcast when she spends the evening with Mike and one of his graduate-school friends.

**100**   The Best of All in the Family (one hour)   December 21, 1974
**Writers:** Bernie West, Michael Ross
**Director:** H. Wesley Kenney
**Guest Star:** Henry Fonda

Henry Fonda hosts an hour-long retrospective of high points from the show's first four years.

**101**   Prisoner in the House                    January 4, 1975
**Writers:** Bud Wiser, Lou Derman, Bill Davenport
**Story:** Bud Wiser
**Director:** H. Wesley Kenney
**Guest Stars:** Cliff Osmond, Sid Chute

A plumber's assistant causes Archie agony when he finds out that the worker is a convict on a work-release program from Sing Sing.

**102**   The Jeffersons Move Up                   January 11, 1975
**Writers:** Don Nicholl, Michael Ross, Bernie West
**Director:** H. Wesley Kenney
**Guest Stars:** Paul Benedict, Franklin Cover, Berlinda Tolbert, Zara Cully

The Bunkers bid a fond farewell to the Jeffersons when their neighbors abandon Queens for the nouveau-riche life in a Manhattan high-rise.

This episode was the pilot for the excruciatingly long-running spinoff series *The Jeffersons*.

**103**   All's Fair                               January 18, 1975
**Writers:** Lloyd Turner, Gordon Mitchell
**Director:** H. Wesley Kenney

Gloria gives Edith a lesson in marriage assertiveness.

**104**   Amelia's Divorce                         January 25, 1975
**Writers:** Lou Derman, Bill Davenport
**Director:** H. Wesley Kenney
**Guest Stars:** George S. Irving, Elizabeth Wilson

Edith is surprised to discover that her cousin Amelia's ideal marriage is rotten to the core.

The writers made sure that O'Connor and Stapleton—masters of the comic take—had plenty of opportunity to practice their exquisite comic reactions on *All in the Family*. When Amelia frankly confides her husband's preoccupation with sex, Edith's discomfited reactions are funnier than any lines she might utter. And the episode closes with a memorable nonverbal scene where Archie and Edith reaffirm the bond of their own marriage by clasping hands in a poignant silence that speaks volumes.

**105** Everybody Does It                                    February 8, 1975
   **Writers:** Lou Derman, Bill Davenport, Susan Ware
   **Director:** H. Wesley Kenney

Archie steals a box of nails from work and finds himself at the center of a household debate on morality.

**106** Archie and the Quiz                                  February 15, 1975
   **Writer:** Michael Morris
   **Director:** H. Wesley Kenney

Archie feels the weight of his own mortality after a magazine quiz on life expectancy gives him another seven years—tops.

**107** Edith's Friend                                       February 22, 1975
   **Writers:** Barry Harmon, Harve Brosten
   **Director:** H. Wesley Kenney
   **Guest Stars:** Tim O'Conner, Jane Rose, Ruth Manning

Edith is reunited with her childhood sweetheart when she returns to her hometown for a wedding.

**108** No Smoking                                           March 1, 1975
   **Writers:** Lou Derman, Bill Davenport
   **Director:** H. Wesley Kenney

The Bunker house is locked in a battle of wills after Mike vows that he can go without food longer than Archie can abstain from smoking.

**109**   Mike Makes His Move                    March 8, 1975
   **Writers:** Lou Derman, Bill Davenport
   **Story:** Robert Arnott
   **Director:** H. Wesley Kenney
   **Guest Stars:** Burt Mustin, Ruth McDevitt, Sherman Hemsley

After a fruitless search for new lodgings, Mike and Gloria agree to rent George Jefferson's old house—even though it means living next door to Archie.

## 1975-76   THE SIXTH SEASON

*Year-End Rating: 30.1 (1st place)*

A fresh stable of writers in the sixth year sets the stage for the family's most notable addition, Mike and Gloria's baby, little Joey Stivic. The nine-pound source of fresh storylines unites the Bunker clan as never before, as they embark on all-new debates over topics ranging from the baby's name to his religious upbringing.

An influx of experienced comedy veterans joins the show's creative staff in the sixth year, including story editors Milt Josefsberg, Larry Rhine, Phil Doran, and Douglas Arango; special program consultants Mel Tolkin and Ben Starr; and producers Lou Derman and Bill Davenport. Their first-rate scripts in the later seasons lack the passionate fire of the early shows, but the fine-tuned performances—and assured direction by Paul Bogart—guarantee well-crafted, if occasionally predictable, entertainment.

Woody Kling and Lou Derman serve as script supervisors, and Hal Kanter, Woody Kling, and Norman Lear share the executive producer's credit over the course of the year.

**110**   The Very Moving Day                    September 8, 1975
   **Writer:** Hal Kanter
   **Director:** Paul Bogart

Gloria is nervous about announcing her unexpected pregnancy because of Mike's stubborn attitude toward overpopulation.

**111**   Alone at Last?                    September 15, 1975
   **Writer:** Hal Kanter
   **Director:** Paul Bogart

Teary farewells turn into fireworks when Mike hits Archie with five years of repressed rage, only to discover that he and Gloria can't move out for another week.

In the sixth season, Carroll O'Connor was able to bring in Paul Bogart as the series's new director. The star had known Bogart since the days of live television, and his arrival marked the beginning of the series's final, most tranquil period.

**112**   Archie the Donor                       September 22, 1975
**Writers:** Bill Davenport, Larry Rhine
**Director:** Paul Bogart
**Guest Stars:** J.A. Preston, Don Randolph, Sorrell Booke

Archie tries to impress his boss by making the maximum contribution to his favorite charity and unwittingly ends up donating his body to medical science.

The producers aired four episodes at the start of the season in which Gloria didn't appear, after Sally Struthers sued to break her contract, which she felt was keeping her from a promising movie career. The problems were smoothed over, and judging by the first project she had to turn down—the ill-fated *Day of the Locust*—the producers probably did her a favor by keeping her tied to the show.

**113**   Archie the Hero                        September 29, 1975
**Writers:** Lou Derman, Bill Davenport
**Director:** Paul Bogart
**Guest Stars:** Lori Shannon, Sandy Kenyon, Billy Halop

Archie gets a rude shock when the tall, classy dame whose life he saved in a taxicab turns out to be a man.

Once again, the celebrated fireworks of Archie's reaction are no more than a theatrical contrivance compared to the script's real charm—the finely observed exchanges between Archie and Edith that authentically capture the tone of a couple who've been married to each other for twenty-six years.

**114**   Mike's Pains                           October 6, 1975
**Writers:** Lou Derman, Milt Josefsberg
**Director:** Paul Bogart
**Guest Star:** Francine Beers

Mike has second thoughts about natural childbirth when he gets queasy at the prospect of standing in the delivery room during Gloria's labor.


**115**   Chain Letter                    October 20, 1975
**Writers:** Lou Derman, Milt Josefsberg
**Story:** Lou Derman
**Director:** Paul Bogart
**Guest Stars:** Robert Guillaume, Beatrice Colen, Billy Halop

Archie's refusal to participate in a chain letter triggers a string of unlikely events.


**116**   Mike Faces Life                    October 27, 1975
**Writers:** Mel Tolkin, Larry Rhine
**Director:** Paul Bogart
**Guest Stars:** George Furth, Diane Shalet

Mike becomes the sole support of a growing family when Gloria loses her job because of her pregnancy.


**117**   Edith Breaks Out                    November 3, 1975
**Writers:** Lou Derman, Bill Davenport
**Director:** Paul Bogart
**Guest Star:** James Hong

Archie feels abandoned after Edith begins to volunteer part-time at the Sunshine Home for the Elderly.


**118**   Grandpa Blues                    November 10, 1975
**Writers:** Mel Tolkin, Larry Rhine
**Story:** John Rappaport
**Director:** Paul Bogart
**Guest Stars:** Sorrell Booke, John Zoller, Greg Mabrey, Tracy Bogart

Archie has difficulty keeping his blood pressure down for a company physical after the family launches into a heavy debate over the baby's name.

**119**   Gloria Suspects Mike                    November 17, 1975
   **Writers:** Lou Derman, Milt Josefsberg
   **Director:** Paul Bogart
   **Guest Star:** Bernadette Peters

Gloria suspects hanky-panky when she meets the beautiful blonde Mike's been tutoring after school hours.

**120**   The Little Atheist                      November 24, 1975
   **Writer:** Lou Derman
   **Director:** Paul Bogart

Thanksgiving dinner becomes a family battleground when Archie discovers that Mike and Gloria don't want to impose the family's religious beliefs on their baby.

**121**   Archie's Civil Rights                   December 1, 1975
   **Writers:** Larry Rhine, Mel Tolkin
   **Director:** Paul Bogart
   **Guest Stars:** Paulene Myers, Frank Campanella, John Alvin, Charles Siebert

Archie gets a lesson in civil liberties when he's arrested for using outlawed tear gas to protect himself against a mugger.

The producers regularly trotted out episodes that were designed to offer piercing insights into social issues, such as this heavy-handed exploration of civil rights and unconstitutional police procedure. Unfortunately, most of these well-intentioned topical episodes were about as subtle as an episode of *Dragnet '67*.

**122**   Gloria Is Nervous                       December 8, 1975
   **Writers:** Milt Josefsberg, Ben Starr
   **Director:** Paul Bogart
   **Guest Stars:** Robin Wilson, Garn Stephens, Suzanne Astor, Madeleine Fisher

The baby is already nine days overdue, and the stress is turning Mike and Gloria into nervous wrecks.

Gloria's miraculous three-month gestation period is not uncommon to sitcom mothers. The medical breakthrough had been observed a full two decades earlier when Lucy Ricardo gave birth a scant six weeks after she first announced her pregnancy.

**123**   Birth of the Baby (Part 1)          December 15, 1975
 **Writers:** Lou Derman, Bill Davenport, Larry Rhine, Mel Tolkin
 **Director:** Paul Bogart
 **Guest Stars:** Herb Voland, Victor Rendina, Allan Melvin

Stuck in a phone booth in an Italian restaurant, Gloria goes into labor while Archie is busy rehearsing for his lodge's minstrel show.

Archie's blackface shenanigans were an unfortunate by-product of the writers' efforts to pad the episode out to two parts; the script also sets a new record for the show's long-standing—and inexplicable—fascination with bathroom humor: No less than three laughs are punched by the sound of a toilet's flush.

**124**   Birth of the Baby (Part 2)          December 22, 1975
 **Writers:** Milt Josefsberg, Ben Starr
 **Director:** Paul Bogart
 **Guest Stars:** Gene Blakely, Barbara Cason, Priscilla Morrill, Sudie Bond, Sharon Ullrick

Archie arrives at the hospital direct from his minstrel show—in blackface—just in time for Gloria's blessed event.

**125**   New Year's Wedding          January 5, 1976
 **Writers:** Lou Derman, Bill Davenport, Milt Josefsberg, Ben Starr
 **Director:** Paul Bogart
 **Guest Stars:** Billy Crystal, Eliot Reid, Joan Copeland, Elaine Princi, Michael Mann, Joe Bratcher, Nancy Stephens, Bibi Osterwald

The Stivics have a spat when Michael volunteers their living room for a wedding ceremony without even consulting Gloria.

**126**   Archie the Baby-Sitter          January 12, 1976
 **Writers:** Lou Derman, Bill Davenport
 **Director:** Paul Bogart
 **Guest Stars:** Jack Somack, Joe Mantell, Ken Menard, Leslie Ackerman, Thad Geer

Archie's buddies form a lullaby quartet when Grandpa Bunker baby-sits Joey on his poker night.

Incredibly, this innocuous episode caused a furor when the network objected to a scene that called for total frontal nudity—the baby's! Despite the censor's objections, the producers trampled another TV taboo and ran Archie's diaper-changing sequence uncut.

**127**  Archie Finds a Friend                    January 26, 1976
   **Writers:** Mel Tolkin, Larry Rhine
   **Director:** Paul Bogart
   **Guest Star:** Jack Gilford

Archie sees a chance to get rich quick when he befriends an old watchmaker who's got a sure-fire invention.

**128**  Mike's Move                              February 2, 1976
   **Writers:** Milt Josefsberg, Ben Starr
   **Director:** Paul Bogart
   **Guest Stars:** Lee Bergere, David Downing

Mike's integrity is put to the test when he loses a teaching position to an equally qualified black candidate.

Archie extracts sweet revenge when he turns the tables on his bleeding-heart son-in-law with a hilarious reworking of the Emma Lazarus inscription on the Statue of Liberty. Archie's version begins, "Send me your poor, your deadbeats, your filthy. . . all of them free to live together in their own separate little sections where they feel safe and break your head if you go in there."

**129**  Archie's Weighty Problem                February 9, 1976
   **Writers:** Mel Tolkin, Larry Rhine
   **Director:** Paul Bogart
   **Guest Stars:** Burt Mustin, Billy Halop

Energetic Justin Quigley inspires Archie to stick with the strict diet his doctor has recommended.

**130**  Love by Appointment                     February 16, 1976
   **Writers:** Lou Derman, Bill Davenport
   **Director:** Paul Bogart

Mike and Gloria's sex life suffers after they have to begin planning their encounters around the baby's feeding schedule.

In another funny and believable talk between mother and daughter,

Struthers shows us how the flighty post-adolescent of the earliest shows has matured—first as a wife, then as a mother, until she finally emerges in later seasons as a woman who doesn't feel completely fulfilled in either of those roles.

**131** Joey's Baptism                                    February 23, 1976
   **Writers:** Milt Josefsberg, Mel Tolkin, Larry Rhine
   **Director:** Paul Bogart
   **Guest Star:** Clyde Kusatsu

After Mike and Gloria refuse to have their son baptized, Archie stubbornly steals away to a church to anoint the infant himself.

**132**   Mike and Gloria's Houseguests              March 1, 1976
   **Writers:** Larry Rhine, Mel Tolkin, Milt Josefsberg
   **Director:** Paul Bogart

A broken furnace forces Archie and Edith to spend a few nights under the Stivics' roof during a power blackout.

**133**   Edith's Night Out                          March 8, 1976
   **Writers:** Lou Derman, Douglas Arango, Phil Doran
   **Director:** Paul Bogart
   **Guest Stars:** Doris Roberts, Scott Brady, Jason Wingreen

Edith abandons her stick-in-the-mud husband to liven things up on her own during an evening out at Kelcy's Bar.

Jason Wingreen would play Harry the bartender for the rest of show's run, and he would also be one of the few holdovers to survive the series's transition to *Archie Bunker's Place* at the end of the ninth season.

## 1976-77    THE SEVENTH SEASON

*Year-End Rating: 22.9 (12th place)*

The fury of the early years has largely evaporated by the seventh season as the writers exploit the rich personalities of the central cast in well-crafted character comedies that take full advantage of the show's rock-solid ensemble.

Mort Lachman joins the staff as executive producer for the show's last three seasons, and Milt Josefsberg takes over as producer. The pair also serve as script supervisors. Larry Rhine and Mel Tolkin are executive story editors, and Douglas Arango and Phil Doran are the seventh-year story editors.

**134**   Archie's Brief Encounter              September 22, 1976
        (Part 1—one hour)
   **Writers:** Mel Tolkin, Larry Rhine
   **Director:** Paul Bogart
   **Guest Stars:** Janis Paige, Scott Brady, Theodore Wilson, André Pavon

Edith leaves Archie when she finds out that he dated a flirtatious waitress while she was volunteering at the Sunshine Home.

**135**   Archie's Brief Encounter (Part 2)      September 29, 1976
   **Writers:** Mel Tolkin, Larry Rhine
   **Director:** Paul Bogart
   **Guest Stars:** Scott Brady, Maxine Elliot, Bella Chronis, Harry Davis

Edith forgives Archie's indiscretion after Mike and Gloria bring the two together for an emotional reunion.

The events of this classic two-parter would color the Bunkers' relationship for some time to come. The subject would arise only on rare occasions—but in the aftermath of Archie's mistake, the couple shared a renewed tenderness that would carry them through the final three seasons.

**136**   The Unemployment Story (Part 1)        October 6, 1976
   **Writers:** Ben Starr, Chuck Stewart
   **Director:** Paul Bogart
   **Guest Stars:** Jinaki, F. Murray Abraham

Archie's self-esteem takes a beating when he loses his job on the loading dock.

**137**   The Unemployment Story (Part 2)        October 13, 1976
   **Writers:** Chuck Stewart, Ben Starr
   **Director:** Paul Bogart
   **Guest Stars:** Gerald Hiken, Neva Patterson, Eliza Garrett, Jeannie Linero, Ellen Travolta

A college grad threatens to commit suicide after he loses a janitor's job to Archie.

**138**  Archie's Operation (Part 1)               October 20, 1976
  **Writers:** Milt Josefsberg, Mort Lachman
  **Story:** Calvin Kelly, Jim Tisdale
  **Director:** Paul Bogart
  **Guest Stars:** Vinnette Carroll, Liz Torres, Milton Selzer

Archie's trip to the hospital is an ethnic nightmare: He's admitted by a Puerto Rican receptionist, treated by a Jewish physician, and is forced to accept a blood transfusion from a black doctor!

Liz Torres makes her first appearance as Teresa Betancourt, who would shortly become the Bunkers' boarder.

**139**  Archie's Operation (Part 2)               October 27, 1976
  **Writers:** Mel Tolkin, Larry Rhine
  **Director:** Paul Bogart
  **Guest Stars:** Vinnette Carroll, Frances Fong, Danny Dayton

Archie recuperates in record time after he's called back to work—with a raise and a promotion.

Danny Dayton appears as Hank Pivnik, one of Archie's pals who would frequent Kelcy's Bar and, later, *Archie's Place*.

**139**  Beverly Rides Again               November 6, 1976
  **Writers:** Phil Doran, Douglas Arango
  **Director:** Paul Bogart
  **Guest Stars:** Lori Shannon, Eugene Roche, Phoebe Dorin, André Pavon

As a practical joke, Archie fixes up one of his drinking buddies with female impersonator Beverly LaSalle.

Lori Shannon returns for another round of tired theatrics as the showgirl Archie once saved with mouth-to-mouth resuscitation.

**141**  Teresa Moves In               November 13, 1976
  **Writer:** Michael Loman
  **Director:** Paul Bogart
  **Guest Stars:** Liz Torres, Alex Colon

The Bunkers take in a boarder to help revive their battered budget.

**142**   Mike and Gloria's Will                November 20, 1976
   **Writers:** Bill Richmond, Gene Perret
   **Director:** Paul Bogart

The Bunkers are stunned to hear that Mike and Gloria plan to appoint another couple as Joey's legal guardians in their will.

**143**   Mr. Edith Bunker                      November 27, 1976
   **Writers:** Mel Tolkin, Larry Rhine
   **Director:** Paul Bogart
   **Guest Stars:** Priscilla Morrill, Phil Leeds, Florence Halop, James Greene, Maxine Elliot, Bella Chronis, Bob Duggan

Edith saves a man's life and becomes the toast of the town, but Archie isn't happy standing in the shadow of her limelight.

**144**   Archie's Secret Passion                December 4, 1976
   **Writer:** Michael Loman
   **Director:** Paul Bogart
   **Guest Stars:** Estelle Parsons, Mike Kellin

Edith discovers that Archie once had a brief encounter with an old high school friend she's invited to dinner.

Estelle Parsons would be typecast as the show's lady of dubious virtue. After playing the woman with a checkered past in this episode, she returned in the ninth season as Barney Hefner's comically wayward wife.

**145**   The Baby Contest                       December 11, 1976
   **Writers:** Larry Rhine, Mel Tolkin
   **Story:** Marion Zola, Ed Haas
   **Director:** Paul Bogart
   **Guest Stars:** Allan Melvin, Danny Dayton, Jason Wingreen

Archie enters Joey in a newspaper's beautiful-baby contest, against the express wishes of Mike and Gloria.

The series had become much less topical in later years, and many stories—like this one—revolved around the classic domestic situation of two married couples who are best friends and next-door neighbors. The show's occasional resemblance to *I Love Lucy*—albeit with the roles reversed and the focus now on the older couple—wasn't entirely coincidental. Many of *All in the Family's* current writers had formerly scripted the redhead's video misadventures. Lou Derman and Bill Davenport even wrote for Lucy's earliest radio sitcom, *My Favorite Husband,* before joining Milt Josefsberg many years later on *Here's Lucy.* And Bob Schiller and Bob Weiskopf, who joined *All in the Family* in the eighth season, were two-fifths of the writing team on the original *I Love Lucy.*

**146**  Gloria's False Alarm                December 18, 1976
   **Writers:** Phil Doran, Douglas Arango
   **Director:** Paul Bogart
   **Guest Star:** Michael Mann

Gloria insists that Mike get the vasectomy he's talked about for years.

**147**  The Draft Dodger                December 25, 1976
   **Writers:** Jay Moriarty, Mike Milligan
   **Director:** Paul Bogart
   **Guest Stars:** Eugene Roche, Renny Temple, Liz Torres

Sparks fly when Mike invites a former draft resister to the Bunkers' Christmas dinner, where the guest of honor is the father of a vet who was killed in Vietnam.

The war returns as a topic of controversy in an unexpected homage to the kitchen-table fireworks of the earliest episodes, now invested with the deeper emotional coloration typical of the show's later period. Instead of contributing to the predictable battle of clashing viewpoints, the bereaved father surprises everyone with an impassioned plea for amnesty.

Try as he might, even Archie can't remain unmoved. He agrees to mull the issue over in his mind and then, in frustration, retreats to the front porch to berate a festive chorus of carolers. But the singing continues, and in the final shot of this classic episode, Archie stands alone, a bewildered Scrooge, unable to snuff out the last candle of hope.

**148**  The Boarder Patrol                January 8, 1977
   **Writers:** Larry Rhine, Mel Tolkin
   **Director:** Paul Bogart
   **Guest Stars:** Patrick Cronin, William Lanteau, Juan De Carlos

The Bunkers return home unexpectedly to find Teresa in bed with her boyfriend.

Much as the producers tried to establish Teresa as the Bunkers' surrogate daughter, the chemistry just wasn't there—and the boarder quietly moved out at the close of the season.

**149**   Archie's Chair                              January 15, 1977
   **Writers:** Phil Doran, Douglas Arango
   **Director:** Paul Bogart
   **Guest Stars:** Michael Pataki, Allan Rich, Doug Robinson, Colin Hamilton, Tyler McVey

Archie's beloved easy chair ends up in an art museum after the repair shop accidentally sells it to a modern artist.

Archie's chair actually did end up in a museum: no less than the Smithsonian Institution. At the request of a Congressional committee, Norman Lear donated the Bunkers' living-room ensemble to the Smithsonian's permanent collection at the close of the eighth season.

**150**   Mike Goes Skiing                           January 22, 1977
   **Writers:** Ben Starr, Chuck Stewart
   **Director:** Paul Bogart
   **Guest Stars:** John Karlen, Rod Loomis, Tom Fitzsimmons, Mark Lonow

Mike asserts his independence by leaving Gloria behind while he joins his friends on a weekend skiing trip.

**151**   Stretch Cunningham, Good-Bye               January 29, 1977
   **Writers:** Phil Doran, Douglas Arango, Milt Josefsberg
   **Director:** Paul Bogart
   **Guest Stars:** Charles Siebert, Jay Gerber

Archie reluctantly agrees to deliver Stretch Cunningham's eulogy, unaware that his departed friend was Jewish.

**152**   The Joys of Sex                            February 5, 1977
   **Writer:** Erik Tarloff
   **Director:** Paul Bogart

Edith sneaks a peek at a best-selling sex manual and decides that her romantic life could stand a little perking up.

Archie's squirming—and Edith's squeamishness—aside, *All in the Family* was the first TV series to openly acknowledge a healthy sexual relationship shared by a middle-aged couple. As incredible as it seems, before the Bunkers, television's married couples—young or old—always slept in twin beds.

**153**   Mike the Pacifist                    February 12, 1977
  **Writers:** Phil Doran, Douglas Arango
  **Director:** Paul Bogart
  **Guest Stars:** Wynn Irwin, Nita Talbot, Sudie Bond, Richard Lawson, William Lanteau, William Pierson

Mike feels guilty for punching a man on the subway, even though he acted in defense of Gloria.

**154** Fire                    February 19, 1977
  **Writers:** Michael Loman, Larry Rhine, Mel Tolkin
  **Director:** Paul Bogart
  **Guest Star:** Roger C. Carmel

Archie tries to collect on a fraudulent insurance claim after a small fire breaks out in the upstairs bathroom.

**155**   Mike and Gloria Split                    February 26, 1977
  **Writers:** Mel Tolkin, Larry Rhine
  **Story:** Mort Lachman, Milt Josefsberg
  **Director:** Paul Bogart

Mike spends a night with Archie after a fight with Gloria.

**156**   Archie the Liberal                    March 5, 1977
  **Writers:** Ben Starr, Chuck Stewart
  **Director:** Paul Bogart
  **Guest Star:** James McEachin

When his lodge comes under fire for discrimination, Archie tries to knock off two quotas at once by courting a black Jew for membership.

**157**   Archie's Dog Day Afternoon                    March 12, 1977
  **Writers:** Chuck Stewart, Ben Starr
  **Story:** Mort Lachman, Milt Josefsberg
  **Director:** Paul Bogart
  **Guest Stars:** Bill Hunt, Vanda Barra, Tracy Bogart

Archie accidentally runs over Barney Hefner's dog.

# 1977-78    THE EIGHTH SEASON
*Year-End Rating: 24.4 (4th place)*

In what was originally conceived as the show's final season, the writers pull out all the stops to create a handful of the series's most memorable dramatic episodes—including the departure of Mike and Gloria at the season's end—many of them scripted by Bob Schiller and Bob Weiskopf, the veteran writing team who signed on as script consultants for the show's final two seasons.

In addition to contributions from the familiar bullpen—including story editors Mel Tolkin and Larry Rhine, and producer Milt Josefsberg—memorable scripts are written by Phil Sharp, Erik Tarloff, Chuck Stewart, and Ben Starr.

**158**   Archie Gets the Business (one hour)          October 2, 1977
   **Writers:** Mel Tolkin, Larry Rhine
   **Director:** Paul Bogart
   **Guest Stars:** Frank Maxwell, Norma Donaldson, Sid Conrad

Archie, desperate to realize his personal dream and buy Kelcy's Bar, forges Edith's signature on mortgage papers.

Archie's graduation from wage earner to entrepreneur opened up a wealth of new story possibilities, even as it changed the essential character of the show. No longer a downtrodden member of the working class, Archie the small businessman had less reason to vent his outrage than in days past, and the show mellowed considerably in its final two seasons.

**159**   Cousin Liz                                October 9, 1977
   **Writers:** Bob Schiller, Bob Weiskopf
   **Story:** Barry Harmon, Harve Brosten
   **Director:** Paul Bogart
   **Guest Star:** K Callan

At the funeral of Edith's cousin Liz, the Bunkers are shocked to learn that she'd been living with a lesbian roommate for years.

**160**   Edith's Fiftieth Birthday (one hour)      October 16, 1977
   **Writers:** Bob Schiller, Bob Weiskopf
   **Director:** Paul Bogart
   **Guest Stars:** David Dukes, Jane Connell, John Brandon, Ray Colella

Edith misses her birthday party when a rapist holds her at gunpoint in her own living room.

Schiller and Weiskopf faced built-in compromises when they chose to depict such a singularly violent crime within the confines of a television comedy, especially when the victim was one of the most beloved figures on prime time. Though the creators were justifiably applauded for their efforts, the episode wasn't entirely successful; the shocking drama and unsettling suspense of the first half hour makes for an uneasy blend with the head-thumping slapstick of Mike and Archie's ill-advised comic relief in the second half hour.

**161**   Unequal Partners                    October 23, 1977
   **Writers:** Chuck Stewart, Ben Starr
   **Director:** Paul Bogart
   **Guest Stars:** Ian Wolfe, Merie Earle, Will Mackenzie

Edith ruins Archie's weekend fishing trip when she stages a wedding in the Bunkers' living room.

**162**   Archie's Grand Opening               October 30, 1977
   **Writers:** Larry Rhine, Mel Tolkin
   **Director:** Paul Bogart
   **Guest Stars:** Sorrel Booke, Joe Petrullo, Paul Larson, Sam Solito, Grace Lee

The family steps in to serve drinks and tend bar at Archie's tavern after his staff deserts him on opening night.

**163**   Archie's Bitter Pill (Part 1)        November 6, 1977
   **Writers:** Mel Tolkin, Larry Rhine, William C. Rader, M.D.
   **Director:** Paul Bogart
   **Guest Stars:** Arny Freeman, A. Martinez

Archie takes a few pep pills to keep pace with the increased demands of running his own business and winds up with an amphetamine addiction.

**164**   Archie's Road Back (Part 2)          November 13, 1977
   **Writers:** Mel Tolkin, Larry Rhine, William C. Rader, M.D.
   **Director:** Paul Bogart
   **Guest Stars:** A. Martinez, MacIntyre Dixon

A despondent Archie retreats to his bedroom, until Harry offers to bail him out with a partnership offer for the bar.

**165**   Archie and the Ku Klux Klan (Part 1)        November 27,1977
**Writers:** Bob Schiller, Bob Weiskopf, Mort Lachman, Milt Josefsberg
**Director:** Paul Bogart
**Guest Stars:** Dennis Patrick, Roger Bowen, Owen Bush

Archie is nominated for membership in a mysterious fraternal order that turns out to be the local branch of the KKK.

**166**   Archie and the Ku Klux Klan (Part 2)        December 4, 1977
**Writers:** Bob Schiller, Bob Weiskopf
**Director:** Paul Bogart
**Guest Stars:** Dennis Patrick, Roger Bowen

Archie devises a plan to prevent the Klan from burning a cross on Mike and Gloria's lawn.

**167**   Mike and Gloria Meet                        December 11, 1977
**Writers:** Bob Schiller, Bob Weiskopf
**Director:** Paul Bogart
**Guest Stars:** Christopher Guest, Priscilla Lopez

A flashback explores Mike and Gloria's first blind date.

Rob Reiner would cast co-star Christopher Guest as one of the leads when he directed the 1984 rock 'n' roll satire *This Is Spinal Tap.*

**168**   Edith's Crisis of Faith (Part 1)           December 18, 1977
**169**   Edith's Crisis of Faith (Part 2)           December 25, 1977
**Writers:** Bob Schiller, Bob Weiskopf (Part 1); Erik Tarloff, Mel Tolkin, Larry Rhine (Part 2)
**Story:** Erik Tarloff
**Director:** Paul Bogart
**Guest Stars:** Lori Shannon, Ron Vernan

Edith's religious faith is shaken after her friend, female impersonator Beverly LaSalle, is brutally murdered by street thugs at Christmas.

**170**   Archie and the Super Bowl                January 15, 1978
   **Writers:** Bob Schiller, Bob Weiskopf
   **Director:** Paul Bogart
   **Guest Stars:** Art Metrano, Louis Guss, Gloria LeRoy, J.J.
   Johnston, Raymond O'Keefe

Archie's Place is robbed on Super Bowl Sunday, the busiest day
of the year.

**171**   The Commercial                          January 8, 1978
   **Writers:** Ben Starr, Ron Bloomberg
   **Story:** Ron Bloomberg
   **Director:** Paul Bogart
   **Guest Stars:** Alan Hamel, Frank Aletter, Darryl Hickman,
   Thomas Middelton

Edith has a chance to appear in a TV commercial but finds herself unable to lie when she begins to doubt the quality of the
sponsor's detergent.

**172**   Aunt Iola's Visit                        January 22, 1978
   **Writer:** Albert E. Lewin
   **Story:** Michael Loman
   **Director:** Paul Bogart
   **Guest Star:** Nedra Volz

Archie refuses to let Edith's elderly aunt move into their spare
bedroom, even after she's been turned away by every other relative.

**173**   Love Comes to the Butcher                February 5, 1978
   **Writer:** Phil Sharp
   **Director:** Paul Bogart
   **Guest Stars:** Theodore Bikel, Sarina C. Grant

Archie is jealous when a lonely butcher lavishes attention on
Edith.

**174**   Two's a Crowd                            February 12, 1978
   **Writer:** Phil Sharp
   **Director:** Paul Bogart

Mike and Archie have a long talk when they find themselves
locked in the storeroom of Archie's Place.

Carroll O'Connor and Rob Reiner are splendid in this compelling exploration of their frequently tempestuous relationship. Locked in the quiet solitude of a cold cellar, each reveals a part of himself that's always been well guarded. And in the shadows of the dark basement, they begin to see each other in a new light. In Archie's touching monologue, he recalls the reverent devotion he always felt toward his father, and then dozes off in sorrow at the painful realization that he never earned the same respect from his own daughter. Michael doesn't say a word, but quietly reaches over to cover him in the warmth of the cellar's lone blanket. The sleeping King Lear never stirs when he finally earns a small gesture of fatherly respect—bestowed not by a daughter but a son.

**175**   Stale Mates                              February 19, 1978
   **Writers:** Larry Rhine, Mel Tolkin
   **Director:** Paul Bogart
   **Guest Stars:** Judy Kahan, Terry Kiser

Mike and Gloria are convinced that the romance has gone out of their marriage when even a weekend in the Poconos fails to re-ignite the spark.

**176**   Archie's Brother                         February 26, 1978
   **Writers:** Larry Rhine, Mel Tolkin
   **Director:** Paul Bogart
   **Guest Star:** Richard Mackenzie

Archie's estranged brother returns, after twenty-nine years, to smooth things over before he enters the hospital for a serious operation.

**177**   Mike's New Job                              March 5, 1978
   **Writers:** Mel Tolkin, Larry Rhine
   **Director:** Paul Bogart
   **Guest Star:** Sherman Hemsley

The Stivics prepare to move to California when Mike is offered a teaching position in Santa Barbara.

**178**   The Dinner Guest                           March 12, 1978
   **Writers:** Mel Tolkin, Larry Rhine
   **Director:** Paul Bogart

Edith is crushed when Mike and Gloria make other plans after she's prepared a special farewell dinner in their honor.

**179**   The Stivics Go West                    March 19, 1978
   **Writers:** Bob Schiller, Bob Weiskopf
   **Director:** Paul Bogart
   **Guest Star:** Clyde Kusatsu

The Bunker house is the scene of many tearful good-byes when
Mike and Gloria finally leave for California.

When the cast concluded taping this classic episode, there was hardly
a dry eye in the house, onstage or off. The sentimental ceremonies that
attended the season's final show were originally planned as a wrap party
for the entire series. When Reiner and Struthers first announced their
intention to leave at the end of the season, Norman Lear couldn't conceive of carrying on without them. "I'm confident you are watching the
last full season of *All in the Family*," he told reporters in January, as he
announced his own plans to leave television and return to the greener
pastures of feature-film production.

Carroll O'Connor was equally adamant about his own retirement.
"Television's like a good neighborhood gone bad," he told columnist
Marilyn Beck, "and I'd like to get out." But that was before CBS stepped
in with an eleventh-hour offer to keep the ratings powerhouse going at
least one more year.

"I don't see why we should deprive the American public of one their
favorite shows," was CBS president Bob Daly's public rationale for luring Carroll O'Connor back to the fold with a salary that exceeded $100,000
per episode—in addition to a lucrative production deal with the network.
The actor helped convince Jean Stapleton to return, and to everyone's
surprise, *All in the Family* entered a ninth and final season—without Mike,
without Gloria, and without Norman Lear.

## 1978-79   THE NINTH SEASON

*Year-End Rating: 24.9 (9th place)*

The show's final—and not entirely unworthy—season is redeemed by
a handful of first-rate scripts, though the Bunkers almost never recover
from the deadening pathos that arrives with the introduction a nine-year-
old on Hauser Street. Even so, the writers manage to explore the ever-
deepening bond between Archie and Edith, who continue to evolve as
the most plausibly romantic couple on television.

Most ninth-year stories are scripted by a talented writing stable that
includes story editors Mel Tolkin and Larry Rhine, producer Milt

Josefsberg, and story consultant Phil Sharp. Script consultants Bob Schiller and Bob Weiskopf once again contribute a number of memorable scripts, as do newcomers Patt Shea and Harriett Weiss.

**180**   Little Miss Bunker                    September 24, 1978
   **Writers:** Mel Tolkin, Larry Rhine
   **Director:** Paul Bogart
   **Guest Stars:** Marty Brill, Bhetty Waldron, Santos Morales, Bern Bennett

Edith's cousin Floyd abandons his nine-year-old daughter, Stephanie, on the Bunkers' doorstep.

Danielle Brisebois, the littlest orphan in Broadway's *Annie,* joined the cast as Edith's niece, Stephanie Mills. The introduction of a child into the Bunker household created a hazardous breeding ground for gross sentimentality at a time when the show's critics were already lambasting Carroll O'Connor for letting Archie go soft in the show's old age. O'Connor later dismissed the criticism in the pages of *TV Guide* when he insisted, "We're not going to have him yell 'coon' every week just so we can keep up the reputation of a socially pungent show."

**181**   End in Sight                          October 1, 1978
   **Writer:** Nate Monaster
   **Director:** Paul Bogart
   **Guest Star:** Phil Leeds

Archie spends a night wallowing in self-pity when an insurance physical reveals an ominous spot on his liver.

**182**   Reunion on Hauser Street              October 8, 1978
   **Writers:** Milt Josefsberg, Phil Sharp
   **Director:** Paul Bogart
   **Guest Stars:** Estelle Parsons, Gloria LeRoy

The Bunkers attempt to reunite Blanche and Barney Hefner after her latest fling with an exterminator fizzles.

**183**   What'll We Do With Stephanie?         October 15, 1978
   **Writers:** Larry Rhine, Mel Tolkin
   **Director:** Paul Bogart
   **Guest Star:** Abbey Lincoln

The Bunkers decide to keep Stephanie after her father fails to reclaim her as promised.

**184**   Edith's Final Respects                    October 22, 1978
   **Writers:** Bob Schiller, Bob Weiskopf
   **Story:** Sam Greenbaum
   **Director:** Paul Bogart
   **Guest Stars:** Howard Morton, Charles Siebert

Edith is the sole mourner at her Aunt Rose's funeral.

**185**   Weekend in the Country                   October 29, 1978
   **Writers:** Phil Sharp, Milt Josefsberg
   **Director:** Paul Bogart
   **Guest Star:** Estelle Parsons

Once again, Archie and Edith try to preserve peace between Barney Hefner and his extremely wayward wife.

**186**   Archie's Other Wife                      November 5, 1978
   **Writers:** Bob Schiller, Bob Weiskopf
   **Director:** Paul Bogart
   **Guest Stars:** Eugene Roche, Harvey Lembeck, Jonelle Allen, James J. Casino

At an American Legion convention, Archie awakens facing a beautiful black airline stewardess who swears they were married the night before.

**187**   Edith Versus the Bank                    November 19, 1978
   **Writers:** Mel Tolkin, Larry Rhine
   **Director:** Paul Bogart
   **Guest Star:** John Harkins

Edith is disillusioned when her bank refuses to grant a loan without her husband's signature.

When she discovers that her husband is as narrow-minded as the bank manager, Edith demands that Archie pay her a token five-dollars-a-week payment for her labors as a housewife. Using her own unique logic, she extracts exactly what she wants from Archie in the end, proving once again that in the realm of common sense, this dingbat has no peer.

**188**   The Return of the Waitress                November 26, 1978
   **Writers:** Milt Josefsberg, Phil Sharp
   **Director:** Paul Bogart
   **Guest Star:** Janis Paige

Edith finally confronts the waitress who tempted Archie's fidelity after Harry unwittingly hires her to work at Archie's Place.

Edith bears no malice toward the waitress, but thanks her for helping to strengthen her union with Archie. He ends the episode with the observation, "Edith, you're a pip." The expression, employed as Archie's most disparaging put-down in the early years, suddenly rings with a tenderness as compelling as Ralph Kramden's classic declaration of devotion, "Baby, you're the greatest."

**189**   Bogus Bills                          December 3, 1978
   **Writers:** Bob Schiller, Bob Weiskopf
   **Director:** Paul Bogart
   **Guest Stars:** Sandy Kenyon, John Finnegan, Charles Hallahan

Edith is arrested for passing phony $10 bills she got from Archie's Place.

**190**   The Bunkers Go West                  December 10, 1978
   **Writers:** Mel Tolkin, Larry Rhine
   **Director:** Paul Bogart

After Mike and Gloria cancel their trip home for Christmas, the Bunkers decide to travel west for the holidays.

**191**   California, Here We Are (one hour)      December 17, 1978
   **Writers:** Milt Josefsberg, Phil Sharp (first half); Bob Schiller, Bob Weiskopf (second half)
   **Director:** Paul Bogart
   **Guest Star:** Cory Miller

The Bunkers arrive in Santa Barbara for Christmas and soon discover that all is not right with Mike and Gloria.

More disturbing than the Stivics' heartbreaking announcement of their separation is Archie's reaction when he discovers that Gloria has been unfaithful to her husband: For the first time in nine years, he turns his back on his daughter and sides with Michael. The script, rife with disturbing details of the petty cruelties that have already poisoned the Stivics' marriage, avoids the easy out of a tidy resolution. Mike and Gloria do effect a spontaneous reconciliation under the tree, but the tentative exchange lacks the conviction of a permanent reunion. They've been through enough to know, as we do, that the optimism of Christmas morning doesn't always stand up to the cold light of the new year.

The script's only nod toward romanticism is suggested by Edith and Archie, who never felt as thankful for the years they've shared together as they did on that eventful Christmas morning.

**192**    A Night at the PTA                    January 7, 1979
   **Writers:** Mel Tolkin, Larry Rhine
   **Director:** Paul Bogart

When Edith develops laryngitis on the eve of her singing debut at Stephanie's PTA recital, Archie steps in to understudy the duet.

**193**    A Girl Like Edith                     January 14, 1979
   **Writers:** Bob Schiller, Bob Weiskopf
   **Director:** Paul Bogart
   **Guest Stars:** Theodore Bikel, Giovanna Pucci

Edith meets butcher Klemmer's new sweetheart, a woman who just happens to be her spitting image.

Edith's Teutonic double is played by Stapleton in a dual role, a technical stunt that would have been impossible to pull off while the show was still taped with a live crowd. The producers had done away with the live studio audience at the start of the ninth season to please O'Connor, who preferred to tape in a cold studio and dub in the laughs later.

**194**    The Appendectomy                      January 21, 1979
   **Writers:** Phil Sharp, Milt Josefsberg
   **Director:** Paul Bogart
   **Guest Stars:** George Wyner, Tracy Bogart

Edith and Archie rush Stephanie to the hospital for an emergency appendectomy.

**195**   Stephanie and the Crime Wave                January 28, 1979
   **Writers:** Larry Rhine, Mel Tolkin
   **Director:** Paul Bogart
   **Guest Star:** Davis Roberts

The Bunkers are at odds over Stephanie's punishment after they
catch her stealing petty items from around the house.

**196**   Barney the Gold Digger                    February 5, 1979
   **Writers:** Bob Schiller, Bob Weiskopf, Phil Sharp, Milt Josefsberg
   **Story:** Winston Moss
   **Director:** Paul Bogart
   **Guest Star:** Peggy Rea

Barney Hefner is suicidal when Blanche finally deserts him, until
Archie fixes him up with an overweight but wealthy widow.

**197**   Stephanie's Conversion                   February 18, 1979
   **Writers:** Patt Shea, Harriet Weiss
   **Director:** Paul Bogart
   **Guest Stars:** Clyde Kusatsu, Michael Mann

Archie is forced to reevaluate his religious prejudice after
Stephanie tries to conceal the fact that she's Jewish.

**198**   Edith Gets Fired                         February 25, 1979
   **Writers:** Patt Shea, Harriet Weiss
   **Story:** Mort Lachman
   **Director:** Paul Bogart
   **Guest Stars:** Angela Clarke, Dolores Sutton, Michael McGuire,
   Leonard Stone, Victor Kilian, Gerald Castillo

Edith loses her job at the Sunshine Home after she honors an in-
valid woman's final wish to be allowed to die with dignity.

**199**   The Best of All in the Family              March 4, 1979
   (ninety-minute special)
   **Director:** Walter Miller
   **Guest Star:** Norman Lear

Norman Lear hosts an affectionate look at the high points of his
ground-breaking TV series.

**200**   The Return of Archie's Brother            March 11, 1979
   **Writers:** Bob Schiller, Bob Weiskopf
   **Story:** Bob Schiller, Bob Weiskopf, Tom Sawyer
   **Director:** Paul Bogart
   **Guest Stars:** Richard Mackenzie, Ellissa Leeds

Archie's brother, Fred, arrives with his latest wife—a child bride of eighteen.

**201**   The Family Next Door                      March 18, 1979
   **Writers:** Mel Tolkin, Larry Rhine
   **Director:** Paul Bogart
   **Guest Stars:** Richard Ward, David Byrd, Isabel Sanford, Janet MacLachlan

Archie hits the roof when Edith rents out the old Jefferson house to a black couple.

**202**   The Return of Stephanie's Father          March 25, 1979
   **Writers:** Mel Tolkin, Larry Rhine
   **Director:** Paul Bogart
   **Guest Stars:** Ben Stack, Victor Kilian, Rick Plastina, Charles Wagenheim, Hugh McPhillips

Stephanie's father, Floyd, finally arrives with a devastating proposition for the Bunkers: They can keep Stephanie if they agree to pay him $1000 cash!

**203**   Too-Good Edith                            April 8, 1979
   **Writers:** Patt Shea, Harriet Weiss
   **Director:** Paul Bogart
   **Guest Star:** George Wyner

Archie is hurt and outraged when Edith tries to hide a serious illness from him.

There's a funny exchange between Archie and Edith in one of the very last episodes that reveals with pristine clarity the underlying optimism of the show. Archie is railing at the top of his lungs—dead-set against befriending the black family that's just moved in next door. Edith patiently waits for him to finish and continues preparing sandwiches for the new neighbors.

Miffed by her lack of sympathy, Archie moans, "You know damn well there's certain things about me I ain't never gonna change. But you keep asking me to make out like I'm gonna."

Edith pauses, then replies with a comical certainty, "That's right."

And so the series ends as it began, with Archie cursing the darkness, as Edith lights a candle and patiently waits for some small sign of progress. Things haven't really changed much since we first met the Bunkers at their twenty-second anniversary party so many years ago. Then, as now, Archie held forth in blustery ignorance as he demanded that Edith stifle herself at the first sign of rebuttal. And yet there is one small—but very encouraging—difference: This time, it's Edith who gets in the last word.

It's a telling irony that, by the time *All in the Family* left the air in 1979, so many of the sweeping societal changes that had taken place during our nine years with the Bunkers had already started to seem like they'd never taken place. The show dawned during the peak of Nixon's reign and reached its inevitable conclusion just as another Republican readied his own assault on the White House.

By the end of the decade, equal opportunity for blacks in television appeared to be just another program trend that had run its course. And for all the vaunted inroads *All in the Family* made in prime-time sophistication, by 1979 the most-watched show in the land was a slight comedy about a bachelor who shared a disarmingly platonic arrangement with a pair of perky female roommates.

Of course, it was Norman Lear himself who warned against pinning too much hope on what was, after all, just a television show. As he admits, "If a couple thousand years of Judeo-Christian ethic have not solved the problems of bigotry and narrow-mindedness, I'd be a fool to think a little half-hour situation comedy is gonna do the trick."

## EMMY AWARDS

The following is a complete listing of the Emmy Awards bestowed on *All in the Family* by the National Academy of Television Arts and Sciences.

**1970-71**    Outstanding Comedy Series
Outstanding New Series
Outstanding Continued Performance by an Actress in a
Leading Role in a Comedy Series: Jean Stapleton

**1971-72**  Outstanding Series: Comedy
Outstanding Continued Performance by an Actor in a
  Leading Role in a Comedy Series: Carroll O'Connor
Outstanding Continued Performance by an Actress in a
  Leading Role in a Comedy Series: Jean Stapleton
Outstanding Performance by an Actress in a Supporting
  Role in Comedy: Sally Struthers (tied with Valerie
  Harper)
Outstanding Directorial Achievement in Comedy: John
  Rich, "Sammy's Visit"
Outstanding Writing Achievement in Comedy: Burt Styler,
  "Edith's Problem"

**1972-73**  Outstanding Comedy Series
Outstanding Writing Achievement in Comedy: Michael
  Ross, Bernie West, Lee Kalcheim, "The Bunkers and the
  Swingers"

**1973-74**  Outstanding Supporting Actor in a Comedy Series: Rob
  Reiner

**1976-77**  Outstanding Lead Actor in a Comedy Series: Carroll
  O'Connor

**1977-78**  Outstanding Comedy Series
Outstanding Writing in a Comedy Series: Bob Schiller, Bob
  Weiskopf, teleplay; Barry Harmon, Harve Brosten, story,
  "Cousin Liz"
Outstanding Directing in a Comedy Series: Paul Bogart,
  "Edith's Fiftieth Birthday"
Outstanding Continuing Performance by a Supporting Actor
  in a Comedy Series: Rob Reiner
Outstanding Lead Actress in a Comedy Series: Jean
  Stapleton
Outstanding Lead Actor in a Comedy Series: Carroll
  O'Connor

**1978-79**  Outstanding Lead in a Comedy Series: Carroll O'Connor
Outstanding Supporting Actress in a Comedy Series: Sally
  Struthers, "California, Here We Are"

# M*A*S*H

·

*War is hell. So is TV.*
—LARRY GELBART

D<small>R</small>. R<small>ICHARD</small> H<small>ORNBERGER</small> figured that his profits from *M\*A\*S\*H*—in surgeon's terms—came to about one gall bladder per episode.

Or about $300 a week, which is what Twentieth Century-Fox Studios promised the small-town doctor—and part-time novelist—when they negotiated the television rights to *M\*A\*S\*H* in 1971. Hornberger, who, under the pen name Richard Hooker, had written the novel that spawned Fox's 1970 hit film *M\*A\*S\*H,* thought it sounded like a fair deal, though he had little reason to believe that the series would last more than a few weeks.

Fortunately, Fred Silverman was somewhat more optimistic. As the man most responsible for the CBS network's prime-time schedule in 1972, Silverman knew that controversy was in—the staggering numbers that *All in the Family* delivered every week left little doubt of that. So, when William Self, the head of the Twentieth Century-Fox TV unit, called CBS to pitch his idea of spinning off a series from the popular *M\*A\*S\*H* movie, the network programmer snapped it up. After all, what could be more controversial than a bawdy, bloody antiwar comedy?

Nothing. And that's what worried producer Gene Reynolds when he was assigned to develop the project. He loved Robert Altman's irreverent movie, but he also knew how easily network meddling could emas-

248

culate a powder keg like *M*A*S*H*. Finally, after CBS promised him a free hand, he decided that it might be worth a try.

He flew to England to work out the details of the pilot script with Larry Gelbart, an expatriate American screenwriter then living in London. "We felt an obligation not to make the series a homogenized imitation of the film," Gelbart recalled. "CBS threw us a terrific curve. They agreed."

After Reynolds flew back to the States, Gelbart crafted a script that was a brilliant subversion of TV's traditional service comedy; in fact, the plotline of Gelbart's initial *M*A*S*H* script would be instantly familiar to anyone who'd ever seen an episode of *McHale's Navy*: a gang of fun-loving Army surgeons stage a drunken bash that's foiled when a strict general drops by for a surprise inspection. But in Gelbart's version, the party doesn't end until the war begins.

The air fills with choppers carrying a precious cargo—the bodies of maimed and wounded men, fresh from the front lines. The hijinks end abruptly as the doctors scrub up to begin their cycle of insanity once again. They stitch and patch the broken soldiers until they're well enough to go back out and get shot at all over again. It was situation comedy as absurdist drama.

It was also a thinly veiled satire of contemporary U.S. foreign policy. Taking a cue from the original film, Gelbart and Reynolds viewed the series as their contribution to the swelling antiwar movement. "We were doing a story about the Korean War, but it was really about Vietnam," explained Reynolds. "A lot of our stories were Vietnam stories."

Apparently untroubled by Reynolds' and Gelbart's edgy approach, CBS wasted little time adding the series to its fall 1972 schedule. But, as Reynolds would discover once the show was in production, not everyone at the network was entirely comfortable with the show's darker ambiguities. At one point CBS suggested that the producers tone down the tense operating-room scenes so as not to offend viewers. That's when Reynolds and Gelbart knew that it was time to assert themselves. "Gene and I decided to offend the network and put in as many such scenes as we could," said Gelbart.

But the series's mixed critical response and lackluster ratings certainly didn't help their case. After the show finished the season slumped in forty-sixth place, the *M*A*S*H* company was almost surprised to hear that they'd actually been renewed for a second year.

The show had been saved by Fred Silverman, who was convinced that the series could make it, if only it was allowed to find its audience. To prove his point, he rescheduled the comedy to a slot where no one could miss it—Saturday nights, following the megahit *All in the Family*. And sure enough, *M*A*S*H* became an instant—if somewhat belated—hit.

"As our ratings climbed," observed Gelbart, "corporate resistance fell." Not surprisingly, Gelbart and Gene Reynolds wasted no time putting their creative liberties to good use. By the end of the third season, the show had tackled a raft of topics that were rarely broached on network TV—including homosexuality, interracial marriage, adultery, military genocide, and transvestitism.

As the content of the shows grew more sophisticated and varied, so did the personnel of the 4077th. Reynolds and his associate producer, former casting director Burt Metcalfe, had assembled a powerful ensemble that included Alan Alda, McLean Stevenson, Gary Burghoff, Larry Linville, Wayne Rogers, and Loretta Swit: all of whom were anxious to grow beyond the limitations that their characters had inherited from the original film. But it was Hawkeye Pierce who emerged as the voice of the 4077th from the very start. Alan Alda radiated intelligence, sensitivity, and the incongruous charm of a class clown—a combination that made him a natural anchor for the series's sincere irreverence.

Gelbart readily confessed his own fondness for the character. "It was the first time that I ever tried writing a character who would speak as I do, act as I do—or at least as the idealized *I* do," he told reporter Marshall Berges. "After years of writing material that would conform with a performer's image, I was able to try molding one to my own."

Ironically, Alda's galvanizing effect on the series also brought about the show's first major rift, when Wayne Rogers made it clear that he wasn't pleased with Hawkeye's growing dominance. Rogers' repeated protests finally ended in a string of bitter, and ultimately unsuccessful, contract negotiations.

"I know who I am and where I'm going," Rogers told a *TV Guide* reporter at the time. "If both CBS and Twentieth Century-Fox burned down tomorrow, I'd retire to a small intellectual community and be a professional student for the rest of my life." At the close of the third season, Rogers walked away from the series and never looked back.

The producers dealt with another contract dispute in a more ingenious fashion, when McLean Stevenson grew restless to break out on his own during the show's second and third years. "I'm tired of being one of six," he complained. "I want to be one of one."

When Stevenson made it clear that he wouldn't be returning for a fourth year, the producers planned Colonel Blake's final appearance in absolute secrecy. When the actor got his copy of the complete script of his farewell episode, he was shocked to discover that Colonel Blake was to be shot down over the Sea of Japan after his final exit. "I felt it was vindictive," he told David Reiss, author of *M*A*S*H: The Exclusive, Inside Story of Television's Most Popular Show*, "that the real motive was to prevent me from doing a show where I might want to continue being Henry Blake, M.D." But after his anger softened, he was forced to admit, "It did make one hell of a show."

To Gelbart and Reynolds, the circumstances of the actor's departure afforded them a rare opportunity to make a statement about war that would carry an emotional impact that viewers wouldn't soon forget. "By killing a cherished character," Gelbart told *Newsweek*, "you can approximate the feeling of losing someone you love."

By the time new recruits Mike Farrell, Harry Morgan, and David Ogden Stiers signed on, there would be less outright silliness and robust sexuality on the show as the producers moved the series away from the madcap antics of the original film.

"We couldn't just keep repeating, 'War is hell, war is hell,'" Burt Metcalfe remarked not long after he and Alan Alda took over the show's supervision in the series's final years. "So we started really exploring the characters and allowing them to evolve."

But as the staff of the 4077th grew more sympathetic in the show's later seasons, there was an ever-present danger that they'd sacrifice the comic bite that gave the series its edge. And indeed, by mid-point in the show's evolution, Margaret Houlihan had left her "Hot Lips" moniker behind, only to emerge as an incongruous humanitarian in tailor-made dungarees; and the show's creeping nobility eventually turned Hawkeye into a insufferable "saint in surgical garb"—exactly the sort of windbag that he would've punctured with the business end of his surgeon's rapier in earlier shows. As Larry Gelbart observed in *People* some years after his departure from the series he helped create, "I'm not a big fan of commercial heart. In a comedy you also have to kick the character with heart in the ass. If you don't, you lose crispness, friction, conflict, drama . . . and comedy, too."

By the tenth season, the cast and writing staff openly acknowledged the creative strain that had set in. "Alan and I find it increasingly difficult to come up with story material," Burt Metcalfe told TV columnist Gary Deeb. "Some of us feel it would be a good idea to end the series while we're still on top in terms of both ratings and quality. But CBS and the studio would like to keep it going a lot longer."

At the end of the tenth year, the cast took a vote to decide the fate of *M*A*S*H*. Jamie Farr, William Christopher, and Harry Morgan put thumbs up, but found themselves outvoted by Alan Alda, David Ogden

Stiers, Loretta Swit, and Mike Farrell—all of whom balked at returning for another year. And so it was decided: the tenth season would be the last year for *M\*A\*S\*H*.

But the executives at Twentieth Century-Fox and CBS approached Alan Alda with a counter-offer. If the actor could convince the cast to return for one final year, the network would allow them to film an abbreviated season of only sixteen episodes, with a grand finale that would be the most ambitious single TV show ever filmed: a final, feature-length farewell episode.

The gambit worked.

Alda couldn't resist the opportunity to cap the series in so grandiose a fashion. At the last minute he swung his vote in favor of doing an eleventh, and unequivocally final, season.

The climactic two-and-one-half-hour episode, "Good-Bye, Farewell and Amen," aired to unprecedented media hoopla and went on to become the single highest-rated program in television history, seen by an incredible 125 million viewers. The demise of the TV series received as much, if not more, attention than had the actual Korean War ceasefire three decades earlier.

Which is an appropriate irony for a show that brought the war into our living rooms in a way that no wire service or news broadcast could hope to. "We weren't kidding ourselves, though," Alan Alda acknowledged once the series had shut down. "We did enough research on war to know there's a vast difference between what we did on the show from 8:00 A.M. to 8:00 P.M. and the people who bled real blood."

But if the TV show was incapable of delivering the wounds of battle in all their graphic horror, the series never flinched in its depiction of the equally violent wounds wrought by boredom, loneliness, and the sorrow that is the inevitable yield of prolonged exposure to human suffering. And yet, even in the bleakest moments, the silliness of a practical joke—or the kindness of a shared affection—would pop up as a hopeful reminder of the indomitability of the human spirit. There were some things, we came to see, even more powerful than the ravages of war.

It was a complex message—both funny and sad. And the show's uncompromising treatment of these conflicting emotions provides a clue to the series's timeless appeal. In their finest half hours, the cast and creators of *M\*A\*S\*H* didn't seem to care whether we laughed or cried—just so long as we never stopped watching.

# A Critical Guide to All 251 Episodes

REGULAR CAST

| | |
|---|---|
| Captain Hawkeye Pierce | Alan Alda |
| Captain Trapper John McIntyre | Wayne Rogers |
| Lieutenant Col. Henry Blake | McLean Stevenson |
| Captain B. J. Hunnicut | Mike Farrell |
| Major Margaret "Hot Lips" Houlihan | Loretta Swit |
| Major Frank Burns | Larry Linville |
| Corporal Radar O'Reilly | Gary Burghoff |
| Colonel Sherman Potter | Harry Morgan |
| Major Charles Winchester | David Ogden Stiers |
| Corporal Max Klinger | Jamie Farr |
| Father John Mulcahy | William Christopher |

FIRST-SEASON SUPPORTING CAST

| | |
|---|---|
| Spearchucker Jones | Timothy Brown |
| Lieutenant Dish | Karen Philipp |
| Nurse Margie Cutler | Marcia Strassman |
| Lieutenant Ginger Ballis | Odessa Cleveland |
| General Hammond | G. Wood |
| Ho-John | Patrick Adiarte |
| Father Mulcahy (pilot episode) | George Morgan |
| Ugly John | John Orchard |
| Nurse Leslie Scorch | Linda Meiklejohn |
| Nurse Nancy Griffin | Lynnette Mettey |
| General Brandon Clayton | Herb Voland |

SUPPORTING CAST

| | |
|---|---|
| Nurse Kellye | Kellye Nakahara |
| Colonel Flagg | Edward Winter |
| Major Sidney Freedman | Allan Arbus |

| | |
|---|---|
| Sergeant Zelmo Zale | Johnny Haymer |
| Igor | Jeff Maxwell |
| Nurse Bigelow | Enid Kent |
| Luther Rizzo | G. W. Bailey |
| Lieutenant Colonel Donald Penobscott | Beeson Carroll, Mike Henry |
| Soon Lee | Rosalind Chao |

STOCK COMPANY

Bobbie Mitchell, Patricia Stevens, Judy Farrell, Tom Dever, Dennis Troy, Abby Nelson, Soon Teck Oh, Jan Jorden, Val Bisoglio

Created by Larry Gelbart, Gene Reynolds
Theme Song ("Suicide Is Painless") by Johnny Mandel
Directors of photography were William Jurgensen, Meredith Nicholson, Dominick R. Palmer
Principal directors were Gene Reynolds, Hy Averback, Jackie Cooper, Don Weis, William Jurgensen, Larry Gelbart, Burt Metcalfe, Charles S. Dubin, Alan Alda, George Tyne, Harry Morgan

## 1972-73    THE FIRST SEASON

*Year-End Rating: 17.5 (46th place)*

In their first season behind the lines of the Korean War, Hawkeye and Trapper John spend considerably more time chasing skirts than patching wounds in the operating room. But by the end of the year, producer Gene Reynolds and co-creator Larry Gelbart have evolved the bawdy and irreverent world of the 4077th mobile army surgical hospital into television's first true black comedy—a simultaneously grim and hilarious vision of war where laughter is the most potent weapon of defense.

In addition to executive story consultant Larry Gelbart's contributions, first-year scripts from Laurence Marks, Carl Kleinschmitt, and Sid Dorfman all help shape the series's early viewpoint. Burt Metcalfe is associate producer of the first four seasons, and William Jurgensen the director of photography for the first five. Stanford Tischler and Fred W. Berger are the show's regular editors for the first four years.

**1**      M*A*S*H Pilot                              September 17, 1972
   **Writer:** Larry Gelbart
   **Director:** Gene Reynolds
   **Guest Stars:** Karen Philipp, Patrick Adiarte, G. Wood, Timothy
   Brown, Linda Meiklejohn, Laura Miller, George Morgan

Iconoclastic Army surgeons Hawkeye Pierce and Trapper John
McIntyre throw a drunken bash to raise money to send their Korean houseboy to a U.S. college.

A remarkable episode that established the show's major characters in
a black comedy of absurd proportions. In one fell blow, the barracks
buffoonery of Sergeant Bilko and Gomer Pyle was rendered hopelessly
and shamefully irrelevant.

Karen Philipp appeared—briefly—as Lieutenant Dish, one of the characters from the film who failed to survive the transition to the small
screen. Timothy Brown's Spearchucker Jones, the 4077th's black surgeon,
was another prominent movie holdover in early episodes; he even bunked
with Hawkeye and Trapper John before he was quietly shipped out midway through the season. Writer Larry Gelbart maintains that the black
doctor was dropped after research revealed that there simply *weren't any*
black surgeons in Korea. But whatever the reason for Spearchucker's
demise, it's clear that the show's writers had no idea where to go with
the blandly written character from the very start.

**2**   To Market, To Market                          September 24, 1972
   **Writer:** Burt Styler
   **Director:** Michael O'Herlihy
   **Guest Stars:** G. Wood, Robert Ito, Jack Soo, John C. Johnson

Hawkeye hopes to replenish dwindling medical supplies by trading Henry's antique desk for a shipment of black-market hydro-
cortisone.

Jack Soo plays a Korean black-marketeer here, though the late character actor would be better remembered as Japanese detective Nick Yemena
on *Barney Miller*.

**3**   Requiem for a Lightweight                      October 1, 1972
   **Writer:** Bob Klane
   **Director:** Hy Averback
   **Guest Stars:** Marcia Strassman, Sorrell Booke, Mike McGirr

Trapper John is sorely mismatched when he faces a massive opponent in an intercamp boxing tournament.

Hawkeye and Trapper John both vie for the attention of Nurse Margie Cutler, whose tour of duty at the 4077th barely outlasts the first season.

**4    Chief Surgeon Who?**                        October 8, 1972
**Writer:** Larry Gelbart
**Director:** E.W. Swackhamer
**Guest Stars:** Linda Meiklejohn, Jack Riley, Sorrell Booke, Timothy Brown, Odessa Cleveland, Jamie Farr

Jealous when Hawkeye is appointed chief surgeon, Frank summons a flabbergasted general to look in on the unorthodox leisure activities of the new head doctor.

There's a gag in this episode about a GI so desperate for a psychiatric discharge that he wears women's clothes—inspired, according to Larry Gelbart, by Lenny Bruce, who attempted a similar gambit to get thrown out of the Navy. The sight gag would eventually blossom into financial security for bit player Jamie Farr, but it very nearly got left on the cutting-room floor. In director E.W. Swackhamer's first cut, he had Farr play the transvestite as an effeminate swish—a cliché that sent the producers scrambling for a retake. Reynolds did reshoot it. The second time the actors played it straight, the bit was much funnier, and in no time at all, Corporal Max Klinger was a fixture on the series.

**5    The Moose**                        October 15, 1972
**Writer:** Laurence Marks
**Director:** Hy Averback
**Guest Stars:** Paul Jenkins, Virginia Lee, Craig Jue, Barbara Brownell, Patrick Adiarte, Tim Brown

Incensed when a GI arrives with a Korean teenager he bought as a slave, Hawkeye conspires to emancipate the girl and restore her self-respect.

The writers often drew stories from actual historical detail, such as this one, in which a Korean family's practice of arcane indentured-servitude rituals spurs the characters to action. The unstinting research paid off: Letters commending or correcting the show's accuracy began to pour in from veteran MASH doctors, most of whom were anxious to share their own wartime experiences. Over the years, these rich and detailed first-hand accounts of war would form the basis for some of the show's strongest episodes.


**6**   Yankee Doodle Doctor                    October 22, 1972
**Writer:** Laurence Marks
**Director:** Lee Philips
**Guest Stars:** Ed Flanders, Bert Kramer, Herb Voland

The doctors rebel when they discover that the Army plans to make a propaganda film glorifying the depressing conditions of war.


**7**   Bananas, Crackers, and Nuts             November 5, 1972
**Writer:** Burt Styler
**Director:** Bruce Bilson
**Guest Star:** Stuart Margolin

Hawkeye acts even crazier than usual after he's denied a weekend pass to Tokyo.


**8**   Cowboy                                  November 12, 1972
**Writer:** Bob Klane
**Director:** Don Weis
**Guest Stars:** Billy Green Bush, Alicia Bond, Rick Moses, Joe Corey

The 4077th copes with a shell-shocked helicopter pilot who turns to violence after Henry denies his discharge back to the States.

Don Weis, one of the first-season directors of *The Andy Griffith Show*, would continue as a *M*A*S*H* director for four of the first six seasons.


**9**   Henry, Please Come Home                 November 19, 1972
**Writer:** Laurence Marks
**Director:** William Wiard
**Guest Star:** G. Wood

When Colonel Blake's transfer to Tokyo leaves Frank Burns in command, Hawkeye and Trapper wage a campaign to get their beloved—and tolerant—commanding officer back in the fold.

**10**    I Hate a Mystery                              November 26, 1972
  **Writer:** Hal Dresner
  **Director:** Hy Averback
  **Guest Stars:** Bonnie Jones, Linda Meiklejohn

Hawkeye decides to play detective when he becomes the chief suspect in a rash of petty thefts.

Hy Averback started out as a radio announcer before he distinguished himself as one of the most prolific television directors of the 1950s and 1960s. He would be the only early *M\*A\*S\*H* director to continue with the show throughout its run.

The producers weren't as happy with some of the other first-year directors, most of whom had made their reputations directing a mixed bag of one-camera sitcoms during the 1960s. After a few run-ins with unsympathetic—or just plain confused—directors, Gelbart, and later Reynolds and Alda, added directing to their other duties. Together they would nurture the show through its first fledgling seasons, along with a handful of returning first-year directors, including Averback, Don Weis, William Wiard, and Jackie Cooper.

**11**    Germ Warfare                              December 10, 1972
  **Writer:** Larry Gelbart
  **Director:** Terry Becker
  **Guest Stars:** Robert Gooden, Karen Philipp, Byron Chung

Frank is the unwitting donor in an emergency blood transfusion when Hawkeye extracts a pint from the major while he sleeps.

**12**    Dear Dad                              December 17, 1972
  **Writer:** Larry Gelbart
  **Director:** Gene Reynolds
  **Guest Stars:** Bonnie Jones, Lizabeth Deen, Gary Van Orman

During a lull in surgery, Hawkeye composes a Christmas letter to his dad describing the simple joys and endless dread of daily life in a war zone.

In one of his earliest attempts to stretch the narrative boundaries of situation comedy, Gelbart allowed the audience to look at life through the surgeon's eyes, as Hawkeye narrates the episode as a letter he's written to his dad. The script was more influential than anyone guessed at the time; it established Hawkeye as the show's empathetic voice, just as Gelbart was discovering his own voice in the character.

**13**   Edwina                                December 24, 1972
   **Writer:** Hal Dresner
   **Director:** James Sheldon
   **Guest Stars:** Arlene Golonka, Linda Meiklejohn, Marcia
   Strassman

The nurses band together to find a date for an accident-prone
nurse.

**14**   Love Story                              January 7, 1973
   **Writer:** Laurence Marks
   **Director:** Earl Bellamy
   **Guest Stars:** Kelly Jean Peters, Indira Danks, Barbara Brownell,
   Jerry Harper

Trapper and Hawkeye offer Radar a crash course in music and lit-
erature when they fix him up with a nurse who's culturally inclined.

Though few were aware of it at the time, four years earlier guest star
Kelly Jean Peters had originated the role of Gloria in the earliest pilot for
the series that would become *All in the Family.*

**15**   Tuttle                                 January 14, 1973
   **Writers:** Bruce Shelly, David Ketchum
   **Director:** William Wiard
   **Guest Stars:** Herb Voland, Mary-Robin Redd, James Sikking

The medics create a fictitious captain so that they can donate his
Army salary to an orphanage.

**16**   The Ringbanger                         January 21, 1973
   **Writer:** Jerry Mayer
   **Director:** Jackie Cooper
   **Guest Stars:** Leslie Nielsen, Linda Meiklejohn

Trapper and Hawkeye conspire to have an overzealous commander shipped back home to protect the troops from his military
enthusiasm.

Director Jackie Cooper was a former child star who had grown up to
star in two successful sitcoms of the 1950s, *The People's Choice* and
*Hennesey,* which he also produced. It was on the latter series that the
actor gave Gene Reynolds—himself a retired child actor—an opportu-

nity to direct. Reynolds returned the favor on *M\*A\*S\*H*, where Cooper would eventually direct the majority of episodes in the series's second year.

**17**     Sometimes You Hear the Bullet                    January 28, 1973
   **Writer:** Carl Kleinschmitt
   **Director:** William Waird
   **Guest Stars:** James Callahan, Ronny Howard, Lynnette Mettey

Hawkeye mourns the sudden death of an old friend on his operating table.

Alan Alda cited this episode as the series's first real groundbreaker. "It was the first time on our show that a sympathetic and charming character had died," the actor wrote in *TV Guide*. It was a breakthrough that was largely lost on the confused executives at CBS, most of whom were unaccustomed to having death sprung on them between the toothpaste commercials of half-hour situation comedy. The producers held their ground by insisting that a soldier's sudden and unexpected death was an entirely appropriate subject for a comedy set in war. When the episode finally aired, it drove yet another nail into the coffin of the superfluous situation comedy of the 1960s.

A decade earlier, writer Carl Kleinschmitt had been a prolific contributor to the original *Dick Van Dyke Show*.

**18**     Dear Dad . . . Again                          February 4, 1973
   **Writer:** Sheldon Keller, Larry Gelbart
   **Director:** Jackie Cooper
   **Guest Stars:** Alex Henteloff, Gail Bowman, Odessa Cleveland

In another letter home, Hawkeye explains how he survives the perverse insanity of war by staying just one step ahead of the butterfly net.

**19**     The Long-John Flap                           February 18, 1973
   **Writer:** Alan Alda
   **Director:** William Wiard
   **Guest Stars:** Kathleen King, Joseph Perry

A coveted pair of long-johns arrive during a Korean cold spell and find their way into more than one *M\*A\*S\*H* footlocker before day's end.

A handful of TV actors had directed episodes of their own series before, and a few had even written scripts that could actually be filmed; but Alan Alda is probably the only actor ever to simultaneously direct, write, and star in a long-running television series. Not surprisingly, his early scripts reflect Gelbart's strong influence, though Alda would quickly develop his own voice, both as a writer and as a director.

**20**   The Army-Navy Game                    February 25, 1973
**Writer:** Sid Dorfman
**Story:** McLean Stevenson
**Director:** Gene Reynolds
**Guest Stars:** Alan Manson, David Doyle, Tom Richards

The medics' enjoyment of the radio broadcast of the Army-Navy game is seriously compromised when an undetonated bomb lands in the middle of camp.

**21**   Sticky Wicket                              March 4, 1973
**Writers:** Laurence Marks, Larry Gelbart
**Story:** Richard Baer
**Director:** Don Weis
**Guest Stars:** Wayne Bryan, Lynnette Mettey, Bonnie Jones

Hawkeye accuses Frank of incompetent surgery, only to discover that one of his own patients has suffered a mysterious relapse.

**22**   Major Fred C. Dobbs                     March 11, 1973
**Writer:** Sid Dorfman
**Director:** Don Weis
**Guest Stars:** Harvey J. Goldenberg

Frank is about to ship out of the 4077th, but Hawkeye and Trapper John trick him into staying on after they discover that his transfer doubles their workload.

The producers hadn't yet quite got their bearings, as this uncharacteristic episode proves. The script violates the basic premise of the characters in an inconsequential plot that veers dangerously into stock sitcom territory. Larry Gelbart would be so embarrassed by this episode that in later years he would remember it as simply "the worst."

**23**   Ceasefire                                        March 18, 1973
**Writers:** Laurence Marks, Larry Gelbart
**Story:** Larry Gelbart
**Director:** Earl Bellamy
**Guest Star:** Herb Voland

The 4077th makes premature plans to dismantle the camp when they hear rumors of a ceasefire.

The producers always kept an eye on the headlines as they fashioned their Vietnam allegory, so it's not entirely coincidental that this episode aired the same week that the United States began withdrawing troops from Vietnam. Surprisingly, the end of the fighting in Southeast Asia had very little effect on the show. The ceasefire might have dulled the show's urgency, but it didn't blunt its message. As Hawkeye observed in a Gelbart script aired two years later, "Wars don't last forever, only war does."

**24**   Showtime                                       March 25, 1973
**Writer:** Robert Klane, Larry Gelbart
**Story:** Larry Gelbart
**Director:** Jackie Cooper
**Guest Stars:** Joey Forman, Harvey Goldenberg, Stanley Clay, Sheila Lauritsen, Oksum Kim

A song-and-dance man performs a USO comedy show in stark counterpoint to the bleak goings on in the operating room.

## 1973-74   THE SECOND SEASON

*Year-End Rating: 25.7 (4th place)*

The comedy's ratings skyrocket after CBS sandwiches it between *All in the Family* and *The Mary Tyler Moore Show* on their Saturday-evening lineup, and the show swiftly rises to the challenge set by such sterling company. Hawkeye continues to anchor the comic drama, but other characters also emerge as distinct and complex personalities in second-year scripts that reveal unexpected depth of feeling in Trapper John, Colonel Blake, and, perhaps most surprising of all, Hot Lips.

Producer Gene Reynolds is officially joined by Larry Gelbart as co-producer. Gelbart also continues to write or polish every script, along with the equally prolific story editor, Laurence Marks. Together and separately, the pair write the majority of the season's episodes, most of which are directed by Jackie Cooper, William Wiard, Don Weis, or Gene Reynolds.

**25**   Divided We Stand                    September 15, 1973
  **Writer:** Larry Gelbart
  **Director:** Jackie Cooper
  **Guest Star:** Anthony Holland

The personnel of the 4077th are on their best behavior when they're visited by an Army observer intent on reassigning the unit.

Gelbart and Reynolds designed this first episode of the new season to serve as an unofficial second pilot; the idea was to reintroduce the show's major characters for the benefit of all the new viewers who would presumably be joining the series in its improved time slot.

**26**   Five O'Clock Charlie               September 22, 1973
  **Writer:** Larry Gelbart, Laurence Marks
  **Story:** Keith Walker
  **Director:** Norman Tokar

Frank is not amused when the camp starts placing bets on a bumbling enemy pilot's attempts to bomb an abandoned dump near the 4077th.

Director Norman Tokar had previously helmed *Leave It to Beaver* from 1957 to 1963.

**27**   Radar's Report                      September 29, 1973
  **Writer:** Laurence Marks
  **Story:** Sheldon Keller
  **Director:** Jackie Cooper
  **Guest Stars:** Joan Van Ark, Allan Arbus, Tom Dever

There's a raving POW loose in the O.R., and an Army psychiatrist tries to determine whether or not Klinger is certifiably nuts.

This is Allan Arbus's first appearance as Army psychiatrist Major Freedman, who would be a frequent guest at the 4077th over the next decade.

**28** For the Good of the Outfit October 6, 1973
**Writer:** Jerry Mayer
**Director:** Jackie Cooper
**Guest Star:** Frank Aletter

After the Army accidentally bombs a local village, Hawkeye and Trapper buck heads with a general when they refuse to cooperate in the military cover-up.

**29** Dr. Pierce and Mr. Hyde October 13, 1973
**Writers:** Alan Alda, Robert Klane
**Director:** Jackie Cooper

Hawkeye's behavior is unrestrained, even by *his* standards, when he refuses to slow his pace after a three-day marathon in the O.R.

**30** Kim October 20, 1973
**Writers:** Marc Mandel, Larry Gelbart, Laurence Marks
**Director:** William Wiard
**Guest Stars:** Leslie Evans, Edgar Raymond Miller, Ray Poss, Maggie Roswell, Momo Yashima

Trapper John decides to adopt an orphaned Korean refugee.

**31** L.I.P. (Local Indigenous Personnel) October 27, 1973
**Writer:** Carl Kleinschmitt
**Director:** William Wiard
**Guest Stars:** Corinne Camacho, Burt Young, Jerry Zaks

The doctors resort to blackmail to persuade a stubborn official who refuses to okay a young GI's marriage to a South Korean woman.

**32** The Trial of Henry Blake November 3, 1973
**Writers:** McLean Stevenson, Larry Gelbart, Laurence Marks
**Director:** Don Weis
**Guest Stars:** Hope Summers, Robert F. Simon, Jack Aaron

The hijinks of the 4077th fall under scrutiny when Colonel Blake faces a military hearing to determine whether he's fit for command.

Flashback sequences depict the 4077th in the throes of near-bacchanalian abandon that serve as a reminder of what a randy bunch the doctors and nurses of the 4077th were in the show's early years, when their libidinous shenanigans served as their chief refuge from the grim realities all around. It's a pity that the medics' carnal urges were tamed as the series developed—their earthier desires often provided the setting for some of the crew's funniest, and most authentic, wartime escapades.

**33**    Dear Dad . . . Three                    November 10, 1973
   **Writers:** Larry Gelbart, Laurence Marks
   **Director:** Don Weis
   **Guest Stars:** Mills Watson, Sivi Aberg, Arthur Abelson

In another letter home, Hawkeye describes his efforts to remove a live grenade from a wounded soldier's chest; and the staff gathers for an impromptu screening of Henry's home movies.

A masterful piece of storytelling begins when the doctors assemble in Blake's office, all prepared to snicker at his quaint home movies. We're encouraged to laugh along with the wisecracking doctors as we watch Henry onscreen—a Midwestern rube posturing and clowning for the shaky camera.

Then we see the screen through Henry Blake's eyes. We see the clumsy shadows of a child's birthday celebration as he does—a sweet and poignant vision of a simple time that suddenly seems so far away.

Blake fights back a tear, as do we. He's come to realize, as we have, that the carefree man dancing up there on the screen is already dead, an early casualty of war. In this short, elegiac sequence, writers Gelbart and Marks eloquently describe the worst war crime of all—the Army's dreadful capacity to smother a man's spirit . . . very, very slowly.

**34**    The Sniper                    November 17, 1973
   **Writer:** Richard M. Powell
   **Director:** Jackie Cooper
   **Guest Stars:** Teri Garr, Marcia Gelman, Dennis Troy

The sanctuary of the compound is threatened when the 4077th is besieged by a lone sniper.

Film actress Teri Garr has a pre-stardom role as one of the nurses in this episode.

**35**   Carry On, Hawkeye                    November 24, 1973
  **Writers:** Bernard Dilbert, Larry Gelbart, Laurence Marks
  **Story:** Bernard Dilbert
  **Director:** Jackie Cooper
  **Guest Stars:** Lynnette Mettey, Gwen Farrell, Marcia Gelman

Hawkeye and Hot Lips are the only medical personnel left standing after a flu epidemic hits the hospital.

The shortage of qualified doctors requires the head nurse to perform surgical duties far beyond her training or abilities, all of which she tackles with patience and stamina. Before the day is done, she has saved a boy's life with her own hands—and gained the first shreds of self-respect that would soon spur major changes for Hot Lips Houlihan.

**36**   The Incubator                    December 1, 1973
  **Writers:** Larry Gelbart, Laurence Marks
  **Director:** Jackie Cooper
  **Guest Stars:** Robert F. Simon, Logan Ramsey, Vic Tayback

Hawkeye and Trapper follow the military chain of command to the very top in their determination to secure an incubator for the compound.

**37**   Deal Me Out                    December 8, 1973
  **Writers:** Larry Gelbart, Laurence Marks
  **Director:** Gene Reynolds
  **Guest Stars:** Pat Morita, Allan Arbus, Edward Winter, John Ritter

Frank tries to prevent the doctors from operating on a wounded military intelligence officer for fear that he'll leak classified information while under sedation.

Edward Winter plays Captain Halloran, a prototype for Colonel Flagg, the malevolent patriot who would be a frequent visitor to the 4077th throughout the first five seasons.

**38**   Hot Lips and Empty Arms                    December 15, 1973
  **Writers:** Linda Bloodworth, Mary Kay Place
  **Director:** Jackie Cooper

Fed up with the limited horizons of her life at the 4077th, Hot Lips requests a transfer to another unit.

Gelbart and Reynolds commissioned a pair of twenty-five-year-old novice writers to script what they'd slated as "Loretta's show." Linda Bloodworth and Mary Kay Place interviewed Loretta Swit for hours before they finally wrote a story that sees Margaret questioning her life, her career, and perhaps most of all, her barren relationship with Frank Burns. By the end of the episode, the first stage of Margaret's evolution is complete. The strident, two-dimensional Army strumpet of the early shows has grown into a thinking, feeling, independent-minded woman.

Mary Kay Place would become better known as an actress, though Linda Bloodworth continued as a scripter for *M*A*S*H* and other television comedies. In 1986, as Linda Bloodworth Thomason, the writer would create and write *Designing Women* for CBS, a series that bore distinct echoes of her work on this early script.

**39**   Officers Only                          December 22, 1973
**Writer:** Ed Jurist
**Director:** Jackie Cooper
**Guest Stars:** Robert F. Simon, Robert Weaver, Clyde Kusatsu

Trapper and Hawkeye disagree with General Mitchell's restricted admissions policy for the new officer's club he's opened at the 4077th.

**40**   Henry in Love                              January 5, 1974
**Writers:** Larry Gelbart, Laurence Marks
**Director:** Don Weis
**Guest Stars:** Katharine Baumann, Odessa Cleveland, Sheila Lauritsen

Henry returns from Tokyo smitten by a cheerleader half his age, convinced that it's the real thing.

**41**   For Want of a Boot                         January 12, 1974
**Writer:** Sheldon Keller
**Director:** Don Weis
**Guest Stars:** Michael Lerner, Suzanne Zenor, Johnny Haymer

Hawkeye exchanges favors with everyone in camp in his efforts to get a new pair of boots.

A classic episode that shows the 4077th as one big, happy family— except that in this clan, everyone's out for himself. The supply sergeant wants his teeth fixed in exchange for the precious boots; the dentist demands a weekend pass for his services; and Radar barters his cooperation for a night with Nurse Murphy! Obviously, this episode occurred *before* Radar became a virgin. The refreshing lack of sentiment in this cynical roundelay typifies the sardonic humor that informed so much of the show's comedy in the early seasons.

**42**    Operation Noselift                          January 19, 1974
   **Writer:** Erik Tarloff
   **Story:** Paul Richards, Erik Tarloff
   **Director:** Hy Averback
   **Guest Star:** Stuart Margolin

Hawkeye and Trapper enlist the aid of an Army plastic surgeon to perform a nose job on a deserving GI.

**43**    The Chosen People                          January 26, 1974
   **Writers:** Laurence Marks, Sheldon Keller, Larry Gelbart
   **Story:** Gerry Renert, Jeff Wilheim
   **Director:** Jackie Cooper
   **Guest Stars:** Pat Morita, Clare Nono, Dennis Robertson, Jay Jay
   Jue, Jerry Fujikawa

A Korean family tries to reclaim the land under the 4077th as their own; and a young woman from the village declares Radar the father of her child.

**44**    As You Were                              February 2, 1974
   **Writers:** Larry Gelbart, Laurence Marks
   **Story:** Gene Reynolds
   **Director:** Hy Averback
   **Guest Star:** Patricia Stevens

The doctors agree to treat Frank's hernia during a lull in the action, only to face a new deluge of wounded while Burns lies incapacitated in post-op.

**45**    Crisis                                   February 9, 1974
   **Writers:** Larry Gelbart, Laurence Marks
   **Director:** Don Weis
   **Guest Stars:** Jeff Maxwell, Alberta Jay

Tempers flare when the 4077th faces a supply shortage of food and fuel during a frigid cold spell.

**46**   George                                    February 16, 1974
**Writers:** John Regier, Gary Markowitz
**Director:** Gene Reynolds
**Guest Stars:** Richard Ely, George Simmons

Hawkeye and Trapper scheme to prevent Frank from having a homosexual private drummed out of the corps.

**47**   Mail Call                                February 23, 1974
**Writers:** Larry Gelbart, Laurence Marks
**Director:** Alan Alda
**Guest Stars:** Dennis Troy, Sheila Lauritsen

Hawkeye can't resist teasing Frank with bogus stock-market tips after the major brags about his keen investments.

**48**   A Smattering of Intelligence             March 2, 1974
**Writers:** Larry Gelbart, Laurence Marks
**Director:** Larry Gelbart
**Guest Stars:** Edward Winter, Bill Fletcher

It's spy versus spy when the CIA's Colonel Flagg decides to get the goods on an Army intelligence agent who's been snooping around the 4077th.

## 1974-75   THE THIRD SEASON

*Year-End Rating: 27.4 (5th place)*

Larry Gelbart and Laurence Marks share third-season scripting chores with Jim Fritzell and Everett Greenbaum, notable additions to an overworked stable of writers that also includes Sid Dorfman and Simon Muntner, among others. Producers Gene Reynolds and Larry Gelbart bolster their third-year story sessions with anecdotes they've gathered during a tour of Korea's 43rd Army Surgical Hospital.

**49**   The General Flipped at Dawn             September 10, 1974
**Writers:** Jim Fritzell, Everett Greenbaum
**Director:** Larry Gelbart
**Guest Stars:** Harry Morgan, Lynnette Mettey, Theodore Wilson, Brad Trumbull, Dennis Erdman

The doctors suspect their new spit-and-polish commander is missing a few marbles after he threatens to move the 4077th out onto the battlefield.

When Harry Morgan's crazed general was shipped off to the Pentagon at the end of this episode, no one guessed that the accomplished character actor would return to the series as Henry Blake's replacement the very next season.

**50**    Rainbow Bridge                        September 17, 1974
   **Writers:** Larry Gelbart, Laurence Marks
   **Director:** Hy Averback
   **Guest Stars:** Mako, Leland Sun, Loudon Wainwright III

McIntyre and Pierce abandon their planned furlough when they travel into enemy territory to retrieve a group of wounded GIs.

**51**    Officer of the Day                     September 24, 1974
   **Writer:** Laurence Marks
   **Director:** Hy Averback
   **Guest Stars:** Edward Winter, Dennis Troy, Jeff Maxwell, Jerry Fujikawa, Tad Horino, Richard Lee Sung, Mitchell Sakamoto, Norman Hamano

While Henry vacations in Seoul, Hawkeye protects a wounded North Korean prisoner from Colonel Flagg, who wants to see the alleged spy executed.

**52**    Iron Guts Kelly                         October 1, 1974
   **Writers:** Larry Gelbart, Sid Dorfman
   **Director:** Don Weis
   **Guest Stars:** James Gregory, Keene Curtis, Byron Chung

A visiting general suffers a fatal heart attack in the throes of passion on Hot Lips' bed, and his loyal aide schemes to give the commander a hero's funeral.

From the general's entrance—pearl-handled pistols at his side—to his final send-off in an ambulance packed with prostitutes, this first-rate effort from Gelbart and Dorfman ranks among the season's best: a sardonic black comedy that employs the medium of laughter to deliver a trenchant message on the folly of those who seek glory in war.

**53   O. R.**                                  October 8, 1974
   **Writers:** Larry Gelbart, Laurence Marks
   **Director:** Gene Reynolds
   **Guest Stars:** Allan Arbus, Bobbie Cleveland, Bobby Herbeck,
   Orlando Dole, Jeanne Schulherr, Roy Goldman, Leland Sun

The staff faces an unrelenting day in the operating theater as casualties continue to mount, with no end in sight.

Set entirely in the O.R., the story builds on the stark drama of life and death as the doctors struggle to save those who can be saved and move the rest out as quickly as possible. It's an uncompromising episode, and though not without humor, it was one of the earliest episodes aired minus a laugh track. Despite the network's early objection to scenes set in the O.R., the producers steadfastly refused to compromise the impact of those sequences by dubbing in canned laughter. "It's hard to imagine the audience belly laughing at bowel surgery," quipped Gelbart.

**54   Springtime**                             October 15, 1974
   **Writers:** Linda Bloodworth, Mary Kay Place
   **Director:** Don Weis
   **Guest Stars:** Alex Karras, Mary Kay Place, Greg Mabrey

In spring, even an enlisted man's fancy turns to romance—a maxim that's borne out when Radar and Klinger are both stung by Cupid's arrow.

Writer Mary Kay Place scripted herself into this episode in the role of Louise, the willing object of Radar's affection. Two years later, the actress would achieve considerable acclaim for her portrayal of Loretta Haggers on *Mary Hartman, Mary Hartman.*

**55   Checkup**                                October 22, 1974
   **Writers:** Laurence Marks
   **Director:** Don Weis
   **Guest Stars:** Jeff Maxwell, Patricia Stevens

The camp throws a teary farewell party for Trapper John when he discovers that his ulcer guarantees him a one-way ticket home.

Though a last-minute technicality spoils Trapper's clean break this time, Hawkeye's stirring—if premature—farewell speech would have to do. There would be no time for more formal good-byes a few months later when Wayne Rogers' leave-taking forced his character's equally abrupt departure at the end of the season.

**56**    Life With Father                        October 29, 1974
    **Writers:** Everett Greenbaum, Jim Fritzell
    **Director:** Hy Averback
    **Guest Star:** Sachiko Penny Lee

Henry suspects his wife may be having an affair; and Father Mulcahy officiates at an infant's circumcision.

This was the second *M\*A\*S\*H* script from Everett Greenbaum and Jim Fritzell, a veteran comedy team with impeccable credits—they'd scripted *Mr. Peepers* in the 1950s and written some of the finest episodes of *The Andy Griffith Show* in the 1960s.

**57**    Alcoholics Unanimous                    November 12, 1974
    **Writers:** Everett Greenbaum, Jim Fritzell
    **Director:** Hy Averback
    **Guest Star:** Bobbie Mitchell

In Henry's absence, Frank uses his executive powers to declare a prohibition at the 4077th.

**58**    There Is Nothing Like a Nurse          November 19, 1974
    **Writers:** Larry Gelbart
    **Director:** Hy Averback
    **Guest Stars:** Molli Benson, Leland Sun, Jeanne Schulherr, Loudon Wainwright III

The compound becomes more hellish than usual when the threat of enemy invasion forces the nurses to evacuate the 4077th.

**59**    Adam's Ribs                            November 26, 1974
    **Writer:** Laurence Marks
    **Director:** Gene Reynolds
    **Guest Stars:** Basil Hoffman, Joe Stern, Jeff Maxwell

Fed up with Army rations, Hawkeye places an order by shortwave to his favorite Chicago barbecue joint: forty pounds of ribs . . . to go.

**60**    A Full, Rich Day                         December 3, 1974
   **Writer:** John D. Hess
   **Director:** Gene Reynolds
   **Guest Stars:** William Watson, Sirri Murad, Curt Lowens

Hawkeye's latest letter home describes a typical day at the 4077th: There's a mad Turk in the operating room, and the doctors have misplaced the body of an officer who may, or may not, be dead.

**61**    Mad Dogs and Servicemen              December 10, 1974
   **Writers:** Linda Bloodworth, Mary Kay Place
   **Director:** Hy Averback
   **Guest Stars:** Michael O'Keefe, Shizuko Hoshi, Arthur Song

Radar tries to find the potentially rabid dog who bit him; and the surgeons treat a corporal suffering from psychosomatic paralysis.

**62**    Private Charles Lamb                     December 31, 1974
   **Writers:** Larry Gelbart, Sid Dorfman
   **Director:** Hy Averback
   **Guest Stars:** Ted Eccles, Titos Vandis, Gene Chronopolous

Radar almost sparks an international incident when he rescues a lamb from the skewer of a Greek regiment's Easter feast.

**63**    Bombed                                   January 7, 1975
   **Writers:** Everett Greenbaum, Jim Fritzell
   **Director:** Hy Averback
   **Guest Stars:** Louisa Moritz, Edward Marshall

The medics continue to operate on incoming wounded, despite a steady barrage that threatens to blow the camp apart at the seams.

**64**    Bulletin Board                           January 14, 1975
   **Writers:** Larry Gelbart, Simon Muntner
   **Director:** Alan Alda
   **Guest Star:** Johnny Haymer

Posted camp activities include a picnic and a Shirley Temple movie.

**65**   The Consultant                              January 21, 1975
  **Writers:** Larry Gelbart, Robert Klane
  **Director:** Gene Reynolds
  **Guest Stars:** Robert Alda, Joseph Maher, Tad Horino

Hawkeye is deeply disappointed when a visiting specialist gets too drunk to perform a vital operation to save a soldier's leg.

Alan Alda's father joins him in this episode, a dramatic vehicle tailor-made for both generations of the acting clan.

**66**   House Arrest                                February 4, 1975
  **Writers:** Jim Fritzell, Everett Greenbaum
  **Director:** Hy Averback
  **Guest Stars:** Mary Wickes, Jeff Maxwell, Dennis Troy

Hawkeye nearly faces a court-martial after he gets carried away during one of his petty squabbles with Frank Burns.

**67**   Aid Station                                 February 11, 1975
  **Writers:** Larry Gelbart, Simon Muntner
  **Director:** William Jurgensen
  **Guest Star:** Tom Dever

Margaret and Hawkeye provide emergency aid at the front lines when they're sent into battle with Corporal Klinger.

Klinger suits up in regular Army fatigues when the chips are down, prefiguring the character's eventual position of responsibility much later in the series. Hot Lips, too, undergoes a change when she earns the men's respect with her cool performance under battle conditions. By the end of the episode, she and Hawkeye raise their mugs in a silent toast that only hints at the major changes yet to come.

**68**   Love and Marriage                           February 18, 1975
  **Writer:** Arthur Julian
  **Director:** Lee Philips
  **Guest Stars:** Soon Teck Oh, Dennis Dugan, Pat Li, Jerry Fujikawa

Trapper and Hawkeye attempt to unite one enlisted man with his pregnant wife and try to prevent another from marrying a Korean prostitute.

**69**   Big Mac                                    February 25, 1975
**Writers:** Laurence Marks
**Director:** Don Weis
**Guest Stars:** Graham Jarvis, Bob Courtleigh, Jeanne Schulherr, Loudon Wainwright III

The camp prepares for a visit from Commanding General Douglas MacArthur.

**70**   Payday                                        March 4, 1975
**Writers:** John Regier, Gary Markowitz
**Director:** Hy Averback
**Guest Stars:** Jack Soo, Eldon Quick, Johnny Haymer, Mary Katherine Peters, Leland Sun, George Holloway, Pat Marshall

Hawkeye is surprised when a military oversight nets him an extra $3000 paycheck.

**71**   White Gold                                   March 11, 1975
**Writers:** Larry Gelbart, Simon Muntner
**Director:** Hy Averback
**Guest Stars:** Edward Winter, Hilly Hicks, Stafford Repp

When valuable supplies of penicillin begin to disappear, the doctors suspect the involvement of CIA operative Colonel Flagg.

**72**   Abyssinia, Henry                             March 18, 1975
**Writers:** Everett Greenbaum, Jim Fritzell
**Director:** Larry Gelbart
**Guest Stars:** Kimiko Hiroshige, Virginia Lee, Cherylene Lee, Ray Poss

With the memory of Colonel Blake's gala farewell party still fresh in their minds, the 4077th is shocked to learn that the commanding officer's plane has just been shot down over the Sea of Japan.

The producers weren't content to simply write Blake out of the series after the actor voluntarily left the show. "Faced with the show-business reality of one of the star players wanting out," Larry Gelbart explained in *The New York Times*, "we looked for a bold solution to his disappearance consistent with the series's view of the wastefulness of war. Angry viewers [later] accused us of trying to make them unhappy, as if the warranty that came with their sets promised them only happy moments of viewing."

## 1975-76   THE FOURTH SEASON

*Year-End Rating: 22.9 (14th place)*

With the departure of Colonel Blake and Trapper John, the series enters a second, more subdued phase, as new recruits B.J. Hunnicut and Colonel Sherman Potter—played by Mike Farrell and Harry Morgan—are integrated into the tightly knit ensemble. The new characters are less zany than their predecessors, and far more noble—a development that gradually affects the tone of the show in this and future seasons.

Larry Gelbart and the team of Jim Fritzell and Everett Greenbaum write most of the season's scripts, with significant contributions from Simon Muntner, Jay Folb, and Burt Prelutsky, among others. Associate producer Burt Metcalfe, cinematographer William Jurgensen, and actor Harry Morgan all make their directing debuts, although most fourth-season shows are directed by Alan Alda, Larry Gelbart, or Gene Reynolds.

**73**   Welcome to Korea (one hour)          September 12, 1975
  **Writers:** Everett Greenbaum, Jim Fritzell, Larry Gelbart
  **Director:** Gene Reynolds
  **Guest Stars:** Robert A. Karnes, Arthur Song, Shirlee Kong

Hawkeye returns from a weekend in Tokyo too late to bid farewell to Trapper, so he welcomes the surgeon's replacement, Captain B.J. Hunnicut, instead.

We first see the new recruit at an airstrip, far from the familiar surroundings of the 4077th, as the producers wisely prevent any direct comparisons with his predecessor. In fact, Trapper John had almost nothing in common with his replacement. An outsider from the start, Trapper was a strong-willed fighter who also served as Hawkeye's chief partner in gambling, whoring, and insubordination.

Of course, by the show's fourth year, the emphasis had drifted away from the surgeons' carnal pursuits; there would be more humanism and less sleeping around from this point forward. The new Hawkeye required a different sort of partner, someone who would complement, rather than compete with, the undisputed anchor of the series. Enter B.J. A gentle family man from Marin County, California, he was undoubtedly one of the most sensitive men drafted into the Korean conflict. He and Hawkeye were a match made in story editors' heaven.

**74**    Change of Command                    September 19, 1975
    **Writers:** Jim Fritzell, Everett Greenbaum
    **Director:** Gene Reynolds

Colonel Potter, the stern new commander of the 4077th, is eyed with suspicion until Hawkeye and B.J. convince him to exercise a certain flexibility in his leadership at the 4077th.

**75**    It Happened One Night                    September 26, 1975
    **Writers:** Larry Gelbart, Simon Muntner
    **Story:** Gene Reynolds
    **Director:** Gene Reynolds
    **Guest Stars:** Christopher Allport, Darren O'Connor

On a bitterly cold night, Frank searches for love letters in Margaret's tent while the head nurse assists the surgeons in a marathon operation.

**76**    The Late Captain Pierce                    October 3, 1975
    **Writers:** Glen Charles, Les Charles
    **Director:** Alan Alda
    **Guest Stars:** Richard Masur, Eldon Quick

After the Army erroneously lists Hawkeye as killed in action, he's tempted to exploit the error for a ticket home.

Hawkeye's ever-widening streak of nobility gets its first clear definition in this episode. The once-irreverent surgeon follows his survival instinct and tries to turn a military error into a one-way ticket home. But his conscience gets the better of him, and at the first sound of arriving choppers carrying wounded, he abandons all common sense and returns to the call of duty in the operating room.

This was written by two brothers, Glen and Les Charles, who later became writer/producers of *Taxi* and, eventually, co-creators of *Cheers*.

**77    Hey, Doc**                                    October 10, 1975
  **Writer:** Rick Mittleman
  **Director:** William Jurgensen
  **Guest Stars:** Frank Marth, Bruce Kirby, Ted Hamilton

The doctors demonstrate the fine art of wheeling and dealing when they perform a series of routine medical favors in exchange for a new microscope.

The tank commander is Frank Marth, a familiar face to *Honeymooners'* fans. As one of Jackie Gleason's stock players, Marth played dozens of roles on that series throughout the mid-1950s.

**78    The Bus**                                     October 17, 1975
  **Writer:** John D. Hess
  **Director:** Gene Reynolds
  **Guest Star:** Soon Teck Oh

The men of the 4077th get stranded in enemy territory when their bus breaks down on the way back from a poker game.

While the other characters demonstrate a previously unseen level of maturity, Frank Burns displays his unfailing selfishness by cowering in the bus and hoarding Hershey bars from the stranded company. Burns' craven character defied growth; whatever decent instincts he may have had were buried too deep in his psychosis for the writers to unearth. Despite Larry Linville's accomplished performance, Burns would remain a one-note character even as the rest of the show outgrew him.

**79    Dear Mildred**                                October 24, 1975
  **Writers:** Everett Greenbaum, Jim Fritzell
  **Director:** Alan Alda

The personnel of the camp bring gifts to their new commander as he writes a letter home to his wife on their wedding anniversary.

**80    The Kids**                                    October 31, 1975
  **Writers:** Jim Fritzell, Everett Greenbaum
  **Director:** Alan Alda
  **Guest Stars:** Ann Doran, Mitchell Sakamoto, Huanani Minn

The compound becomes a temporary refuge and maternity ward when a local orphanage is shelled.

**81**   Quo Vadis, Captain Chandler?               November 7, 1975
   **Writers:** Burt Prelutsky
   **Director:** Larry Gelbart
   **Guest Stars:** Allan Arbus, Edward Winter, Alan Fudge

A guilt-plagued bombardier with a messiah complex arrives—
arousing the interest of both Army psychiatrist Major Freedman
and the CIA's Colonel Flagg.

Major Freedman's reassuring voice of reason frequently contrasted
with the maniacal ravings of the chillingly dispassionate Colonel Flagg
in their joint appearances, though Freedman eventually proved a more
durable character. The Army psychiatrist would figure prominently in
the series long after the writers retired the spy from active duty.

**82**   Dear Peggy                                 November 11, 1975
   **Writers:** Jim Fritzell, Everett Greenbaum
   **Director:** Burt Metcalfe
   **Guest Stars:** Ned Beatty, Dennis Troy

In a letter to his wife, B.J. describes Hawkeye's attempt to break
the world record for Jeep stuffing as well as his own efforts to rescue a patient from Frank's inept surgery.

**83**   Of Moose and Men                           November 21, 1975
   **Writers:** Jay Folb
   **Director:** John Erman
   **Guest Stars:** Johnny Haymer, Lois Foraker, Jeff Maxwell

Hawkeye's in deep when he splatters mud on an angry colonel;
and B.J. counsels Sergeant Zale after his Stateside wife admits a
lapse in fidelity.

**84**   Soldier of the Month                       November 28, 1975
   **Writers:** Linda Bloodworth
   **Director:** Gene Reynolds
   **Guest Stars:** Johnny Haymer

Colonel Potter sponsors a "soldier of the month" contest to boost
sagging morale; and Frank comes down with a raging fever.

**85**   The Gun                                    December 2, 1975
   **Writers:** Larry Gelbart, Gene Reynolds
   **Director:** Burt Metcalfe
   **Guest Star:** Warren Stevens

Frank steals a wounded colonel's vintage Colt .45.


**86**   Mail Call Again                           December 9, 1975
   **Writers:** Jim Fritzell, Everett Greenbaum
   **Director:** George Tyne

Letters from home arrive with bad news for Frank: His wife knows
about Margaret.


**87**   The Price of Tomato Juice              December 16, 1975
   **Writers:** Larry Gelbart, Gene Reynolds
   **Director:** Gene Reynolds
   **Guest Star:** James Jeter

Radar engages in elaborate negotiations to secure regular rations
of tomato juice for Colonel Potter.


**88**   Dear Ma                                  December 23, 1975
   **Writers:** Everett Greenbaum, Jim Fritzell
   **Director:** Alan Alda
   **Guest Stars:** Redmond Gleeson, Byron Chung, John Fujioka

A camp-wide foot inspection is one of the subjects of Radar's letter home.


**89**   Der Tag                                     January 6, 1976
   **Writers:** Everett Greenbaum, Jim Fritzell
   **Director:** Gene Reynolds
   **Guest Stars:** Joe Morton, John Voldstad, George Simmons,
   William Grant

Colonel Potter convinces Hawkeye and B.J. to treat Frank with a
touch of kindness.

**90**   Hawkeye                                              January 13, 1976
   **Writers:** Larry Gelbart, Simon Muntner
   **Director:** Larry Gelbart
   **Guest Stars:** Philip Ahn, Shizuko Hoshi, June Kim, Susan
   Sakimoto

Hawkeye seeks help from a family of uncomprehending Koreans
after he's wounded in a Jeep accident on the road to camp.

Hawkeye has to stay alert until help arrives to treat his concussion, so
he embarks on a nonstop stream-of-consciousness monologue that lasts
the length of the program. Gelbart wasn't sure that the one-man script
would play, but he later admitted that he was excited by the risk: "For
me, the least satisfying episodes were the ones that we *knew* would work."
Apparently, this one did—the experiment earned Emmy Awards for the
writers and cinematographer William Jurgensen.

**91**   Some 38th Parallels                             January 20, 1976
   **Writers:** John Regier, Gary Markowitz
   **Director:** Burt Metcalfe
   **Guest Stars:** George O'Hanlon, Jr., Lynnette Mettey, Richard Lee
   Sung, Ray Poss

A headstrong colonel insists on retrieving the bodies of soldiers
killed in action, regardless of the risk to those still living; and
Frank auctions off the camp garbage to local scavengers.

**92**   The Novocain Mutiny                             January 27, 1976
   **Writers:** Burt Prelutsky
   **Director:** Harry Morgan
   **Guest Stars:** Ned Wilson, Johnny Haymer, Patricia Stevens

In temporary command during Colonel Potter's absence, Frank
lodges formal charges against Hawkeye for mutiny.

**93**   Smilin' Jack                                      February 3, 1976
   **Writers:** Larry Gelbart, Simon Muntner
   **Director:** Charles S. Dubin
   **Guest Stars:** Robert Hogan, Dennis Kort, Michael A. Salcido,
   Alba Francesca

The doctors try to ground a diabetic chopper pilot who's determined to set a military record for carrying in the greatest number
of wounded.

Inspired by their Army research, the producers were anxious to emphasize the efforts of the chopper pilots. "They play a much bigger role than we realized," Gelbart observed on his return from a trip to Korea, "and they're more romantic than doctors." During the fourth year, the producers wove the helicopters into storylines—with a vengeance. They soon realized that the choppers were a device more wisely used sparingly, but not before it got to the point where the poor medics couldn't go to the latrine without getting buzzed by the untimely arrival of those damn choppers.

**94**   The More I See You                         February 10, 1976
   **Writers:** Larry Gelbart, Gene Reynolds
   **Director:** Gene Reynolds
   **Guest Stars:** Blythe Danner, Mary Jo Catlett

When his medical-school sweetheart is transferred to the 4077th, Hawkeye is anxious to relive the exquisite pain all over again.

**95**   Deluge                                     February 17, 1976
   **Writers:** Larry Gelbart, Simon Muntner
   **Director:** William Jurgensen

An unexpected border advance by the Chinese results in a flood of casualties far beyond the capacity of the overworked 4077th.

**96**   The Interview                              February 24, 1976
   **Writers:** Larry Gelbart
   **Director:** Larry Gelbart
   **Guest Star:** Clete Roberts

A documentary look at the lives and work of the men and women of the 4077th, as seen through the eyes of a U.S. war correspondent.

Larry Gelbart was convinced he'd run out of storylines for the series, until Gene Reynolds suggested that they create a quasi-documentary as the season's final episode. The writer fashioned a script based on the actors' actual responses to a series of questions about the war, and then surprised them with additional unrehearsed questions, which were added after the cameras began to roll. Clete Roberts, a Southern California newsman and former war correspondent, was enlisted to conduct the interview.

The results were edited, in black and white, into one of the show's most effective stylistic departures. A passionate and often chilling look at war through the eyes of reasonable men and women who find themselves stuck in a most unreasonable situation, "The Interview" sums up perfectly Gelbart's four years with the show. The writer retired from the series after this valedictory episode, exhausted but proud.

## 1976-77    THE FIFTH SEASON

*Year-End Rating: 25.9 (4th place)*

In the fifth season, the show continues to explore the comic depths of military absurdity, but with a new seriousness of purpose. Margaret's marriage caps a season of major growth for most of the show's characters, with the notable exception of Frank Burns.

By now, the production values on the show exceed those of any sitcom in prime time; the lighting, editing, and cinematography are all first-rate, and the show looks more like a feature film than a weekly series. Still, die-hard fans would miss the grittiness of the early years and wonder if the high-gloss finish was really an improvement over the messy, often disjointed style that matched so perfectly the show's often messy and disjointed subject matter.

Burt Metcalfe signs on as producer, joined by Allan Katz and Don Reo. Gene Reynolds becomes executive producer, and writer Jay Folb handles story duties as the new executive story editor.

**97**   Bug Out (one hour)                                September 21, 1976
  **Writers:** Jim Fritzell, Everett Greenbaum
  **Director:** Gene Reynolds
  **Guest Stars:** Richard Lee Sung, Frances Fong, Don Eitner, Barry Cahill, Peter Zapp, James Lough, Eileen Saki, Ko-Ko Tani

Hawkeye, Radar, and Margaret are left behind to care for critical patients when the 4077th moves out to avoid a threatened invasion.

**98**   Margaret's Engagement                          September 28, 1976
  **Writer:** Gary Markowitz
  **Director:** Alan Alda

Margaret returns from Tokyo engaged, and the entire camp eagerly awaits Frank's response.

Margaret's engagement came as a direct result of Loretta Swit's desire to develop her character's identity separate from Frank Burns. The producers acknowledged that she'd outgrown her childish relationship with Burns by introducing her offscreen romance with Donald Penobscott—leaving poor Frank to fend for himself.

**99**   Out of Sight, Out of Mind                    October 5, 1976
   **Writers:** Ken Levine, David Isaacs
   **Director:** Gene Reynolds
   **Guest Stars:** Tom Sullivan, Judy Farrell, Enid Kent, Dudley Knight, Michael Cedar

Hawkeye sees the world with a clearer focus when he is temporarily blinded in an accident.

Writers Ken Levine and David Isaacs were newcomers who had already contributed numerous scripts to *The Jeffersons*, *The Tony Randall Show*, and *Joe and Sons*. After two seasons as *M\*A\*S\*H* story editors and three seasons on *Cheers*, they would create Mary Tyler Moore's short-lived 1986 comeback series, *Mary*.

**100**   Lieutenant Radar O'Reilly                    October 12, 1976
   **Writers:** Everett Greenbaum, Jim Fritzell
   **Director:** Alan Rafkin
   **Guest Stars:** Sandy Kenyon, Johnny Haymer, Raymond Chao

Radar wins a promotion in a poker game, but finds that life as a lieutenant doesn't agree with him.

**101**   The Nurses                    October 19, 1976
   **Writer:** Linda Bloodworth
   **Director:** Joan Darling
   **Guest Stars:** Linda Kelsey, Gregory Harrison, Mary Jo Catlett, Carol Lawson Locatell, Patricia Sturges

Margaret discovers a gap between herself and the nursing staff when one of them defies her to spend the night with her newly-wed husband.

This tale of Hot Lips' relationship with her nurses is a departure that draws attention to how few stories were told from the nurses' point of view. The situation improved somewhat as avowed feminist Alan Alda gained more creative control, but the circumstance of these women stranded in a forgotten corner of the war suggest a wealth of story possibilities that were largely overlooked.

**102**   The Abduction of Margaret Houlihan          October 26, 1976
   **Writers:** Allan Katz, Don Reo
   **Story:** Gene Reynolds
   **Director:** Gene Reynolds
   **Guest Stars:** Edward Winter, June Kim, Le Quynh, Susan
   Bredhoff

When Major Houlihan ventures into the village to help deliver a
baby, Frank causes a panic by announcing that she's been kidnapped.

Before they signed on as *M*A*S*H* writer/producers, Don Reo and
Allan Katz had written or produced shows as disparate as *Mary Tyler
Moore, All in the Family, Cher, Laugh-In*, a Lily Tomlin special, and *Rhoda*.


**103**   Dear Sigmund                              November 9, 1976
   **Writer:** Alan Alda
   **Director:** Alan Alda
   **Guest Stars:** Allan Arbus, Charles Frank, Bart Braverman, Sal
   Viscuso, J. Andrew Kenny, Jennifer Davis

Psychiatrist Sidney Freedman tries to escape his deep depression
by spending a few days observing the therapeutic antics of the
4077th at close range.


**104**   Mulcahy's War                             November 16, 1976
   **Writer:** Richard Cogan
   **Director:** George Tyne
   **Guest Stars:** Brian Byers, Ric Mancini, Richard Foronjy, Ray
   Poss

Father Mulcahy goes AWOL to experience battlefield conditions
firsthand.


**105**   The Korean Surgeon                        November 23, 1976
   **Writer:** Bill Idelson
   **Director:** Gene Reynolds
   **Guest Stars:** Soon Teck Oh, Robert Ito, Larry Hama, Richard
   Russell Ramos, Dennis Troy

B.J. and Hawkeye cover up the identity of a skilled North Korean
surgeon who's anxious to save lives on either side of the battle.

**106**   Hawkeye Get Your Gun                    November 30, 1976
  **Writer:** Jay Folb
  **Story:** Gene Reynolds, Jay Folb
  **Director:** William Jurgensen
  **Guest Stars:** Mako, Richard Doyle, Jae Woo Lee, Thomas
  Botosan, Phyllis Katz, Carmine Scelza

Colonel Potter and Hawkeye wage their own war of ideals when
Pierce refuses to fire at enemy soldiers during an ambush.

In this story, Reynolds and Folb touch on the two seemingly irrecon-
cilable sides of Colonel Potter—the surgeon and the career soldier. As a
physician, he shares with his draftee doctors the common goal of allevi-
ating human suffering. Yet his rank and career status imply his underlying acceptance of the military machinery that's ultimately responsible
for the suffering in the first place.

**107**   The Colonel's Horse                     December 7, 1976
  **Writers:** Jim Fritzell, Everett Greenbaum
  **Director:** Burt Metcalfe

The doctors treat Margaret and the colonel's horse when they
each fall prey to very different maladies.

**108**   Exorcism                                December 14, 1976
  **Writer:** Joy Folb
  **Story:** Gene Reynolds, Jay Folb
  **Director:** Alan Alda
  **Guest Stars:** Virginia Ann Lee, James Canning, Phillip Ahn

Everything that *can* go wrong *does* after Colonel Potter removes
a Buddhist good-luck talisman from the compound.

**109**   Hawk's Nightmare                        December 21, 1976
  **Writer:** Burt Prelutsky
  **Director:** Burt Metcalfe
  **Guest Stars:** Allan Arbus, Patricia Stevens, Sean Roche

After a series of unsettling dreams, Hawkeye wonders if he hasn't
finally cracked up.

**110**  The Most Unforgettable Characters       January 4, 1977
  **Writers:** Ken Levine, David Isaacs
  **Director:** Burt Metcalfe
  **Guest Star:** Jeff Maxwell

Radar records his impressions for a correspondence course in creative writing; and B.J. and Hawkeye stage a feud for Frank's benefit on his birthday.

**111**  Thirty-Eight Across       January 11, 1977
  **Writers:** Jim Fritzell, Everett Greenbaum
  **Director:** Burt Metcalfe
  **Guest Stars:** Dick O'Neill, Oliver Clark

Radar's signals get crossed when his shortwave call for help on a crossword puzzle summons a Navy admiral expecting a dire emergency.

**112**  Ping-Pong       January 18, 1977
  **Writers:** Sid Dorfman
  **Director:** William Jurgensen
  **Guest Stars:** Richard Narita, Frank Maxwell, Sachiko Penny Lee

Colonel Potter confronts an old Army buddy whose military incompetence has already cost too many lives on the battlefield.

**113**  End Run       January 25, 1977
  **Writer:** John D. Hess
  **Director:** Harry Morgan
  **Guest Stars:** Henry Brown, Johnny Haymer

Hawkeye tries to raise a former all-American football player's morale after the GI loses a leg; and Klinger and Sergeant Zale settle a feud in the boxing ring.

**114**  Hanky-Panky       February 1, 1977
  **Writer:** Gene Reynolds
  **Director:** Gene Reynolds
  **Guest Star:** Ann Sweeny

B.J. is plagued by guilt when his tender consolation of a nurse ends in a one-night stand.

**115**   Hepatitis                                February 8, 1977
   **Writer:** Alan Alda
   **Director:** Alan Alda
   **Guest Star:** Barbara James

Father Mulcahy is quarantined with infectious hepatitis; and Hawkeye suffers psychosomatic back pain.

Alda's script was inspired by real life. Actor William Christopher's own bout with hepatitis caused him to miss a good many days of work that season.

**116**   The General's Practitioner                February 15, 1977
   **Writer:** Burt Prelutsky
   **Director:** Alan Rafkin
   **Guest Stars:** Edward T. Binns, Leonard stone, Suesie Elene

Hawkeye chafes under his new appointment as personal physician to a general; and Radar copes with the unexpected arrival of a baby to a Korean war bride.

**117**   Movie Tonight                            February 22, 1977
   **Writers:** Gene Reynolds, Don Reo, Allan Katz, Jay Folb
   **Director:** Burt Metcalfe
   **Guest Stars:** Enid Kent, Judy Farrell, Jeffrey Kramer

When technical problems beset the screening of Colonel Potter's favorite film, the camp improvises a talent show in defiance of the obstreperous projector.

**118**   Souvenirs                                March 1, 1977
   **Writer:** Burt Prelutsky
   **Story:** Burt Prelutsky, Reinhold Weege
   **Director:** Joshua Shelley
   **Guest Stars:** Michael Bell, Brian Dennehy, Scott Mulhern

Frank buys a priceless antique vase from a shady junk dealer as a war memento.

**119**   Post-Op                                    March 8, 1977
**Writer:** Ken Levine, David Isaacs
**Story:** Gene Reynolds, Jay Folb
**Director:** Gene Reynolds
**Guest Stars:** Hilly Hicks, Sal Viscuso, Andy Romano

An acute shortage of blood complicates another marathon tour of
duty for the doctors in O.R.

The chilling battle stories told by the recuperating soldiers were culled
from firsthand accounts and interviews with veterans of both Vietnam
and the Korean War. Producer Gene Reynolds acknowledged the series's
debt to its sources: "At least sixty percent of the plots dealing with medical
or military incidents were taken from real life. These guys gave us details we never would have thought of. They kept us honest."

**120**   Margaret's Marriage                        March 15, 1977
**Writers:** Everett Greenbaum, Jim Fritzell
**Director:** Gene Reynolds
**Guest Stars:** Beeson Carroll, Judy Farrell, Lynne Marie Stewart,
Ray Poss, Kellye Nakahara

Donald Penobscott arrives at the 4077th to marry Margaret in an
improvised ceremony that calls for something borrowed—a wedding dress from Klinger—and something blue: best-man Frank
Burns.

As Margaret flies off on her honeymoon, blissfully unaware of the cruel
tricks that fate—and the show's writers—have in store, it spells the end
for Frank Burns. He could hardly continue on the series once Margaret's
marriage altered permanently his one tenuous connection to reality.

Actor Larry Linville breathed a sigh of relief when he decided not to
renew his contract. "I wasn't tired of playing Frank Burns," he explained,
"I was tired of playing *only* Frank Burns."

"After Gelbart left," the actor told writer Suzy Kalter in *The Complete
Book of M*A*S*H*, "it was easier to run Frank into a scene, dump on him,
get a laugh, and run him out the door." It was quite a letdown for the
actor who understood so well the character's dark function in the comedy of military absurdity. As Linville once described Frank Burns in the
pages of *TV Guide*: "He personified the psychosis of war itself—mindless, random, hostile one moment, silly the next."

## 1977-78    THE SIXTH SEASON

*Year-End Rating: 23.3 (8th place)*

The war continues for a sixth year of contained madness as the 4077th welcomes David Ogden Stiers in the role of Major Charles Winchester III, a skilled surgeon and vituperative adversary for B.J. and Hawkeye. With the departure of Frank Burns, the ratio of slapstick to drama of the early years has reversed. Stories in this third phase of *M*A*S*H* often sacrifice belly laughs for the sake of the characters' emotional growth.

Gene Reynolds ceases day-to-day involvement to become a special creative consultant for the remainder of the run—a title he shares with Alan Alda, reflecting the actor's growing involvement behind the scenes. Burt Metcalfe continues as producer. Executive story editor Jay Folb oversees the sixth season's scripts, along with story editors Ken Levine and David Isaacs, and Ronny Graham, who signs on as a special program consultant.

**121**   Fade Out, Fade In (one hour)              September 20, 1977
   **Writers:** Jim Fritzell, Everett Greenbaum
   **Director:** Hy Averback
   **Guest Stars:** James Lough, Raymond Singer, Tom Stovall, Rick Hurst, Robert Symonds, William Flatley, Joseph Burns, Barbara James

Frank is shipped home after he goes bonkers in Tokyo, leaving the 4077th to wonder if his replacement—the skilled, articulate, and thoroughly strident Major Winchester—is much of an improvement.

Burt Metcalfe hired the classically trained David Ogden Stiers after spotting him on *The Mary Tyler Moore Show*, where the actor played Mary's station manager during the final season. The producer knew immediately that he'd found the man to play the William F. Buckley of the 4077th. "David has this unique quality," he told *TV Guide*. "He can be lovably unlovable."

For all his pomposity, Winchester finally gains our sympathy when he musters a humble, if grudging, admiration for the skill of the 4077th's surgeons. The new doctor may be insufferable, but he's not unlikable. Metcalfe's hunch to replace Frank Burns with a more formidable adversary was a master stroke. With Winchester, the show's central triangle achieved a parity that made the balanced ensemble of the final years possible.

**122**   Fallen Idol                                           September 27, 1977
   **Writer:** Alan Alda
   **Director:** Alan Alda
   **Guest Stars:** Frances Fong, Robin Riker, Larry Gilman, Roy Goldman

Radar comes to the painful realization that Hawkeye is only human after the surgeon's performance is compromised by a hangover.

Ironically, by the sixth season, Hawkeye had already lost most of the flaws that had rendered him so human in the first place. In the following seasons, Alda and the writers gradually purged the doctor of his remaining excesses: Hawkeye's womanizing was reduced to a series of half-hearted one-liners that rarely rated so much as a bemused smile from the disinterested nurses; his onscreen drinking would be severely curtailed; and even the selfish outrage that once fueled his most elaborate practical jokes would be sublimated to the service of his frequently self-righteous antiwar protests.

**123**   Last Laugh                                            October 4, 1977
   **Writers:** Everett Greenbaum, Jim Fritzell
   **Director:** Don Weis
   **Guest Stars:** James Cromwell, Robert Karnes, John Ashton

The Army questions B.J.'s medical credentials as a result of an elaborate practical joke staged by one of his old college chums.

**124**   War of Nerves                                         October 11, 1977
   **Writer:** Alan Alda
   **Director:** Alan Alda
   **Guest Stars:** Allan Arbus, Michael O'Keefe, Peter Riegert

Major Freedman arrives as a casualty, just in time to offer therapeutic advice to the squabbling staff of the 4077th.

**125**   The Winchester Tapes                    October 18, 1977
   **Writers:** Everett Greenbaum, Jim Fritzell
   **Director:** Burt Metcalfe
   **Guest Stars:** Thomas Carter, Kimiko Hiroshige

Charles is the butt of B.J.'s merciless practical jokes, even as he dictates a letter pleading with his influential father to get him a transfer home.

There is a playful degree of heat generated when Margaret and Winchester discover their meeting of the minds, but of course, nothing comes of it. The writers are too smart to limit the characters with an ongoing romantic involvement.

**126**   The Light That Failed                    October 25, 1977
   **Writer:** Burt Prelutsky
   **Director:** Charles S. Dubin
   **Guest Stars:** Enid Kent, Gary Erwin, Philip Baker Hall

The M*A*S*H crew play amateur sleuths when they try to determine whodunit in a mystery novel that arrives minus the final page.

**127**   In Love and War                    November 1, 1977
   **Writer:** Alan Alda
   **Director:** Alan Alda
   **Guest Stars:** Kieu Chinh, Susan Krebs, Soorah Ahn, Enid Kent

Hawkeye finds a brief respite from the war when he romances an aristocratic South Korean woman who shelters the local orphans in her home.

In the final scene, Hawkeye and Margaret raise a toast to the flickering flame of romance in war. She drinks to a temporary reunion with her estranged newlywed husband, while Hawkeye raises his glass to a love he knows he'll never see again. It's a wistful moment that defines perfectly the romantic pessimism that would underlie many of the best shows in later seasons.

**128**   Change Day                          November 8, 1977
    **Writer:** Laurence Marks
    **Director:** Don Weis
    **Guest Stars:** Phillip Ahn, Noel Toy, Glenn Ash, Richard Lee Sung

Winchester concocts a scheme to profit from the hapless villagers when the Army announces a scrip exchange.

**129**   Images                              November 15, 1977
    **Writer:** Burt Prelutsky
    **Director:** Burt Metcalfe
    **Guest Stars:** Susan Blanchard, Larry Block, John Durren

Against everyone's better judgment, Radar is determined to sharpen his image with a tattoo.

**130**   The M*A*S*H Olympics                November 22, 1977
    **Writers:** Ken Levine, David Isaacs
    **Director:** Don Weis
    **Guest Stars:** Mike Henry, Michael McManus

Inspired by the 1952 Helsinki games, Potter organizes his own Olympics for the men and women of the 4077th.

Mike Henry appears as Margaret's husband, Lieutenant Colonel Donald Penobscott. The character's only other appearance on the show was at his wedding, when he was played by a different actor, Beeson Carroll.

**131**   The Grim Reaper                     November 29, 1977
    **Writer:** Burt Prelutsky
    **Director:** George Tyne
    **Guest Stars:** Charles Aidman, Jerry Hauser, Kellye Nakahara

Hawkeye is aghast at a military strategist's enthusiastic predictions of incoming casualty figures.

**132**   Comrades in Arms (Part 1)          December 6, 1977
    **Writer:** Alan Alda
    **Director:** Burt Metcalfe
    **Guest Stars:** Jon Yune, James Saito

Lost behind enemy lines, Hawkeye and Margaret form a personal truce and seek shelter in a roadside hut.

This two-parter was the only episode of *M\*A\*S\*H* to be jointly directed, by Alan Alda and Burt Metcalfe—though a Directors Guild rule required them each to take individual credit for one of the two separate episodes.

**133** Comrades in Arms (Part 2) December 13, 1977
   **Writer:** Alan Alda
   **Director:** Alan Alda
   **Guest Stars:** Jon Yune, James Saito, Doug Rowe

Margaret and Hawkeye seek solace from enemy fire in each other's arms and end up, briefly, as lovers.

A pivotal episode for the head nurse. Her night with Hawkeye signaled the end of their comic enmity and foreshadowed her divorce from Penobscott, setting the stage for her final evolution as a confident and secure member of the 4077th family.

**134** The Merchant of Korea December 20, 1977
   **Writers:** Ken Levine, David Isaacs
   **Director:** William Jurgensen
   **Guest Star:** Johnny Haymer

When B.J. and Hawkeye are unable to repay loans to Winchester, he extracts petty favors from the pair until they're forced to even the score over poker chips.

**135** The Smell of Music January 3, 1978
   **Writers:** Jim Fritzell, Everett Greenbaum
   **Director:** Stuart Miller
   **Guest Stars:** Jordan Clarke, Nancy Steen, Lois Foraker, Richard Lee Sung

Hawkeye and B.J. wage a battle of wills with their bunkmate when they refuse to bathe until Winchester ceases his agonizing French-horn practice.

**136** Patent 4077 January 10, 1978
   **Writers:** Ken Levine, David Isaacs
   **Director:** Harry Morgan
   **Guest Stars:** Keye Luke, Brenda Thomson, Harry Gold, Pat Stevens

Klinger loses Margaret's wedding ring; and the doctors commission a peddler of cheap jewelry to build a surgical clamp.

**137**   Tea and Empathy             January 17, 1978
    **Writer:** Bill Idelson
    **Director:** Don Weis
    **Guest Stars:** Bernard Fox, Neil Thompson, Sal Viscuso

Klinger and Father Mulcahy volunteer to retrieve a stolen cache of penicillin from the black market.

**138**   Your Hit Parade             January 24, 1978
    **Writer:** Ronny Graham
    **Director:** George Tyne
    **Guest Stars:** Ronny Graham, William Kux, Ken Michelman

Radar plays disc jockey to keep spirits from sagging when the 4077th is deluged with an overflow of wounded from other M\*A\*S\*H units.

**139**   What's Up, Doc?             January 30, 1978
    **Writer:** Larry Balmagia
    **Director:** George Tyne
    **Guest Stars:** Charles Frank, Lois Foraker, Kurt Andon

Hawkeye performs delicate rabbit surgery to determine if Margaret is pregnant; and Klinger is the willing hostage of a mad GI who demands passage to Ohio.

**140**   Mail Call Three             February 6, 1978
    **Writers:** Everett Greenbaum, Jim Fritzell
    **Director:** Charles S. Dubin
    **Guest Stars:** Oliver Clark, Jack Grapes, Carmine Scelza, Terri Paul

A tardy sack of mail brings a batch of misdelivered love letters to Hawkeye and a Dear John letter for Klinger, from his wife, Laverne.

The unfortunate corporal had married Laverne Esposito in a short-wave ceremony during the third season, but never did get to Toledo to consummate the union.

**141**   Temporary Duty                          February 13, 1978
   **Writer:** Larry Balmagia
   **Director:** Burt Metcalfe
   **Guest Stars:** George Lindsey, Marcia Rodd

The camp is enlivened by the arrival of a boisterous surgeon on
temporary assignment to the 4077th.


**142**   Potter's Retirement                     February 20, 1978
   **Writer:** Laurence Marks
   **Director:** William Jurgensen
   **Guest Stars:** George Wyner, Peter Hobbs, Ken White

Colonel Potter discovers that somebody down there doesn't like
him when unflattering reports of his command are filed by someone in his own unit.


**143**   Dr. Winchester and Mr. Hyde             February 27, 1978
   **Writers:** Ken Levine, David Isaacs, Ronny Graham
   **Director:** Charles S. Dubin
   **Guest Stars:** Chris Murney, Joe Tornatore, Ron Max, Rod Gist

Winchester falls prey to drug abuse when he relies on self-pre-
scribed amphetamines to help him through a long tour of duty.


**144**   Major Topper                             March 27, 1978
   **Writers:** Allyn Freeman
   **Director:** Charles S. Dubin
   **Guest Stars:** Hamilton Camp, Andrew Bloch, Donald Blackwell,
   Peter Zapp, Paul Linke, John Kirby, Michael Mann, Kellye
   Nakahara

The doctors resort to placebos when the morphine supply is contaminated; and Klinger has competition when a new nut is introduced into the 4077th.


## 1978-79   THE SEVENTH SEASON

*Year-End Rating: 25.4 (7th place)*


The creative staff rises to the challenge of keeping the series fresh as
the ensemble undergoes a slight, but perceptible shift. Actor Gary

Burghoff had chosen to limit Radar's involvement to thirteen appearances a year, and Alan Alda occasionally spent more time behind the camera than in front of it. As the leading players regrouped, it naturally followed that supporting characters like Corporal Klinger and Father Mulcahy would blossom during the later years of the show.

Executive story editors Ken Levine and David Isaacs write a third of the season's stories, with multiple script contributions from story editor Larry Balmagia, story consultant Ronny Graham, Alan Alda, Mitch Markowitz, and Tom Reeder.

**145**  Commander Pierce                September 18, 1978
  **Writer:** Ronny Graham
  **Director:** Burt Metcalfe
  **Guest Stars:** James Lough, Andrew Massett, Jan Jorden

The 4077th is astonished when Hawkeye becomes a petty tyrant and military bureaucrat after he's appointed temporary camp commander.

**146**  Peace on Us                September 25, 1978
  **Writers:** Ken Levine, David Isaacs
  **Director:** George Tyne
  **Guest Stars:** Kevin Hagen, Hugh Gillan

Hawkeye, frustrated by the lack of progress at the Panmunjom peace talks, decides to make a personal plea to the diplomats.

**147**  Lil                October 2, 1978
  **Writer:** Sheldon Bull
  **Director:** Burt Metcalfe
  **Guest Stars:** Carmen Mathews, W. Perren Page

Colonel Potter develops a more-than-casual interest in a spirited Army nurse who visits the 4077th on an inspection tour.

Radar, ever the guardian on morality, keeps a watchful eye on the happily married colonel, as he did under similar circumstances for Henry Blake in the third season's "Henry in Love."

**148**   Our Finest Hour (one hour)                    October 9, 1978
**Writers:** Ken Levine, David Isaacs, Larry Balmagia, Ronny
Graham
**Director:** Burt Metcalfe
**Guest Star:** Clete Roberts

War correspondent Clete Roberts returns for a fresh documentary
look at the lives of the doctors and nurses of the *M\*A\*S\*H*
4077th.

This reprise of "The Interview" sums up the show's middle period,
much as that previous pseudo-documentary put a cap on the first four
years. Not surprisingly, there's very little here that wasn't expressed with
equal eloquence in the earlier show.

**149**   The Billfold Syndrome                          October 16, 1978
**Writers:** Ken Levine, David Isaacs
**Director:** Alan Alda
**Guest Stars:** Kevin Geer, Allan Arbus

Major Sidney Freedman treats a shell-shocked medic who has
completely forgotten who he was before the war.

**150**   None Like It Hot                               October 23, 1978
**Writers:** Ken Levine, David Isaacs, Johnny Bonaduce
**Director:** Tony Mordente
**Guest Stars:** Ted Gehring, Johnny Haymer, Jan Jorden

Hawkeye and B.J. receive a mail-order bathtub during a heat
wave and then try to keep a few dozen interlopers away from
their portable oasis.

**151**   They Call the Wind Korea                       October 30, 1978
**Writers:** Ken Levine, David Isaacs
**Director:** Charles S. Dubin
**Guest Stars:** Tom Dever, Paul Cavonis, Randy Stumpf

Klinger and Winchester provide emergency medical care to a
truckload of wounded Greeks after a Manchurian windstorm
strands them on the road to Seoul.

**152**   Major Ego                                    November 6, 1978
   **Writer:** Larry Balmagia
   **Director:** Alan Alda
   **Guest Stars:** Greg Mullavey, David Dean, Frank Pettinger,
   Phyllis Katz

Charles basks in the spotlight when his medical handiwork becomes the subject of a feature story in *Stars and Stripes.*

**153**   Baby, It's Cold Outside                     November 13, 1978
   **Writer:** Gary David Goldberg
   **Director:** George Tyne
   **Guest Stars:** Terry Wills, Teck Murdock, David Dramer, Jan
   Jorden

Winchester is well insulated in a polar snowsuit as a GI fights to
survive exposure during a record-breaking cold snap.

**154**   Point of View                               November 20, 1978
   **Writer:** Ken Levine, David Isaacs
   **Director:** Charles S. Dubin
   **Guest Stars:** Brad Gorman, Marc Baxley, Edward Gallardo, Jan
   Jorden, Hank Ross, David Stafford, Paul Tuerpe

The efforts of the doctors and nurses of the 4077th are examined
from the perspective of a wounded soldier made mute by a throat
injury.

The writers' recent efforts to deepen the characters from the inside
out pay off splendidly in this classic episode that lets us see them from
the outside looking in. From the winning charm of Margaret's bedside
manner to the disarming compassion of Hawkeye's wisecracks, the dignity and warmth of the 4077th crew are revealed with a clarity uncol-
ored by the cloying sentimentality that would sink so many of the series's
later efforts in this vein.

**155**   Dear Comrade                                November 27, 1978
   **Writer:** Tom Reeder
   **Director:** Charles S. Dubin
   **Guest Stars:** Sab Shimono, Larry Block, Robert Clotworthy

A Communist spy goes undercover as Winchester's houseboy to
gather intelligence on the 4077th's superior record of medical
success.

**156**   Out of Gas                         December 4, 1978
   **Writer:** Tom Reeder
   **Director:** Mel Damski
   **Guest Stars:** Justin Lord, Byron Chung, Johnny Haymer

Father Mulcahy and Winchester are the unlikely emissaries sent
to barter for black-market supplies of much-needed sodium pen-
tothal.

**157**   An Eye for a Tooth                 December 11, 1978
   **Writer:** Ronny Graham
   **Director:** Charles S. Dubin
   **Guest Star:** Peter Palmer

When Father Mulcahy is passed over for promotion yet again, he
decides to attract attention by sneaking off on an emergency
chopper mission.

**158**   Dear Sis                           December 18, 1978
   **Writer:** Alan Alda
   **Director:** Alan Alda
   **Guest Stars:** Lawrence Driscoll, Patrick Driscoll, Jo Ann Thomp-
   son, W. Perren Page

In a Christmas letter to his sister, Mulcahy laments his inability to
help the GIs in ways more concrete than just the spiritual.

William Christopher, the actor who played Father Mulcahy, commented on the strength of the *M\*A\*S\*H* ensemble when he told a reporter,
"It's heartening to work on this show because I know my time will come
each year and there will be a show in which my character is expanded."
He hit a jackpot in the seventh year when these three consecutive episodes cast him in the spotlight.

**159**   B.J. Papa San                      January 1, 1979
   **Writer:** Larry Balmagia
   **Director:** James Sheldon
   **Guest Stars:** Dick O'Neill, Mariel Aragon, Chao-Li Chi, Stephen
   Keep, Johnny Haymer, Richard Furukawa, Shizuko Hoshi

B.J. devotes himself to a destitute Korean family in an attempt to
fill the void caused by his own separation from his wife and
daughter.

**160**  Inga                                      January 8, 1979
   **Writer:** Alan Alda
   **Director:** Alan Alda
   **Guest Stars:** Mariette Hartley, Phyllis Katz, Mark Favara

A twinge of jealousy quickly develops into pigheaded sexism when Hawkeye refuses to be outdone by a beautiful Swedish doctor.

Not surprisingly, this was one of Alan Alda's all-time favorite scripts. When it won an Emmy, the writer/actor/director gleefully cartwheeled to the podium to accept the award. Alda's confirmed feminism was never so pronounced, or frankly anachronistic, as in this story that revealed how far Hawkeye had come since the days of his amorous liaisons in the mattress-supply room—and how much further he had yet to travel.

**161**  The Price                                 January 15, 1979
   **Writer:** Erik Tarloff
   **Director:** Charles S. Dubin
   **Guest Stars:** Miko Mayama, Yuki Shimoda, Ken Mochizuki, Dennis Sakamoto

Hawkeye and B.J. shield a young Korean draft dodger; and Potter's horse becomes a source of pride to an aged South Korean war hero.

**162**  The Young and the Restless                January 22, 1979
   **Writer:** Mitch Markowitz
   **Director:** William Jurgensen
   **Guest Star:** James Canning

Elder statesmen Potter and Winchester are dazzled—and intimidated—by the accomplished surgical technique of a young Army medical instructor.

**163**  Hot Lips Is Back in Town                  January 29, 1979
   **Writers:** Larry Balmagia, Bernard Dilbert
   **Story:** Bernard Dilbert, Gary Markowitz
   **Director:** Charles S. Dubin
   **Guest Stars:** Peggy Lee Brennan, Walter Brooke, Jan Jorden

Major Houlihan, her sour marriage behind her, asserts her new independence when she rebuffs the advances of a general; and Radar is smitten by a new nurse.

**164**   C*A*V*E                                February 5, 1979
**Writers:** Larry Balmagia, Ronny Graham
**Director:** William Jurgensen
**Guest Stars:** Basil Hoffman, Mark Taylor, Charles Jenkins

The 4077th is driven underground, literally, when heavy shelling forces the camp to relocate temporarily in a cave.

**165**   Rally 'Round the Flagg, Boys                February 14, 1979
**Writer:** Mitch Markowitz
**Director:** Harry Morgan
**Guest Stars:** Edward Winter, Neil Thompson, Bob Okazaki

Colonel Flagg returns to the 4077th to investigate Hawkeye's alleged Communist sympathies.

**166**   Preventative Medicine                      February 19, 1979
**Writer:** Tom Reeder
**Director:** Tony Mordente
**Guest Stars:** James Wainwright, Larry Jenkins

B.J. takes issue when Hawkeye prescribes unnecessary surgery for an overzealous commander to prevent him from jeopardizing the lives of more boys in battle.

The filming of this episode offers a glimpse into the writers' fluid approach to M*A*S*H story material. In the original script, both doctors colluded in the bogus appendectomy—a breach of medical ethics that actor Mike Farrell found morally reprehensible. Alda disagreed, and the actors launched into a heated onstage debate, which producer Metcalfe noted and later incorporated in to the final script. As the producer observed, "It was better than what any writer alone could have done to improve the show."

**167**   A Night at Rosie's                         February 26, 1979
**Writers:** Ken Levine, David Isaacs
**Director:** Burt Metcalfe
**Guest Stars:** Keye Luke, Joshua Bryant, Joseph Di Reda

Hawkeye drowns his sorrows in an evening at Rosie's Bar, and one by one, the rest of the camp joins him.

Levine and Isaacs wrote this story "like a little play," just so they could place the characters in a fresh setting that everyone hadn't already seen a thousand times.

**168**   Ain't Love Grand                              March 5, 1979
   **Writers:** Ken Levine, David Isaacs
   **Director:** Mike Farrell
   **Guest Stars:** Kit McDonough, Sylvia Chang, Eileen Saki,
   Michael Williams, Judy Farrell

Charles develops an infatuation for an earthy Korean call girl; and Klinger is amazed to find himself the object of a new nurse's fancy.

**169**   The Party                                    March 12, 1979
   **Writers:** Burt Metcalfe, Alan Alda
   **Director:** Burt Metcalfe

B.J. refuses to let an evacuation dampen plans for the grand party he's arranged for the staff's relatives back home in the States.

Burt Metcalfe's first *M*A*S*H* script gave the producer new respect for his scripters—he would later compare writing to visiting the dentist. He and Alda dictated the entire second act of this episode into a tape recorder over an Italian dinner at Anna's restaurant in Los Angeles, a watering hole that frequently played host to the writers' brainstorming sessions.

## 1979-80   THE EIGHTH SEASON

*Year-End Rating: 25.3 (4th place)*

Radar O'Reilly's decampment near the top of the eighth season sets the stage for Klinger's emergence as a more believable, three-dimensional central figure. The now fully balanced ensemble is poised for the series of rich character studies that will comprise the best episodes of the show's final seasons.

Burt Metcalfe is executive producer for the final four seasons, and Stanford Tischler is the associate producer. John Rappaport and Jim Mulligan sign on as producers, and Dennis Koenig is the season's story editor. Thad Mumford and Dan Wilcox are the executive story editors. Ronny Graham continues as program consultant, and Charles S. Dubin is the staff director in season eight.

**170**   Too Many Cooks                    September 17, 1979
   **Writer:** Dennis Koenig
   **Director:** Charles S. Dubin
   **Guest Stars:** John Randolph, Ed Begley, Jr.

The staff is forced to reevaluate their opinion of a bumbling foot soldier after he works wonders in the mess tent kitchen.

**171**   Are You Now, Margaret?             September 24, 1979
   **Writers:** Thad Mumford, Dan Wilcox
   **Director:** Charles S. Dubin
   **Guest Stars:** Lawrence Pressman, Jennifer Davis, Jeff Maxwell

A witch-hunting Congressional investigator tries to uncover Communist sympathies in Margaret's youthful past.

Thad Mumford and Dan Wilcox had written scripts, together and separately, for *Maude, Alice, The Electric Company, America 2-Night,* as well as the miniseries *Roots II.* The hardworking story editors would eventually become producers during the show's final two seasons.

**172**   Guerrilla My Dreams                 October 1, 1979
   **Writer:** Bob Colleary
   **Director:** Alan Alda
   **Guest Stars:** Mako, Joshua Bryant, Huanani Minn, George Kee Cheung, Marcus Mukai, Connie Izay

Hawkeye tries to prevent a South Korean officer from interrogating a wounded woman being held at the 4077th as an enemy guerrilla.

**173**   Good-Bye, Radar (Part 1)            October 8, 1979
   **Writers:** Ken Levine, David Isaacs
   **Director:** Charles S. Dubin
   **Guest Stars:** Marilyn Jones, Johnny Haymer, Michael O'Dwyer, Richard Lee-Sung, Tony Cristino, Arell Blanton

Radar returns from furlough to discover that he's been discharged to help out at home after a family crisis.

Gary Burghoff decided to leave the series at the end of the seventh year, complaining that the monotony of the series had taken its toll.

Though few tears were shed when the hotheaded actor finally left, CBS coerced him to return for this two-part farewell episode that was scheduled to take advantage of the November ratings sweeps period.

**174** Good-Bye, Radar (Part 2)       October 15, 1979
  **Writers:** Ken Levine, David Isaacs
  **Director:** Charles S. Dubin
  **Guest Stars:** Lee de Broux, Whitney Rydbeck, David Dozer

Radar's gala farewell party is upstaged by the unexpected arrival of incoming wounded, leaving the corporal to say his good-byes in silence to an empty camp.

Writers Levine and Isaacs successfully avoid the mawkish in their approach to Radar's farewell scene by opting for a more compelling treatment that allows the little corporal only a muted last hurrah. The war arrives—an uninvited guest at his good-bye party—and suddenly everyone is back to the business of battle, with not a single tear shed. The character's final moments at the 4077th are moving, yet refreshingly devoid of gushing sentiment. Now, if only they hadn't dragged out that teddy bear for the final coda . . .

**175** Period of Adjustment       October 22, 1979
  **Writers:** Jim Mulligan, John Rappaport
  **Director:** Charles S. Dubin
  **Guest Stars:** Jeff Maxwell, Eileen Saki, Gwen Farrell

B.J. feels the pangs of homesickness when he hears how his toddler daughter mistook Radar for her soldier daddy; and Klinger finds it rough going when he takes over as company clerk.

**176** Nurse Doctor       October 29, 1979
  **Writers:** Sy Rosen, Thad Mumford, Dan Wilcox
  **Story:** Sy Rosen
  **Director:** Charles S. Dubin
  **Guest Star:** Alexandra Stoddart

The camp is in the midst of a drought, but Father Mulcahy finds himself in plenty of hot water he rebuffs the affections of a young nurse.

**177**   Private Finance                          November 5, 1979
   **Writer:** Dennis Koenig
   **Director:** Charles S. Dubin
   **Guest Stars:** Shizuko Hoshi, Denice Kumagi, Mark Kologi, Joey
   Pento, Philip Simma, Art Evans

Hawkeye debates whether to send a dead soldier's black-market
profits home to the boy's parents; and Klinger's offer of financial
support to a young Korean girl is misinterpreted by her mother.

**178**   Mr. and Mrs. Who?                      November 12, 1979
   **Writer:** Ronny Graham
   **Director:** Burt Metcalfe
   **Guest Stars:** Charlotte Nevins, James Keane

Charles returns from a lost weekend in Tokyo, stinging from a
hangover—and the possibility that he may have gotten married.

**179**   The Yalu Brick Road                    November 19, 1979
   **Writer:** Mike Farrell
   **Director:** Charles S. Dubin
   **Guest Stars:** Soon Teck Oh, G.W. Bailey

After Klinger's Thanksgiving feast yields a harvest of food poison-
ing, Hawkeye and B.J. are sidetracked on their way to retrieve an
antibiotic antidote.

**180**   Life Time                               November 26, 1979
   **Writers:** Alan Alda, Walter D. Dishell, M.D.
   **Director:** Alan Alda
   **Guest Star:** Kevin Brophy

The surgeons race the clock when a soldier's medical complications force them to complete his delicate heart operation within
twenty minutes.

An onscreen clock creates arresting suspense as it ticks off in real time
as the half-hour progresses.

The episode's script was co-written by Alda and Walter Dishell, the
show's medical adviser. The story is 100 percent medically plausible—
one of the more remarkable examples of the painstaking research that
went into almost every script. Dishell actually kept a 1953 medical text-

book in his office to ensure that the surgeons' procedures were never anachronistic, and a registered Army nurse was always on the set to oversee the accuracy of triage and O. R. sequences.


**181**  Dear Uncle Abdul                    December 3, 1979
   **Writers:** John Rappaport, Jim Mulligan
   **Director:** William Jurgensen
   **Guest Stars:** Kelly Ward, Richard Lineback, Alexander Petale

With all his new responsibilities, Klinger barely has time to write a letter home to his family in Toledo.


**182**  Captains Outrageous                  December 10, 1979
   **Writers:** Thad Mumford, Dan Wilcox
   **Director:** Burt Metcalfe
   **Guest Stars:** Eileen Saki, John Orchard, Sirri Murad, G.W. Bailey, Paul Cavonis, Momo Yashima, Jo Ann Thompson

Members of the staff tend bar after Rosie gets hurt during one of their brawls; and Father Mulcahy skeptically awaits news of his long-awaited promotion.


**183**  Stars and Stripe                     December 17, 1979
   **Writer:** Dennis Koenig
   **Director:** Harry Morgan
   **Guest Star:** Joshua Bryant

B.J. and Winchester form a tempestuous partnership to write an article for a medical journal; and Hot Lips is reunited with a macho front-line boyfriend.


**184**  Yessir, That's Our Baby              December 31, 1979
   **Writer:** Jim Mulligan
   **Director:** Alan Alda
   **Guest Stars:** Howard Platt, William Bogert, Yuki Shimoda, Elizabeth Farley

The 4077th plays adoption agency when the staff tries to find a home for an unwanted Amer-Asian baby abandoned on their doorstep.

**185**   Bottle Fatigue                                    January 7, 1980
   **Writers:** Thad Mumford, Dan Wilcox
   **Director:** Burt Metcalfe
   **Guest Stars:** Shelley Long, David Hirokane, Shari Saba

Hawkeye's huge bar bill convinces him to go on the wagon; and Charles frets when his sister plans to marry beneath her station.

As he struggles to release his grip on demon rum, Hawkeye examines his last boisterous, irredeemable, and purely selfish habit—and completes the final stages of his character's transformation. The lusty, hard-drinking, quick-witted, and fallibly human doctor who'd been drafted eight seasons earlier has finally emerged as the walking, talking conscience of humanity—the Jiminy Cricket of the Korean War.

**186**   Heal Thyself                                    January 14, 1980
   **Writer:** Dennis Koenig
   **Story:** Dennis Koenig, Gene Reynolds
   **Director:** Mike Farrell
   **Guest Star:** Edward Herrman

Hawkeye and B.J. are delighted with a temporary surgeon who fills in for the ailing Winchester, until the new medic begins to crack under the strain.

**187**   Old Soldiers                                    January 21, 1980
   **Writer:** Dennis Koenig
   **Director:** Charles S. Dubin
   **Guest Stars:** Jane Connell, Sally Imamura, Jason Autajay

Colonel Potter toasts his old Army buddies after he finds out that he's the last survivor of his World War I battalion.

**188**   Morale Victory                                    January 28, 1980
   **Writer:** John Rappaport
   **Director:** Charles S. Dubin
   **Guest Stars:** James Stephens, G.W. Bailey, Connie Izay

Potter challenges B.J. and Hawkeye to boost camp morale; and Winchester tries to lift the spirits of a pianist who has a paralyzed hand.

**189**   Lend a Hand                        February 4, 1980
   **Writer:** Alan Alda
   **Director:** Alan Alda
   **Guest Stars:** Robert Alda, Anthony Alda, Daren Kelly, Shari
   Saba

Hawkeye volunteers for an emergency mission on the front lines
only to find himself paired up with an abrasive medical consultant he'd locked horns with earlier.

Robert Alda returns to reprise his role as the medical consultant Dr.
Borelli, who previously appeared in the third year. Alan's brother, Anthony, completes the family portrait in a small role as the medic who
referees the bickering physicians.

**190**   Good-Bye, Cruel World             February 11, 1980
   **Writers:** Thad Mumford, Dan Wilcox
   **Director:** Charles S. Dubin
   **Guest Stars:** Clyde Kusatsu, Allan Arbus, Philip Bruns, James
   Lough, David Cramer

Dr. Freedman treats a wounded Asian-American war hero who
would rather commit suicide than return home.

**191**   Dreams                            February 18, 1980
   **Writer:** Alan Alda
   **Story:** Alan Alda, James Jay Rubinfier
   **Director:** Alan Alda
   **Guest Stars:** Ford Rainey, Robin Haynes, Catherine Bergstrom,
   Fred Stuthman, Kurtis Sanders, Ray Lynch, Connie Izay

The staff's worst fears and most desperate frustrations are explored
as they daydream during short catnaps away from the rigors of
surgery.

B.J.'s dream features the first appearance of his wife, Peg, played by
Catherine Bergstrom.

**192**   War Co-Respondent                 March 3, 1980
   **Writer:** Mike Farrell
   **Director:** Mike Farrell
   **Guest Stars:** Susan Saint James, Brad Wilkin, Calvin Levels

B.J. wrestles with his conscience when he nearly forsakes his marriage for an infatuation with an attractive war correspondent.

Susan Saint James is the reporter who tempts B.J. She'd been Rock Hudson's TV wife for six seasons of NBC's *McMillan and Wife* when she joined the sitcom camp as one half of *Kate and Allie* on CBS in 1984.

**193**   Back Pay                                    March 10, 1980
   **Writers:** Thad Mumford, Dan Wilcox, Dennis Koenig
   **Director:** Burt Metcalfe
   **Guest Stars:** Sab Shimono, Peter Kim, Jerry Fujikawa, G.W. Bailey, Richard Herd, Roy Goldman

Hawkeye bills the Army $38,000 for his services to protest the profits that civilian doctors are reaping from their contributions to the war effort.

**194**   April Fools                                 March 24, 1980
   **Writer:** Dennis Koenig
   **Director:** Charles S. Dubin
   **Guest Stars:** Pat Hingle, G.W. Bailey, Roy Goldman, Jennifer Davis

Potter warns the camp to be on their best behavior when a hard-boiled colonel schedules his inspection during the 4077th's April Fool's Day festivities.

## 1980-81   THE NINTH SEASON

*Year-End Rating: 25.7 (4th place)*

After nearly 200 episodes, the characters are superbly defined, but the irony is inescapable: As the years mount, these well-drawn and articulate characters are rapidly running out of things to say.

Dan Wilcox and Thad Mumford are the ninth season's executive script consultants, and Dennis Koenig is the executive story editor. John Rappaport returns as producer, and Gene Reynolds, Alan Alda, and Ronny Graham continue to serve as special creative and story consultants.

**195** The Best of Enemies                                          November 17, 1980
  **Writer:** Sheldon Bull
  **Director:** Charles S. Dubin
  **Guest Stars:** Mako, Steven Lum

A North Korean soldier forces Hawkeye to perform an emergency roadside operation on his buddy.

**196** Letters                                                      November 24, 1980
  **Writer:** Dennis Koenig
  **Director:** Charles S. Dubin
  **Guest Stars:** Richard Paul, Eileen Saki, Larry Cedar, Michael Currie, Shari Saba

Members of the 4077th share their impressions of war in response to letters from fourth graders in Hawkeye's hometown.

**197** Cementing Relationships                                      December 1, 1980
  **Writers:** David Pollack, Elias Davis
  **Director:** Charles S. Dubin
  **Guest Stars:** Joel Brooks, Alan Toy, Mel Harris

A jilted Italian soldier is smitten by Margaret; and Klinger pours a cement floor in the operating room to fight the spread of germs.

**198** Father's Day                                                 December 8, 1980
  **Writer:** Karen L. Hall
  **Director:** Alan Alda
  **Guest Stars:** Andrew Duggan, Jeffrey Kramer, Art Le Fleur, Roy Evans

Margaret has trouble pretending she's a chip off the old block when her dad, blood-and-guts "Howitzer" Al Houlihan, arrives for a visit.

**199** Death Takes a Holiday                                        December 15, 1980
  **Writer:** Mike Farrell
  **Director:** Mike Farrell
  **Guest Stars:** G.W. Bailey, Keye Luke, Yoshiko Hoover

Christmas at the 4077th finds the surgeons struggling to keep a mortally wounded soldier alive, even if it's only through the holiday.

**200**   A War for All Seasons                    December 29, 1980
   **Writers:** Dan Wilcox, Thad Mumford
   **Director:** Burt Metcalfe
   **Guest Stars:** Carl Freed, Laurie Bates, Jeff Maxwell

On New Year's Eve, the staff looks back on the highlights of 1951: The doctors invent an artificial kidney machine; Mulcahy plants a garden; and Margaret takes up knitting.

**201**   Your Retention, Please                    January 5, 1981
   **Writer:** Erik Tarloff
   **Director:** Charles S. Dubin
   **Guest Stars:** Barry Corbin, Sam Weisman, Jeff Maxwell

Klinger is so depressed by news that his ex-wife plans to remarry, he re-enlists for an additional six-year hitch.

By this time Klinger had already given up on his section-eight discharge, and with it, his wardrobe of Twentieth Century-Fox originals.

**202**   Tell It to the Marines                    January 12, 1981
   **Writer:** Hank Bradford
   **Director:** Harry Morgan
   **Guest Stars:** Stan Wells, Michael McGuirre, Denny Miller, James Gallery

Winchester takes command during Potter's absence; and B.J. and Hawkeye try to convince the Marines to grant a hardship discharge to an immigrant soldier.

**203**   Taking the Fifth                    January 19, 1981
   **Writers:** Elias Davis, David Pollack
   **Director:** Charles S. Dubin
   **Guest Stars:** Charles Hallahan, Judy Farrell, Margie Impert, Susan Berger

Hawkeye uses a bottle of vintage wine to lure unsuspecting nurses into his den; and Potter tries to secure a different sort of anesthetic when the Army threatens to ban a painkiller.

Alda and the writers have a bit of fun with Hawkeye's bygone reputation as a ladies' man. Hawkeye, once the rooster of the henhouse, is reduced to posting a notice on the nurses' bulletin board practically begging for a volunteer.

**204**   Operation Friendship                    January 26, 1981
**Writer:** Dennis Koenig
**Director:** Rena Down
**Guest Stars:** Tim O'Connor, Gwen Farrell

Klinger saves Winchester's life when an explosion rocks the operating room; and B.J. is reluctant to reveal the extent of his injuries after the blast.

**205**   No Sweat                              February 2, 1981
**Writer:** John Rappaport
**Director:** Burt Metcalfe
**Guest Stars:** W. Perren Page, Jeff Maxwell, Kellye Nakahara

Margaret develops a case of prickly heat—just one of the indignities suffered by the 4077th staff during another unendurably hot night.

**206**   Depressing News                       February 9, 1981
**Writers:** Dan Wilcox, Thad Mumford
**Director:** Alan Alda
**Guest Stars:** William Bogert, David Dozer, Albert Insinnia

Klinger's Army newspaper reports on Hawkeye's monument to military stupidity: a giant tower made from a half million erroneously shipped tongue depressors.

**207**   No Laughing Matter                    February 16, 1981
**Writers:** Elias Davis, David Pollack
**Director:** Burt Metcalfe
**Guest Stars:** Robert Symonds, Mae Hi, Nathan Jung

Hawkeye wagers that he can go a full day without a wisecrack; and Winchester finally confronts the major who exiled him to the 4077th.

**208**   Oh, How We Danced                     February 23, 1981
**Writer:** John Rappaport
**Director:** Burt Metcalfe
**Guest Stars:** Yuki Shimoda, Arlen Dean Snyder, Catherine Bergstrom, Michael Choe, Jennifer Davis

Winchester is sent to inspect sanitary conditions on the front lines while the rest of the camp plans a surprise anniversary party for B.J.

**209**   Bottoms Up                             March 2, 1981
**Writer:** Dennis Koenig
**Director:** Alan Alda
**Guest Stars:** Gail Strickland, Shari Saba, Kellye Nakahara

One of Margaret's nurses tries to hide a severe drinking problem; and Hawkeye is scorned after a practical joke he plays on Winchester backfires.

**210**   The Red/White Blues                  March 9, 1981
**Writers:** David Pollack, Elias Davis
**Director:** Gabriel Beaumont
**Guest Stars:** Roy Goldman, Jeff Maxwell, Kellye Nakahara

Colonel Potter nearly blows his stack when his well-intentioned colleagues begin to mollycoddle him in an effort to lower his blood pressure before his upcoming physical.

**211**   Bless You, Hawkeye                   March 16, 1981
**Writers:** Dan Wilcox, Thad Mumford
**Director:** Nell Cox
**Guest Stars:** Allan Arbus, Barry Schwartz

When Hawkeye can't stop an apparently psychosomatic sneezing fit, psychiatrist Sidney Freedman digs into the surgeon's past for a clue to the unusual malady.

**212**   Blood Brothers                           April 6, 1981
**Writers:** Elias Davis, David Pollack
**Director:** Harry Morgan
**Guest Stars:** Patrick Swayze, Ray Middleton, G.W. Bailey

Hawkeye is overcome by the devotion of a terminally ill GI for his critically wounded buddy.

**213**   The Foresight Saga                    April 13, 1981
**Writers:** Elias Davis, David Pollack
**Director:** Charles S. Dubin
**Guest Stars:** Rummel Mor, Philip Sterling, Jeff Maxwell

The 4077th is given a gift of fresh-grown vegetables by a grateful Korean; and Potter questions the veracity of an upbeat letter from Radar.

**214**   The Life You Save                         May 4, 1981
**Writers:** John Rappaport, Alan Alda
**Director:** Alan Alda
**Guest Stars:** G.W. Bailey, Val Bisoglio

After Charles is nearly felled by a sniper's bullet, he develops a philosophical obsession with death.

## 1981-82   THE TENTH SEASON

*Year-End Rating: 22.3 (10th place)*

Stories in the tenth year again focus on the personalities of the central characters, who are forced, by the thinning plot lines, to explore situations that range from the mundane—poker games, petty thefts, and toothaches—to the bizarre: in one episode a goat swallows a $22,000 payroll.

The creative staff for the final two seasons includes John Rappaport, now the supervising producer; and Thad Mumford, Dan Wilcox, and Dennis Koenig, the new producers. Elias Davis and David Pollack are the executive script consultants, and Karen Hall is story editor in the tenth year, and executive story editor for the final season.

**215**   That's Show Biz (one hour)              October 26, 1981
**Writers:** Elias Davis, David Pollack
**Director:** Charles S. Dubin
**Guest Stars:** Gwen Verdon, Gail Edwards, Danny Dayton, Karen Landry, Amanda McBroom

A touring USO show brings an unexpected touch of vaudeville to the 4077th when the star showgirl requires an emergency operation.

**216**   Identity Crisis                         November 2, 1981
**Writers:** Dan Wilcox, Thad Mumford
**Director:** David Ogden Stiers
**Guest Stars:** Dirk Blocker, Squire Fridell, Joe Pantoliano

Father Mulcahy counsels a GI who is plagued by guilt.

**217**    Rumor at the Top               November 9, 1981
**Writers:** David Pollack, Elias Davis
**Director:** Charles S. Dubin
**Guest Stars:** Nicholas Pryor, Jeff Maxwell, Roy Goldman

The latest scuttlebutt affects everyone's behavior when a visiting emissary is rumored to be recruiting for a new *M\*A\*S\*H* unit.

**218**    Give 'Em Hell, Hawkeye          November 16, 1981
**Writers:** Dennis Koenig
**Director:** Charles S. Dubin
**Guest Stars:** Stefan Gierasch, Ed Vasgersian, Tom Kindle

Hawkeye writes a heartfelt letter to President Harry Truman to protest the continued fighting in Korea.

**219**    Wheelers and Dealers           November 23, 1981
**Writers:** Dan Wilcox, Thad Mumford
**Director:** Charles S. Dubin
**Guest Stars:** Anthony Charnota, Tony Becker, Chris Petersen

On the eve of a big poker game, B.J.'s pride is bruised when he finds out that his wife is working as a waitress; and Potter takes driving lessons from Klinger.

**220**    Communication Breakdown        November 30, 1981
**Writer:** Karen L. Hall
**Director:** Alan Alda
**Guest Stars:** James Saito, Byron Chung, Abby Nelson

Winchester infuriates the camp when he hoards his Stateside newspapers; and Hawkeye reunites two Korean brothers who have been fighting on opposite sides of the war.

**221**    Snap Judgment (Part 1)            December 7, 1981
**Writer:** Paul Perlove
**Director:** Hy Averback
**Guest Star:** Peter Hobbs

The military police think they've solved a rash of thefts at the 4077th when they apprehend Klinger with Hawkeye's stolen camera.

**222**   Snappier Judgment (Part 2)          December 14, 1981
    **Writer:** Paul Perlove
    **Director:** Hy Averback
    **Guest Star:** Peter Hobbs

B.J. and Hawkeye resolve to clear Klinger's name after he chooses
Winchester to defend him at his military court-martial.


**223**   'Twas the Day After Christmas          December 28, 1981
    **Writers:** David Pollack, Elias Davis
    **Director:** Burt Metcalfe
    **Guest Stars:** Michael Ensign, Leo Lewis, Val Bisoglio

To boost post-Yuletide morale on December 26, Potter has the
officers and enlisted men exchange jobs for the day.


**224**   Follies of the Living—Concerns          January 4, 1982
       of the Dead
    **Writer:** Alan Alda
    **Director:** Alan Alda
    **Guest Stars:** Kario Salem, Randall Patrick, Jeff Tyler

In a fever dream, Klinger communicates with the spirit of a dead
soldier who stays on to witness his own last rites.


**225**   The Birthday Girls          January 11, 1982
    **Writer:** Karen L. Hall
    **Director:** Charles S. Dubin
    **Guest Stars:** Jerry Fujikawa, Kellye Nakahara

Margaret's birthday plans are spoiled when she and Klinger get
stranded on a desolate roadside; and the surgeons assist in the
delivery of a calf.


**226**   Blood and Guts          January 18, 1982
    **Writer:** Lee H. Grant
    **Director:** Charles S. Dubin
    **Guest Stars:** Gene Evans, Brett Cullen, Stoney Jackson

Hawkeye is outraged when a sensationalistic war correspondent
reports irresponsible GI stunts as tales of military valor.

**227**    A Holy Mess                              February 1, 1982
  **Writers:** Elias Davis, David Pollack
  **Director:** Burt Metcalfe
  **Guest Stars:** Cyril O'Reilly, David Graf, Val Bisoglio

An AWOL officer seeks sanctuary behind Father Mulcahy's robes.

**228**    The Tooth Shall Set You Free             February 8, 1982
  **Writers:** Elias Davis, David Pollack
  **Director:** Charles S. Dubin
  **Guest Stars:** Tom Atkins, Jason Bernard, John Fujioka, Larry
  Fishburne

Charles faces a tooth extraction; and the doctors suspect prejudice when an inordinate number of black casualties are brought
in from a single unit.

**229**    Pressure Points                          February 15, 1982
  **Writer:** David Pollack
  **Director:** Charles S. Dubin
  **Guest Stars:** Allan Arbus, John O'Connell, Gene Pietragallo,
  William Rogers, Roy Goldman

Potter sends for the Army psychiatrist when he loses confidence
in his own surgical abilities; and Winchester loses patience with
his bunkmates' sloppiness.

**230**    Where There's a Will, There's a War     February 22, 1982
  **Writers:** Elias Davis, David Pollack
  **Director:** Alan Alda
  **Guest Stars:** Dennis Howard, Larry Ward, Jim Borelli, James
  Emery

Hawkeye draws up a will under heavy shelling at the front lines.

**231**    Promotion Commotion                      March 1, 1982
  **Writer:** Dennis Koenig
  **Director:** Charles S. Dubin
  **Guest Stars:** John Matuszak, Jim Reid Boyce, Deborah Harmon,
  Cameron Dye, Richard Fullerton

Winchester, Pierce, and Hunnicut find themselves in the sticky
position of having to decide which enlisted men to recommend
for promotion.

**232** Heroes                              March 15, 1982
**Writers:** Thad Mumford, Dan Wilcox
**Director:** Nell Cox
**Guest Stars:** Pat McNamara, Earl Boen, Britt Leach, Matthew Faison

Hawkeye is the golden boy of the world press when he treats a celebrity prize fighter for a stroke.

**233** Sons and Bowlers                    March 22, 1982
**Writers:** Elias Davis, David Pollack
**Director:** Hy Averback
**Guest Stars:** Dick O'Neill, William Lucking, Roger Hampton

Hawkeye anxiously awaits word on his father's Stateside operation as his cohorts engage the Marines in a bowling tournament.

**234** Picture This                        April 5, 1982
**Writer:** Karen L. Hall
**Director:** Burt Metcalfe
**Guest Stars:** John Fujioka, Jeff Maxwell

Potter's attempts to assemble the crew for a family portrait are thwarted by a feud between bunkmates Pierce, Hunnicut, and Winchester.

**235** That Darn Kid                       April 12, 1982
**Writer:** Karen L. Hall
**Director:** David Ogden Stiers
**Guest Stars:** George Presnell, John P. Ryan, Tom Kindle

Klinger's goat eats the 4077th's $22,000 payroll, leaving paymaster Hawkeye holding the bag.

## 1982-83   THE ELEVENTH SEASON

*Year-End Rating: 22.6 (3rd place)*

With the show's research and story sources completely exhausted after eleven years—and most of the cast restless to move on—the long-running series calls it quits in one final season that culminates in the most highly anticipated TV program of all time: the last episode of *M*A*S*H*.

**236**   Hey, Look Me Over                          October 25, 1982
   **Writer:** Alan Alda
   **Director:** Susan Oliver
   **Guest Stars:** Kellye Nakahara, Peggy Feury, Perry Lang,
   Deborah Harmon

Hawkeye watches Nurse Kellye brighten a wounded GI's final
moments and comes to appreciate the nurses' vital contribution to
the healing process.

Kellye Nakahara had played Nurse Kellye since the very first year,
when she signed on as a background extra and never left.

The show kept a regular crew of actresses on the payroll to play the
various nurses who staffed the operating room from week to week—
and each got a crash course in actual triage and O.R. techniques on their
first day of shooting. Less obvious is the company of recurring actors
who played background GIs or wounded soldiers—and sometimes both.
More than one battlefield casualty reappears miraculously in the mess
tent in a later episode—a hungry Lazarus, courtesy of the Screen Actors
Guild.

**237**   Trick or Treatment                          November 1, 1982
   **Writer:** Dennis Koenig
   **Director:** Charles S. Dubin
   **Guest Stars:** George Wendt, Richard Lineback, Andrew Clay,
   James Lough

The 4077th Halloween party hosts an unexpected guest after Father Mulcahy works an apparent miracle during the reading of a
soldier's last rites.

George Wendt already seems typecast as a drunken reveler—the rotund actor had just been cast to occupy a regular barstool at Sam's place
on NBC's *Cheers*.

**238**   Foreign Affairs                          November 8, 1982
   **Writers:** David Pollack, Elias Davis
   **Director:** Charles S. Dubin
   **Guest Stars:** Melinda Mullins, Jeffrey Tambor, Soon Teck Oh,
   Byron Chung

The Army tries to get a North Korean pilot to defect; and Charles gets a rude shock when he falls for a French nurse with an unacceptable past.

**239** The Joker Is Wild                    November 15, 1982
   **Writers:** John Rappaport, Dennis Koenig
   **Director:** Burt Metcalfe
   **Guest Stars:** Clyde Kusatsu, David Haid

Hawkeye's guard is up when B.J. threatens to pull off the most elaborate practical joke in the compound's history.

**240** Who Knew?                    November 22, 1982
   **Writers:** David Pollack, Elias Davis
   **Director:** Harry Morgan
   **Guest Stars:** Kellye Nakahara, Enid Kent

Hawkeye volunteers to deliver the eulogy for a dead nurse and belatedly discovers her deep feelings for him.

The surgeon had dallied with the nurse on a few harmless evenings but never considered that her attraction for him might be serious. His eulogy, colored by this guilt, makes for the strangest farewell of the entire season: The feminist Hawkeye bids adieu to the womanizing cad that was once Hawkeye Pierce.

**241** Bombshells                    November 29, 1982
   **Writers:** Dan Wilcox, Thad Mumford
   **Director:** Charles S. Dubin
   **Guest Stars:** Gerald O'Laughlin, Allen Williams, Stu Charno

Charles and Hawkeye start a rumor that Marilyn Monroe plans to visit the 4077th; and B.J. feels responsible when he's unable to rescue a wounded soldier.

**242**   Settling Debts                    December 6, 1982
**Writers:** Dan Wilcox, Thad Mumford
**Director:** Mike Switzer
**Guest Stars:** Guy Boyd, Jeff East

Hawkeye and the crew surprise Colonel Potter with a party to commemorate Mildred's final payment on the couple's mortgage.

**243**   The Moon Is Not Blue              December 13, 1982
**Writer:** Larry Balmagia
**Director:** Charles S. Dubin
**Guest Stars:** Hamilton Camp, Sandy Helberg, Jan Jorden

With the camp facing prohibition and a severe medical-supply shortage during another heat wave, Hawkeye resolves to lift morale by importing a racy new movie.

**244**   Run for the Money                 December 20, 1982
**Writers:** Mike Farrell, David Pollack, Elias Davis
**Director:** Nell Cox
**Guest Stars:** Thomas Calloway, Mark Anderson, Phil Brock, William Schilling, Robert Alan Browne

When an Olympic runner assigned to the 4077th fails to materialize, Father Mulcahy must save the camp's honor in a high-stakes footrace against the 8063rd.

**245**   U.N. the Night and the Music      January 3, 1983
**Writers:** David Pollack, Elias Davis
**Director:** Harry Morgan
**Guest Stars:** George Innes, Kavi Raz, Dennis Holahan, David Packer

A United Nations delegation—a Swede, a Hindu, and a British officer—tours the 4077th, and each leaves a lasting effect on the men and women of the camp.

The show's reputation for seamlessly blending comedy and drama began to suffer as the years advanced. Here, B.J.'s dramatic decision to amputate a young GI's leg—all dark lighting and slow, ponderous line readings—is awkwardly juxtaposed with a ludicrous slapstick sequence where Colonel Potter learns to stand on his head.

The onscreen sparks shared by Margaret and her handsome Swede ignited an offscreen romance that eventually led to the marriage of Loretta Swit and actor Dennis Holahan.

**246**   Strange Bedfellows                       January 10, 1983
  **Writer:** Mike Farrell
  **Director:** Karen L. Hall
  **Guest Stars:** Dennis Dugan, Benjamin F. Wilson

The 4077th faces a sleepless night as Charles's snoring keeps B.J. and Hawkeye from counting sheep; and Colonel Potter discovers that his son-in-law has had an affair.

**247**   Say No More                             January 24, 1983
  **Writer:** John Rappaport
  **Director:** Charles S. Dubin
  **Guest Stars:** John Anderson, Michael Horton, Chip Johnson, James Karen

A military strategist refuses to accept responsibility for the war games that have mortally wounded his own son; and Margaret develops laryngitis.

**248**   Friends and Enemies                     February 7, 1983
  **Writer:** Karen L. Hall
  **Director:** Jamie Farr
  **Guest Star:** John McLiam

Colonel Potter must decide whether to blow the whistle on an old Army chum whose military follies are costing boys their lives.

**249**   Give and Take                           February 14, 1983
  **Writer:** Dennis Koenig
  **Director:** Charles S. Dubin
  **Guest Stars:** Craig Wasson, G.W. Bailey, Derek Wong

A wounded GI learns a painful lesson when he forms a recovery-room friendship with the enemy soldier he's critically wounded.

**250**   As Time Goes By                    February 21, 1983
    **Writers:** Dan Wilcox, Thad Mumford
    **Director:** Burt Metcalfe
    **Guest Stars:** Rosalind Chao, G.W. Bailey, Michael Swan, Mark
    Herrier, Jeff Maxwell

Hawkeye and Margaret encapsulate the breadth of their wartime
experience when they bury souvenirs as a reminder for future
generations.

Actually the last episode filmed, "As Time Goes By" offers an economical alternative to the unwieldy behemoth that eventually closed the
series the following week. Margaret briefly, almost nostalgically, re-
emerges as the spitfire patriot who "sees the world through khaki-col-
ored glasses," and Hawkeye goes out, as always, the cynical romantic.
The pair bury their memories along with the hatchet in a classic episode
that strikes a near-perfect balance of sentiment, statement, and smiles.


**251**   Good-Bye, Farewell and Amen        February 28, 1983
         (2 1/2-hour special)
    **Writers:** Alan Alda, Burt Metcalfe, John Rappaport, Thad
    Mumford, Dan Wilcox, David Pollack, Elias Davis, Karen L.
    Hall
    **Director:** Alan Alda
    **Guest Stars:** Allan Arbus, Rosalind Chao, G.W. Bailey, Shari
    Saba, Jeff Maxwell, Gwen Farrell, Kellye Nakahara, Roy
    Goldman

The men and women of M*A*S*H discover that a peace treaty
doesn't vanquish the horrors of war overnight. Hawkeye suffers a
nervous breakdown when he tries to suppress memories of a hei-
nous atrocity; and Charles teaches a group of Chinese prisoners to
play a Mozart quintet, only to see them killed in the last gasp of
fighting.

At last, the armistice is signed, and the weary medics regroup for final farewells as they face their inevitable futures. Klinger makes plans to
stay in Korea with his native bride; Charles returns to Boston as he bids
Margaret adieu with a book of Browning and a kiss; and Hawkeye and
B.J. deliver their first—and only—full military salute to Colonel Potter
before each embarks on his own private journey back to a blessed sanity.

Larry Gelbart envisioned a different scenario for the final episode. In the *Los Angeles Times*, he described what he saw as the only logical conclusion to so many seasons of televised war: "I wanted the camera to pull back and back and back, and I wanted to hear a director say, 'Cut,' and see the cast embrace and say good-bye." Then, Alan Alda would turn, face the camera, and say directly to the audience:

No matter how we tried, we could give you only an idea of what it was like. The blood was a pale imitation. This is only a show. War is not this manageable . . . or this entertaining.

Not surprisingly, that ending was never even considered.

## EMMY AWARDS

The following is a complete listing of the Emmy Awards bestowed on *M*A*S*H* by the National Academy of Television Arts and Sciences.

**1973-74**  Outstanding Comedy Series
Outstanding Lead Actor in a Comedy Series: Alan Alda
Actor of the Year, Series: Alan Alda
Outstanding Directing in Comedy: Jackie Cooper, "Carry On, Hawkeye"

**1974-75**  Outstanding Directing in a Comedy Series: Gene Reynolds, "O.R."

**1975-76**  Outstanding Directing in a Comedy Series: Gene Reynolds, "Welcome to Korea"
Outstanding Film Editing for Entertainment Programming: Stanford Tischler, Fred W. Berger, "Welcome to Korea"

**1976-77**  Outstanding Continuous Performance by a Supporting Actor in a Comedy Series: Gary Burghoff
Outstanding Directing in a Comedy Series: Alan Alda, "Dear Sigmund"

**1978-79**  Outstanding Writing in a Comedy Series: Alan Alda, "Inga"

**1979-80**  Outstanding Supporting Actor in a Comedy Series: Harry Morgan
Outstanding Supporting Actress in a Comedy Series: Loretta Swit

**1981-82**  Outstanding Lead Actor in a Comedy Series: Alan Alda
Outstanding Supporting Actress in a Comedy Series:
  Loretta Swit

CBS didn't think anyone would accept Lucille Ball as the wacky wife of Desi Arnaz's Cuban bandleader, but their stubborn determination yielded "I Love Lucy," television's very first classic sitcom.

Jackie Gleason, Audrey Meadows, Art Carney, Joyce Randolph—the cast of "The Honeymooners"—a classic that remains as funny on the third, fourth, even tenth viewing as it was the first time around.

A sense of dingy reality permeated every fiber of the series, from Norton's battered felt hat to the Kramden's Depression-era kitchen. "Make it real," Gleason told his writers. "If it i

BUY
S. SAVINGS BONDS
the Payroll Savings Plan Today

Even stronger than the Kramden's conjugal ties—and perhaps more crucial to the show's chemistry—was the spiritual bond shared by lodge brothers Ralph and Ed.

Wiry, even-tempered, reasonably satisfied with his life, Art Carney's Ed Norton was everything Ralph Kramden was not—and yet, it was in Norton's childlike devotion that Kramden found strength.

Mary Tyler Moore, Dick Van Dyke, Larry Mathews—the Petries—on "The Dick Van Dyke Show," an undisputed masterpiece in the admittedly thin annals of television art.

"It was like a lovely party you never wanted to end," recalls Morey Am-sterdam, pictured here with Rose Marie, Van Dyke, and Tyler Moore—the nucleus of one of TV's great ensembles.

The producers considered casting Johnny Carson, but finally chose Dick Van Dyke to play Rob Petrie because he seemed shy, like a writer. Mary Tyler Moore landed the role of Laura after Carl Reiner heard her say hello . . . like a real person.

Mary Tyler Moore as associate news producer Mary Richards. For the first time television showed us a beautiful young woman who was single by choice, not chance.

"The Mary Tyler Moore Show" family: Gavin MacLeod, Mary Tyler Moore, Ted Knight, Valerie Harper, Edward Asner, Cloris Leachman. In later seasons they were joined by Betty White and Georgia Engel (right). Each would probably agree that they did the best work of their careers on the series.

The episodes that defined and explored Mary's friendship with Rhoda Morgenstern—many of them script-ed by women writers—often carried a sharp sting of truth.

Mary Richards' compassion for her boss set the stage for one of the most graceful love affairs in popular fiction: the unconsummated romance between Mary and Lou.

Mary looks on as Ted Baxter, played by Ted Knight, comforts Ed Asner's Lou Grant. Each member of the cast represented the perfect marriage of actor and role.

All in the Family's Jean Stapleton, Carroll O'Connor, Sally Struthers, and Rob Reiner as America's noisiest neighbors, the Archie Bunker clan of Queens, New York.

Long-suffering Edith Bunker appeals to Archie, who was once described by his creator as "basically a horse's ass." Somehow this incongruous pair made an absolutely convincing married couple.

It's hard to imagine a different pair of actors in the roles of Gloria and Mike Stivic, but Sally Struthers and Rob Reiner were actually the third couple to play those parts.

The unkempt original cast of CBS's bawdy, brawling—and initially low-rated—antiwar comedy, M*A*S*H (clockwise, from the left): Larry Linville, Wayne Rogers, Gary Burghoff, Mac-Lean Stevenson, Alan Alda, Loretta Swit.

Jamie Farr models another hand-me-down from the Twentieth Century-Fox wardrobe department. Klinger's efforts to get thrown out of the military were inspired by writer Larry Gelbart's recollection of how Lenny Bruce attempted a similar gambit to get discharged from the Navy.

There was more sentiment than slapstick in later seasons, but after eleven years the 4077th staff had developed into TV's most fully defined character ensemble (*left to right, from the top*): William Christopher, Jamie Farr, Mike Farrell, Henry Morgan, Loretta Swit, David Ogden Stiers, Alan Alda.

The cast of *The Bob Newhart Show*—Marcia Wallace, Bob New-hart, Peter Bonerz, Suzanne Pleshette, Bill Daily—inhabitants of a surreal universe that frequently resembled Alice's Wonderland.

The Hartleys' unabashed sexuality gave the series a distinctive, sophisticated edge, but writers admit that they were equally tickled by the comic possibilities of the situation. Chuckled one of the show's creators, "It was funny to imagine Newhart in bed."

Tom Poston makes a guest appearance as Bob's old friend, the Peeper. The irony was that Bob's cast of crazies behaved as if they were the most well-adjusted characters on television.

The members of Barney Miller's detective squad—Jack Soo, Steve Landesberg, Ron Glass, Hal Linden, James Gregory, Max Gail, Ron Carey—were seldom afraid to share the spotlight with the host of bit players who gave the show its heart.

Abe Vigoda's Detective Fish proved so popular that ABC (and Vigoda himself) insisted that his character be given a spinoff, a request that producer Danny Arnold resisted for two seasons.

Unlike most TV supercops, the Twelfth Precinct detectives usually came up short in their struggles with the unrelenting stress of police work, a fact that caused law-enforcement agencies to applaud Barney Miller as the most realistic show on television.

The first-season cast of *Taxi*, worthy heirs of the MTM legacy (*clockwise, from top left*): Randall Carver, Andy Kaufman, Judd Hirsch, Tony Danza, Danny DeVito, Jeff Conaway, Marilu Henner.

Like Latka, Christopher Lloyd's Reverend Jim Ignatowski also hailed from a far-distant reality—in Jim's case, the faraway land of the 1960s.

Danny DeVito's Louie De Palma squares off with Marilu Henner's Elaine Nardo. Venal, disagreeable, dishonest, the pint-sized dispatcher quickly rose to the status of co-star in an ensemble loaded with memorable characters.

Funny, sophisticated, unpredictable, "Cheers" outlashed an initial season of dismal ratings to emerge as one of the top comedies of the 1980s (*left to right, from the top*): Shelly Long, Ted Danson, Woody Harrelson, Rhea Perlman, George Wendt, John Ratzenberger.

In later seasons, the gang at Cheers grew to embrace an emotionally overwrought bar manager, Rebecca Howe, and a pair of overeducated analysts, Dr. Frasier Crane and his wife, Lilith Sternin-Crane. Front row, left to right: George Wendt, Kirstie Alley, Ted Danson, John Ratzenberger. Back row, left to right: Rhea Perlman, Woody Harrelson, Kelsey Grammer, Bebe Neuwirth.

The most turbulent affair on prime time—the love story of Sam and Diane—offered a frequently harrowing look at the dark underside of modern romance.

# THE BOB NEWHART SHOW

·

*The show was so often
overlooked because it was
always in Mary's shadow.*
—GLEN CHARLES

MARY was a smash.

Her show was not just a hit, but a hit with class. And at CBS—the self-styled Tiffany's of television—class was valued almost as highly as ratings. That Mary Tyler Moore was able to deliver both made her very special, perhaps even one of a kind. And yet, who could blame the network for inquiring if there were any more at home like her?

"There was a strong feeling that if that show's working, there might be another one there," remembers Alan Wagner, the network's head of new program development during that fertile period in the early 1970s. "The place was bubbling with creative enthusiasm." Late in *Mary's* first year, the CBS executive casually approached two of that show's most prolific contibutors to see if they would be interested in writing a series of their own.

David Davis and Lorenzo Music were flattered—and excited. The prospect of creating a series of your very own is every TV writer's dream. But it would have to wait—they were too busy writing and producing *Mary Tyler Moore* to give much thought to anything beyond next week's show. The writers found themselves in the ironic position of having an open invitation to pitch a show to the network—and not a single idea for a series.

As their fateful appointment with Alan Wagner loomed closer, David Davis had an inspiration. "We don't have to come up with any ideas at all," he told his partner. "Let's just ask CBS what stars they've already signed for the fall. Then, we'll just volunteer to create a brand-new show for any one of them."

But, as the writers sat down on the wide couch that faced Alan Wagner's executive swivel chair, they couldn't help but notice that he already seemed less enthusiastic than he had when they'd first met.

"Before we even start, I've gotta tell you—it's not a very good time for this meeting," began Wagner. "We've already spent this season's budget for new development, so even if I absolutely love it, there's no way we could act on your idea just now."

Music and Davis were relieved. "Oh, that's okay," answered Music, "'cause we don't really have any ideas."

The executive leaned forward in his chair, suddenly intrigued. "Tell me more."

Davis explained how they'd hoped to create a brand-new series for one of CBS's contract stars, and Wagner stopped him midsentence. It was a good plan, but it had one flaw: The network hadn't signed a star to an exclusive contract in years. "We don't work that way anymore," he explained. But still, his curiosity piqued, he leaned back and posed a question. "If you *could* tailor a show to any star in the world—anyone you wanted—who would it be?"

It didn't take the writers long to answer that one. Without a pause, they answered in unison.

"Bob Newhart."

The writers left the meeting with the network's go-ahead to write a pilot for a new series called *The Bob Newhart Show*.

"We were very interested in Newhart," recalls Wagner. "I felt he was an essentially untried television performer with great potential. He'd tried one variety show ten years earlier—hardly enough to make a fair assessment." The executive was also aware that Newhart's manager, Arthur Price, had experienced great success with another of his clients who had done quite well in television—a perky actress named Mary Tyler Moore.

Even so, convincing the successful comic to settle down to the weekly grind of series television would not be easy. Newhart was an established nightclub star whose comedy albums had sold in the millions. As for television, he still shuddered at the thought of his first series, an award-winning 1961 variety show that somehow failed to make it past a single season. The first *Bob Newhart Show* had left the star convinced that weekly television was simply not for him.

But David Davis and Lorenzo Music were determined to prove him wrong.

In fact, they'd already tried twice before. One of the team's first scripts had been a *Love, American Style* episode that they'd custom-tailored to the button-down style of Bob Newhart. He turned it down. They later wrote a love-struck tax auditor into one of the earliest *Mary Tyler Moore* scripts—a plum role created especially for the accountant-turned-comic. Once again, Newhart passed, and the part went to Paul Sand.

"It wasn't that he didn't like our scripts," quipped Lorenzo Music. "I think he just didn't want to learn all those lines." In fact, Newhart had long respected Music's ability to capture him on paper. When the comic was a guest on *The Smothers Brothers Comedy Hour* in the late 1960s, Music—along with Carl Gottlieb—created a monologue that featured Newhart as a harried air-traffic controller. The star liked the piece so much that he bought it and used it in his nightclub act for years.

Davis and Music were confident that they'd have no trouble creating a series that would fit the star's unique style. The hardest part would be finding the time to write it in between all their other duties as writer/ producers on *Mary Tyler Moore*. At last, the writers decided that their only hope might be to head for the beach.

"We went to Santa Barbara to figure the show out, just to get away from the phones and the families," is how Lorenzo Music described the ordeal. "We decided to take as long as it needed, and we set up a tough schedule. We'd get up at six in the morning and eat breakfast. Then we'd sit on the beach all day long and write. We wouldn't even eat—we just had Cokes for lunch. After four days, we'd written the pilot for *The Bob Newhart Show*."

They brought the script back to Alan Wagner in Hollywood, who loved it. He asked the writers how soon they could start shooting it as the pilot for the new series. Very soon, they assured him. Just as soon as they talked Newhart into doing it.

Once again, Alan Wagner leaned forward in his executive chair. "Oh," he ventured, "I thought you had him already."

"No," confessed Davis. "Not yet. We didn't want to approach him until we had a series commitment. But *now* we've got something to offer him."

As the writers turned to leave, the executive stopped them. "Well, don't worry—we like this pilot. Even if you *can't* get Newhart, we'll still do the series. We'll just try to find someone else."

Finding a replacement for Bob Newhart was a casting quandary that they would never have to face. The star liked their script as much as the network had. As Newhart recalled, "It was the first one I'd read where I didn't say, 'It's a good idea, but what do we do for show number two?'" The quality of the material, and the fact that Mary Tyler Moore had found such uncompromised success in the television medium, finally eased the star's lingering hesitations about signing on to do another series. "I kept saying no, it was kind of reflex," explained Newhart. "Then one day I asked myself why."

There was no arguing that the show Davis and Music created was different from anything the star had seen before. Bob would play psychologist Robert Hartley, an occupation the writers chose after going through an entire telephone directory. "Luckily it was in Santa Barbara, and they've got a skinny little phone book," recalls Lorenzo Music. "When we found 'psychologist,' we thought it sounded right. We figured out that Bob listens funny, so we wanted to find a job where he could listen to all sorts of people. As a psychologist, Bob could still be the guy everyone knew him to be—an accountant from Chicago who was kinda Catholic and kinda shockable."

They even set his practice in Chicago—geographically, anyway. For at times, the universe of *The Bob Newhart Show* more closely resembles something out of *Alice in Wonderland*.

Bob and Emily Hartley lived in a jabberwocky world that wasn't bound by conventional laws of psychology or logic. You never quite knew what to expect. Ordinary take-out burgers might come swathed in an entire ream of butcher paper. An elevator door could open to reveal a black militant businessman with a Great Dane named Whitey; an empty shaft; or a giggling family of all-Americans straight out of Norman Rockwell. And face a truckload of zucchini on this show, as one of Bob's patients had the misfortune to do, and you're as good as gone.

Yet somehow, all of this strange behavior was enacted by a cast of utterly believable characters whom we actually cared about. Like *The Mary Tyler Moore Show*, the series was populated by witty, sincere people who daily faced the irrational realities of ordinary life.

But the distance between Mary's Minneapolis and Bob's Chicago was far wider than the length of the state of Wisconsin. If *The Mary Tyler Moore Show* was offbeat, *The Bob Newhart Show* was positively surreal. While Mary and her friends fought a valiant if invariably losing struggle to maintain sanity in an absurd world, Bob and his extended family accepted absurdity as the natural order of things. In many ways, Bob and his loonies were among the most well-adjusted characters on television.

The show's undercurrent of preposterous logic was actually an outgrowth of Newhart's own clearly defined comic persona. The performer whose nightclub act routinely featured one-sided conversations with Abraham Lincoln, Sir Walter Raleigh, and King Kong was certainly no stranger to surrealism. "Comedy," Newhart once observed, "is my way of bringing logic to an illogical situation."

Of course, if all the show had to offer had been quirky characters and bizarre situations, it probably wouldn't have lasted the season. Over the life of the series, the show's many creators understood that their incredible flights of fancy could work only if one part of Bob Hartley's life remained rooted in a solid, wholesome reality—which is where the Hartleys' marriage came in. "Every one of the show's producers was committed to showing a good, sound, healthy adult marriage on television," commented long-time producer Michael Zinberg. And the casting of Suzanne Pleshette was crucial to that goal.

"We were trying to get away from the standard TV wife," David Davis recalled. To his surprise, he and Music discovered the perfect candidate when they happened to spy Pleshette as a guest on Johnny Carson's *Tonight Show*. "There she was, just what we were looking for." Adds Music, "She was sharp and sexy and hip and outspoken, and we said that's the woman for Bob."

And there can be little doubt that Pleshette's unapologetic sensuality gave the show a distinctive, sophisticated edge. And once the writers began to explore the realities of the couple's married life, it wasn't long before they and the Hartleys had dealt a critical blow to the prime-time puritanism that still dictated separate beds for even the happiest of married couples—an arrangement that was doomed from the first time Bob and Emily climbed between the covers of their king-size bed. By openly acknowledging that a couple on the far side of thirty could still enjoy a healthy, hearty sex life, the cast and creators of *The Bob Newhart Show* made it clear that this was a situation comedy for grown-ups.

"We were selling class and charm and wit," David Davis told *TV Guide's* Dwight Whitney. And the show didn't stray far from that principle throughout six seasons that saw contributions from some of television's most talented creators, including producers Tom Patchett and Jay Tarses, Martin Cohan, Gordon and Lynne Farr, and Glen and Les Charles; as well as directors Alan Rafkin, Peter Baldwin, Peter Bonerz, and Michael Zinberg.

Finally, after six years, Newhart decided to call it quits. "We hadn't slipped in any way," observed the star. "The show was still funny. Which was the time to get off."

Like *The Mary Tyler Moore Show* a year before, the series voluntarily left the air after contributing some of situation comedy's finest half hours.

But unlike its more illustrious counterpart, the passing of *Bob Newhart* didn't launch a spate of news articles or a flood of awards. "I was very proud of our show," Newhart told *The New York Times*, "but chagrined that the show and the people on it were never truly acknowledged by the TV industry—not one Emmy."

Perhaps it would be some consolation to the star that a good many of his show's writers and producers would go on to craft some of the finest situation comedies of the following decade, including *Taxi* and *Cheers*, to name only two top-drawer comedies that owed a considerable debt to the off-kilter comic anarchy pioneered by the unassuming little show that was always in Mary's shadow.

But finally, perhaps Bob Newhart himself summed it up best when he paid tribute to the show's fine acting ensemble—though he might just as well have been talking about any of the show's many creators. "We had so many good people—Suzanne Pleshette, Billy Daily, Marcia Wallace, Peter Bonerz, and the rest, and they all made it look too easy!"

# A Critical Guide to All 142 Episodes

|                                       |                  |
|---------------------------------------|------------------|
| Martha Hartley (Bob's mother)         | Martha Scott     |
| Gordon Borden (Howard's brother)      | William Redfield |
| Debbie Flett (Carol's fill-in)        | Shirley O'Hara   |
| Eddie, the Mailman                    | Bill Quinn       |

Created by David Davis, Lorenzo Music
Music by Pat Williams
Theme Song ("Home to Emily") by Lorenzo and Henrietta Music
Directors of photography were Paul Uhl, Edward E. Nugent (final year)
Principal directors were Alan Rafkin, Peter Bonerz, Peter Baldwin, Jay
    Sandrich, Michael Zinberg, Dick Martin

## 1972-73   THE FIRST SEASON

*Year-End Rating: 21.8 (16th place)*

The life and times of Chicago psychologist Bob Hartley and his wife, Emily, are chronicled by series creators David Davis and Lorenzo Music, who serve as executive producers for the first three seasons. They are also the first season producers, along with Bill Idelson. Michael Zinberg is the associate producer for the initial three years.

Primary directors in the premiere season are Jay Sandrich—on loan from *Mary Tyler Moore*—and Alan Rafkin, one of the show's most prolific directors. Freshman-year scripts are contributed by a handful of MTM's best writers, including Davis and Music, Charlotte Brown, Jerry Mayer, Martin Cohan, Tom Patchett, and Jay Tarses.

**1**   Fly the Unfriendly Skies                  September 16, 1972
**Writers:** David Davis, Lorenzo Music
**Director:** Jay Sandrich
**Guest Stars:** Penny Marshall, Patricia Smith, Noam Pitlik, Jack Riley, Florida Friebus

Bob tries to help Emily overcome her paralyzing fear of planes by inviting her to join his "Fear of Flying" therapy group on a short flight to New York.

The series begins with a nod toward tradition, as Bob walks in the front door and doffs his hat, as sitcom husbands had been doing since the days when father knew best. And yet, over the course of our first short visit, things get curiouser and curiouser as we enter the peculiar universe of Bob Hartley, a rational man—a psychologist, no less—who finds himself moored in a surrealistic universe where the only prevailing logic is the serendipity of the absurd.

**2    Tracy Grammar School,**                 September 23, 1972
       **I'll Lick You Yet**
**Writers:** Carl Gottlieb, George Yanock
**Director:** Jay Sandrich
**Guest Stars:** King Moody, Larry Gelman, Patricia Smith

Bob puts Emily's third graders to sleep when he attempts to explain the nuances of psychology on career day at Tracy Grammar School.

The episode hints at the show's casual attitude toward the Hartley's decidedly grown-up relationship. Always affectionate, and often demonstrative, Emily can't resist teasing her husband unmercifully. At one point she surprises Bob with a triple-strength kiss outside his office before she disappears into the elevator.

"It was funny to imagine Newhart in bed," chuckled writer Lorenzo Music, who quickly realized that the Hartleys' obvious physical attraction to each other added a new dimension to Newhart's firmly established persona. "Bob could just as easily have been a loser on a date, but Emily gave him sexuality. If someone as hip and sexy as her saw something in him, he *must* have had something special. We didn't ever have to show it—you just knew it was there."

**3    Tennis, Emily?**                 September 30, 1972
**Writers:** David Davis, Lorenzo Music
**Director:** Alan Rafkin
**Guest Stars:** Peter Brown, Barbara Barnett, Pay Lysinger

Bob treats a handsome tennis pro who complains that every woman he meets makes a pass at him—including Emily.

**4    Mom, I L-L-Love You**                 October 7, 1972
**Writers:** Dick Clair, Jenna McMahon
**Director:** Alan Rafkin
**Guest Stars:** Martha Scott, Marilyn Child, Patricia Smith

Despite the difficulty he has talking to his mother, Bob finally resolves to tell her how much he cares for her.

**5**   Goodnight, Nancy                    October 21, 1972
**Writer:** Susan Silver
**Director:** Jay Sandrich
**Guest Stars:** Penny Fuller, Richard Schaal, James B. Sikking,
Patricia Smith

Emily is surprised to find herself acting like a typical jealous wife
when one of Bob's old girlfriends pays a visit.

**6**   Come Live With Me                   October 28, 1972
**Writer:** Jerry Mayer
**Director:** Alan Rafkin
**Guest Stars:** Eugene Troobnik, John Fielder

Emily decides to get involved when Carol has trouble deciding
whether to move in with her new boyfriend.

John Fiedler makes his first appearance as the self-effacing Mr.
Peterson.

**7**   Father Knows Worst                  November 4, 1972
**Writers:** Tom Patchett, Jay Tarses
**Director:** Alan Rafkin
**Guest Stars:** Moosie Drier, Alice Borden

Howard is convinced that he's failed as a father when Howie, Jr.,
begins spending most of his time with Jerry Robinson.

**8**   Don't Go to Bed Mad                 November 11, 1972
**Writer:** Gene Thompson
**Director:** Alan Rafkin

The Hartleys spend a sleepless night after they agree not to rest
until they've settled a raging dispute over Bob's Monday-night
football habit.

The petty annoyances that continually dogged Bob and Emily's domestic life depicted the day-to-day struggles of real-life marriage with
perceptive, and always comic, accuracy. The Hartleys were as romantic
as any prime-time couple since Rob and Laura Petrie—but that didn't
mean that they always had to get along. Come to think of it, Bob and
Emily probably aren't all that different from what Rob and Laura might
have been like ten years later—the approximate length of time between
the debut of *The Dick Van Dyke Show* and *Bob Newhart*'s premiere in 1972.

**9    P-I-L-O-T**                                November 18, 1972
**Writers:** David Davis, Lorenzo Music
**Director:** Jay Sandrich
**Guest Stars:** Louise Lasser, Patricia Smith, William Redfield

Frustrated by their inability to conceive a child, the Hartleys decide to become adoptive parents.

This uncharacteristic episode is actually a re-edited version of the show's pilot film, which bore very little resemblance to the characters and settings we would come to know in the series. In the original pilot, Bob and Emily managed their apartment complex in addition to their other jobs; Howard Borden hadn't even been invented; and Jerry was a swinging psychologist who shared an office suite with Bob!

"We thought we needed other interests for Bob at home, so we made him manager of a condominium," explained creator Lorenzo Music. But the idea was dropped when CBS executives complained that people wouldn't know what a condo was. "We joked that they were afraid the public might get it confused with something high school boys buy at the drugstore to carry around in their back pockets. And they agreed!"

After the series went into production, new scenes incorporating some of the show's more familiar elements were edited into the original pilot, and some of the existing footage was dropped. For obvious reasons, a more characteristic episode was substituted for the series debut, and this odd hybrid was quietly slipped in during the show's ninth week.

**10    Anything Happen While I Was Gone?    November 25, 1972**
**Writer:** Martin Cohan
**Director:** Jay Sandrich
**Guest Star:** Elaine Giftos

Jerry announces his engagement to a beautiful but domineering oral hygienist he's just met.

**11    I Want to be Alone**                    December 2, 1972
**Writer:** Jerry Mayer
**Director:** Alan Rafkin
**Guest Stars:** Archie Hahn, Bernie Kopell, Alan Hewitt, Patricia Smith

Howard is worried that the Hartleys are splitting up after Bob moves into a hotel room for a few days of peace and quiet.

This episode contains the final appearance of Patricia Smith as Emily's neighbor, Margaret Hoover, a homespun mother of two who was meant to serve as Emily's comic counterpoint—until the writers recognized the character as a needless plot contrivance. "There was so much going on down at the office that we didn't need her," writer Lorenzo Music confessed. "We couldn't get a Rhoda out of it."

**12**    Bob and Emily and Howard                December 9, 1972
         and Carol and Jerry
   **Writer:** Charlotte Brown
   **Director:** Peter Baldwin

With Emily's help, Carol's momentary infatuation with Howard leads to a romance that ends almost before it begins.

**13**    I Owe It All to You . . .                December 16, 1972
         But Not That Much
   **Writer:** Martin Cohan
   **Director:** Alan Rafkin

Bob gains a patient but loses a friend when Jerry suddenly decides to become a paying customer.

**14**    His Busiest Season                       December 23, 1972
   **Writers:** David Davis, Lorenzo Music
   **Director:** Peter Baldwin
   **Guest Stars:** Harvey J. Goldenberg, Florida Friebus, King Moody, Ray Montgomery

Bob foolishly attempts to raise sagging holiday spirits by inviting his group to an impromptu Christmas party at his apartment.

**15**    Let's Get Away From It Almost            January 6, 1973
   **Writers:** Tom Patchett, Jay Tarses
   **Director:** Jay Sandrich
   **Guest Stars:** Chuck McCann, Joyce Van Patten, Allen Garfield

The Hartleys flee the city to get away from it all, only to spend the worst vacation of their life in a rundown ski lodge.

**16**   The Crash of Twenty-Nine Years Old         January 13, 1973
   **Writer:** Charlotte Brown
   **Director:** Alan Rafkin
   **Guest Stars:** Renee Lippin, Jack Bender, Dan Barrows

Depressed by the approach of her twenty-ninth birthday, Carol decides to quit her job and expand her horizons beyond the reception area.

During her three seasons with the series, Charlotte Brown would script some of the show's funniest moments, but her greatest contribution would be the keen insight she brought to the characterizations of the show's women: Emily; Bob's sister, Ellen; and especially Carol. In Brown's early scripts, Carol emerges as a vulnerable, impulsive, and painfully sincere young woman. More than any other character, Carol was capable of growth and change; throughout her long journey of star-crossed romances and her countless attempts to break out of her receptionist's cage, we never stopped rooting for her.

**17**   The Man With the Golden Wrist            January 20, 1973
   **Writer:** Bill Idelson
   **Director:** Alan Rafkin
   **Guest Stars:** Larry Gelman, Mimi Torchin, Michael Lerner

Bob refuses to wear the expensive gold watch Emily gave him for his birthday after he discovers how much she paid for it.

**18**   The Two Loves of Dr. Hartley            January 27, 1973
   **Writer:** Gene Thompson
   **Director:** George Tyne
   **Guest Star:** Emmaline Henry

Emily is more than slightly concerned when one of Bob's patients falls hopelessly in love with him.

**19**   Not With My Sister You Don't            February 3, 1973
   **Writer:** Frank Buxton
   **Director:** Alan Rafkin
   **Guest Stars:** Heather Menzies, Mel Stewart

Howard does his best to hide his swinging lifestyle from his younger sister when she arrives to spend a week in the big city.

**20**   A Home Is Not Necessarily a House         February 10, 1973
**Writers:** David Davis, Lorenzo Music
**Director:** Peter Baldwin
**Guest Stars:** Jenna McMahon, Dick Clair, Petty Palivoda

Howard is crestfallen when Bob and Emily make plans to move into their dream house.

MTM writers Jenna McMahon and Dick Clair make a cameo appearance as the other couple interested in the Hartley's house.

**21**   Emily, I'm Home—Emily?              February 17, 1973
**Writer:** Martin Cohan
**Director:** Rick Edelstein
**Guest Star:** Alma Beltran

Bob feels abandoned at home when Emily begins a full-time job at the Board of Education.

**22**   You Can't Win 'Em All              February 24, 1973
**Writer:** Bill Idelson
**Director:** Jerry London
**Guest Stars:** Vern E. Rowe, Jim Watkins, Larry Gelman

Bob basks in reflected glory when he counsels the Chicago Cubs' star pitcher out of a losing streak.

By the time he signed on as producer of *The Bob Newhart Show*, Bill Idelson was already a respected practitioner of quality TV comedy. At various times in his career, he had written scripts for such distinguished sitcoms as *The Andy Griffith Show*, *The Odd Couple*, *M\*A\*S\*H*, and *The Dick Van Dyke Show*—where he also appeared as Sally's boyfriend, Herman Glimscher.

**23**   Bum Voyage                         March 3, 1973
**Writers:** Austin and Irma Kalish
**Director:** Martin Cohan
**Guest Stars:** Archie Hahn, Pat McCormick

Bob resists Emily's plans for a two-month cruise because he's convinced that his group couldn't survive that long without him.

**24**   Who's Been Sleeping on My Couch?         March 10, 1973
   **Writer:** Jerry Mayer
   **Director:** Alan Rafkin
   **Guest Stars:** Renee Lippin, Herbie Faye

Jerry turns to Bob for solace in the aftermath of another failed romance, but it's a date with Carol that finally sets him straight.

## 1973-74    THE SECOND SEASON

*Year-End Rating: 22.3 (12th place)*

The peculiar logic of the *Newhart* universe continues to evolve as the offbeat individuals in Bob's therapy group emerge as a steady source of story ideas in the second year. Tom Patchett and Jay Tarses contribute the bulk of the season's scripts, along with Jerry Mayer and Charlotte Brown, among others.

Producer Martin Cohan is a key architect of this emerging universe, along with writers Patchett and Tarses, who serve as the season's story consultants. Peter Baldwin directs more than a third of the year's episodes, along with Jay Sandrich, George Tyne, Alan Rafkin, Jerry London, Peter Bonerz, and Don Bustany.

**25**   Last TV Show                      September 15, 1973
   **Writer:** Charlotte Brown
   **Director:** Jay Sandrich
   **Guest Stars:** Jack Riley, Florida Friebus, John Fiedler, Renee Lippin, Noam Pitlik, Don Dandridge

Bob reluctantly accepts an invitation to hold a group session on live television.

The group insists that Bob schedule the TV appearance, and he bows to their will—only to find himself betrayed on live television when they freeze up, leaving him fifty-six minutes to fill with stories of his Air Force days, his stint as a soprano in the boys' choir, and those wonderful summers on his Uncle Ned's farm. It was a stock MTM situation—Mary Richards often found herself in similar straits—but no performer ever communicated the divine comedy of devastating anxiety quite so well as Bob Newhart.

**26**   Motel                                        September 22, 1973
   **Writers:** Tom Patchett, Jay Tarses
   **Director:** Jay Sandrich
   **Guest Stars:** Zohra Lampert, Barbara Brownell

Bob gets an unexpected taste of Jerry's swinging lifestyle when the bachelor fixes him up with a local girl during an ill-fated trip to Peoria.

**27**   Backlash                                     September 29, 1973
   **Writer:** Susan Silver
   **Director:** George Tyne
   **Guest Star:** Michael Conrad

Emily begins to wonder if they'll ever take a vacation when Bob calls off their trip to Mexico because of sudden back pain.

Emily is especially anxious to get away from it all, convinced that a few romantic nights south of the border will increase their odds of finally conceiving a baby. Her maternal yearnings surfaced in two or three of the earliest shows, but Newhart maintained that adding a child to the cast would dilute the show's adult appeal, and Emily's urgent longing was reduced to no more than a poignant subtext in later seasons.

**28**   Somebody Down Here Likes Me          October 6, 1973
   **Writer:** Peter Myerson
   **Director:** Jerry London
   **Guest Star:** John McMartin

Bob feels responsible when the minister he's been treating decides to leave the church.

**29**   Emily in for Carol                       October 13, 1973
   **Writer:** Jerry Mayer
   **Director:** Alan Rafkin
   **Guest Stars:** Howard Platt, Rhoda Gemignani, Teri Garr

Despite Bob's strenuous objections, the doctors on his floor insist on hiring Emily as receptionist while Carol's on vacation.

**30**   Have You Met Miss Dietz?          October 20, 1973
   **Writer:** Bill Idelson
   **Director:** George Tyne
   **Guest Stars:** Mariette Hartley, David Fresco

Bob is caught in the middle of an unpleasant rivalry between his best friends when Emily's newly divorced girlfriend dates Howard and Jerry at the same time.

**31**   Old Man Rivers          October 27, 1973
   **Writer:** Martin Cohan
   **Director:** Martin Cohan
   **Guest Stars:** Jeff Corey, Don Fenwick

Carol thinks she's found happiness at last—with a doctor who's thirty years her senior.

Bob's receptionist is embarrassed to admit that she plans to have a butterfly tattoo removed from a place where no gentleman would see it anyway. But by a telepathy unique to the characters on *The Bob Newhart Show*, both Howard and Jerry know about the tattoo without having to be told. How they came by such intimate knowledge is a provocative question that's never explained—and perhaps it's better that way.

**32**   Mister Emily Hartley          November 3, 1973
   **Writer:** Charlotte Brown
   **Director:** Jerry London
   **Guest Stars:** Bill Quinn, Claudette Nevins, Tom Patchett, Jay Tarses

Bob suffers from wounded pride when he discovers that Emily's IQ is a full twenty points higher than his.

Writers Patchett and Tarses, who began their careers as stand-up comics, make cameo appearances as a waiter and one of the guests at the cocktail party for geniuses.

**33**   Mutiny on the Hartley          November 10, 1973
   **Writers:** Tom Patchett, Jay Tarses
   **Director:** Peter Baldwin
   **Guest Star:** Henry Corden

Bob's therapy group stages a rebellion to protest a five-dollar rate increase.

**34**   I'm Okay, You're Okay,                  November 17, 1973
So What's Wrong?
**Writer:** Earl Barret
**Director:** George Tyne
**Guest Star:** Katherine Helmond

Bob and Emily consult a marriage counselor to help them through a lull in their married life.


**35**   Fit, Fat, and Forty-One                 November 24, 1973
**Writers:** Bill Idelson, Harvey Miller
**Director:** Peter Baldwin
**Guest Stars:** Bruce Kirby, Lilyan Chauvin, Bob Ridgely, Ron Glass

Bob resolves to lose eight pounds by his forty-first birthday, but he quickly finds the regimen of dieting almost unbearable.


**36**   Blues for Mr. Borden                    December 1, 1973
**Writers:** Tom Patchett, Jay Tarses
**Director:** Jerry London
**Guest Stars:** Moosie Drier, Julius Harris

Howard goes on a bender when he discovers that his ex-wife is engaged to be remarried—to a pilot.

The episode contains one of the series's most memorable throwaway gags, involving Jerry and a Great Dane. The high-strung dentist hears an imposing black man bark out the command to "Sit, Whitey!," which Jerry does—before he realizes that the order was intended for the man's perversely named dog, Whitey.


**37**   My Wife Belongs to Daddy                December 8, 1973
**Writer:** Jerry Mayer
**Director:** Jerry London
**Guest Stars:** John Randolph, Ann Rutherford

Emily is delighted when her parents pay a visit, but Bob is discouraged when he discovers that there's no way to compete with his charismatic father-in-law.

**38**   T. S. Elliot                          December 15, 1973
   **Writers:** Gerry Renert, Jeff Wilheim
   **Director:** Peter Baldwin
   **Guest Stars:** Shirley O'Hara, Robert Riesel, Shizuko Hoshi

Bob arranges for Carol to date Mr. Carlin—and they hit it off so
well that Elliot immediately begins making wedding plans.

**39**   I'm Dreaming of a Slight Christmas      December 22, 1973
   **Writers:** Tom Patchett, Jay Tarses
   **Director:** Peter Baldwin
   **Guest Stars:** Gene Blakely, John Fiedler, Larry Gelman

A power failure traps Bob in his office on Christmas Eve.

**40**   Oh, Brother                          January 5, 1974
   **Writer:** Martin Cohan
   **Director:** Peter Baldwin
   **Guest Star:** Raul Julia

Jerry's brother arrives with a surefire plan for starting his own den-
tal practice—he'll steal his patients from his older brother.

**41**   The Modernization of Emily            January 12, 1974
   **Writer:** Charlotte Brown
   **Director:** Peter Baldwin
   **Guest Stars:** Sharon Gless, Bill Miller, J.J. Barry

Emily is on a youth kick, convinced that she can stave off the advancing years by donning an embarrassing new wardrobe of T-
shirts and tight blue jeans.

In a moment that's painfully funny, Emily opens a present bought for
her at the House of Tacky—only to discover that Carol's idea of a gag
gift is a tasteless spangled T-shirt, the same one that Emily's got on! Her
insecurity and dread of encroaching middle age reveal a chink in Emily's
usually well-adjusted outlook, but the bittersweet humor of Charlotte
Brown's sympathetic script refuses to betray the character's basic integrity. In the end, Emily forsakes the tacky fringes and denim as she finally
accepts the wisdom that comes along with the wrinkles.

**42**    The Jobless Corps                          January 19, 1974
   **Writers:** Tom Patchett, Jay Tarses
   **Director:** Peter Baldwin
   **Guest Stars:** Millie Slavin, Howard Hesseman

Howard joins Bob's out-of-work workshop after he loses his job at the airline.

Under writers Patchett and Tarses, the series found some of its biggest laughs in the perversely comic outlook of the downtrodden and maladjusted members of Bob's group. In 1983, the same writers would carry their formula to sidesplitting extremes when they created *Buffalo Bill*, which revolved around the most maladjusted protagonist in sitcom history: Buffalo Bill, a petty, egocentric, thoroughly reprehensible, and irresistibly hilarious talk-show host. Come to think of it, he might have fit into one of Bob's groups very nicely.

Howard Hesseman debuts as the out-of-work television writer, Mr. Plager.

**43**    Clink Shrink                              January 26, 1974
   **Writers:** Paul B. Lichtman, Howard Storm
   **Director:** Peter Bonerz
   **Guest Stars:** Henry Winkler, Len Lessor

Bob wonders whether he should accept an expensive gift from his newest patient, a recently paroled ex-con who served time for armed robbery.

When supporting player Bonerz wasn't on camera, he was behind the scenes, observing the directors. "It sure beats waiting around drinking coffee," he once quipped. The producers finally sanctioned the actor's ambitions to step behind the camera with this episode. Bonerz adapted to his new role magnificently—he would eventually direct more *Bob Newhart* shows than any other director.

**44**    Mind Your Own Business                    February 2, 1974
   **Writers:** Tom Patchett, Jay Tarses
   **Director:** Alan Rafkin
   **Guest Stars:** Ron Rifkin, Katharine Dunfee, Lou Cutell

Bob isn't sure he's cut out for the world of high finance after his new business manager puts him on a restricted budget of $50 a week.

**45**   A Love Story                        February 9, 1974
   **Writer:** Martin Cohan
   **Director:** Peter Bonerz
   **Guest Stars:** Pat Finley, Martha Scott, Renee Lippin

It's love at first sight when Howard meets Bob's sister, Ellen, despite one slight complication—she's already engaged to another man.

When Emily tries to coax the pair together, Bob observes—with deadpan accuracy—that her matchmaking has "sunk to a new low." But Howard's childlike determination wins out, and the befuddled bachelor experiences his finest triumph when the blushing bride interrupts his ironing with the news that she's called off her wedding.

**46**   By the Way . . . You're Fired        February 16, 1974
   **Writers:** Barbara Gallagher, Sybil Adelman
   **Director:** Peter Baldwin
   **Guest Stars:** Richard Schaal, Larry Gelman, Jill Jaress, Gene Blakely, Howard Platt

Carol's work suffers when she loses her head over her latest beau—a kook who recites half-baked epiphanies over lunch.

**47**   Confessions of an Orthodontist       February 23, 1974
   **Writers:** Tom Patchett, Jay Tarses
   **Director:** Peter Baldwin
   **Guest Stars:** Roger Perry, Teri Garr

Jerry surprises Bob with the startling confession that he's hopelessly in love with Emily.

**48**   A Matter of Principal                March 2, 1974
   **Writers:** Ray Jessel, Arnie Kogen
   **Director:** Don Bustany
   **Guest Stars:** Milton Selzer, Michael Conrad

Emily defies her school board by refusing to let an undeserving student skip a grade.

## 1974-75    THE THIRD SEASON

*Year-End Rating: 22.4 (17th place)*

The romance between Howard and Bob's sister, Ellen, played by Pat Finley, provides fresh perspective in the domestic storyline, as producers Tom Patchett and Jay Tarses usher the show into its most inventive period. Jerry Mayer is the season's story consultant, and Alan Rafkin directs many of the episodes—most of which are written by Patchett and Tarses, Charlotte Brown, and Jerry Mayer.

**49**   Big Brother Is Watching              September 14, 1974
  **Writer:** Charlotte Brown
  **Director:** Robert Moore
  **Guest Star:** Pat Finley

Bob puts a damper on Howard's blossoming romance with Ellen when he refuses to let his sister move in with the navigator.

**50**   The Battle of the Groups             September 21, 1974
  **Writers:** Tom Patchett, Jay Tarses
  **Director:** Alan Rafkin
  **Guest Stars:** Howard Hesseman, Daniel Travanti, Lenore Woodward, Millie Slavin

Bob has his hands full when he joins two therapy groups together for a marathon weekend session at a mountain retreat.

**51**   The Great Rimpau Medical Arts        September 28, 1974
       Co-Op Experiment
  **Writers:** Coleman Mitchell, Geoffrey Neigher
  **Director:** George Tyne
  **Guest Stars:** Merie Earle, Larry Gelman, Howard Platt, Julie Payne, Tom Lacy

Jerry organizes a medical co-op so that the doctors can exchange services without charge, a plan that Bob discovers works better in conception than execution.

**52  The Separation Story**                    October 5, 1974
**Writers:** Tom Patchett, Jay Tarses
**Story:** Bob Garland
**Director:** Peter Bonerz
**Guest Stars:** Richard Stahl, Carl Gottlieb

After Emily moves into a dormitory to bone up for her master's degree, rumors of the Hartleys' separation begin to buzz.

The inflatable-furniture salesman was played by Carl Gottlieb, the screenwriter of *Jaws* and *The Jerk*, and also one of the show's earliest writers.

**53  Sorry, Wrong Mother**                    October 12, 1974
**Writer:** Charlotte Brown
**Director:** Jay Sandrich
**Guest Stars:** Moosie Drier, Pat Finley, John Ritter

Even after she plies him with gifts and ice cream, Ellen can't seem to earn the approval of Howard's son.

The family tensions are played out in the unlikely setting of a razzle-dazzle straw-hat ice-cream parlor, which is also the scene of one of Bob's most unforgettable comic nightmares, as towering plates of Hazelnut Hoohas, Hot 'n' Heavy Fandangoes, and Banana Fofana Splits are served up by an unrestrained waiter with the tableside manner of Rip Taylor. Hoping to avoid all the embarrassing hoopla, Bob orders an unassuming scoop of plain vanilla, only to find himself besieged by a cadre of singing waiters chanting, "Single scooper, single scooper, this man is a party pooper," as he tries to melt into the brightly checkered tablecloth.

**54  The Gray Flannel Shrink**                    October 19, 1974
**Writer:** Jerry Mayer
**Director:** Peter Bonerz
**Guest Stars:** John Anderson, Edward Winter, Jerry Fogel

Bob abandons his practice for the corporate world when he accepts a position as resident shrink for a major insurance company.

**55**    Dr. Ryan's Express                    October 26, 1974
   **Writers:** Tom Patchett, Jay Tarses
   **Director:** Alan Rafkin
   **Guest Stars:** Shirley O'Hara, Lucien Scott, Paula Victor, Maxine
   Stuart

Jerry hires a supremely incompetent temporary receptionist who
makes a mess of Bob's well-ordered office routine.

**56**    Brutally Yours, Bob Hartley          November 2, 1974
   **Writer:** John Rappaport
   **Director:** Alan Rafkin
   **Guest Stars:** Lawrence Pressman, Rose Gregario

Bob resolves to be completely honest and open with everyone he
encounters, and in no time at all he's alienated his wife and most
of his friends.

**57**    Ship of Shrinks                      November 9, 1974
   **Writers:** Coleman Mitchell, Geoffrey Neigher
   **Director:** Alan Rafkin
   **Guest Stars:** David L. Lander, Bobby Ramsen, Pat Finley

Bob is embarrassed to face his professional colleagues after a psychology article he wrote is published with revisions that he thinks
make him look foolish.

**58**    Life Is a Hamburger                  November 16, 1974
   **Writer:** Jerry Mayer
   **Director:** George Tyne
   **Guest Star:** Richard Schaal

Carol happily announces her engagement to the oddball poet
she's been dating, even though her friends are convinced that
he's a loser.

**59**    An American Family                   November 23, 1974
   **Writer:** Charlotte Brown
   **Director:** Peter Bonerz
   **Guest Stars:** Barnard Hughes, Martha Scott, John Randolph, Ann
   Rutherford

The Hartleys' plans for a festive Thanksgiving dinner are dashed
when Bob's mother locks horns with Emily's dad.

**60**   We Love You . . . Good-Bye          November 30, 1974
**Writer:** Charlotte Brown
**Director:** Peter Bonerz
**Guest Stars:** Rhoda Gemignani, Ann Weldon

Bob gets drummed out of his own women's consciousness-raising group after Emily reveals the truth about his less-than-enlightened behavior at home.

**61**   Jerry Robinson Crusoe              December 7, 1974
**Writer:** Erik Tarloff
**Director:** Alan Rafkin
**Guest Star:** Gail Strickland

The call of the wild beckons Jerry when a free-spirited girlfriend convinces him to chuck his practice and move to the South Seas.

**62**   Serve for Daylight                 December 14, 1974
**Writer:** Jerry Mayer
**Director:** Alan Rafkin
**Guest Stars:** Larry Gelman, Howard Platt, Paula Shaw

Bob is determined to win the tennis trophy in the doctors' annual tournament, but gets quickly discouraged when he's paired with Emily in a doubles match.

**63**   Home Is Where the Hurt Is          December 21, 1974
**Writers:** Tom Patchett, Jay Tarses
**Director:** Alan Rafkin
**Guest Star:** Bill Quinn

The Hartleys spend a dismal Christmas Eve as Carol shares her unhappy memories of past holidays.

**64**   Tobin's Back in Town               January 4, 1975
**Writer:** Michael Zinberg
**Director:** Peter Bonerz
**Guest Stars:** Fred Willard, Catherine Bacon

Howard worries that he might lose Ellen when her jilted fiancé returns to reclaim her.

Ellen's suede-and-leather Lothario is Fred Willard, best remembered for his stint as the dim-witted co-host of *Fernwood 2-Night*.

**65**   Think Smartly—Vote Hartley                January 11, 1975
   **Writers:** Coleman Mitchell, Geoffrey Neigher
   **Director:** Bob Finkel
   **Guest Stars:** George Wyner, Lillian Garrett, Quinn Redeker

Emily's friends convince Bob to run for chairman of the school board.

**66**   The Way We Weren't                        January 18, 1975
   **Writer:** Roger Beatty
   **Director:** James Burrows
   **Guest Stars:** Wayne Tippit, Joseph Sicari, Casey Connors, David Knapp

Emily is determined to figure out why Bob is so reluctant to discuss a mysterious former girlfriend.

**67**   A Pound of Flesh                          January 25, 1975
   **Writer:** Jerry Mayer
   **Director:** Alan Rafkin
   **Guest Stars:** Merie Earle, Dick Wilson

Jerry is in a huff after Bob refuses to lend him money to buy a new motorcycle.

**68**   My Business Is Shrinking                  February 1, 1975
   **Writers:** Arnie Kogen, Ray Jessel
   **Director:** Alan Rafkin
   **Guest Stars:** Phillip R. Allen, Timothy Blake, Ray Stewart, Mary Jo Catlett, Ron McIlwain

Bob joins another psychologist's therapy group to work his way through a temporary depression.

**69**   The New Look                              February 8, 1975
   **Writers:** Gordon and Lynne Farr
   **Director:** Peter Bonerz
   **Guest Stars:** Cliff Norton, Marcia Lewis, Oliver Clark

Bob can't seem to find a comfortable spot in his own living room after Emily redecorates their apartment with antique furniture.

**70**   Bob Hits the Ceiling                    February 15, 1975
**Writer:** Phil Davis
**Director:** Jay Sandrich
**Guest Stars:** Cynthia Harris, Mike Henry, Al Stellone

Bob reluctantly agrees to counsel one of Emily's friends through her marital difficulties.

**71**   Emily Hits the Ceiling                  February 22, 1975
**Writer:** Jerry Mayer
**Director:** James Burrows
**Guest Stars:** George Wyner, Howard Hesseman, Susan Davis, Lillian Garrett, Tom Newman

The Hartleys are drafted into service as counselors when a group of Emily's friends decide to start a summer camp.

**72**   The Ceiling Hits Bob                     March 8, 1975
**Writers:** Tom Patchett, Jay Tarses
**Director:** Alan Rafkin
**Guest Stars:** Bill Quinn, Jess Nadelman, Lucien Scott, Pat Finley

The ceiling in Bob's office falls in—and the rest of his world threatens to follow when Ellen and Howard announce that they're moving to New York, and Carol starts to look for a new job.

## 1975-76   THE FOURTH SEASON

*Year-End Rating: 20.7 (26th place)*

Bob welcomes two significant additions to the family in the fourth season—Tom Poston arrives as Cliff Murdoch in the first of the Peeper's many appearances; and Carol meets, courts, and marries travel agent Larry Bondurant, played by actor—and sometime director—Will Mackenzie.

Michael Zinberg is appointed producer in midseason, after producers Tom Patchett and Jay Tarses assume the duties of executive producers. Gordon and Lynne Farr are the season's story consultants; and Peter Bonerz, Michael Zinberg, and James Burrows are the most prominent of the season's directors.

**73**   The Longest Good-Bye                    September 13, 1975
   **Writers:** Tom Patchett, Jay Tarses
   **Director:** James Burrows
   **Guest Star:** Tom Poston

Emily is less than impressed by Bob's legendary college chum, the Peeper—an inveterate jokester who arrives to spend a day and then stays a week.

**74**   Here's Looking at You, Kid                    September 20, 1975
   **Writers:** Gordon and Lynne Farr
   **Director:** Peter Bonerz
   **Guest Stars:** Pat Finley, Richard Balin, Vern E. Rowe, Don Nagel

Howard looks to Bob for moral support when he proposes to Ellen at a crowded restaurant.

Ellen didn't think the time was right for marriage, a decision shared by the show's producers. As Howard reclaimed his bachelor status in the final seasons, Bob's sister was reluctantly written out of the series.

**75**   Death of a Fruitman                    September 27, 1975
   **Writers:** Tom Patchett, Jay Tarses
   **Director:** Peter Bonerz
   **Guest Stars:** Renee Lippin, John Fiedler, Florida Friebus

The group is angry at Mr. Gianelli for missing their fourth anniversary party, until they find out he was crushed to death beneath a truckload of zucchini.

Noam Pitlik would meet a somewhat happier fate than his character when the actor cut back on his performing commitments to become the full-time director of *Barney Miller*.
   Gianelli's ludicrous demise foreshadowed the funeral of Chuckles the Clown on *The Mary Tyler Moore Show* the following month. Although the episodes have little in common beyond similarly silly treatment of the same subject matter, a comparison of the two offers a revealing look at how divergent the two shows really were. When WJM's kiddie-show host

was trampled by a rogue elephant, the newsroom came to a halt as the staff registered shock—and, ultimately, laughter—at the ridiculous details of the clown's passing. The fruitman's death is no less absurd, and yet Bob and his group accept the circumstances of his demise with almost existential calm. On *The Bob Newhart Show*, life itself was such an absurd proposition that death—even death by zucchini—was taken in stride.

**76**   Change Is Gonna Do Me Good              October 4, 1975
   **Writers:** Gordon and Lynne Farr
   **Director:** John Erman
   **Guest Star:** Brian Byers

In an effort to shake Bob out of his domestic rut, Emily suggests that they exchange household duties.

The husband-and-wife writing team of Gordon and Lynne Farr gave a boost to the continuing saga of the Hartleys in a series of fine fourth- and fifth-season scripts. "We wanted to develop Emily," recalled Lynne Farr, "so we made sure she spent as little time in the kitchen as possible."

**77**   The Heavyweights              October 11, 1975
   **Writers:** Tom Patchett, Jay Tarses
   **Director:** Bob Claver
   **Guest Stars:** Cliff Osmond, Marcia Lewis, Larry Gelman

Carol gets roped into a date with an obnoxious tubbo from Bob's overweight workshop.

**78**   Carol's Wedding              October 18, 1975
   **Writers:** Gordon and Lynne Farr
   **Director:** Michael Zinberg
   **Guest Stars:** Will Mackenzie, Robert Casper

Bob is skeptical when Carol announces that she's getting married to Larry Bondurant, a travel agent she met less than twelve hours earlier.

**79**    Shrinks Across the Sea                    October 25, 1975
   **Writers:** Phil Doran, Douglas Arango
   **Director:** Bob Claver
   **Guest Stars:** Rene Auberjonois, Françoise Ruggieri, Richard
   Foronjy

Bob and Emily host a visiting French psychologist, who arrives in
the company of another man's wife.

**80**    What's It All About, Albert?                    November 1, 1975
   **Writer:** Phil Davis
   **Director:** Michael Zinberg
   **Guest Star:** Keenan Wynn

Convinced that his psychological counseling has done none of his
patients a bit of good, Bob seeks inspiration from his old college
professor.

His college mentor is no help at all. But, grasping at straws, Bob discovers a new approach to therapy in the movie *Born Free* and urges his
patients to follow the example of Elsa the lioness and return to their wild
state.

**81**    Who Is Mr. X?                    November 8, 1975
   **Writer:** Bruce Kane
   **Director:** Peter Bonerz
   **Guest Stars:** Jennifer Warren, Alan Manson, Claudette Duffy

A seemingly innocuous talk-show host uses Bob as bait when she
decides to do a hatchet job on the entire field of psychology.

Once again, Bob finds himself humiliated before the unyielding gaze
of the entire city—and this time he's in trouble from the very start. Says
host Ruth Corley, by way of introduction, "It's been said that today's
psychologist is nothing more than a con man, a snake-oil salesman flim-
flamming innocent people, peddling cures for everything from nail bit-
ing to a lousy love life—and I agree. We'll ask Dr. Hartley to defend
himself after these messages."

**82**    Seemed Like a Good Idea at the Time    November 15, 1975
**Writers:** Tom Patchett, Jay Tarses
**Director:** Richard Kinon
**Guest Stars:** Titos Vandis, Ruth McDevitt, Phillip R. Allen

Bob forms an unlikely alliance when he goes into partnership with a well-heeled playboy psychologist.

**83**    Over the River and Through the Woods November 22, 1975
**Writer:** Bruce Kane
**Director:** James Burrows
**Guest Stars:** Janet Meshad, David Himes

When Emily flies home for Thanksgiving, Bob joins Jerry, Howard, and Mr. Carlin for a bachelor's feast of Chinese food and beer.

**84**    Fathers and Sons and Mothers            November 29, 1975
**Writer:** Arnold Kane
**Director:** James Burrows
**Guest Stars:** William Daniels, Martha Scott, Lucien Scott

Bob's mother drops by for an extended visit and begins to drive her son crazy within moments of her arrival.

**85**    The Article                        December 6, 1975
**Writer:** Eric Tarloff
**Director:** Michael Zinberg
**Guest Stars:** Pat Finley, Ellen Weston, Bobby Ramsen, Jack O'Leary, Howard Platt

Bob and Jerry have second thoughts after they agree to let Ellen do a newspaper feature on the drama of life in a big-city medical building.

**86**    A Matter of Vice-Principal            December 13, 1975
**Writers:** Gordon and Lynne Farr
**Director:** Peter Bonerz
**Guest Stars:** Lawrence Pressman, Kristina Holland, Frances Lee McCain, Nora Marlowe

Emily suddenly finds herself embroiled in grammar school politics when she gets promoted to vice-principal ahead of a teacher with greater seniority.

**87**    Bob Has to Have His Tonsils Out,        December 20, 1975
          So He Spends Christmas Eve in the Hospital
**Writers:** Tom Patchett, Jay Tarses
**Director:** James Burrows
**Guest Stars:** Graham Jarvis, Merie Earle

Bob faces another depressing holiday when he's forced to undergo an emergency tonsillectomy on Christmas Eve.

**88**    No Sale                                     January 3, 1976
**Writer:** Michael Zinberg
**Director:** Eddie Ryder
**Guest Star:** Malcolm Atterbury

Bob and Jerry are investment partners in one of Carlin's shady real-estate deals—this one hinges on evicting an old man from a slum tenement.

**89**    Carol at 6:01                              January 10, 1976
**Writers:** Gordon and Lynne Farr
**Director:** Peter Bonerz
**Guest Star:** Will Mackenzie

Carol turns to Bob for help when she begins to feel smothered by her new husband's overly lavish attentions.

**90**    Warden Gordon Borden                       January 17, 1976
**Writers:** Gordon and Lynne Farr
**Director:** James Burrows
**Guest Stars:** William Redfield, Pat Finley

Howard is upset by the arrival of his sibling rival, Gordon—his brother has always taken things from him, and now he's got his eye on Ellen.

William Redfield plays Howard's possessive brother, Gordon. The actor had originally been cast as the Hartleys' annoying next-door neighbor in the series's original pilot film—a role that was dropped, ironically, when the show was revamped to include the navigator next door, Howard Borden.

**91**   My Boy Guillermo                    January 24, 1976
   **Writer:** Sy Rosen
   **Director:** Alan Myerson
   **Guest Stars:** Gail Strickland, Matthew Laborteaux

Jerry's globe-hopping girlfriend returns to tempt him out of his rut with an offer of marriage and an instant family.

Story editors Gordon and Lynne Farr received this script in the mail from a hopeful writer who was then working at a Palo Alto, California, Goodwill Store. "We liked it so much we actually bought it—which was almost never done," recalls Lynne Farr. "And then we invited him to sit in on the rewrite, which was also never done. Afterward, we told him we needed another story editor for the next season and asked him if he was willing to leave his job at the Goodwill. His jaw nearly hit the floor, he was so excited."

**92**   Duke of Dunk                    January 31, 1976
   **Writers:** Douglas Arango, Phil Doran
   **Director:** Peter Bonerz
   **Guest Star:** Anthony Costello

Bob counsels an egocentric basketball superstar in the fine art of team playing.

**93**   Guaranteed Not to Shrink                    February 7, 1976
   **Writer:** Sy Rosen
   **Director:** James Burrows
   **Guest Stars:** Will Mackenzie, Claudia Bryar, Paul Bryar

Carol becomes an overnight psychoanalyst when she enrolls in a night school psychology course.

This episode contains a priceless and hilariously authentic husband-and-wife exchange when Bob starts to describe a brilliant old girlfriend who was so unambitious that she settled, tragically, for an unchallenging job as a mere schoolteacher. Of course, Bob's barely finished his sentence before he's stopped cold by the withering glare of his wife—the schoolteacher. Bob next bungles a tactful retreat when he attempts to salvage the thought midsentence by amending it to "she finally settled for being a . . . school." By then, of course, it's already too late—and Bob is forced to spend the rest of the episode in a doghouse of his own design.

**94** Birth of a Salesman February 14, 1976
**Writer:** Sy Rosen
**Director:** John C. Chulay
**Guest Star:** Oliver Clark

After Bob counsels Mr. Herd to be more assertive, the milquetoast takes the advice to heart and slaps Bob with a lawsuit.

**95** The Boy Next Door February 21, 1976
**Writer:** Hugh H. Wilson
**Director:** Peter Bonerz
**Guest Star:** Moosie Drier

Howard's ex-wife grants him custody of their son, but Bob and Emily end up spending more time with Howie than his dad does.

Hugh Wilson—a prolific second-generation MTM writer/producer— would eventually distinguish himself as creator of *WKRP in Cincinnati* in 1978.

**96** Peeper—Two February 28, 1976
**Writers:** Tom Patchett, Jay Tarses
**Director:** Michael Zinberg
**Guest Stars:** Tom Poston, Veronica Hamel, Sally Stark, Barbara Ellen Levene

When the Peeper returns in sullen spirits after his wife leaves him, Jerry decides to reacquaint Bob's old chum with the swinging singles' scene.

## 1976-77 THE FIFTH SEASON

*Year-End Rating: 19.0 (45th place)*

Bob Hartley confronts another season of unparalleled comic anxiety in fifth-year stories by Gordon and Lynne Farr, Hugh Wilson, Gary David Goldberg, and Sy Rosen, who is also the season's story consultant. Producers Gordon and Lynne Farr and Michael Zinberg return as custodians of this fine madness, along with executive producers Tom Patchett and Jay Tarses.

**97**   Enter Mrs. Peeper                      September 25, 1976
   **Writers:** Gordon and Lynne Farr
   **Director:** Michael Zinberg
   **Guest Stars:** Tom Poston, Jean Palmerton, Jay Tarses, Charles
   Thomas Murphy

Bob encounters an unexpected change in the Peeper when the incorrigible joker adopts a more serious outlook after his second marriage.

**98**   Caged Fury                             October 2, 1976
   **Writers:** Gordon and Lynne Farr
   **Director:** Michael Zinberg
   **Guest Star:** Will Mackenzie

The Hartleys miss their own bicentennial party after Emily accidentally locks them in the basement storage room.

**99**   Some of My Best Friends Are . . .      October 9, 1976
   **Writer:** Hugh Wilson
   **Director:** Alan Myerson
   **Guest Star:** Leonard Stone

Howard undergoes a behavior-modification treatment to cure his unhealthy dependence on Bob and Emily.

The strange triangle of Bob, Emily, and Howard defied simple description. The perennially jet-lagged navigator was the Hartleys' best friend and neighbor, but also something more—as Bob discovers after one of his colleagues cures Howard's dependency by turning him into a joyless, self-sufficient bore.

Things just aren't the same without Howard around. Finally, Bob and Emily set a trap—with home-cooked mashed potatoes and roast beef as bait—to lure the old Howard back into blissful dependency, having come to the sobering conclusion that they need him as much as he needs them. Howard, the childlike dreamer, filled a void in the childless couple's life that gave the reciprocal devotion they shared an understated, and quite touching, subtext in the rich fabric of this deceptively simple show.

**100**   Still Crazy After All These Years          October 16, 1976
   **Writers:** Pat Jones, Donald Reiker
   **Director:** James Burrows
   **Guest Stars:** Howard Hesseman, Florida Friebus, John Fiedler,
   Renee Lippin

Bob's group is stunned when Mr. Plager admits that he's a homosexual.

**101**   The Great Rent Strike                     October 23, 1976
   **Writer:** David Lloyd
   **Director:** John C. Chulay
   **Guest Star:** Jack Riley

Bob organizes a rent strike to protest the abominable conditions
in his high-rise, only to discover that Mr. Carlin is the new owner
of his building.

**102**   Et Tu, Carol                              October 30, 1976
   **Writer:** Gary David Goldberg
   **Director:** Alan Myerson
   **Guest Stars:** Shirley O'Hara, Larry Gelman, Howard Platt

Bob faces the nightmare of adjusting to a new secretary after
Carol drops him from her work roster.

**103**   Send This Boy to Camp                     November 6, 1976
   **Writer:** David Lloyd
   **Director:** Michael Zinberg
   **Guest Stars:** Sorrell Booke, Michael LeClair, Tierre Turner

Bob and Jerry plan an exciting camping trip for a pair of orphans,
but the foursome never gets any farther than a downtown parking
lot.

**104**   A Crime Most Foul                         November 13, 1976
   **Writer:** Sy Rosen
   **Director:** John C. Chulay
   **Guest Stars:** Oliver Clark, Florida Friebus, John Fiedler

No one is above suspicion when Bob's expensive new tape recorder turns up missing—not even Emily.

Bob explains his obsession to recover the stolen recorder by rationalizing how he never got over the theft of his boyhood harmonica—the one he used when he played "Pop Goes the Weasel," just like Al of the Harmonicats. Bob's rambling autobiographical anecdotes rarely provided any real insight into the character's formative years, but the cockeyed wisdom and slippery irony of these vignettes was the closest we'd come to a definition of the world according to Bob.

**105**   The Slammer                              November 20, 1976
   **Writers:** Gordon and Lynne Farr
   **Director:** Michael Zinberg
   **Guest Stars:** Tom Poston, Bobby Ramsen, Lucy Lee Flippin, Jean Palmerton, David Himes, Kim O'Brien

A nostalgic visit to their old college bar turns sour when Bob and the Peeper are booked on vice charges by a pair of undercover policewomen.

**106**   Jerry's Retirement                        November 27, 1976
   **Writer:** Hugh Wilson
   **Director:** Alan Myerson
   **Guest Stars:** John Randolph, Howard Morris

Bob questions the wisdom of Jerry's sudden decision to quit his practice and live off the profits of his real estate investments.

**107**   Here's to You, Mrs. Robinson              December 4, 1976
   **Writers:** Gordon and Lynne Farr
   **Director:** James Burrows
   **Guest Stars:** Lucy Landau, Fred D. Scott, Steve Anderson

The newly retired Jerry sets off on a worldwide quest to find his natural parents.

**108**   Breaking Up Is Hard to Do                 December 11, 1976
   **Writer:** Sy Rosen
   **Director:** Peter Bonerz
   **Guest Stars:** John Holland, Martha Scott

Bob is shocked to discover that his parents have separated after forty-seven years of married life.

**109** Making Up Is the Thing to Do December 25, 1976
   **Writers:** Gordon and Lynne Farr
   **Director:** Harvey Medlinsky
   **Guest Stars:** Barnard Hughes, Martha Scott, Will Mackenzie

Bob invites his feuding parents to Christmas dinner in the hope that the warm Yuletide spirit will bring the pair back together.

**110** Love Is the Blindest January 8, 1977
   **Writer:** Gary David Goldberg
   **Director:** Will Mackenzie
   **Guest Star:** Mary Ann Chinn

Mr. Carlin invents a colorful string of tall tales about himself to impress his love-struck new secretary.

**111** The Ironwood Experience January 15, 1977
   **Writer:** Phil Davis
   **Director:** Peter Bonerz
   **Guest Star:** Max Showalter

Bob's lecture at the Ironwood Institute for Interpersonal Relationships gets off to an unexpected start when the audience arrives in the nude.

**112** Of Mice and Men January 22, 1977
   **Writer:** Bruce Kane
   **Director:** Peter Bonerz
   **Guest Stars:** John Fiedler, Oliver Clark, Betty Kean, Inga Neilsen

Bob invites Emily to participate in a role-playing session with the repressed men in his consciousness-raising group for hen-pecked husbands.

**113** Halls of Hartley January 29, 1977
   **Writer:** Michael Zinberg
   **Director:** James Burrows
   **Guest Stars:** Richard Libertini, Craig Wasson, Addison Powell, Tresa Hughes

Fed up with the pressures of urban life, Bob applies for a position on the faculty of a small rural college.

**114**   The Heartbreak Kidd                    February 5, 1977
   **Writer:** Sy Rosen
   **Director:** Dick Martin
   **Guest Star:** Tovah Feldshuh

An enthusiastic psychology major develops a schoolgirl crush on Bob during her student internship.

Dick Martin began a very successful career as a TV comedy director with this episode, after an auspicious start as one-half of Rowan and Martin, the comedy team that hosted NBC's *Laugh-In*. He came to the series by way of Newhart, who introduced him to producer Michael Zinberg—with typical understatement—as "a friend of mine who wants to become a director."

**115**   Death Be My Destiny                    February 12, 1977
   **Writer:** Sy Rosen
   **Director:** Michael Zinberg
   **Guest Stars:** Oliver Clark, Lieux Dressler, Tom Patchett

Bob is convinced that he's living on borrowed time after he narrowly escapes death in a freak elevator accident.

Producer Tom Patchett appears in a cameo as Mr. Death.

**116**   Taxation Without Celebration                    February 19, 1977
   **Writer:** Sy Rosen
   **Director:** Peter Bonerz
   **Guest Stars:** Vince Martorano, Will Mackenzie, Drew Michaels

Bob has a choice of honoring the income tax deadline *or* his anniversary when he discovers that they both fall on the same day.

**117**   Desperate Sessions                    February 26, 1977
   **Writers:** Michael Zinberg, Martin Davidson
   **Director:** Dick Martin
   **Guest Stars:** Robert Pine, Walker Edmiston

Bob is held hostage by an affable robber he befriended in the lobby of his bank.

**118**   The Mentor                              March 5, 1977
  **Writer:** Gary David Goldberg
  **Director:** Michael Zinberg
  **Guest Star:** Will Mackenzie

Bob inspires Carol's husband to start his own travel agency, never suspecting that Larry would set up shop right outside his office.

**119**   Shrinking Violence                      March 12, 1977
  **Writer:** Sy Rosen
  **Director:** Peter Bonerz
  **Guest Stars:** Robert Ridgely, Florida Friebus, Oliver Clark

When Emily has difficulty venting her anger at a belligerent auto mechanic, Bob decides to show her how it's done.

**120**   You're Having My Hartley                March 19, 1977
  **Writers:** Gordon and Lynne Farr
  **Director:** Peter Bonerz
  **Guest Stars:** Tom Poston, Jean Palmerton, Bobby Ramsen

Bob has barely recovered from Carol's announcement that she's going to have a baby when he finds out that Emily is also expecting a visit from the stork.

This episode was written after Bob announced his intention to retire the series at the end of the fifth year. But by the time it was filmed, the star had decided to return for one final year—and a last-minute rewrite was required to explain away Emily's pregnancy as a dream.

"In the original story, she really was pregnant," recalls writer Lynne Farr. "Bob always said he wouldn't do the show with a baby, but when he announced he wasn't coming back for a sixth year, we decided to have some fun and see how far we could go before he changed his mind." Newhart—who'd long maintained that the Hartleys could get along very nicely without children—cringed at the thought of introducing "baby humor" in the show's final year.

"When Bob first saw the script at the Monday-morning reading, he refused to do it as written—and all of a sudden we didn't have a script," remembers Farr. "We spent a frantic night trying to save the story before we finally just turned the whole thing into a dream. And even after all that, it was actually a pretty good show."

## 1977-78    THE SIXTH SEASON

*Year-End Rating: 16.2 (67th place)*

By the time Bob Newhart reconsidered his earlier decision to end the series after the fifth year, most of the show's longtime staff had already moved on to other projects. But despite the loss of so many key writers and producers, the show's final and most inconsistent season is redeemed by a handful of memorable and funny episodes.

Executive producer Michael Zinberg assembled a sixth-season staff that included producers Glen Charles and Les Charles, story editor Lloyd Garver, and executive script consultant Tom Tenowich. Directing chores are divided almost equally between Peter Bonerz, Michael Zinberg, and Dick Martin, who also serves as creative consultant in the show's final year.

**121**   Bob's Change of Life                    September 24, 1977
**Writers:** Glen Charles, Les Charles
**Director:** Peter Bonerz
**Guest Star:** Martha Scott

Bob faces a mid-life crisis when he and Emily decide to move to a new apartment.

**122**   Ex-Con Job                              October 1, 1977
**Writer:** Ziggy Steinberg
**Director:** Michael Zinberg
**Guest Stars:** Bert Rosario, H. B. Haggerty, Allen Case, Taurean Blacque

Bob's newest therapy group has a unique set of problems—all five are freshly paroled ex-convicts.

**123**   A Jackie Story                          October 8, 1977
**Writer:** Lloyd Garver
**Director:** Michael Zinberg
**Guest Stars:** Hope Alexander Willis, Sam Kwasman

Bob treats a schizophrenic ventriloquist and his dummy; and Jerry is convinced that his beautiful new girlfriend is too good for him.

**124**   Who Was That Masked Man?                    October 15, 1977
    **Writers:** Glen Charles, Les Charles
    **Director:** Dick Martin
    **Guest Stars:** John Fiedler, Toni Lamond, Florida Friebus

After his wife kicks him out, Mr. Peterson finds an unlikely soulmate in Mr. Carlin.

**125**   Carlin's New Suit                             October 22, 1977
    **Writer:** Andrew Smith
    **Director:** Dick Martin
    **Guest Stars:** Loni Anderson, Mark Lenard, Sparky Marcus, Pat Cranshaw

Carlin decides to take advantage of a bogus paternity suit to pal around with the son he never had.

Loni Anderson would soon make waves as the sultry receptionist of MTM's *WKRP in Cincinnati*.

**126**   A Day in the Life                            October 29, 1977
    **Writers:** Kathy Donnell, Madelyn Dimaggio Wagner
    **Director:** Dick Martin
    **Guest Stars:** Richard Stahl, Bud Kenneally, Joan Kenneally, Rob Kenneally, Pamm Kenneally

Bob accepts a spur-of-the-moment invitation to Mardi Gras and then has but a single day to convince his patients that they can survive a week without him.

**127**   My Son the Comedian                        November 12, 1977
    **Writer:** David Lloyd
    **Director:** Dick Martin
    **Guest Stars:** Moosie Drier, Bobby Ramsen, Elizabeth Kerr, Johnny West

Howard laughs at all his son's jokes, until Howie decides to quit high school to pursue a career as a professional comedian.

**128**   You're Fired, Mr. Chips          November 19, 1977
   **Writer:** Lloyd Garver
   **Director:** Peter Bonerz
   **Guest Stars:** Ralph Bellamy, Richard Roat, Howard Witt

Bob hires his old college professor to help out with his practice
and then faces the unenviable task of firing his mentor when
things don't work out.

**129**   Shallow Throat          November 26, 1977
   **Writer:** Earl Pomerantz
   **Director:** Dick Martin
   **Guest Stars:** Richard Libertini, Frank Maxwell, J. Jay Saunders,
   Lorrie Gia, Alan Haufrect, Julienne Wells

Bob convinces a closed-mouthed patient to open up but wishes
he'd left well enough alone when the man's confession makes
him an accessory to larceny.

**130**   A Girl in Her Twenties          December 3, 1977
   **Writer:** Laura Levine
   **Director:** Peter Bonerz
   **Guest Stars:** Mildred Natwick, Sondra Currie, J.J. Johnston,
   Macon McCalman

While Bob's away on business, Emily becomes better acquainted
with an eccentric neighbor—an elderly woman who's perfectly
content to live her life in the past.

As a condition of his return to the series's final year, Newhart's sixth-
season contract allowed him to sit out five of the final twenty-two shows.
Emily takes the spotlight in this episode, as well as in "Grizzly Emily,"
"Emily Carlin, Emily Carlin," "It Didn't Happen One Night," and "Crisis in Edukation," while Bob makes only token appearances in all five.

**131**   Grand Delusion          December 17, 1977
   **Writer:** Lloyd Garver
   **Director:** Dick Martin
   **Guest Stars:** Morgan Fairchild, F. William Parker, Michael Evans

On the evening of their tenth anniversary, Bob and Emily imagine how their lives might have been different had they each married someone else.

**132**   'Twas the Pie Before Christmas          December 24, 1977
   **Writer:** Phil Davis
   **Director:** Dick Martin
   **Guest Stars:** Florida Friebus, John Fiedler, Rik Pierce

Bob's group decides to boycott his Christmas party after they each discover a rate increase notice that was accidentally included with their Christmas cards.

**133**   Freudian Ship                          January 7, 1978
   **Writer:** Earl Pomerantz
   **Director:** Peter Bonerz
   **Guest Stars:** John Crawford, Jeff Donnell

Even though he and Emily are supposed to be enjoying themselves on a ten-day pleasure cruise, Bob can't seem to resist solving other people's problems.

**134**   Grizzly Emily                          January 14, 1978
   **Writer:** Laura Levine
   **Director:** Peter Bonerz
   **Guest Stars:** Barnard Hughes, Alice Nunn, Bob Yerkes

Emily is one disgruntled camper after Bob's father insists that she stay behind to cook and clean while he and Howard go fishing.

**135**   Son of Ex-Con Job                      January 21, 1978
   **Writer:** Lloyd Garver
   **Director:** Dick Martin
   **Guest Stars:** Bert Rosario, Wyatt Johnson, Taurean Blacque, Norman Parker, Ric Mancini, Allen Case

Unable to find work on the outside, the parolees from Bob's ex-con therapy group decide to go into business for themselves.

**136**   Group on a Hot Tin Roof                January 28, 1978
   **Writer:** Andrew Smith
   **Director:** Michael Zinberg
   **Guest Stars:** Howard Hesseman, Jerry Devine, Florida Friebus, John Fiedler, Frank Ashmore, Ty Wilson, Lou Cutell, Amzie Strickland

Mr. Plager invites Bob's group to see his play—a turgid World War I drama with characters who bear more than a passing resemblance to the other members of the group.

**137**   Emily Carlin, Emily Carlin              February 4, 1978
   **Writer:** Laura Levine
   **Director:** Peter Bonerz
   **Guest Stars:** Karen Ericson, Michael Alldredge, Woody Skaggs,
   Carole Shelyne Barry

Carlin convinces Emily to attend his high school reunion posing
as his wife, and then takes shameless advantage of the situation.

**138**   Easy for You to Say                  February 11, 1978
   **Writer:** Andrew Smith
   **Director:** Dick Martin
   **Guest Stars:** Jerry Fogel, K.C. Martel, J.R. Miller

Bob treats Ralph Alfalfa, a stuttering radio personality who dreams
of hosting a children's TV show.

**139**   It Didn't Happen One Night            February 18, 1978
   **Writer:** Laura Levine
   **Director:** Dick Martin
   **Guest Star:** David Hedison

The Hartleys' friends assume the worst when Emily renews her
friendship with a handsome old boyfriend while Bob's away on
business.

**140**   Carole Ankles for Indie-Prod          March 4, 1978
   **Writer:** Lloyd Garver
   **Director:** Mark Tinker
   **Guest Stars:** Madeleine Fisher, John Terry Bell, Mert Rich, Joe
   George

Bob and Jerry are shocked when Carol announces that she's quit-
ting to accept a better job offer—working as personal assistant to
Mr. Carlin!

Director Mark Tinker, the son of MTM founder Grant Tinker, was also
associate producer of the final two seasons of *The Bob Newhart Show*. He
would later produce MTM's *The White Shadow* and *St. Elsewhere*.

**141**   Crisis in Edukation                     March 11, 1978
   **Writer:** Earl Pomerantz
   **Director:** Peter Bonerz
   **Guest Stars:** Edward Andrews, Robert Costanzo, Jan Fisher,
   Patricia Stevens, Bill Zuckert, Brian Miller, Delores Albin

Emily is left to fend off a group of irate parents after her principal
skips town to avoid the brewing protest.

**142**   Happy Trails to You                      April 1, 1978
   **Writers:** Glen Charles, Les Charles, Lloyd Garver
   **Directors:** Michael Zinberg, Peter Bonerz
   **Guest Stars:** Bobby Ramsen, Bill Quinn, Florida Friebus, John
   Fiedler

Jerry, Howard, and Carol exchange tearful farewells at the
Hartleys' good-bye party after Bob accepts a teaching job at a
small college in Oregon.

When the show went off the air, it seemed almost unimaginable that
Bob would trade in the hustle and bustle of the big city for the bucolic
pace of small-town life. And yet, four years later, Newhart reappeared
in a new MTM series set, coincidentally, in a small town. Before *Newhart*
premiered in 1982, the star actually considered returning to his former
stomping grounds. "At one time," Newhart told *TV Guide*, "I thought of
simply picking up the old show four years later. I think it might have
worked."

Perhaps. But given the unlikelihood of any such officially sanctioned
postscript, fans of *The Bob Newhart Show* can always take solace in the
show's continued afterlife in nightly rerun syndication. For it's there that
the infectious wit and cockeyed wisdom of Bob and Emily and Carol,
Jerry and Howard will continue to illuminate the late-night landscape as
long as there are people willing to smile in the darkness.

But for many of those who'd made *The Bob Newhart Show* a regular
part of their Saturday-night agenda for six years, the satisfying finality
of the last show sealed the wit and warmth of Bob, Emily, and Howard
forever into a single time and place. And then the show vanished, like a
strange dream, with no imaginable postscript.

For them, it's consolation enough to know that sooner or later the show
will appear—mysteriously, and without warning—in reruns on late-night
television. And that when it does, it will never fail to bring a smile in the
darkness.

# BARNEY MILLER

·

*That squad room was the end
result of twenty-six years of
analysis.*
—DANNY ARNOLD, *Barney
Miller* creator

THE FAILED PILOT for *Barney Miller* was already dead by the time the
president of ABC and his lieutenants sat down to lunch with the hottest
TV director in Hollywood. But John Rich was determined that it wouldn't
stay buried.

Martin Starger, Barry Diller, and Michael Eisner—the reigning powers at ABC—had invited the director to their executive dining room to
woo him into their camp in time for the 1974 season. But Rich didn't
want to talk comedy. After four years at the helm of *All in the Family*, he
was in no hurry to lock himself into another series.

In fact, the only show he *would* talk about was a great pilot that his
friend Danny Arnold had just made—a comedy about a compassionate
New York cop named Barney Miller.

Danny Arnold's quirky concept for a cop show had been around, in
one form or another, for years. At NBC in 1970, he pitched *Jacobi's Turf*—
a proposed vehicle for character actor Lou Jacobi, who would play a
bedraggled Jewish patrolman who served as protector and father-con-
fessor to residents of a tough Manhattan precinct. The network thought
that it sounded too ethnic. Despite Arnold's solid credits as a producer—
*That Girl*, *Bewitched*, and *My World and Welcome to It*—NBC politely turned
him down.

Danny Arnold put the concept on hold, but he refused to abandon it. He was convinced that the cops 'n' robbers shoot-'em-ups that had been a staple of prime time since the 1950s barely scratched the rich vein of material that lurked below the surface. "I wanted to turn the standard detective drama inside out," Arnold recalled, "I wanted to peer into the lives of cops who are stuck in an out-of-the-way precinct in a job that's really fundamentally boring."

It was fertile ground. And Danny Arnold wasn't the only one who thought so. In 1974 an agent introduced him to another writer who had an idea for a humanistic cop show of his own.

Ted Flicker, a comedy director best known for the dark satire of his 1968 feature, *The President's Analyst*, had been working on a concept for a police drama about a Jewish detective who operated in the sunny climes of California. Arnold, who by this time had secured a development deal with ABC, proposed a collaboration—but he insisted that they each drop the details of their original concepts and start fresh. "They're not going to buy a Jewish detective in the San Fernando Valley any more than they bought him in New York."

They came up with a new half-hour pilot for ABC called *The Life and Times of Barney Miller*. The detective was still Jewish, but the creators had decided not to draw attention to his background. "The name Miller was an attempt to be ethnic and non-ethnic at the same time," recalled Arnold. ABC's insistence on casting the resolutely non-ethnic Abby Dalton as Barney's wife further obscured the detective's ethnic origins. But it didn't much matter whether he was Jewish or not—because ABC wasn't really all that interested in Barney in the first place.

The network's research showed that Hal Linden—imported from New York for the title role—tested "dull." And besides, the precinct comedy had so many characters and storylines that it just seemed confusing. The ABC executives aired the pilot once—buried late in the summer of 1974— and then promptly forgot about it.

Until John Rich mentioned the show again during lunch.

In that instant, the unsold pilot took on a new significance. In the eyes of Starger, Diller, and Eisner, *Barney Miller* had suddenly become a potential trump card in their plan to lure the most successful TV director in Hollywood over to their side.

And Martin Starger wanted Rich badly. For the network boss who'd let *All in the Family* slip through his fingers five years earlier, nabbing the director who had finally shepherded that comedy through its first four seasons would provide a much-needed salve for the executive's still-wounded pride. ABC was determined to lure John Rich into the fold, even if they had to revive a dead pilot to do it.

When ABC's Barry Diller finally commissioned four *Barney Miller* scripts, Danny Arnold was convinced that the network had decided to make the relatively small investment, in his words, "just to shut me up." So it came as a complete surprise to the producer when network honcho Michael Eisner called and asked him to start production on *Barney Miller*.

But there was a catch. The network insisted that John Rich direct.

"They really wanted John on the team," Danny Arnold remembered. "And I knew he was good. But I like to run my own show." The director had almost exactly the same reservations about the producer. Rich had worked with Arnold on *My World and Welcome to It* and knew the seasoned TV veteran to be a brilliant producer. But the powerful director had also envisioned running his own show, not signing on as part of a network package deal with another creator who could be just as stubborn and single-minded as he. Rich finally agreed to direct the first two episodes of the new series, if only to get the project off and running.

And, as expected, the creative sparks began to fly from the very first day of production. The director insisted on shooting the new comedy on videotape, straight through, like a one-act play—the technique he'd perfected on *All in the Family*. "Danny went crazy," Rich remembered.

"I was horrified!" Arnold says with a laugh. The one-time film editor hated to lose the editing options that are sacrificed in a live-on-tape production setting. "You had no control over moments you might want to extend. To do even minimal editing, we had to physically take the tape to this tiny facility that Rich had set up in some guy's apartment! Those first two shows were such a horrifying experience that I vowed never to shoot live on tape again."

The two sample episodes were hardly enough to boost the network's confidence in the fledgling series, but ABC finally gave *Barney Miller* the go-ahead anyway. Actually, they had little choice. ABC's 1974 lineup had been a disaster, and the network desperately needed new half-hour comedies to replace the early failures of their the fall schedule. And so *Barney Miller*, already primed and ready to roll into production, was hastily slated as a mid-season replacement to debut in January 1975.

But the budget-conscious network made one firm demand: The show would continue to be shot before a live audience on cost-effective videotape. ABC had no intention of footing the bill for the financial extravagance of film stock just to suit the aesthetic whims of Danny Arnold.

Arnold cringed. He knew that he'd never be able to capture the dark, downbeat squalor of an urban squad room using the bright, flat lighting that was customarily employed in live-on-tape production. Arnold finally solved the problem by devising one of the most complex and unusual shooting techniques ever attempted for a TV situation comedy.

Instead of taping the whole show straight through, Arnold and his directors painstakingly adjusted the lighting for each separate scene, just as they would if they were shooting a movie. When they were satisfied that they had captured the best take of a scene, they would move on to the next shot. The show's live studio audience was actually superfluous to the process, since most of the real work was accomplished in painstaking set-ups that were recorded well after the audience had already gone home. Eventually, the producer abandoned the use of a studio audience altogether. The method produced striking results. *Barney Miller* would be justly celebrated for its moody, evocative atmosphere. But few realized that to achieve this look, the cast and crew labored under a grueling shooting schedule that frequently lasted far into the night. Actor Ron Glass remembered, "There were some days I didn't make it home until six the next morning."

The long hours didn't faze Danny Arnold. He approached the series with the enthusiasm of a man possessed, attacking every aspect of *Barney Miller*'s production with a fanatic's attention to detail. "You have to live with a show all the time," he insisted. And there were long stretches when he did just that—working, eating, and sleeping in the studio for days at a time.

But his greatest obsession was writing. With his partner and co-producer, Chris Hayward, Arnold personally wrote—or rewrote, sometimes line by line—nearly every script produced during the show's first two seasons. So great was the producer's enthusiasm that he would frequently storm onto the set with his latest story revisions and act out all the parts himself. It was a performance for which Danny Arnold was particularly well suited.

"They're all a part of me," the writer confessed. "Barney was the compassionate, moral guy I always thought I should be. Wojo was well meaning, but sometimes pretty irresponsible. Harris's narcissism, Dietrich's sardonic point of view, Yemena's weakness for horses—all a part of my own private paranoia. My analyst, a big fan of the show, once told me, 'You don't know how thrilled I am that I protected your paranoia all these years.'"

To bring these characters to life, the producer hired an ensemble of seasoned veterans that included Hal Linden, Abe Vigoda, Jack Soo, Barbara Barrie, and James Gregory, and paired them with relative newcomers Ron Glass, Max Gail, Greg Sierra, and, eventually, Steve Landesberg and Ron Carey. But fine as they were, the show frequently rested on the shoulders of the guest stars and bit players—that endless parade of kooks, con men, and lost souls that gave the series its heart.

"The show was a great platform," observed Arnold. "Anyone in the world could walk—or be dragged—into that station house." And in the simple democracy of the Twelfth Precinct, no one was ever denied a forum, no matter how unpopular—or absurd—his or her viewpoint.

There was the Indian who wanted to die in Central Park, and the Gypsy who vandalized the novelty shop of a Nazi war criminal. The squad room hosted foot fetishists, spies, and librarians; mad bombers, prostitutes, and, once, even a werewolf.

They came to the Twelfth Precinct for different reasons—some demanding justice, others looking for hope; while still others sought nothing more than a few moment's escape from their loneliness. But, no matter why they came, they rarely left unchanged.

*Barney Miller* was an instant hit with the critics, who applauded the show's slightly mocking approach to topics like teenage prostitution, urban terrorism, and mental illness—subjects that were seldom touched in prime time, and rarely with such wit and compassion. *Time* and *Newsweek* gave the series glowing write-ups, and before long, the show began to amass a faithful and ever-growing audience. By the end of its first full season, the series emerged as a consistent—though rarely spectacular—ratings winner.

In fact, the quiet success of *Barney Miller* was one of the secrets of the show's surprising longevity. The show staked out a comfortable niche, and as long as it delivered the same dependable ratings, ABC was content to leave it alone. The network recognized that *Barney Miller* was in a class by itself—a situation comedy for connoisseurs.

Remarkably, thanks to enormous creative contributions from writers Tony Sheehan, Chris Hayward, Reinhold Weege, Frank Dungan, and Jeff Stein—and director Noam Pitlik—the series was able to retain its almost cultlike following throughout eight prime-time seasons. And when the station house was finally shuttered at the end of the eighth season, it wasn't for lack of ratings.

"We were a topical show that was running out of topics," confessed writer Jeff Stein. "We had the choice of floating on forever, like *The Love Boat*, or going out with a little dignity. We decided to go out with dignity."

In the course of 168 well-crafted comic plays—each a model of clockwork precision that appears effortless in execution—the show's cast and creators chronicled the entire range of human behavior in stories that could be hilarious or chilling, and were often both. Considering the show's depth of wit and the breadth of its intelligence, it's probably not surprising that *Barney Miller* attracted a large and devoted following in its initial run. Indeed, even in reruns, the show's unfailing humor and affectionate view of humanity, in all of its colors, continues to attract new viewers almost every day.

Given time, it might just make connoisseurs of us all.

# A Critical Guide to All 168 Episodes

REGULAR CAST

| | |
|---|---|
| Captain Barney Miller | Hal Linden |
| Detective Sergeant Phil Fish | Abe Vigoda |
| Detective Sergeant Chano Amenguale | Gregory Sierra |
| Detective Stan Wojciehowicz | Maxwell Gail |
| Detective Sergeant Nick Yemena | Jack Soo |
| Detective Sergeant Ron Harris | Ron Glass |
| Inspector Frank Luger | James Gregory |
| Detective Sergeant Arthur Dietrich | Steve Landesberg |
| Officer Carl Levitt | Ron Carey |
| Elizabeth Miller | Barbara Barrie |
| Elizabeth Miller (pilot episode) | Abby Dalton |

SUPPORTING CAST

| | |
|---|---|
| Lieutenant Scanlon | George Murdock |
| Marty | Jack DeLeon |
| Bernice Fish | Florence Stanley |
| Detective Janice Wentworth | Linda Lavin |
| Detective Roslyn Licori | Mari Gorman |
| Arnold Ripner | Alex Henteloff |
| Detective Maria Battista | June Gable |
| Inspector Kelly | Dick O'Neill |
| Detective Eric Dorsey | Paul Lieber |
| Officer Kogan | Milt Kogan |
| Detective Wilson | Rod Perry |
| Detective Mike Lovatelli | Art Metrano |
| Perlita Avilar (Luger's wife) | Carina Afable |
| Rachel Miller (Barney's daughter) | Anne Wyndham |
| David Miller (Barney's son) | Michael Tessier |

STOCK COMPANY

Stanley Brock, Paul Lichtman, Richard Stahl, Philip Sterling, Phil Leeds,
    Jack Somack, Stuart Pankin, Kenneth Tigar, Miriam Byrd Netherly,
    Florence Halop, Phil Bruns, Candy Azzara, Doris Roberts, Oliver
    Clark, Ivor Francis, Stefan Gierasch, Michael Tucci, Walter Janowitz,
    Howard Platt, John Dullaghan, J.J. Barry, Peter Hobbs, Peggy Pope,
    Richard Libertini, Don Calfa, David Clennon, Ralph Manza, Dino
    Natali, Rod Colbin, Todd Susman, Walter Olkewicz
Created by Danny Arnold, Theodore J. Flicker
Music by Jack Elliot, Allyn Ferguson
Principal directors were Danny Arnold, Noam Pitlik

## 1974    THE PILOT EPISODE

**Pilot**   The Life and Times of Barney Miller          August 22, 1974
    **Writers:** Danny Arnold, Theodore J. Flicker
    **Director:** Theodore J. Flicker
    **Guest Stars:** Abby Dalton, Anne Wyndham, Val Bisoglio, Henry
    Beckman

A day in the life of Captain Barney Miller, a compassionate family man and chief detective in a colorful Greenwich Village precinct—where today he comes face-to-face with a gun-wielding
junkie.

The series's original filmed pilot, it aired only once—as an unsold pilot
on *Just for Laughs,* an ABC summer anthology series. Abby Dalton is
Barney's wife, Liz, the role played by Barbara Barrie when the script was
rewritten—and reshot—for *Barney Miller*'s debut five months later.

## 1975    THE FIRST SEASON

*Year-End Rating: 14.7 (70th place)*

The detectives of New York's Twelfth Precinct assemble for their first
season under the exhaustive stewardship of executive producer Danny
Arnold, who, along with producer Chris Hayward, would write the bulk
of the stories during the first two seasons. Lila Garrett serves as executive script consultant during the first year, and associate producer duties are shared by Tim Steele and Mark Goode.

**1**   Ramon                                    January 23, 1975
**Writers:** Danny Arnold, Theodore J. Flicker
**Director:** Bill Davis
**Guest Stars:** Chu Chu Malave, Michael Moore, Buddy Lester,
John Hawker

Barney tries to reason with a frightened young junkie who holds
the Twelfth Precinct at bay with a small handgun.

Faced with a wild-eyed gunman, the first thing Barney does is introduce himself! He disarms the scared felon with a simple act of respect—
standard procedure at the Twelfth Precinct, where for the next eight seasons, lawbreaker and victim alike would be treated with an empathy
rarely seen on TV cop shows.

**2**   Experience                                    January 30, 1975
**Writer:** Steve Gordon
**Director:** Danny Arnold
**Guest Stars:** Jack DeLeon, Rod Perry, Alex Henteloff, Jane Dulo,
Ray Sharkey, Milt Kogan, Noam Pitlik

Fish worries that he's getting too old for his job; a mad bomber
leaves a live charge in the squad room; and the detectives arrest a
gay shoplifter.

Though Danny Arnold was credited as director of this episode, it was
actually the second—and final—episode directed by John Rich. "We col-
laborated on that episode," explained Arnold. "And John's tough. He
knew what he wanted, and I knew what I wanted—but they weren't always the same thing. In the end, John didn't think it represented his work,
so he chose not to have his name on it."

Actually the issue of who got final credit for writing and directing various episodes would be a constant source of frustration for the producer.
"Those credits were dictated by strict union rules," insists Arnold. "In
many, many cases, the writing and directing credits that appear on *Barney
Miller* have nothing to do with authorship or the actual work that was
done on the show. They give a false impression that is very unfair to those
who actually made substantial contributions to *Barney Miller*."

The episode marks the first appearance of Alex Henteloff as Arnold
Ripner, the disreputable ambulance chaser who would plague the men
of the Twelfth for the next eight years; Jack DeLeon plays Marty, the gay
thief who would also make his share of return visits. Not so for Rod

Perry's Detective Wilson, a black member of the squad who failed to make the precinct's permanent roster.

**3    Snow Job**                                    February 6, 1975
**Writers:** Ron Friedman, Danny Arnold, Chris Hayward
**Story:** Dick Morgan
**Director:** Richard Kinon
**Guest Stars:** Ron Feinberg, Richard Stahl, Ted Noose, Paul Lichtman, Reid Cruickshanks

A department store entrusts their cash payroll to Wojo for safe-keeping during a blizzard; and a despondent flasher attempts suicide in the precinct's bathroom.

**4    Graft**                                       February 13, 1975
**Writers:** Danny Arnold, Chris Hayward
**Story:** Lila Garrett, Sanford Krinski
**Director:** Noam Pitlik
**Guest Stars:** Dick O'Neill, Buddy Lester, Derrel Maury

Chano investigates a rash of obscene phone calls; and Inspector Kelly arrives, intent on snooping out corruption in the Twelfth.

The episode contains one of a handful of scenes that took place in Barney's kitchen. Though the show had been designed to place equal emphasis on the policeman's home and work life, it quickly became apparent that the domestic scenes diluted the central focus of the squad room. In the early years, the writers made a few strained attempts to bring Liz down to the precinct. But, as producer Tony Sheehan observed, "There were only so many times we could have Liz drop in to have lunch or bring Barney a flower." With few exceptions, Barney's wife finally evolved into an offscreen presence throughout most of the series.

**5    The Courtesans**                              February 20, 1975
**Writers:** Jerry Davis, Danny Arnold, Chris Hayward, Sybil Adelman
**Story:** Sanford Krinski, Jerry Davis
**Director:** Noam Pitlik
**Guest Stars:** Nancy Dussault, Naomi Stevens, Audrey Christie, Rosana Soto, Shannon Christie, Lavell Roby

Barney's daughter wants to move out on her own; and a call girl rejects Wojo's tender efforts to reform her.

**6**  Stakeout                    February 27, 1975
**Writer:** Danny Arnold
**Director:** John Rich
**Guest Stars:** Lou Jacobi, Ed Barth, Brett Sommers, Vic Tayback, Marjorie Bennett, Florence Stanley, Lucille Meredith, Jo Jo Malone, Peter Carew

Fish, Barney, and Wojo are visited by a parade of curious neighbors when they attempt a stakeout in an abandoned apartment.

Though broadcast as the seventh episode, this script, directed by John Rich, was actually the first regular Barney Miller episode shot.

**7**  Bureaucrat                    March 6, 1975
**Writers:** Richard Baer, Danny Arnold, Chris Hayward
**Director:** Bob Finkel
**Guest Stars:** David Wayne, Elliot Reid, Milt Kogan, Milton Selzer, Claudio Martinez

A drunken bureaucrat finds himself behind bars; Wojo has the l ocal deli closed for minor health-code infractions; and Chano nabs the twelve-year-old burglar who robbed his apartment.

**8**  Ms. Cop                    March 13, 1975
**Writers:** Danny Arnold, Chris Hayward
**Director:** Noam Pitlik
**Guest Stars:** Linda Lavin, Howard Platt, Wynn Irwin

The detectives are put off by the determined lady cop who arrives on temporary transfer to the Twelfth; and Chano gets the goods on an obscene caller.

Linda Lavin's Detective Janice Wentworth would be reassigned to the Twelfth for a stay of duty that lasted throughout the show's second year.

**9**  Vigilante                    March 20, 1975
**Writers:** Danny Arnold, Chris Hayward
**Story:** Howard Albrecht, Sol Weinstein
**Director:** Noam Pitlik
**Guest Stars:** Titos Vandis, Gabe Dell, Marla Gibbs, Lee de Broux, Milt Kogan, Nick Holt

An elderly vigilante defends his neighborhood against muggers; Luger complains that Barney's squad isn't despised enough by the citizenry; and Wojo arrests a transvestite teamster.

James Gregory's gruff but avuncular Inspector Luger was inspired by Danny Arnold's friend Barney Ruditsky, a roaring-twenties racket-buster whose life was immortalized on *The Lawless Years*, an NBC cop show that ran from 1959 to 1961. Oddly enough, Jim Gregory played Ruditsky in that series as well.

**10**   The Guest                                March 27, 1975
   **Writers:** Danny Arnold, Chris Hayward, William Taub
   **Director:** Noam Pitlik
   **Guest Stars:** Herb Edelman, Jack DeLeon, Ed McCready, Milt Kogan

Wojo eats a poisoned sandwich that was intended for their prisoner, a nervous mob accountant; and Chano sets up a narcotics buy—with the detectives' own cash.

**11**   Escape Artist                             April 10, 1975
   **Writers:** Howard Leeds, Danny Arnold, Chris Hayward
   **Director:** Noam Pitlik
   **Guest Stars:** Roscoe Lee Browne, Leonard Frey, Danny Dayton, Judson Pratt, Reid Cruickshanks

The Twelfth plays host to a philosophical escape artist; Harris begins work on a police novel; and a crazy inventor attempts to fly.

Harris's literary leanings provide one of the show's most durable storylines—the eventual publication of *Blood on the Badge* in the sixth year would provide the author with both joy and anguish throughout the show's last three seasons.

**12**   Hair                                      April 17, 1975
   **Writers:** Ron Pearlman, Danny Arnold, Chris Hayward
   **Story:** Jerry Ross
   **Director:** Allen Baron
   **Guest Stars:** Michael Lembeck, Henry Beckman, Florence Stanley, Charles Fleischer

A long-haired loner from narcotics is transferred to the Twelfth Precinct; and Bernice is alarmed when Fish spends an afternoon investigating a massage parlor.

**13**   The Hero                                        May 1, 1975
   **Writers:** Danny Arnold, Chris Hayward
   **Director:** Noam Pitlik
   **Guest Stars:** Todd Bridges, Cal Gibson

Chano is involved in a shoot-out with a pair of armed robbers;
and Liz brings in a twelve-year-old who tried to rob her with a
stick.

## 1975-76   THE SECOND SEASON

*Year-End Rating: 19.0 (38th place)*

As executive producer, Danny Arnold continues to perform and su-
pervise a wide array of creative tasks in the second year. Arne Sultan
joins Chris Hayward as producer for the show's first full season, and
Noam Pitlik is established as the show's primary director, a distinction
he will maintain throughout most of the series's run.

**14**   Doomsday                              September 11, 1975
   **Writers:** Danny Arnold, Chris Hayward, Arne Sultan
   **Director:** Noam Pitlik
   **Guest Stars:** William Windom, J.J. Barry, Steve Landesberg

A nervous human bomb threatens to blow himself up to protest
the sorry state of Western civilization; the plumbing conks out;
and Wojo arrests a bogus priest.

The guest cast is made up of friends, old and new. William Windom
had starred in Danny Arnold's 1969 comedy *My World and Welcome to It;*
J.J. Barry probably spent more time in the Twelfth Precinct's cage than
any other actor; and Steve Landesberg would be invited back to play
Sergeant Dietrich the following season.

**15**   The Social Worker                     September 18, 1975
   **Writers:** Danny Arnold, Chris Hayward, Arne Sultan
   **Director:** Noam Pitlik
   **Guest Stars:** Art Metrano, Herbie Faye, Alex Henteloff

The detectives book a master forger, but Barney is preoccupied
with worry after Liz begins her new job as a social worker on the
streets of the South Bronx.

**16**    The Layoff                                    September 25, 1975
**Writers:** Danny Arnold, Chris Hayward, Arne Sultan
**Director:** Noam Pitlik
**Guest Stars:** Bob Dishy, Oliver Clark, Candy Azzara, Sandra Deel, Milt Kogan

New York City's cash crunch forces Barney to lay off Chano, Harris, and Wojo; a manicurist stabs her client; and an unemployed stockbroker turns purse-snatcher.


**17**    Ambush                                        October 2, 1975
**Writers:** Danny Arnold, Chris Hayward, Arne Sultan
**Director:** Noam Pitlik
**Guest Stars:** David Doyle, Dick O'Neill, Milt Kogan

Barney is offered a new job in Florida; and the men are shocked to discover that bystanders failed to assist after Yemena was shot in an ambush.


**18**    Heat Wave                                     October 9, 1975
**Writers:** Danny Arnold, Chris Hayward
**Story:** Danny Arnold, Chris Hayward, Arne Sultan
**Director:** Noam Pitlik
**Guest Stars:** Linda Lavin, Janet Ward, Harold Oblong, Gloria Calomee, Paul Lichtman, Angelo Gnazzo

Wojo and Wentworth go undercover to lure a rapist into the open; and a wife reports her husband for assault and battery.


**19**    The Arsonist                                  October 16, 1975
**Writer:** Tony Sheehan
**Director:** Noam Pitlik
**Guest Stars:** Roger Bowen, Jack Somack, Leonard Stone, Steve Franken

The detectives suspect arson after a rash of fires; and Chano arrests a man for shooting a subway candy machine.

The first script by Tony Sheehan, a prolific writer whose eventual contribution to the series would be incalculable. Sheehan was hired on the basis of a spec script he'd written for *M\*A\*S\*H*—in longhand, on a legal pad—while still a student at UCLA. Larry Gelbart recommended him to Danny Arnold, who hired the talented young scribe as story editor. During his long tenure on the show, he would be a credited author on more than sixty *Barney Miller* teleplays, and an uncredited contributor to scores of others.

**20** Grand Hotel October 23, 1975
**Writers:** Danny Arnold, Chris Hayward, Arne Sultan
**Story:** Chris Hayward, Danny Arnold
**Director:** Noam Pitlik
**Guest Stars:** Linda Lavin, Robert Mandan, Adam Arkin, Queenie Smith, Beatrice Colen, Joe Medalis, Arnold Soboloff

Wojo and Wentworth pose as a wealthy couple to flush out a burglary ring in a luxury hotel; and a college student is arrested for registering with his underage girlfriend.

The smoldering romance between Wojo and Wentworth was actually part of Danny Arnold's grand plan to please ABC's insatiable appetite for a spinoff series, preferably starring Fish. The producer refused—why jeopardize the chemistry of *Barney Miller* by pulling Fish out of the squad room for his own series? Instead, Arnold's novel solution proposed pulling *all of the detectives* out of the squad room—one at a time—for a separate anthology series that each week would examine the private life of a different member of the squad. Wentworth and Wojo's romance was projected as the basis for one storyline; and alternating episodes might pick up Barney's life at home with Liz, or perhaps the camera would follow Fish home to a house full of wayward foster kids. Unfortunately, the producer abandoned the project as too ambitious for *Barney Miller*'s already overworked staff, though he did salvage the latter storyline as the basis for the *Fish* spinoff, which finally aired two years later.

**21** Discovery October 30, 1975
**Writers:** Tom Reeder, Danny Arnold, Chris Hayward
**Director:** Lee Bernhardi
**Guest Stars:** Jack DeLeon, Ray Stewart, Norman Rice, Philip Sterling

The department's computers declare Fish dead; and an impostor harasses neighborhood gays while posing as a detective from the Twelfth Precinct.

**22**   You Dirty Rat                          November 13, 1975
   **Writers:** Arne Sultan, Danny Arnold, Chris Hayward
   **Story:** Arne Sultan
   **Director:** Noam Pitlik
   **Guest Stars:** Ned Glass, J. Pat O'Malley, Franklyn Ajaye, Val
   Bisoglio, Del Vecchio

A hungry rat is the suspect when two pounds of marijuana come
up missing from the evidence locker; and a vagrant spends the
night in a department store.

**23**   Horse Thief                            November 20, 1975
   **Writer:** Tony Sheehan
   **Director:** Noam Pitlik
   **Guest Stars:** Ron Masak, Jack Dodson, Liam Dunn, Bruce
   Solomon, Judy Cassmore

A hansom-cab driver's horse is stolen during the Bicentennial celebration; and a canny streetwalker uses patriotic souvenirs to
mask her trade.

**24**   Rain                                   November 27, 1975
   **Writer:** Tony Sheehan
   **Story:** Danny Arnold, Chris Hayward
   **Director:** Noam Pitlik
   **Guest Stars:** Sidney Miller, Phil Leeds, Paul Lichtman

The squad room ceiling springs a leak; and the officers are forced
to put up with a steady stream of bad jokes from an incarcerated
comedian.

**25**   Fish                                   December 4, 1975
   **Writer:** Danny Arnold, Chris Hayward, Herbert Baker
   **Director:** Noam Pitlik
   **Guest Stars:** Doris Belack, Steve Landesberg, Emily Levine,
   Darryl Seman

Fish worries about his job when a new detective is assigned to
the precinct after his doctor puts him on restricted duty.

Stand-up comic Steve Landesberg debuts as Sergeant Arthur Dietrich,
a one-shot tryout whose low-key appeal made him a natural for the squad
room ensemble. He would be added to the precinct's permanent roster
the following season.

**26** Hot Dogs December 11, 1975
**Writer:** Tony Sheehan
**Story:** Arne Sultan, Danny Arnold, Chris Hayward
**Director:** Lee Bernhardi
**Guest Stars:** Jonelle Allen, Nellie Bellflower, David L. Lander, Howard Honig

A pair of eager lady cops makes an overzealous drug bust; and a confused husband identifies his missing wife with a dime-store photo of Jean Harlow.

**27** Protection December 18, 1975
**Writer:** Tom Reeder
**Story:** Danny Arnold, Chris Hayward, Tom Reeder
**Director:** Noam Pitlik
**Guest Stars:** Jack Somack, Ralph Manza, Ray Sharkey

A protection racket springs up amid rumors that the precinct is about to be shuttered; and a local hood confesses to a crime that can't be proven.

**28** Happy New Year January 8, 1976
**Writers:** Danny Arnold, Chris Hayward, Arne Sultan
**Director:** Bruce Bilson
**Guest Stars:** Edith Diaz, Johnny Lamotta

The precinct hosts a suicidal man on New Year's Eve; and Wojo delivers a pregnant shoplifter's baby.

Edith Diaz also played the very expectant Puerto Rican mother who gave birth in a crowded elevator on *All in the Family* exactly four years earlier.

**29** Sniper January 22, 1976
**Writers:** Tom Reeder, Danny Arnold, Chris Hayward
**Director:** Lee Bernhardi
**Guest Stars:** Charlotte Rae, Jay Robinson, Sully Boyar

A space-age travel agent bilks a couple out of the cost of a round-trip to Saturn; and Wojo and Luger are targets of a sniper outside the station house.

**30**    Fear of Flying                      January 29, 1976
   **Writer:** Reinhold Weege
   **Director:** Lee Bernhardi
   **Guest Stars:** Jack Riley, Valerie Curtin, Charles Murphy

Wojo must overcome his fear of flying when he's chosen to accompany an extradited bigamist to Cleveland.

Writer Reinhold Weege would become a major force in the show's
middle years, first as a prolific writer and story editor, and finally as
producer in the fifth year. He learned his lessons well: His 1984 NBC
series, *Night Court*, owed a considerable debt of inspiration to *Barney
Miller*.

**31**    Block Party                       February 12, 1976
   **Writer:** Tom Reeder
   **Director:** Noam Pitlik
   **Guest Stars:** Larry Bishop, Linda Lavin, George Murdock,
   Stanley Brock

Wentworth stops an assassin at a block party, but is frustrated
when Chano gets all the credit.

**32**    Massage Parlor                    February 19, 1976
   **Writer:** Tony Sheehan
   **Director:** Dennis Steinmetz
   **Guest Stars:** Linda Lavin, Florence Halop, Meg Wyllie, Kenneth
   Tigar, Charles Frank, Janet Ruff, Opal Euard

Wentworth goes undercover in a massage parlor and gets the
goods on a bewildered midnight cowboy; and an elderly woman
is arrested for mugging.

This would be Linda Lavin's last appearance as Detective Wentworth.
The actress left *Barney Miller* to star in *Alice*, the long-running CBS series
that would premiere the following season.

**33**    The Psychiatrist                  February 26, 1976
   **Writers:** Tony Sheehan, Danny Arnold, Chris Hayward
   **Story:** Greg Tiefer
   **Director:** Noam Pitlik
   **Guest Stars:** Fred Sadoff, Neil J. Schwartz, Martin Garner

Wojo's aggressive tendencies come under the scrutiny of a psychiatrist who insists that the officer is unfit to carry a gun.

**34**   The Kid                                    March 4, 1976
**Writers:** Tony Sheehan, Danny Arnold, Chris Hayward
**Director:** Stan Lathan
**Guest Stars:** Charles Murphy, Arny Freeman, Angelina Estrada, Jose Flores

A good Samaritan returns to retrieve the unclaimed cash he turned in a month earlier; and Fish is smitten by the mother of a teenage pickpocket.

**35**   The Mole                                   March 18, 1976
**Writers:** Danny Arnold, Chris Hayward, Reinhold Weege
**Director:** Mark Warren
**Guest Stars:** Dean Santoro, Richard Russell Ramos, Ron Carey, Severn Darden

Fish agonizes over an upcoming operation; and Harris and Wojo track a burglar through the sewers.

Ron Carey plays the subterranean thief who would return to the precinct as the uniformed cop Officer Carl Levitt at the start of the following season. The episode also marks the final appearance of Greg Sierra's Chano. The actor eventually resurfaced in *AES Hudson Street*, a short-lived attempt by *Barney Miller*'s creator to duplicate the chemistry of the Twelfth Precinct in a hospital emergency room.

The producers were confident that the series could withstand the loss of major characters like Chano—and eventually, Fish. As Danny Arnold observed, "The squad room itself is as much a personality as any of the characters. Our audience buys the situation, and change is part of it."

## 1976-77   THE THIRD SEASON

*Year-End Rating: 22.2 (17th place)*

The precinct undergoes its only major personnel shake-down in season three, when Gregory Sierra's Chano and Linda Lavin's Wentworth leave the series and are replaced by new recruits Dietrich, Levitt, and briefly, Detective Maria Battista, played by Ron Carey, Steve Landesberg, and June Gable, respectively. Producer Chris Hayward also departs at the close of season two, bound for greener pastures and, perhaps, shorter hours elsewhere.

Danny Arnold serves as producer in the show's third year. Story editor Tony Sheehan is credited on most of the season's scripts; and there are multiple submissions from Reinhold Weege, Tom Reeder, and Danny Arnold. Jerry Ross is the executive script consultant.

**36** Evacuation                                      September 23, 1976
   **Writer:** Danny Arnold
   **Story:** Chris Hayward, Danny Arnold
   **Director:** Noam Pitlik
   **Guest Stars:** Joe Petrullo, Denise Miller, Paul Lichtman, Kenneth Mars

Wojo decides to beef up evacuation procedures for New York's eleven million citizens; and a young thief finds a friend in Fish.

**37** Quarantine (Part 1)                             September 30, 1976
   **Writer:** Tony Sheehan
   **Director:** Lee Bernhardi
   **Guest Stars:** Paula Shaw, Jack DeLeon, Ray Stewart, Arthur Peterson, David Darlow, Michael Kerns, Dennis Spiegelman

The station house is filled to capacity when authorities place it under quarantine because an ailing burglar may have smallpox.

**38** Quarantine (Part 2)                             October 7, 1976
   **Writer:** Tony Sheehan, Danny Arnold
   **Director:** Noam Pitlik
   **Guest Stars:** Paula Shaw, Jack DeLeon, Ray Stewart

The continued threat of smallpox forces an unlikely gathering of characters to spend the night in the Twelfth Precinct.

The underlying tension of a medical quarantine provides the ideal setting for a classic *Barney Miller* episode. The precinct emerges as a downtrodden Grand Hotel, with crackling dialogue flying nonstop among the disparate personalities suddenly forced together for a long night in very close quarters. Despite his initial resistance, Wojo comes to accept Marty and his gay lover; Inspector Luger learns to lighten up; and the writers even grant Fish a few privileged moments as the weary detective forms a tender platonic bond with an imperturbable prostitute— and for at least one night in his life, someone calls him Phil.

**39**   Bus Stop                                October 14, 1976
**Writers:** Tony Sheehan, Danny Arnold, Reinhold Weege, Jerry
Ross
**Story:** Reinhold Weege, Chris Hayward, Danny Arnold
**Director:** Noam Pitlik
**Guest Stars:** Candy Azzara, Phil Bruns, Sal Viscuso, Florence
Halop, Joe George, Howard Honig

A holdup man robs a busload of commuters and then faces their
fury as they storm the precinct house.

**40**   The Election                            October 21, 1976
**Writer:** Tom Reeder
**Director:** Lee Bernhardi
**Guest Stars:** Brett Somers, Richard Venture, Gilbert Green, Steve
Landesberg

On Election Day, a jailed shoplifter demands his right to cast a
ballot; and the officers confront a husband who refuses to let his
wife vote.

**41**   Werewolf                               October 28, 1976
**Writers:** Reinhold Weege, Tony Sheehan, Danny Arnold,
Seymour Blicker
**Story:** Seymour Blicker, Tony Sheehan
**Director:** Noam Pitlik
**Guest Stars:** Kenneth Tigar, Janet MacLachlan, Queenie Smith,
Jon Lormer

The usual loonies arrive during the full moon, including a man
who swears he's turning into a werewolf.

**42**   The Recluse                          November 11, 1976
**Writers:** Reinhold Weege, Danny Arnold
**Story:** Chris Hayward, Reinhold Weege
**Director:** Bruce Bilson
**Guest Stars:** Arnold Soboloff, Ivor Francis, Florence Stanley,
Denise Miller, John Cassisi

A doomsayer shares the cell with a recluse who hid in his apartment for three decades to avoid jury duty.

**43**   Non-Involvement                        November 18, 1976
   **Writers:** Reinhold Weege
   **Story:** Chris Hayward, Danny Arnold, Reinhold Weege
   **Director:** Bruce Bilson
   **Guest Stars:** Mike Kellin, Ron Feinberg, June Gable, Oliver
   Clark, Alex Henteloff, Lucille Meredith

Wojo arrests a man for refusing to interfere when he witnessed a
mugging in progress.

June Gable appears as Detective Maria Battista, a short-lived addition
to the precinct's ranks. "Every once in a while we'd bring in someone
new, to shake things up. But it never seemed to work out," explained
writer Tony Sheehan. "We had such a tight group that the newcomer always seemed like an outsider. It was very hard to get them past that point."

**44**   Power Failure                        December 9, 1976
   **Writers:** Tony Sheehan, Danny Arnold
   **Story:** Reinhold Weege, Danny Arnold, Tony Sheehan
   **Director:** Noam Pitlik
   **Guest Stars:** Susan Brown, Arny Freeman, Stefan Gierasch, Paul
   Lichtman

During a blackout, the station plays host to a suspect with a split
personality.

**45**   Christmas Story                        December 23, 1976
   **Writers:** Tony Sheehan, Reinhold Weege
   **Director:** Bruce Bilson
   **Guest Stars:** Nobu McCarthy, Jay Gerber, John Morgan Evans

Fish goes undercover as Santa Claus; Barney reluctantly invites
Luger to spend Christmas with his family; and Nick falls under the
spell of an Oriental call girl.

**46**   Hash                        December 30, 1976
   **Writer:** Tom Reeder
   **Director:** Noam Pitlik
   **Guest Stars:** Ed Peck, Walter Janowitz, George Perina, Michael
   Tucci

It's a giddy evening at the Twelfth when the detectives sample
Wojo's girlfriend's brownies before anyone realizes that her recipe
included an ample portion of hashish.

**47**   Smog Alert                          January 6, 1977
**Writer:** Reinhold Weege
**Story:** Chris Hayward, Danny Arnold
**Director:** Bruce Bilson
**Guest Stars:** Lee Kessler, Alan Haufrect, June Gable

Fish bears up during a first-stage smog alert; and a suicidal
woman strikes up a relationship with an obscene-graffiti artist.


**48**   Community Relations                 January 13, 1977
**Writers:** Tony Sheehan, Dennis Koenig, Larry Balmagia
**Story:** Tony Sheehan, Winston Moss
**Director:** Noam Pitlik
**Guest Stars:** David Tress, Ralph Manza, Joseph Perry, Judson
Morgan

A homeless old man confronts his former landlord with a musket;
and a lawyer accuses Barney of harassment after he books a blind
shoplifter.


**49**   The Rand Report                     January 20, 1977
**Writer:** Reinhold Weege
**Story:** Roland Kibbee, Reinhold Weege
**Director:** Noam Pitlik
**Guest Stars:** Martin Garner, Anna Berger, John William Evans

Wojo resigns the force in protest after the department releases a
critical study that recommends that the detectives return to uniformed patrol.


**50**   Fire '77                            January 27, 1977
**Writer:** Tony Sheehan
**Director:** Bruce Bilson
**Guest Stars:** Sal Viscuso, Howard Platt, K Callan, Russell Shan-
non

A suicidal couple is delighted when flames threaten to engulf the
squad room after an arsonist sets fire to the station house.

**51**   Abduction                    February 3, 1977
**Writer:** Tom Reeder, Tony Sheehan, Reinhold Weege
**Director:** Bruce Bilson
**Guest Stars:** Buddy Lester, Vivi Janiss, Rod Colbin, Jane Alice Brandon, David Clennon, Florence Stanley

Nick's bookie is brought in; and a suburban couple turns to Barney for help after they kidnap their daughter back from a religious cult.

**52**   Sex Surrogate                February 10, 1977
**Writers:** Tony Sheehan, Dennis Koenig, Larry Balmagia
**Story:** Jerry Ross, Tony Sheehan
**Director:** Noam Pitlik
**Guest Stars:** Eugene Elman, Doris Roberts, Marilyn Sokol, Billy Barty

A middle-aged woman shoots her husband for seeing a sexual surrogate; and Harris suffers the ultimate indignity when he's attacked by a gang of delinquents who ruin his suit.

**53**   Moonlighting                 February 17, 1977
**Writer:** Reinhold Weege
**Director:** Noam Pitlik
**Guest Stars:** George Pentecost, Cal Gibson, John Dullaghan, Jan Stuart Schwartz

Barney discovers that Harris has been moonlighting; Dietrich arrests a priest for fencing stolen goods; and a numbers racketeer uses a retarded boy as a runner.

**54**   Asylum                       February 24, 1977
**Writers:** Roland Kibbee, Tony Sheehan, Reinhold Weege, Danny Arnold
**Director:** Alex March
**Guest Stars:** Ion Teodorescu, Michael Panaieff, David Clennon, Louis Zito, Jack DeLeon

Wojo runs afoul of diplomatic protocol when he offers political asylum to a Russian defector; and the squad room's old friend Marty violates his probation with a half ounce of marijuana.

**55**    Group Home                              March 10, 1977
    **Writers:** Tony Sheehan, Danny Arnold
    **Story:** Dennis Koenig, Larry Balmagia
    **Director:** Lee Bernhardi
    **Guest Stars:** George Murdock, Don Calfa, Florence Stanley,
    John Cassisi

The squad tracks a mad bomber who's threatened to blow up an
Army recruiting office; and Fish has to dress as a woman when
it's his turn for mugging detail.

The running joke of the mugging detail afforded the audience at least
one good belly laugh every season, as each member of the squad took
his turn in drag.

**56**    Strike (Part 1)                         March 24, 1977
    **Writer:** Reinhold Weege
    **Story:** Dennis Koenig, Larry Balmagia
    **Director:** Jeremiah Morris
    **Guest Stars:** Peter Hobbs, Peggy Pope

A woman is robbed by her computer date; and the detectives
must decide whether to honor an unauthorized policeman's
strike.

**57**    Strike (Part 2)                         March 31, 1977
    **Writers:** Reinhold Weege, Tony Sheehan, Danny Arnold
    **Story:** Dennis Koenig, Larry Balmagia
    **Director:** Danny Arnold
    **Guest Stars:** Peter Hobbs, Peggy Pope

Inspector Luger fills in for the striking detectives; and the woman
who was robbed by her computer date refuses to press charges.

## 1977-78    THE FOURTH SEASON

*Year-End Rating: 21.4 (17th place)*

Abe Vigoda's Detective Fish retires from active duty at the top of the
fourth season, as the series moves into its fertile middle period, with no
creative drop-off in sight. Tony Sheehan is promoted to producer, and
Reinhold Weege assumes the duties of story editor, though both will
continue to write most of the show's scripts. Other memorable fourth-

year stories are contributed by Dennis Koenig, Larry Balmagia, Tom Reeder, and executive producer Danny Arnold.

**58**    Good-Bye, Mr. Fish (Part 1)                September 15, 1977
    **Writers:** Reinhold Weege, Danny Arnold
    **Director:** Danny Arnold
    **Guest Stars:** Stanley Brock, Arny Freeman, Jack Somack, Gregory V. Karliss

Barney tries to quell a neighborhood vigilante group; and Fish fails to arrive for work on his retirement day.

**59**    Good-Bye, Mr. Fish (Part 2)                September 22, 1977
    **Writer:** Reinhold Weege
    **Director:** Danny Arnold
    **Guest Stars:** Larry Gelman, Timothy Jerome, Florence Stanley

Fish arrives for work as usual, refusing to acknowledge his forced retirement from the department.

The long-suffering detective had been dividing his time between the squad room and *Fish*, the spinoff that began the previous February, despite resistance from Danny Arnold, who preferred to keep Abe Vigoda's blues bottled up as a potent source of laughter in the squad room. It was a decision Vigoda protested with vigor. "I found myself with a very unhappy actor on my hands," Arnold remembers. "Abe would walk around the set like a man in shock. Who was I to deprive an actor of this once-in-a-lifetime break? Finally I said, 'Okay—just stay through the third year of *Barney Miller*, and we'll go with your show, too.'" With this episode, the senior detective retires to pursue his fortunes full-time in the spinoff that, ironically, lasted only thirty-four episodes.

**60**    Bugs                                        September 29, 1977
    **Writers:** Dennis Koenig, Larry Balmagia, Tony Sheehan
    **Director:** David Swift
    **Guest Stars:** Sammy Smith, Mari Gorman, Paula Shaw, Robert Costanzo, Lavell Roby

The detectives discover that someone has planted electronic bugs throughout the squad room.

**61**   Corporation                           October 6, 1977
**Writers:** Lee H. Grant, Tony Sheehan, Danny Arnold
**Story:** Lee H. Grant
**Director:** Hal Linden
**Guest Stars:** David Dukes, Fran Ryan, Vernon Weddle

A vigilante environmentalist who's been sabotaging a chemical plant faces the corporation's high-powered lawyer.


**62**   Burial                               October 20, 1977
**Writer:** Michael Russnow
**Director:** Danny Arnold
**Guest Stars:** Sy Kramer, Jack Kruschen, Abe Vigoda

After a suspect steals his best friend's corpse and refuses to tell anyone where he's hidden it, Fish returns to help Barney find the body.


**63**   Copy Cat                             October 27, 1977
**Writers:** Douglas Wyman, Tony Sheehan
**Director:** Jeremiah Morris
**Guest Stars:** Don Calfa, Norman Bartold, Don Sherman, John Dullaghan

Prime time's cops and robbers provide inspiration for a criminal who mimics the felonies of TV police shows; and a drunk attempts armed robbery without a gun.


**64**   Blizzard                            November 3, 1977
**Writer:** Tony Sheehan
**Director:** Danny Arnold
**Guest Stars:** Alex Henteloff, Lou Cutell, Lewis Charles, Tom Henschell

The officers are unable to remove a corpse from the station house during a blizzard; and an eccentric swears that the snow is the start of a new ice age.

**65**   Chase                                    November 17, 1977
   **Writers:** Tom Reeder, Danny Arnold, Reinhold Weege
   **Director:** Jeremiah Morris
   **Guest Stars:** Luis Avalos, George Murdock, Marya Small, Joey
   Aresco, George Loros

Wojo wrecks a taxi that he borrows to chase a robbery suspect;
and Lieutenant Scanlon enlists the help of a drug pusher to test
the detectives' honesty.


**66**   Thanksgiving Story                       November 24, 1977
   **Writer:** Reinhold Weege
   **Director:** David Swift
   **Guest Stars:** Ian Wolfe, George Skaff, Tom Lacy, Susan Davis,
   Anita Dangler, Kip King

The automat is the scene of a chaotic dinner when three mental
patients sit down to a Thanksgiving feast.


**67**   Tunnel                                   December 1, 1977
   **Writers:** Tony Sheehan, Michael Russnow
   **Story:** Michael Russnow
   **Director:** David Swift
   **Guest Stars:** Leonard Stone, J.J. Barry, Jay Gerber

Wojo gets buried underground on the trail of a burglar who's dig-
ging into the diamond exchange; and Harris desperately looks for
a new apartment in Manhattan.


**68**   Atomic Bomb                              December 15, 1977
   **Writers:** Tom Reeder, Reinhold Weege
   **Director:** Noam Pitlik
   **Guest Stars:** Phil Leeds, Karl Bruck, Stephen Pearlman, Al
   Ruscio, Will Seltzer, John Getz

The FBI arrives to investigate a college student who built a working nuclear bomb for his physics class project.

**69**   The Bank                                     January 5, 1978
   **Writer:** Tony Sheehan
   **Director:** Noam Pitlik
   **Guest Stars:** Sandy Sprung, Peter Jurasik, Jodie Mann

A man with a vasectomy wreaks havoc when he accuses the owner of a sperm bank of destroying his only remaining sperm sample.


**70**   The Ghost                                    January 12, 1978
   **Writer:** Reinhold Weege
   **Director:** Lee Bernhardi
   **Guest Stars:** Nehemiah Persoff, Titos Vandis, Kenneth Tigar, Caroline McWilliams

The detectives are skeptical of a man's claim that he's being pestered by a poltergeist, until a string of unexplainable occurrences gives them pause.


**71**   Appendicitis                                 January 19, 1978
   **Writer:** Tony Sheehan
   **Director:** Noam Pitlik
   **Guest Stars:** Jack Bernardi, Michael Durrell

An aging bounty hunter and a sugar addict are the precinct's latest guests; and Yemena is rushed to the hospital after an appendicitis attack.


**72**   Rape                                         January 26, 1978
   **Writer:** Dennis Koenig
   **Director:** Noam Pitlik
   **Guest Stars:** Michael Pataki, Joyce Jameson, William Bogert, Dick Balduzzi, Linda Dano

A woman accuses her husband of raping her; Yemena is thrilled that New York has legalized off-track betting; and a master of disguise embarks on a crime spree.

**73**    Eviction (Part 1)                              February 2, 1978
   **Writers:** Tom Reeder, Reinhold Weege
   **Director:** Noam Pitlik
   **Guest Stars:** Dave Madden, Rosana Soto, Felipe Turich

Barney refuses to comply with the court-ordered eviction of the impoverished residents of a condemned hotel.


**74**    Eviction (Part 2)                              February 9, 1978
   **Writers:** Tom Reeder, Reinhold Weege
   **Director:** Noam Pitlik
   **Guest Stars:** Dave Madden, George Kirby, John Clavin, Donna Bacalia

Barney intermediates when a SWAT team is dispatched to remove the stubborn occupants of a condemned hotel.


**75**    Wojo's Problem                               February 23, 1978
   **Writer:** Tony Sheehan
   **Director:** Max Gail
   **Guest Stars:** Ray Girardin, Henry Slate, Mari Gorman, Stanley Brock

Wojo's problem is a case of temporary impotence; the squad faces the jealous husband of their new female detective; and a wheelchair-bound shoplifter escapes.

Mari Gorman debuts as Detective Roslyn Licori. Like those of her predecessors, her assignment to the precinct would be temporary.


**76**    "Quo Vadis?"                                    March 2, 1978
   **Writer:** Tony Sheehan
   **Story:** Douglas Wyman, Tony Sheehan
   **Director:** Alex March
   **Guest Stars:** Ivy Bethune, Barbara Barrie

An irate woman demands the closing of an art gallery's nude-painting exhibit; and marital problems between Barney and Liz reach a standoff.

**77**   Hostage                                        March 23, 1978
  **Writer:** Reinhold Weege
  **Story:** Reinhold Weege, Chris Hayward
  **Director:** Hal Linden
  **Guest Stars:** Earle Towne, Oliver Clark, Don Calfa

A prisoner holds the precinct hostage; Harris finds an apartment in the Village; and a ventriloquist is held responsible for his dummy's lewd remarks.

**78**   Evaluation                                      May 4, 1978
  **Writer:** Larry Balmagia
  **Director:** Noam Pitlik
  **Guest Stars:** Richard Libertini, Kay Medford, Eugene Elman

Barney must file an evaluation on each of the men; a mom-and-pop porno store is vandalized; and Dietrich books a kook who insists he has no name, only a number.

**79**   The Sighting                                    May 11, 1978
  **Writer:** Tony Sheehan
  **Story:** Reinhold Weege, Carol Gary
  **Director:** Alex March
  **Guest Stars:** Doris Roberts, Peter Hobbs, Jack Bannon

Wojo's excuse for tardiness is that he was up late the night before tracking a UFO; and a woman reports her husband for turning all their possessions into gold.

**80**   Inauguration                                    May 18, 1978
  **Writers:** Reinhold Weege, Carol Gary
  **Director:** Alex March
  **Guest Stars:** Philip Sterling, Basil Hoffman, Florence Hallop

Harris has to decide whether to leave the squad after he's offered a job in the mayor's office.

## 1978-79   THE FIFTH SEASON

*Year-End Rating: 22.8 (15th place)*

Fifth-year producers are Tony Sheehan and Reinhold Weege, who also serve as the season's uncredited story editors. And once again, Danny

Arnold is the series's executive producer and uncredited script consultant. Notable additions to the show's small stable of writers include Wally Dalton and Shelley Zellman, and Frank Dungan and Jeff Stein, two prolific teams who make their initial contributions in the fifth year.

**81**	Kidnapping (one hour)	September 14, 1978
**Writers:** Reinhold Weege, Danny Arnold, Tony Sheehan
**Director:** Noam Pitlik
**Guest Stars:** Fred Sadoff, Beverly Sanders, Todd Susman, Barrie Youngfellow, Ralph Manza, John O'Connell

A department-store magnate is held for ransom by a political extremist; and Wojo arrests a prostitute and her john—an Arkansas traveler.

**82**	The Search	September 21, 1978
**Writers:** Bob Colleary, Tony Sheehan
**Story:** Bob Colleary
**Director:** Noam Pitlik
**Guest Stars:** Jenny O'Hara, Bruce Kirby, Arny Freeman

Television's Mr. Science is in the holding tank; Harris shaves his mustache for mugging detail; and the detectives help a woman find her father after twenty-eight years.

**83**	Dog Days	September 28, 1978
**Writer:** Reinhold Weege
**Director:** Noam Pitlik
**Guest Stars:** Rosalind Cash, Joseph Perry

Wojo is bitten by a possibly rabid German shepherd when he attempts to bust an illegal dogfight ring; and Barney has the blues over his impending separation.

**84**	The Baby Broker	October 5, 1978
**Writer:** Tony Sheehan
**Director:** Noam Pitlik
**Guest Stars:** Frederic Cook, Phoebe Dorin, Michael Durrell, Ivor Francis, Martine Getty

A couple tries to prevent a pregnant German girl from leaving the country by claiming that she's carrying *their* baby.

The intriguing premise of an unscrupulous lawyer's attempts to sell an as-yet-unborn infant to a childless couple—only to have the young mother change her mind—yields an archetypal *Barney Miller* situation: A question of morality is confused by the poignancy of human desire. And, not surprisingly, the law is a woefully ill-equipped arbiter. The jokes—and as always, there are plenty—each reveal something new about the characters and situation as the story dictates its own tentative, if far from happy, conclusion. The childless couple, now likely to remain that way, find some consolation in the pain they share; the single mother is offered scant encouragement by Dietrich; and, ironically, the lawyer who engineered the whole mess is the only one to walk away scot-free. As in all the series's best scripts, the offbeat subject matter suggests no easy answers—and, refreshingly, the show's creators would never presume to impose any.

**85**  Accusation                      October 12, 1978
  **Writers:** Wally Dalton, Shelley Zellman
  **Director:** Max Gail
  **Guest Stars:** George Murdock, Eugene Elman, Ruth Warshawsky, Michael Tucci, Miriam Byrd Netherly

A lonely woman accuses Dietrich of making indecent advances; and Yemena arrests a rabbi for running a gambling operation in his synagogue.

**86**  The Prisoner                    October 19, 1978
  **Writers:** Reinhold Weege, Wally Dalton, Shelley Zellman
  **Director:** Noam Pitlik
  **Guest Stars:** Jeff Corey, Peggy Pope, Bruce Glover, Henry Jones

A newly released parolee discovers that he was happier behind bars; and the detectives book a burglar's widow when she decides to carry on the family trade.

**87**  Loan Shark                      November 2, 1978
  **Writer:** Tony Sheehan
  **Story:** Judith Anne Nielsen, Richard William Beban, Mario Roccuzzo, Bob Colleary
  **Director:** Noam Pitlik
  **Guest Stars:** Boris Aplon, Lewis Charles, Larry B. Scott, Mario Roccuzzo

After twenty years on the force, Yemena unexpectedly rebels; a tattoo artist refuses to remove his handiwork from a timid client; and Harris counsels a savvy teenage loan shark.


**88   The Vandal**                                    November 9, 1978
   **Writers:** Dennis Koenig, Tony Sheehan
   **Director:** Noam Pitlik
   **Guest Stars:** Jay Gerber, Howard Honig, Christopher Lloyd

A disgruntled TV fan assaults a network programmer in a coffee shop; and Levitt is the detectives' chief suspect when the squad room is vandalized.

The psychopathic vandal is played by Christopher Lloyd, soon to make his debut as Reverend Jim Ignatowski on *Taxi*.


**89   The Harris Incident**                          November 30, 1978
   **Writers:** Wally Dalton, Shelley Zellman, Reinhold Weege
   **Director:** Noam Pitlik
   **Guest Stars:** Ed Peck, Michael Lombard, Marilyn Chris, Rick Waln

Harris is shot at by a pair of prejudiced patrolmen who assume that he's a felon because of his skin color; and a stockbroker is arrested for panhandling.


**90   The Radical**                                   December 7, 1978
   **Writer:** Tony Sheehan
   **Story:** Lee H. Grant
   **Director:** Noam Pitlik
   **Guest Stars:** Corey Fischer, Stuart Pankin, Craig Richard Nelson

Inspector Luger locks horns with a radical fugitive from the 1960s underground; and Harris collars a rotund and very defensive burglar.

**91**   Toys                                    December 14, 1978
   **Writers:** Wally Dalton, Shelley Zellman, Tony Sheehan
   **Story:** Wally Dalton, Shelley Zellman
   **Director:** Noam Pitlik
   **Guest Stars:** Zachary Berger, Barbara Barrie, Walter Janowitz,
   Sidney Lassick

Barney has little cause to be jolly as he faces his first holiday
since his separation from Liz with a claustrophobic thief and a
pair of feuding toymakers.

The long-running storyline that ended in Barney's trial separation from
Liz didn't sit well with a sizable portion of the show's loyal audience,
and they made their opinions known. Producer Tony Sheehan recalls,
"We got letters telling us, 'Don't do this! They have the best marriage on
television.' But the funny thing is, she wasn't even *on* the show anymore!
We came up with the separation storyline to bring Barbara back—because we liked her and loved using her character—but before that, they
hadn't seen Liz in years! And still we got all these letters about what a
wonderful marriage they had."

**92**   The Indian                              January 4, 1979
   **Writer:** Reinhold Weege
   **Story:** Richard William Beban, Judith Anne Nielsen, Reinhold
   Weege
   **Director:** Noam Pitlik
   **Guest Stars:** Charles White Eagle, Phil Leeds, Richard Stahl,
   Dino Natali

A foot fetishist steals a woman's shoes right off her feet; and Wojo
befriends an aged Indian who wants to be allowed to die quietly
in Central Park.

Wojo, easily the most openly compassionate of all the detectives, refuses to abandon the old man at Bellevue. Instead, he returns to the park,
where he sits with the Indian in silent vigil, until, at last, the brave dies—
as he wished, in peace. When the detective later explains how he defied
procedure, Barney can't help but forgive him. Wojo broke the rules but
respected a higher order, and, as the Captain realizes, there are some
things that just aren't covered in the police manual.

**93**   Voice Analyzer                                January 11, 1979
  **Writers:** James Bonnet, Reinhold Weege
  **Story:** James Bonnet
  **Director:** Noam Pitlik
  **Guest Stars:** George Murdock, Phil Roth, Allan Rich, Barry Pearl

Suspicious Lieutenant Scanlon tries to root out corruption with the aid of a voice-activated lie detector; and a furrier files a fraudulent burglary report.

**94**   The Spy                                       January 18, 1979
  **Writer:** Tony Sheehan
  **Director:** Noam Pitlik
  **Guest Stars:** Philip Sterling, Estelle Omens, Stanley Brock, Flip Reade

A mime is charged with disorderly conduct; and an unemployed—and extremely paranoid—spy holds the squad room hostage.

**95**   Wojo's Girl (one hour)                        January 25, 1979
  **Writers:** Tony Sheehan, Danny Arnold
  **Director:** Noam Pitlik
  **Guest Stars:** Darlene Parks, Michael Conrad, Philip Bruns, Lewis Arquette, Peter Hobbs, Doris Roberts

A man threatens to leave his wife to become a soldier of fortune; and Wojo moves in with his new girlfriend, a reformed prostitute.

**96**   Middle Age                                    February 1, 1979
  **Writers:** Reinhold Weege, Danny Arnold
  **Story:** Wally Dalton, Shelley Zellman
  **Director:** Noam Pitlik
  **Guest Stars:** Nehemiah Persoff, Richard Libertini, Raleigh Bond, Kres Mersky

Barney worries about his encroaching middle age; a Hassidic diamond trader is robbed; and a decathlon hopeful is arrested for disorderly conduct.

**97**   The Counterfeiter                         February 8, 1979
**Writers:** Frank Dungan, Jeff Stein, Reinhold Weege
**Director:** Max Gail
**Guest Stars:** Jack Riley, J. Pat O'Malley, George Pentecost,
Susan Davis

Harris is delighted by the story potential of a colorful old counterfeiter; and a man assaults the plastic surgeon who operated on his wife.

**98**   Open House                              February 15, 1979
**Writers:** Wally Dalton, Shelley Zellman, Tony Sheehan
**Director:** Noam Pitlik
**Guest Stars:** Allan Miller, Christopher Lloyd, David Fresco,
Carmen Filipi

A psychiatrist refuses to divulge the name of a known arsonist in his care; and the Twelfth Precinct holds an open house that attracts only vagrants.

**99**   Identity                                 March 1, 1979
**Writer:** Tom Reeder
**Director:** Noam Pitlik
**Guest Stars:** Jack Somack, Don Calfa, David Clennon, Kip King

The Justice Department requests immunity for a thief who's been given a new identity in a witness-relocation program; and Dietrich saves Harris's life.

Harris, burdened by the enormity of his debt to Dietrich, blows off steam by admonishing a subway crazy with a terse outline of the precinct's minimum requirement for its guests: "I don't care if you're psychotic—just don't *whine* about it."

**100**   Computer Crime                         March 15, 1979
**Writer:** Calvin Kelly
**Story:** Calvin Kelly, Dennis Koenig
**Director:** Max Gail
**Guest Stars:** Mabel King, Barry Gordon, Rod Colbin, Roger
Brown

Dietrich apprehends a white-collar embezzler; and Harris is flabbergasted by a black doctor who claims to be cursed by voodoo.

**101**   Graveyard Shift                  May 10, 1979
    **Writer:** Tony Sheehan
    **Director:** Noam Pitlik
    **Guest Stars:** Paul Lawrence Smith, Raymond Singer, Lee Kessler

Late-night visitors to the precinct include an irate tourist and an insomniac who's convinced that he'll be possessed by a succubus once he dozes off.

**102**   Jack Soo, a Retrospective          May 17, 1979
    **Writers:** Various
    **Director:** Noam Pitlik

The cast offers an affectionate tribute to the late Jack Soo by reviewing Sergeant Nick Yemena's more memorable moments at the Twelfth Precinct.

Producer Danny Arnold had known Korean-American actor Jack Soo since they'd both performed stand-up on the same Midwestern nightclub circuit in the late forties—before Soo made his Broadway splash in *Flower Drum Song* in the fifties. The producer's loyalty to the actor was so great that he refused to authorize a new photo to commemorate the show's fifth anniversary once Soo had gone into the hospital. "Nothing goes out without Jack," the producer insisted. "Use the old shots."

## 1979-80    THE SIXTH SEASON

*Year-End Rating: 20.9 (21st place)*

The show moves smoothly into a sixth year, despite major behind-the-scenes upheavals. After suffering a heart attack late in the fifth season, executive producer Danny Arnold would strictly curtail his active involvement for the duration of the sixth and seventh years. Director Noam Pitlik joins Tony Sheehan as producer, and associate producer Gary Shaw takes on the duties of co-producer for the remainder of the series's run. The team of Frank Dungan and Jeff Stein contributes most of the year's scripts—along with Tony Sheehan, when they sign as the new story editors.

**103** Inquisition September 13, 1979
**Writer:** Tony Sheehan
**Story:** Jim Tisdale, Calvin Kelly
**Director:** Noam Pitlik
**Guest Stars:** George Murdock, Dino Natali, Norman Bartold,
Peter Jurasik, David Darlow

An angry citizen takes an ax to a department-store Muzak machine; and Scanlon starts a witch-hunt to root out an anonymous gay officer in the Twelfth Precinct.

**104** The Photographer September 20, 1979
**Writer:** Bob Colleary
**Director:** Noam Pitlik
**Guest Stars:** Sal Viscuso, Kenneth Tigar, Phil Leeds, Anita
Dangler

A charming mugger poses as a photographer to lure his victims; and a would-be messiah scolds the Eighth Avenue pimps for debasing the harlots.

The detectives calmly accept the arrival of a streetwise Christ with healthy skepticism—though none are prepared to dismiss the possibility that he might *actually be* what he claims. It's a tacit acknowledgment that not even miracles are outside the realm of possibilities in the Twelfth Precinct.

**105** Vacation September 27, 1979
**Writers:** Frank Dungan, Jeff Stein
**Director:** Noam Pitlik
**Guest Stars:** Bruce Kirby, Jack Bernardi, Ben Slack

Nobody's very happy when Barney posts the annual vacation schedule; and two brothers feud when one refuses to donate a kidney to his ailing sibling.

**106** The Brother October 4, 1979
**Writers:** Wally Dalton, Shelley Zellman
**Director:** Noam Pitlik
**Guest Stars:** Gary Imhoff, John Christy Ewing, Elise Caitlin

A monk suspects foul play when one of his novitiates vanishes during a weekend in New York; and it's Dietrich's turn to crossdress for mugging detail.

**107**   The Slave                                October 18, 1979
  **Writers:** Frank Dungan, Jeff Stein
  **Director:** Noam Pitlik
  **Guest Stars:** Manu Tupou, Sumant, Peg Shirley, Stanley Kamel

The detectives are shocked to discover that a chauffeur involved in a minor traffic accident is actually a slave indentured to a Burmese diplomat.


**108**   Strip Joint                              November 1, 1979
  **Writers:** Jaie Brashar, Frank Dungan, Jeff Stein
  **Director:** Noam Pitlik
  **Guest Stars:** Todd Susman, Rosana Soto, Walter Janowitz, Diana Canova, James Cromwell

A man is convinced that he's overdue to explode in spontaneous combustion; and a bookseller complains that a new strip joint is ruining his business.


**109**   The Bird                                 November 8, 1979
  **Writers:** Frank Dungan, Jeff Stein
  **Story:** Frank Dungan, Jeff Stein, Richard Beban, Judith Nielsen
  **Director:** Noam Pitlik
  **Guest Stars:** Michael Lombard, Martin Garner, Miriam Byrd Netherly

Harris's publisher insists that he obtain signed releases from the detectives; Wojo's new parrot dies; and a suicide hot-line operator decides to end it all.


**110**   The Desk                                 November 22, 1979
  **Writers:** Frank Dungan, Jeff Stein
  **Director:** Noam Pitlik
  **Guest Stars:** Don Calfa, Jeff Corey, Alex Henteloff, Fred Sadoff

A partial lobotomy turns a master thief into a mindless zombie; and an Amish man is unable to use the telephone to call for help after he's been mugged.

**111**   The Judge                              December 6, 1979
**Writers:** Frank Dungan, Jeff Stein, Tony Sheehan
**Director:** Noam Pitlik
**Guest Stars:** Peggy Pope, Philip Sterling

A judge assaults an attorney with his gavel; and a confused day-time-drama devotee reports dastardly deeds from TV soap operas as if they really happened.

**112**   The DNA Story                         December 13, 1979
**Writer:** Rich Reinhart
**Story:** Rich Reinhart, Jaie Brasher
**Director:** Noam Pitlik
**Guest Stars:** Kay Medford, Jack Kruschen, A. Martinez, Stefan Gierasch, Raymond Singer

A dangerous disease culture is missing from a research lab; and a woman insists that her husband has been replaced by a clone.

**113**   The Dentist                           December 27, 1979
**Writers:** Frank Dungan, Jeff Stein
**Director:** Noam Pitlik
**Guest Stars:** Oliver Clark, Jenny O'Hara, Arthur Malet, Estelle Omens

A dentist is accused of taking advantage of his female patients; and Wojo books a man accused of disturbing the peace by making noises with his hands.

**114**   People's Court                        January 3, 1980
**Writers:** Frank Dungan, Jeff Stein
**Director:** Noam Pitlik
**Guest Stars:** Michael Tucci, Howard Honig, Rod Colbin, Ralph Manza, Helen Verbit

A census taker breaks into an apartment to count the uncooperative residents; and a burglar is kept locked in a basement cell by a vigilante tenants' group.

**115** Vanished (Part 1) January 10, 1980
**Writers:** Tony Sheehan, Frank Dungan, Jeff Stein
**Director:** Noam Pitlik
**Guest Stars:** Elaine Giftos, John Dullaghan

Harris mysteriously vanishes during his undercover assignment as a vagrant; and a woman seeking a man to father her child considers candidates Dietrich and Wojo.

**116** Vanished (Part 2) January 17, 1980
**Writers:** Tony Sheehan, Frank Dungan, Jeff Stein
**Director:** Noam Pitlik
**Guest Stars:** Leonard Frey, David Fresco, Elaine Giftos, John Dullaghan, Ralph Olivia

Harris uncovers the secret of the shanghaied hobos; and Luger accepts a demotion in order to stay on the force past his official retirement date.

**117** The Child Stealers January 24, 1980
**Writers:** Frank Dungan, Jeff Stein
**Director:** Noam Pitlik
**Guest Stars:** Joanna Miles, Ray Stewart, Jack DeLeon, Dino Natali, Richard Libertini

A divorced father reclaims custody of his son by kidnapping him; and the precinct is visited by a man who claims to be from the twenty-first century.

**118** Guns January 31, 1980
**Writers:** Rich Reinhart, Tony Sheehan, Frank Dungan, Jeff Stein
**Director:** Noam Pitlik
**Guest Stars:** Jack Dodson, Madison Arnold, Mario Roccuzzo, David Paymer

Luger is despondent with his new assignment in the Twelfth; a man robs a liquor store with a duelist's pistol; and a citizen steals a TV from the police vault.

**119**   Uniform Day                      February 7, 1980
**Writers:** Richard Beban, Judith Nielsen
**Director:** Noam Pitlik
**Guest Stars:** Leonard Stone, Michael Alaimo, Stuart Pankin

Natty Sergeant Harris refuses to buckle under to a department edict that requires all detectives to dress in full uniform one day a year.

**120**   Dietrich's Arrest (Part 1)        February 28, 1980
**Writers:** Tony Sheehan, Frank Dungan, Jeff Stein
**Director:** Noam Pitlik
**Guest Stars:** George Murdock, Candice Azzara, Peter Hobbs

A lottery winner causes a riot by tossing money from a window; and Dietrich is arrested for participating in an antinuclear protest rally.

**121**   Dietrich's Arrest (Part 2)         March 6, 1980
**Writers:** Tony Sheehan, Frank Dungan, Jeff Stein
**Director:** Noam Pitlik
**Guest Stars:** George Murdock, Kay Medford, Allan Miller

Harris books Dietrich for his participation in the illegal protest; and a nuclear engineer is arrested for splashing atomic water on the demonstrators.

"With Dietrich, you're never quite sure just who he is or why he does things," Tony Sheehan told *TV Guide*. Despite his unflappable wit and carefully guarded irreverence, Dietrich surprised no one when he willingly faced a jail sentence in support of his principles. The writers merely cultivated the enigmatic quality that deadpan Steve Landesberg brought to the role, and as a result, the precinct's resident intellectual remained something of a paradox right to the end of the series. "We kind of like it that way," confessed Sheehan.

**122**   The Architect                              March 27, 1980
   **Writers:** Tony Sheehan, Frank Dungan, Jeff Stein
   **Story:** Calvin Kelly, Jim Tisdale
   **Director:** Noam Pitlik
   **Guest Stars:** Paul Lieber, Chu Chu Malave, Norman Bartold,
   Jesse Aragon, David Clennon

An architect, unhappy with the changes carried out on a building
he designed, threatens to bomb the structure.

As the clock ticks away on the time bomb, the squad room is a pressure cooker. And, as the producers had long since discovered, tension in
a life-or-death situation creates the perfect climate for black humor. When
a pair of hapless gunmen storm into the precinct at the height of the bomb
scare, Barney patiently explains that he's busy, and that they'll just have
to sit down and wait their turn.


**123**   The Inventor                                May 1, 1980
   **Writers:** Frank Dungan, Jeff Stein, Tony Sheehan
   **Director:** Noam Pitlik
   **Guest Stars:** Ben Piazza, Arny Freeman, Dan Frazer

Wojo tries to recall the details of a forgotten case while under
hypnosis; and an inventor is accused of stealing the plans for his
own invention.


**124**   Fog                                          May 8, 1980
   **Writers:** Frank Dungan, Jeff Stein, Tony Sheehan
   **Story:** Mark Brull
   **Director:** Noam Pitlik
   **Guest Stars:** J.J. Barry, Sidney Lassick, Robert Levine, William
   Dillard

A street musician assaults a string quartet that tried to move in on
his corner; and once again, Barney is turned down for deputy inspector.

A thick fog enshrouds the station for one of the most downbeat episodes of the entire series. His optimism spent after another rejection for
the deputy inspector's rank, Barney finally faces the grim futility of his
job. "It's getting harder and harder to keep a sense of purpose around
here," he grieves. "We bring people in, we ship 'em out. Nothing

changes." After the other detectives fail to raise his bitter spirits, it's finally the mournful melody of the street musician's slow blues that draws the detective away from his gloom. As the sublime melancholy of the lonely horn fills the corners of Barney's own private dread, he rises to join his fellow detectives in the squad room. While outside his window, the fog only grows thicker.

## 1980-81    THE SEVENTH SEASON

*Year-End Rating: 18.4 (33rd place)*

The sixth-season creative team—producers Noam Pitlik and Tony Sheehan and story editors Frank Dungan and Jeff Stein—reprise their roles in the seventh year, with an able assist in the script department from newcomers Jordan Moffett and Nat Mauldin.

**125**   Homicide (Part 1)                       October 30, 1980
   **Writers:** Frank Dungan, Jeff Stein
   **Director:** Noam Pitlik
   **Guest Stars:** Harold J. Stone, Marjorie Bennett, Jack Somack,
   Allyn Ann McLerie, Al Ruscio, Tricia O'Neill

The detectives book a man who admits that he killed his barber after a bad haircut; and a woman decides to cancel the murder contract she put out on her husband.

**126**   Homicide (Part 2)                       November 6, 1980
   **Writers:** Frank Dungan, Jeff Stein
   **Director:** Noam Pitlik
   **Guest Stars:** Ben Piazza, Tricia O'Neill, Harold J. Stone, Allyn
   Ann McLerie, Michael Alaimo, Jack Somack

The detectives attempt to find the hapless husband before the hit man does; and Harris makes a pass at the station's new crime photographer.

The Twelfth Precinct's temporary reassignment as a homicide-only squad created a near-panic among the show's most vocal fans. "Boy, did we get letters on that," writer Frank Dungan recalls. "People were so scared it was going to be permanent."

**127**   The Delegate                          November 13, 1980
   **Writer:** Jim Tisdale
   **Director:** Noam Pitlik
   **Guest Stars:** Phil Leeds, Bob Dishy, Bonnie Bartlett, Don
   Sherman, Tom Henschel

The precinct discovers an impostor in their ranks; and a vagrant
claims he came to town as a delegate to the 1976 Democratic
Convention and never left.

**128**   Dorsey                                November 27, 1980
   **Writer:** Tony Sheehan
   **Director:** Noam Pitlik
   **Guest Stars:** Paul Lieber, Michael Lombard, Darrell Zwerling,
   Cal Gibson, Andrew Bloch

The squad's new member insinuates that the detectives are all on
the take; and a refugee from a no-smoking clinic complains that
their methods are hazardous to his health.

Paul Lieber—previously seen as one of the gunmen in "The Architect" episode—arrives as Dorsey, yet another short-lived addition to the
squad's roster.

**129**   Agent Orange                         December 11, 1980
   **Writer:** Tony Sheehan
   **Director:** Noam Pitlik
   **Guest Stars:** Paul Lieber, Peter Hobbs, Doris Roberts, Michael
   Currie, Joe Regalbuto, Louis Giambalvo, Lyman Ward, Robert
   Phalen

A woman complains when her apartment building goes nudist;
and a confused vet blames his condition on exposure to the resi-
due of germ warfare in Vietnam.

**130**   Call Girl                            December 18, 1980
   **Writers:** Frank Dungan, Jeff Stein
   **Director:** Noam Pitlik
   **Guest Stars:** Paul Lieber, Arthur Malet, Paul Kent, Tasha
   Zemrus, Sarina C. Grant, Nancy Bleier

Dorsey plays big brother to a young prostitute; Harris solicits
stock tips from a well-heeled call girl; and Dietrich explores the
new celibacy.

**131**  Resignation                                    January 8, 1981
**Writers:** Frank Dungan, Jeff Stein
**Director:** Noam Pitlik
**Guest Stars:** Allan Rich, Steve Franken, Peter Elbling, Mario Roccuzzo

Dietrich is plagued by guilt after he's forced to use his gun to stop a robbery; and a playwright assaults an incompetent actor.

Unlike most TV supercops, the very human detectives of the Twelfth often came up short in their struggle against the unrelenting stress of police work. And yet, law enforcement agencies everywhere applauded the series as the most realistic cop show on television. The New York Police Department even conferred honorary membership on Barney's squad, prompting the unintended irony of Los Angeles police chief Daryl Gates's quip, "We view *Barney Miller* as a comedy, but my colleagues in New York think of it as a documentary."

**132**  Field Associate                                January 15, 1981
**Writer:** Jordan Moffet
**Director:** Noam Pitlik
**Guest Stars:** Jeffrey Tambor, Ned Glass, Florence Halop

Someone in the precinct has been leaking incriminating information to Internal Affairs; and a burglar celebrates his fiftieth year in crime.

**133**  Movie (Part 1)                                 January 22, 1981
**Writers:** Frank Dungan, Jeff Stein
**Director:** Noam Pitlik
**Guest Stars:** Arny Freeman, Dino Natali, George Murdock, Dennis Howard

A veteran radio journalist roughs up an insipid TV news anchor; and Harris scripts a porno-movie spectacular as part of an undercover vice operation.

**134**  Movie (Part 2)                                 January 29, 1981
**Writers:** Frank Dungan, Jeff Stein
**Director:** Noam Pitlik
**Guest Stars:** Jay Gerber, Ralph Manza, J.J. Barry, Norman Bartold

Harris proudly screens his overbudget hard-core spectacular; a blind man is mugged; and a overzealous charity collector stages a holdup.

**135** The Psychic                                              February 5, 1981
**Writers:** Tony Sheehan, Frank Dungan, Jeff Stein
**Director:** Noam Pitlik
**Guest Stars:** Kenneth Tigar, Fred Sadoff, Rod Colbin, Larry Hankin, Robert Burgos

A linguist vandalizes a billboard to protest improper grammar in advertising; and a psychic foils a purse snatcher—*before* the crime is committed.

**136** Stormy Weather                                           February 12, 1981
**Writer:** Nat Mauldin
**Director:** Noam Pitlik
**Guest Stars:** Phyllis Frelich, Robert Costanzo, Seymour Bernstein, Peter Wolf

Wojo plunges into the Hudson in pursuit of a looter; and Barney confronts a deaf woman with an unusual occupation—she's a hooker.

**137** The Librarian                                            February 19, 1981
**Writers:** Tony Sheehan, Frank Dungan, Jeff Stein
**Director:** Noam Pitlik
**Guest Stars:** Allan Miller, Titos Vandis, Miriam Byrd Netherly, Zachary Berger, James Gallery

A librarian employs artillery to enforce order in her reading room; and a Gypsy is arrested for continually harassing the owner of a novelty store.

In one of the series's most chilling images, the kindly old man who sells whoopee cushions and dribble glasses is identified as a Nazi war criminal—even as a set of windup teeth chatter away on the desk. As always, the bizarre juxtaposition is not without humor—but when Harris finally reaches down to snap the toy teeth shut, there is no laugh track to break the eerie pall of silence that blankets the squad room.

On *Barney Miller*, even canned laughter was used as a creative element in the producers' palette. The series hadn't been taped before a live studio audience since the third year, when the show's creators decided that they could more carefully orchestrate their curious blend of comedy and drama without the wild card of audience reaction—as this particular episode certainly bears out.

**138**  Rachel                                                  February 26, 1981
   **Writers:** Tony Sheehan, Frank Dungan, Jeff Stein
   **Director:** Noam Pitlik
   **Guest Stars:** Anne Wyndham, Stanley Brock, Alex Henteloff, Chu Chu Malave

The owner of a sports store rigs a lethal trap to catch a burglar; shyster Arnold Ripner sues Harris for libel; and Wojo asks Barney's daughter for a date.

**139**  Contempt (Part 1)                                       March 12, 1981
   **Writers:** Frank Dungan, Jeff Stein
   **Director:** Noam Pitlik
   **Guest Stars:** Dale Robinette, Larry Gelman, William Windom, Maggie Brown, John Dullaghan

Barney is charged with contempt of court when he refuses to name an informant; and a man complains that he was refused service at a restaurant because he's ugly.

**140**  Contempt (Part 2)                                       March 19, 1981
   **Writers:** Frank Dungan, Jeff Stein
   **Director:** Noam Pitlik
   **Guest Stars:** Jack Murdock, Maggie Brown, J.J. Barry, John Dullaghan, William Windom

Harris assumes command of the precinct after Barney is jailed for his contempt citation.

**141**  The Doll                                                March 26, 1981
   **Writer:** Tony Sheehan
   **Story:** Jordan Moffet, Nat Mauldin
   **Director:** Noam Pitlik
   **Guest Stars:** A. Martinez, Philip Bruns, Oliver Clark, Dee Croxton

An expensive antique doll is kidnapped for ransom; a naive optician buys a bogus ticket to ride the NASA space shuttle; and Luger puts Barney in his will.

**142**   Lady and the Bomb                         April 9, 1981
  **Writer:** Lee H. Grant
  **Director:** Noam Pitlik
  **Guest Stars:** Abe Vigoda, Peggy Pope, Howard Mann, Judson
  Morgan, James Murtaugh, Ben Freedman

Sergeant Fish drops in for a visit; Arnold Ripner wins his libel suit
against Harris; and a woman threatens to blow up the precinct
with a homemade bomb.

**143**   Riot                                      April 30, 1981
  **Writers:** Frank Dungan, Jeff Stein
  **Story:** Greg Giangregorio
  **Director:** Noam Pitlik
  **Guest Stars:** Nehemiah Persoff, Howard Platt, Susan Tolsky, Victor
  Brant, Pat McNamara

A group of Hasidic Jews rally to protest the department's ineffec-
tiveness; and a pair of urban survivalists are found living in steam
tunnels beneath the city.

**144**   The Vests                                 May 7, 1981
  **Writer:** Nat Mauldin
  **Director:** Noam Pitlik
  **Guest Stars:** Don Calfa, Alice Hirson, Warren Munson

The detectives are issued bulletproof vests; and Luger collects
background information for the detectives' official obituaries.

**145**   The Rainmaker                             May 14, 1981
  **Writers:** Frank Dungan, Jeff Stein
  **Story:** Paul Hunter, Frank Dungan, Jeff Stein
  **Director:** Noam Pitlik
  **Guest Stars:** J. Pat O'Malley, Beatrice Colen, Leonard Stone

An eccentric stages a rainmaking ceremony in Washington
Square; and Wojo, Harris, and Dietrich all eye an opening in the
vice squad.

**146**   Liquidation                                     May 21, 1981
  **Writers:** Frank Dungan, Jeff Stein
  **Director:** Noam Pitlik
  **Guest Stars:** Walter Olkewicz, Martin Garner, James Cromwell

Harris liquidates everything he owns to pay off the $320,000 judgment Arnold Ripner was awarded in his libel suit against the detective.

## 1981-82   THE EIGHTH SEASON

*Year-End Rating: 15.7 (54th place)*

After seven and a half seasons, Danny Arnold decides to retire the Twelfth Precinct at the conclusion of the eighth season, marking the end of one of the longest unbroken streaks of top-flight writing, acting, and direction in the history of the situation comedy.

Producers Frank Dungan and Jeff Stein continue as story editors in the eighth season, and their considerable story contributions are augmented by memorable scripts from Nat Mauldin, Jordan Moffet, and Tony Sheehan, among others. Gary Shaw continues as co-producer; Gennaro Montanino, Danny Arnold, Lee Lochhead, and Bruce Bilson direct most of the year's episodes; and Roland Kibbee joins Danny Arnold as executive producer for the final year.

**147**   Paternity                                    October 29, 1981
  **Writer:** Nat Mauldin
  **Director:** Danny Arnold
  **Guest Stars:** Rebecca Holden, Dana Gladstone, Stephan Gierasch

A beauty queen has her purse snatched; an angry moviegoer vandalizes a theater for showing snuff films; and Wojo is slapped with a paternity suit.

**148**   Advancement                                  November 5, 1981
  **Writers:** Frank Dungan, Jeff Stein
  **Director:** Danny Arnold
  **Guest Stars:** Martin Garner, Anna Berger, Howard Honig, Mario Roccuzzo, Philip Simms

Luger asks for Barney's help in composing a letter to his prospective wife; Harris signs another book deal; and a lottery winner threatens the couple who lost his winning ticket.

**149**   The Car                                    November 12, 1981
   **Writer:** Nat Mauldin
   **Director:** Bruce Bilson
   **Guest Stars:** Joseph Regalbuto, Patrick McNamara, Larry Gelman, Alice Backes

An overzealous sanitation officer pulls a gun on a litterbug; Levitt performs an act of heroism; and a car thief confesses—twenty-five years after the fact.

**150**   Possession                               November 19, 1981
   **Writers:** Tom Reeder, Roland Kibbee
   **Director:** Bruce Bilson
   **Guest Stars:** Kenneth Tigar, Susan Peretz, Allan Miller, Phil Rubenstein

A police chaplain performs an impromptu exorcism; and a full-figured wife assaults her husband for forcing her into a pair of designer jeans.

**151**   Stress Analyzer                          November 26, 1981
   **Writer:** Nat Mauldin
   **Director:** Bruce Bilson
   **Guest Stars:** Florence Halop, Phil Leeds, James Cromwell, Ann Guilbert, James Murtaugh, Rod Colbin

A Peace Corps recruiter goes berserk at a job fair; and Barney is distraught when an electronic stress analyzer indicates that Dietrich has been shot in action.

**152**   Games                                   December 10, 1981
   **Writer:** Jordan Moffet
   **Director:** Gennaro Montanino
   **Guest Stars:** Philip Sterling, Carol Rossen, Vernon Weddle, Trinidad Silva, Warren Munson, John O'Leary, Sarah Kennedy

A WAC supplements her meager Army salary by soliciting in Greenwich Village; and a video-game chip manufacturer is accused of spying for the KGB.

**153** Homeless                              December 17, 1981
**Writers:** Jordan Moffet, Frank Dungan, Jeff Stein
**Director:** Lee Lochhead
**Guest Stars:** Stanley Brock, Don Calfa, Ben Piazza, David
Clennon, Paul Stolarsky, Zane Buzby, Mari Gorman, Walter
Janowitz

The homeless flock to the Twelfth Precinct at Christmas; a livid
greeting-card writer loses his job; and a local merchant rousts a
vagrant with a cattle prod.

**154** The Tontine                              January 7, 1982
**Writer:** Nat Mauldin
**Story:** Nat Mauldin, Dick Wesson
**Director:** Homer Powell
**Guest Stars:** Ivor Francis, Ian Wolfe, Jay Robinson, Jane Dulo,
Lou Cutell, Dennis Lipscomb

One of the last two survivors of an old-world tontine decides to
do himself in so that his cousin can enjoy the benefits of the pact.

**155** Examination Day                          January 14, 1982
**Writer:** Jordan Moffet
**Director:** Gennaro Montanino
**Guest Stars:** Jack Kruschen, Lyman Ward, Louis Giambalvo

The detectives are forced back into uniform while the rest of the
force takes the sergeant's exam.

**156** The Clown                                January 21, 1982
**Writer:** San Simon
**Director:** Alan Bagmen
**Guest Stars:** Walter Olkewicz, Howard Platt, Philip Bruns, J.J.
Barry, Michael Tucci

A mugger singles out street clowns; and a bureaucrat alleviates
jail overcrowding by quietly releasing a hundred inmates on
Madison Avenue in the dead of night.

A pair of storylines that could have come straight from the screaming
headlines of the New York tabloids—and probably did. "We got a lot of
ideas from the *New York Post* and the *New York Daily News*," writer Jeff

Stein confessed. "We'd look at the other papers, but we never found much we could use in the *New York Times*."

**157**  Chinatown (Part 1)                          February 4, 1982
   **Writers:** Frank Dungan, Jeff Stein
   **Director:** Danny Arnold
   **Guest Stars:** Chao-Li Chi, George Murdock, Fred Sadoff, Joanna Barnes, Leonard Stone

Lieutenant Scanlon falls for a wealthy mugging victim; a restaurateur breaks into his own restaurant; and a Chinese waiter is an uncooperative witness to murder.

**158**  Chinatown (Part 2)                         February 11, 1982
   **Writers:** Frank Dungan, Jeff Stein
   **Director:** Danny Arnold
   **Guest Stars:** Chao-Li Chi, Joanna Barnes, Phil Diskin, Peter Pan, George Murdock

Dietrich and Harris stake out their murder suspect at a Chinese restaurant.

**159**  Hunger Strike                              February 18, 1982
   **Writer:** Tony Sheehan
   **Story:** Tony Sheehan, Stephen Neigher
   **Director:** Tony Sheehan
   **Guest Stars:** Nora Meerbaum, Larry Gelman, Stanley Kamel, Ion Teodorescu

A prisoner stages a hunger strike to end nuclear arms; Dietrich aids an elderly psychiatric patient; and Barney refuses his latest nomination for promotion to deputy inspector.

**160**  Arrival                                    February 25, 1982
   **Writer:** Jordan Moffet
   **Director:** Lee Lochhead
   **Guest Stars:** Carina Afable, Andrew Bloch, Alan Oppenheimer

Luger finally meets the Manilan he's been courting by mail; a genius turns to petty crime; and a man is mugged by an elderly woman.

**161**   Obituary                                March 11, 1982
**Writer:** Nat Mauldin
**Director:** Gennaro Montanino
**Guest Stars:** Barney Martin, Richard Stahl, Phil Diskin, Will
Seltzer, Peggy Pope

An angry citizen complains when the newspaper prints his premature obituary; and a modern-day Robin Hood steals surplus chickens from a government warehouse.


**162**   Inquiry                                 March 26, 1982
**Writers:** Frank Dungan, Jeff Stein
**Director:** Gennaro Montanino
**Guest Stars:** Michael Lombard, Bonnie Bartlett, Allan Rich,
Barry Gordon

An angry parent assaults the admissions director of a private kindergarten; and Wojo faces a police inquiry for using excessive
force in a recent arrest.


**163**   Old Love                                  April 2, 1982
**Writer:** Philip Jayson Lasker
**Director:** Hal Linden
**Guest Stars:** Sharon Spelman, Mitch Kreindel, Ben Hammer,
Mario Roccuzzo, Audrey Christie

A former child star assaults his agent with a telephone; a good Samaritan is charged with assault; and Dietrich spends the afternoon
with a college sweetheart.


**164**   Altercation                               April 9, 1982
**Writer:** Tony Sheehan
**Director:** Alan Bergmann
**Guest Stars:** Alex Henteloff, Todd Susman, Miriam Byrd
Netherly, Rod Colbin, Robert Pastorelli

Harris punches Arnold Ripner when the lawyer threatens another
libel suit; and a mugging victim reveals that she's carried the
torch for Barney since 1966.

**165**  Bones                                    April 29, 1982
  **Writers:** Jordon Moffet, Nat Mauldin
  **Story:** Jordon Moffet, Nat Mauldin, Lee H. Grant
  **Director:** Max Gail
  **Guest Stars:** Howard Platt, Ivor Francis, Pancito Gomez, Mark
  Banks, Luis Avalos

The precinct's plumbing goes out again; a scoutmaster apprehends a mugger; and a militant Indian retrieves his tribe's ancestral bones from a museum exhibit.

**166**  Landmark (Part 1)                          May 6, 1982
  **Writer:** Tony Sheehan
  **Director:** Tony Sheehan
  **Guest Stars:** Susan Tolsky, Philip Sterling, James Gallery, Al
  Ruscio

The Twelfth is declared a national landmark; a former political
hostage decides to emigrate back to South America; and an unemployed man is robbed at an automatic teller machine.

**167**  Landmark (Part 2)                         May 13, 1982
  **Writers:** Frank Dungan, Jeff Stein
  **Director:** Danny Arnold
  **Guest Stars:** Helen Verbit, Florence Halop, James Murtaugh,
  Carina Afable

Dietrich arrests the head of a professional crime school, along
with a pair of his unlikely graduates; Luger tries to squirm out of
his marriage commitment; and the Twelfth Precinct is sold to a
real estate developer.

**168**  Landmark (Part 3)                         May 20, 1982
  **Writers:** Frank Dungan, Jeff Stein, Tony Sheehan
  **Director:** Danny Arnold
  **Guest Stars:** Carina Afable, George Murdock, Walter Janowitz,
  Ray Stewart, John Dullaghan, Jack DeLeon, Mari Gorman,
  Stanley Brock, J.J. Barry, Earl Boen, Oliver Clark, Ralph Manza,
  Meshach Taylor, Judson Morgan, F. William Parker

The squad room fills with familiar faces who arrive to pay last respects to the departing detectives; and Barney bids a fond fare-

well to the men and women—past and present—who made up
the illustrious roster of the Twelfth Precinct.

Producer Danny Arnold once singled out the station house itself as
the most important personality in the drama of *Barney Miller*. And indeed, of all the sad farewells in that final episode, no single image evoked
the sense of passing as eloquently as the sight of those dingy old walls,
now stripped bare and waiting for the first inevitable blow of the
rehabber's hammer.

During their time together, the detectives of the Twelfth Precinct endured the ravages of fire, death, depression, and maddening bureaucracy.
They were laid off, arrested, seduced, shanghaied, and even haunted;
they survived bomb threats, snipers, rabid dogs, and corrupt politicians.
But in the show's final—and fitting—irony, after eight years, the ol' one-
two was done in by a real estate speculator.

It was a fate that could happen only in New York.

## EMMY AWARDS

The following is a complete listing of the Emmy Awards bestowed on
*Barney Miller* by the National Academy of Television Arts and Sciences.

**1978-79**  Outstanding Directing in a Comedy Series: Noam Pitlik,
"The Harris Incident"

**1979-80**  Outstanding Writing in a Comedy Series: Bob Colleary,
"The Photographer"

**1981-82**  Outstanding Comedy Series

# TAXI

·

*It was* not *a lotta one liners
about crazy New York cabbies.
It was about lives, the human
condition.*
—JUDD HIRSCH

A FEW WEEKS before the premiere of *Taxi*, Ed. Weinberger made a bold prediction. "I think we're going to deliver a hit."

In the business of TV comedy, such prophecy is always risky conjecture. And yet, coming from one of four producers who'd just shepherded *The Mary Tyler Moore Show* through seven seasons of prime time, the writer's confident assertion could be seen as something greater than a mere boast. For Weinberger, whose brash optimism matched that of his producing partners James L. Brooks, Stan Daniels, and David Davis, it was a declaration of independence.

Until recently, the four writers had formed the inner circle of MTM Productions' creative brain trust. Together or separately, they had been instrumental in the development of every important series produced by the company during its glory days, including *Mary Tyler Moore*, *Bob Newhart*, *Rhoda*, and *Lou Grant*. But by 1978, they'd left to start their own independent production unit at Paramount Studios.

"It was a staggering blow," MTM president Arthur Price told journalist Paul Weingarten. "None of those guys ever came and said we're a group now, and this is what we want to do, can you match it? I just got a phone call, 'We'd like to come up and see you,' and they came up and they laid it on us and they were gone."

"They felt like the sons had betrayed them, and I understand those feelings," recalled Ed. Weinberger. James Brooks also acknowledged the difficulty of leaving the shop where he and his partners had experienced so much creative freedom. "I can't tell you how perfect it was there, and it couldn't stay that way."

After the team retired *Mary Tyler Moore*—a tough act to follow, even for its creators—Ed. Weinberger and his partner, Stan Daniels, sat back and waited for something to happen. "We had no plans after *Mary*," explained Weinberger, "and nobody made us any offers. So we went to see our agents, who proposed that we go to ABC and see if we could pick up some commitments. Somewhere along the line, Jim and Dave came along, and we all joined together. It was as simple as that."

Of course, the producers were also aware that creating shows under their own banner made a lot of sense from a financial standpoint as well. "The people with the greatest desire to see us move were our agents," admitted Brooks. Which isn't surprising, since the talent brokers stood to profit immensely from their clients' independence. As co-owners of the shows they wrote and produced, the profits that would accrue to Brooks, Weinberger, Daniels, and Davis after syndication could be astounding.

And so, after their inevitable departure from MTM, the producers moved onto the Paramount backlot. They hung up a shingle that read John Charles Walters Productions—no such person existed, but they thought it sounded classy—and signed a contract with ABC, which guaranteed that at least two of their new series would go on the air, without pilots.

Brooks, Daniels, Davis, and Weinberger had done all right for themselves. They had their own production facility and as much creative freedom as they could hope for. All they needed now was a premise for a hit comedy.

And Jim Brooks had one, though at that point it was really little more than a hunch. "All I had was a magazine article and an idea," Brooks recalled. "Nothing else." But he figured that was a start, so he got the network on the phone and pitched his idea. "They liked it. They bought it."

Within twenty-four hours, four of the best creative minds in television were hard at work on a new comedy called *Taxi*.

The idea of a TV series set in a taxi garage had actually originated about a year earlier, when Brooks and Jerry Belson—a co-creator of ABC's *Odd Couple*, and a regular writer on the original *Dick Van Dyke Show*— convinced MTM to option an article they'd seen in *New York* magazine. The story, which was written by the soon-to-be celebrated novelist and screenwriter Michael Tolkin, offered a glimpse into the days and nights of the Dover Cab Company, a New York taxi garage that served as a way station for aspiring actors, writers, and other creative types who were waiting for their dreams to come true.

Brooks and Belson thought that they might develop the material into a one-camera show that could be shot on actual New York locations. But, eventually, both writers moved on to other projects, and *Taxi* was all but forgotten—until Jim Brooks revived it as the perfect vehicle for the creative talents at John Charles Walters.

Daniels, Davis, and Weinberger warmed to the idea instantly. For one thing, the show would be about men.

Of course, the guys had nothing against women on television. But after seven seasons of *Mary Tyler Moore* and another half dozen concurrent seasons of *Phyllis* and *Rhoda*, they were growing weary of exploiting the comic potential in the daily struggles of modern single women in a middle-class milieu. "We felt we'd explored that world," explained Ed. Weinberger. "But *Taxi* was a blue-collar situation, and it was about guys. That really appealed to us."

As anxious as they were to get started, there was still one slight hitch. Before they could proceed, the producers had to consult their old boss. Technically, MTM had a prior claim to the concept, since the company still retained the rights to the original magazine piece that had inspired the series. But after a quick phone call, MTM's Grant Tinker gave *Taxi* his blessings, and—with customary generosity—sold Brooks and company the rights to the article for $1500, exactly what MTM had paid for it in the first place.

The series quickly took shape, and before long the producers began scouting for a suitable leading man. As the sympathetic anchor for most of the show's action, the producers recognized that the character of cabbie Alex Reiger would have to be played by a comic actor versatile enough to handle the role's considerable dramatic demands as well.

It didn't take long to narrow the choice down to one—Judd Hirsch.

"We wrote the part of Alex Reiger with Judd Hirsch in mind," recalled Ed. Weinberger. But convincing the successful film and stage actor to commit his creative energies to a weekly situation comedy would not be easy. "I told my agent to pass the offer by," Hirsch confided. "I'd *done* TV, you know?" The actor was referring to the bitter taste left by CBS's cancellation of *Delvecchio*—Hirsch's well-regarded 1976 cop show—after barely a season.

The producers continued to court the actor, and he continued to play hard to get. But finally, after Hirsch got a look at the show's first script, he would require little further encouragement. Just as the producers had hoped, the actor responded to the unmistakable quality of the words they'd put on the page.

Drawing from a wide palette of inspiration, the creators had taken the intelligent humanism they'd perfected on *Mary Tyler Moore*, added a dollop of the surreal wackiness that Dave Davis favored on *The Bob Newhart Show*, and then dropped the whole strange brew into an atmospheric blue-collar setting in which Ralph Kramden might have felt entirely at home. The potent blend that resulted fused the hip sophistication of MTM-style humor with the vintage situational comedy of traditional shows like *The Honeymooners*.

And at the center of it all was Alex—the cab company's resident Everyman, and the only practical thinker in the entire garage. Like any good cabbie, he had a philosophical observation to relieve any situation that might confront one of his beleaguered colleagues—though he was usually at a loss when it came to facing one of his own dark quandaries.

Of course, not everyone at the Sunshine Cab Company fell prey to the clouds of existential angst that so frequently darkened the skies above the garage—dispatcher Louie De Palma, for one, was rarely tormented by questions of a moral or philosophical nature. On the contrary, the thoroughly disagreeable dispatcher was unfailingly venal, selfish, and—most annoying of all—far and away the most well-adjusted character in the garage. There he sat in his cage, far above the rabble, like a malevolent Wizard of Oz, bluffing everyone into thinking that he was far more omniscient than his pint-sized stature could ever allow.

The character actually began his life as a much smaller supporting role. But that changed the minute casting director Joel Thurm read the script and cautioned the producers, "Don't cast that part until you meet Danny DeVito!"

"Danny and the material met head-on," declared Ed. Weinberger, recalling the actor's audition. "Before he even got to his car, we were on the phone to his agent. And his part eventually grew from a page and a half in the first script until he became, in effect, the show's co-lead."

The producers rounded out their talented ensemble with a cast that included Marilu Henner, Tony Danza, Jeff Conaway, Randall Carver, and, most memorably, comedian Andy Kaufman.

Brooks, Daniels, Davis, and Weinberger carefully built an equally talented behind-the-scenes crew as well. Former MTM staffer James Burrows was signed to direct the series, and Glen and Les Charles were lured over from MTM to produce the show and head the writing staff.

Before long, *Taxi* attracted some of the finest writing talent in the industry. And the show continued to develop a new stable of young writers, many of whom eventually carried the show's tradition of quality with them when they went on to produce some of the best TV comedy of the 1980s. As Les Charles observed, "It was a terrific group of writers. Probably as good as any show has ever had at one time."

With a nucleus of creative talent like that, the producers thought, there was no reason why the show shouldn't be a resounding success. And, for a time at least, it was.

Buoyed by an advantageous time slot on ABC's powerhouse Tuesday comedy night, the series finished its first two seasons in the top twenty. But after ABC moved the show to Wednesday night, the network was surprised to notice a sharp drop in ratings during the third season. They eventually shuttled the series to Thursday, where it did even worse.

By the end of the fourth year, the series had slumped its way into fifty-third place, at which point ABC canceled the show—despite the fact that *Taxi* had won the Emmy for best comedy series in each of its first three seasons. Of course, no one argued that the show lacked quality; the network simply felt that the series had lost the power to pull in the big numbers.

And then, just when it looked as if *Taxi* had run its course, an odd thing happened. Very important people suddenly began to take a keen interest in the show's survival.

And, by a strange twist of fate, one of them was Grant Tinker.

By 1981, Tinker had left the top post at MTM to accept a job as head of the NBC network, where he shook things up by inaugurating a downright radical policy of quality programming. After ABC orphaned *Taxi*, Tinker declared that his network would give the series a second chance. He topped a competing bid from the Home Box Office pay-TV channel—which also coveted the prestigious comedy—and *Taxi* parked at NBC for its fifth year.

Alas, the show's renaissance would be short-lived. The comedy's ratings didn't show much improvement on NBC, and it was unceremoniously canceled at the end of the season.

But even after two cancellations, *Taxi* was still not easily forgotten.

The following September, the Academy of Television Arts and Sciences once again honored the show with a cluster of Emmy Awards, as it had during each of the show's previous four seasons, prompting Judd Hirsch to quip, "Don't they know we've been canceled?" When he rose to accept his own award as best actor in a comedy, Hirsch introduced a note of rancor to the stately proceedings by criticizing the priorities of an industry that would choose to honor a series that it couldn't afford to keep alive.

"If you can't get it out of your mind," he intoned, "if you have to keep giving laurels to us, then you should put it back on the air."

But this time, there would be no last-minute reprieve.

Even so, the show's creators certainly had no cause for regret. In *Taxi*, they had crafted something pretty rare—a television comedy with heart, humor, and a genuine point of view. *Taxi* placed a premium on the value of dreams, but never let us forget that there's more to life than chasing rainbows.

It was a philosophy Brooks, Daniels, Davis, and Weinberger must've taken to heart. The four writers set out with a dream—to deliver a hit series. But, five seasons and 113 episodes later, it was obvious that they had finally accomplished a great deal more.

# A Critical Guide to All 113 Episodes

| | |
|---|---|
| Alex Reiger | Judd Hirsch |
| Louie De Palma | Danny DeVito |
| Elaine Nardo | Marilu Henner |
| Bobby Wheeler | Jeff Conaway |
| Jim Caldwell Ignatowski | Christopher Lloyd |
| Tony Banta | Tony Danza |
| Latka Gravas | Andy Kaufman |
| Simka Dahblitz Gravas | Carol Kane |
| Zena Sherman | Rhea Perlman |
| John Burns (lst season) | Randall Carver |
| Jeff Bennett | J. Alan Thomas |

SUPPORTING CAST

| | |
|---|---|
| Tommy, the Waiter | T.J. Castronova |
| Jason Nardo (Elaine's son) | Michael Hershewe, |
| | David Mendenhall |
| Jennifer Nardo (Elaine's daughter) | Melanie Gaffin |
| Phyllis Consuelos (Alex's ex-wife) | Louise Lasser |
| Cathy Consuelos (Alex's daughter) | Talia Balsam |
| Greta Gravas (Latka's mother) | Susan Kellermann |
| Tom Caldwell (Jim's brother) | Walter Olkewicz |
| Ivan Reiger (Alex's father) | Jack Gilford |

Created by James L. Brooks, Stan Daniels, David Davis, Ed. Weinberger
Music and theme song ("Angela") by Bob James
Directors of photography were Edward E. Nugent, Ken Peach
Principal directors were James Burrows, Noam Pitlik

436

## 1978-79    THE FIRST SEASON

*Year-End Rating: 24.9 (9th place)*

*Taxi*'s ragtag ensemble springs to life in first-season stories that detail the aspirations and frustrations of the colorful gang at New York's Sunshine Cab Company. First-season scripts are written under the watchful eyes of executive producers James L. Brooks, Stan Daniels, David Davis, and Ed. Weinberger, with significant contributions from producers Glen Charles and Les Charles, and writers Earl Pomerantz and Barry Kemp, among others.

James Burrows directs practically all premiere-season episodes, as he will continue to do throughout the show's first four years. Bud Cherry is the first year's associate producer, and James L. Brooks receives a credit as executive consultant.

**1**   Like Father, Like Daughter                September 12, 1978
**Writers:** James L. Brooks, Stan Daniels, David Davis, Ed.
Weinberger
**Director:** James Burrows
**Guest Stars:** Talia Balsam, Jill Jaress

With all the cabbies in tow, Alex drives to Miami for a surprise reunion with the daughter he hasn't seen in fifteen years.

One of the best-written—and most economical—opening episodes ever devised for a situation comedy. In the space of a single half hour, the writers skillfully introduce each fully developed character in the cast of seven, with time left over for the touching sequence where Alex finally meets his estranged teenage daughter in the lobby of the Miami airport. Father and daughter attempt to compress the scattered emotions of fifteen lost years into a few short minutes in a wholly satisfying blend of comedy and pathos that would be the hallmark of this most sophisticated situation comedy.

**2**   One-Punch Banta                           September 19, 1978
**Writer:** Earl Pomerantz
**Director:** James Burrows
**Guest Stars:** Carlos Palomino, Allan Arbus

Tony's lucky punch during a sparring round earns him a once-in-a-lifetime bout with World Champion Carlos Navarone.

Actor Tony Danza had actually been a struggling New York middle-weight before he turned to acting. Ironically, his greatest success in the ring came after he'd hung up his gloves to join *Taxi*, when a canny promoter arranged for the celebrity to box his last match in New York's Madison Square Garden after the conclusion of the show's first season.

**3    Blind Date                              September 26, 1978**
**Writer:** Michael Leeson
**Director:** James Burrows
**Guest Star:** Suzanne Kent

Alex, stuck on a date with an overweight and overbearing woman, refuses to let her bitterness spoil their evening.

**4    Bobby's Acting Career                    October 5, 1978**
**Writers:** Ed. Weinberger, Stan Daniels
**Director:** James Burrows
**Guest Stars:** Taurean Blacque, John Lehne, Michael Mann, Robert Phalen

Bobby's self-imposed deadline to land an acting job is about to expire, and the struggling actor has no prospects in sight.

**5    Come As You Aren't                       October 10, 1978**
**Writers:** Glen Charles, Les Charles
**Director:** James Burrows
**Guest Stars:** Andra Akers, William Bogert, Paula Victor, Clyde Kusatsu, Treva Silverman

Elaine convinces Alex to be her date at a fancy party and then insists that he not tell anyone that they both work as cabbies.

The shy young woman who leaves the party on Latka's arm is actually Emmy Award-winning writer Treva Silverman in a rare cameo appearance.

**6    The Great Line                           October 17, 1978**
**Writer:** Earl Pomerantz
**Director:** James Burrows
**Guest Stars:** Ellen Regan, Dolph Sweet, Sheila Rogers

John develops second thoughts after he finds himself married to a girl he met at Mario's the night before.

**7**    High School Reunion                    October 24, 1978
**Writer:** Sy Rosen
**Director:** James Burrows
**Guest Stars:** Joanna Cassidy, Arlene Golonka, Sandy Holt,
Pierrino Mascarino

Ashamed of what his classmates might think of him, Louie convinces Bobby to attend the dispatcher's twentieth high-school reunion in his place.

**8**    Paper Marriage                         October 31, 1978
**Writers:** Glen Charles, Les Charles
**Story:** Barton Dean
**Director:** James Burrows
**Guest Stars:** Christopher Lloyd, Rita Taggart, James Randolph

Latka gets a disillusioning view of American mating rituals when
he marries a call girl to qualify for U.S. citizenship.

The ceremony is presided over by the Reverend Jim Ignatowski, an
ordained minister and bona fide relic of the 1960s, who is recruited from
Mario's Bar and Grill. "He wasn't intended to be a permanent character," recalled writer Glen Charles. "But," adds executive producer Ed.
Weinberger, "from the first minute Christopher Lloyd hit the stage, he
was destined to stay. That very night, we all agreed we had to get him
on the show."

**9**    Money Troubles                         November 14, 1978
**Writer:** Earl Pomerantz
**Director:** James Burrows
**Guest Star:** Ellen Regan

After John's wealthy in-laws move to Florida, he and his new wife
turn to Alex for a friendly—and sizable—loan.

Ellen Regan returns as John's young wife, Suzanne.

**10**    Men Are Such Beasts                    November 21, 1978
**Writers:** Ed. Weinberger, Stan Daniels
**Director:** James Burrows
**Guest Stars:** Gail Edwards, George Reynolds

Tony tries to dump his possessive girlfriend after she takes a job
at the cab company just to be near him.

**11**    Memories of Cab 804 (Part 1)          November 28, 1978
**Writer:** Barry Kemp
**Director:** James Burrows
**Guest Stars:** Scoey Mitchell, Rod Browning, Chris Barnes

After John wrecks cab 804, the cabbies pay tribute to the beloved taxi with fond recollections of memorable shifts spent behind its wheel.

**12**    Memories of Cab 804 (Part 2)          December 5, 1978
**Writer:** Barry Kemp
**Director:** James Burrows
**Guest Stars:** Tom Selleck, Mandy Patinkin, Regie Baff

The cabbies' vigil continues as Elaine recalls an unusual date she had in 804, and Alex recounts how the cab once served as a makeshift maternity ward.

Elaine's handsome stranger is played by Tom Selleck, in a role that predated his prime-time success in *Magnum, P.I.* by two years.

The sequence where Alex delivers a baby in the backseat of cab 804 while the anxious dad peers over his shoulder demonstrates the show's wide emotional range. The story effortlessly switches gears from high comedy to a moment of compelling drama without missing a beat.

The nervous papa was played by Mandy Patinkin, a New York actor who had been the producers' first choice for the role of *Taxi*'s struggling thespian, long before Jeff Conaway landed the part. Patinkin turned it down, perfectly content to remain in Manhattan, where he achieved continued success on stage and in feature films.

**13**    A Full House for Christmas          December 12, 1978
**Writer:** Barry Kemp
**Director:** James Burrows
**Guest Star:** Richard Foronjy

Alex and Louie team up in a high-stakes poker game against the dispatcher's disreputable brother, Nick.

Richard Foronjy was a last-minute replacement in the role of Louie's brother. *Taxi* cast member Andy Kaufman had originally been set to play Nick De Palma in the guise of Tony Clifton, the lounge-lizard character that Kaufman often used to warm-up his nightclub act. As part of the joke, the conceptual performer maintained that he and Tony were actually two different people. It seemed a harmless-enough stunt, until things took an ugly turn on the first day of rehearsal, when Kaufman refused to drop the obnoxious character, onstage or off.

As spoiled nightclub performer Tony Clifton, Kaufman ordered cases of liquor delivered to his trailer on the Paramount lot, where he holed up with a pair of ladies he'd brought along for companionship. By the third day, he refused to show up for rehearsals—venturing out of his trailer just long enough to heap abuse on fellow actors, stagehands, and anyone else who dared cross his supposedly temperamental path.

Executive producer Ed. Weinberger finally summoned Kaufman to his office, where the comic meekly suggested that Tony Clifton be fired, preferably on the soundstage and in front of the entire crew—a request to which the producer gladly complied. "It was all part of Andy's theater," remembers producer Glen Charles. "But it was not as much fun as it sounds. It was a very troubled week."

**14**   Sugar Mama                              January 16, 1979
**Writers:** Glen Charles, Les Charles
**Director:** James Burrows
**Guest Stars:** Ruth Gordon, Herb Vigran, Aharon Ipale

Alex's conscience bothers him after he accepts cash and extravagant gifts from an eccentric old woman who rides in his cab for companionship.

**15**   Friends                                 January 30, 1979
**Writer:** Earl Pomerantz
**Director:** James Burrows
**Guest Stars:** Liz Miller, J. Alan Thomas

Tony ends his friendship with Bobby after the irresponsible actor accidentally allows Tony's beloved pet goldfish to die.

**16**   Louie Sees the Light                    February 6, 1979
**Writer:** Ruth Bennett
**Director:** James Burrows
**Guest Stars:** John Dukakis, Fay Hauser

Louie resolves to mend his irascible ways after he survives a nerve-racking operation.

**17**    Elaine and the Lame Duck                February 13, 1979
   **Writers:** Glen Charles, Les Charles
   **Director:** James Burrows
   **Guest Stars:** Jeffrey Tambor, Susan Heldfond, Rusdi Lane

Alex fixes Elaine up with an inept Congressman, convinced that an evening with the fiery redhead will do wonders for the legislator's sagging confidence.

Elaine eventually decides to sleep with the hapless politician, only to face an awkward morning-after scene when she realizes that her therapeutic solution has caused more problems than it's solved. The series's depiction of Elaine as a single, sexually independent woman was a refreshing breakthrough for situation comedy. Unfortunately, television tastes were receding so rapidly that the show's mature sophistication would have little direct impact on the increasingly childish sitcoms of the era.

**18**    Bobby's Big Break                       February 15, 1979
   **Writer:** Barry Kemp
   **Director:** James Burrows
   **Guest Stars:** Amanda McBroom, Michele Conaway

Bobby tears up his hack license after he lands a part on a soap opera, but his grandiose exit soon proves premature.

**19**    Mama Gravas                             February 27, 1979
   **Writers:** Glen Charles, Les Charles
   **Director:** James Burrows
   **Guest Star:** Susan Kellermann

Latka demands that Alex marry his mother after the cabbie's date with the lusty Brunhilde ends in an evening of spirited "nik nik."

The garage's peculiar mechanic was largely the creation of Andy Kaufman, who was cast in the show after the producers saw him hold a nightclub audience spellbound in his persona as a stuttering, painfully shy immigrant. Recognizing a good thing at once, the producers simply threw a pair of white coveralls on the character, named him Latka Gravas, and wrote him into the very first show. The show's writers loved Latka, whose strange language and behavior afforded them ample opportunity for offbeat explorations of his surreal world.

**20**   Alex Tastes Death and Finds              March 6, 1979
         a Nice Restaurant
  **Writer:** Michael Leeson
  **Director:** James Burrows
  **Guest Stars:** James Staley, Byron Webster

After Alex is nearly killed by a mugger, he abandons the garage
to become a waiter in a four-star restaurant.

**21**   Hollywood Calling                        May 8, 1979
  **Writers:** Glen Charles, Les Charles
  **Director:** James Burrows
  **Guest Stars:** Martin Mull, Joey Aresco

The cabbies are star-struck when a Hollywood producer arrives to
absorb background for a movie based on life in a New York taxi
garage.

Comedian Martin Mull was fondly remembered for his portrayal of
twin brothers Garth and Barth Gimble on Norman Lear's *Mary Hartman,
Mary Hartman* and its spinoffs, *Fernwood 2-Night* and *America 2-Night*.

**22**   Substitute Father                        May 15, 1979
  **Writer:** Barry Kemp
  **Director:** James Burrows
  **Guest Stars:** Michael Hershewe, David Knapp, Suzanne Carney

The cabbies become substitute daddies when Elaine leaves her
nine-year-old in their care after she's suddenly called out of town.

This episode marked the final appearance of cabbie John Burns. The
character was dropped as the producers pared the ensemble in preparation for the arrival of Jim Ignatowski in the second season. As producer
Ed. Weinberger observed, "We just had too many people. We couldn't
write for everybody."

## 1979-80   THE SECOND SEASON

*Year-End Rating: 22.4 (13th place)*

Danny DeVito's Louie and Andy Kaufman's Latka each discover romance
in season two, and the cabbies recruit Christopher Lloyd's Jim Ignatowski
into their ranks in the year's third episode. Once again, producers Glen

Charles and Les Charles contribute some of the season's finest scripts, along with Earl Pomerantz, executive script consultant Barry Kemp, and program consultant Ken Estin. Ian Praiser and Howard Gewirtz are the story editors, and Richard Sakai is associate producer for the second and third seasons. James L. Brooks, Stan Daniels, and Ed. Weinberger serve as executive producers for the remainder of the show's run.

**23**   Louie and the Nice Girl                    September 11, 1979
   **Writer:** Earl Pomerantz
   **Director:** James Burrows
   **Guest Star:** Rhea Perlman

Louie is petrified at the prospect of falling in love with a girl he's sure is too good for him.

Kind-hearted candy girl Zena Sherman was played by Rhea Perlman, DeVito's real-life girlfriend. Louie's romance with Zena barely lasted through season four, but the real-life couple finally did tie the knot three years later in an impulsive ceremony conducted during a *Taxi* lunch break.

**24**   Honor Thy Father                          September 18, 1979
   **Writers:** Glen Charles, Les Charles
   **Director:** James Burrows
   **Guest Stars:** Jack Gilford, Ian Wolfe, Richard Beauchamp

Alex is strangely unmoved by news of his father's heart attack.

**25**   Reverend Jim: A Space Odyssey             September 25, 1979
   **Writers:** Glen Charles, Les Charles
   **Director:** James Burrows
   **Guest Star:** Kenneth Kimmins

The cabbies help a refugee from the 1960s find sanctuary behind the wheel of a taxi.

The Reverend Jim Caldwell Ignatowski—he added Ignatowski to his family name, we later discovered, because he thought it meant "Star Child"—was a comic creation of practically unlimited potential. There was no concept too bizarre, no drug too potent, and no experience too outlandish for Jim. He had experienced life in ways the other cabbies could barely imagine, yet he remained an innocent who drew our sympathy as easily as our laughter. When Tony angrily confronts Jim with the bitter accusation that he fought in Vietnam so that burnouts like him could stay home and get loaded at protest rallies, the philosophical Ignatowski can only stammer a heartfelt, and utterly sincere, "Thank you."

**26** Nardo Loses Her Marbles October 2, 1979
**Writer:** Earl Pomerantz
**Director:** James Burrows
**Guest Stars:** Tom Ewell, Paula Victor, Mary Woronov, Robert Picardo, William Callaway

Alex suggests that Elaine seek professional help when the stress of holding down two jobs while raising a pair of kids begins to take a toll on her sanity.

In a low moment, Elaine decides that sleeping with Alex might be the most expedient form of therapy—an offer that he shuns, to his instant regret. The sexual tension that developed over the course of their relationship was rarely addressed with such candor, though it remained a compelling subtext that colored their friendship throughout the life of the series.

**27** Reluctant Fighter October 9, 1979
**Writer:** Ken Estin
**Director:** James Burrows
**Guest Stars:** Marc Danza, Armando Muniz, Michael V. Gazzo

Tony has a chance to fight the retired champ but loses heart when he discovers that his opponent has dedicated his victory to a handicapped child.

**28** Wherefore Art Thou, Bobby? October 16, 1979
**Writer:** Barry Kemp
**Director:** James Burrows
**Guest Star:** Michael Horton

Bobby is stunned when an inexperienced actor fresh off the bus lands a plum role on his very first audition.

**29** The Lighter Side of Angela Matusa October 23, 1979
**Writer:** Earl Pomerantz
**Director:** James Burrows
**Guest Stars:** Suzanne Kent, Phil Rubenstein, Dick Miller

Alex's overweight blind date returns, now a hundred pounds thinner and ready for serious romance.

**30**    A Woman Among Friends                    October 30, 1979
   **Writer:** Ken Estin
   **Director:** James Burrows
   **Guest Star:** Constance Forslund

Tony and Bobby compete for the attentions of a woman who seems to have fallen for both of them.


**31**    The Great Race                         November 6, 1979
   **Writer:** Glenn Gordon Caron
   **Director:** James Burrows
   **Guest Stars:** James Hong, Jean Owens Hayworth, Fred Stuthman, Scott Brady, Craig T. Nelson, Bob Levine, Julie Payne, Milt Oberman, Kres Mersky

The cabbies place their bets when Louie and Alex compete to see who can book the most money in a single shift.

Writer Glenn Gordon Caron would eventually mastermind *Moonlighting*, the cross-genre detective spoof that premiered on ABC in 1985.


**32**    The Apartment                          November 13, 1979
   **Writer:** Barry Rubinowitz
   **Director:** James Burrows
   **Guest Stars:** Nancy Steen, Dick Butkus, Mike Binder

Latka blows his entire life savings on a luxury penthouse after he assumes that the $3000 monthly rent is a one-time charge.


**33**    Alex's Romance                         November 20, 1979
   **Writers:** Ian Praiser, Howard Gewirtz
   **Director:** Ed. Weinberger
   **Guest Star:** Dee Wallace

Alex surprises everyone—including himself—when he falls in love with an out-of-work actress.

Actress Dee Wallace would find plenty of work in feature films, including a starring role in Steven Spielberg's *E.T.*

**34**   Latka's Revolting                    November 27, 1979
**Writers:** Glen Charles, Les Charles
**Director:** James Burrows
**Guest Star:** Lenny Baker

Latka hears the patriotic call when revolution breaks out in his homeland.

**35**   Elaine's Secret Admirer                 December 4, 1979
**Writer:** Barry Kemp
**Director:** James Burrows
**Guest Star:** Michael Delano

Elaine is determined to find out which of the cabbies has been leaving anonymous love poems in her locker.

**36**   Louie Meets the Folks                  December 11, 1979
**Writer:** Barry Kemp
**Director:** James Burrows
**Guest Stars:** Rhea Perlman, Camila Ashland, John Becher

Nervous at the prospect of meeting Zena's parents for the first time, Louie pays Alex $500 to come along for moral support.

**37**   Jim Gets a Pet                         December 18, 1979
**Writer:** David Lloyd
**Director:** James Burrows

Jim makes a killing at the track and then buys the winning horse to take home as a pet.

**38**   Tony and Brian                          January 8, 1980
**Writer:** Ken Estin
**Director:** James Burrows
**Guest Star:** Marc Danza

Tony wants to adopt his foster child officially, but the canny youngster would rather take his chances with a wealthy couple.

Tony's foster child was played by Danza's real-life eight-year-old, Marc Antony Danza.

**39**     Guess Who's Coming for Brefnish          January 15, 1980
   **Writer:** Barry Kemp
   **Director:** James Burrows
   **Guest Stars:** Carol Kane, Frank Ashmore

Latka's whirlwind romance with a strange girl from his home country sours after he discovers that she's from a socially inferior class.

When Carol Kane was hired to play Simka, the actress received a crash-course in Latka-language when Andy Kaufman invited her to dinner and then refused to let her speak English during the meal. "It is the perfect way to learn a language," observed the actress. "Andy made it up and got a very specific sound to it. You just open your mouth and dive in."

**40**     What Price Bobby?          January 22, 1980
   **Writer:** Ken Estin
   **Director:** James Burrows
   **Guest Star:** Susan Sullivan

Bobby hits it off with an influential agent who seems more confident of his talents in bed than on the stage.

**41**     Shut It Down (Part 1)          January 29, 1980
   **Writers:** Howard Gewirtz, Ian Praiser
   **Story By:** Mark Jacobson, Michael Tolkin
   **Director:** James Burrows

Shop steward Elaine faces a dilemma when Louie agrees to meet the cabbies' labor demands—in exchange for a date.

**42**     Shut It Down (Part 2)          February 5, 1980
   **Writers:** Howard Gewirtz, Ian Praiser
   **Director:** James Burrows

Elaine's date with Louie goes as badly as expected, until the dispatcher surprises her with an uncharacteristic display of human feelings.

**43**   Alex Jumps Out of an Airplane                February 26, 1980
   **Writer:** Ken Estin
   **Director:** James Burrows

After he survives a death-defying ski jump, Alex develops a daredevil's addiction to thrills.


**44**   Art Work                                     March 4, 1980
   **Writers:** Glen Charles, Les Charles
   **Director:** James Burrows
   **Guest Star:** Marvin Newman

Elaine convinces the cabbies to pool their money to bid on undervalued artwork at a gallery auction.


**45**   Fantasy Borough (Part 1)                     May 6, 1980
   **Writer:** Barry Kemp
   **Director:** James Burrows
   **Guest Stars:** Eric Sevareid, Herve Villechaize, Warren Munson

A visit from *Fantasy Island*'s Herve Villechaize prompts each of the cabbies to share their own private fantasies.


**46**   Fantasy Borough (Part 2)                     May 13, 1980
   **Writer:** Barry Kemp
   **Director:** James Burrows
   **Guest Stars:** Herve Villechaize, Lassie

Alex has difficulty imagining a fantasy with a happy ending; and Elaine envisions herself belting a Broadway showstopper in the dreary garage.

Lassie makes a cameo appearance as Louie's pet collie in the dispatcher's far-fetched fantasy that he's wealthy and well-liked.

# 1980-81    THE THIRD SEASON

*Year-End Rating: 17.1 (53rd place)*

*Taxi* rolls into a strong third season under the guidance of executive producers James L. Brooks, Stan Daniels, and Ed. Weinberger, and producers Glen Charles and Les Charles, who continue to contribute noteworthy scripts, along with David Lloyd, executive script consultant Barry Kemp, and executive story editor Ken Estin.

**47    Louie's Rival**                              November 19, 1980
**Writer:** Ken Estin
**Director:** James Burrows
**Guest Stars:** Rhea Perlman, Richard Minchenberg

Louie is crushed when Zena drops him for the bartender at Mario's.

**48    Tony's Sister and Jim**                      November 26, 1980
**Writer:** Michael Leeson
**Director:** James Burrows
**Guest Stars:** Julie Kavner, Andrew Block

Tony tries to match Alex up with his wacky sister—who only has eyes for Jim.

Tony's sister was played by Julie Kavner, best remembered for her stint as Brenda Morgenstern, the title character's younger sister on *Rhoda*.

**49    Fathers of the Bride**                       December 3, 1980
**Writer:** Barry Kemp
**Director:** James Burrows
**Guest Stars:** Louise Lasser, Talia Balsam, Carlo Quinterio

Alex—enraged that he wasn't invited to his daughter's New York wedding—crashes the fancy reception and confronts his estranged wife.

In addition to hosting one of the brightest acting ensembles in television history, *Taxi* also managed to attract some of Hollywood's finest character players as recurring guest stars. Carol Kane, Jack Gilford, and

Andrea Marcovicci were all well established before they made repeat appearances on the series, as was Louise Lasser, who would return as Alex's loopy ex-wife in a handful of later episodes.

**50** Elaine's Strange Triangle                December 10, 1980
 **Writer:** David Lloyd
 **Director:** James Burrows
 **Guest Star:** John David Carson

Alex and Tony fix Elaine up with a handsome stranger, only to discover that her new beau is actually more attracted to Tony.

**51** Going Home                December 17, 1980
 **Writers:** Glen Charles, Les Charles
 **Director:** James Burrows
 **Guest Stars:** Victor Buono, Barbara Deutsch, Walter Olkewicz, Dick Yarmy

Jim's wealthy father dispatches a private eye to the garage to coax his son into a long-overdue reconciliation.

**52** The Ten Percent Solution                January 7, 1981
 **Writer:** Pat Allee
 **Director:** James Burrows
 **Guest Stars:** Sarina C. Grant, Ed. Weinberger, Jim Staskell

Bobby decides to manage Tony's budding acting career on a lark, but soon develops a bad case of professional jealousy.

Series creator Ed. Weinberger has a brief cameo as—what else?—one of the producers at Tony's audition.

**53** The Call of the Mild                January 21, 1981
 **Writer:** Katharine Green
 **Director:** James Burrows
 **Guest Star:** Harvey Vernon

Inspired by Bobby's rugged beer commercial, the cabbies retreat to the wilderness for a survival weekend.

**54**    Latka's Cookies                    February 5, 1981
**Writers:** Glen Charles, Les Charles
**Director:** James Burrows
**Guest Star:** Wally "Famous" Amos

Latka decides to market his own line of cookies using a special old-world recipe that includes at least one highly illegal ingredient.

**55**    Thy Boss's Wife                    February 12, 1981
**Writer:** Ken Estin
**Director:** James Burrows
**Guest Stars:** Eileen Brennan, Stephen Elliot

Louie has difficulty resisting temptation when the boss's wife casts a lustful eye in his direction—even though he knows that the affair may cost him his job.

**56**    The Costume Party                  February 19, 1981
**Writer:** David Lloyd
**Director:** James Burrows
**Guest Stars:** Hector Britt, Louie Guss, Michael Klingher

The cabbies plan to hobnob with the stars when they crash what they assume is Woody Allen's masquerade ball.

**57**    Elaine's Old Friend                February 26, 1981
**Writers:** Susan Linder, Nancy Lane
**Director:** Jeff Chambers
**Guest Stars:** Martha Smith, John Considine

Elaine makes a date with her old high-school rival and then cons Alex into posing as her imaginary boyfriend—a worldly Columbia University professor.

**58**    Out of Commission                  March 12, 1981
**Writer:** Sam Simon
**Director:** James Burrows
**Guest Stars:** Carmine Caridi, Al Ruscio, Jesse Goins, Jimmy Lennon

Tony refuses to abandon his career in the ring, even after the boxing commission revokes his license.

**59**    Zen and the Art of Cab Driving          March 19, 1981
     **Writers:** Glen Charles, Les Charles
     **Director:** Will Mackenzie
     **Guest Stars:** Nicholas Hormann, Michael Mann

The cabbies are mystified when Jim embarks on a mysterious quest for absolute perfection.

Jim goes to enormous expense to set up an elaborate bank of TVs and satellite receivers in his small apartment—a foolhardy extravagance that causes the other cabbies to scoff. And yet, none of them can resist the hypnotic lure of Jim's video Medusa, and the show closes with a curious meditation on our own love-hate relationship with the tube, as each of the cabbies sits frozen, staring at their world through Jim's electronic windows.

**60**    Louie's Mother                          March 26, 1981
     **Writer:** Katharine Green
     **Director:** James Burrows
     **Guest Star:** Julia DeVito

Louie throws a party to celebrate his independence after his elderly mother moves out to enter a retirement home.

Louie's spry mom was played by Julia DeVito, the actor's real-life mother.

**61**    Bobby's Roommate                         April 9, 1981
     **Writer:** Earl Pomerantz
     **Director:** James Burrows

Alex and Tony suspect Bobby's motives when he offers to let Elaine stay at his apartment after she loses her own place.

**62**    Louie Bumps Into an Old Lady            April 16, 1981
     **Writer:** David Lloyd
     **Director:** James Burrows
     **Guest Stars:** Iris Korn, Sam DeFazio, Jay F. Riley, Lane Brody, Joe Medalis

Louie is slapped with a million-dollar lawsuit by a kindly old woman he accidentally ran down with his cab.

**63**    Bobby and the Critic              April 30, 1981
**Writer:** Barry Kemp
**Director:** James Burrows
**Guest Star:** John Harkins

Bobby performs a turgid one-man show for a vengeful theater critic who carries a personal grudge against the actor.

**64**    On the Job (Part 1)            May 7,1981
**Writers:** Dennis Danziger, Ellen Sandler
**Director:** James Burrows
**Guest Stars:** Robert Balderson, Bill Wiley, John O'Leary, Carmine Caridi, Alice Hirson, John Petlock, Robin Pearson Rose

A month after the cab company goes bankrupt, the drivers reunite to exchange tales of their employment experiences in the outside world.

Tony lands a job as a loan shark's enforcer; Elaine finds work as a secretary; and, as a door-to-door salesman, Jim nearly destroys a condo when he attempts to demonstrate a new high-powered vacuum cleaner.

**65**    On the Job (Part 2)           May 14, 1981
**Writers:** Dennis Danziger, Ellen Sandler
**Director:** James Burrows
**Guest Stars:** Clint Young, Claire Malis, Al Lewis, Michael McGuire, Dana Halsted

The cabbies continue to recount harrowing tales of their new jobs.

Before they return to the shelter of the garage, Louie discovers his calling in the stock market; Bobby plays the Easter Bunny at children's birthday parties; and Alex lands a job as a night watchman.

**66**    Latka the Playboy             May 21, 1981
**Writers:** Glen Charles, Les Charles
**Director:** James Burrows
**Guest Stars:** George Wendt, Robin Klein

Tired of striking out with the ladies, shy Latka adopts the split personality of smooth-talking ladies' man Vic Ferrari.

## 1981-82    THE FOURTH SEASON
*Year-End Rating: 15.8 (53rd place)*

Fourth-season producers Ken Estin, Howard Gewirtz, and Ian Praiser write many of the year's scripts, along with executive script consultant David Lloyd, executive story editor Sam Simon, and Glen Charles and Les Charles, who are credited as executive consultants in the fourth year. Richard Sakai is co-producer, and James L. Brooks is billed as executive creative consultant.

**67**    Jim the Psychic                                October 8, 1981
   **Writer:** Barry Kemp
   **Story:** Holly Holmberg Brooks
   **Director:** James Burrows
   **Guest Stars:** Diane Peterson, Kiva Dawson

The cabbies prepare for the worst when Jim's latest premonition foretells doom for Alex.

This episode was based on a story submitted by Holly Holmberg Brooks, the wife of executive producer James L. Brooks.

**68**    Vienna Waits                                  October 15, 1981
   **Writer:** Ken Estin
   **Director:** Howard Storm
   **Guest Stars:** Reuven Bar-Yotam, Gary Phillips, Warwick Sims, Cassandra Gava, Patch Mackenzie

Alex is worried that Elaine might cramp his style during a trip to Europe, but she ends up adapting to the romantic climate far better than he does.

Alex and Elaine's occasional attraction resurfaces in a lovely scene where they both agree that, after four years of helping each other through good times and bad, their bond may actually be strong enough to withstand a single night as lovers.

**69**    Mr. Personalities                             October 22, 1981
   **Writers:** Ian Praiser, Howard Gewirtz
   **Director:** Howard Storm
   **Guest Stars:** Barry Nelson, Bernadette Birkett, Wendy Goldman

The cabbies convince Latka to see a psychiatrist after his playboy persona threatens to take over his entire personality.

**70**    Jim Joins the Network                    October 29, 1981
**Writer:** David Lloyd
**Director:** Noam Pitlik
**Guest Stars:** Martin Short, Melendy Britt

A spineless network executive taps Jim as a silent partner after the cabbie's programming hunches prove unerringly correct.

**71**    Louie's Fling                    November 5, 1981
**Writer:** Sam Simon
**Director:** James Burrows
**Guest Stars:** Andrea Marcovicci, Rhea Perlman

Louie takes advantage of Zena's emotionally unstable girlfriend Emily.

After he exploits Emily, Louie still can't resist entertaining the fantasy that she's in love with him—a dream that comes tumbling down when, like Chaplin's drunken benefactor in *City Lights,* she sobers up in the cold morning light to declare him disgusting. And yet, despite Louie's despicable behavior, our sympathy goes out to this misguided devil who is brave—or foolish—enough to act out his own mischievous fantasies.

**72**    Like Father, Like Son                    November 12, 1981
**Writer:** David Lloyd
**Director:** James Burrows
**Guest Stars:** Jack Gilford, Barbara Babcock

Alex gets involved in a bizarre triangle when he finds himself in romantic competition with his own irrepressible father.

**73**    Louie's Mom Remarries                    November 19, 1981
**Writer:** Earl Pomerantz
**Director:** James Burrows
**Guest Stars:** Julia DeVito, Jerry Fujikawa

Louie hits the roof when his mother asks his blessing for her marriage to an elderly Japanese man.

**74**   Fledgling                              November 26, 1981
   **Writer:** Ken Estin
   **Director:** James Burrows
   **Guest Star:** Paul Sand

Elaine tries to convince a severely agoraphobic artist to venture outside his studio for the first time in years.

**75**   Of Mice and Tony                       December 10, 1981
   **Writers:** Glen Charles, Les Charles
   **Director:** James Burrows
   **Guest Stars:** Ernie Hudson, John Christy Ewing

Tony's dream of managing an up-and-coming young boxer crumbles when a syndicate of well-to-do doctors makes his fighter a better offer.

Writers Ian Praiser and Howard Gewirtz make cameo appearances as two of the well-heeled doctors.

**76**   Louie Goes Too Far                     December 17, 1981
   **Writer:** Danny Kallis
   **Director:** Michael Lessac
   **Guest Stars:** Allen Williams, Noni White

Louie's days at the Sunshine Cab Company appear numbered when Elaine files charges against him for spying on her through a peephole in the ladies' room.

**77**   I Wanna Be Around                      January 7, 1982
   **Writers:** Glen Charles, Les Charles
   **Director:** James Burrows
   **Guest Star:** J. Alan Thomas

Louie prepares for an imagined apocalypse by recruiting a survival squad for his bomb shelter.

**78**   Bobby Doesn't Live Here Anymore        January 14, 1982
   **Writers:** Glen Charles, Les Charles
   **Director:** James Burrows
   **Guest Star:** Jeff Conaway

Bobby returns to suffer Louie's taunts one last time as he prepares to move on to brighter horizons in Hollywood.

**79**   Nina Loves Alex                    January 21, 1982
  **Writer:** David Lloyd
  **Director:** Joan Darling
  **Guest Stars:** Charlaine Woodard, John Mengatti, Audrey Berindey

An optimistic cabbie launches a romantic campaign to attract Alex, who finds himself fiercely uninterested in the ingratiating young actress.

A superb comic script that captures the essence of Alex's tragic inability to synchronize head and heart. At his most caustic, he dismisses his would-be companion as a naive fool: "She's like every actress or Hindu I've ever met!" The inevitable turnaround comes when Alex consoles Nina after her first defeat, and he finally comes to recognize his attraction to her despair. He inspires her to strike out on her own, only to find himself standing alone once more at the top of the stairs.

**80**   Tony's Lady                    January 28, 1982
  **Writer:** Ken Estin
  **Director:** Michael Zinberg
  **Guest Stars:** Rebecca Holden, Joel Brooks, John Calvin

Tony lands a job as chauffeur for a wealthy young woman and soon finds himself falling in love with the untouchable beauty.

**81**   Simka Returns                    February 4, 1982
  **Writers:** Ian Praiser, Howard Gewirtz
  **Director:** Michael Zinberg
  **Guest Star:** Carol Kane

Latka discovers an unlikely rival for Simka's affections when she falls under the spell of his alter-ego, Vic Ferrari.

Carol Kane had already appeared in more than a dozen films when she approached Jim Brooks for advice on whether she should do television. The executive producer's response was to offer her the role of Latka's girlfriend in a third-year episode. "It went through the roof," he remembers, which brought about Simka's reprise in this episode—an appearance that would earn the actress an Emmy.

**82**   Jim and the Kid                    February 11, 1982
  **Writer:** David Lloyd
  **Director:** Michael Zinberg
  **Guest Stars:** Tony La Torre, Rebecca Clemons, Mark Harrison

After Tony brings a runaway into the Sunshine garage, Jim decides to raise the wayward kid as his own son.

**83**   Take My Ex-Wife, Please           February 18, 1982
  **Writers:** Ian Praiser, Howard Gewirtz
  **Director:** Noam Pitlik
  **Guest Stars:** Louise Lasser, Candi and Randi Brough, Alex Rodine

Alex is frantic when his ex-wife develops an unexplainable attraction to Louie De Palma.

**84**   The Unkindest Cut                  February 25, 1982
  **Writer:** Sam Simon
  **Story:** Barbara Duncan
  **Director:** Noam Pitlik
  **Guest Stars:** Ted Danson, Gela Jacobsen, Karen Anders

Louie and Alex extract revenge on a snooty hairdresser who has bilked Elaine out of $225 for a perfectly hideous hairstyle.

During a lull in shooting, director Jim Burrows asked guest star Ted Danson if he might be interested in reading for a part in a new series the director was developing with Glen and Les Charles. The show was called *Cheers*, and Danson walked off with the lead role.

**85**   Tony's Comeback                    March 4, 1982
  **Writer:** Sam Simon
  **Director:** Michael Lessac
  **Guest Stars:** Bubba Smith, Naomi Stevens

An unemployed pro football player inspires Tony to attempt a boxing comeback.

**86**    Elegant Iggy                                    March 18, 1982
  **Writer:** Ken Estin
  **Director:** Noam Pitlik
  **Guest Stars:** Fran Ryan, Nina Van Pallandt, Robert Denison

Elaine prepares for the most embarrassing night of her life when Jim escorts her to an elegant dinner party hosted by an influential society matron.


**87**    The Wedding of Latka and Simka          March 25, 1982
  **Writers:** Howard Gewirtz, Ian Praiser
  **Director:** James Burrows
  **Guest Stars:** Carol Kane, Dr. Joyce Brothers, Susan Kellermann, Vincent Schiavelli, Peter Elbing

Latka and Simka's marriage plans fall in doubt when the pair fails to pass the bizarre rituals of their old-world wedding ceremony.


**88**    Cooking for Two                              April 8, 1982
  **Writers:** Ken Estin, Sam Simon
  **Director:** James Burrows

Jim proves a most unwelcome houseguest when he sleeps through a fire that reduces Louie's apartment to cinders.


**89**    The Road Not Taken (Part 1)              April 29, 1982
  **Writers:** Sam Simon, Ken Estin
  **Director:** James Burrows
  **Guest Stars:** J. Pat O'Malley, Wendy Phillips, Tom Hanks, Eugene Roche, Charles Cioffi, Michael A. Salcido

The cabbies recall crucial turning points in their own lives when they help Elaine face a momentous decision of her own.

Film star Tom Hanks has a role as one of Jim's college chums in a hilarious flashback that reveals the cabbie's first fateful brush with mind-expanding drugs.

**90**   The Road Not Taken (Part 2)              May 6, 1982
**Writers:** Ian Praiser, Howard Gewirtz
**Director:** James Burrows
**Guest Stars:** Susan Kellermann, Max Wright, Jill Jaress, David
Mendenhall, Melanie Gaffin, Matthew Faison

Despite all the well-meaning advice from her fellow cabbies,
Elaine still can't decide whether she wants to pull up stakes and
move to Seattle.

Flashbacks reveal Latka's tearful farewell to his frigid homeland on
the eve of his emigration to America, and a second vignette reveals Alex's
final confrontation with the petty tyranny of office politics.

## 1982-83   THE FIFTH SEASON

*Year-End Rating: 13.2 (73rd place)*

As the show moves to NBC for a fifth season, producers Ken Estin,
Sam Simon, and Richard Sakai attempt to rejuvenate the series by introducing new romantic interests for Louie, Tony, and Elaine. But despite
their efforts, the show is canceled at the close of the fifth year.

David Lloyd is executive script consultant in the final season, and
Katharine Green serves as the season's executive story editor. Harvey
Miller signs on as executive consultant, and James L. Brooks continues
as executive creative consultant and executive producer, along with Stan
Daniels and Ed. Weinberger.

**91**   The Shloogel Show              September 30, 1982
**Writers:** Ken Estin, Sam Simon
**Director:** Noam Pitlik
**Guest Stars:** Marcia Wallace, Carlene Watkins, Wallace Shawn,
Anne DeSalvo, Murphy Cross

Latka and Simka attempt to match each of the cabbies with their
ideal partner when they stage a massive blind date at Mario's.

Jim finally meets Marcia Wallace—his TV idol since her days as a co-
star of *The Bob Newhart Show*. The actress played herself in the producers' sly homage to that classic comedy.

Three of the cabbies' blind dates resurfaced in later episodes of the
season. Anne DeSalvo would return as Tony's streetwise girlfriend, Vicki;
Elaine later introduced bookish Arnie—played by Wallace Shawn—to

the kids; and Murphy Cross played Louie's date, Judy, the irrepressible blind girl whose sight would be restored by the end of the season.

**92**    Jim's Inheritance                              October 7, 1982
   **Writer:** Ken Estin
   **Director:** Noam Pitlik
   **Guest Stars:** Dick Sargent, F. William Parker

Jim stands to inherit millions from his father's estate, but only if he can legally prove his sanity.

**93**    Alex Goes off the Wagon                       October 14, 1982
   **Writer:** Danny Kallis
   **Director:** Noam Pitlik

Alex falls prey to his old gambling addiction after a lucky night in Atlantic City, and Jim is the only one who can help.

**94**    Scenskees From a Marriage (Part 1)          October 21, 1982
   **Writers:** Ian Praiser, Howard Gewirtz
   **Director:** Noam Pitlik
   **Guest Stars:** Allyce Beasley, Peter Elbing, Vincent Schiavelli

After spending the night snowbound with a woman cabbie, Latka lands in hot water when Simka discovers how the pair managed to stay warm.

**95**    Scenskees From a Marriage (Part 2)          October 28, 1982
   **Writers:** Ian Praiser, Howard Gewirtz
   **Director:** Noam Pitlik

To even the score with her wayward husband, old-world tradition dictates that Simka must choose a lover from among Latka's workmates.

**96**    Crime and Punishment                        November 4, 1982
   **Writer:** Katharine Green
   **Director:** Stan Daniels
   **Guest Stars:** J. Alan Thomas, Allen Goorwitz, Martin Garner

Louie persuades Jeff to cover for him after the boss discovers his petty thievery, a favor that costs the hapless junior dispatcher his job.

**97**   Alex the Gofer                    November 11, 1982
   **Writer:** David Lloyd
   **Director:** Michael Lessac
   **Guest Stars:** Matthew Laurence, David Paymer, Caren Kaye

Alex is thrilled to land a job in show business, even though he winds up as no more than an errand boy for a pair of arrogant young producers.


**98**   Louie's Revenge                    November 18,1982
   **Writer:** Sam Simon
   **Director:** Stan Daniels
   **Guest Stars:** Andrea Marcovicci, Charlie Stavola

Louie plans to extract revenge on Emily—the unbalanced woman who turned on him after their ill-fated fling—but ends up falling for her all over again.


**99**   Travels With My Dad                    November 25, 1982
   **Writer:** Barton Dean
   **Director:** Michael Zinberg
   **Guest Stars:** Donnelly Rhodes, Dick Miller, Wendell Wright

Tony's seafaring father returns from his travels to offer his son a job on a Chinese freighter.


**100**   Elaine and the Monk                    December 2, 1982
   **Writer:** David Lloyd
   **Director:** Danny DeVito
   **Guest Star:** Mark Blankfield

Elaine falls for a guy who's fun-loving, sensitive, and bright—and also due back at the monastery in exactly one week.

As he prepares to renew his vows of silence, Elaine and her beau share a last dance—choreographed by Debbie Allen, one of the stars of TV's *Fame*.

**101**   Zena's Honeymoon                    December 9, 1982
  **Writer:** David Lloyd
  **Director:** Richard Sakai
  **Guest Stars:** Rhea Perlman, Peter Jurasik

Louie is broken-hearted to hear that Zena is getting married, especially since he always hoped she'd come crawling back to him.

Zena Sherman's exit from *Taxi* was inevitable after Rhea Perlman moved to a neighboring Paramount soundstage to begin her new life as irascible waitress Carla Tortelli on *Cheers*.

**102**   Get Me Through the Holidays         December 16, 1982
  **Writers:** Ken Estin, Sam Simon
  **Director:** Michael Zinberg
  **Guest Star:** Louise Lasser

Alex's ex-wife attempts a holiday reconciliation to dispel her Yuletide loneliness.

**103**   Louie Moves Uptown                  January 22, 1983
  **Writer:** David Lloyd
  **Director:** Michael Zinberg
  **Guest Stars:** Gayle Hunicutt, Penny Marshall, Nelson Welch,
  Lois DeBanzie

Louie plans to move into an exclusive Manhattan co-op apartment, if he can win the approval of a panel of pompous tenants.

*Laverne and Shirley* star Penny Marshall plays herself in a delightful cameo where she tries to convince the co-op board that acting in a situation comedy is a legitimate profession.

**104**   Alex's Old Buddy                    January 29, 1983
  **Writers:** Ken Estin, Sam Simon
  **Director:** Richard Sakai
  **Guest Stars:** Judith Marie Bergan, John Hancock

Alex comes to terms with the imminent death of his oldest friend—his aged family dog, Buddy.

**105**   Sugar Ray Nardo                    February 5, 1983
   **Writer:** Katharine Green
   **Director:** Danny DeVito
   **Guest Stars:** David Mendenhall, Brad Kester, Michael Alldredge

Elaine is upset when her son abandons his oboe lessons to study boxing with Tony.

**106**   Celebration of Taxi (one hour)          March 23, 1983
   **Writers:** Various
   **Directors:** Various

A retrospective of highlights from the first four seasons of *Taxi.*

**107**   Alex Gets Burned by an Old Flame       March 30, 1983
   **Writer:** Barton Dean
   **Director:** Harvey Miller
   **Guest Star:** Cathie Shiriff

Alex falls for a lady lawyer who still carries the torch for Jim.

**108**   Louie and the Blind Girl                 April 6, 1983
   **Writer:** Larry Anderson
   **Director:** Noam Pitlik
   **Guest Stars:** Murphy Cross, David Young

Louie's blind girlfriend has her sight restored, but the dispatcher worries that she may have second thoughts about him once she sees what he looks like.

Over five seasons, it became necessary to soften Louie's rough edges from time to time. It's too horrible to imagine what might have happened if the leering, slobbering Louie from the show's first year had been left at the bedside of a blind girl! But even at his sweetest, Louie oozed a palpably disreputable charm—there was always that sly twinkle in Danny DeVito's eyes that warned you not to trust him.

**109**   Arnie Meets the Kids                    April 13, 1983
   **Writer:** John Markus
   **Director:** Richard Sakai
   **Guest Stars:** Wallace Shawn, Melanie Gaffin, David Mendenhall, Wendy Jewell

Elaine's new beau tries to win her kids' affection by bribing them with cash and gifts.

**110**    Tony's Baby                                     April 20, 1983
   **Writer:** Dari Daniels
   **Director:** Richard Sakai
   **Guest Stars:** Anne De Salvo, Keenan Wynn

On the eve of a big match, Tony is shocked to learn that his girl-friend is expecting a baby.

**111**    Jim's Mario's                                     May 18, 1983
   **Writers:** Ken Estin, Sam Simon
   **Director:** Danny DeVito
   **Guest Star:** Walter Olkewicz

The cabbies pitch in to make a success of Mario's after Jim buys the restaurant against his family's better judgment.

**112**    A Grand Gesture                                  May 25, 1983
   **Writers:** Ken Estin, Sam Simon
   **Director:** Noam Pitlik
   **Guest Stars:** Jeff Thomas, Vincent Schiavelli, Scatman Crothers, Tom Villard, Tracey Walter, Melanie Gaffin

Jim concocts a novel plan to share the wealth when he offers each of the cabbies a thousand-dollar bill to be given away to whomever he or she sees fit.

**113**    Simka's Monthlies                                June 15, 1983
   **Writer:** Holly Holmberg Brooks
   **Director:** Harvey Miller

Latka worries when Simka's behavior suddenly grows erratic on the eve of her final meeting at the Bureau of Immigration.

This would be the last first-run episode of *Taxi*.

Despite the protests of Judd Hirsch and other cast members, the series quietly expired in the late spring of 1983—a tragic victim of audience indifference. "The show still had a lot of life in it," producer Ed. Weinberger maintains. "We probably could have gone another two years." Maybe so. But times were changing.

By the early 1980s, the progressive era that spawned Archie Bunker, Hawkeye, and Mary Richards had already faded from the public consciousness. Given the country's shifting tastes, perhaps it's best that *Taxi* ran out of gas when it did—before the free-spirited misfits of the Sunshine garage fell completely out of step with the times. At least this way,

Jim Ignatowski would never have to face the indignity of mandatory drug-testing.

In any event, there was very little chance of another revival for a show that had already been canceled by two networks. In the end, diehard fans would find their only consolation in syndicated reruns—where, freed from the pressures of network ratings battles, the show would flourish. And now that everyone's stopped paying so much attention to the meter, *Taxi* just may run forever.

## EMMY AWARDS

The following is a complete listing of the Emmy Awards bestowed on *Taxi* by the National Academy of Television Arts and Sciences.

**1978-79**  Outstanding Comedy Series
Outstanding Lead Actress in a Comedy for a Continued or Single Performance in a Regular Series: Ruth Gordon, "Sugar Mama"
Outstanding Achievement in Film Editing: M. Pam Blumenthal, "Paper Marriage"

**1979-80**  Outstanding Comedy Series
Outstanding Directing in a Comedy Series: James Burrows, "Louie and the Nice Girl"
Outstanding Achievement in Film Editing: M. Pam Blumenthal, "Louie and the Nice Girl"

**1980-81**  Outstanding Comedy Series
Outstanding Lead Actor in a Comedy Series: Judd Hirsch
Outstanding Supporting Actor in a Comedy Series: Danny DeVito
Outstanding Directing in a Comedy Series: James Burrows, "Elaine's Strange Triangle"
Outstanding Writing in a Comedy Series: Michael Leeson, "Tony's Sister and Jim"
Outstanding Achievement in Film Editing: M. Pam Blumenthal, Jack Michon, "Elaine's Strange Triangle"

**1981-82**  Outstanding Lead Actress in a Comedy Series: Carol Kane, "Simka Returns"
Outstanding Supporting Actor in a Comedy Series: Christopher Lloyd
Outstanding Writing in a Comedy Series: Ken Estin, "Elegant Iggy"

**1982-83**  Outstanding Lead Actor in a Comedy Series: Judd Hirsch
Outstanding Supporting Actress in a Comedy Series:
  Carol Kane
Outstanding Supporting Actor in a Comedy Series:
  Christopher Lloyd

# CHEERS

·

*In* Cheers, *nobody slips on the banana peel.*
—JIM BURROWS, director and
executive producer of *Cheers*

IN THE GLORY DAYS OF 1974, Glen and Les Charles knew that there was simply no better place to spend a Saturday night than in front of the TV.

For a brief spell during the glory days of the early 1970s, the benevolent programmers at CBS had thoughtfully scheduled *All in the Family*, *M\*A\*S\*H*, and *both* the *Bob Newhart* and the *Mary Tyler Moore* shows to run back-to-back, one right after the other, each and every Saturday night. For confirmed fans of situation comedy, the network's Saturday evening schedule would provide a particularly exhilarating evening's entertainment. But for the two brothers who would one day mastermind *Cheers*, watching that lineup of television would prove to be nothing less than a revelation.

Back then, Glen was an advertising copywriter, and Les worked part-time as a junior high school teacher. They had no experience in television, but both recognized the quiet revolution that was taking place in our living rooms in the early 1970s. After a mindless decade of witches, genies, and talking horses, television suddenly seemed capable of delivering bright, literate comedy that you could laugh at without feeling embarrassed. It was a time when many of the funniest writers in show business had chosen television as their preferred medium of expression.

To Glen and Les Charles, writing for TV seemed like a perfectly plausible alternative to the deadend careers they'd each fallen into. Getting paid lots of money to write scripts that made people laugh—well, how hard could that really be?

And with no more preparation than that, they sat down and began to write.

"We were so eager to get into the business," recalled Les Charles, "we wrote a script for every comedy on the air. Then we started in on dramas." Within a few months they had submitted full scripts—unsolicited, on speculation—to every major program supplier in Hollywood. "We blanketed the town with spec scripts."

Glen Charles later remarked, incredulously, "We even wrote a spec script for *Gunsmoke!*"

But, unlike thousands of other hopeful young writers who've employed that gambit before and since, the brothers' efforts took a fairy-tale twist when one of their scripts found its way to a story editor's desk at MTM Productions and landed them a job. By chance, there happened to be a couple of immediate openings on *Phyllis*—a troubled *Mary Tyler Moore* spinoff that had recently undergone a major format overhaul—and the brothers were hired to write for the show. And it would not be long before they found themselves producing the series.

On their first major assignment, the writers had lucked into a golden opportunity to learn the TV business from the inside out. As fate would have it, one of the key directors on *Phyllis* was Jim Burrows, a soft-spoken man who shared the brothers' low-key sense of humor. And by odd coincidence, he, too, had been lured to Hollywood by the siren song of *The Mary Tyler Moore Show*.

The son of Pulitzer Prize-winning playwright Abe Burrows, James had stage-managed Mary Tyler Moore's ill-fated 1967 Broadway debut in *Holly Golightly*. Years later, after Mary returned to television in her own hit series, Burrows wrote a letter congratulating the star on her new success. The letter found its way to the desk of Mary's then-husband, Grant Tinker, who was running MTM at that time. Always on the lookout for new talent, the executive offered the bright young stage manager a job as a novice director at MTM.

Tinker's instincts were right on target. Burrows proved to be a quick study—before long he was directing episodes of MTM's top comedies, including *Phyllis*, *Rhoda*, and *The Bob Newhart Show*. His work drew compliments from the company's top creators, including James L. Brooks, Ed. Weinberger, Stan Daniels, and David Davis—all of whom were about to split off from MTM to produce shows under their own banner. When they left, they asked Burrows—and the Charles brothers—to come along to help write, produce, and direct a new comedy series called *Taxi*.

One of the finest comedies of the late 1970s, *Taxi* proved a worthy heir to the MTM legacy—due, in no small part, to the contributions of Burrows and the Charles brothers. "It was a great experience," Les Charles remembered. Between them, Burrows and the Charles brothers wrote, produced, or directed nearly every episode of the show's first three seasons. But finally, the talented threesome longed to move on.

"It just wasn't *our* show," Les Charles explained. "We felt we were ready to do something of our own."

Apparently, so did Brandon Tartikoff. The young NBC programming chief fancied himself a connoisseur of TV comedy, and he made it a point to keep careful tabs on the industry's most promising writers and directors. Naturally, when Tartikoff heard that the director and head writers of *Taxi* had formed their own production company, he urged his boss, NBC honcho Fred Silverman, to grab them—before somebody else did.

Silverman didn't hesitate to heed his top programmer's advice. He snagged Charles, Burrows, and Charles by offering to finance their first series—with a guarantee that NBC would buy no fewer than thirteen episodes, regardless of the show's initial ratings. It was a promise that the executive would not personally carry out. In 1981—no longer the golden boy of network television—Fred Silverman was ousted from the presidency of NBC.

In his place, the network appointed Grant Tinker.

"We're looking for *quality*" was the new NBC president's edict to programmers and producers alike. After a decade of producing many of the finest shows in prime time at MTM Productions, Tinker declared his intention to apply those same high standards to the program practices of an entire broadcast network. And Charles, Burrows, and Charles were delighted when the executive chose to inaugurate his new policy by giving the green light to the show they'd been brainstorming for well over a year by then—a comedy set in a bar called Cheers.

"We wanted to do an ensemble show, like *M*A*S*H* or *Taxi*, rather than a family story," Glen Charles told *TV Guide*. "At first we thought of setting it in a hotel, to bring a lot of different types of people together." But when they realized that most of the show's action would take place in the bar, they dropped the hotel premise entirely and moved the show to a neighborhood saloon in Boston. As Les Charles observed, "It's much easier to write when you put all your characters in one room. Anytime you need a joke, you've got someone there who can do it."

On *Taxi*, Burrows and the brothers Charles had learned that atmosphere was a key ingredient in a character-driven comedy, and so they were determined that Cheers would look, sound—and even smell—just like a genuine neighborhood watering hole. Glen Charles even traveled to the Bull and Finch—an actual tavern on the Boston Commons—to find a model for the working bar that they would construct on a soundstage at Paramount Studios.

The ensemble cast was assembled with no less attention to detail. The denizens of *Cheers* would be comprised of a cast of experienced players—most of them new to series television—who would immediately meld into a close-knit ensemble. Rhea Perlman, who'd been Louie De Palma's girlfriend for three years on *Taxi*, landed the part of the bar's wisecracking waitress Carla. George Wendt and John Ratzenberger were cast as Cheers's steadiest customers—Norm, a rotund and harmless boozer; and Cliff, a proud U.S. Mail carrier who dazzled no one with his bottomless font of useless knowledge. Finally, Nick Colasanto was chosen to play Coach Ernie Pantusso, the addled but avuncular bartender who afforded the show's usually sardonic proceedings an irresistibly soft center.

But it was the central relationship played out by Shelley Long and Ted Danson that provided the producers with their greatest challenge. "We wanted to create a show around a Katharine Hepburn/Spencer Tracy-type relationship," Burrows told a *New York Times* reporter. Perhaps. But in creating the discordant pairing of Sam and Diane, the producers were at least equally inspired by the benign friendship of *The Mary Tyler Moore Show*'s Mary Richards and Lou Grant.

As longtime fans of *The Mary Tyler Moore Show*, Glen and Les Charles were always frustrated that the news director and his associate producer were never allowed an opportunity to let their underlying passion surface throughout seven seasons of that classic series. "Lou and Mary were essentially the same at the end as they were at the beginning. We didn't want that," Les Charles insisted. "Our key concern was not to get stuck in a rut. We didn't want to set up a situation and just ride it out for however long the show was on."

There was certainly no danger of that. From their very first meeting in *Cheers*'s premiere episode, it's almost impossible to keep up with Sam and Diane as they set off on the maddeningly convoluted path that the producers have mapped out for them.

Abandoned at Cheers while her fiancé goes off to find a wedding ring, Diane is both repelled and enchanted by the uncouth bartender whose girlfriends casually call to remind him that he's "a magnificent pagan beast." The evening doesn't end until Diane has spent what is easily the most hellish—and exciting—night of her life.

When she finally faces the harsh truth—that her would-be suitor *has* stranded her at Cheers—the prim English Lit major immediately reverts into just another poor wretch "with no one in the world to turn to but some stranger who mixes drinks." Naturally, Sam takes advantage of the opening to launch the first assault in what will become prime time's most protracted seduction. Leaning over the bar, he tenders a job offer, confident that she'll accept, since the phrase "magnificent pagan beast" has never left her mind.

And, despite her protests, there's a glint in Diane's eye that tells us he's right—it hasn't.

It was a remarkable beginning. Funny, unpredictable, sophisticated—and a dismal failure in the ratings. "It looked pretty bleak for a while," Glen Charles commented, recalling the show's early ratings. "The one encouraging thing was that the people at the network were very much fans of the show."

Grant Tinker and Brandon Tartikoff were still convinced that NBC could capture an audience by taking the high road to prime time. For them, *Cheers* had become a source of personal, as well as professional, pride. Both executives *watched* the show. They both *liked* the show. So, despite barely measurable ratings, there was no way they could *cancel* the show—not after the quality-programming campaign they'd pitched to their eager affiliate stations.

In October the executives held their breath and ordered the nine additional episodes needed to round out a full season of *Cheers*. They were confident that the show would find its audience by the end of the season. It had to.

Eventually, it did—if only by a nose.

Buoyed by a barrage of favorable press and excellent word of mouth—once viewers finally did tune in, they almost invariably became loyal, nearly evangelical fans—*Cheers* inched its way up the Nielsen chart throughout the rest of the season, a few agonizing points at a time. Finally, in August, after a flood of Emmy nominations proffered the industry's official endorsement, Tinker's faith in the series was vindicated when—to the amazement of skeptics throughout the industry—*Cheers* finally broke into Nielsen's top ten.

But for Jim Burrows and the brothers Charles, the ratings breakthrough and the cartload of Emmy nominations the series gathered for its first season represented only one measure of success. Not long after they began production on the show's second season, Glen and Les Charles discovered a very different—but no less significant—indication that they must be doing something right.

They noticed a large pile of *Cheers* sample scripts stacked near their secretary's desk. Many had been submitted—on spec—from hopeful young writers who had obviously watched the show and been inspired enough to take a crack at writing an episode themselves. Getting paid lots of money to write scripts that made people laugh—well, how hard could that really be?

The two brothers, who certainly knew the answer, could only chuckle as they returned to work on the next *Cheers* script.

# A Critical Guide to All 270 Episodes

SUPPORTING CAST

| | |
|---|---|
| Esther Clavin | Frances Sternhagen |
| Nick Tortelli | Dan Hedaya |
| Loretta Tortelli | Jean Kasem |
| Anthony Tortelli | Timothy Williams |
| Annie Tortelli | Mandy Ingber |
| Gino Tortelli | Josh Lozoff |
| Serafina Tortelli | Leah Remini |
| Eddie LeBec | Jay Thomas |
| Evan Drake | Tom Skerritt |
| Robin Colcord | Roger Rees |
| Don Santry | Tom Berenger |
| Margaret O'Keefe | Annie Golden |
| John Allen Hill | Keene Curtis |
| Mr. Gaines | Richard Doyle |
| Dr. Sumner Sloan | Michael McGuire |
| Henri Fourchette | Anthony Cistaro |
| Gary | Robert Desiderio, Joel Polis |
| Harry the Hat | Harry Anderson |
| Andy Andy | Derek McGrath |
| Father Barry | Eric Christmas |
| Bud, the Fire Inspector | Robert Machrey |

Created by Les Charles, James Burrows, Glen Charles
Music by Craig Safan
Theme ("Where Everybody Knows Your Name") by Judy Hart Angelo,
   Gary Portnoy, sung by Gary Portnoy
Director of photography was John Finger
Principal director was James Burrows

## 1982-83    THE FIRST SEASON

*Year-End Rating: 13.1 (75th place)*

The friendliest bar in Boston opens its doors to a comic assortment of chronic misfits and eccentric regulars in a first year written under the careful supervision of Glen Charles, Les Charles, and first-year co-producers Ken Levine and David Isaacs. Along with executive story editor David Lloyd, they will contribute the bulk of scripts for the first season.

The freshman year is produced by Glen Charles, James Burrows, and Les Charles. Burrows also directs every episode, as he will—with a few exceptions—for each of the seasons to follow. Tim Berry is the series's associate producer.

**1   Give Me a Ring Sometime**                    September 30, 1982
**Writers:** Glen Charles, Les Charles
**Director:** James Burrows
**Guest Stars:** Michael McGuire, John P. Navin, Jr., Erik Holland, Ron Frazier

On the eve of her intended elopement, Diane Chambers sits on a Cheers barstool and watches her life crumble before her eyes.

"Where better than here to study life in all its facets?" Diane asks, rationalizing why she has stooped to accept Sam's offer of a job as a cocktail waitress. "People meet in bars, they part, they rejoice, they suffer, they come here to be with their own kind."

It's a flimsy rationale from a perennial student who is suddenly confronted with the fact that her entire life has prepared her for nothing more challenging than serving drinks in a bar. In her shallow appraisal of Cheers, Diane even misses the irony that Sam and the gang have offered her sanctuary—even though they have just met—while the man with whom she planned to spend her life didn't think twice about dumping her on their doorstep. Though she complains that her stay at Cheers is a form of purgatory, Diane, too, has come to Cheers to be with her own kind. She just doesn't know it yet.

**2   Sam's Women**                    October 7, 1982
**Writer:** Earl Pomerantz
**Director:** James Burrows
**Guest Stars:** Donna McKechnie, Donnelly Rhodes, Angela Aames

Diane chides Sam for dating women of limited intellect; and a visitor to Cheers demands to speak to the former owner.

The show's producers were well acquainted with writer Earl Pomerantz from his many contributions to *Taxi* during their own tenure on the series.

**3**   The Tortelli Tort                        October 14, 1982
**Writer:** Tom Reeder
**Director:** James Burrows
**Guest Stars:** Ron Karabatsos, Stephen Keep

Sam is slammed with a lawsuit after Carla assaults an outspoken Yankees fan who dared to wander into Cheers.

**4**   Sam at Eleven                          October 21, 1982
**Writers:** Glen Charles, Les Charles
**Director:** James Burrows
**Guest Stars:** Fred Dryer, Harry Anderson, Rick Dees, Julie Brown

During a TV interview with a local sportscaster, Sam reveals how much he misses the spotlight of his major-league days.

The loudmouth sportscaster was played by Fred Dryer, who, along with film star William Devane, had been a contender for the role of Sam Malone in *Cheers's* original casting sessions.

**5**   The Coach's Daughter                   October 28, 1982
**Writer:** Ken Estin
**Director:** James Burrows
**Guest Stars:** Allyce Beasley, Philip Charles MacKenzie, Tim Cunningham

Coach meets his daughter's fiancé, an obnoxious salesman who's so thoroughly detestable that even the Coach can't stand him.

Philip Charles MacKenzie would become better known as the flighty Donald on *Brothers*, cable TV's first sitcom; and Allyce Beasley found much greater renown as Miss DiPesto, the gal Friday of *Moonlighting*.

**6**   Any Friend of Diane's                  November 4, 1982
**Writers:** Ken Levine, David Isaacs
**Director:** James Burrows
**Guest Stars:** Julia Duffy, Macon McCalman

An old school chum of Diane's arrives at Cheers and hankers for an afternoon of lustful abandon with Sam.

Julia Duffy, who, along with film star Lisa Eichhorn was one of the actresses considered for the part of Diane in the series's early development, soon landed the plumb role of Stephanie, the self-absorbed maid on *Newhart*.

**7** Friends, Romans, Accountants                     November 11, 1982
**Writers:** Ken Levine, David Isaacs
**Director:** James Burrows
**Guest Stars:** James Read, Kenneth Kimmins, Peter Van Norden

After a disastrous office party at Cheers, Norm tries to score points with his boss by fixing him up with Diane.

Norm succeeds only in losing his job—which helps explain how he was able to spend so much time at the bar. Norm, *Cheers's* all-purpose underachiever, was based on a real-life guzzler Les Charles remembered from his days as a bartender in college.

**8** Truce or Consequences                     November 18, 1982
**Writers:** Ken Levine, David Isaacs
**Director:** James Burrows
**Guest Star:** Jack Knight

Carla calls a truce with Diane to reveal a shocking secret.

**9** The Coach Returns to Action                     November 25, 1982
**Writer:** Earl Pomerantz
**Director:** James Burrows
**Guest Star:** Murphy Cross

Sam participates in an unwitting rivalry with Coach when both have designs on the same woman.

**10** Endless Slumper                     December 2, 1982
**Writer:** Sam Simon
**Director:** James Burrows
**Guest Stars:** Christopher McDonald, Anne Haney

Sam becomes an accident-prone wreck after he lends his good-luck charm to a Red Sox pitcher who's stuck in a slump.

**11**    One for the Book                    December 9, 1982
  **Writer:** Katharine Green
  **Director:** James Burrows
  **Guest Stars:** Boyd Bodwell, Ian Wolfe

An aging doughboy holds a lonely World War I reunion in Cheers; and a novice monk comes looking for one last night of debauchery before he checks into the monastery.

**12**    The Spy Who Came in for a Cold One    December 16,1982
  **Writer:** David Lloyd
  **Director:** James Burrows
  **Guest Stars:** Ellis Rabb, Robert Evan Collins, Kurtis Woodruff

The gang at Cheers copes with an inveterate liar who's convinced Diane that he's a poet, while Carla is certain he's really a spy.

**13**    Now Pitching: Sam Malone              January 6, 1983
  **Writers:** Ken Levine, David Isaacs
  **Director:** James Burrows
  **Guest Stars:** Barbara Babcock, Luis Tiant, Richard Hill, Paul Vaughn

Sam feels used when an attractive theatrical agent lands him a string of lucrative commercial endorsements in exchange for his romantic favors.

After Diane and Sam debate the barkeeper's options, Coach arrives to offer Sam his own no-nonsense solution—along with a well-placed kick in the pants. For all his confusion, the simple-minded Coach was often the only person in Cheers capable of straightforward thought. Glen and Les Charles admitted that their model for Coach Ernie Pantusso was baseball's legendary Yogi Berra, who was also well known for the peculiar logic of his public utterances.

**14**    Let Me Count the Ways                January 13, 1983
  **Writer:** Heide Perlman
  **Director:** James Burrows
  **Guest Stars:** Mark King, Jack Knight, Steve Hanafin

Distraught over the death of her housecat, Diane finds few shoulders to cry on at Cheers during a Celtics game.

The script, the first of many written by Rhea Perlman's sister, Heide, opens with a precredit "teaser" scene, as did every episode of the series. Here, Diane arrives, bursting with enthusiasm after attending an Indian film festival—only to leave screaming in abject defeat a moment later, after Coach and Carla describe their own favorite Indian film, *Fort Apache*. Given the soap-operatic overtones of the show's continuing narrative line, the producers designed the opening teaser as a hook that would serve as an instant introduction to the show and its characters for the uninitiated—a useful weapon in the uphill ratings battle the series faced during the first year.

**15** Father Knows Last                           January 20, 1983
   **Writer:** Heide Perlman
   **Director:** James Burrows
   **Guest Stars:** Mark King, Jack Knight

Diane attempts to prevent an injustice when Carla schemes to convince an unwitting computer programmer that he's the father of her baby.

**16** The Boys in the Bar                          January 27, 1983
   **Writers:** Ken Levine, David Isaacs
   **Director:** James Burrows
   **Guest Stars:** Alan Autry, Harry Anderson, John Furey, Michael Kearns, Kenneth Tigar, Lee Ryan, Jack Knight, Tom Babson

After Sam publicly supports an old teammate who has just come out of the closet, the regulars are convinced that Cheers is turning into a trendy gay hangout.

**17** Diane's Perfect Date                        February 10, 1983
   **Writer:** David Lloyd
   **Director:** James Burrows
   **Guest Stars:** Derek McGrath, Gretchen Corbett, Doug Sheehan

Sam unwittingly fixes Diane up with a man who was just released from a prison for the criminally insane.

The date begins when the ex-offender refuses to eat in an Italian restaurant where he once killed a waitress—and goes downhill from there. Andy Andy would return to Cheers about once a year over the next few seasons.

**18**    No Contest                              February 17, 1983
  **Writer:** Heide Perlman
  **Director:** James Burrows
  **Guest Stars:** Charlie Stavola, Renee Gentry, Paul Vaughn,
  Thomas "Tip" O'Neill, Tessa Richarde, Sharon Peters

Diane attempts to sabotage the Miss Boston Barmaid contest after
she discovers that Sam entered her in the competition without her
knowledge.

The cameo appearance of Bostonian *Cheers* fan, Speaker of the House
Thomas "Tip" O'Neill, was a stunt designed to draw attention—and viewers—to the show during the first fledgling season.


**19**    Pick a Con. . . Any Con                 February 24, 1983
  **Writer:** David Angell
  **Director:** James Burrows
  **Guest Stars:** Harry Anderson, Reid Shelton

Sam convinces Cheers's resident con man to stage an elaborate
sting to retrieve Coach's money from a traveling card shark.

Stand-up comic and magician Harry Anderson—soon to be the star of
*Night Court*—was typecast as Harry the con man.


**20**    Someone Single, Someone Blue              March 3, 1983
  **Writer:** David Angell
  **Director:** James Burrows
  **Guest Stars:** Glynis Johns, Duncan Ross, Dean Dittman, Paul
  Willson

Diane and Sam plan a marriage of convenience to protect her
mother's fortunes from a bizarre stipulation in her late father's will.

Diane's mother is played by British stage and film actress Glynis Johns,
in the first *Cheers* episode scripted by David Angell, who would become
one of the show's chief contributors.

**21**   Showdown (Part 1)                            March 24, 1983
**Writers:** Glen Charles, Les Charles
**Director:** James Burrows
**Guest Stars:** George Ball, Alan Koss, Paul Vaughn, Deborah
Shelton

Sam can't conceal his resentment of his visiting brother—a rich and
talented charmer with something to offer everyone, especially
Diane.

**22**   Showdown (Part 2)                            March 31, 1983
**Writers:** Glen Charles, Les Charles
**Director:** James Burrows
**Guest Stars:** Lois DeBanzie, Helen Page Camp, Peggy Kubena

Sam's brother sweeps Diane off her feet with an invitation to Paris,
but the waitress finds it harder to leave Cheers than she imagined.

"We didn't want to have two people just flirting with each other ad
infinitum," explained Les Charles. So he and his brother, Glen, planned
this season's finale—a quirky cliff-hanger that ends with the lovers poised
on the brink of consummating their season-long tryst. It's an unlikely
romantic encounter that begins when Sam pledges his feelings under
duress—Diane has threatened to run her fingernails on the chalkboard
if he doesn't—and ends with the lovers locked in a violent embrace. At
least for the time being.

## 1983-84   THE SECOND SEASON

*Year-End Rating: 16.6 (34th place)*

Sam and Diane's well-contained passion finally bubbles to the surface when the pair form a tentative romantic alliance during the second
season. Once again, the producers are Glen Charles, James Burrows, and
Les Charles. The second-year story editors are David Angell and Heide
Perlman. David Lloyd serves as executive script consultant, a function
he will serve throughout most of the show's remaining seasons.

**23**   Power Play                                  September 29, 1983
   **Writers:** Glen Charles, Les Charles
   **Director:** James Burrows
   **Guest Stars:** Alan Koss, Paul Vaughn

The gang at Cheers doesn't hold much hope for Sam and Diane's newly blossomed romance after Sam returns to Cheers early on the night of their first date.

"You've made my life a living hell," Sam complains, brushing aside the stuffed toys that litter the scene of their intended carnal pleasure. "I didn't want you to think I was easy," Diane retorts, setting the comic tone for the bumpy romance that ensues throughout the second season. The show's loyal fans were delighted to see Sam and Diane in each other's arms at last, but the couple's petty insecurities and power plays nearly doom the affair before it's begun.

**24**   Little Sister, Don'tcha                     October 13, 1983
   **Writer:** Heide Perlman
   **Director:** James Burrows
   **Guest Stars:** Paul Vaughn, Paul Willson, Jerry Prell

Cliff falls for Carla's identical twin, a mousy woman who's actually more like her sister than anyone guesses.

Early on, Coach proclaims Cheers "a romantic bar. As many people fall in love here as get sick." But before the night is over, it's Cliff and Norm who declare their devotion—to each other! After Norm warns Cliff away from Carla's sister, the bewildered postman confesses that Normie is the best friend he's ever had—though the two do stop short of actually hugging. As Cliff points out, it's not like Norm pulled him from a burning car or anything. Rhea Perlman also plays Carla's twin sister, Annette Lozupone.

**25**   Personal Business                           October 20, 1983
   **Writer:** Tom Reeder
   **Director:** James Burrows

Norm and Diane each decide to expand their horizons, but for very different reasons.

**26**   Homicidal Ham                                          October 27, 1983
   **Writer:** David Lloyd
   **Director:** James Burrows
   **Guest Stars:** Severn Darden, Derek McGrath, Paul Vaughn,
   Alan Koss

Andy Andy returns to Cheers with a new career goal—he wants to
be an actor.

Diane's criminally maladjusted blind date is up to his old tricks when
he performs a strikingly realistic interpretation of the murder scene from
*Othello*, with Diane as his unsuspecting Desdemona.

**27**   Sumner's Return                                        November 3, 1983
   **Writer:** Michael J. Weithorn
   **Director:** James Burrows
   **Guest Star:** Michael McGuire

To compete with Diane's brainy former beau, Sam tries to finish
*War and Peace* in five days.

**28**   Affairs of the Heart                                   November 10, 1983
   **Writer:** Heide Perlman
   **Director:** James Burrows
   **Guest Star:** Don Amendolia

Carla rebuffs her latest suitor, convinced that any guy who's interested in her must have something wrong with him.

**29**   Old Flames                                             November 17, 1983
   **Writer:** David Angell
   **Director:** James Burrows
   **Guest Stars:** Fred Dryer, Elizabeth McIvor

An overbearing sportscaster wagers that he can put an end to Sam
and Diane's romance within twenty-four hours.

**30**   Manager Coach                                          November 24, 1983
   **Writer:** Earl Pomerantz
   **Director:** James Burrows
   **Guest Stars:** Herb Mitchell, Elliott Scott, Corey Feldman,
   Martin Davis

Coach undergoes a startling personality transformation when he
volunteers to manage a Little League team.

**31**   They Called Me Mayday                    December 1, 1983
   **Writer:** David Angell
   **Director:** James Burrows
   **Guest Stars:** Dick Cavett, Walter Olkewicz, Ed Quinlan

Dick Cavett inspires Sam to write his memoirs; and Norm fumes when Vera dates his old high-school rival.

Broke, unemployed, and homeless after his separation from Vera, Norm has evolved into an almost heroically pathetic character. At his lowest ebb, he actually takes up full-time residence in his home-away-from-home when he secretly camps out in Sam's office after closing hours.

**32**   How Do I Love Thee, Let Me               December 8, 1983
         Call You Back
   **Writer:** Earl Pomerantz
   **Director:** James Burrows
   **Guest Star:** Harry Anderson

Diane insists on a week's separation from Sam to allow them both time to reevaluate the depth of their commitment.

**33**   Just Three Friends                       December 15, 1983
   **Writer:** David Lloyd
   **Director:** James Burrows
   **Guest Star:** Markie Post

Diane refuses to believe that her best friend finds Sam completely irresistible.

**34**   Where There's a Will                     December 22, 1983
   **Writer:** Nick Arnold
   **Director:** James Burrows
   **Guest Stars:** George Gaynes, Alan Koss

The gang at Cheers lifts the gloom of a terminally ill customer, and in return he leaves them $10,000 in a hastily scrawled will.

**35**   Battle of the Exes                       January 5, 1984
   **Writers:** Ken Estin, Sam Simon
   **Director:** James Burrows
   **Guest Stars:** Dan Hedaya, Jean Kasem

Carla's insensitive ex-husband invites her to his wedding, which she attends with Sam in tow.

Dan Hedaya gives flesh to the previously only imagined horrors of Carla's ex-husband, Nick Tortelli, who would soon develop semi-regular status in the Cheers cosmos.

**36   No Help Wanted**                              January 12, 1984
  **Writer:** Max Tash
  **Director:** James Burrows
  **Guest Star:** Barbra Horan

Feeling sorry for Norm, Sam reluctantly hires the unemployed accountant to do Cheers's income tax return.

**37   And Coachie Makes Three**                     January 19, 1984
  **Writer:** Heide Perlman
  **Director:** James Burrows
  **Guest Star:** Eve Roberts

When Coach begins to spend his every waking moment with Sam and Diane, they decide to fix him up with an eligible woman of his own.

**38   Cliff's Rocky Moment**                        January 26, 1984
  **Writer:** David Lloyd
  **Director:** James Burrows
  **Guest Stars:** Sam Scarber, Peter Iacangelo

Tired of hearing Cliff's opinions on everything under the sun, a Cheers patron finally challenges the verbose mailman to a fight.

**39   Fortune and Men's Weights**                   February 2, 1984
  **Writer:** Heide Perlman
  **Director:** James Burrows
  **Guest Star:** Tim Cunningham

Diane worries that the uncanny predictions of an antique fortune-teller's scale might end the spell—and spell the end—for her and Sam.

The couple convince themselves that their fate rests on the very next card drawn from the fortune-teller's slot, but the cryptic legend reads, "Machine empty. Order more fortunes today." The screen goes black before they have time to comprehend the message, and we are left on our own to ponder their fate—at least for another week.

As the comedy traces the peaks and valleys in the continuing saga of

Sam and Diane, their epic courtship begins to take on nearly operatic proportions. The show's creators admit a far greater debt to soap opera than Wagner, but still insist they never planned to carry the romance to such extremes when they started. "Initially there was no master plan," Glen Charles confessed, "but when it began to look like the show might actually stay on the air a second year, we knew we'd have to chart their relationship over a period of time. Now, at the start of every year, we sit down and figure out where we want Sam and Diane to be at the beginning, the middle, and the end of the season."

**40**    Snow Job                              February 9, 1984
   **Writer:** David Angell
   **Director:** James Burrows
   **Guest Star:** James Gallery

Cliff is jealous of Norm's new friendship; and Sam concocts a farfetched story so that he can slip away for a weekend skiing trip in Vermont.

**41**    Coach Buries a Grudge                  February 16, 1984
   **Writer:** David Lloyd
   **Director:** James Burrows

Coach mourns the passing of an old friend until he discovers that the cad was once romantically involved with his wife.

**42**    Norman's Conquest                      February 23, 1984
   **Writer:** Lissa Levin
   **Director:** James Burrows
   **Guest Star:** Anne Schedeen

The guys egg Norm into making a play for an attractive woman who's hired him to audit her books.

**43**    I'll Be Seeing You (Part 1)               May 3, 1984
   **Writers:** Glen Charles, Les Charles
   **Director:** James Burrows
   **Guest Stars:** Christopher Lloyd, Steve Giannelli

A temperamental artist offers to paint Diane's portrait, convinced that he can reveal the inner turmoil that Sam has inflicted on her soul.

Christopher Lloyd, late of *Taxi*, plays Philip Semenko, the haughty painter who comes between Sam and Diane.

**44**   I'll Be Seeing You (Part 2)                    May 10, 1984
   **Writers:** Glen Charles, Les Charles
   **Director:** James Burrows
   **Guest Star:** Christopher Lloyd

Diane jeopardizes her relationship with Sam when she poses for a portrait against Sam's express wishes.

Once again, the Charles brothers script a darkly funny season finale. This one ends with the lovers pitched in a nose-pulling, slapstick stand-off that's as harrowing as it is hilarious. "This is it!" Diane declares in comic desperation. "We have sunk as low as two human beings can sink. There is no degradation left!" Only after she's stormed out of Cheers for good does Sam allow himself to be taken in by the fragile melancholy of her oil portrait. In the episode's final, sad moment, the barman—who rebelled so violently against Diane's cultural superiority—now finds his only solace in the quiet appreciation of a work of art.

## 1984-85   THE THIRD SEASON

*Year-End Rating: 19.7 (13th place)*

*Cheers's* love story forms a triangle in the third season when Kelsey Grammer is introduced as Diane's new beloved, Dr. Frasier Crane. Producers for the third year are Ken Estin and Sam Simon; Heide Perlman is the season's executive story consultant; and David Angell serves as executive story editor. Glen Charles, James Burrows, and Les Charles will serve as executive producers for the remainder of the series's run.

**45**   Rebound (Part 1)                        September 27, 1984
   **Writers:** Glen Charles, Les Charles
   **Director:** James Burrows
   **Guest Stars:** Kelsey Grammer, Duncan Ross

Coach tries to reunite Sam and Diane after he sees the shambles their lives have become in the wake of their soured romance.

In flashback, Cliff reveals how Sam and Diane spent their summer vacation: Sam went back to the bottle and has emerged a boorish drunk, while Diane spent her hiatus in a rest home after a nervous breakdown. Though alcoholism and mental instability seem unlikely subjects for comedy, the wisecracking gang at Cheers keeps the bleaker aspects of this latest wrinkle in comic perspective. Diane also reveals a newly blossomed romance with her hapless psychoanalyst, Frasier Crane, played by Kelsey Grammer—who makes his debut as *Cheers's* latest regular character in this episode.

**46**    Rebound (Part 2)                              October 4, 1984
   **Writers:** Glen Charles, Les Charles
   **Director:** James Burrows
   **Guest Stars:** P.J. Soles, Kelsey Grammer

Diane's analyst helps Sam get back on the wagon; and Diane reluctantly returns to Cheers.

**47**    I Call Your Name                              October 18, 1984
   **Writers:** Peter Casey, David Lee
   **Director:** James Burrows
   **Guest Star:** Sam Scarber

Frasier turns the tables on his patient when he seeks advice from Sam; and Cliff faces the wrath of a vengeful co-worker.

**48**    Fairy Tales Can Come True                     October 25, 1984
   **Writer:** Sam Simon
   **Director:** James Burrows
   **Guest Star:** Bernadette Birkett

Cliff attends a masquerade party dressed as a suave ladykiller and discovers that sometimes clothes do make the man.

**49**    Sam Turns the Other Cheek                     November 1, 1984
   **Writer:** David Lloyd
   **Director:** James Burrows
   **Guest Stars:** Kim Lankford, Carmen Argenziano

Sam accidentally shoots himself in the rear while tussling with an irate husband and then builds his blunder into a tale of barside valor.

**50**    Coach in Love (Part 1)                        November 8, 1984
   **Writer:** David Angell
   **Director:** James Burrows
   **Guest Stars:** Bette Ford, Ellen Regan

Coach and Sam make a play for a mother and daughter who wander into Cheers—and by the end of the evening, Coach finds himself engaged.

**51**   Coach in Love (Part 2)         November 15, 1984
**Writer:** David Angell
**Director:** James Burrows
**Guest Star:** Bette Ford

Coach refuses to believe that his new fiancée has dumped him just because she won a fortune in the state lottery.

**52**   Diane Meets Mom         November 22,1984
**Writer:** David Lloyd
**Director:** James Burrows
**Guest Star:** Nancy Marchand

Diane encounters unexpected wrath when she meets Frasier's mother for the first time.

**53**   An American Family         November 29, 1984
**Writer:** Heide Perlman
**Director:** James Burrows
**Guest Stars:** Dan Hedaya, Jean Kasem

Carla is unexpectedly cooperative when her loutish ex-husband returns to demand custody of their son.

**54**   Diane's Allergy         December 6, 1984
**Writer:** David Lloyd
**Director:** James Burrows

Diane is convinced that the source of her sudden acute allergy can only be Frasier.

**55**   Peterson Crusoe         December 13, 1984
**Writer:** David Angell
**Director:** James Burrows
**Guest Stars:** Howard Goodwin, Michael Griswold, John Marzilli

Diane bests Carla in an extemporaneous waitress competition; and Norm decides to chuck it all and start a new life in Bora Bora.

**56**   A Ditch in Time                    December 20, 1984
   **Writer:** Ken Estin
   **Director:** James Burrows
   **Guest Stars:** Carol Kane, Larry Harpel

Despite Diane's warnings, Sam gets involved with an unbalanced young woman who makes marriage plans after their very first date.

**57**   Whodunit?                          January 3, 1985
   **Writer:** Tom Reeder
   **Director:** James Burrows
   **Guest Stars:** James Karen, Kelsey Grammer, Ernie Sabella

Frasier is appalled when one of his most respected colleagues admits that he's smitten with Carla.

After rebuffing the professor's advances and, finally, his proposal of marriage, the flinty barmaid offers a sad and sweet description of the white knight she's certain will one day walk through Cheers's door. Sweet, because it reveals the Tasmanian devil of a waitress as a misty-eyed dreamer; and sad, because—with a few minor adjustments—the man she describes could be Sam.

**58**   The Heart Is a Lonely Snipe Hunter      January 10, 1985
   **Writer:** Heide Perlman
   **Director:** James Burrows
   **Guest Stars:** Alan Koss, Tim Cunningham, Kelsey Grammer

Diane pressures the guys into taking Frasier along on a camping trip, where they can't resist having a little fun at the gullible psychiatrist's expense.

**59**   King of the Hill                    January 24, 1985
   **Writer:** Elliot Shoenman
   **Director:** James Burrows
   **Guest Stars:** John Hancock, David Paymer, Larry Harpel, Steve Giannelli

Sam reveals a vicious competitive streak when he returns to the mound in a charity ball game and then wages a marathon Ping-Pong match with Diane.

**60**   Teacher's Pet                              January 31, 1985
   **Writer:** Tom Reeder
   **Director:** James Burrows

While Coach studies diligently for a night school course, Sam discovers that his own grade-point average rises sharply once he begins dating the teacher.

**61**   The Mail Goes to Jail                      February 7, 1985
   **Writer:** David Lloyd
   **Director:** James Burrows
   **Guest Stars:** Debi Richter, Troy Evans, Nick De Mauro, Al Rosen

Norm is charged with postal theft after he substitutes on Cliff's route as a favor to the ailing postman; and Diane gets wedged into a broken heating vent.

Trapping Diane in an air duct was one of the more creative solutions concocted to conceal Shelley Long's blooming pregnancy. The producers toyed with the idea of making Diane Chambers an unwed mother in the third season, until reason prevailed. "I don't think America would have stood for it," explained Glen Charles. "We figured Sam had to be the father, and the more we considered *that*, the less acceptable it seemed."

**62**   Behind Every Great Man                     February 21, 1985
   **Writers:** Ken Levine, David Isaacs
   **Director:** James Burrows
   **Guest Star:** Alison La Placa

For his latest conquest, Sam sets his sights on an attractive reporter who's doing an in-depth survey of the Boston singles scene.

**63**   If Ever I Would Leave You                  February 28, 1985
   **Writers:** Ken Levine, David Isaacs
   **Director:** James Burrows
   **Guest Stars:** Dan Hedaya, Jean Kasem

After his new wife dumps him to go on tour with a singing group called the Grinning Americans, Carla's ex-husband turns over a new leaf to win the waitress back.

**64**    The Executive Executioner                    March 7, 1985
**Writer:** Heide Perlman
**Director:** James Burrows
**Guest Stars:** Richard Roat, Larry Harpel

After Norm is charged with the task of firing one of his fellow employees, he discovers a hidden talent as a corporate hatchet man.

**65**    Bar Bet                                      March 14, 1985
**Writer:** Jim Parker
**Director:** James Burrows
**Guest Stars:** Michael Richards, Laurie Walters, Thomas W. Babson

In the aftermath of a long-forgotten drunken bet, Sam stands to lose Cheers unless he can meet—and marry—Jacqueline Bisset by midnight.

**66**    Cheerio Cheers                               April 11, 1985
**Writer:** Sam Simon
**Director:** James Burrows

Diane decides to leave Cheers when Frasier is offered a job at the University of Bologna.

In a scene that generated more erotic heat than is usually registered on a situation comedy, Sam bids Diane farewell with a good-bye embrace that neither is anxious to release. Though the couple's separation bore the earmarks of classic melodrama, Diane's sudden trip to Europe was actually motivated by the writers' desire to conceal the actress's problematic pregnancy. "We thought it would be easier to sit her down behind sidewalk cafés," confided producer Glen Charles.

**67**    The Bartender's Tale                         April 18, 1985
**Writer:** Sam Simon
**Director:** James Burrows
**Guest Stars:** Lila Kaye, Camilla More, Rhonda Shear, Tim Cunningham

To avoid any more on-the-job romantic entanglements, Carla insists that Sam hire a dowdy older woman as Cheers's new waitress.

**68**   The Belles of Saint Clete's                May 2, 1985
**Writer:** Ken Estin
**Director:** James Burrows
**Guest Stars:** Camila Ashland, Kate Zentall

Carla is hot for revenge when the high school teacher who once made her life miserable wanders into Cheers.

**69**   Rescue Me                May 9, 1985
**Writer:** Ken Estin
**Director:** James Burrows
**Guest Stars:** Martin Ferrero, James V. Christy, Dan Galliani, Susan Kase

Diane calls from Europe, hoping that Sam will talk her out of accepting Frasier's sudden marriage proposal.

## 1985-86   THE FOURTH SEASON

*Year-End Rating: 23.7 (5th place)*

In the fourth year, Woody Harrelson joins *Cheers's* staff as the new bartender, Woody Boyd. Peter Casey and David Lee are the season's producers, along with Heide Perlman and David Angell. Writers Cheri Eichen and Bill Steinkellner are the executive story consultants for season four.

**70**   Birth, Death, Love, and Rice                September 26, 1985
**Writer:** Heide Perlman
**Director:** James Burrows
**Guest Star:** Woody Harrelson

Sam tracks Diane to a convent, where she's taken to scrubbing floors in penance for the reckless debauchery of her recent European spree.

Frasier Crane, dumped by Diane and now at *his* lowest ebb, has finally earned a place at Cheers, where he will spend the better part of the fourth season nursing his wounds.

**71**    Woody Goes Belly Up                    October 3, 1985
   **Writer:** Heide Perlman
   **Director:** James Burrows
   **Guest Star:** Amanda Wyss

Woody begins a mysterious eating binge after his hometown girl-friend pays a surprise visit.

After Nick Colasanto's death in the third season, the producers tackled the delicate challenge of replacing the well-loved actor who had become firmly identified with the role of Cheers's bartender. Newcomer Harrelson's Woody Boyd bore little outward resemblance to Colasanto. Yet, like the Coach before him, the new bartender provided *Cheers* with a marshmallow center that took the sting off the show's occasionally bitter sarcasm. As Les Charles observed, "Our humor tends to have a hard edge. On *Cheers,* if you take that sweet and innocent guy away, it gets a little dark in the bar."

**72**    Someday My Prince Will Come        October 17, 1985
   **Writers:** Tom Seeley, Norman Gunzenhauser
   **Director:** James Burrows
   **Guest Star:** Frank Dent

After she creates a lively fantasy life about the owner of a lost jacket, Diane rashly arranges a blind date with her imagined Prince Charming.

**73**    The Groom Wore Clearasil            October 24, 1985
   **Writers:** Peter Casey, David Lee
   **Director:** James Burrows
   **Guest Stars:** Timothy Williams, Mandy Ingber, John Ingle, Sherilyn Fenn

Carla hopes that the allure of Sam's bachelor lifestyle will dissuade her teenage son from his premature marriage plans.

**74**    Diane's Nightmare                      October 31, 1985
   **Writer:** David Lloyd
   **Director:** James Burrows
   **Guest Stars:** Derek McGrath, Nancy Cartwright

Diane dreams that the ex-con who once tried to strangle her is hiding out in Cheers's cellar.

The long-running saga of Andy Andy apparently comes to an end when the maladjusted murderer returns to Cheers as a healthy and honorable citizen. Alas, as it turns out, the unlikely events are merely part of a dream-within-a-dream that also features Diane's unlikely fantasy of Sam as a culture vulture with a pipe and smoking jacket.

**75    I'll Gladly Pay You Tuesday**                 November 7, 1985
**Writers:** Cheri Eichen, Bill Steinkellner
**Director:** James Burrows
**Guest Star:** William Lanteau

Sam is understandably upset when Diane borrows $500, only to squander the cash on an Ernest Hemingway first edition.

**76    2 Good 2 Be 4 Real**                          November 14, 1985
**Writers:** Peter Casey, David Lee
**Director:** James Burrows
**Guest Stars:** Michael Alaimo, Don Lewis

The guys concoct an imaginary lonely hearts pen pal for Carla, but the ruse backfires when she rejects a real life prospect in favor of her dream date.

**77    Love Thy Neighbor**                           November 21, 1985
**Writer:** David Angell
**Director:** James Burrows
**Guest Stars:** Miriam Flynn, Ernie Sabella, John F. Dryer, Carolyn Ann Clark

Norm and his neighbor's wife jump to conclusions about their spouses; and Diane is incensed when Sam describes her as his "former love bunny" on a radio show.

Even when confronted with his wife's adultery, Norm maintains his usual aplomb, though he does eventually leave his barstool—a sure sign of emotional upheaval for the uncommonly sedentary drinker. The burly accountant actually reveals a wistful side when he tells Woody a tender anecdote about the football game where he first set eyes on the cheer-leader he would one day marry. But Woody is more interested in who won the game—a gag, typical of *Cheers*, that undercuts the sentiment at the precise moment before it grows leaden.

David Angell's script is refreshing in another way. Somehow, he's fashioned a script about adultery without resorting to any of the idiotic clichés that have rescued errant sitcom wives from their husbands' wrath since the dawn of the cathode ray tube: Vera *wasn't* secretly planning Norm's surprise party; she *wasn't* mistakenly overheard rehearsing lines from a play; nor was the man she'd been seeing really a TV producer planning to spotlight Norm on *This Is Your Life*. She actually was planning to cheat on poor Norm, but everything is resolved so that Norm, Vera, and the neighbor's wife are all allowed their full measure of dignity.

**78**   From Beer to Eternity                    November 28, 1985
  **Writers:** Peter Casey, David Lee
  **Director:** James Burrows
  **Guest Star:** Joel Polis

When Woody freezes up during the crucial frame of the Cheers bowling tournament, Diane takes it upon herself to rescue the bar's wounded pride.

**79**   The Barstoolie                           December 5, 1985
  **Writers:** Andy Cowan, David S. Williger
  **Director:** James Burrows
  **Guest Stars:** Dick O'Neill, Claudia Cron

Diane joins Sam and his new girlfriend on their first date; and Cliff is reunited with his long-lost father.

**80**   Don Juan Is Hell                         December 12, 1985
  **Writer:** Phoef Sutton
  **Director:** James Burrows
  **Guest Stars:** Kenneth Tigar, Steve Minor

Sam is flattered when Diane's psychology class observes him as a case study in modern human sexuality.

**81**   Fools and Their Money                    December 19, 1985
  **Writer:** Heide Perlman
  **Director:** James Burrows
  **Guest Stars:** Paul Willson, Al Rosen

Inspired by his success in the Cheers football pool, Woody bets his entire life savings on an impossible long shot.

**82**   Take My Shirt, Please                          January 9, 1986
   **Writer:** David Lloyd
   **Director:** James Burrows
   **Guest Stars:** Robert Symonds, Frances Bey

Sam's ego takes a beating when he donates his retired baseball jersey to a charity auction—and no one bids on it.


**83**   Suspicion                                      January 16, 1986
   **Writer:** Tom Reeder
   **Director:** James Burrows
   **Guest Star:** Hamilton Camp

As part of her latest psychology experiment, Diane dupes the gang at Cheers—and then faces the anxiety of awaiting their certain revenge.


**84**   The Triangle                                   January 23, 1986
   **Writer:** Susan Seeger
   **Director:** James Burrows

To lift Frasier's sagging spirits from a deep depression, Sam and Diane agree to pose as lovers once more—with dire consequences.


**85**   Cliffie's Big Score                            January 30, 1986
   **Writer:** Heide Perlman
   **Director:** James Burrows

Cliff's in double trouble when Diane and Carla each consent to be his date for the mailman's ball.


**86**   Second Time Around                             February 6, 1986
   **Writers:** Cheri Eichen, Bill Steinkellner
   **Director:** Tom Lofaro
   **Guest Stars:** Jennifer Tilly, Bebe Neuwirth, Lou Fant

Sam's campaign to salvage Frasier's shrinking self-respect takes an unexpected turn after the bartender fixes him up with a woman who is guaranteed to be a sure thing.

**87**   The Peterson Principle                February 13, 1986
**Writers:** Peter Casey, David Lee
**Director:** James Burrows
**Guest Stars:** Chip Zien, Daniel Davis

Norm discovers that a co-worker is having an affair with the boss's wife and wonders if he should use the information to gain a promotion.

**88**   Dark Imaginings                February 20, 1986
**Writer:** David Angell
**Director:** James Burrows
**Guest Stars:** Pamela Bach, Tim Dunigan, Christine Dickinson Lisa Vice, Jeré Fields

Sam refuses to acknowledge that he's not as spry as he once was, until he lands in the hospital from injuries he got on the racquetball court.

**89**   Save the Last Dance for Me                February 27, 1986
**Writer:** Heide Perlman
**Director:** James Burrows
**Guest Stars:** Dan Hedaya, Jean Kasem, Hal Landon, Jr., Nick Dimitri, Sinara Stull

Carla wants to win a dance contest in her old neighborhood so badly that she's willing to consider a temporary reunion with her ex-husband, Nick Tortelli.

The writers frequently alluded to Carla's Terpsichorean passion—an enthusiasm shared by actress Rhea Perlman, who regularly devoted one lunch hour a week to tap-dance lessons on the studio lot.

**90**   Fear Is My Co-Pilot                March 13, 1986
**Writers:** Cheri Eichen, Bill Steinkellner
**Director:** James Burrows
**Guest Star:** Joseph Whipp

Sam and Diane get a chance to live dangerously when a daredevil pilot abandons them at the controls of his plane in midair.

**91**   Diane Chambers Day                     March 20, 1986
   **Writer:** Kimberly Hill
   **Director:** James Burrows

To brighten Diane's spirits, the gang at Cheers grudgingly attends an evening at the opera.

**92**   Relief Bartender                       March 27, 1986
   **Writer:** Miriam Trogdon
   **Director:** James Burrows

Sam takes on a new bartender and then reluctantly gives Woody notice when he discovers that he can't afford to keep them both.

**93**   Strange Bedfellows (Part 1)            May 1, 1986
   **Writer:** David Angell
   **Director:** James Burrows
   **Guest Stars:** Kate Mulgrew, David Paymer, Max Wright, Brad Burlingame, Carolyn Ann Clark, Mike Hagerty

Carla and Diane are each concerned when Sam's fling with a brash lady politician starts to develop into something more serious.

Diane had good reason to fret: Kate Mulgrew's Janet Eldridge was the first woman to pose a real threat to her relationship with Sam. "We wanted Sam genuinely involved with someone other than Diane," explained writer Glen Charles. "Rather than just having them *say* they loved each other, we let it run three episodes so that it would mean a little more."

**94**   Strange Bedfellows (Part 2)            May 8, 1986
   **Writer:** David Angell
   **Director:** James Burrows
   **Guest Stars:** Kate Mulgrew, David Paymer, Max Wright, Senator Gary Hart

Janet reveals a jealous streak when she insists that Sam fire Diane and sever his ties with the barmaid once and for all.

The character of strong, confident Janet Eldridge brings out colors we hadn't before seen in Diane—or in Carla either. Rarely have our sympathies for Diane been so deeply felt as when we spy her huddling under the bar after she overhears Sam's resolution to dump her—abandoned and painfully alone. Oddly, Sam echoes a similar emotion in the show's closing moments. After Diane has made the first of her grand exits, he cranes his neck for one last, longing glance at the woman who has haunted his every waking hour for the previous four years.

**95**    Strange Bedfellows (Part 3)                    May 15, 1986
  **Writer:** David Angell
  **Director:** James Burrows
  **Guest Stars:** Kate Mulgrew, David Paymer

After Sam and Diane create a public scene during Janet's press conference, the councilwoman develops serious doubts about her future with the bartender.

Diane stages her most grandiose exit yet in a scene that slyly encapsulates the slapstick sadomasochism that has plagued their relationship from the start. As the TV cameras roll, Diane storms out of the bar—dragging Sam after her by the neck—before she abruptly slams the door on him, and Cheers, forever.
  Or at least until the start of the next season.
  In the show's final moments, Sam picks up the phone to tender a weary marriage proposal to the unseen voice on the other end. Of course, the cliff-hanger leaves us dangling—but few fans of the show were surprised at the top of the fifth year when Sam greeted Diane to replay for another season the sublime agony that only those two seemed to understand.

## 1986-87    THE FIFTH SEASON

*Year-End Rating: 27.2 (3rd place)*

After her fourth-season debut in the role of Frasier's flinty romantic foil, Dr. Lilith Sternin, Bebe Neuwirth becomes a permanent fixture at the bar in season five, which opens with Sam's ill-fated proposal of marriage to Diane—and ends, not surprisingly, with Sam and Diane more than a few steps shy of their proposed trip down the aisle. David Angell, Peter Casey, and David Lee are producers for year five, which is co-produced by Tim Berry. Prominent members of the show's writing staff for the season include executive script consultant Bob Ellison, executive story consultants Cheri Eichen and Bill Steinkellner, story editors Janet Leahy, Phoef Sutton, and Jeff Abugov, and creative consultant Tom Tenowich.

**96** The Proposal               September 25, 1986
**Writers:** Peter Casey, David Lee
**Director:** James Burrows

The gang at Cheers tries to guess the identity of Sam's fiancée-to-be; and the anxious bartender looks for the perfect spot to pop the question once again.

**97** The Cape Cad             October 2, 1986
**Writers:** Andy Cowan, David Williger
**Director:** James Burrows
**Guest Stars:** Brenda Strong, William Garson, Don Perry, Sid Conrad, Kathryn White

Diane develops second thoughts about spurning Sam's marriage proposal after she discovers that he plans to spend a romantic weekend with another woman.

**98** Money Dearest            October 9, 1986
**Writer:** Janet Leahy
**Director:** James Burrows
**Guest Stars:** Frances Sternhagen, Richard Erdman, Paul Willson, Tom Babson

Hoping to find a quick end to his own financial woes, Cliff fixes his mother up with a wealthy suitor.

Broadway star Frances Sternhagen logs the first of many appearances in the role of Cliff's canny old mom, Esther Clavin. Though the actress had by then appeared in a number of feature films—including a memorable turn in 1981's *Outland*, which also featured John Ratzenberger in a small role—Sternhagen's reputation rested primarily on her New York stage work, which included starring roles in the Broadway productions of *On Golden Pond*, *Equus*, and *The Good Doctor*, among many others. According to *Cheers* producer Peter Casey, the show's cast and creative staff were justifiably proud that *Cheers* was so frequently able to attract actors of Sternhagen's stature to its guest cast list. "The show was so well-respected," recalls Casey, "that we found out we could get actors of an extremely high caliber to play these parts when they'd come up." Indeed, in the show's later years, *Cheers* casting director Jeff Greenberg would come to rely increasingly on Broadway-trained actors such as Keene Curtis, Harvey Fierstein, Marilyn Cooper, and Sada Thompson to fill the show's constant demand for solid guest stars and supporting players.

**99**  Abnormal Psychology October 16, 1986
  **Writer:** Janet Leahy
  **Director:** James Burrows
  **Guest Stars:** Richard Herkert, Steve Giannelli, Alan Koss, Tim Cunningham

Frasier is distraught to discover that his opponent on a TV debate is to be none other than Dr. Lilith Sternin, an overbearing colleague whom he once dated.

According to producer Peter Casey, the addition of Bebe Neuwirth to the show's regular cast was a foregone conclusion from the moment the actress walked on stage for a short scene in the fourth-year episode "Second Time Around." "I don't think her scene was more than two or three pages," notes Casey, recalling Neuwirth's earliest appearance in the role of Dr. Lilith Sternin. "But she and Frasier were just funny right off the bat. Her deadpan delivery of everything in this sort of emotionless analytic tone was just perfect. So we brought her back for this second episode, which was also very funny. And by that time we knew we really had something going there."

**100**  House of Horrors with Formal October 30, 1986
     Dining and Used Brick
  **Writer:** David Angell
  **Director:** James Burrows

Carla discovers that the house she bought on Cliff's recommendation may be haunted.

**101**  Tan 'n Wash November 6, 1986
  **Writers:** Cheri Eichen, Bill Steinkellner
  **Director:** James Burrows
  **Guest Stars:** Paul Willson, Steve Giannelli

The Cheers gang seems headed for financial disaster after they invest in Norm's latest business venture, a combination coin-op laundry and tanning salon.

**102**   Young Doctor Weinstein                    November 13, 1986
   **Writer:** Phoef Sutton
   **Director:** James Burrows
   **Guest Stars:** Kristi Somers, Dennis Robertson, Barry Laws,
   Joseph Kell, Julian Barnes, Josh Clark, Paul Lukather, Melinda
   Cordell, J.J. Wall

In his desperation to impress Diane, Sam is reduced to imperson-
ating a prominent surgeon in order to snag dinner reservations at
an exclusive Boston restaurant.

**103**   Knights of the Scimitar                    November 20, 1986
   **Writer:** Jeff Abugov
   **Director:** James Burrows
   **Guest Stars:** J. Eddie Peck, Stephen Vinovich, Bill DeLand

Cliff nominates Norm for membership in his lodge; and Sam is
skeptical of Diane's claim that she's met a handsome new suitor.

**104**   Thanksgiving Orphans                    November 27, 1986
   **Writers:** Cheri Eichen, Bill Steinkellner
   **Director:** James Burrows

Norm's skill in the culinary arts proves somewhat lacking when
he's pressed into service as chef at the gang's ill-fated Thanksgiving
feast.

**105**   Everyone Imitates Art                    December 4, 1986
   **Writer:** Heide Perlman
   **Director:** James Burrows
   **Guest Star:** Michael Holden

Diane is sick with envy when a poetry journal that has repeatedly
rejected her work agrees to publish Sam's first poem.

**106**   The Book of Samuel                    December 11, 1986
   **Writer:** Phoef Sutton
   **Director:** James Burrows
   **Guest Stars:** Amanda Wyss, Katherine McGrath, John Brace,
   Pamela Hedges, Barbara Chase, Steve Giannelli

Diane plots to make Woody's hometown sweetheart jealous after
the fickle girlfriend arrives at Cheers with her new fiancé in tow.

**107**   Dance, Diane, Dance                    December 18, 1986
   **Writer:** Jeff Abugov
   **Director:** James Burrows
   **Guest Stars:** Marilyn Lightstone, Dan Gerrity

Frasier's efforts to shield Diane from her ballet teacher's criticism backfire when the deluded barmaid decides to quit her job and pursue a full-time career as a dancer.

**108**   Chambers v. Malone                      January 8, 1987
   **Writer:** David Angell
   **Director:** James Burrows
   **Guest Stars:** Tom Troupe, Tom Babson, Hugh Maguire, Glen Vernon, Michael Keys Hall

Sam winds up facing assault charges after Diane rejects his latest proposal of marriage.

**109**   Diamond Sam                            January 15, 1987
   **Writer:** David Angell
   **Director:** James Burrows
   **Guest Star:** Al Rosen

Sam assumes that he's saved a bundle when he buys a cut-rate copy of the engagement ring that Diane's had her eye on, though he soon discovers that the cheaper bauble was no bargain.

**110**   Spellbound                             January 22, 1987
   **Writer:** Kimberly Hill
   **Director:** James Burrows
   **Guest Stars:** Dan Hedaya, Jean Kasem

Carla referees a marital dispute between her ex-husband and his wife, Loretta, who's decided that she's ready to dump the philandering Lothario once and for all.

When it was first broadcast, "Spellbound" was intended to serve as an unofficial introduction to *The Tortellis*, a short-lived *Cheers* spinoff that premiered in the time slot immediately following this episode's original network airing. But in spite of the auspicious circumstances surrounding its launch, *The Tortellis* soon proved a disappointment to all involved, and the series was quickly canceled—with few regrets—at the end of a single half-season on the air.

**111**   Never Love a Goalie (Part 1)          January 29, 1987
    **Writers:** Ken Levine, David Isaacs
    **Director:** James Burrows
    **Guest Stars:** Jay Thomas, Marc Arnott

Carla falls for the star goalie of the Boston Bruins hockey team; and Diane serves jury duty in a murder trial.

Los Angeles radio personality Jay Thomas joins the cast in the recurring role of hockey star Eddie LeBec, who would continue to make occasional appearances on the show through the end of the seventh season. A few years later, Thomas would land a starring role on *Love & War*, which would premiere on CBS in the fall of 1992.

**112**   Never Love a Goalie (Part 2)          February 5, 1987
    **Writers:** Ken Levine, David Isaacs
    **Director:** James Burrows
    **Guest Stars:** Jay Thomas, Brent Spiner, Suzanne Collins, William B. Jackson, Laura Waterbury, Linda Hoy

Superstitious Carla is convinced that she's the cause of Eddie's losing streak; and the defendant in Diane's murder trial pays a visit to Cheers.

The defendant in Diane's murder trial is played by Brent Spiner, who would soon discover far greater celebrity in the role of Lieutenant Commander Data on *Star Trek: The Next Generation*, which would premiere in first-run syndication in October, 1987.

**113**   One Last Fling          February 12, 1987
    **Writers:** Cheri Eichen, Bill Steinkellner
    **Director:** James Burrows
    **Guest Stars:** Tim Holland, Peter Schreiner, Marc Arnott, Tim Cunningham, Steve Giannelli, Larry Harpel, Alan Koss, Hugh Maguire

Diane grants Sam twenty-four hours to sow the last of his wild oats as an unattached bachelor.

**114**   Dog Bites Cliff                              February 18, 1987
   **Writer:** Joanne Pagliaro
   **Director:** James Burrows
   **Guest Stars:** Anita Morris, Steve Giannelli

Cliff thinks twice about suing the attractive owner of a dog that
took a nip at him; and Diane prepares to spend a week of quiet
meditation at a Buddhist monastery.


**115**   Dinner at Eight-ish                          February 26, 1987
   **Writer:** Phoef Sutton
   **Director:** James Burrows
   **Guest Stars:** Al Rosen, Doris Grau, Zetta Whitlow

Frasier and Lilith celebrate their first week of successful cohabita-
tion by inviting Sam and Diane to join them for an ill-fated
evening of dinner and conversation.


**116**   Simon Says                                    March 5, 1987
   **Writers:** Peter Casey, David Lee
   **Director:** James Burrows
   **Guest Stars:** John Cleese, Ray Underwood

Diane is only too eager to seek prenuptial advice from an emi-
nent marriage counselor, until he reveals his prognosis for her future life with Sam.

According to producer Peter Casey, who co-wrote "Simon Says" with
his partner, David Lee, former Monty Python mainstay John Cleese created quite a stir in the show's executive offices when he made it known
that he was interested in appearing on an episode of *Cheers*. "Glen and
Les and Jimmy were huge fans of *Fawlty Towers*," explains Casey, "so
they were thrilled to have him on the show." The episode, which was
tailor-made to suit the considerable comic abilities of its guest star, is
thought by many to be among the show's very best. "It was one of my
all-time favorites," admits Casey. "We all really enjoyed that one." And
apparently, the show's creative staff wasn't alone in their positive assessment of the episode—the following September, the Academy of Television Arts and Sciences would voice their approval by awarding Cleese
an Emmy Award for his performance in this episode.

**117**   The Godfather, Part III                    March 19, 1987
  **Writers:** Chris Cluess, Stuart Kreisman
  **Director:** James Burrows
  **Guest Stars:** Cady McClain, Joe Colligan, Al Rosen

Sam is certain that he's entrusted his goddaughter to a perfect gentleman when he allows Woody to take her out on the town— a decision he soon comes to regret.

**118**   Norm's First Hurrah                        March 26, 1987
  **Writers:** Andy Cowan, David S. Williger
  **Director:** Thomas Lofaro
  **Guest Stars:** Tegan West, Neil Zevnik

Norm's extravagant descriptions of his new job fall under unexpectedly close scrutiny when the gang decides to pay him a surprise visit at work.

**119**   Cheers: The Motion Picture                 April 2, 1987
  **Writer:** Phoef Sutton
  **Director:** Tim Berry
  **Guest Stars:** Doris Grau, Al Rosen

The gang shoots an improbably upbeat home movie of Woody's life at as a sop to the barman's skeptical small-town parents.

**120**   A House is Not a Home                      April 30, 1987
  **Writer:** Phoef Sutton
  **Director:** James Burrows
  **Guest Stars:** Billie Bird, Douglas Seale, Stephanie Walski, Marc Smollin, Stefanie Mason, Lou Bonacki, Penny Krompier

Sam and Diane buy their dream house, only to discover that it comes already furnished with another couple's dreams.

**121**   I Do, Adieu                                May 7, 1987
  **Writers:** Glen Charles, Les Charles
  **Director:** James Burrows
  **Guest Stars:** Michael McGuire, Walter Addison, Steve Giannelli

Sam and Diane's matrimonial plans are foiled by the eleventh-hour return of Diane's old beau, Dr. Sumner Sloan, who arrives with a tempting proposition for his former student.

Buoyed by the positive reception to her breakthrough performance opposite Bette Midler in the 1987 feature *Outrageous Fortune*, Shelley Long made the decision to leave her role on *Cheers* at the close of show's fifth season, a move that was designed to allow the actress more time to devote to her burgeoning big-screen career. In response, the show's writers crafted this fifth-year closer, which features the return of Diane's one-time mentor, Sumner Sloan, who arrives to tempt the barmaid away with the promise of a book contract. And so it is not with a bang, but a whimper, that Diane Chambers finally abandons the security of that charmed circle where everybody knows her name, ready at last to face the grand challenges that she imagines await her beyond the bar's swinging doors.

It was an extremely clever exit premise, not the least because it left the door open just wide enough to justify Diane's return should the show's producers ever want—or need—to bring the character back. And, according to producer Peter Casey, the inevitability of Diane's return in the series's final episode was an all but foregone conclusion in the minds of executive producers Jim Burrows and Glen and Les Charles. "I think they did want to leave that door open," recalls Casey, "if only because they were far-sighted enough to know that when they finally did wrap the show, they knew they were going to want to wrap things up with Diane, too."

## 1987-88   THE SIXTH SEASON

*Year-End Rating: 23.4 (3rd place)*

Kirstie Alley arrives in the role of bar manager Rebecca Howe at the start of season six, thus inaugurating a new era in the show's narrative evolution—an era that is launched under the watchful gaze of *Cheers* creators Glen Charles, James Burrows, and Les Charles, who will continue to serve as the show's executive producers throughout the remaining seasons. Other prominent architects of the show's sixth-season refurbishing include returning producers David Angell, Peter Casey, and David Lee, executive script consultants Cheri Eichen and Bill Steinkellner, creative consultant David Lloyd, executive script consultant Bob Ellison, and executive story editor Phoef Sutton. Tim Berry returns as the show's co-producer, and Mary Fukuto moves into the role of associate producer, a position she will maintain throughout the remainder of the show's long run.

**122**   Home Is the Sailor                         September 24, 1987
      **Writers:** Glen Charles, Les Charles
      **Director:** James Burrows
      **Guest Stars:** Jay Thomas, Jonathan Stark, Al Rosen, Steve Giannelli

Broke and depressed, Sam returns home from an ill-fated sailing trip to discover that his beloved watering hole is no longer the place it once was.

Upon his return to Cheers, the bartender has difficulty figuring out what to make of the bar's new no-nonsense manager—a quandary that had the show's writers equally stymied. "When Glen and Les Charles wrote the first episode with Kirstie," notes sixth-season producer Peter Casey, recalling the writing staff's equally difficult acclimation to the show's latest addition, "they saw Rebecca as a very cool character, a strong woman—or at least someone who put up the façade of being a strong businesswoman." Perhaps a little too strong, suggests Casey, who recalls that, as initially envisioned, Rebecca's steely edges made the character a less-than-perfect match for the more relaxed comic atmosphere that prevailed at the bar. "To be really honest," admits Casey, "we were having trouble figuring out where we were gonna plumb the humor from this character after the first five episodes that she was in."

To their great relief, explains Casey, the writers finally experienced a major breakthrough in their understanding of the character a few weeks later, during production of the season's sixth episode, "Paint Your Office." "There's a scene in that one where Rebecca finally opens up to Norm. They have a nice little chat, and you finally see that there is a soft side to her character. Once we saw that Rebecca was indeed a little insecure about what she was doing, the character started to open up."

In the view of *Cheers* writer Dan Staley, who would join the show's writing staff in season eight, the most significant element in Rebecca's comic evolution fell into place only after the show's producers discovered—and quickly learned to exploit—their leading lady's unique facility for stage crying. "At some point," observes Staley, "they discovered that Kirstie could cry a hundred different ways—all of them very funny. That's when they found out that Kirstie was actually very good at playing slapstick. And that's when they began to retool the character to fit these new colors." And so began a character evolution that would, as Staley notes, eventually prove quite dramatic. "If you look at the Rebecca character toward the end of the show and compare her to the character that was introduced in the sixth season, it's almost like you're seeing two different people."

**123**   "I" On Sports                              October 1, 1987
   **Writers:** David Isaacs, Ken Levine
   **Director:** James Burrows
   **Guest Stars:** Fred Dryer, Catherine MacNeal, J. Stephen Coyle

Sam jeopardizes his already tenuous standing at Cheers when he accepts an opportunity to moonlight as a TV sportscaster.

Fred Dryer reprises his role as sportscaster Dave Richards, a character who first appeared on one of the show's earliest episodes. Since losing the part of Sam Malone to Ted Danson in the show's original casting sessions, Dryer had become well-known to prime-time audiences as the star of NBC's long-running adventure series *Hunter*.

**124**   Little Carla, Happy at Last (Part 1)        October 15, 1987
   **Writers:** Cheri Eichen, Bill Steinkellner
   **Director:** James Burrows
   **Guest Stars:** Jay Thomas, Timothy Williams, Mandy Ingber, Janet Brandt

Carla and Eddie's wedding plans appear to be jinxed after the superstitious pair accidentally catch sight of each other before the ceremony.

**125**   Little Carla, Happy at Last (Part 2)        October 22, 1987
   **Writers:** Cheri Eichen, Bill Steinkellner
   **Director:** James Burrows
   **Guest Stars:** Jay Thomas, Timothy Williams, Mandy Ingber, Ron Husmann

Sam is determined to defy the jinx that's cast a pallor over Carla's wedding plans; and Rebecca anxiously awaits the arrival of the bar's corporate manager.

**126**   The Crane Mutiny                            October 29, 1987
   **Writer:** David Angell
   **Director:** James Burrows
   **Guest Stars:** Ralph Peduto, Tim Cunningham, Alan Koss

Norm and Cliff convince a gullible Frasier that Rebecca has designs on him.

**127**   Paint Your Office                    November 5, 1987
   **Writers:** Peter Casey, David Lee
   **Director:** James Burrows

Norm begins to see Rebecca in a more sympathetic light after he moves behind the scenes to paint her private office.

**128**   The Last Angry Mailman                November 12, 1987
   **Writers:** Ken Levine, David Isaacs
   **Director:** James Burrows
   **Guest Stars:** Frances Sternhagen, Kevin Dunn, Don Sparks

Cliff vows to defend his house from the wrecker's ball, despite his mother's apparent eagerness to let the bricks fall where they may.

**129**   Bidding on the Boys                   November 19, 1987
   **Writer:** David Lloyd
   **Director:** Thomas Lofaro
   **Guest Stars:** Sharon Barr, Gary Beach

Sam and Woody are talked into offering themselves up as bachelors-for-bid at a Cheers charity auction.

**130**   Pudd'n Head Boyd                     November 26, 1987
   **Writers:** Cheri Eichen, Bill Steinkellner
   **Director:** James Burrows
   **Guest Stars:** Anne Pitoniak, John Paragon, Brigitte

Amateur thespian Woody is delighted to land the part of Mark Twain, until he discovers that his convincing portrayal has attracted the attentions of an elderly patron at Cheers.

**131**   A Kiss Is Still a Kiss                December 3, 1987
   **Writer:** David Lloyd
   **Director:** James Burrows
   **Guest Stars:** Tom Skerritt, Harry Anderson

Rebecca calls on Sam to serve as her escort when she attends her boss's latest corporate bash.

*Night Court* star Harry Anderson returns in his occasional role as the bar's resident flim-flam man, Harry the Hat. The episode also features

Tom Skerritt's debut as Rebecca's unrequited love interest, Evan Drake. An actor best-known for playing offbeat leading men in such films as *M\*A\*S\*H* and *Alien*, Skerritt would eventually earn an Emmy award for his portrayal of small-town sheriff Jimmy Brock on the CBS drama series *Picket Fences*.

**132**   My Fair Clavin                          December 10, 1987
   **Writer:** Phoef Sutton
   **Director:** James Burrows
   **Guest Stars:** Karen Akers, Philip Arthur Ross

Cliff gives his date a beauty makeover that proves more effective than either of them expected; and Rebecca's nerves get frayed after she resolves to quit smoking.

**133**   Christmas Cheers                        December 17, 1987
   **Writers:** Cheri Eichen, Bill Steinkellner
   **Directors:** James Burrows, Thomas Lofaro
   **Guest Stars:** Jayne Modean, Harry Frazier, Michael Donavon O'Donnell, Hal Havins, Joseph V. Perry

Seasonal Santa Norm gathers a gaggle of his unruly fellow Kringles at Cheers; and Sam searches for an eleventh-hour gift for Rebecca.

**134**   Woody for Hire Meets Norman              January 7, 1988
          of the Apes
   **Writer:** Phoef Sutton
   **Director:** Tim Berry
   **Guest Stars:** Robert Urich, Paddi Edwards, Betty Vaughn

Cliff enlists an orangutan's help in making a monkey of Norm; and Woody tries to convince his skeptical pals at the bar that he's landed a role on *Spenser: For Hire*.

*Spenser: For Hire* star Robert Urich appears as himself.

**135**   And God Created Woodman                  January 14, 1988
   **Writer:** Jeffrey Duteil
   **Director:** John Ratzenberger
   **Guest Stars:** Peter Hansen, Jude Mussetter

Havoc ensues when Rebecca hires Sam and Woody to help out at a fancy dinner party that she's catering for her company's chairman of the board.

**136**   Tale of Two Cuties                        January 21, 1988
   **Writers:** Cheri Eichen, Bill Steinkellner
   **Director:** Michael Zinberg
   **Guest Stars:** Tom Skerritt, Mandy Ingber, Timothy Williams, Bobbie Eakes, Paul Willson

A love-struck Annie Tortelli fills in for her mother-in-law during Carla's latest maternity leave.

**137**   Yacht of Fools                           February 4, 1988
   **Writer:** Phoef Sutton
   **Director:** Thomas Lofaro
   **Guest Stars:** Tom Skerritt, Dorothy Parke, Tom Astor, Eddie Frierson, Dominic Hoffman

Sam entertains fantasies of romance on the high seas when he and Rebecca set sail for a weekend cruise on Evan Drake's yacht.

**138**   To All the Girls I've Loved Before       February 11, 1988
   **Writers:** Ken Levine, David Isaacs
   **Director:** James Burrows
   **Guest Stars:** Karen Witter, Deke Anderson, Peter Schreiner, Hugh Maguire, Tom Babson

Frasier wrestles with a bad case of cold feet on the eve of his marriage.

**139**   Let Sleeping Drakes Lie                  February 18, 1988
   **Writer:** David Lloyd
   **Director:** James Burrows
   **Guest Stars:** Tom Skerritt, Cec Verrell, Jay Bell

When Evan Drake hires Norm to paint his bedroom, Rebecca spots a golden opportunity to indulge in a little judicious snooping.

**140**   Airport V                                    February 25, 1988
   **Writers:** Ken Levine, David Isaacs
   **Director:** George Wendt
   **Guest Stars:** Jay Thomas, Peter Elbling, Robert Starr, Carol
   Navratil, Pete Gonneau, Michelle Davidson, Peter Schreiner,
   Tom Babson, Al Rosen, Copper Neal

   Frasier tries to cure Carla's fear of flying; and Rebecca frets over an
   important restaurant critic's review of the bar.

**141**   The Sam in the Gray Flannel Suit              March 3, 1988
   **Writers:** Cheri Eichen, Bill Steinkellner
   **Director:** Tim Berry
   **Guest Stars:** Tom Skerritt, Pamela Bowen, Vincent Howard,
   George Shannon

   Rebecca is dismayed to discover that Evan Drake has offered Sam
   an executive promotion that she'd had her eye on.

**142**   Our Hourly Bread                             March 10, 1988
   **Writer:** Susan Herring
   **Director:** Andy Ackerman
   **Guest Stars:** Thomas Ryan, Ron Boussom, Erik Menyuk

   When Rebecca pleads poverty in answer to Sam and Woody's request for a raise, the bartenders resolve to improve the bar's financial profile by organizing a raffle.

**143**   Slumber Party Massacred                      March 24, 1988
   **Writer:** Phoef Sutton
   **Director:** James Burrows
   **Guest Stars:** Jay Thomas, Elizabeth Ruscio, Mandy Ingber,
   Timothy Williams, Cynthia Songe

   Rebecca and Lilith stage a slumber party in an ill-fated attempt to
   lift Carla's sagging spirits.

**144**   Bar Wars                                     March 31, 1988
   **Writers:** Ken Levine, David Isaacs
   **Director:** James Burrows
   **Guest Stars:** Wade Boggs, Robert Desiderio, Tom Rosqui, Greg
   Collins, Phil Morris

The Cheers regulars recruit Boston Red Sox player Wade Boggs to help them wrest the bar's prized bowling trophy back from their arch-rivals at Gary's Old Towne Tavern.

The show's otherwise nearly unblemished record of casting continuity was slightly tarnished when the producers cast actor Robert Desiderio in the role of Gary for this episode, despite the fact that the character had been played by a different actor—Joel Polis—in an earlier episode. Actually, the show's producers had every intention of bringing the original actor back for Gary's second appearance, until it was discovered—after the show had already been locked into the schedule—that Joel Polis was already booked that week. All of which left the producers little choice but to cast the equally capable Robert Desiderio, who would continue to trade off the role of Gary with Polis through the remainder of the show's run.

**145**   The Big Kiss-Off                                   April 28, 1988
   **Writers:** Ken Levine, David Isaacs
   **Director:** James Burrows
   **Guest Stars:** Carol Francis, Hugh Maguire, Alan Koss, Al Rosen

Woody and Sam lock horns in an unlikely competition to determine who can be first to steal a kiss from the unsuspecting Rebecca.

**146**   Backseat Becky, Up Front                            May 5, 1988
   **Writers:** Cheri Eichen, Bill Steinkellner
   **Director:** James Burrows
   **Guest Stars:** Tom Skerritt, Ron Barker, Vincent Howard, George Shannon, Al Rosen

Sam helps a lovelorn Rebecca express her true feelings to the soon-to-be-departing Evan Drake.

## 1988-89   THE SEVENTH SEASON

*Year-End Rating: 22.3 (4th place)*

Cupid's arrow finds its mark behind the bar in season seven, when Jackie Swanson arrives in the role of heiress Kelly Gaines, who will come to play an increasingly large role in bartender Woody's romantic life over the course of the show's remaining seasons. Behind the scenes, longtime producers David Angell, Peter Casey, and David Lee are promoted to supervising producer status for the season, which is produced by Cheri Eichen and Bill Steinkellner, and co-produced by Tim Berry. Other notable contributors to the show's seventh-season scripting sessions include co-producer Phoef Sutton, executive story editors Brian Pollack and Mert Rich, executive script consultant Bob Ellison, and creative consultant David Lloyd.

**147**   How to Recede in Business                    October 27, 1988
   **Writer:** David Angell
   **Director:** James Burrows
   **Guest Stars:** Brian Bedford, Peter Schreiner, Al Rosen, Robert Pescovitz, Tim Cunningham

   Sam receives a promotion in the wake of the bar's latest management shake-up, while Rebecca finds herself left out in the cold.

**148**   Swear to God                    November 3, 1988
   **Writer:** Tom Reeder
   **Director:** James Burrows
   **Guest Stars:** Eric Christmas, Kim Johnston Ulrich, Shanna Reed

   Playboy Sam struggles to live up to a celibacy vow he made during a moment of rash judgment; and Woody is cast as an unlikely understudy for the role of Moses.

   Eric Christmas makes his debut as the bar's resident clergyman, Father Barry, who would continue to drop into the bar on an as-needed basis throughout the show's remaining seasons.

**149**   Executive Sweet                    November 10, 1988
   **Writer:** Phoef Sutton
   **Director:** James Burrows
   **Guest Stars:** Alex Nevil, Gerald Hiken, Nathan Purdee, David Schall

   In a desperate attempt to ward off the unwanted advances of her underage boss, Rebecca convinces Sam to pose as her steady beau.

**150**   One Happy Chappy in a Snappy        November 17, 1988
          Serape
**Writers:** Cheri Eichen, Bill Steinkellner
**Director:** James Burrows
**Guest Stars:** Alex Nevil, Gerald Hiken, Fred Asparagus, Marco
Hernandez, Loren Farmer

Rebecca's elaborate scheme to keep her unwanted suitor at bay
begins to unravel when Sam is dispatched to tend bar at a remote
Mexican resort.

**151**   Those Lips, Those Ice              November 24, 1988
**Writers:** Peter Casey, David Lee
**Director:** James Burrows
**Guest Stars:** Jay Thomas, Isa Anderson, Alan Koss, Hugh
Maguire

Carla is convinced that Eddie is having an affair with a figure skater
from an ice show.

**152**   Norm, Is That You?                 December 8, 1988
**Writers:** Cheri Eichen, Bill Steinkellner
**Director:** James Burrows
**Guest Stars:** Jane Sibbett, George Deloy, B.J. Turner, Craig
Branham, Al Rosen

Norm frets over the ribbing he'll get from the gang at the bar after
he accepts a string of lucrative assignments as an interior decorator.

**153**   How to Win Friends and Electrocute   December 15, 1988
          People
**Writer:** Phoef Sutton
**Director:** James Burrows
**Guest Stars:** Robert Benedetti, Steve Bean, Ed Wright, Shirley
Prestia, Andrew Lowery

Cliff goes to shocking extremes when he embarks on an ill-fated
self-improvement campaign.

**154**   Jumping Jerks                          December 22, 1988
   **Writers:** Ken Levine, David Isaacs
   **Director:** James Burrows
   **Guest Stars:** J. Kenneth Campbell, Thomas Sanders, Hugh
   Maguire, Peter Schreiner

The guys at the bar put their courage to the test when they take to
the skies for a death-defying skydiving excursion.

**155**   Send in the Crane                          January 5, 1989
   **Writer:** David Lloyd
   **Director:** James Burrows
   **Guest Stars:** Sandahl Bergman, Chelsea Noble, Patricia
   Morison

Rebecca taps Frasier to play the clown at a children's party; and
Sam is forced to choose between an attractive woman and her
equally fetching daughter.

**156**   Bar Wars II: The Woodman Strikes Back     January 12, 1989
   **Writers:** Ken Levine, David Isaacs
   **Director:** James Burrows
   **Guest Stars:** Joel Polis, Robert O'Reilly, Greg Collins, Vincent
   Pantone, Time Winters

Woody is the bar's designated mixer when Cheers competes
against Gary's Old Towne Tavern in a Bloody Mary making
contest.

**157**   Adventures in Housesitting                 January 19, 1989
   **Writers:** Patricia Niedzialek, Cecile Alch
   **Director:** James Burrows
   **Guest Star:** Michael Currie

Rebecca hopes to curry favor with her boss by volunteering to
dogsit his prize-winning pooch.

**158**   Please Mr. Postman                          February 2, 1989
   **Writers:** Mert Rich, Brian Pollack
   **Director:** James Burrows
   **Guest Stars:** Annie Golden, Howard Mungo

Romance blossoms in the post office when Cliff's new postal
trainee develops a crush on him.

Annie Golden makes her debut as Cliff's new sweetheart, Maggie O'Keefe. The love-struck postal worker would continue to pay occasional visits to the bar throughout the show's remaining seasons.

**159**   Golden Boyd                                    February 6, 1989
   **Writers:** Cheri Eichen, Bill Steinkellner
   **Director:** James Burrows
   **Guest Stars:** Jackie Swanson, Tyrone Power, Jr., Richard Doyle, Gary Bergher

After Woody is bested by a blueblood during a party scuffle, the bartender plots to salvage his flagging self-respect by making a play for the wealthy bully's date.

Jackie Swanson arrives in the role of Woody's fiancée-to-be, heiress Kelly Gaines. Actor Richard Doyle also logs the first of many appearances as Kelly's father, Mr. Gaines.

**160**   I Kid You Not                                 February 16, 1989
   **Writer:** Rob Burton
   **Story:** Rick Beren
   **Director:** James Burrows
   **Guest Stars:** Jarrett Lennon, Jackie Swanson

Frasier and Lilith test their parenting skills when they babysit Carla's precocious six-year-old son.

Child actor Jarrett Lennon is introduced in the first of his occasional appearances as Carla's child prodigy, Ludlow.

**161**   Don't Paint Your Chickens                    February 23, 1989
   **Writers:** Ken Levine, David Isaacs
   **Director:** James Burrows
   **Guest Stars:** Stefan Gierasch, Lisa Aliff, Sarah Marshall, Ralph Meyering, Jr.

Determined to prove her management skills, Rebecca signs on as marketing consultant for Norm's painting business; and Sam struggles to keep pace with a fitness-obsessed woman.

**162**   The Cranemakers                              March 2, 1989
   **Writer:** Phoef Sutton
   **Director:** Andy Ackerman
   **Guest Star:** James R. Winker

A newly pregnant Lilith decides to become one with nature when she and Frasier embark on a woodland retreat; and Rebecca presses Woody to take a well-deserved vacation.

**163**   Hot Rocks                                   March 16, 1989
   **Writers:** Ken Levine, David Isaacs
   **Director:** James Burrows
   **Guest Stars:** Admiral William J. Crowe, Jr., Al Rosen

Rebecca flies in the face of protocol when she accuses a visiting government dignitary of pocketing her diamond earrings.

Admiral William J. Crowe, Chairman of the Joint Chiefs of Staff, appears as himself.

**164**   What's Up, Doc?                             March 30, 1989
   **Writers:** Brian Pollack, Mert Rich
   **Director:** James Burrows
   **Guest Star:** Madolyn Smith Osborne

Sam implies that he's struggling with a bout of impotence in an effort to invoke the sympathies of Frasier's attractive psychology colleague, an expert on human sexual dysfunction.

**165**   The Gift of the Woodi                       April 6, 1989
   **Writer:** Phoef Sutton
   **Director:** James Burrows
   **Guest Stars:** Jackie Swanson, Bruce French, Richard Doyle, Vaughn Armstrong

Woody runs afoul of Kelly's materialistic tendencies when he tries to present her with a heartfelt musical tribute in lieu of a more tangible birthday gift.

**166**   Call Me, Irresponsible                      April 13, 1989
   **Writers:** Dan O'Shannon, Tom Anderson
   **Director:** James Burrows
   **Guest Stars:** Jay Thomas, Ann Guilbert, Fredric Cook

Carla worries that Eddie, on the road with the team, will forget their second wedding anniversary.

Actress Ann Guilbert, fondly remembered for her role as Millie Helper on *The Dick Van Dyke Show*, contributes a cameo in the show's opening teaser.

**167**   Sisterly Love                                      April 27, 1989
  **Writer:** David Lloyd
  **Director:** James Burrows
  **Guest Stars:** Marcia Cross, Richmond Harrison

Sam attempts to soothe a long-standing rift between Rebecca and her sister Susan.

Rebecca's feuding sibling is played by Marcia Cross, who would eventually return to prime time—with a vengeance—in the role of the decidedly deranged Dr. Kimberly Shaw on the Fox-TV melodrama *Melrose Place*.

**168**   The Visiting Lecher                                May 4, 1989
  **Writer:** David Lloyd
  **Director:** James Burrows
  **Guest Stars:** John McMartin, Joanna Barnes, Fabiana Udenio, Nicholas Miscusi

The gang suspects that Rebecca may be crying "wolf" in more ways than one when she insists that a visiting authority on marital fidelity has been making passes at her.

## 1989-90    THE EIGHTH SEASON

*Year-End Rating: 22.7 (3rd place)*

Rebecca continues her star-crossed search for romance in season eight, when Roger Rees arrives to play the lovelorn bar manager's latest romantic foil, corporate raider Robin Colcord. Cheri Eichen, Bill Steinkellner, and Phoef Sutton serve as co-executive producers for the year, which is produced by Tim Berry and co-produced by the show's longtime film editor and sometime director, Andy Ackerman. Also on board for season eight are executive story consultants Brian Pollack and Mert Rich, executive story editors Dan O'Shannon and Tom Anderson, and creative consultants David Lloyd, Ken Levine, and David Isaacs.

**169**   The Improbable Dream (Part 1)        September 21, 1989
   **Writers:** Cheri Eichen, Bill Steinkellner
   **Director:** James Burrows
   **Guest Stars:** Roger Rees, Tony DiBenedetto

Rebecca's romantic fantasies are ignited by the arrival of a fabulously wealthy Wall Street raider, Robin Colcord.

Roger Rees debuts in the role of Robin Colcord, who would figure prominently in the show's storylines through the middle of the ninth season.

**170**   The Improbable Dream (Part 2)        September 28, 1989
   **Writers:** Cheri Eichen, Bill Steinkellner
   **Director:** James Burrows
   **Guest Stars:** Roger Rees, Webster Williams, Valerie Hartman

It's Sam who starts having nightmares when Rebecca's dreams of a romantic interlude with Robin Colcord appear to be coming true.

**171**   A Bar Is Born        October 12, 1989
   **Writer:** Phoef Sutton
   **Director:** James Burrows
   **Guest Stars:** Roger Rees, Tony DiBenedetto

Sam is determined to open a bar of his own, despite the fact that the site he's chosen for his new watering hole has clearly seen better days.

**172**   How to Marry a Mailman        October 19, 1989
   **Writers:** Brian Pollack, Mert Rich
   **Director:** James Burrows
   **Guest Stars:** Roger Rees, Annie Golden, Webster Williams

Cliff suffers a bout of temporary blindness when his post-office paramour returns from Canada with serious plans for their future together.

**173**   The Two Faces of Norm                    October 26, 1989
   **Writer:** Eugene B. Stein
   **Director:** Andy Ackerman
   **Guest Stars:** Eric Allan Kramer, Cynthia Stevenson, Rob Moran,
   Gordon Hunt, Mark Knudsen, J.C. Victor, Kristen Citron,
   Jacqueline Alexandra Citron

   Norm transforms himself into a tyrant in an effort to whip his
   painting crew into shape; and Sam suffers a bout of separation
   anxiety after he sells his cherished Corvette.

**174**   The Stork Brings a Crane                  November 2, 1989
   **Writer:** David Lloyd
   **Director:** Andy Ackerman
   **Guest Stars:** Victoria Hoffman, Monty Ash, Laura Robinson,
   Raymond L. Flynn

   The bar's 100th anniversary festivities go up for grabs after Lilith
   unexpectedly goes into labor.

   Boston's Mayor Raymond Flynn appears as himself.

**175**   Death Takes a Holiday on Ice             November 9, 1989
   **Writer:** Ken Levine
   **Director:** James Burrows
   **Guest Stars:** Anne De Salvo, Eric Christmas, Kevin Conroy,
   Thomas Haden-Church

   Carla is stunned by the news that Eddie has met his maker in a
   bizarre hockey accident, but the real shocker comes when she
   discovers that she may not be his only surviving widow.

   The following season, guest star Thomas Haden-Church would resur-
   face in the role of maintenance man Lowell Mather on *Wings*, the long-
   running NBC sitcom created by *Cheers* producers David Angell, Peter
   Casey, and David Lee.

**176**   For Real Men Only                        November 16, 1989
   **Writers:** David Pollack, Elias Davis
   **Director:** James Burrows
   **Guest Stars:** Michael Currie, Jay Robinson, Rick Podell, Michael
   Holden, Gilbert Girion, Melanie Kinnaman

Frasier flinches at the thought of witnessing the bris of his infant son; and Carla tries to convince Eddie's hockey team to retire her late husband's number.

**177**   Two Girls for Every Boyd                    November 23, 1989
     **Writers:** Dan O'Shannon, Tom Anderson
     **Director:** James Burrows
     **Guest Stars:** Jackie Swanson, Jeffrey Richman, Lisa Kudrow, Mark Kubr

Woody is skittish about kissing his leading lady in a production of *Our Town*; and the guys at the bar stage a beard-growing competition.

Guest star Lisa Kudrow would eventually land a featured role in the ensemble of *Friends*, which would debut under the direction of *Cheers* co-creator Jim Burrows in the fall of 1994.

**178**   The Art of the Steal                    November 30, 1989
     **Writer:** Sue Herring
     **Director:** James Burrows

Rebecca and Sam spend a disquieting evening as unwitting prisoners of Robin Colcord's elaborate home-security system.

**179**   Feeble Attraction                    December 7, 1989
     **Writers:** Dan O'Shannon, Tom Anderson
     **Director:** Andy Ackerman
     **Guest Stars:** Cynthia Stevenson, Michael Holden, John Pappas

Norm is unsettled by the discovery that he's become the object of his former secretary's romantic obsessions.

Norm's secretary is played by Cynthia Stevenson, reprising the role she'd played in "The Two Faces of Norm" a few months earlier. The actress would go on to play a choice role in the 1992 film *The Player*, before returning to prime time as a star of the 1995 series *Hope & Gloria*.

**180**   Sam Ahoy                    December 14, 1989
     **Writer:** David Lloyd
     **Director:** James Burrows
     **Guest Stars:** Roger Rees, Tim Cunningham, Patrick Maguire, Stephen Burks

Sam faces a seagoing surprise when he borrows Robin Colcord's yacht to compete in a local regatta and finds Rebecca stowed away in the hold.

**181**   Sammy and the Professor                January 4, 1990
   **Writers:** Brian Pollack, Mert Rich
   **Director:** James Burrows
   **Guest Stars:** Alexis Smith, Stack Pierce, Dietrich Bader

Rebecca is unnerved by Sam's romantic involvement with her business professor; and Carla faces an IRS audit.

**182**   What Is . . . Cliff Clavin?                January 18, 1990
   **Writers:** Dan O'Shannon, Tom Anderson
   **Director:** Andy Ackerman
   **Guest Stars:** Alex Trebek, Greg E. Davis, Bernard Kuby, Johnny Gilbert

Cliff tries game-show emcee Alex Trebek's patience when the pontifical postman is booked as a quiz-show contestant on *Jeopardy*.

Quizmaster Alex Trebek and *Jeopardy* announcer Johnny Gilbert appear as themselves.

**183**   Finally (Part 1)                January 25, 1990
   **Writers:** Ken Levine, David Isaacs
   **Director:** James Burrows
   **Guest Stars:** Roger Rees, Bill Medley, Gail O'Grady, Crystal Carson

Rebecca is forced to revise her plans for a romantic evening alone with Robin after the mercurial millionaire invites Sam to tag along on their date.

Guest star Gail O'Grady would eventually earn considerable acclaim for her portrayal of Donna Abandando, the outspoken administrative assistant on *NYPD Blue*, which would debut on ABC in the fall of 1993.

**184**   Finally (Part 2)                          February 1, 1990
**Writers:** Ken Levine, David Isaacs
**Director:** James Burrows
**Guest Stars:** Roger Rees, Bill Medley, Valerie Karasek, Gilbert
Girion, Alan Koss, Carol Robbins

Still flying high after her date with Robin Colcord, Rebecca's spirits tumble abruptly back to earth when she discovers her unfaithful millionaire in the arms of another woman.

Pop singer Bill Medley—one-half of the musical Righteous Brothers—
appears as himself in both installments of this two-part episode.

**185**   Woody or Won't He?                        February 8, 1990
**Writers:** Brian Pollack, Mert Rich
**Director:** Andy Ackerman
**Guest Stars:** Jackie Swanson, Melendy Britt, Bill Geisslinger,
Richard Doyle, Robert Gallo

Woody is at his wit's end when he begins to suspect that Kelly's
mother has designs on him; and Cliff is determined to get the
better of the bar's mechanical bull.

**186**   Severe Crane Damage                       February 15, 1990
**Writers:** Dan O'Shannon, Tom Anderson
**Director:** Andy Ackerman
**Guest Stars:** Phyllis Katz, Lorelle Brina, Donna Fuller, Marsha
Kramer, Marti Muller, Audrey Rapoport

Sam creates quite a stir when he appears on a local talk show
with Lilith to promote her new pop psychology book, *Good Girls,
Bad Boys.*

**187**   Indoor Fun with Sammy and Robby           February 22, 1990
**Writer:** Phoef Sutton
**Director:** Andy Ackerman
**Guest Stars:** Roger Rees, Mark Arnott, Tim Cunningham, Peter
Schreiner

Rebecca's plans for a perfect romantic date with Robin are de-
railed when the millionaire is side-tracked by a childish game of
one-upsmanship with Sam.

**188**　Fifty-Fifty Carla　　　　　　　　　March 8, 1990
　　**Writer:** David Lloyd
　　**Director:** James Burrows
　　**Guest Stars:** Roger Rees, Anne De Salvo, Steve Devorkin,
　　Michael Holden

Carla agrees to split her late husband's estate with his other widow, until she discovers that Eddie was carrying a substantial life-insurance policy when he died.

**189**　Bar Wars III: The Return of Tecumseh　　March 15, 1990
　　**Writers:** Ken Levine, David Isaacs
　　**Director:** James Burrows
　　**Guest Stars:** Robert Machray, Tim Donoghue, Phil Therrien

The theft of the bar's wooden Indian mascot kicks off the latest skirmish in the gang's ongoing war with the guys at Gary's Old Towne Tavern.

**190**　Loverboyd　　　　　　　　　　　March 29, 1990
　　**Writers:** Brian Pollack, Mert Rich
　　**Director:** James Burrows
　　**Guest Stars:** Jackie Swanson, Richard Doyle, Tony
　　DiBenedetto, Trish Ramish

Woody suffers premature separation anxiety when Kelly announces her intention to continue her schooling in France.

**191**　The Ghost and Mrs. LeBec　　　　　April 12, 1990
　　**Writers:** Dan Staley, Rob Long
　　**Director:** James Burrows
　　**Guest Stars:** Georgia Brown, Kevin Conroy, Michael Rupert

Carla consults a mystic after her dead husband's ghost pays an unexpected visit.

**192**　Mr. Otis Regrets　　　　　　　　April 19, 1990
　　**Writers:** Ken Levine, David Isaacs
　　**Director:** Andy Ackerman
　　**Guest Stars:** Christine Cavanaugh, Eric Bruskotter, Colin Wells,
　　Barry Zajac

Sam irritates Rebecca with his boast that he's had a romantic encounter with her arch-rival on an elevator.

**193**   Cry Hard (Part 1)                              April 26, 1990
   **Writers:** Dan O'Shannon, Tom Anderson
   **Director:** James Burrows
   **Guest Stars:** Roger Rees, Jonathan McMurtry, Eden Bodnar

Rebecca is crestfallen to discover that Robin Colcord has been using her as an unwitting accomplice in a ruthless game of corporate espionage.

**194**   Cry Harder (Part 2)                             May 3, 1990
   **Writers:** Cheri Eichen, Bill Steinkellner, Phoef Sutton
   **Story:** Bill Steinkellner
   **Director:** James Burrows
   **Guest Stars:** Roger Rees, Jonathan McMurtry, Ron Canada, Peter Schreiner, Michael Holden, Christopher Darga, James Nardini

Rebecca faces her bleak romantic prospects after Robin Colcord is indicted on insider trading charges; and, after being richly rewarded for his own role in bringing Robin's crimes to light, Sam offers the distraught bar manager a compassionate shoulder to cry on.

## 1990-91   THE NINTH SEASON

*Year-End Rating: 21.3 (1st place)*

Sam meets a worthy foil when Keene Curtis is introduced in the role of restaurateur John Allen Hill in the show's ninth season, which is once again co-executive produced by Cheri Eichen, Bill Steinkellner, and Phoef Sutton. Tim Berry and Andy Ackerman are producers for the year, which is co-produced by Larry Balmagia, Brian Pollack, Mert Rich, Dan O'Shannon, and Tom Anderson. Other important players on the show's ninth-season roster include story editors Dan Staley and Rob Long, creative consultants David Lloyd, Ken Levine, and David Isaacs, and executive script consultant Bob Ellison.

**195**   Love Is a Really, Really              September 20, 1990
         Perfectly Okay Thing
   **Writer:** Phoef Sutton
   **Director:** James Burrows
   **Guest Stars:** Roger Rees, Eric Christmas, Edmund Gaynes, Christopher Abraham

Sam struggles hard to remain discreet about what went on behind closed doors during his spontaneous romantic interlude with Rebecca.

**196**   Cheers Fouls Out                           September 27, 1990
   **Writer:** Larry Balmagia
   **Director:** James Burrows
   **Guest Stars:** Roger Rees, Kevin McHale, Joel Polis, James Hornbeck, James Nardini, Lee Vines

The players from Gary's Old Towne Tavern cry foul when Sam recruits a basketball pro to play on the Cheers team as the rival bars prepare to face each other on the court.

Boston Celtics star Kevin McHale appears as himself.

Though not officially numbered as such, this episode would serve as the fourth installment in the "bar wars" series that had been launched with Ken Levine and David Isaacs' eponymously titled sixth-season entry, "Bar Wars"—an episode that was itself inspired by Peter Casey and David Lee's fourth-season show, "From Beer to Eternity."

**197**   Rebecca Redux                           October 4, 1990
   **Writers:** Phoef Sutton, Bill Steinkellner, Cheri Eichen
   **Story:** Bill Steinkellner
   **Director:** James Burrows
   **Guest Stars:** Bryan Clark, Perry Anzilotti, Randy Pelish, Timothy Fall, Tony DiBenedetto, Peter Schreiner, Stanley Bennett Clay, Paul Cira

Rebecca takes a dim view of her post-Cheers employment prospects after she's forced to accept part-time work as an auto-show model.

**198**   Where Nobody Knows Your Name                           October 11, 1990
   **Writers:** Dan O'Shannon, Tom Anderson
   **Director:** Andy Ackerman
   **Guest Stars:** Roger Rees, Arsenio Hall, Catherine MacNeal, Ron Ulstad, Paul Willson

Rebecca tries to play it cool when her rival for Robin Colcord's attentions boasts about her own lock on the jailed financier's affections.

Talk-show host Arsenio Hall contributes a cameo appearance, as himself, in this episode.

**199**    Ma Always Liked You Best           October 18, 1990
    **Writers:** Dan O'Shannon, Tom Anderson
    **Director:** Andy Ackerman
    **Guest Stars:** Frances Sternhagen, Rocky LaPorte, John Posey, Paul Willson, Peter Schreiner, Ken Foree, James F. Dean

Cliff's mother takes a shine to Woody, whom she fancies to be the son she never had.

**200**    Grease                           October 25, 1990
    **Writers:** Brian Pollack, Mert Rich
    **Director:** James Burrows
    **Guest Stars:** Sheldon Leonard, John Reger

Norm launches a campaign to keep his favorite local eatery from closing its doors.

The legendary actor and television pioneer Sheldon Leonard guest stars as Sid Nelson, the feisty proprietor of Norm's favorite all-beef restaurant, The Hungry Heifer.

**201**    Breaking in Is Hard to Do          October 31, 1990
    **Writers:** Ken Levine, David Isaacs
    **Director:** Andy Ackerman
    **Guest Stars:** Roger Rees, Clive Rosengren, John Boyle, Edward Penn, Paul Willson, Philip Perlman

Rebecca schemes to arrange an unscheduled conjugal visit with the incarcerated Robin Colcord; and Frasier and Lilith cope with the demands of parenting a gifted child.

Rhea Perlman's real-life dad, Philip Perlman, logs his first credited appearance on the show with this episode. Perlman's elderly barfly, Phil, would be a fixture at the bar throughout the show's remaining seasons.

**202**    The Cheers 200th Anniversary Special     November 8, 1990
       (one hour)
    **Writers:** Cheri Eichen, Bill Steinkellner, Phoef Sutton
    **Directors:** James Burrows, Andy Ackerman

Political pundit John McLaughlin hosts a retrospective look at highlights of the show's first eight and a half seasons.

Designed to commemorate the filming of the show's 200th episode, this hour-long special was anchored by an in-depth panel discussion with the series's creators, as well as most of the show's past and current cast, including Shelley Long.

**203** Bad Neighbor Sam                    November 15, 1990
   **Writers:** Cheri Eichen, Bill Steinkellner
   **Director:** James Burrows
   **Guest Stars:** Keene Curtis, Carl Mueller, Sandy Edgerton, Tamara Mark, Phil Perlman, E.E. Bell, Aileen Fitzpatrick, Fred Slyter

Sam finds himself caught up in a feud with the haughty owner of Melville's restaurant, John Allen Hill.

Keene Curtis—best known for his long-running role as Little Orphan Annie's Daddy Warbucks in the Broadway warhorse *Annie*—debuts in the role of John Allen Hill in the 200th *Cheers* episode filmed.

**204** Veggie Boyd                    November 22, 1990
   **Writers:** Rob Long, Dan Staley
   **Director:** James Burrows
   **Guest Stars:** Tom Everett, Debbie Gregory, John Cervenka, Philip Perlman, Michael Holden, Tony DiBenedetto

Woody lands a job as spokesperson in a commercial for a new vegetable drink; and know-it-all Cliff faces unexpected competition from the bar's new trivia napkins.

**205** Norm and Cliff's Excellent Adventure    December 6, 1990
   **Writers:** Ken Levine, David Isaacs
   **Director:** James Burrows
   **Guest Stars:** Tom Klunis

Norm and Cliff ferment a feud between Sam and Frasier; and Woody finds himself addicted to a televised home-shopping show.

**206**    Woody Interruptus               December 13, 1990
     **Writers:** Dan Staley, Rob Long
     **Director:** James Burrows
     **Guest Stars:** Jackie Swanson, Anthony Cistaro, Michael Keenan, Douglas MacHugh, Paul Willson, Tony DiBenedetto

Woody's girlfriend Kelly returns from overseas with an attractive Frenchman in tow; and Cliff decides to have his brain cryogenically preserved after his death.

Anthony Cistaro debuts in the role of Frenchman Henri Fourchette, who would continue to make regular appearances at the bar throughout the show's remaining seasons.

**207**    Honor Thy Mother                 January 3, 1991
     **Writers:** Brian Pollack, Mert Rich
     **Director:** James Burrows
     **Guest Stars:** Sada Thompson, Keene Curtis, Oceana Marr, Josh Lozoff, Carol Ann Susi, Randy Pelish

Carla rebels against her domineering mother after the dotty matriarch issues an impossible deathbed decree.

Carla's eccentric Mama Lozupone is played by Sada Thompson, a veteran character actress best-remembered by TV audiences for her portrayal of Kate Lawrence on ABC's mid-'70s dramatic series *Family*.

**208**    Achilles' Hill                      January 10, 1991
     **Writers:** Ken Levine, David Isaacs
     **Director:** Andy Ackerman
     **Guest Stars:** Keene Curtis, Valerie Mahaffey, Eric Christmas

Sam hopes to get John Allen Hill's goat by romancing the restaurateur's unsuspecting daughter; and Carla is convinced that the bar's foosball table is possessed.

**209**    Days of Wine and Neuroses (Part 1)      January 24, 1991
     **Writers:** Mert Rich, Brian Pollack
     **Director:** James Burrows
     **Guest Stars:** Calvin Jung, Paul Willson, Shad Willingham, Kristine Knudson

Rebecca debates the wisdom of accepting an ill-timed marriage proposal from Robin Colcord; and Frasier fancies himself a crooner after the bar installs a karaoke machine.

**210**   Wedding Bell Blues (Part 2)                    January 31, 1991
   **Writers:** Dan O'Shannon, Tom Anderson
   **Director:** James Burrows
   **Guest Stars:** Roger Rees, Bobby Hatfield, Ray Stricklyn, Paul
   Willson, Ron Abel, George Case

In spite of her initial doubts, Rebecca appears surprisingly gung ho
as the hour of her wedding approaches.

The singer Bobby Hatfield, formerly of The Righteous Brothers, appears
as himself.

**211**   I'm Getting My Act Together and            February 7, 1991
      Sticking It in Your Face
   **Writers:** Dan Staley, Rob Long
   **Director:** Andy Ackerman
   **Guest Stars:** Jeff McCarthy, Paul Willson, Jan Gan Boyd

Rebecca struggles to recover from her break-up with Robin; and
Frasier attempts to regale the gang with a reading from Dickens.

**212**   Sam Time Next Year                         February 14, 1991
   **Writer:** Larry Balmagia
   **Director:** James Burrows
   **Guest Stars:** Barbara Feldon, Mike Dukakis, Roger Eschbacher,
   Gibby Brand, Don Took

Sam finds himself unexpectedly incapacitated on the eve of his annual Valentine's Day tryst with an old girlfriend.

Sam's anniversary waltz partner is played by Barbara Feldon, who
co-starred as Agent 99 on the long-running 1960s sitcom *Get Smart*.
Former Democratic presidential candidate Mike Dukakis also logs a brief
appearance in the episode's pre-credit teaser.

**213**   Crash of the Titans                        February 21, 1991
   **Writers:** Dan Staley, Rob Long
   **Director:** James Burrows
   **Guest Stars:** Keene Curtis, Jeremiah Morris, Paul Willson,
   Philip Perlman, Tony DiBenedetto, Peter Schreiner, Adele
   Baughn, Anadel Baughn

Rebecca and Sam compete for John Allen Hill's favor after word
leaks out that the bar's long-term lease may be up for grabs.

**214**   It's a Wonderful Wife                    February 28, 1991
   **Writer:** Sue Herring
   **Director:** James Burrows
   **Guest Stars:** Keene Curtis, Anthony Cistaro, Heather Lee, Peter
   Schreiner, Tony DiBenedetto

The bar celebrates Frasier's birthday, but it looks as though the
party may be over for Norm when his wife, Vera, lands a job
upstairs at Melville's.

The voice of Norm's wife is provided by George Wendt's real-life
spouse, Bernadette Birkett. The actress had earlier appeared on the
show—in a different role—in the third-season episode "Fairy Tales Can
Come True."

**215**   Cheers Has Chili                         March 14, 1991
   **Writers:** Cheri Eichen, Bill Steinkellner, Phoef Sutton
   **Director:** Andy Ackerman
   **Guest Stars:** Robert Machray, Peter Schreiner, Stanley Bennett
   Clay

Sam is skeptical of Rebecca's latest marketing brainstorm, an ill-
conceived plan to transform the bar's pool room into a chili
parlor.

**216**   Carla Loves Clavin                       March 21, 1991
   **Writers:** Dan Staley, Rob Long
   **Director:** James Burrows
   **Guest Stars:** Danté Di Loreto, Nathan Davis, Jessie Scott, Paul
   Willson

Carla is forced to observe an uneasy truce with Cliff after she discovers that the postman has been chosen to serve as a judge in
the annual Miss Boston Barmaid contest.

**217**   Pitch It Again, Sam                      March 28, 1991
   **Writers:** Dan O'Shannon, Tom Anderson
   **Director:** James Burrows
   **Guest Stars:** Michael Fairman, Henry Woronicz, Zachary Ben-
   jamin, James Reynolds, Peter Kevoian, Michael Cannizzo, Joel
   Anderson, Victoria Barrett, Leanne Griffin

One of Sam's old baseball rivals shows up to challenge the
former pitcher to one final battle on the mound.

**218**  Rat Girl                                         April 4, 1991
**Writers:** Ken Levine, David Isaacs
**Director:** James Burrows
**Guest Stars:** Paul Willson, Beth Toussaint, Cheryl Lynn Bruce,
Andre Miripolsky, Peter Schreiner

Lilith grieves the passing of her favorite lab rat; and rotund Cheers
regular Paul is taken aback by the unexpected advances of an
attractive young woman.

**219**  Home Malone                                     April 25, 1991
**Writers:** Dan O'Shannon, Tom Anderson
**Director:** Andy Ackerman
**Guest Stars:** Jackie Swanson, Anthony Cistaro, Kevin and
Christopher Graves, Paul Willson, Peter Schreiner, Philip
Perlman, Gary Lee Davis, Norm Compton, Steve Hulin

Sam plays part-time papa when Frasier and Lilith draft him into
service as Frederick's babysitter; and Woody has his hands full
when Kelly lands a part-time job at the bar.

**220**  Uncle Sam Wants You                             May 2, 1991
**Writers:** Dan Staley, Rob Long
**Director:** James Burrows
**Guest Stars:** Pete Willcox, Kevin and Christopher Graves, Tress
MacNeille, Paul Willson

Sam is surprised to discover that playing surrogate dad to Frasier's
kid has put him in touch with his own latent parental yearnings.

## 1991-92   THE TENTH SEASON

*Year-End Rating: 17.6 (4th place)*

Although Sam and Rebecca indulge a sudden urge to become parents
in the show's tenth season, it's Woody and Kelly who finally tie the knot
in the season's grand finale. Les Charles, Glen Charles, and James Burrows continue to serve in their ongoing capacity as executive producers
in season ten, when they are joined by fellow executive producers Cheri
Eichen, Bill Steinkellner, and Phoef Sutton. Dan O'Shannon and Tom
Anderson are supervising producers in the tenth season, which is produced by Tim Berry and co-produced by Dan Staley and Rob Long. Also

returning to the show's masthead are creative consultants David Lloyd, Ken Levine, and David Isaacs and executive script consultant Bob Ellison.

**221**   Baby Balk                                    September 19, 1991
   **Writers:** Dan O'Shannon, Tom Anderson
   **Director:** James Burrows
   **Guest Star:** Bruce Wright

Prospective parents Sam and Rebecca seek pre-natal advice from Lilith and Frasier when they discover that the road to conception is somewhat rockier than anticipated.

**222**   Get Your Kicks on Route 666              September 26, 1991
   **Writers:** Dan O'Shannon, Tom Anderson
   **Director:** James Burrows
   **Guest Stars:** Anthony Addabbo, Paul Willson

The guys embark on an ill-advised road trip; and Carla's cousin Frankie finds temporary employment at the bar.

**223**   Madame LaCarla                              October 3, 1991
   **Writer:** Phoef Sutton
   **Director:** Tom Moore
   **Guest Stars:** Georgia Brown, Jeffrey Richman, Jim Brochu, Barry Zajac, Peter Schreiner

Carla is surprised to discover that her soon-to-retire mystic advisor has chosen the barmaid to serve as her successor in the fortune-telling trade.

**224**   The Norm Who Came to Dinner              October 10, 1991
   **Writers:** Dan O'Shannon, Tom Anderson
   **Director:** Tom Moore
   **Guest Stars:** Paul Willson, Peter Schreiner, Philip Perlman

Frasier and Lilith find themselves saddled with an unwanted house guest when Norm is laid low by a back injury while painting their living room.

**225**  Ma's Little Maggie                    October 17, 1991
  **Writers:** Tracy Newman, Jonathan Stark
  **Director:** James Burrows
  **Guest Stars:** Frances Sternhagen, Annie Golden, Paul Willson

Cliff's mother takes an unexpected shine to her son's girlfriend; and Rebecca's latest attempt to increase her fertility leaves Sam cold.

**226**  Unplanned Parenthood                  October 24, 1991
  **Writers:** Dan Staley, Rob Long
  **Director:** James Burrows
  **Guest Stars:** Jackie Swanson, Leah Remini, Josh Lozoff, Jarrett Lennon, Phillip Perlman, Paul Willson, Risa Littman, Thomas Tulak, Danny Kramer, Sabrina Wiener

Sam and Rebecca get a first-hand look at the harsh realities of parenthood when they babysit Carla's unruly brood; and Cliff volunteers to direct Woody's latest home movie.

**227**  Bar Wars V: The Final Judgment        October 31, 1991
  **Writers:** Ken Levine, David Isaacs
  **Director:** James Burrows
  **Guest Stars:** Robert Desiderio, Rick Cramer, Paul Willson, Phil Perlman, Christopher and Kevin Graves

The gang wonders if the latest prank in their ongoing war with Gary's Old Towne Tavern might actually have scared arch-rival Gary into an early grave.

**228**  Where Have All the Floorboards Gone?    November 7, 1991
  **Writers:** Ken Levine, David Isaacs
  **Director:** James Burrows
  **Guest Stars:** Kevin McHale, Lynn McHale, Glenn Ordway, Philip Perlman, Paul Willson, Tim Cunningham

The Boston Celtics' Kevin McHale is driven to distraction after the gang drags him into a barside debate over the number of bolts in the floorboards of the Boston Garden.

Basketball star Kevin McHale and his wife, Lynn, appear as themselves.

**229**   Head Over Hill                        November 14, 1991
   **Writers:** Dan Staley, Rob Long
   **Director:** John Ratzenberger
   **Guest Stars:** Keene Curtis, Paul Willson, Jordan Lund, Ken
   Magee, Philip Perlman, Peter Schreiner

Sam accuses Carla of sleeping with the enemy after the randy
barmaid enjoys a fling with John Allen Hill.

**230**   A Fine French Whine                   November 21, 1991
   **Writers:** Dan Staley, Rob Long
   **Director:** James Burrows
   **Guest Stars:** Jackie Swanson, Anthony Cistaro, Sonje Fortag, Jeff
   Heston, Paul Willson, Peter Foxon Miker, Nancy Arnold, Ron
   Ray, Bill Gratton

Woody is forced to put his engagement plans on hold while Kelly
debates the wisdom of entering into a paper marriage with her
French friend, Henri.

**231**   I'm Okay, You're Defective             December 5, 1991
   **Writers:** Dan Staley, Rob Long
   **Director:** James Burrows
   **Guest Stars:** Paul Willson, Julie Lloyd, Donald Hotton, John
   Serembe, Rob Neukirch, Philip Perlman

Sam begins to doubt his own ability to deliver the goods when
Rebecca returns from her fertility specialist with a glowing medical report.

**232**   Go Make                              December 12, 1991
   **Writer:** Phoef Sutton
   **Director:** James Burrows
   **Guest Stars:** Ric Coy, Gerry Gibson, Sharon Case, Stephen
   Preusse, Paul Willson

Sam and Rebecca re-evaluate their baby-making plans after they
spend an eye-opening weekend at a honeymoon retreat.

According to *Cheers* producer Dan Staley, Sam and Rebecca's half-
hearted run at parenthood was doomed well before the couple finally
decided to throw in the towel at the conclusion of this episode. "Nobody

liked that story arc," recalls Staley. "It was such a bizarre idea, that two people who weren't romantically involved would suddenly decide to have a baby together. It was hard to find the comedy in that situation— it just seemed like one of those ideas that might make sense in Hollywood circles, but went right over the head of everybody else in the country." Under the circumstances, it's hardly surprising that there was little debate over the producers' decision to jettison the storyline with this episode. "By that time," observes Staley, "it was obvious to everyone that the story arc wasn't going to work, so we just decided to end it there. It was over fast, but I still get chills thinking about some of those shows."

**233**   Don't Shoot . . . I'm Only the Psychiatrist   January 2, 1992
  **Writer:** Kathy Ann Stumpe
  **Director:** James Burrows
  **Guest Stars:** Keene Curtis, David A. Levy, Steve Nevil, Harvey Evans, Paul Willson, Michael Holden, Philip Perlman, Richard Doran

Barber Woody bungles his attempt to give Sam a trim; and Norm and Cliff wreak havoc with Frasier's therapy group.

**234**   No Rest for the Woody   January 9, 1992
  **Writers:** Tracy Newman, Jonathan Stark
  **Director:** James Burrows
  **Guest Stars:** Celeste Holm, Jackie Swanson, Richard Doyle, Sy Richardson, Paul Willson, Marc Epstein

Dead tired from working the graveyard shift, Woody practically has to be propped up for his first meeting with Kelly's grandmother.

Hollywood veteran Celeste Holm plays Grandmother Gaines.

**235**   My Son, the Father   January 16, 1992
  **Writers:** Dan Staley, Rob Long
  **Director:** James Burrows
  **Guest Stars:** Keene Curtis, Josh Lozoff, Paul Willson, Philip Perlman, Neal Lerner

Carla is stunned when her son announces that he plans to enter the priesthood; and Cliff takes his stand-up act to a local comedy club.

**236**   One Hugs, the Other Doesn't                   January 30, 1992
  **Writers:** Cheri Eichen, Bill Steinkellner
  **Director:** James Burrows
  **Guest Stars:** Emma Thompson, Christopher and Kevin Graves,
  Paul Willson, Thomas Tulack, Danny Kramer, Edward Joseph
  Derham, Jonathan Daniel Harris, Jennifer Williams

Lilith is none too pleased when an old flame of Frasier's who has
made good as a children's singer invites the psychiatrist and his
family to one of her recitals.

Future Oscar winner Emma Thompson guest stars as the children's
troubadour, Nanny Gee. The original material sung by Thompson's character was composed for the episode by *Cheers* musical director, Craig
Safan, along with writers Cheri Eichen and Bill Steinkellner.

**237**   A Diminished Rebecca With                    February 6, 1992
      a Suspended Cliff
  **Writers:** Dan O'Shannon, Tom Anderson
  **Director:** James Burrows
  **Guest Stars:** Harry Connick, Jr., Raye Birk, Paul Willson, Jim
  Norton

Woody's visiting cousin finds himself hopelessly smitten by
Rebecca; and Cliff protests the postal service's adoption of non-
traditional uniforms.

Singer Harry Connick, Jr., guest stars as Woody's visiting cousin.

**238**   License to Hill                              February 13, 1992
  **Writers:** Ken Levine, David Isaacs
  **Director:** James Burrows
  **Guest Stars:** Keene Curtis, Paul Willson, Philip Perlman,
  Stephen Rowe, Frank M. Schuller, Lenny Citrano, Nancy
  Stephens, Robert Gossett, Ralph P. Martin

Rebecca struggles to placate a roomful of thirsty patrons after she
discovers that the bar's liquor license has lapsed.

**239**   Rich Man, Wood Man                           February 20, 1992
  **Writer:** Daniel Palladino
  **Director:** James Burrows
  **Guest Stars:** Jackie Swanson, Jarrett Lennon, Vili Kraljevic

After spending a vacation in merrie olde England with Kelly, Woody returns to Cheers a changed man; and Sam shows no mercy when he agrees to act as Frasier's personal trainer.

**240** Smotherly Love                    February 27, 1992
**Writer:** Kathy Ann Stumpe
**Director:** James Burrows
**Guest Stars:** Marilyn Cooper, Wes Stern, Rebecca Staab, Fredd Wayne, Paul Willson

Frasier tries to convince Lilith to stand up to her overbearing mother; and Rebecca casts a dispassionate eye at Norm's bulging bar tab.

Lilith's domineering mother, Betty Sternin, is played by veteran stage actress Marilyn Cooper, whose long list of Broadway credits included starring roles in *Woman of the Year*, *Brighton Beach Memoirs*, and *Broadway Bound*, among many others.

**241** Take Me Out to the Ballgame          March 26, 1992
**Writer:** Kathy Ann Stumpe
**Director:** James Burrows
**Guest Stars:** John Finn, Anthony Starke, Paul Willson, Philip Perlman, Lance Slaughter, Michael Wiseman

Sam attempts a major-league comeback; and Frasier is in danger of winding up in the dog house after he misplaces Lilith's pet lab rat, Whiskers.

**242** Rebecca's Lover . . . Not          April 23, 1992
**Writers:** Tracy Newman, Jonathan Starke
**Director:** James Burrows
**Guest Stars:** Harvey Fierstein, Jackie Swanson, Kirby Tepper, Peter Kelleghan, Ben Mittleman, Philip Perlman, Paul Willson, Joel Fredericks, Jana Robbins, Barry Zajac

Rebecca launches an ill-considered campaign to rekindle the very cold embers of an old high-school romance; and Sam mourns the loss of his stolen car.

Rebecca's high-school flame is played by Harvey Fierstein, the playwright and star of the acclaimed Broadway hit *Torch Song Trilogy*, which was later made into a film of the same name, with Fierstein reprising his leading role.

**243**   Bar Wars VI: This Time It's For Real          April 30, 1992
   **Writers:** Ken Levine, David Isaacs
   **Director:** Rick Beren
   **Guest Stars:** Harry Guardino, Senator John Kerrey, J.C. Quinn,
   Bari K. Willerford, Larry Brandenburg, Paul Willson, Larry
   Paulsen, Cleto Augusto

The Cheers gang wonders if the mysterious new owner of Gary's
Old Towne Tavern might actually be an organized-crime boss.

Veteran actor Harry Guardino plays tough guy Frank Carpaccio. Also
featured in a cameo role is U.S. Senator John Kerrey.

**244**   Heeeeeere's Cliffy                          May 7, 1992
   **Writers:** Ken Levine, David Isaacs
   **Director:** James Burrows
   **Guest Stars:** Johnny Carson, Doc Severinsen, Frances
   Sternhagen, Joshua Mostel, Paul Willson, Nicolas Mize, Angel
   Harper

Norm convinces Cliff that Johnny Carson plans to use one of the
postman's one-liners on *The Tonight Show*, a bluff that backfires
when Cliff books passage to Burbank to watch the taping.

Johnny Carson and *Tonight Show* bandleader Doc Severinsen appear
as themselves.

**245**   An Old-Fashion Wedding (one hour)          May 14, 1992
   **Writer:** David Lloyd
   **Director:** James Burrows
   **Guest Stars:** Jackie Swanson, Milo O'Shea, Richard Doyle,
   Colleen Morris, Mark Voland, Daniel Gerroll, Richard Merson

Despite odds that seem hopelessly weighted in favor of disaster,
best man Sam is determined to see that Woody and Kelly's wedding ceremony proceeds without a snag.

## 1992-93   THE ELEVENTH SEASON

*Year-End Rating: 16.1 (8th place)*

After a nearly unprecedented run of eleven prime-time seasons, the
creators of *Cheers* finally decide to call it quits with a record-length vale-

dictory season that will ultimately increase the show's already bulging comic inventory by no less than twenty-eight all-new half hours. Executive producers for the show's farewell season are Dan O'Shannon and Tom Anderson, who share the title with the show's creators, Glen Charles, James Burrows, and Les Charles. Dan Staley and Rob Long are co-executive producers for the show's final season, which is produced by Tim Berry and co-produced by Tom Leopold. Other notable contributors to the show's eleventh-season story sessions include executive story consultant Rebecca Parr Cioffi, story consultant Kathy Ann Stumpe, and story editors Fred Graver and Sue Herring. And rounding out the show's writing staff for season eleven are executive script consultant Bob Ellison and veteran creative consultants David Lloyd, Ken Levine, and David Isaacs.

**246** The Little Match Girl September 24, 1992
**Writers:** Dan Staley, Rob Long
**Director:** James Burrows
**Guest Stars:** Jackie Swanson, Keene Curtis, Robert Machray, Amanda Carlin, Peter Keleghan, Peter Kevoian

Rebecca tries to lay the blame on faulty wiring after she accidentally sets fire to the bar.

**247** The Beer Is Always Greener October 1, 1992
**Writer:** Tom Leopold
**Director:** James Burrows
**Guest Stars:** Jackie Swanson, Glenn Shadix, Matthew Glave, Julia Montgomery, Rosa Nevin, Paul Willson, Alan Koss, Tim Cunningham, Philip Perlman, Spencer Beglarian

Carla discovers far greener pastures—and substantially increased tips—when she lands a temporary job at another bar during Cheers's post-fire rehabilitation.

**248** The King of Beers October 8, 1992
**Writer:** Dan O'Shannon
**Director:** John Ratzenberger
**Guest Stars:** Cliff Bemis, Cameron Thor, Paul Willson, Joe Costanza, Bradford English, William Long, Jr., Mirron E. Willis

Norm thinks that he's found his dream job when he signs on as beer taster for a local brewery; and Rebecca tries her luck on the bar's new slot machine.

**249**   The Magnificent Six                        October 22, 1992
   **Writer:** Sue Herring
   **Director:** James Burrows
   **Guest Stars:** Anthony Cistaro, Eddie Jones, Sondra C. Baker,
   Jennifer Gatti, Jeri Gale, Leilani Jones, Patricia Clipper, Maria
   Pecci, Tim Cunningham, Alan Koss, Philip Perlman

Sam pits his homegrown charms against Henri's continental
savoir-faire when the two playboys vie for the unofficial title of
"world's greatest ladies' man."

**250**   Do Not Forsake Me, O My Postman          October 29, 1992
   **Writers:** Ken Levine, David Isaacs
   **Director:** James Burrows
   **Guest Stars:** John Mahoney, Annie Golden, Derek McGrath,
   Cameron Watson, Paul Willson, Tim Cunningham, Jack Kenny,
   Leland Orser, Steve Giannelli

Maggie O'Keefe returns to Cheers with startling news for Cliff—
he's going to be a father; and Rebecca commissions a songwriter
to compose an advertising jingle for the bar.

The episode's teaser features Derek McGrath in a reprise of his role as
Andy Andy, the ex-con who made life miserable for Diane Chambers in
the show's early years. Another familiar face in the episode's guest cast
is John Mahoney, who appears here as jingle writer Sy Flembeck; the
actor would be reunited with at least one of the show's cast members
the following season, when Mahoney would land the part of Frasier's
dad, Martin, on the *Cheers* spinoff series *Frasier*.

**251**   Teaching With the Enemy                  November 5, 1992
   **Writer:** Tom Anderson
   **Director:** James Burrows
   **Guest Stars:** Don Gibb, Larry Brandenburg, Barry Zajac, Philip
   Perlman, Michael Buchman Silver

Rebecca can hardly believe her eyes when she spies Frasier's
wife, Lilith, in the arms of another man.

**252**   The Girl in the Plastic Bubble          November 12, 1992
   **Writer:** Dan O'Shannon
   **Director:** James Burrows
   **Guest Stars:** Peter Vogt, Brian Smiar, Tim Cunningham, Patrick
   Shea

Frasier is ready to toss himself from a ledge after Lilith informs him that she plans to spend the coming year in an underground biosphere with her new lover.

**253** Ill Gotten Gaines · November 19, 1992
**Writer:** Fred Graver
**Director:** James Burrows
**Guest Stars:** Keene Curtis, Jackie Swanson, Richard Doyle, Robert Cornthwaite, Sondra Currie, Christopher and Kevin Graves, John Valentine, Thomas Tulak, Danny Kramer, Sabrina Wiener

Kelly's father is convinced that Woody is trying to blackmail him; and Rebecca's Thanksgiving feast for the gang goes predictably awry.

**254** Feelings . . . Whoa, Whoa, Whoa · December 3, 1992
**Writer:** Kathy Ann Stumpe
**Director:** Rick Beren
**Guest Stars:** Keene Curtis, Jackie Swanson, Erick Avari, Paul Willson, Tim Cunningham, Philip Perlman, Eric A. Payne

Carla is reluctant to reveal her true feelings after John Allen Hill suffers a heart attack.

**255** Daddy's Little Middle-Aged Girl · December 10, 1992
**Writer:** Rebecca Parr Cioffi
**Director:** James Burrows
**Guest Stars:** Robert Prosky, Jackie Swanson

Rebecca's dictatorial father commands her to move back to San Diego; and Woody and Kelly attempt to iron out the kinks in their own living arrangements.

One-time *Hill Street Blues* co-star Robert Prosky is cast as Rebecca's tyrannical father, Navy Captain Franklin Howe. The part was actually a homecoming of sorts for the well-known character actor, who had some years earlier been offered the part of Coach in the show's original pilot. But though scheduling difficulties forced the actor to forfeit the role—which was eventually played to great effect by Nick Colasanto—the show's producers were only too pleased to invite the actor back to the bar when this plumb guest-starring role finally presented itself a decade later. Also present in the episode's guest cast is Ethel Kennedy, who contributes a cameo in the show's teaser.

**256**   Love Me, Love My Car                 December 17, 1992
  **Writer:** David Lloyd
  **Director:** James Burrows
  **Guest Stars:** Dana Delany, Shane Sweet, Toni Elizabeth White,
  Amanda Costello

Sam is determined to get his Corvette back from the widow of the
man who bought it from him; and Rebecca becomes attached to
the pig that Woody plans to cook for Christmas dinner.

Dana Delany, late of ABC's Vietnam-era series *China Beach*, guest stars
as the widow who inherits Sam's car.

**257**   Sunday Dinner                          January 7, 1993
  **Writer:** Fred Graver
  **Director:** James Burrows
  **Guest Stars:** Kristen Cloke, David Froman, Marilyn Rockafellow,
  Jonathan Emerson, Toby Ganger, Charles Esten, Colin Drake,
  Ruth Engel, Paul Willson, Laura Gardner, George Milan, Rich-
  ard Danielson, Chris and Kevin Graves, Tim Cunningham, Alan
  Koss

Frasier mistakes his secretary's intentions after she invites him to
her house for Sunday dinner; and Norm and Cliff videotape a
family reunion.

**258**   Norm's Big Audit                       January 14, 1993
  **Writer:** Tom Leopold
  **Director:** John Ratzenberger
  **Guest Stars:** Sharon Barr, Paul Willson, Tim Cunningham,
  Steve Giannelli, Alan Koss

A determined IRS auditor makes a play for Norm; and Sam attempts to prevent the gang from watching one of his old games
on TV.

Sharon Barr, who had previously guest starred as one of the bachelor-
bidders in the sixth-year episode "Bidding on the Boys," returns to play
the IRS agent in this episode—one of the rare instances where the show's
producers violated their own long-standing "one actor-one role" casting
rule.

**259**   It's a Mad, Mad, Mad, Mad Bar          January 21, 1993
  **Writer:** Rebecca Parr Cioffi
  **Director:** James Burrows
  **Guest Stars:** Roger Rees, Robert Machray

A newly destitute Robin Colcord returns to Cheers hoping to retrieve a cache of money he'd stashed there before his arrest.


**260**   Loathe and Marriage          February 4, 1993
  **Writers:** Ken Levine, David Isaacs
  **Director:** James Burrows
  **Guest Stars:** Jean Kasem, Dan Hedaya, Keene Curtis, Jackie Swanson, Leah Remini, Josh Lozoff, Dennis Cockrum, Barry Zajac

Carla's daughter, Serafina, ferments a minor family crisis when she insists that her wayward father, Nick, be allowed to give her away at her upcoming wedding.


**261**   Is There a Doctor in the Howe? (Part 1)     February 11, 1993
  **Writer:** Kathy Ann Stumpe
  **Director:** James Burrows
  **Guest Stars:** Paul Willson, Tera Hendrickson, Tim Cunningham, Alan Koss, Peter Schreiner

Still reeling from the shock of his recent marital difficulties, Frasier turns to Rebecca for romantic consolation.


**262**   The Bar Manager, the Shrink, (Part 2)     February 18, 1993
       His Wife and Her Lover
  **Writer:** Kathy Ann Stumpe
  **Director:** James Burrows
  **Guest Stars:** Keene Curtis, Peter Vogt, Paul Willson

Lilith pays a surprise call on Frasier, with her newly deranged fiancé—now armed and dangerous—not far behind.

Guest star Peter Vogt returns in the role of Lilith's slightly off-center paramour, Dr. Louis Pascal.

**263**   The Last Picture Show                    February 25, 1993
   **Writers:** Fred Graver
   **Director:** James Burrows
   **Guest Stars:** Pat Hingle, Michael Winters, Nick Oleson

Carla and Rebecca contemplate mutiny after Sam leaves the bar's former owner in charge; and Cliff leads the guys on a nostalgic excursion to a local drive-in theater.

Veteran character actor Pat Hingle plays the bar's former proprietor, Gus O'Malley.


**264**   Bar Wars VII: The Naked Prey             March 18, 1993
   **Writers:** Ken Levine, David Isaacs
   **Director:** James Burrows
   **Guest Stars:** Harry Anderson, Robert Desiderio, Paul Willson, Maurice Roëves, Jayson Kane

Sam enlists the help of con man Harry the Hat in the latest round of the bar's ongoing feud with the denizens of Gary's Old Towne Tavern.

Longtime *Night Court* star Harry Anderson once again reprises his occasional role as the bar's resident bamboozler, Harry the Hat.


**265**   Look Before You Sleep                    April 1, 1993
   **Writer:** Rebecca Parr Cioffi
   **Director:** James Burrows
   **Guest Stars:** Frances Sternhagen, Peter MacNicol, Keene Curtis, Bernadette Birkett, Gordon Clapp, Deirdre Imershein

Sam embarks on an increasingly futile search for a bed to sleep in after he accidentally locks his house keys in the bar.

Film star Peter MacNicol guest stars as the hotel clerk in this episode. Also featured in the episode's supporting cast is Gordon Clapp, who would figure prominently in the ensemble cast of ABC's *NYPD Blue* the following season.

**266**  Woody Gets an Election                         April 22, 1993
   **Writers:** Dan O'Shannon, Tom Anderson, Dan Staley, Rob Long
   **Director:** James Burrows
   **Guest Stars:** Jackie Swanson, Spanky McFarland, Philip Baker
   Hall, Peri Gilpin, Clarke Gordon, Paul Willson, LaTanya
   Richardson, Stephen Parr, Jerry Penacoli

Frasier nominates Woody for a city council seat as a prank, only
to find himself amazed when the bartender's campaign actually
begins to gain momentum.

Former *Our Gang* star Spanky McFarland contributes a cameo in this
episode. Also featured in the guest cast is Peri Gilpin, who would reap-
pear as Frasier's able assistant, Roz, on *Frasier* the following season.

**267**  It's Lonely on the Top                         April 29, 1993
   **Writer:** Heide Perlman
   **Director:** James Burrows
   **Guest Stars:** Jackie Swanson, Philip Perlman, Paul Willson

Carla is overwhelmed by remorse in the wake of a recent romantic indiscretion, until Sam bolsters her waning self-confidence
with a surprising revelation of his own.

Filmed out of broadcast sequence, this show bears the distinction of
being the last-produced episode of *Cheers*.

**268**  Rebecca Gaines, Rebecca Loses (one hour)       May 6, 1993
   **Writer:** David Lloyd
   **Director:** James Burrows
   **Guest Stars:** Frances Sternhagen, Jackie Swanson, Richard
   Doyle, George Hearn, Robert Cornthwaite, Paul Willson, Calvin
   Remsberg, Renata Scott

Rebecca jumps to the conclusion that Kelly's father has designs
on her; and the gang suspects foul play when Cliff's mother appears to have vanished without a trace.

**269**   The Guy Can't Help It                    May 13, 1993
   **Writers:** David Angell, Peter Casey, David Lee
   **Director:** James Burrows
   **Guest Stars:** Tom Berenger, Sharon Lawrence, Paul Willson,
   Gilbert Lewis, Bradford Bancroft, Steve Kehela

Rebecca wonders if she's finally found Mr. Right when she begins
dating a plumber; and Sam makes a break with the past when he
joins a support group for sexual compulsives.

Film actor Tom Berenger, best-remembered for his starring role in the
1986 Oscar winner *Platoon*, is well-cast as Rebecca's earthy romantic interest, Don Santry. Also featured in this episode's guest roster is Sharon
Lawrence, who would land a choice role in the cast of ABC's *NYPD Blue*
the following season.

**270**   One for the Road (two-hour special)        May 20, 1993
   **Writers:** Glen Charles, Les Charles
   **Director:** James Burrows
   **Guest Stars:** Shelley Long, Tom Berenger, Jackie Swanson, Mike
   Ditka, Kim Alexis, Mark Harelik, Anthony Heald, Paul Willson,
   Mitchell Lichtenstein, Tim Cunningham, Steve Giannelli, Alan
   Koss

When Diane Chambers turns up for an unexpected visit, Sam is
determined to convince his former fiancée that he's discovered
domestic bliss at last; and Rebecca finds a happy denouement to
her own romantic woes when her whirlwind courtship with
plumber Don Santry leads to matrimony.

Originally intended to run in a one-hour time slot, the last episode's
running time was expanded by an additional half-hour during the show's
final production week, after it became clear to all concerned that trying
to wrap up eleven seasons' worth of loose ends in anything less than an
hour and half would've proved a difficult task indeed. It's unlikely that
the show's producers received any argument on that decision from the
programmers at NBC, who rather shrewdly positioned the show's 97-
minute grand finale as the centerpiece of "Last Call," the gala two-hour
spectacular that would serve as the show's last hurrah on prime time.
The series's closing night festivities were kicked off with a special twenty-
two minute *Cheers* mini-retrospective hosted by NBC sports announcer
Bob Costas.

By the time *Cheers* left the air at the close of the 1992-93 prime-time season, the series had long since distinguished itself as one of the most popular programs in the history of the medium. But perhaps the greatest measure of the show's lasting legacy can be seen in its ongoing influence on the better comedies that dot today's prime-time landscape, where *Cheers's* trademark blend of high comedy and understated wit continues to inform and inspire situation comedies as varied in texture and approach as *Murphy Brown, Roseanne, Seinfeld, Friends,* and, of course, *Frasier.*

None of which should come as a surprise to readers of the present volume, who will by this point have little difficulty recognizing *Cheers's* unique status as the latest link in a comic dynasty that stretches at least as far back as *I Love Lucy.* And, as *Cheers* marches forth to assume its rightful place in the hallowed company of the medium's most-beloved classics, it's not hard to imagine Sam Malone standing up at the end of his bar to lead a toast.

Raise your mugs, he might propose, and toast the Ricardos and the Kramdens; here's to the Petries, the Bunkers, and the Hartleys. To all those TV families who, in good times or bad, never failed to leave their porch lights burning.

To the cabbies at Sunshine Taxi and the staff of the WJM Six O'Clock News; to the die-hard detectives of the Twelfth Precinct, and the tireless surgeons of the 4077th. To all the misfits and miscreants who beckoned us to join their gang on those nights when we had nothing better to do. It was an invitation we found hard to resist—even when we did have better things to do. And, finally, a toast to all those sitting at the bar. To tomorrow's classics, and all those reruns yet to come.

Cheers.

## EMMY AWARDS

The following is a listing of the Emmy Awards bestowed on *Cheers* by the National Academy of Television Arts and Sciences.

**1982-83**   Outstanding Comedy Series
Outstanding Lead Actress in a Comedy Series: Shelley Long
Outstanding Directing in a Comedy Series: James Burrows, "Showdown (Part 2)"
Outstanding Writing in a Comedy Series: Glen Charles, Les Charles, "Give Me a Ring Sometime"
Outstanding Individual Achievement/Graphic Design and Title Sequences: James Castle, Bruce Bryant

**1983-84**   Outstanding Comedy Series
Outstanding Supporting Actress in a Comedy Series: Rhea
  Perlman
Outstanding Writing in a Comedy Series: David Angell,
  "Old Flames"
Outstanding Film Editing for a Series: Andrew Chulack,
  "Old Flames"

**1984-85**   Outstanding Supporting Actress in a Comedy: Rhea
  Perlman
Outstanding Live and Tape Sound Mixing and Sound
  Effects for Series:   Douglas Gray, Michael Ballin, Thomas
  Huth, Sam Black, "The Executive Executioner"

**1985-86**   Outstanding Supporting Actress in a Comedy: Rhea
  Perlman
Outstanding Sound Mixing for a Comedy Series: Michael
  Ballin, Robert Douglas, Douglas Gray, Thomas
  Huth, "Fear Is My Co-Pilot"

**1986-87**   Outstanding Guest Performer in a Comedy Series: John
  Cleese, "Simon Says"
Outstanding Sound Mixing for a Comedy Series: Michael
  Ballin, Bob Douglas, Doug Grey, Tom Huth,
  "The Proposal"

**1987-88**   Outstanding Editing for a Comedy Series, Multi-Camera
  Production: Andy Ackerman, "The Big Kiss-Off"

**1988-89**   Outstanding Comedy Series
Outstanding Supporting Actor in a Comedy Series: Woody
  Harrelson
Outstanding Supporting Actress in a Comedy Series: Rhea
  Perlman

**1989-90**   Outstanding Lead Actor in a Comedy Series: Ted Danson
Outstanding Supporting Actress in a Comedy Series: Bebe
  Neuwirth
Outstanding Sound Mixing in a Comedy Series or Special:
  Robert Crosby, Jr., Thomas Huth, Bobby Douglas, "The
  Stork Brings a Crane"

**1990-91**   Outstanding Comedy Series
Outstanding Lead Actress in a Comedy Series: Kirstie Alley
Outstanding Supporting Actress in a Comedy Series: Bebe

Neuwirth
Outstanding Directing in a Comedy Series: James Burrows,
"Woody Interruptus"

**1992-93**  Outstanding Lead Actor in a Comedy Series: Ted Danson
Outstanding Editing for Series, Multi-Camera Production:
Robert Bramwell, "One for the Road"

# Appendix A

.

---

## The Critics' Choice Poll

---

In early 1985, forty-five professional television critics were polled by the author to determine the classic comedies that would become the subject of this book. Here are the results of that poll, listed in order of the critics' preferences.

### THE TOP TV SITCOMS OF ALL TIME AS DETERMINED BY THE NATION'S TV CRITICS—1985

| | |
|---|---|
| 1 | *The Mary Tyler Moore Show* |
| 2 | *All in the Family* |
| 3 | *I Love Lucy* |
| 4 | *M\*A\*S\*H* |
| 5 | *The Dick Van Dyke Show* |
| 6 | *The Honeymooners* |
| 7 | *Barney Miller* |
| 8 | *Cheers* |
| 9 | *The Bob Newhart Show* |
| 10 | *Taxi* |

### RUNNERS-UP

| | |
|---|---|
| 11 | *The Phil Silvers Show* |
| 12 | *The Andy Griffith Show* |
| 13 | *Get Smart* |
| 14 | *Soap* |
| 15 | *United States* |

# Appendix B

.

---

# Critical Choices

---

The following is a complete list of the critics who responded to the Critics' Choice Poll, along with their newspaper or syndicate affiliation at the time of the poll, and a complete list of their choices for the best - and worst - situation comedies of all time.

GLENN ALBIN *Interview* Magazine (New York, N.Y.)

BEST    *Green Acres, The Burns and Allen Show, Mary Hartman, Mary Hartman, Get Smart, Bewitched*

WORST   *Happy Days, Three's Company, Welcome Back, Kotter, Family Ties, Facts of Life*

JON ANDERSON *Chicago Tribune* (Chicago, Ill.)

BEST    *I Love Lucy, The Honeymooners, The Dick Van Dyke Show, The Mary Tyler Moore Show, Mr. Peepers*

WORST   *My Mother the Car, Rango, The Munsters, We Got It Made, AKA Pablo*

KEN BECK *The Tennessean* (Nashville, Tenn.)

BEST    *The Andy Griffith Show, Car 54, Where Are You?, Sanford and Son, Get Smart, The Mary Tyler Moore Show*

WORST   *Family Affair, The Partridge Family, Sugar Time, The Doris Day Show, Maude*

**JEFF BORDEN** *The Columbus Dispatch* (Columbus, Ohio)

BEST     *Barney Miller, M\*A\*S\*H, Cheers, I Love Lucy, The Associates*

WORST    *Three's Company, The Jeffersons, My Mother the Car, Carter Country, Ball Four*

**RUTH BUTLER** *Grand Rapids Press* (Grand Rapids, Mich.)

BEST     *M\*A\*S\*H, The Mary Tyler Moore Show, The Phil Silvers Show, The Dick Van Dyke Show, Barney Miller*

WORST    *Laverne and Shirley, Three's Company, AKA Pablo, The Jeffersons, The Hathaways*

**STUART D. BYKOFSKY** *Philadelphia Daily News* (Philadelphia, Pa.)

BEST     *The Mary Tyler Moore Show, All in the Family, I Love Lucy, Get Smart, Barney Miller*

WORST    *Laverne and Shirley, Joanie Loves Chachi, The Ropers, The Ted Knight Show, Three's Company*

**JOHN CARMAN** *Atlanta Journal and Constitution* (Atlanta, Ga.)

BEST     *The Mary Tyler Moore Show, The Honeymooners, The Bob Newhart Show, Cheers, United States*

WORST    *The Roller Girls, The Ropers, Punky Brewster, Gilligan's Island, Coed Fever*

**KENNETH R. CLARK** *Chicago Tribune* (Chicago, Ill.)

BEST     *The Mary Tyler Moore Show, The Dick Van Dyke Show, All in the Family, The Honeymooners, I Love Lucy*

WORST    *Open All Night, Gimme a Break, Ozzie and Harriet, The Flying Nun, Gilligan's Island*

**JERRY COFFEY** *Fort Worth Star-Telegram* (Fort Worth, Tex.)

BEST     *The Dick Van Dyke Show, All in the Family, I Love Lucy, The Honeymooners, M\*A\*S\*H*

WORST    *The Tammy Grimes Show, The Debbie Reynolds Show, Mr. T and Tina, Me and the Chimp, Lotsa Luck*

JEAN COLLOHAN *American Film Magazine* (Washington, D.C.)

BEST   *All in the Family, I Love Lucy, Dobie Gillis, The Odd Couple, The Mary Tyler Moore Show*

WORST   *Punky Brewster, The Ted Knight Show, Bosom Buddies, Me and the Chimp, Hello Larry*

DAVID CUTHBERT *New Orleans Times-Picayune-States-Item* (New Orleans, La.)

BEST   *I Love Lucy, The Mary Tyler Moore Show, The Bob Newhart Show, The Dick Van Dyke Show, All in the Family*

WORST   *When Things Were Rotten, The Brady Bunch, Family Affair, I Married Joan, Hogan's Heroes*

GARY DEEB *News America Syndicate* (Chicago, Ill.)

BEST   *The Honeymooners, Barney Miller, All in the Family, The Mary Tyler Moore Show, I Love Lucy*

WORST   *Three's Company, Joanie Loves Chachi, Flo, Mr. T and Tina, What's Happening*

MICHAEL DOUGAN *San Francisco Examiner* (San Francisco, Calif.)

BEST   *All in the Family, M\*A\*S\*H, The Mary Tyler Moore Show, Paul Sand in Friends and Lovers, The Dick Van Dyke Show*

WORST   *We Got It Made, Three's Company, My Mother the Car, Petticoat Junction, The Flying Nun*

DAVID DRAKE *Columbus Citizen-Journal* (Columbus, Ohio)

BEST   *The Dick Van Dyke Show, The Honeymooners, The Mary Tyler Moore Show, The Andy Griffith Show, The Bob Newhart Show*

WORST   *Roller Girls, CPO Sharkey, Mr. T and Tina, Hello Larry, Coed Fever*

RICK DU BROW *Los Angeles Herald Examiner* (Los Angeles, Calif.)

BEST   *The Honeymooners, Barney Miller, All in the Family, The Mary Tyler Moore Show, The Phil Silvers Show*

WORST   *Hello Larry, Me and the Chimp, Camp Runamuck, The Mothers-In-Law, Blansky's Beauties*

MIKE DUFFY *Detroit Free Press* (Detroit, Mich.)

BEST    *The Honeymooners, The Phil Silvers Show, The Mary Tyler Moore Show, Taxi, Bosom Buddies*

WORST    *Hello Larry, My Mother the Car, The Jeffersons, Three's Company, I'm Dickens, He's Fenster*

PETER FARRELL *The Oregonian* (Portland, Ore.)

BEST    *M\*A\*S\*H, Cheers, All in the Family, Barney Miller, United States, Soap*

WORST    *Mr. Smith, Three's Company, Condo, The New Odd Couple, Laverne and Shirley*

JUDY FLANDER *United Features Syndicate* (New York, N.Y.)

BEST    *The Mary Tyler Moore Show, Buffalo Bill, The Cosby Show, I Love Lucy, United States, All in the Family*

WORST    *The Ropers, Three's Company, The Jeffersons, Carter Country, Hogan's Heroes*

BARRY GARRON *Kansas City Star* (Kansas City, Mo.)

BEST    *All in the Family, M\*A\*S\*H, The Mary Tyler Moore Show, Odd Couple, The Dick Van Dyke Show*

WORST    *The Brian Keith Show, The McLean Stevenson Show, Joanie Loves Chachi, Ozzie's Girls, My Mother the Car*

TONY GENTILE *Newsday* (Long Island, N.Y.)

BEST    *I Love Lucy, The Honeymooners, The Mary Tyler Moore Show, All in the Family, Taxi*

WORST    *Mr. T and Tina, My Mother the Car, The Dumplings, The Montefuscos, Mama Malone*

MARC GUNTHER *Hartford Courant* (Hartford, Conn.)

BEST    *The Honeymooners, The Mary Tyler Moore Show, M\*A\*S\*H, I Love Lucy, All in the Family*

WORST    *We Got It Made, The Flying Nun*

### RICHARD HACK *Hollywood Reporter* (Hollywood, Calif.)

BEST   *The Mary Tyler Moore Show, Cheers, I Love Lucy, The Courtship of Eddie's Father, M\*A\*S\*H*

WORST   *My Mother the Car, Punky Brewster, Me and the Chimp, Welcome Back, Kotter, United States*

### KEN HOFFMAN *Phoenix Gazette* (Phoenix, Ariz.)

BEST   *Cheers, Taxi, The Honeymooners, Police Squad, All in the Family*

WORST   *Roller Girls, The Pruitts of Southampton, The McLean Stevenson Show, Facts of Life, Joanie Loves Chachi*

### BARBARA HOLSOPPLE *Pittsburgh Press* (Pittsburgh, Pa.)

BEST   *M\*A\*S\*H, The Mary Tyler Moore Show, All in the Family, Barney Miller, The Lucy Show*

WORST   *Me and the Chimp, Blansky's Beauties, Mr. T and Tina, The Mothers-In-Law, My Mother the Car*

### NOEL W. HOLSTON *Orlando Sentinel* (Orlando, Fla.)

BEST   *Barney Miller, The Mary Tyler Moore Show, The Bob Newhart Show, M\*A\*S\*H, The Andy Griffith Show*

WORST   *Mr. T and Tina, The Ropers, Coed Fever, Baby, I'm Back, Lotsa Luck*

### TOM JICHA *Miami News* (Miami, Fla.)

BEST   *All in the Family, Cheers, The Honeymooners, M\*A\*S\*H, Soap*

WORST   *The Hathaways, The McLean Stevenson Show, The Ropers, Three's a Crowd, Rango*

### BILL LANE *World News Syndicate* (Los Angeles, Calif.)

BEST   *Archie Bunker's Place, I Love Lucy, The Jeffersons, Amos 'n Andy, Sanford and Son, The Bill Cosby Show*

WORST   *Baby, I'm Back, Barney Miller, Alice (without Flo), Bridget Loves Bernie, The Monkees*

SYLVIA F. LAWLOR *Allentown Call-Chronicle* (Allentown, Pa.)

BEST  *The Mary Tyler Moore Show, All in the Family, The Dick Van Dyke Show, M\*A\*S\*H, Barney Miller, Cheers*

WORST  *San Pedro Beach Bums, Holmes and Yoyo, Busting Loose, In the Beginning, 90 Bristol Court*

JIM LYNCH *JDL Syndicate* (Boca Raton, Fla.)

BEST  *Barney Miller, All in the Family, Cheers, The Dick Van Dyke Show, Taxi*

WORST  *Laverne and Shirley, Three's Company, Mr. Ed, Gilligan's Island, Bosom Buddies*

JACK MAJOR *Providence Journal-Bulletin* (Providence, R.I.)

BEST  *The Dick Van Dyke Show, The Bob Newhart Show, I Love Lucy, Barney Miller, Fernwood 2-Night*

WORST  *Don't Call Me Charlie, Mama Malone, In the Beginning, Apple Pie, Ball Four*

LEE MARKSBURY *Fresno Bee* (Fresno, Calif.)

BEST  *I Love Lucy, M\*A\*S\*H, The Mary Tyler Moore Show, Laverne and Shirley, The Andy Griffith Show*

WORST  *Filthy Rich, I Dream of Jeannie, Three's Company, My Mother the Car, CPO Sharkey*

JOHN D. MILLER *South Bend Tribune* (South Bend, Ind.)

BEST  *M\*A\*S\*H, I Love Lucy, The Dick Van Dyke Show, All in the Family, Soap*

WORST  *The Ropers, The Beverly Hillbillies, My Mother the Car, We Got It Made, Hello Larry*

WALLY PATRICK *Asbury Park Press* (Asbury Park, N.J.)

BEST  *All in the Family, Buffalo Bill, The Mary Tyler Moore Show, Taxi, Leave It to Beaver*

WORST  *Mr. T and Tina, The ABC Evening News with Barbara Walters and Harry Reasoner*

JON-MICHAEL REED *United Features Syndicate* (New York, N.Y.)

BEST *The Mary Tyler Moore Show, Kate and Allie, The Dick Van Dyke Show, The Burns and Allen Show, The Bob Newhart Show*

WORST *AfterM\*A\*S\*H, Jennifer Slept Here, Hello Larry, Car 54, Where Are You? The Hathaways*

HAROLD SCHINDLER *Salt Lake City Tribune* (Salt Lake City, Utah)

BEST *Barney Miller, You'll Never Get Rich (The Phil Silvers Show), M\*A\*S\*H, F-Troop, The Dick Van Dyke Show*

WORST *Buffalo Bill, Detective School, Fish, My Mother the Car, The New Odd Couple*

TOM SHALES *Washington Post* (Washington, D. C.)

BEST *I Love Lucy, The Honeymooners, All in the Family, You'll Never Get Rich (The Phil Silvers Show), The Mary Tyler Moore Show*

WORST *Buffalo Bill, Just Our Luck, My Little Margie, Gimme a Break, Hello Larry*

RICK SHEFCHIK *Saint Paul Pioneer Press-Dispatch* (Saint Paul, Minn.)

BEST *The Dick Van Dyke Show, M\*A\*S\*H, The Mary Tyler Moore Show, I Love Lucy, Green Acres*

WORST *It's About Time, Hello Larry, The Tammy Grimes Show, Coed Fever, Benson*

DWIGHT SILVERMAN *San Antonio Light* (San Antonio, Tex.)

BEST *The Honeymooners, All in the Family, Get Smart, The Mary Tyler Moore Show, M\*A\*S\*H*

WORST *My Mother the Car, The Brady Bunch, The Flying Nun, Gilligan's Island, The Partridge Family*

STEVE SONSKY *Miami Herald* (Miami, Fla.)

BEST *All in the Family, The Mary Tyler Moore Show, I Love Lucy, The Honeymooners, The Bob Newhart Show*

WORST *The McLean Stevenson Show, Condo, My Mother the Car, Hogan's Heroes, Hello Larry*

VINCE STATEN *Louisville Times* (Louisville, Ky.)

BEST    *The Mary Tyler Moore Show, The Andy Griffith Show, The Dick Van Dyke Show, The Phil Silvers Show, M\*A\*S\*H*

WORST   *Alice, Mama Malone, The Ropers, The Waverly Wonders, My Mother the Car*

GUS STEVENS *San Diego Tribune* (San Diego, Calif.)

BEST    *Barney Miller, Taxi, WKRP in Cincinnati, M\*A\*S\*H, The Mary Tyler Moore Show*

WORST   *Hello Larry, My Mother the Car, Mr. T and Tina, Car 54, Where Are You? The Girl With Something Extra*

KARL VICK *Saint Petersburg Times* (Saint Petersburg, Fla.)

BEST    *The Andy Griffith Show, The Dick Van Dyke Show, The Mary Tyler Moore Show, All in the Family, Cheers*

WORST   *Ball Four, The Six O'Clock Follies, Carter Country, Brothers and Sisters, Far Out Space Nuts*

KEITH WATSON *Houston Post* (Houston, Tex.)

BEST    *I Love Lucy, All in the Family, Cheers, The Dick Van Dyke Show, Taxi*

WORST   *The Brady Bunch, Webster, Punky Brewster, Petticoat Junction, It's Not Easy*

RON WEISKIND *Pittsburgh Post-Gazette* (Pittsburgh, Pa.)

BEST    *All in the Family, M\*A\*S\*H, The Mary Tyler Moore Show, The Honeymooners, Cheers*

WORST   *Gilligan's Island, Three's a Crowd, Three's Company, Ball Four, Green Acres*

BOB WISEHART *Sacramento Bee* (Sacramento, Calif.)

BEST    *The Dick Van Dyke Show, I Love Lucy, M\*A\*S\*H, The Mary Tyler Moore Show, The Honeymooners*

WORST   *Gilligan's Island, My Mother the Car, Three's Company, The Hathaways, The Jeffersons*

# Appendix C

.

---

## For Further Research

---

Museum of Television and Radio, 25 West 52nd Street, New York, NY 10019
  An extensive and ever-growing collection of classic radio and television programs is the highlight of this invaluable research facility. Write for visitor or membership information.

*The Television Index*
  A trade newsletter that provides the broadcast industry with complete, in-depth network program listings each week. Subscription information: Editor in chief, 40-29 27th Street, Long Island City, NY 11101

*TV Collector: The Bi-monthly for Collectors of Television Material*
  Reviews, articles, and episode guides to the best of vintage television. Subscription information: Diane L. Albert, Editor, Dept. CS, P.O. Box 1088, Easton, MA 02334

*TV Guide*
  The best single source for background on TV and television programming. Subscription information: TV Guide, Box 600, Radnor, PA 19080

# Appendix D

.

---

# Who's Who

---

This short biographical glossary is designed to provide a quick reference to the careers of the writers, directors, producers, and network executives who appear most prominently in this book. The credits listed are by no means complete, but are included to suggest some of the more interesting sideroads that these colorful creators embarked on before—or after—they made their most significant contributions to the classic situation comedy.

HARRY ACKERMAN   CBS vice president of programming in the early 1950s. A key figure in the genesis of *I Love Lucy*, he later executive produced a string of long-running sitcoms, including *Bachelor Father*, *Hazel*, and *Bewitched*, among many others.

DESI ARNAZ   Executive producer of *I Love Lucy*. At one time the head of Desilu Studios, he retired in the early 1960s, only to return as executive producer of *The Mothers-in-Law* in 1967.

DANNY ARNOLD   Creator, with Theodore Flicker, and producer of *Barney Miller*. A former film editor, he was a staff writer for Rosemary Clooney and Tennessee Ernie Ford in the 1950s, and later served as story editor on *The Real McCoys*, produced *Bewitched* and *That Girl*, and was executive producer of *My World and Welcome to It*.

WILLIAM ASHER   Most prominent director of *I Love Lucy*. He would continue as a top sitcom producer/director on *Bewitched* in the 1960s and as a regular director of *Alice* in the late 1970s.

PETER BALDWIN   Director of *The Dick Van Dyke Show*. A top TV director, he joined the MTM stable in the early 1970s, where he directed numerous episodes of *The Mary Tyler Moore Show* and *The Bob Newhart Show*, among many others.

JERRY BELSON   Prolific contributor, with partner Garry Marshall, to *The Dick Van Dyke Show*. Among many distinguished credits, he created and wrote—with Marshall—TV's *Odd Couple* and directed a handful of classic *Mary Tyler Moore* episodes.

PETER BONERZ   Director of *The Bob Newhart Show*. He began as an improvisational actor but emerged from *Bob Newhart* as one of the most sought-after directors in the field.

JAMES L. BROOKS   Co-creator of *The Mary Tyler Moore Show* and *Taxi*. One of the central forces in the comedy renaissance of the 1970s, the prolific writer was one of the creators of *Rhoda*, *Lou Grant*, *Room 222*, and one of the few sitcom writers to successfully branch out into feature films, though he occasionally continues to devote his energies to television, including 1987's *Tracey Ullman Show* and *The Simpsons*.

ALLAN BURNS   Co-creator of *The Mary Tyler Moore Show*. A prominent TV comedy writer in the 1960s, he began—with partner Chris Hayward—as a scripter for Jay Ward's *Bullwinkle Show* and was one of the founding writers at MTM, where he also created *Rhoda*, *Lou Grant*, and *The Duck Factory*, among others.

JAMES BURROWS   Co-creator of *Cheers*. The son of playwright Abe Burrows, the one-time Broadway stage manager was one of the brightest young directors at MTM in the mid-seventies before he was tapped as full-time director of *Taxi* in 1978.

BOB CARROLL AND MADELYN PUGH MARTIN DAVIS   Co-creators and writers of *I Love Lucy*. In addition to their credits as executive producers on *Alice* and *Private Benjamin*, the team that practically invented the TV sitcom also created *The Tom Ewell Show*, *The Lucy Show*, and *The Mothers-in-Law*.

GLEN CHARLES AND LES CHARLES   Co-creators of *Cheers*. With their impeccable credentials as writers for *M\*A\*S\*H*, *The Mary Tyler Moore Show*, and *The Bob Newhart Show*, the brothers were a perfect choice to serve as producers and head writers for the first three seasons of *Taxi*.

MARC DANIELS   The original director of *I Love Lucy*, he left that series in 1952 to direct *I Married Joan*. The veteran TV pioneer eventually signed on as staff director of *Alice* in the late 1970s.

STAN DANIELS   Producer and writer of *The Mary Tyler Moore Show*. A prolific writer who also co-created—with Ed. Weinberger—a long line of TV comedies in the 1970s, including *Doc*, *Phyllis*, *The Betty White Show*, as well as *Taxi* and *The Associates*, among others.

DAVID DAVIS   Creator, with Lorenzo Music, of *The Bob Newhart Show*, and co-creator of *Taxi*. He began his career as a youthful director of *Dobie Gillis*, later moved into production on *He and She*, and teamed up with Lorenzo Music to write and produce early episodes of *The Mary Tyler Moore Show*.

MADELYN PUGH MARTIN DAVIS   (see Bob Carroll)

SAM DENOFF AND BILL PERSKY   Prominent writers on *The Dick Van Dyke Show*. Among their many other writing and production credits, the team went on to create *That Girl*, *Good Morning World*, and *Lotsa Luck*.

THEODORE FLICKER   Creator, with Danny Arnold, of *Barney Miller*. He moved from improvisational theater into television comedy in the 1960s, where he earned writing or directing credits on *The Dick Van Dyke Show*, *The Andy Griffith Show*, and *I Dream of Jeannie*, among many others.

JIM FRITZELL AND EVERETT GREENBAUM   Writers for *M*A*S*H*. The veteran writers had contributed scripts to a long line of first-rate comedies, including *Mr. Peepers* in the early 1950s and *The Andy Griffith Show* a decade later.

LARRY GELBART   With Gene Reynolds, developed *M*A*S*H* for television. Among his many other credits, he created *United States* for TV, authored *Sly Fox* for Broadway, and wrote *Tootsie* for the big screen.

EVERETT GREENBAUM   (see Jim Fritzell)

CHRIS HAYWARD   Prolific writer for *Barney Miller*. Created—with one-time partner Alan Burns—a string of sixties comedies, including *My Mother the Car*, and *The Munsters*, before teaming with Danny Arnold on *Barney Miller* and *Joe Bash*.

DAVID ISAACS AND KEN LEVINE   Executive story editors on *M*A*S*H*. The team also served as writers and co-producers of *Cheers* before they created Mary Tyler Moore's underrated comeback series, *Mary*, in 1985.

BARRY KEMP   Frequent contributor to *Taxi*. He later created MTM's *Newhart*.

MORT LACHMAN   Executive producer on *All in the Family*. A longtime writer for Bob Hope and producer of numerous TV spectaculars, the veteran writer also produced *Archie Bunker's Place* and *One Day at a Time* for Norman Lear, among many others.

NORMAN LEAR   Creator of *All in the Family*. The producer responsible for more ground-breaking comedy series than any other creator in television, his credits include *Mary Hartman, Mary Hartman*, *Maude*, and *All That Glitters*, among others.

SHELDON LEONARD   Executive producer of *The Dick Van Dyke Show*. A major figure in the evolution of quality TV comedy, he produced or created a large and distinguished family of sitcoms in the 1950s and 1960s, including *Make Room for Daddy*, *The Andy Griffith Show*, and *The Real McCoys*, among others.

KEN LEVINE   (see David Isaacs)

DAVID LLOYD   Story editor and writer for *The Mary Tyler Moore Show*. He also contributed numerous first-rate scripts to *The Bob Newhart Show*, *Taxi*, and *Cheers* and was creator of ABC's *Mr. Sunshine* and cable TV's *Brothers*.

GARRY MARSHALL   Prolific contributor, with Jerry Belson, to *The Dick Van Dyke Show*. He later created TV's *Odd Couple* and *Happy Days*, which became the cornerstone of a formidable comic dynasty in the late 1970s.

BURT METCALFE   Executive producer of *M*A*S*H*. A former actor and studio casting agent, he later directed and produced numerous episodes of the series and created—with Larry Gelbart—*AfterM*A*S*H*.

LORENZO MUSIC   Creator, with David Davis, of *The Bob Newhart Show*. A former folk singer, he was a staff writer on *The Smothers Brothers Comedy Hour* before he teamed up with David Davis to write many of the best early *Mary Tyler Moore* scripts, which led to the team's assignment to develop and produce *Rhoda*.

DON NICHOLL, MICHAEL ROSS, AND BERNIE WEST   Producers of *All in the Family*. After contributing many of the best scripts during that show's early years, the team later developed *Three's Company* for ABC.

JESS OPPENHEIMER  Co-creator and producer of *I Love Lucy*. He returned to weekly TV in 1969, when he created *The Debbie Reynolds Show*, a series that bore a distinct resemblance to his earlier classic.

JERRY PARIS  Director of *The Dick Van Dyke Show*. The former actor would eventually be reunited with Dick Van Dyke writer Garry Marshall as a regular director of *The Odd Couple* and staff director on *Happy Days*.

TOM PATCHETT AND JAY TARSES  Influential writers and producers of *The Bob Newhart Show*. They went on the create MTM's *The Tony Randall Show* before they hit their stride with the underrated classic *Buffalo Bill* in the early 1980s. Patchett was later a co-creator of *Alf* for NBC.

BILL PERSKY  (see Sam Denoff)

NOAM PITLIK  Director of *Barney Miller*. After a successful acting career that included a regular part on *The Bob Newhart Show*, he directed many later episodes of *Taxi* before signing on as staff director of *Mr. Belvedere*.

ALAN RAFKIN  Director of *The Bob Newhart Show*. A respected director with hundreds of sitcom episodes to his credit, including a handful of *Dick Van Dyke* shows and numerous installments of Norman Lear's *One Day at a Time*.

CARL REINER  Creator of *The Dick Van Dyke Show*. After that series, the writer-director embarked on a very successful career as an actor and director in feature films, though he did return to television as creator of *The New Dick Van Dyke Show* in the early 1970s and as executive producer and star of *Good Heavens* in 1976.

GENE REYNOLDS  Producer of *M\*A\*S\*H*. The former child actor was an NBC casting director in the 1950s and later directed series as varied as *Peter Gunn*, *The Andy Griffith Show*, *My Three Sons*, and *Hogan's Heroes* before he established his reputation as a top-flight producer on shows like *Room 222* and *Lou Grant*.

JOHN RICH  Director of *The Dick Van Dyke Show* and producer/director of *All in the Family*. A top producer and director whose credits list *Our Miss Brooks*, *Gunsmoke*, *My World and Welcome to It*, *On the Rocks*, *Mr. Sunshine*, and *MacGyver*, among many others.

MICHAEL ROSS  (see Don Nicholl)

JAY SANDRICH  Director of *The Mary Tyler Moore Show* and *The Bob Newhart Show*. After an apprenticeship as assistant director on *I Love Lucy* and *The Danny Thomas Show*, he directed an astounding array of distinguished series, including most episodes of *He and She*, *Soap*, and *The Cosby Show*, all in addition to his highly influential work at MTM in the early 1970s.

BOB SCHILLER AND BOB WEISKOPF  Prolific contributors to *I Love Lucy* and *All in the Family*. Their numerous other TV credits include shows as varied as *Pete and Gladys*, *All in the Family*, and *Maude*.

TONY SHEEHAN  Producer of *Barney Miller*. One of the most prolific contributors to that long-running series, he later signed on as executive producer of *Mr. Belvedere*.

FRED SILVERMAN  The only broadcast executive to head the entertainment divisions of all three networks. Throughout the 1970s, he was an instrumental figure in the genesis of *M\*A\*S\*H*, *Rhoda*, *Maude*, *Taxi*, *Cheers*, and *United States*, among many others.

LEONARD STERN  Writer, with Sydney Zelinka, of *The Honeymooners*. He later scripted *The Phil Silvers Show*, produced *Get Smart*, and created *He and She*, a little-seen but highly influential series of the late 1960s.

JAY TARSES   (see Tom Patchett)

ALAN WAGNER   Vice president of CBS Development from 1967 to 1973. As the executive in charge of new program development, he nurtured *The Bob Newhart Show*, *All in the Family*, *The Mary Tyler Moore Show*, and *M\*A\*S\*H*, among others.

REINHOLD WEEGE   Producer and writer of *Barney Miller*. He later created and produced NBC's *Night Court*.

ED WEINBERGER   Writer and producer of *The Mary Tyler Moore Show*. A prolific writer who was also involved in the creation of *Taxi*, 1969's *The Bill Cosby Show*, as well as *The Cosby Show*, *Doc*, *Phyllis*, *The Betty White Show*, and *Amen*, among others.

BOB WEISKOPF   (see Bob Schiller)

BERNIE WEST   (see Don Nicholl)

ROBERT WOOD   President of CBS from 1969 to 1976. The executive changed the face of modern television comedy when he added *All in the Family* and *The Mary Tyler Moore Show* to the network's schedule in the early 1970s.

MICHAEL ZINBERG   Executive producer of *The Bob Newhart Show*. He also wrote or directed various episodes of that series, *The Mary Tyler Moore Show*, and *Taxi*, among others.

# Bibliography

.

---
# General
---

Bedell, Sally. *Up the Tube: Prime Time TV in the Silverman Years.* New York: Viking, 1981.

Brooks, Tim and Earle Marsh. *The Complete Directory to Prime Time TV Network Shows: 1946-Present.* New York: Ballantine, 1979.

Brown, Les. *Les Brown's Encyclopedia of Television.* New York: Zoetrope, 1982.

_____. *Television: The Business Behind the Box.* New York: Harvest Books/ Harcourt Brace Jovanovich, 1971.

Christensen, Mark, and Cameron Stauth. *The Sweeps: Behind the Scenes in Network TV.* New York: Morrow, 1984.

Eisner, Joel, and David Krinsky. *Television Comedy Series: An Episode Guide to 153 TV Sitcoms in Syndication.* Jefferson, N.C.: McFarland, 1984.

Gitlin, Todd. *Inside Prime Time.* New York: Pantheon, 1985.

Halliwell, Leslie. *Halliwell's Film Guide.* New York: Scribner's, 1982.

_____, with Philip Purser. *Halliwell's Television Companion.* 2d ed. London: Granada, 1982.

Javna, John. *Cult TV: A Viewer's Guide to the Shows America Can't Live Without.* New York: St. Martin's, 1985.

Katz, Ephraim. *The Film Encyclopedia.* New York: Perigee/Putnam, 1982.

McNeil, Alex. *Total Television: A Comprehensive Guide to Programming from 1948 to the Present.* 2d ed. New York: Viking/Penguin, 1984.

Mitz, Rick. *The Great TV Sitcom Book.* New York: Perigee/Putnam, 1983.

Newcomb, Horace, and Robert S. Alley. *The Producer's Medium: Conversations with Creators of American TV.* New York: Oxford University Press, 1983.

Scheuer, Stephen H. *Who's Who in Television and Cable.* New York: Facts on File, 1983.

Steinberg, Cobbett. *TV Facts: Revised and Updated.* New York: Facts on File, 1983.

Terrace, Vincent. *Encyclopedia of Television Series, Pilots and Specials.* New York: Zoetrope, 1985.

# Chapter Notes

*Classic Sitcoms* contains the most complete guide ever published to ten of America's favorite television comedies. To ensure accuracy, and to keep the information consistent from show to show, the credits that appear in this book were copied—whenever possible—directly from the on-screen credits broadcast at the beginning and end of each of the better than fifteen hundred episodes listed.

The original network airdates were gathered from weekly listings in *TV Guide* and *The Television Index* and then, whenever possible, compared with original production or syndication company records. The names that appear in the cast listings—prominent guest stars as well as obscure bit players—were drawn from all of the above sources, and reviewed with input from one or more of the individuals whose expertise on the various programs in this book is acknowledged elsewhere.

Of course, despite every effort to check and double-check the information gathered between these covers, the author is aware that errors and inconsistencies are inevitable in a work of this scope. Sharp-eyed readers who spot obvious mistakes are invited to submit their corrections or suggestions to the author in care of the publisher, or directly via e-mail to <vince@lafn.org>.

Of the hundreds of books and magazine articles consulted during the preparation of this book, the following were particularly useful in providing quotes and invaluable background material.

## "I LOVE LUCY"

Andrews, Bart. *The "I Love Lucy" Book*. Garden City, N.Y.: Dolphin/Doubleday, 1985.

Arnaz, Desi. *A Book*. New York: Morrow, 1976.

"Dialogue With Lucille Ball," American Film Institute, *Dialogue on Film*.

McGrath, Douglas. "I Love Lucy" The Collector's Edition." Program notes, CBS Video Library, 1986.

MacKenzie, Alex C., Jr. "A Descriptive Analysis of the Factors That Influenced the Creation of Selected Television Programs, 1946-76." Ph.D. thesis, available from University Microfilms International, Ann Arbor, Mich.

O'Flaherty, Terrence. "TV Will Never Be Quite the Same Again." *TV Guide*, July 6, 1974.

Whitney, Dwight. "We Wrote the Baby Into the Story. We Had To." *TV Guide,* March 31, 1973.

## "THE HONEYMOONERS"

Crescenti, Peter, and Bob Columbe. *The Official Honeymooners Treasury: To the Moon and Back With Ralph, Norton, Alice and Trixie.* New York: Perigee Books/ Putnam, 1985.
McCrohan, Donna. "The Honeymooners Classic 39." *Reruns Magazine,* no. 22, Spring 1986.
_____. *The Honeymooners Companion: The Kramdens and the Nortons Revisited.* New York: Workman, 1978.
_____, and Peter Crescenti. *The Honeymooners Lost Episodes.* New York: Workman, 1986.
Shanley, J. P. "Electronicam Said to Cut Costs." *The New York Times,* September 4, 1955.
Stump, Al. "It Was Chaos. Crazy!" *TV Guide,* January 24, 1976.
Zehme, Bill. "Jackie Gleason: The Playboy Interview." *Playboy,* August 1986.

## "THE DICK VAN DYKE SHOW"

Gehman, Richard. "Laurie Petrie Is Mary Tyler Moore. Or Is She?" *TV Guide,* May 23, 1964.
Lewis, Jerry D. "Carl Reiner: Laughs for Stage, Screen, and Dick Van Dyke." *TV Guide,* January 4, 1964.
Novelli, Rebecca. "Great Shows: The Dick Van Dyke Show." *Emmy Magazine,* Summer 1979.
Raddatz, Leslie. "They've Got No Kick Coming." *TV Guide,* March 27, 1965.
_____. "You Don't Give a Desk a Name Because It Has No Moving Parts." *TV Guide,* February 26, 1966.
Rich, John. Interview with the author, October 1986.
Symposium with Morey Amsterdam, Sheldon Leonard, Rose Marie, Carl Reiner, and John Rich. Academy of Television Arts and Sciences, Hollywood, Calif., November 1986.
Tharp, Richard. "The Dick Van Dyke Show." *Reruns Magazine,* no. 14, July 1982, and no. 17, July 1983.
Weissman, Ginny, and Coyne Steven Sanders. *The Dick Van Dyke Show: Anatomy of a Classic.* New York: St. Martin's, 1983.
"What's a Dick Van Dyke?" *TV Guide,* December 9, 1961. Uncredited.
"Who Is That Cutie Playing His Wife?" *TV Guide,* June 2, 1962. Uncredited.

## "THE MARY TYLER MOORE SHOW"

Barber, Rowland. "We Are All Pussycats Here." *TV Guide,* February 8, 1975.
Davidson, Bill. "There Was Mary Tyler Moore . . ." *TV Guide,* May 19, 1973.
Ephron, Nora. "A Fond Farewell to the Funniest Show on Television." *Esquire,* February 1977.
Newcomb, Horace, and Robert S. Alley. *The Producer's Medium.* New York: Oxford University Press, 1983.

Pattison, Jim. "The Mary Tyler Moore Show." *Movie Collector's World*, November 30, 1984.

Torgerson, Ellen. "Mary Marrying Lou, Sue Ann Carried Off by King Kong, Ted Baxter as Cronkite's Assistant . . ." *TV Guide*, March 18, 1977.

Weingarten, Paul. "The Kitten That Roared." *Chicago Tribune Magazine*, December 1, 1985.

Whitney, Dwight. "Mary , It Needs One Beat of Wistfulness." *TV Guide*, February 26, 1972.

————. "You've Come a Long Way, Baby." *TV Guide*, September 19, 1970.

## "ALL IN THE FAMILY"

Adler, Richard P. *All in the Family: A Critical Appraisal.* New York: Praeger, 1979.

Barber, Rowland. "Bellowing, Half-Baked, Fire-Breathing Bigotry." *TV Guide*, Mary 29, 1971.

Beck, Marilyn. "Archie Wants Out, But . . ." Syndicated column, November 4, 1977.

Davidson, Bill. "Trouble in Paradise (Part One)," *TV Guide*, April 6, 1974.

————. "The Uprising in Lear's Kingdom (Part Two)," *TV Guide*, April 13, 1974.

"Dialogue on Film: Norman Lear." *American Film Magazine*, June 1977.

Kaufman, Dave. "Archie a Lovable Bigot, Says Lear." *Daily Variety*, August 3, 1971.

Lear, Norman. Interview with the author, December 1986.

MacKenzie, Alex C., Jr. "A Descriptive Analysis of the Factors That Influenced the Creation of Selected Television Programs, 1946-76." Ph.D. thesis, available from University Microfilms International, Ann Arbor, Mich.

O'Connor, Carrol. "I Regret Nothing Except My Own Anger." *TV Guide*, September 22, 1979.

Rich, John. Interview with the author, October 1986.

Turan, Kenneth. "Archie and Edith and Meathead and Gloria: A Family Journal." *TV Guide*, September 3, 1983.

Whitney, Dwight. "An American Institution Rolls On." *TV Guide*, January 6, 1979.

## "M*A*S*H"

Alda, Alan. "My Favorite Episodes." *TV Guide*, February 12, 1983.

Berges, Marshall. "Home Q & A: Pat & Larry Gelbart." *Los Angeles Times Magazine*, July 16, 1978.

Corliss, Richard, with Denise Worrell. "M*A*S*H, You Were a Smash." *Time*, February 28, 1983.

Darrach, Brad, with Suzanne Adelson. "M*A*S*H, Goodbye, Farewell and Amen . . ." *People*, March 7, 1983.

Davidson, Bill. "CLASH." *TV Guide*, January 24, 1976.

————. "Vintage Year for Wayne."*TV Guide*, November 2, 1974.

Deeb, Gary. "Crash Course for "M*A*S*H?" Syndicated column, January 5, 1982.

Gelbart, Larry. "Its Creator Says Hail and Farewell to "M*A*S*H." *The New York Times*, February 27, 1983.

_____. "A Mash Note to CBS' "M*A*S*H." Los Angeles*Times*, November 3, 1972.

Johnston, David. "The Interplay's the Thing." *TV Guide*, January 5, 1980.

Kalter, Suzy. *The Complete Book of "M*A*S*H*. New York: Abrams, 1984.

Metcalfe, Burt. Interview with the author, August 1986.

Raddatz, Leslie. "Cocktail Hour Starts at 4:30." *TV Guide*, August 24, 1974.

Reiss, David S. *M*A*S*H: The Exclusive, Inside Story of TV's Most Popular Show.* Indianapolis: Bobbs-Merrill, 1983.

Walters, Harry F., with Janet Huck. "Farewell to the M*A*S*H Gang." *Newsweek*, February 28, 1983.

## "THE BOB NEWHART SHOW"

Berges, Marshall. "Home Q & A: The Bob Newharts." *Los Angeles Times Magazine*, September 14, 1975.

Davidson, Bill. "The Suzanne Pleshette Show." *TV Guide*, December 16, 1972.

Farr, Lynne. Interview with the author, December 1986.

Feuer, Jane, Paul Kerr, and Tise Vahimagi. *MTM Quality Television*. London: BFI Books/ The British Film Institute, 1984.

Lochte, Dick. "Friendship by Appointment Only." *TV Guide*, May 11, 1974.

Music, Lorenzo. Interview with the author, November 1986.

Stabiner, Karen. "For Bob Newhart, Affection Is Still the Essence of Successful Comedy." *The New York Times*, December 26, 1982.

Wagner, Alan. Interview with the author, November 1986.

Whitney, Dwight. "Still Button-Down, But No Longer Buttoned Up." *TV Guide*, January 20, 1973.

Witbeck, Charles. "Bob Newhart's New Success." Los Angeles *Herald-Examiner*, December 30, 1972.

Zinberg, Michael. Interview with the author, November 1986.

## "BARNEY MILLER"

Arnold, Danny. Interview with the author, November 1986.

Bedell, Sally. *Up the Tube*. New York: Viking, 1981.

Burke, Tom. "As Japanese as Nathan Detroit." *TV Guide*, July 16, 1977.

DuBrow, Rick. "Danny Arnold Is Back on the Beat." Los Angeles *Herald-Examiner*, November 12, 1985.

Dungan, Frank. Interview with the author, November 1986.

Hano, Arnold. "The Only Actor Ever Named After a Gas Tank." *TV Guide*, July 19, 1975.

Rich, John. Interview with the author, October 1986.

Russell, Dick. "Barney Miller's Secret Weapon." *TV Guide*, July 7, 1979.

_____. "The World's Gonna Catch Up With Steve Landesberg." *TV Guide*, November 26, 1977.

Sheehan, Tony. Interview with the author, November 1986.

Stein, Jeff. Interview with the author, November1986.

Whitney, Dwight. "The Man Is an Actor." *TV Guide*, February 7, 1976.

## "TAXI"

Boyer, Peter. "NBC: A Night of Triumph." Los Angeles *Times*, September 26, 1983.

Burke, Tom. "'Taxi' Puts Him in the Driver's Seat." *TV Guide*, April 28, 1979.

Charles, Glen, and Les Charles. Interview with the author, October 1986.

Clark, Kenneth R. "'Taxi' Picks Up Kane; Vice Versa?" *UPI*, December 3, 1982.

Hicks, Jack. "He Loves to Get Hate Mail." *TV Guide*, June 6, 1981.

Shaw, Ellen Torgerson. "When Latka Says 'Bisha ga ba ba' - She Knows What to Do." *TV Guide*, April 30, 1983.

Weingerger, Ed. Interview with the author, December 1986.

Weingarten, Paul. "The Kitten That Roared." *Chicago Tribune Magazine*, December 1, 1985.

Zinberg, Michael. Interview with the author, November 1986.


## "CHEERS"

Burrows, James. Interview with the author, February, 1988.

Casey, Peter. Interview with the author, May, 1995.

Charles, Glen, and Les Charles. Interview with the author, October 1986.

Christensen, Mark, and Cameron Stauth. *The Sweeps: Behind the Scenes in Network TV*. New York: Morrow, 1984.

Gregory, Fred. "Every Day Is a Shelley Long Improvisation." *TV Guide*, March 26, 1986.

Jorgensen, Eric, and Kevin Treu. "Mega List of *Cheers* Episodes." Internet Usenet groups on-line database, 1995.

Keister, Edwin, Jr. "Expect Some Tears With Your 'Cheers.'" *TV Guide*, October 9, 1982.

Kerr, Peter. "NBC Comedy 'Cheers' Turns Into a Success." *The New York Times*, November 29, 1983.

Staley, Dan. Interview with the author, May, 1995.

Stauth, Cameron. "'Cheers,' The Hit That Almost Missed." *Esquire*, February 1984.

Sutton, Phoef. Interview with the author, May, 1995.

# Episode Guide Index

577

# About the Author

Vince Waldron is the author of *The Official Dick Van Dyke Show Book* and co-author, with pop legend Ronnie Spector, of the singer's autobiography, *Be My Baby.* He has served as a comedy consultant to the BBC and was special program advisor on The Museum of Television and Radio's ABC-TV special, *Great Television Moments, What We Watched.* He lives in Los Angeles.